Scientists on Gaia

Scientists on Gaia

Edited by Stephen H. Schneider and Penelope J. Boston

The MIT Press
Cambridge, Massachusetts
London, England

This book was set in 10 pt. Times Roman by Compset,
Inc. and was printed and bound in the United States of
America.

Library of Congress Cataloging-in-Publication Data

Scientists on Gaia / edited by Stephen Schneider and
Penelope Boston.
    p. cm.
  "Papers delivered at the American Geophysical
Union's annual Chapman Conference in March,
1988"—
  Includes bibliographical references and index.
  ISBN 0-262-19310-8
  1. Gaia hypothesis—Congresses. 2. Geobiology—
Congresses.
I. Schneider, Stephen Henry. II. Boston, Penelope
J. III. American Geophysical Union.
QH331.S375 1991   72358
550—dc20   91-344
                                        CIP

Contents

VI   Mechanisms: Carbon and Biomass

44

Preface

For more than a century students of the evolution of the living and nonliving parts of the Earth have known that life influences the physical and chemical characteristics of the planet. Nevertheless, the dominant paradigm in earth sciences has been that inexorable inorganic forces, such as changing energy output from the Sun, collisions of the Earth with extraterrestrial bodies, continental drift, or orbital element variations have been the principal driving forces behind climate change, and that life is more buffeted by these forces than the reverse. About twenty years ago, James Lovelock and Lynn Margulis coined the phrase the *Gaia hypothesis* to suggest not only that life has a greater influence on the evolution of the Earth than is typically assumed across most earth science disciplines but also that life serves as an active control system. In fact, they suggest that life on Earth provides a cybernetic, homeostatic feedback system, leading to stabilization of global temperature, chemical composition, and so forth.

When first introduced in the early 1970s, the Gaia hypothesis attracted the most attention from theologians interested in the possibility that the Earth controlled its environment on purpose (i.e., teleological implications), from those looking for "oneness" in nature, and from those defending polluting industries, for whom the Gaia hypothesis provided a convenient excuse whereby some collective set of natural processes would largely offset any potential damages from human disturbance to earth systems. Although none of these aspects was underlined in the scientific work of Lovelock and Margulis, these nonscientific side issues diverted attention in the scientific community away from a serious analysis of the Gaia hypothesis and its implications. By the mid 1980s, Gaia advocates and detractors began a series of critiques and countercritiques, often carried out through third parties such as television documentary producers. One of us (Schneider), having been party to such a debate, came to realize the absurdity of the situation in which an interesting and controversial idea like the Gaia hypothesis was being debated largely in nonscientific forums, if at all. Schneider discussed this unfortunate circumstance with Juan Roederer of the University of Alaska, a prominent member of the American Geophysical Union (AGU). Dr. Roederer suggested that an AGU-sponsored Chapman Conference be convened on the Gaia hypothesis, and he further recommended that Dr. Glenn Shaw of the University of Alaska, who had already published some interesting ideas on biogenic sulfur, the sulfur cycle, and its potential for climate control, help organize the meeting. Shaw and Schneider began to formulate an agenda and a proposal in 1986. It soon became apparent that biological expertise was needed, for which the advice of one of us (Boston, a microbial ecologist) was sought. It became clear in a matter of weeks that Boston's contribution to the planning process was fundamental, and thus she joined Shaw and Schneider as coconveners of the meeting.

The proposal to the AGU for a Chapman Conference was not accepted without scientific detractors. It was deemed controversial, and several objections were raised to it both within the AGU council and by outside scientists. It is to the credit of that council that despite some of these criticisms, many of them based on the early perceptions of the Gaia hypothesis as nonscience, the council approved holding a Chapman Conference on the subject, provided outside funding was obtained. We gratefully acknowledge the efforts of Hassan Virji, of the Climate Dynamics section of the Atmospheric Science Division of the National Science Foundation, not only for his section's contribution to the Chapman Conference but also for serving as the organizer at the National Science Foundation (NSF) for obtaining funds from other sections of NSF. That principal grant made the meeting possible. However, widespread interest across a dozen disciplines of science and philosophy was represented at the meeting, and this broad interest led to a full week's agenda, which created another financial burden. Since the coconveners were anxious to have state-of-the-art reviews of the many disciplines relevant to the study of the biological, chemical, geological, and climatic aspects of Earth's evolution, as well as to have many graduate students attend a meeting that would treat so many diverse subjects in depth, it was important to bring a substantial number of students and others without travel funds to the meeting. Our financial crisis was resolved at the eleventh hour by the generous intercession of Dr. Charles Zracket from the MITRE Corporation, whose timely grant allowed us to fund, at least partially, all the graduate students and invited overview paper authors who were able to attend. Finally, producing typescripts of verbal transcripts also required grant assistance, for which we gratefully acknowledge Dr. Shelby Tilford of the Office of Space Science and Applications, Earth Science and Applications Division of the National Aeronautics and Space Administration, whose support made it possible for this volume to be produced.

The meeting itself, held in March 1988 in San Diego, was an illustrious event. Review papers were presented on the Gaia hypothesis, on a Darwinian critique of the Gaia hypothesis, on various physical, chemical, and biological processes that are organic or inorganically driven, on models of stable and unstable systems, on carbon-oxygen-nitrogen-sulfur cycles, on soil processes, mineral weathering, fire effects, Earth-asteroid or comet collisions, epistemology (i.e., a session on the philosophy of science), and a political perspective from Congressman George Brown.

Such a diversity of papers, such a multiplicity of topics, jargon, styles, and scientific approaches produced a meeting that taxed the interdisciplinary skills of all participants. Some talks were differential equation–ladened, whereas others assumed a knowledge of nineteenth-century evolutionary theory or twentieth-century philosophy of science. Panel discussion sections at the end of each of these sections helped clarify unclear issues or allowed focus on basic concepts.

This volume also suffers, admittedly, from the inclusion of heterogeneous papers with differing jargon, presentation styles, and content, and it requires some analytic skill for full comprehension by the reader. Although we have not included discussion sessions in this volume, we did insist that the papers be "dejargonized" to the extent possible. The papers include a wide range of presentational styles, from *Scientific American* style, popularized presentations to that which fits the standards of technical journals. Some of the material across this spectrum of presentational styles overlaps, and we hope enough material is covered in different ways to allow this volume to be useful for both scientifically interested nonscientists as well as professional readers. Moreover, since this volume appears almost three years after the initial meeting, much has been learned since the San Diego event in 1988. While this delay is regrettable, in that a comprehensive reader on Gaia science was not immediately available in the wake of the enthusiasm generated by the Chapman Conference, it is advantageous because the discoveries of the subsequent three years and the growing body of literature are accounted for in this volume. We believe the delay will be amply compensated for by the updated information contained in most chapters in this volume. In any case, compiling articles from so diverse a group necessitated a long delay, which we opportunistically used to ask the authors to keep their papers current to the winter of 1991.

Finally, we wish to acknowledge once again the efforts of the AGU in sponsoring the Chapman Conference, Glenn Shaw in helping us with the initial proposal, Mary Rickel of the National Center for Atmospheric Research (NCAR) for handling much of the administrative detail in advance of the meeting, at the meeting, and for a heroic effort in reading galley proofs and keeping track of missing figures and a myriad of loose ends in preparing this volume, and not least the NSF, MITRE Corporation, and the National Aeronautics and Space Administration for their financial support. In addition, we wish to thank Susan Mikkelson for her efforts in transcribing the tapes from the meeting. We also thank NCAR for contributing some of Schneider's and Rickel's time without overhead, as well as for allowing use of the mails and other amenities of NCAR—which is sponsored by NSF.

Stephen H. Schneider*
National Center for Atmospheric Research**
P.O. Box 3000
Boulder, Colorado   80307

Penelope J. Boston*
Complex Systems Research Inc.
P.O. Box 11320
Boulder, Colorado   80301

*Any opinions, findings, conclusions, or recommendations expressed in this article are those of the authors and do not necessarily reflect the views of the NSF.
**The National Center for Atmospheric Research is sponsored by the National Science Foundation.

Introduction

I Gaia: An Overview

At the outset it is necessary to describe what the Gaia hypothesis is. The best and most appropriate way to accomplish that task, we believe, is to do it in the words of its progenitors, James Lovelock and Lynn Margulis. Each presented a paper at the first session of the Chapman Conference, and their papers are the first to appear in the introductory section. At the San Diego meeting, presentation of their Gaian perspective was followed by a Darwinian critique by Paul R. Ehrlich of Stanford University. His very different view of the coevolution of organic and inorganic processes provides a strong counterpoint to Gaian philosophy, and it focuses the debate that took place at the meeting and subsequently. Ehrlich's paper is followed by a general article describing a number of potential processes in which biogenic influences relevant to the Gaia hypothesis could manifest themselves.

II Philosophical Foundations of Gaia

It is most unusual for physical or biological scientists to have philosophers of science at their meetings, let alone to have an entire evening session devoted to epistemology. Yet this session proved to be one of the most intense and stimulating intellectual evenings we have ever attended at a scientific forum. Largely divergent views were aired, by James Kirchner, a philosopher and physicist at the Energy and Resources Group at the University of California at Berkeley, and by David Abram, a philosopher from State University of New York at Stony Brook. Kirchner cited the historical evolution of Margulis' and Lovelock's thoughts on Gaia, categorizing not one but five hypotheses, from weak to strong, critiquing some as already known and challenging others as either untestable or extreme. He concludes that the most radical version of Gaia (i.e., the theory that the planet is capable of self-control) is more likely a metaphor than a hypothesis. Abram, on the other hand, challenges most biogeophysical science as "mechanical" and suggests that the Gaia hypothesis represents an "organic" alternative. To be frank, Abram's paper was controversial in the review process. We asked him to shorten and sharpen the piece, which he did, but not to the satisfaction of all the reviewers. We believe the reader, rather than the reviewers or editors, should decide on the merit of his arguments, particularly given the controversial nature of his views. John Visvader introduces the philosophical debate with a historical commentary on Gaia on the context of epistemological scholarship. We are indebted to David Hawkins for helping to organize and run the session and for helping to translate some of the philosophical language into familiar terms that natural scientists could more easily digest.

III Theoretical Foundations of Gaia

What are the properties of Gaia and how do they fit in with other well-established principles of natural science? The papers in the section on theoretical foundations of the Gaia hypothesis address this knotty, central arena for disagreement. The players may have different opinions about Gaia, but all are sizing her up next to the Procrustean bed of science-as-we-know-it. How well does she fit . . . and how many toes have to be severed to make the necessary adjustments?

Chapters in this part explain ecological and climate fundamentals, devise several tests for possible Gaian processes, and explore the realm of hypothetical climate-life feedbacks on make-believe planets.

IV Mechanisms: Sulfur

In the mid-1980s, James Lovelock visited the University of Washington in Seattle and met with an interdisciplinary team of scientists, including cloud microphysical chemist Robert Charlson, sulfur cycle biogeochemist Meinrat Andreae, and climate theorist Stephen Warren. Together they conceived a potential biogenic feedback process whereby dimethylsulfide produced in some phytoplankton escapes into the oceans and eventually is chemically transformed into atmospheric sulfur dioxide. Sulfur dioxide then is later chemically converted to sulfuric acid droplets that can serve as cloud condensation nuclei in the sparsely polluted oceanic regions of the Earth. Such nuclei can multiply substantially the number of droplets in a cloud, which in turn increases the reflectivity of the cloud, in ways that could affect the climate. It had been suggested in 1983 by Glenn Shaw that the Gaian mechanisms might operate through the Earth's sulfur cycle by involving biologically produced particles of sulfuric acid. Shaw was hesitant to extend this suggestion to cloud-climate modulation because of the complex nonlinear connectivity that exists between the acid droplets and the cloud properties, a topic summarized in his chapter. Charlson, on the other hand, discusses the cloud nuclei component. Ken Caldeira of New York University discusses evolutionary aspects of planktonic dimethyl sulfide production, and Meinrat Andreae reviews the global sulfur cycle in this context. This area of research, which involves substantial possibilities for hypothesis testing and experimental validation, has evolved substantially since the 1988 San Diego meeting, and these papers recount that debate in the light of what is known as of the end of 1990.

V Mechanisms: Oxygen

One of the critical gases under the control of life is oxygen. The production of oxygen by photosynthesizing organisms is unquestioned among earth scientists, but what happens to that oxygen once emitted depends on inorganic processes such as weathering and other chemical transformations, as well as oceanic and atmospheric circulation and temperatures. Fires, if they transform organic matter to charcoal, a relatively inert form of carbon, can increase oxygen by burying carbon. Robert Berner of Yale University and Heinrich Holland of Harvard, in particular, discuss not only oxygen but the biogeochemical processes and methods that are used for carbon cycle analysis as well.

VI Mechanisms: Carbon and Biomass

On a world of carbon-based life forms, where else to look for Gaian mechanisms than carbon itself? This most ubiquitous and massive of biogeochemical cycles has countless subcycles turning at vastly different rates through the ages. If you do geology, you see the big slow cycles of mountains and oceans. If you do biology, you see the little, fast cycles of a microbe, a plant, or a whole population. Meeting participants bravely tried to drop their own cherished disciplinary blinders and see this massive cycle as others see it.

The chapters in this section span the geological timeline from the early history of our planet and life, 3.5 to 4 billion years ago, to the thousands-of-year timescales of glacial intervals. In addition, several contributors consider the relationship of carbon to biomass and biological evolution, certainly carbon's most elegant and complex manifestation.

VII Other Mechanisms

Gaian principles can extend not only to the dominant biogeochemical cycles, the Big Three already discussed, but also to any other material and energy cycling processes on Earth. The section on other mechanisms offers a sampler of how Gaian processes may or may not involve trace gases, silica in the oceans, humus and biomineralization, weathering, fire, and even the cell walls of plants!

VIII Gaia, Catastrophes, and Other Planets

If Gaia works on Earth during the general course of evolution, what happens when something disrupts business-as-usual wandering asteroids or comet nuclei, for instance? Just how robust is a Gaian system to outside perturbation from astronomical forces and what would it take to overwhelm it?

If Gaia works on Earth, is it a one-shot success story, or can Gaian principles be generalized to other planets in our Solar System or other planets in the Galaxy? To be truly generalizable, Gaian principles would have to be shown to be naturally emerging properties of planetary biological systems in the same way that we imagine (but have no current evidence for) life to be a naturally emerging property of matter in the universe. The chapters in the section on Gaia, catastrophes, and other planets deal with these intriguing, logical, but far-flung ramifications of the Gaia hypothesis.

IX Political Implications

Part of the controversy associated with the Gaia hypothesis in the early 1970s was that some people argued that if biological homeostasis were a reality, then human pollution might be offset by a controlling biota. However, as the chapters in this volume amply demonstrate, not only is it premature to judge the extent to which biological homeostasis has been validated, it also appears that many of the processes by which such feedback might exist take place in geological timescales. Clearly, the rate at which civilization is modifying the atmosphere and environmental landscape is so rapid relative to many of these processes that substantial global change will probably occur during the twenty-first century. Although understanding in quantitative terms the extent to which biological, physical, or chemical processes might damp or enhance the effect of any human disturbance to the environment is the goal of global change research, we believe it will be decades at least before such quantitative knowledge is at hand. Therefore, whether to risk radically modifying the Earth in pursuit of human goals is not a scientific question per se; rather, it is a fundamental political value choice that weighs the immediate benefits of population or economic growth versus the potential environmental or societal risk of a rapidly altered Earth. As Congressman George Brown's article, delivered and edited by Anthony Scoville, amply demonstrates, that choice is both risky and one that is increasingly weighing on the minds of decision makers as the buildup of greenhouse gases, deforested lands, and other environmental disturbances continues with the waning of the twentieth century.

Penelope J. Boston   Stephen H. Schneider

List of Contributors

David Abram   State University of New York at Stony Brook

M.O. Andreae   Max Planck Institut für Chemie

Robert A. Berner   Yale University

William D. Bischoff   Wichita State University
Collette D. Burke

Penelope J. Boston   Complex Systems Research Corporation
Starley L. Thompson   National Center for Atmospheric Research

George E. Brown, Jr.   House of Representatives, U.S. Congress
Anthony Ellsworth Scoville

Ken Caldeira   New York University

Robert J. Charlson   University of Washington

Robert B. Chatfield   NASA Ames Research Center

Paul Ehrlich   Stanford University

David J. Erickson III   National Center for Atmospheric Research

John Harte   University of California at Berkeley

B. Henderson-Sellers   University of New South Wales
A. Henderson-Sellers   Macquarie University
S.M.P. Benbow   University of Liverpool
K. McGuffie   University of Technology, Sydney

Heinrich D. Holland   Harvard University

Ralph Keeling   National Center for Atmospheric Research

Jeffrey T. Kiehl   National Center for Atmospheric Research

John J. Kineman   National Oceanic and Atmospheric Administration

James W. Kirchner   University of California at Berkeley

Lee F. Klinger   National Center for Atmospheric Research

G.H. Kolmaier   Johann Wolfgang Goethe University
Matthias Lüdeke
Alex Janecek
Günther Benderoth
Jürgen Kindermann
Axel Klaudius

Lee R. Kump   Pennsylvania State University
Tyler Volk   New York University

Daniel A. Lashof   Natural Resources Defense Council

Glen B. Lesins   Dalhousie University

Joel S. Levine   NASA Langley Research Center

James E. Lovelock   Cornwall, England

Patrick MacCarthy   Colorado School of Mines
James A. Rice   South Dakota State University

Paul S. Mankiewicz   The Gaia Institute

Lynn Margulis   University of Massachusetts
Gregory Hinkle

Christopher P. McKay   NASA Ames Research Center
Carol R. Stoker

Diane M. McKnight   U.S. Geological Survey

Michael A. Palecki   State University of New York at Buffalo

Michael R. Rampino   New York University

Jennifer M. Robinson   Pennsylvania State University

Manfred Schidlowski   Max Planck Institut für Chemie

David Schwartzman   Howard University
John Evans   U.S. Geological Survey
Harold Okrend   Howard University
Soe Aung   Howard University

Glenn E. Shaw   University of Alaska

Walter Shearer   United Nations University

Raymond Siever   Harvard University

John F. Stolz   Duquesne University

John Visvader   College of the Atlantic

James C.G. Walker   University of Michigan

Andrew J. Watson   Marine Biological Association of the United Kingdom
Linda Maddock

G.R. Williams   University of Toronto

Thomas R. Worsley   Ohio University
R. Damian Nance
Judith B. Moody   J. B. Moody and Associates

Scientists on Gaia

I
Gaia: An Overview

James E. Lovelock
1
Geophysiology—The Science of Gaia

There is growing recognition of the inadequacy of the separated disciplinary approach for the solution of planetary-scale problems. To understand even the atmosphere, which is the simplest of the planetary compartments, knowledge of geophysics is not enough; chemistry and biology are also needed. It might seem that research teams that included experts in each different discipline would resolve the problem, but anyone who has attended gatherings of experts knows that each expert speaks but does not or cannot listen. What might help would be a broader-based general science that provided an environment within which the separate disciplines could interact.

In many ways, contemporary concerns arising from the consequences of changes made by humans in the composition of the atmosphere and the nature of the land surface and biota echo similar concerns raised about the human body early in the development of medicine. In the late nineteenth century, the sciences of biochemistry and microbiology were well advanced but largely disconnected and not very helpful to those with disease. Advances in medicine were, however, vastly enabled by the existence of the general science of physiology, a science that was at once transdisciplinary and also recognized the essentially emergent properties of a living organism. If one were interested in how we maintain our core temperatures at 37°C, a biochemical approach to the problem would be fruitless. Temperature regulation is a systems control problem and within the remit of physiology. But by starting with physiology, the biochemical aspects involving, for example, oxidative metabolism, then fit naturally into place.

This chapter puts forward an analogous earth science geophysiology as the transdisciplinary environment for studying planetary-scale problems, particularly problems involving a wide range of disciplines and for which it is postulated although not proved that emergent properties exist. That is, for practical purposes it may be useful to consider the earth as if it were a living organism.

Before the nineteenth century, scientists were comfortable with the notion of a living earth. One of them was James Hutton, who has often been called the father of geology. Lecturing before the Royal Society of Edinburgh in 1785, Hutton said, "I consider the Earth to be a superorganism and that its proper study should be by physiology." He belonged to the Circulation Society, a scientific society that was inspired by the discoveries of physiology such as the circulation of the blood and the connection between oxygen and life. He applied these ideas to his view of the hydrological cycle and the movements of the nutritious elements of the earth.

James Hutton's wholesome view of the Earth was discarded early in the last century. I think this may have been a consequence of a growing interest in origins and in evolutionary theories for both earth and life scientists. For biologists, there was Darwin's great vision of the evolution of the species of organisms by natural selection. For geologists, there was the wholly independent theory that the evolution of the material environment was simply a matter of chemical and physical determinism.

The divorce of the earth and life sciences in the nineteenth century was inevitable. Not only was there a rapid increase in the supply of information about the earth as exploration and exploitation developed, but the techniques for studying organisms were very different from those for studying the ocean, the air, and the rocks. It must have been an exciting period of science. Few were inclined to stand back and take a broader view or try to keep alive Hutton's superorganism theory. What is remarkable is not the division of the sciences but that two distinct and very different theories of evolution could coexist even until today.

The reason the division has endured is, I think, a mutual acceptance by earth and life scientists of the anaesthetic notion of adaptation. Biologists have assumed that the physical and chemical world evolves according to rules laid down in the geology or the biogeochemistry department of their university and that the details of this material evolution, although interesting, need not concern them in their quest to understand the evolution of the organisms. Biologists are comfortable with the notion that whatever happens to the environment, organisms will *adapt*.

In a similar way, earth scientists were happy to accept without question their biological colleagues' idea of adaptation because it freed them of any need to constrain their earth models on account of the needs of organisms. After all, there were organisms living in hot springs at 100°C and others at the freezing point: a wide enough range for climatologists.

Adaptation is a dubious notion, for in the real world the environment, to which organisms are adapting, is determined by their neighbors' activities, rather than by the blind forces of chemistry and physics alone. In such a world, changing the environment could be part of the game, and it would be absurd to suppose that organisms would refrain from changing their material environment if by so doing they could leave more progeny. In his time, of course, Darwin did not know, as we do now, that the air we breathe, the oceans, and the rocks are all either the direct products of living organisms or else have been greatly modified by their presence. In no way do organisms simply "adapt" to a dead world determined by physics and chemistry alone. They live in a world that is the breath and bones of their ancestors and that they are now sustaining.

It was not until the present century that a minority opinion led by the Russian scientist, Vernadsky (1945), saw that the separation of the earth and life sciences had become too extreme. Vernadsky was the father of the modern science of biogeochemistry. He and his successors, like Hutchinson (1954) and Redfield (1958), recognized that life and the physical environment interact, that gases like oxygen and methane are biological products. Where they differ from proponents of the Gaia hypothesis is that they still accepted, without question, the dogma of mainstream biology, which is that organisms simply adapt to changes in their material environment, without then considering the consequences of such an adaptation in an environment modified by the organisms themselves. Vernadsky's worldview has been developed and expanded in co-

evolutionary theory and in biogeochemical models. Coevolution is rather like a platonic friendship. Biologists and geologists remain friends but never move on to an intimate, close coupled, relationship. Coevolution theory includes no active regulation of the chemical composition and climate of the earth by the system comprising the biota and their material environment; most importantly, it does not see the earth as alive in any sense, nor even as a physiological system.

What Is Gaia

Like coevolution, Gaia rejects the apartheid of Victorian biology and geology, but it goes much further. Gaia theory is about the evolution of a tightly coupled system whose constituents are the biota and their material environment, which comprises the atmosphere, the oceans, and the surface rocks. Self-regulation of important properties, such as climate and chemical composition, is seen as a consequence of this evolutionary process. Like living organisms and many closed-loop self-regulating systems, it would be expected to show emergent properties; that is, the whole will be more than the sum of the parts. This kind of system is notoriously difficult, if not impossible, to explain by cause-and-effect logic, as practicing inventors know to their cost. It is doubtful also if the fashionable and trendy Popperian falsification tests, so valuable for theories in physics, are really applicable to such systems. Consider, for example, the problem faced by someone unfamiliar with earth-based life of designing a test to show that a Lombardy poplar tree was alive. These trees are all males and, hence, can be propagated only by cuttings—90% or more of a fully grown tree is dead wood and dead bark, with just a thin skin of living tissue around the circumference of the wood. Then there is the question, "What does the word *alive* mean?" Biologists studiously avoid trying to answer it.

When biochemists examine a live animal, they know that many of its reactions and processes can be adequately described by simple deterministic physics and chemistry. But they also accept the legitimacy of physiology. They know that for an intact animal, homeostasis, the automatic regulation of temperature, and chemical composition, although it involves chemistry, are emergent properties. Such properties require physiology for their explanation and understanding. I think that the same can be said of the earth. If it is a superorganism, then explaining its reactions and processes requires physiology as well as chemistry and physics.

Evidence for Gaia

The first mention of Gaia was a brief paper in *Atmospheric Environment* (Lovelock, 1972). Earlier work in connection with the National Aeronautics and Space Administration planetary exploration program had suggested that atmospheric compositional evidence could provide prima facie evidence for the existence of life on a planet (Hitchcock and Lovelock 1967). Briefly, a dead planet would have an atmosphere characteristic of the abiological steady state and not far from chemical equilibrium. By contrast, a planet with life would be obliged to use its atmosphere as a transfer medium for waste products and raw materials. Such a use of the atmosphere would introduce disequilibrium among the chemical components, and this might reveal the presence of life. When the terrestrial planets are compared, Mars and Venus are found to have atmospheres dominated by carbon dioxide and close to the abiological steady state. Earth, by contrast, has an atmosphere in which profoundly incompatible gases such as methane and oxygen coexist. This disequilibrium reveals the presence of life. The persistence of the disequilibrium at a steady state for periods much longer than the residence times of the gases suggests the presence of an active control system regulating atmospheric composition. As we may soon discover, the unregulated injection of methane could be seriously destabilizing. Figure 1.1 illustrates the fluxes of gases through the Earth's present atmosphere in comparison with the fluxes expected of a dead Earth.

Until the San Diego meeting, Gaia theory had received little or no financial or other support from the scientific establishment. About five scientists worldwide worked on the topic part time. In such circumstances, it was not practical to strive hard to develop tests for the existence or otherwise of Gaian systems. It seemed better to go into the world and collect information, inspired by the predictions from the theory. Whether it was right or wrong seemed to matter less than that the quest was objective. A good example of this was the expedition in 1972 aboard the research ship Shackleton from the United Kingdom to Antarctica and back to seek the presence of sulfur and iodine compounds in the ocean and determine whether it was possible to transfer these elements from the sea to the air and,

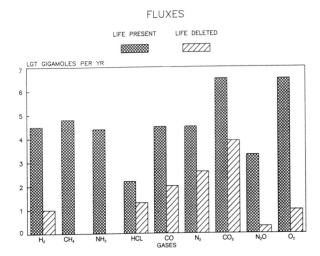

Figure 1.1 The fluxes of gases through the present atmosphere compared with the fluxes of the same gases expected for a dead Earth. The vertical scale is in logarithmic decade units of gigamoles per year.

hence, back to the land surfaces. This voyage found that the gases dimethylsulfide, methyl iodide, and carbon disulfide were ubiquitous throughout the ocean environment. It is relevant to note that before the expedition, peer review committees argued that the search for such compounds was pointless. This was a time when research funds were freely available, yet the expedition was not supported.

A more practical approach is to make models of Gaia and then see how well they can be mapped onto the observed systems. But the feedback loops linking life with its environment are so numerous and so intricate that there seems little chance of quantifying or of understanding them. It occurred to me late in 1981 to reduce the environment to a single variable, temperature, and the biota to a single species, daisies.

Imagine a planet like the Earth; it travels at the Earth's orbit around a star of the same mass and composition as our Sun. This planet spins like the Earth, but its atmosphere has few clouds and a constant low concentration of greenhouse gases. In these circumstances, the mean surface temperature is given by the Stephan-Boltzman expression of the balance between the radiation received from the star and the heat lost by radiation from the planet to space; the albedo of the planet determines its temperature. Assume that this planet is well seeded with daisies whose growth rate is a simple parabolic function of temperature, and that it is well watered and that nutrients are not limited. In these circumstances, it is easy to predict the area of the planet

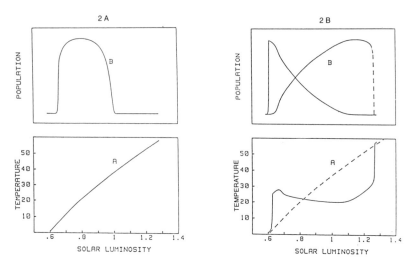

Figure 1.2 Models of the evolution of Daisyworld according to conventional wisdom (**A**) and to geophysiology (**B**). The upper panels illustrate daisy populations in arbitrary units; the lower panels, temperatures in degrees Celsius. Going from left to right along the horizontal axis, the star's luminosity increases from 60% to 140% of that of our own Sun. *A* illustrates how the physicists and the biologists in complete isolation calculate their view of the evolution of the planet. According to this conventional wisdom, the daisies can only respond or adapt to changes in temperature. When it becomes too hot for comfort, they will die. But in the Gaian Daisyworld (*B*), the ecosystem can respond by the competitive growth of the dark and light daisies and regulates the temperature over a wide range of solar luminosity. The dashed line in the lower panel in *B* shows how the temperature would rise on a lifeless Daisyworld.

covered by daisies from a knowledge of the mean surface temperature and equations taken from population biology. Figure 1.2A illustrates the evolution of this simple system when two different-colored daisy species are present, one dark and one light according to conventional wisdom.

The upper panel of the figure shows the response of daisies to temperature; daisies do not grow below 5° or above 40° but grow best at 22.5°C. The lower panel illustrates the evolution of the mean surface temperature as the star increases in luminosity, a smooth monotonic temperature increase.

In figure 1.2B, the same system is modeled as a close-coupled physiology. When the surface temperature reaches 5°, daisy seeds germinate. During the first season, dark-colored daisies will be at an advantage, because they will be warmer than the planetary surface. Light-colored daisies will be at a disadvantage, because by reflecting sunlight they will be cooler than the surface. At the end of the season, many more dark daisy seeds will remain in the soil. When the next season begins, dark daisies will flourish and soon warm, not just themselves, but their locality and, as they spread, the region and eventually the whole planet. The figure illustrates an explosive growth of both temperature and dark daisy population. The spread of dark daisies will eventually be limited by their decline in growth rate

at temperatures above 22.5°C and by competition from light-colored daisies. As the star evolves, the dark and light daisy populations adjust according to the simple population biology equations of Carter and Prince (1981). The planetary temperature moves from just above the optimum for daisy growth at low solar luminosity to just below the optimum at high solar luminosity. Eventually the output of heat from the star is too great for regulation, and the plants die.

This simple model is a graphic illustration of a geophysiological process. The only criticism so far received has been the suggestion by biologists that in a real world there would be daisy species that "cheated," that is, took advantage by saving the energy needed to make the dark or light pigment and so took over the planet and returned the system to the model illustrated in figure 1.1. Figure 1.3 is a model in which daisies having a neutral color, that of the bare planetary surface, are included. In this experiment, even when the neutral-colored daisies were given a 5% increase in growth rate, there was no indication of a planetary takeover or failure of regulation. At low temperatures, only dark daisies are fit to grow; at high temperatures, only light daisies are fit. Neutral daisies grow only when there is little need for regulation. An important point here illustrated is that Gaia theory and coevolution are

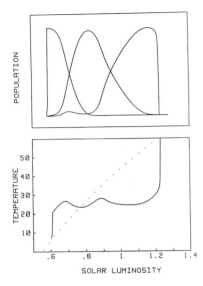

Figure 1.3 The evolution of the climate on a three-species Daisyworld with dark, gray, and light daisies present. By comparison, the dashed line in the lower panel represents the temperature evolution in the absence of life.

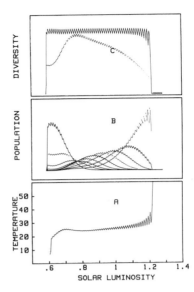

Figure 1.4 The evolution of the climate on a ten-species Daisyworld. The lower panel illustrates planetary temperature, the dashed curve for no life present, and the solid line with daisies. The middle panel shows the populations of the twenty different-colored daisies, with the darkest appearing first (left) and the lightest last (right). The upper panel illustrates diversity, seen to be maximum when the system temperature is closest to optimum.

not always mutually exclusive. Organisms do not strive ostentatiously to regulate their environment when regulation is not needed.

Figure 1.4 illustrates a model that included ten different-colored daisy species, their albedos ranging in evenly spaced steps from dark to light. The regulation of the mean surface temperature (lower panel) is more accurate than in the two- and three-species models. The middle panel shows the populations of the different-colored daisies and the upper panel the diversity index of the ecosystem as the model evolved.

The stable coexistence of three or more species in a population biology model is contrary to the experience of modelers in that field of science. Models of the competition of three or more species, like the three-body problem of astrophysics, tend to be unstable and chaotic. The stability of Daisyworld is even more remarkable given that no attempt was made to linearize the equations used in the model. Not only is the model naturally stable, but it will resist severe perturbations, such as the sudden death of half or more of all the daisies, and then recover homeostasis when the perturbation is removed. The models can include herbivores to graze the daisies and carnivores to cull the grazers without significant loss of stability.

Another scientist like James Hutton was Alfred Lotka, the father of theoretical ecology. Like Hut-

ton, Lotka saw the science he founded develop in a way that he never expected or intended. The unwise isolation of biology from geology has led population biology into a mathematical cul-de-sac where the phenomena of complex dynamics are investigated rather than ecology. For over sixty years, theoretical ecology has ignored Alfred Lotka's wise advice. In his book, *Physical Biology,* written in 1925, he said that

this fact deserves emphasis. It is customary to discuss the "evolution of a species of organisms." As we proceed we shall see many reasons why we should constantly take in view the evolution, as a whole, of the system (organism plus environment). It may appear at first sight as if it should prove a more complicated problem than the consideration of a part only of the system. But it will become apparent, as we proceed, that the physical laws governing evolution in all probability take on a simpler form when referred to the system as a whole than to any portion thereof.

It is not so much the organism or the species that evolves, but the entire system, species plus environment. The two are inseparable.

Daisyworld, as I have described it, is just an invention, a demonstration model to illustrate how I thought Gaia worked and why foresight and planning need not be invoked to explain automatic regulation. But as we shall see when the details are fleshed out, it becomes a generality and a theoretical basis for Gaia. I would like to think of it as the kind of model Alfred Lotka had in mind but could not develop, because in his day there were no computers to carry out the immense task that the hand calculation of even a simple daisy model requires.

Andrew Watson and I (1984) described the mathematical basis of Daisyworld in *Tellus*. But at the time, neither of us realized its unusual properties nor the extent to which it is an expression of the general theory of Gaia. The paper explains the essential mechanism by which homeostasis is maintained. The Daisyworld thermostat has no set point; instead the system always moves to a stable state in which the relationship between daisy population and planetary temperature and that between temperature and daisy growth converge. The systems seek the most comfortable state rather like a cat as it turns and moves before settling.

Inventions often work well but are difficult to explain. Engineers and physiologists have long been aware of the subtleties of feedback. Homeostasis is possible only when feedback is applied at the right amplitude and phase and when the system time constants are appropriate. Both positive and negative feedback can lead to stability or instability according to the timing of their application.

Theoretical ecology models, notorious for their intractable mathematics, would not surprise an engineer who would see them in his words as "open-loop systems," in which feedback was applied or happened by chance in an arbitrary manner. By contrast, geophysiological models, such as Daisyworld, include feedback, negative and positive, in a coherent manner. They are as a consequence robust and stable and happily accommodate any number of nonlinear equations and still prefer to relate with stable attractors.

Figure 1.5 compares the unstable and chaotic behavior (lower panel) of a model of an ecosystem of daisies, rabbits, and foxes according to population biology with the calm stability of the same ecosystem (upper panel) when feedback from the environment is included, as in a Daisyworld.

But what of biogeochemical box models? Are these any more stable? Ann Henderson-Sellers drew my attention to a paper that suggested that biogeochemical models were also prone to chaotic

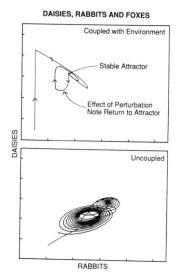

Figure 1.5 Comparison of the stability of a Daisyworld that included rabbits to eat the daisies and foxes to cull the rabbits (upper panel) with the instability of a population biology model of daisies, rabbits, and foxes (lower panel). The model in the upper diagram included environmental feedback; that in the lower diagram did not.

behavior or to an unusual sensitivity to the choice of initial conditions. Geophysiology seems to be a way to avoid these distractions. The concluding model is of the period at the end of the Archean when oxygen first began to dominate the chemistry of the atmosphere. During the long period of the Archean, the biosphere was run by bacteria. The primary producers were cyanobacteria, and the oxygen they made was almost entirely used up to oxidize reducing compounds such as ferrous iron and sulfides present in and continuously released to the environment. The organic matter of the cyanobacteria was most probably digested by methanogens. In the Archean period, cyanobacteria would be like the white daisies of Daisyworld, tending to cool by removing carbon dioxide, and the methanogens would be like the dark daisies, tending to warm by adding methane to the atmosphere. A geophysiological model constructed this way settles down to a constant climate and bacterial population and sustains an atmosphere where methane is the dominant redox gas and traces only of oxygen are present. The continuous leak of carbon to the sediments and perhaps also hydrogen to space would have slowly driven the system oxidizing until quite suddenly oxygen became the dominant atmospheric gas.

In this model, as in Daisyworld, a key factor is the function that set the bounds of the environment

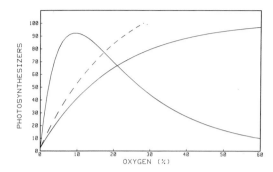

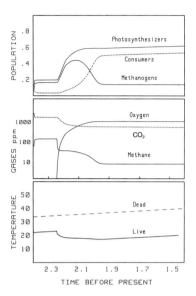

Figure 1.6 The effect of oxygen on the growth of organisms (solid line) and the effect of the presence of organisms on the abundance of oxygen (dashed line). Where the two curves intersect is the level of oxygen at which the system regulates.

for the biota. The same parabolic relationship between growth and temperature was used as in the daisy models but, in addition, a similar function was introduced for oxygen. Figure 1.6 shows how the growth of an ecosystem might increase as oxygen rises from zero. Oxygen increases the rate of rock weathering and, hence, the supply of nutrients, and also increases the rate of carbon cycling through oxidative metabolism. Too much oxygen is, however, toxic. The bounds for oxygen in the figure are set by two simple exponential relationships describing nutrition and toxicity.

Other bounds, such as those set by the limitations of pH, ionic strength, and the supply of nutrients, could have been included. Hutchinson saw the niche as a hypervolume negotiated among the species. In a similar way, I see the physical and chemical bounds to growth form a hypervolume whose surface intersects that of the hypervolume expressing the environmental effects of the species.

The model included geochemical data on the carbon dioxide cycle taken from Holland's book (1984). The rate of weathering was assumed to be a function of the biomass as well as of the abundance of oxygen and carbon dioxide. Figure 1.7 illustrates (in the lower window) the regulation of the temperature: constant during the Archean but falling to a lower steady state in the Proterozoic period after the appearance of oxygen as a dominant gas. The fall in temperature is due to the removal of most of the methane greenhouse effect. The middle window shows the abundances of the three gases—methane, carbon dioxide, and oxygen—during the evolution of the model. The upper panel shows the populations of the three main ecosystems: cyanobacteria, methanogens, and consumers.

Figure 1.7 Model of the transition from the Archean to the Proterozoic period. Lower panel shows climate with a lifeless world (dashed line) compared with a live world (solid line). Note the sudden fall of temperature when oxygen appears. The middle panel shows the abundance of atmospheric gases, carbon dioxide (dashed line), oxygen, and methane (solid lines). The upper panel illustrates the changes in population of the ecosystems as the transition is entered and passed. Note how both photosynthesizers and methanogens increase when oxygen first appears and how methanogens fall back to a steady level when the oxygen-breathing consumers (dashed line) become established.

Like Daisyworld, this model is just an invention and is not intended to describe the real world of those remote times. What it does illustrate is the remarkable mathematical stability of geophysiological models. Climate, three ecosystems, and three gases are regulated simultaneously and while the model is being continuously perturbed by an increasing solar luminosity. The stable homeostasis of the system is independent of a wide range of initial conditions and other perturbations. Perhaps most usefully, the values of the environmental quantities, temperature, and gas abundances it predicts are always realistic for the organisms. My purpose in making the model was to illustrate how I think Gaia works.

I do not disagree with those who propose that some, or even a large proportion, of the total regulation of any chosen earth property can be explained by deterministic chemistry and physics. Living systems use chemistry economically; they do not strive ostentatiously to do better than blind chemistry or physics—there is no need. The point about Gaia is that it offers a new way of looking at the earth and makes predictions that can be tested experimentally. Had it not been for the curiosity stimulated by thoughts on the mechanisms of Gaia, none of the important trace gases—dimethyl sulfide, carbon disulfide, methyl iodide, and chloride—would not have been sought and found when they were.

To conclude, Gaia theory provokes us to think about three things:

1. Life is a planetary-scale phenomenon. There cannot be sparse life on a planet. It would be as unstable as half of an animal. Living organisms must regulate their planet, otherwise the ineluctable forces of physical and chemical evolution would render it uninhabitable.

2. Gaia theory adds to Darwin's great vision. There is no longer any need to consider the evolution of the species separately from the evolution of their environment. The two processes are tightly coupled as a single indivisible process. It is not enough to say that the organism that leaves the most progeny succeeds. Success also depends on coherent coupling between the evolution of the organism and the evolution of its material environment.

3. Lastly, it may turn out that the gift of Gaia theory to geophysics is the reduction of Alfred Lotka's insight to practice. It may provide a new way to look at the earth mathematically that joyfully accepts the nonlinearity of nature without being overwhelmed by the limitations imposed by the chaos of complex dynamics.

References

Carter, R.N., and Prince, S.D. 1981. Epidemic models used to explain biographical distribution limits. *Nature*, 213, 644–645.

Charlson, R.J., Lovelock, J.E., Andreae, M.O., and Warren, S.J. 1987. Ocean phytoplankton, atmospheric sulfur, cloud albedo and climate. *Nature*, 326, 655–661.

Hitchcock, D.R., and Lovelock, J.E. 1967. Life detection by atmospheric analysis. *Icarus*, 7, 149–159.

Holland, H.D. 1984. *The Chemical Evolution of the Atmosphere and the Oceans*. Princeton, NJ: Princeton University Press, 539.

Hutchinson, G.E. 1954. *Biochemistry of the terrestrial atmosphere. The Solar System*. Chapter 8. Kuiper, Ed., Chicago: The University of Chicago Press.

Hutton, J. 1788. Theory of the Earth; or an investigation of the laws observable in the composition, dissolution, and restoration of land upon the globe. *Royal Society of Edinburgh, Transactions*, 1, 209–304.

Lovelock, J.E. 1972. Gaia as seen through the atmosphere. *Atmospheric Environment*, 6, 579–580.

Lovelock, J.E., Maggs, R.J., and Rasmussen, R.A. 1972. Atmospheric dimethylsulphide and the natural sulphur cycle. *Nature*, 237, 452–453.

Margulis, L., and Lovelock, J.E. 1974. Biological modulation of the Earth's atmosphere. *Icarus*, 21, 471–489.

Redfield, A.C. 1958. The biological control of chemical factors in the environment. *American Scientist*, 46, 205–221.

Vernadsky, V. 1945. The biosphere and the noosphere. *American Scientist*, 33, 1–12.

Watson, A.J., and Lovelock, J.E. 1983. Biological homeostasis of the global environment: The parable of Daisyworld. *Tellus*, 35B, 284–289.

Lynn Margulis and Gregory Hinkle

2
The Biota and Gaia: 150 Years of Support for Environmental Sciences

Though often held up as "pure" and "independent," our science is indelibly embedded in the language, religion, and social organization of our past. As a society we define our scientific goals through spending priorities revealed, for instance, in the funding of grants. When we compare the state of funding for environmental science in the mid-nineteenth century (and the underlying aims of the granting institutions at that time), we find remarkable, albeit disturbing similarities in the funding of science in the United States late in the twentieth century.

The Hypothesis

The Gaia hypothesis is a recombinant derived from the lively imagination of James E. Lovelock and the National Aeronautics and Space Administration's (NASA)'s search for life on Mars (Lovelock, 1988). Indeed, without planetary biology, the new science comparing Earth with its nearest neighbors, Mars and Venus, Lovelock would likely never have invented Gaia. As an answer to our more vocal critics, a more subversive and perhaps more appropriate title for this chapter would be "Gaia, Greed, and Glory" with the subtitle "Grants and Gaia." The chapter is divided into two sections. First, we applaud Jim Lovelock and his recognition that the "Earth is alive." We reaffirm Gaia as a creative, scientifically productive hypothesis. However, we express the Gaia hypothesis in an alternate way and assume the role of unofficial spokespeople for the silent majority of life on Earth, the microbes. Second, we discuss the past 150 years or so of financial support for "Gaian studies."

Rather than state "Earth is alive," a phrase that confuses many and offends others, we prefer to say that Gaia is a hypothesis about the planet Earth, its surface sediments, and its atmosphere. We describe the Gaia hypothesis as follows: the Earth's surface is anomalous with respect to its flanking planets, Mars and Venus. The surface conditions of Mars and Venus can be adequately comprehended by physics and chemistry. With respect to certain attributes, the Earth is, from the vantage of physics and chemistry alone, inexplicable. The Earth's physical and chemical anomalies, given new concrete knowledge about Mars and Venus, have become obvious. They include the presence of highly reactive gases (including oxygen, hydrogen, and methane) coexisting for long times in the atmosphere, the stability of the Earth's temperature (i.e., the long-term presence of liquid water) in the face of increasing solar luminosity, and the relative alkalinity of the oceans. The pH of the Earth is anomalously high. When compared with its barren neighbors, Earth's surface chemistry is aberrant with respect to its reactive gases, its temperature, and its alkalinity. These discordant chemical and physical conditions have been maintained over geologic periods of time. Lovelock's concept, with which we entirely agree, is that the biota (i.e., the sum of all the live organisms at any given time), interacting with the surface materials of the planet, maintains these particular anomalies of temperature, chemical composition, and alkalinity. Therefore to understand the Earth's surface we must understand the biota and its properties; we can no longer rely only on physical sciences for a description of the planet.

We have today thirty million distinguishable types of organisms (this may underestimate the number of living species by a factor of 100 or more). Each organism interacts with its local environment. Each organism requires the activities of other organisms not only for obtaining water, minerals, nutrients, and food, but also for removing its solid, liquid, and gaseous wastes. No individual, no matter how large or small, lives in a vacuum, nor can any feed off its own wastes. Indeed, every organism interacts with one or another gas; that is, each takes up one or more kinds of gas from the atmosphere and each emits a different quality and quantity of gas to the atmosphere. All metabolizing organisms exchange gases at all times. Many types, especially bacteria, protists, and plants, interact directly with surface rocks and minerals; many soil or mud-dwelling animals such as earthworms or brachio-pods produce, remove, or dramatically change the properties of sediment. The Gaia hypothesis forces us to consider the cumulative, that is, global, effects of these local phenomena. How can a diverse biota, for such a long period of time, maintain within certain limits the temperature, the reactive gas composition, and the acidity and alkalinity of the Earth's surface? Though much remains to be done, Gaian mechanisms of regulation are now being recognized and studied (Charlson et al., 1987; Barlow and Volk, 1990). The greatest hindrance to the study of Gaia is the fragmentation of science into a proliferating number of disciplines, departments, buildings, journals, and societies. Of course, physics, especially geophysics, chemistry, atmospheric sciences, astronomy, engineering, software and instrument development, and still other scientific fields are absolutely essential to the study of the planets. While we have long recognized that these disciplines are required for the study of Mars and Venus, the Gaia hypothesis forces us to conclude that to study the Earth, the results and insights from all of the subfields of biology, especially microbiology, are required. The conclusion is inescapable: geophysicists and atmospheric scientists must study biology and biologists must know something of geophysics and atmospheric science. For too long, we have had atmospheric chemists wondering "Where does all that methane come from?," and biologists ignorant of "Where all that methane goes."

Earth-based and space-borne studies of cloud-covered Venus have described a very dry planet surrounded by a CO_2-rich atmosphere (>95%) with dense mists of sulfuric acid. Ignoring the claims of American space scientists that the surface of Venus was too harsh an environment for the cameras, detectors, and other equipment of a soft-landing remote sensor, the Soviets have successfully landed at least sixteen *Venera* spacecraft on the surface of Venus. Their *Venera* results have confirmed what was inferred from telescopic, ground-based astronomical studies: Venus with its dry, CO_2 atmosphere, containing sulfate-particle–induced clouds, has an oxidized surface. When we train our analyzers on Mars we are again impressed by the extraordinary dryness of the red planet and the greater than 95% relative concentration of CO_2 in the Martian atmosphere. (Despite humanity's industrious ef-

forts, the Earth's concentration of atmospheric CO_2 is still < 0.04%). And whereas the Earth's surface has water-deposited sedimentary rocks over about 70% of its surface, Mars' surface has very little evidence for water-deposited sediments except for some exceedingly ancient dry "river" beds. Indeed, the loose regolith over most of the surface of Mars is presumably the product of meteoritic impact craters and volcanic debris. From the *Viking* landers and orbiters in 1975 and 1976, the results from ground-based telescope studies have been confirmed: Mars, like Venus, is a dry, CO_2-rich, thoroughly oxidized world. Both planets lack organic matter, they are dead—or they never harbored life at all.

If we look at the Earth with the same sort of space-borne, remote-sensing technologies, we are first aware of the great abundance of water on the surface. We can carefully choose places like the island of Hawaii, however, where a regolith of volcanic debris dominates and the evidence for life is not at first glance obvious (figure 2.1). Were only a simple camera lowered from space onto such bleak Earth environs, there would be no palpable evidence for the presence of life. Knowing this, Lovelock, in his first glimpse of Gaia, recognized that through its exchange of gases, the biota—regardless of its visible structure—leaves an imprint on the composition of the atmosphere. The cumulative effect of the biota's gas exchanges are planetary-scale chemical anomalies. As Lovelock tried to explain to his colleagues, these anomalies are the signature of life (Hitchcock and Lovelock, 1967; Lovelock, 1972). Whereas Venus and Mars presumably were formed from stellar media of very similar composition as the Earth, both are now dry, CO_2 planets with only trace quantities of water and oxygen in their atmospheres. The atmospheres of both Venus and Mars contain nitrogen as N_2 in relative gas con-

Figure 2.1 Hawaiian scene: the Earth without life? (Photo courtesy of Carmen Aguilar-Diaz.)

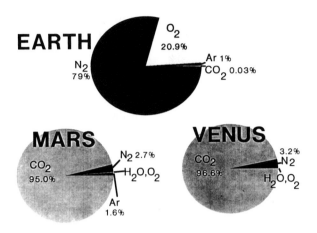

Figure 2.2 Earth, Venus, and Mars: relative concentrations of atmospheric gases.

centrations of < 3% (figure 2.2). Venus and Mars, as Lovelock is fond of saying, have atmospheres composed of "spent" gases. The gases (CO, CO_2, N_2) are "spent" in the sense that they no longer react with each other because they already have reacted. The atmospheres of Mars and Venus can be modeled without any obnoxious intrusion by biology. When the same analysis is extended to the Earth, many anomalies surface: Earth's atmosphere contains 20% oxygen (O_2), an explosively reactive compound (figure 2.2). The 80% nitrogen gas (N_2) in the Earth's atmosphere forms a reactive mixture with the 20% oxygen; when sparked by lightning, oxygen and nitrogen form the stable ion nitrate. Because there are many lightning storms at any one time, abundant opportunity for the atmospheric formation of nitrate (NO_2) exists on Earth. Yet the molecular species N_2 and O_2 prevail (table 2.1). Furthermore, these and many other chemical anomalies have existed in Earth's atmosphere for at least a billion years. Not only is the Earth's atmosphere an inherently reactive mixture, but the CO_2 concentration is astonishingly low (<0.04%). As CO_2 has been pumped out of the Earth's atmosphere and into calcium carbonate, the concentration of gaseous CO_2 has decreased, probably by

several orders of magnitude since the formation of the planet. Calcium and magnesium carbonates form fossiliferous limestone and dolomite, the majority of which were generated from the remains of shelly organisms. Unlike Mars and Venus, Earth has an atmosphere inexplicable without an awareness of the biological production and sequestration of such mobile elements as hydrogen, carbon, oxygen, and nitrogen.

Earth's atmosphere can be explained; only a certain set of elements are distributed in a chemically bizarre fashion. The set includes carbon, hydrogen, sulfur, phosphorus, nitrogen, and others, including many metals. The explanation is related to the fact that these elements strongly interact with life. That the Earth's atmosphere is not explicable by chemistry and physics alone is one of Lovelock's great insights. Given 20% oxygen in our atmosphere, there are what first appear to be inane quantities of other gases: too much nitrogen, far too much methane (by more than thirty-six orders of magnitude), far too much nitrous oxide, far too much ammonia, far too much methyl iodide, and far too much hydrogen (table 2.2). We could continue listing these; at last count over forty biogenic gases have been measured in the Earth's atmosphere (Levine, 1989). Since all of these compounds are burned by molecular oxygen in the atmosphere, there must be a constant and mammoth output or the concentrations of all these gases would soon be undetectably minute. What produces these enormous quantities of nitrogen, methane, hydrogen, nitrous oxide, and ammonia? The correct answer to all such questions is "bacteria." Some of these processes are exclusively bacterial: others are derived through bacterial interactions with other organisms. Nitrate is reduced to nitrogen and nitrous oxide by bacteria; methanogenesis is limited to certain anaerobic bacteria; ammonia is formed by bacterial breakdown of urea and uric acid; seaweeds or possibly their surface bacteria emit methyl iodide; hydrogen is a product of bacterial fermentation. The answer to the question of what produces the anomalous chem-

Table 2.1 Anomalous Atmosphere of Earth: Comparison of Planetary Atmospheres

	Venus	Earth	Mars	Units
CO_2	98	0.03	95	%
N_2	1.7	79	2.7	%
O_2	trace	21	0.13	%
H_2O	0.003	3000	0.00001	Meters
Pressure	90	1	0.0064	Bars
Temperature	477	17	−47	°C

Table 2.2 The Atmosphere Problem*

Gas	Abundance	Expected Equilibrium Concentration	Discrepancy	Residence Time (y)	Output (10^6 tons/y)
Nitrogen	0.8	10^{-10}	10^9	3 × 10^6	1000
Methane	1.5 × 10^{-6}	<10^{-35}	10^{29}	7	2000
Nitrous oxide	3 × 10^{-7}	10^{-20}	10^{13}	10	600
Ammonia	1 × 10^{-8}	<10^{-35}	10^{27}	.01	1500
Methyl iodide	1 × 10^{-12}	<10^{-35}	10^{23}	.001	30
Hydrogen	5 × 10^{-7}	<10^{-35}	10^{23}	2	20

*Assumes 20% oxygen.

istry of our atmosphere is almost always bacteria. Like the honey or wax of a beehive, the Earth's atmosphere, though certainly not alive, is largely a byproduct of life.

The principal anomalies of the present Earth relative to our neighbors are: too much atmospheric oxygen and too little CO_2. On Venus, the CO_2 is virtually all in the atmosphere, giving the planet an atmosphere ninety times as dense as the Earth's. The tenuous atmosphere of Mars (0.6 mbar) is mostly CO_2 as well, but whether carbonate rocks are present on the surface of the red planet is unknown (table 2.1). Since Earth, Venus, and Mars all started some 4.5 billion years ago with roughly the same chemical make-up, the lack of CO_2 in the Earth's atmosphere today suggests that a depletion of atmospheric CO_2 has been occurring throughout geologic time. (In fact, the long-term decrease in CO_2 will soon, geologically speaking, broach an environmental crisis for most plants [the C3 plants] as carbon becomes their limiting nutrient [Lovelock and Whitfield, 1982]). CO_2 has not disappeared from the Earth; removed from the air, most of the CO_2 can be accounted for by the biogenic precipitation into the sediments, many of which have been diagenetically altered to form marble, dolomite, and other carbon-containing rocks. These rocks were and are produced by the activities of microorganisms removing atmospheric CO_2 while producing molecular oxygen in the process of oxygenic photosynthesis. Given dilute concentrations of the proper salts, air, and of course light and water, oxygenic photosynthesizers sequester CO_2 and produce oxygen. This phenomenon is explicable by biology and completely unpredicted by the blind laws of chemistry.

Darwin recognized that all populations given unlimited resources had the capacity to grow exponentially. He called the many "checks" that keep all populations from ever reaching their reproductive potential "natural selection." However, Darwin failed to recognize the enormous impact the growth of populations have on their environment—that the environmental effects of growing and metabolizing populations of organisms are themselves potent agents of natural selection. In accentuating the direct competition between individuals for resources as the primary selection mechanism Darwin (and especially his followers) created the impression that the environment was simply a static arena for "nature, red in tooth and claw" (Tennyson, 1850). Darwin thus emphasized the separation of organisms from their environment. From bacteria to redwood trees, phytoplankton to beavers, the growth and metabolism of all organisms modify their environment. The Russian scientist Vladimir I. Vernadsky (1863–1945), who initiated the field of biogeochemistry, recognized that the divorce of the environment and the biota was artificial. Like most of his work, Vernadsky's comprehension of the interplay between the environment and the biota is almost unknown in the West. With the important exceptions of the great American ecologist G. Evelyn Hutchinson and the founder of biomineralization science, H.A. Lowenstam, few Western scientists recognized the inceptive contributions made by Vernadsky to modern ecological thought. By insisting on the competition between organisms as the main source of selection and by ignoring the chemical reciprocity between the biota and its environment, neo-Darwinists have amplified these errors of omission.

Of course Darwin's grand vision was not wrong, only incomplete. Ignorant of ecology, biogeochemistry, and geology, neo-Darwinism relinquished the ability to ask meaningful questions about the effects the evolution of life has had on the planet Earth. Neo-Darwinism's current funk over altruism reflects a failure to comprehend that every organism is dependent on a huge diversity of life as a source of respiratory gas, water, and food and as a sink for waste products. Do the planktonic algae in the oceans (those that release the sulfide gases that later seed the atmosphere with sulfate particles that act as condensation nuclei for cloud germination) act altruistically? Are cyanobacteria "public-spirited" in ridding themselves of their wastes—metabolically produced oxygen that happens to be necessary for the continued existence of all oxygen-respiring organisms? Are those bacteria that do not produce sulfide gases or oxygen "cheaters" and thus at a reproductive advantage? Richard Dawkins's (1982) claim that the Gaia hypothesis cannot be true because there is no evidence for competition between Earth, Venus, and Mars is reflective of neo-Darwinism's preoccupation with the romantic, Victorian conception of evolution as a prolonged and bloody battle. As a hypothesis, Gaia integrates the evolution of the biota with the well-documented transformations in the surface and atmospheric chemistry of the planet through geologic time. That the Gaia concept cannot be framed by the stilted terminology of neo-Darwinistic population biology is not surprising since Gaia is a hypothesis based in sciences that neo-Darwinism proudly ignores.

The study of Gaia intrinsically involves disciplines as disparate as atmospheric chemistry and microbial physiology. Lacking the social means to focus on the Earth as a living planet, we have just recently recognized the need for a mission to planet Earth. Without such interdisciplinary activities, most Gaian phenomena will remain unstudied. Indeed, the current division into disciplines often impedes science; as Lovelock has noted in his term "academic apartheid," "disciplinary science" interferes with an orderly study of the Earth as a planet. This kind of impedance is less familiar to the community of planetary scientists who have worked together to investigate Mars or Venus as entire objects of study. But such well-planned planetary-scale scientific collaboration has never been the case in the fragmented study of the history of Earth.

Although many details remain to be worked out, the Gaia phenomenon is a collective property of the growth, activities, and death of the myriad of populations that comprise the biota. Gaia involves exponential growth rates of living populations, and feedback related to the tendency of all life to respond to changes in the environment and to die when conditions exceed limits of survival. Sensory systems (to light, water, gravity, gas concentrations, pH, oxidation-reduction states, etc.) are diverse and well characterized in many organisms. The amplification of responses to changes in the en-

vironment in this feedback system lies in the exponential reproductive potential of all populations. The diversity of metabolic responses of organisms to environmental cues is related to the resiliency and change through time. The properties of living systems depend crucially on their history. They establish their own regulatory system which is maintained within their boundaries. These features make autopoietic (living) systems different from cybernetic ones.

Gaia and Grants

In the 1820s, the Bridgewater Treatises were commissioned by Reverend Francis Henry Egerton VIII, Earl of Bridgewater. A noble clergyman, according to Gillespie (1957), Egerton assiduously neglected his parish. A champion of science, the Earl of Bridgewater charged the executors of his will, the Archbishop of Canterbury, the Bishop of London, and the President of the Royal Society, with the duty of selecting eight scientific authors capable of demonstrating (here we quote Bridgewater's will) "the Power, the Wisdom and the Goodness of God, as manifest in the Creation, illustrating such work by all reasonable arguments, as for instance, the variety and formation of God's creatures in the animal, vegetable, and mineral kingdom; the effect of digestion, and thereby of conversion; the construction of the hand of man and an infinite variety of other arguments; as also by discoveries ancient and modern, in arts, sciences, and the whole extent of literature.[1] (Gillespie, 1957). Bridgewater's money and will supported many scientific activities. The Bridgewater Treatises were intended to offer a working epitome for the main branches of the natural sciences. The Treatises were expected to demonstrate the higher meaning of the order of nature and to ennoble empirical discovery into morality. These Treatises, products of the best British minds of the day, were to bring out the evidence of unity and design. The arguments were to show that a single-minded universe could not have risen by chance; it was statistically impossible for such an infinity of occurrences to work together for good without divine direction. Necessity established, it remained only to demonstrate benevolence—that is, to paraphrase the well-known Oxonian William Buckland (a founder of university geology courses

[1]All quotes referring to these Bridgewater Treatises are taken from Charles Coulston Gillespie's wonderful book *Genesis & Geology*.

of study): God's benevolence was shown via the proximity of Britain's iron ore to her coal and limestone. The Providence who ordained that the vegetable cycle coincided with the solar year was that same Providence who furnished man with a hand to work and a codfish with an eye that could see underwater. Since he gave money for these activities, Lord Bridgewater was greatly successful in obtaining the finest scientists in the British Isles to work on "the wisdom and the goodness of God, as manifest in the creation." Here we briefly discuss the contributions of five of the eight scientists whose work Bridgewater funded.

Professor and Reverend William Buckland was assigned geology and mineralogy. His appointment was to describe the clever position of the Earth in the solar system and the Deity's adequacy in his production of his durable creations. According to Buckland, "In all these we find such undeniable proofs of a nicely balanced adaptation of means to ends." We believe Buckland's interpretation of the word *adaptation* has not changed since 1830. Buckland continues, "Of wise foresight and benevolent intention and infinite power, that he must be blind indeed, who refuses to recognize in them the proofs of the most exalted attributes of the Creator." Buckland, in acceding to the wishes of his "granting agency," was trying to demonstrate a system of perpetual destruction followed by continual renovation that at all times tended to increase—in his terms—the aggregate of "animal enjoyment" over the entire surface of the "terraqueous globe."

Peter Mark Roget was dealt animal and vegetable physiology. He did not like to use the word *God* because he found it indecorous. Instead, he said, "In order to avoid the too frequent, and consequently irreverent, introduction of the Great Name of the SUPREME BEING into the familiar discourse on the operations of his power, I have . . . followed this common usage of implying the term *nature* as a synonym, expressive of the same power." The Reverend William Whewell was assigned astronomy and general physics. Whewell wrote that it was "impossible to exclude from our conception of this wonderful system, the idea of a harmonizing, a preserving, a contriving, an intending Mind of a Wisdom, a Power, and Goodness far exceeding the limits of our thoughts." So Whewell not only succeeds in finding what he was looking for, but he couches his conclusions in the same words as his request from the granting agency.

William Prough, according to Gillespie (1957),

was an important chemist. He was handed chemistry, meteorology, and the function of digestion. He said because we know comparatively little about chemistry and its laws, it is more apt to represent the Deity as a free agent. Chemistry demonstrates that all preceding creations were only anticipatory to the creation and governance of man or, he asks, ". . . What would have been the use of this elaborate design without man as its ulterior object."

William Kirby was assigned "the animal kingdom." He felt he was particularly fortunate in the ease with which the manifestation of the power and wisdom of goodness of God can be shown because—he thought—the animal kingdom offered conclusive demonstration of both the Fall of Man and the subsequent exertions of Creative Power. No one could suppose—he noted—that Adam and Eve in their pristine state of glory were prey to such disgusting later creations as lice, fleas, and intestinal worms, which now befall the sinner's lot! (Gillespie, 1957).

These were the criterion for the selection of science projects in the 1820s. We now cite from a published booklet of the United States National Science Foundation's (NSF's) guidelines for criterion for the selection of research projects in 1988.

1. Intrinsic merit. This is the most important criterion according to the National Science Foundation. This criterion is used to assess the likelihood that the research will lead to new discoveries or fundamental advances within its field of science.

2. Utility or relevance. This refers to the likelihood that the research can contribute to the achievement of an extrinsic goal, one in addition to that of the research field itself, and can thereby serve as the basis for new or improved technology.

3. Effect of the research. The research should contribute to a better understanding of improvement of the quality, distribution or effectiveness of the nation's [the United States] scientific and engineering research, education, and manpower base.

So, although we have dropped loyalty to God and Christianity, we still have loyalty to the field and loyalty to the nation as the two highest criteria. Just these three short statements show the intrinsic contradictions in pleasing the granting agencies and working on the Gaia hypothesis.

4. Integration. The National Science Foundation looks forward to "using and integrating the re-

sources of all institutions in the support of science and engineering in their contributions to society and to this nation."

Indeed, the overall guidelines are less objectionable than those in given fields—and of course any investigator must apply through some given field of study. Here, for example is a short version of guidelines to the NSF subfield "population biology and physiological ecology," which Lovelock has told us is intrinsic to Gaian studies of the atmosphere because of the role of exponential population growth in Gaian control systems. The purpose of the field of population biology and physiological ecology is to find the genetic basis for "adaptive traits." Adaptive traits adapt organisms as means to an end, according to William Buckland. The term *adaptation* is still prominent in the 1988 brochure. The atmosphere, in the organization of the NSF, has nothing to do with population biology and physiological ecology. These sciences, very far away from biology, are classified as belonging to the study of the physics, chemistry, and dynamics of the earth's upper and lower atmosphere, If the earth's lower atmosphere is deeply involved with microbiology and population biology but the charge to atmosphericists is to study the physics, chemistry, and dynamics of the earth's lower atmosphere, and to ignore all of biology, how can one submit proposals to study gaian phenomena and be funded? It is not possible. The guidelines go on to endorse research providing further insights into the physical and chemical characteristics and processes that produce such geological features as hydrocarbon and ore deposits. Throughout the meetings of the Chapman conference of the American Geophysical Union, reference was repeatedly made to the concept that coal, hydrocarbon gas, and many types of ore deposits are related to evolutionary biology, especially microbiology. The ignorance of these interrelationships is institutionalized by those who make scientific policy at the NSF and other governmental agencies responsible for funding science in the United States.

Our points are: (1) Gaian science is ignored because there is no way to apply for financial support that will involve integrated study; and (2) we have legacies of religious, social, and historical points of view that have not disappeared just because it is 1991. These legacies are so intrinsic to our thinking and the way we attend to our scientific business that unless we are aware of our social embeddedness as scientists, we simply cannot proceed with

the science required to verify or reject the Gaia hypothesis.

Vladimir Vernadsky always thought in global terms, although not, of course, in modern language; certainly he did not compare directly the surface features of Earth, Venus, and Mars. Vernadsky wrote, not in Russian, but in the *Transactions of the Connecticut Academy of Sciences,* a key paper on biogeochemistry (1944). Just before he died, in 1945, he published a paper in a magazine well known to most scientists, Sigma Xi's *The American Scientist.* G. Evelyn Hutchinson, professor at Yale University and a colleague of George Vernadsky, Vladimir's son, introduced Vernadsky's paper to this journal. These two contributions, one to the *Transactions of the Connecticut Academy of Sciences* and the other to *The American Scientist* together present in English the general intellectual outlook of one of the most remarkable scientific leaders of the present century (Grinevald, 1988). Thus Vernadsky's vision, which preceded, of course, Lovelock's development of the Gaia concept, was not ignored merely because his work was unavailable in English. Although most of his books were published in Russian, Vernadsky's "The Biosphere" has been available in French since 1929. Furthermore, he wrote, "In everyday life, one used to speak of man as an individual living and moving freely about our planet, freely building up his history until recently the historians and the students of the humanities and to a certain extent even the biologists consciously failed to reckon with the natural laws of the biosphere, the only terrestrial envelope within which life can exist. Basically man cannot be separated from it; it is only now that this solubility begins to appear clearly and in precise terms before us. Man is geologically connected with the biosphere, its material, and energetic structure. Actually no living organisms exist on Earth in a state of freedom. All organisms are connected indissolubly and uninterruptedly first of all, through nutrition and respiration, and secondly, with the circumambience material and its energetic medium" (Vernadsky, 1945).

We anticipate with enthusiasm the recognition of Lovelock's worldview of the environment modulated by life and Vernadsky's worldview of life as a geological force by the NSF, NASA, National Center for Atmospheric Research (NCAR), Department of Energy, Department of Defense, Office of Naval Research, and private foundations on which we scientists depend—as Buckland depended on the Earl of Bridgewater—for our funding. We wait, that is, for the era of the Gaian biosphere and its appropriately funded science to arrive (Sagan, 1988, 1990).

Notes

Criteria for the selection of research projects by the NSF taken from the National Science Board policy statement NSB-79-100. p. 9

References

Barlow, C., and Volk, T. 1990. Open systems living in a closed biosphere: A new paradox for gaia debate. *BioSystems,* 23, 371–384.

Charlson, R.J., Lovelock, J.E., Andreae, M.O., and Warren, S.G. 1987. Oceanic phytoplankton, atmospheric sulphur, cloud albedo and climate. *Nature,* 326, 655–661.

Dawkins, R. 1982. *The Extended Phenotype.* San Francisco: W.H. Freeman & Co.

Gillespie, C.C. 1957. *Genesis & Geology.* Cambridge, Mass.: Harvard University Press.

Grinevald, J. 1988. A history of the idea of the biosphere. In: Bunyard, P., and Goldsmith, E., eds. *Gaia: the Thesis, the Mechanisms and the Implications. Proceedings of the First Annual Camelford Conference on the Implications of the Gaia Hypothesis.* Wadebridge, Cornwall, UK: Quintrell & Co. Ltd.

Hitchcock, D.R., and Lovelock, J.E. 1967. Life detection by atmospheric analysis. *Icarus,* 7, 149–159.

Levine, J.S. 1989. Photochemistry of biogenic gases. In: Rambler, M.B., Margulis, L., and Fester, R., eds. *Global Ecology. Towards a Science of the Biosphere.* San Diego, CA: Academic Press, 51–74.

Lovelock, J.E. 1972. Gaia as seen through the atmosphere. *Atmospheric Environment,* 6, 579–580.

Lovelock. J.E. 1988. *The Ages of Gaia.* New York: W.W. Norton, Co.

Lovelock, J.E., and Whitfield, M. 1982. Life span of the biosphere. *Nature,* 296, 561–563.

Sagan, D. 1988. What Narcissus saw: The oceanic "I"/ "EYE". In: Brockman, J., ed. *The Reality Club.* New York: Lynx Books,

Sagan, D. 1990. *Biospheres. Metamorphosis of Planet Earth.* New York: McGraw-Hill Publishing Co.

Tennyson, A. 1850. In memoriam, stanza 4.

Vernadsky, V.I. 1929. *La Biosphere.* Expurgated version translated under the title *The Biosphere.* 1986. Oracle, AZ: Synergetic Press.

Vernadsky, V.I. 1944. Problems of biogeochemistry. Translated by George Vernadsky, edited and condensed by G. Evelyn Hutchinson. *Transactions of the Connecticut Academy of Arts and Science,* 35, 483–517.

Vernadsky, V.I. 1945. The biosphere and the noosphere. *The American Scientist,* 33, 1–12.

Paul Ehrlich

3

Coevolution and Its Applicability to the Gaia Hypothesis

Steve Schneider has removed the idea of coevolution from its strict biological context to apply it to the coevolution of climate and life.[1] It is perfectly fair and reasonable for him to say that climate and life have coevolved. The organisms of the planet have had an enormous impact on the evolution of the atmosphere, and reciprocally, the evolution of the biosphere has obviously had an enormous impact on biological evolution. But, trouble begins if you start to think that the two kinds of coevolution are really all that similar. It is a useful heuristic device to speak of coevolution in this context, but the nonphysical parts of the biosphere do not evolve in the same sense that the biological parts do.

Because it is often discussed in connection with Gaia and often misunderstood, I would like to start with a brief outline of the topic of coevolution as viewed by biologists. Coevolution focuses on what people have long known was occurring but have largely ignored: the reciprocal evolutionary interactions of ecologically intimate species.

I started to work in this area serendipitously. Peter Raven and I were talking about the different plants that were attacked by the larvae of different butterflies. Although it did not occur to us at first, butterflies and plants are the most thoroughly understood series of eaters and eaten. The reason is simple: butterfly collectors want perfect specimens. Perfect specimens are obtained by discovering the food plant of the butterfly's caterpillars, collecting the caterpillars, and feeding them that plant. The caterpillars grow up and form pupae within which they are transformed into beautiful butterflies. As soon as the butterfly's wings are fully extended, they are killed, making perfect specimens. Therefore, it is very important for butterfly collectors to know the food plants of caterpillars, and an extensive literature exists on that subject. Peter and I soon noticed when surveying that literature that plant biochemistry, in particular the array of "secondary compounds" present, seemed to determine which plants got eaten by whom. Until that

time, it was thought that those energy-rich compounds were excretory products!

These plant biochemicals are now recognized to be primarily defenses against the organisms that eat plants from inside or from out—beetles, butterflies, buffalo, bacteria, fungi, viruses, and so on. We make enormous use of these compounds ourselves as spices, medicines, industrial products, insecticides, and mind-blowing drugs.

A quarter of a century ago Peter and I wrote a paper on coevolution of which we are inordinately proud. It more or less established the now-booming field of coevolutionary studies and is probably the best-known paper either of us have written. But the reason we are proud is that we did all the research and wrote the paper without looking at a single organism, alive or dead. We looked only in the literature, which proves the Ehrlich-Raven hypothesis that, if you want to write a well-known paper, you should "study books and not nature."

Peter and I thought we had invented the concept, but I subsequently discovered that Darwin had had much the same idea. In fact, I would not be surprised if Jim Lovelock searched Darwin's work from end to end and found that Darwin was prescient about Gaia, too.

Let me quote some of the things Darwin said that are strictly about coevolution: "When we look at the plants and bushes clothing an entangled bank, we are tempted to attribute their proportional numbers and kinds to what we call chance. But how false a view is this." He then goes on to talk about ancient Indian mounds in the southern United States covered with tangled vegetation, and he said, "What a struggle between the several kinds of trees must here have gone on during the long centuries, each annually scattering its seeds by the thousands; what war between insect and insect—between insects, snails, and other animals with birds and beasts of prey—all striving to increase, and all feeding on each other or on the trees or their seeds and seedlings, or on other plants which first clothed the ground and thus checked the growth of the trees! Throw up a handful of feathers, and all must fall to the ground according to definite laws; but how simple is this problem compared to the action and reaction of innumerable plants and animals which have determined, in the course of centuries, the proportional numbers and kinds of trees now growing on the old Indian ruins!"[2]

The interactions of predators and prey, of competitors, of mutualists, of hosts and parasites, and so forth, "all striving to increase," are now recognized as a major driving force in evolution.

I think the contribution of our butterfly-plant work was of the same general kind as Jim Lovelock's and Lynn Margulis' contribution with the Gaia hypothesis. There have been many arguments about the exact nature of coevolution—how diffuse is it? How often is there actually a one-to-one coupling? Are coevolutionary interactions normally stabilizing or destabilizing?—and so forth. But what our paper did was to make ecologists recognize that relationships between plant and herbivore, host and parasite, competitor and competitor, and so forth, involve reciprocal evolutionary interactions. Before the discipline of coevolution began to develop rapidly about twenty-five years ago, parasitologists characteristically looked at hosts, including human hosts, as unchanging entities. They sometimes studied the evolution of parasites, but not in a context of evolving host defenses. Entomologists looked at host-plant choice in insects, but did not think about the defensive evolutionary responses of plants.[3]

I think that the Gaia hypothesis, in a similar way, has brought home to scientists and laypeople alike the great importance of interactions between the living and nonliving parts of the biosphere. It is making people think about a lot of things they would not have considered without the hypothesis. So whether the weak or strong form of a hypothesis (or neither) is right does not make much difference. Hypotheses in science are things to test; and if Gaia induces a lot of scientists to work on the interactions between the physical earth and the planet's biota, it will have served an important purpose even if it is totally incorrect.

Now let me say a few things about coevolution and Gaia. Although coevolution has been used in a broader sense, strictly speaking, it concerns interactions between evolving populations of organisms. Both physical-chemical systems evolve and organisms evolve, but the two evolve in very different ways. When strictly coevolutionary interactions are considered, one must think in terms of arrays of selection coefficients and how the selection coefficients on each side of the reciprocal interactions change each other. Coevolution must be analyzed in terms of differential reproduction. Differential reproduction of genetic types (genotypes) in which the differentials are too high to be assigned to chance events is the key to how biological systems evolve. It is the process of natural selection.

When detailed analyses of coevolutionary relationships are done, there are a lot of complications. For example, there is reason to believe that coevolutionary interactions in which each player gains a net benefit are much less likely to occur than coevolutionary interactions based on attack and defense or simply competition. Mutualistic coevolution requires more unusual circumstances than the less cooperative sorts.

Another thing to remember in applying coevolutionary thinking to Gaia is that most coevolutionary relationships undoubtedly end with a loser. What we call *selectional races* occur, and one can only observe those now in progress. A plant may be free of the attack of caterpillars because it has been successful in building up its chemical defenses. We would not even know the selectional race had occurred, because the losing butterflies are extinct. In other cases, the plants may have been unsuccessful. Butterflies or other insects may have evolved the ability to detoxify the plant defenses, the plants failed to evolve new ones fast enough, and disappeared.

It is an error to take a too-benign view of nature. There is a tendency to assume that organisms create environments that are good for themselves. To field biologists, that is far from self-evident. For instance, if the temperature and pattern of rainfall is just right, populations of the butterflies in our group studies explode in size. They then completely defoliate and destroy their annual host plants, which have a very small seed bank. That butterfly population then may become extinct. In fact, extinction of populations is a very common phenomenon in the systems we have worked with. A simple mathematical exercise that determines the extinction rates of populations can be used to predict how long it will be before the entire species disappears too. One cannot say that coevolution is itself stabilizing or destabilizing, because it may be either, and changes in other factors may alter the balance. Nor can one claim that organisms coevolve with their environments to make those environments more hospitable, although that may sometimes be a result.

The coevolutionary development of a benign terrestrial environment has been compared to the evolution of benign microclimates inside ant nests. It is quite true that ants do make and maintain nests that produce favorable environmental conditions for themselves, but the analogy is otherwise fallacious. Ants and nests did not coevolve any more than you and your hair coevolved. An ant colony is, in essence, an individual—a reproductive unit. The nest can be thought of as a nonliving part of the colonial individual, just as your hair is nonliving. Climatically regulated ant nests are the result of a selective process in which billions of ant colonies with less well regulated domiciles perished. Our Earth's evolutionary past is not littered with the remains of billions of other planets where life did not manage to coevolve successfully with its physical environment.

The essence of biological evolution is self-replication with variation and then differential reproduction of the variants, which also replicate themselves. That is really all there is to the creative aspect of the process. There are no similar mechanisms in the physical world. The closest are some superficially similar processes in crystals, but they are not really comparable to what occurs in living systems. Life in that sense is a very special thing. You could talk about ocean currents and a sand bar coevolving. The ocean current affects the sand bar. As the sand bar changes, it affects the ocean current. But it is not the same thing as the coevolution of, say, hosts and parasites.

Another analogy may make the distinction clearer. For a long time now, the interior of Australia has been dry. Every once in a while, it gets a lot of rain. When that happens, a large depression fills with water and Lake Eyre appears. But the area is hotter than hell, and Lake Eyre evaporates away. It has not found any way to replicate itself, and there is no variant offspring of Lake Eyre that is more resistant to evaporation and able to persist through the drought.

Various Australian organisms, such as certain insects, some parrots, and some reptiles, *have* evolved in response to the drought-flood cycles. Because they are self-replicating with variation and subject to differential reproduction, organisms can evolve forms that can survive those hideous droughts in the middle of Australia. Lakes, lacking those attributes, have not evolved persistent forms.

So again, there is a very important difference between two biological systems coevolving and a biological system "coevolving" with a physical system or two physical systems "coevolving" with each other. In the first case, there are evolutionary rules that permit detailed analysis. The other two cases simply are analogies; very educational as long as one does not carry them too far. That is why in the context of Gaia, I find myself taking a reductionist position; the idea that life evolves in a way to make the planet more hospitable for itself collapses for want of a mechanism.

It seems to me crystal clear and indisputable that the weak form of the Gaia hypothesis is very strongly supported. There has been an enormous impact on the physical character of the planet by the organisms of the planet. Obviously, there also are homeostatic aspects to the system, as are described in other chapters in this volume. There clearly are many interesting negative feedback loops, as well. Nonetheless, I find it very hard to believe that the physical Earth in some direct or even indirect sense is evolving to make life comfortable for the organisms on it.

As has been pointed out by others, if we were a bunch of anaerobes meeting at that time long ago when photosynthetic organisms were poisoning us with oxygen, we would have a different view. I doubt we would have thought the planet was making things comfortable for life when we had to retreat to termite guts or deep in the muck under swamp waters to survive.

I think that the same thing can be said today when we have one species that is now using or coopting at least 25% of the planet's net primary productivity. I see no signs that we, as the dominant organisms on the planet, are in any way acting to make it more hospitable for life. Many mechanisms have tended to make the planet more hospitable, but I just do not see these mechanisms as having evolved with that as a goal. In fact, if I were to propose a non-Gaia hypothesis, it would be that life has been extremely fortunate. Serendipitously, a lot of negative feedback loops have developed that have so far prevented *Homo sapiens* or life itself from disappearing. I think this is an equally interesting hypothesis. Perhaps the experiment of life on Earth just hasn't been running that long, and has already had some bad moments. One of these days, life will run out of luck.

When one looks around the universe and asks, "Is there a lot of other life out there"? nobody has the first clue. When we are feeling good about ourselves, we think life must be everywhere, and, during a period of shortage, we think life is confined to Earth. Nobody knows the answer, but maybe life is very, very scarce simply because most planetary systems have not serendipitously accumulated enough negative feedback mechanisms to support life as long as Earth has.

The challenge for those who wish to support the strong version of the Gaia hypothesis is to discover some process by which the planet could have accumulated homeostatic mechanisms that favor life. By what process could Earth have learned to sense that state of the biosphere and acquire the "goal" of keeping its biota alive? It is not enough just to have some negative feedback loops that help keep the planet hospitable and to note that life has persisted so far. For the strong version of the Gaia hypothesis to be supported, how Earth could have evolved the characteristics of an organism must be elucidated.

Notes

I thank Anne Ehrlich, Jonathan Roughgarden, and Peter Vitousek for helpful comments on this manuscript.

1. e.g., Schnieder, S.H., and Londer, R. 1984. *The Coevolution of Climate and Life.* San Francisco: Sierra Club Books.

2. Darwin, C. 1859. *The Origin of Species.* London: John Murray, 74–75.

3. For access to the literature of coevolution see Thompson, J.N., 1982. *Interaction and Coevolution.* New York: Wiley; and D.J. Futuyma and M. Slatkin, eds. 1983. *Coevolution.* Sunderland, Mass.: Sinauer.

Walter Shearer

4

A Selection of Biogenic Influences Relevant to the Gaia Hypothesis

Interactions between the biota and the geosphere are fundamental to the Gaia hypothesis (Lovelock and Margulis, 1974). Although examples of the influence of the geosphere on the biota, such as the effects of climate, soil, and hydrology on the distribution of biomes and individual floral and faunal species, are well known, far fewer are the processes so far identified by which the biota can influence climate, soil, and hydrology. Yet the existence of biogenic influences on the environment is essential to the Gaia hypothesis. Furthermore, if homeostasis occurs as postulated, the biotic agents must be connected with the environment through a negative feedback loop.

Research continues to uncover evidence that points to the existence of several previously unsuspected biogenic influences. I have assembled here an inventory of the stronger and more interesting cases of such influences, including those that have been only postulated as well as those that are supported by some evidence. In addition, the interesting and relevant evidence of plant-to-plant communication is considered as one of the many possible information linkages in the biosphere.

In reviewing some of the biogenic influences whose existence is not in doubt or that have been suspected for some time, one obvious set concerns vegetation. The presence and type of vegetation cover are recognized to have a significant influence on such physical parameters as albedo, surface roughness, atmospheric humidity (through evapotranspiration), and rainfall, and thus on climate and soil erosion. Similarly the biota can influence the nutrient composition of soil.

Looking more closely at one of these parameters, it is generally believed that tropical moist forest controls to some extent the regional water cycle. In nonforested areas, rain water is primarily recycled, through run-off and rivers that flow to the sea, where it evaporates and forms clouds that can then redeposit the water as rain. The tropical forest short-circuits this process and influences the temperature and humidity of its environment with large leaf surfaces that intercept the rainwater and provide areas for it to evaporate (while also directly cooling the leaves) into clouds that can produce more rain and shield the forest from radiation. This reduces the air temperature in the forest and prevents it from drying out. From experimental determinations of the water balance in a test basin in the Amazon region (Franken et al., 1982; Leopoldo et al., 1984; and Salati and Vose, 1984), it appears that in that region on the average about half of the rain is evapo-transpired back into the atmosphere, about 25% is intercepted by foliage and immediately evaporated from leaf surfaces, and the remaining quarter flows out of the basin as runoff.

Deacon (1979) has proposed another biogenic influence in the marine environment. It involves the suppression of wave action by coral through the production of a lipid substance containing cetyl palmitate (Benson and Muscatine, 1974) that hydrolyzes to form two powerful surfactants on the ocean surface, thereby altering the surface tension and thus the intensity of wave action. These alterations have been observed in the vicinity of coral reefs as surprisingly small wind stress on the water over a fringing reef (Hicks et al., 1974) and as anomalous wavelengths of ocean waves in satellite remote-sensing images (Lovelock, 1988).

It might be useful to recall the biogenic influences of global proportions that Lovelock (1979), and in some cases others, have proposed. One is the probability that trees and other vegetation, as well as bacteria, are engaged in keeping the atmospheric oxygen concentration within tolerable limits by adjusting their metabolism and therefore oxygen expiration in response to the current oxygen concentration. A second is the possibility of control of the salt concentration in the oceans by corals that build reefs that form lagoons wherein large quantities of salts are trapped as the seawater evaporates.

The views expressed in this article are those of the author and are not necessarily those of either the United Nations or the United Nations University.

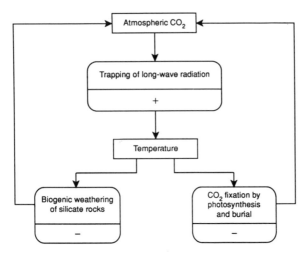

Figure 4.1 Major features of feedback loops for biogenic control of climatic temperature. Measurable physical quantities are in rectangular boxes and processes that change these quantities are in rounded boxes. The sign in a rounded box indicates whether the quantity in the rectangular box immediately downstream increases (+) or decreases (−) for an increase in the quantity in the rectangular box immediately upstream as a result of the process indicated.

Finally, there is the proposal regarding the involvement of CO_2 and the biogenic weathering of rock in global temperature regulation (Lovelock and Watson, 1982; Lovelock and Whitfield, 1982), shown schematically in figure 4.1. The terrestrial and marine biota are sensitive to temperature change and react by changing their rates of CO_2 uptake directly or indirectly from the atmosphere (with subsequent long-term burial) and the rate of CO_2 removed due to biologically induced weathering of silicate rocks. The atmospheric CO_2 concentration then determines the temperature, because the efficiency of long-wave radiation trapping in the atmosphere depends on the atmospheric CO_2 concentration.

Some attention has been given to the question of how vegetation and CO_2 interact. The response of terrestrial vegetation to changes in atmospheric CO_2 concentration, both directly on growth and through climate, is unclear due in part to the effect of clouds. Idso et al. (1987) have reported from experiments with three terrestrial and two floating aquatic plant species that the effect of CO_2 concentration on plant growth is dependent on air temperature. For a doubling of the current CO_2 concentration, plant growth is enhanced with increasing mean daily temperature above 18.5°C but is reduced when the temperature is below this critical value. Another major consideration has been raised by Mooney et al. (1987): it is unclear how the veg-

etation decomposition rate varies with changes in atmospheric CO_2 concentration. Although the decomposition rate could increase with CO_2 enrichment, it might decrease if vegetation growth is nutrient limited. This decrease would be the result of the production of plant tissues with higher carbon-to-nutrient ratios under such conditions leading to lower rates of nutrient release with an ultimate decrease in productivity.

Vegetation is known to be the source of numerous gases. In addition to water, carbon dioxide, and oxygen, the following relatively stable gases are produced: methane, nitrous oxide, and carbonyl sulfide. In addition, more reactive gases such as isoprene, terpenes, carbon monoxide, the oxides of nitrogen (NO_x), ammonia, hydrogen sulfide, dimethylsulfide, methyl mercaptan, and carbon disulfide are generated by vegetation. The impacts of most of these gases on the environment have not been unraveled, but some of them could play key roles in environmental control, at least on the local scale.

Acid Rain from Tropical Forest Ants

Graedel and Eisner (1988) have estimated that in the Amazon basin, where many of the world's approximately 3×10^{14} formicine ants live, these ants should produce about 5×10^{11} g of formic acid annually and be responsible for about 25% of the acid in rain that falls there (Anon., 1987). It is not yet clear what geophysiological control function ant-generated mildly acidic rain might play. One possibility (figure 4.2) is the promotion of the decomposition and recycling of vegetation. Although there

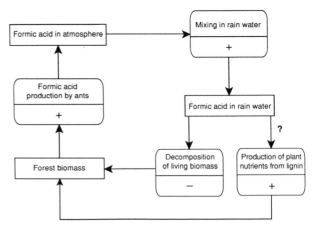

Figure 4.2 Possible feedback loop for the control of acid rain production by formicine ants in tropical forests. (See figure 4.1 for explanation of conventions used.)

are many biological agents that rapidly decompose foliage, formic acid in rain could serve a useful role in accelerating the breakdown of lignin and thereby liberating nutrients that would promote plant growth. Obviously, excess acid rain could adversely affect the living vegetation and, indirectly through the food cycle, reduce the ant population and thus formic acid production. According to this view, formicine ant activity, which results in the dispersion of formic acid largely as a byproduct of defense and communication, indirectly promotes the decomposition and recycling of lignin in dead wood. However, this positive feedback loop is restrained by the simultaneous formic acid control of the living biomass, including the food eaten by the ants. More research on the tropical forest ecosystem will be needed to evaluate the plausibility of this mechanism in the context of the other possibilities that exist.

Dimethylsulfide from Marine Phytoplankton

The most exciting recent proposal of a biogenic influence on the environment concerns the possibility that cloud albedo over the open oceans is influenced by algae that produce dimethylsulfide (DMS) (Charlson et al., 1987), as outlined schematically in figure 4.3. In effect the phytoplankton would be able to protect themselves from excessive insolation or sea surface temperature, such as might occur as a result of atmospheric carbon dioxide enrichment.

In order for negative feedback to be established, warmer seas or greater irradiance below the clouds would have to stimulate phytoplankton to flourish and increase their production of the DMS they release. Once in the atmosphere the DMS oxidizes producing submicroscopic aerosols of sulfate salts. These aerosols serve as nuclei for the condensation of water droplets in clouds over the ocean, so that the size of droplets decreases as the number of nuclei increases. The cloud albedo is higher for clouds composed of small droplets, so the incoming solar radiation and the sea surface temperature are reduced. When the temperature decreases excessively, DMS production would have to be relaxed, thereby increasing cloud droplets and allowing the clouds to transmit more sunlight to the sea surface. In fact, it is not clear whether increased water temperature and increased insolation result in increased DMS production by the phytoplankton.

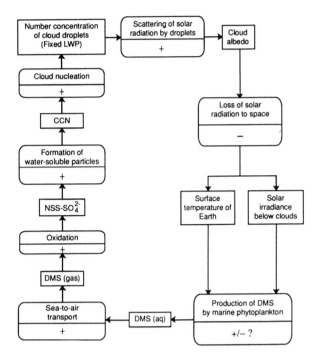

Figure 4.3 Main features of a possible feedback loop involving marine phytoplankton in the control of temperature using cloud cover. (From Charlson et al., 1987). LWP: liquid water path, NSS: non-sea salt, CCN: cloud condensation nuclei. (See figure 4.1 for explanation of conventions used.)

Although nutrients, especially nitrogen, generally limit phytoplankton growth, Lovelock (1988) has also pointed out that the algae also benefit from the rain produced from the clouds. Compounds of nitrogen that the algae need for growth are carried down in the falling raindrops, and the rain increases wind velocity, which stirs surface waters, thereby providing the algae with access to nutrients from the lower ocean layers.

All processes in the main feedback loop have not been measured to determine if the system is actually functioning with negative feedback. The major uncertainties seem to be (1) whether the response of marine plankton to increased sea surface temperature or insolation is to increase or decrease the total DMS production, and (2) the relative production of cloud droplets by cloud condensation nuclei from biologically generated DMS and by salt particles in the marine atmosphere. However, recent studies (Bates et al., 1987) have found a seasonal and latitudinal correlation between DMS fluxes and the numbers of cloud nuclei in the marine atmosphere. This is a relatively easily tested hypothesis and one that has done much to attract attention to the important potential of biogenic influences on the environment, especially for global-scale climate control.

Chlorocarbons Produced by Fungi

Natural sources of chloromethane are responsible for generating annually about five million tons and one quarter of the ozone-depleting chloromethane in the stratosphere. Among these natural sources, the richest source is the wood-rotting bracket fungi of the cosmopolitan genera *Phellinus* and *Inonotus*. Harper (1986) has recently identified twenty-seven species of these fungi, which live on trees and organic litter in tropical and temperate forests, as producers of chloromethane, which they use to forcibly discharge their basidiospores as part of the process of reproduction. He found that about half of these species are able to convert more than 10% of the sodium chloride in their medium to chloromethane. Although the chlorocarbons have a half-life of about three years, they can still produce chlorine in the stratosphere that catalytically decomposes the ozone there. By reducing the solar ultraviolet radiation–intercepting ozone layer, the fungi may threaten the forest biomass on which they depend by exposing it to increased ultraviolet irradiation. In this way, the negative feedback loop shown in figure 4.4 would restrict their numbers and the chloromethane flux. In this case, the biotic agents, the fungi, seem to be able to influence the environment but to no obvious advantage for themselves.

Stimulation of Precipitation by Bacteria

For more than a decade, workers (Schnell, 1975a; Schnell and Vali, 1976; Vali et al., 1976; Maki and Willoughby, 1978; Lindow et al., 1978; Schnell et al., 1981; Yankofsky et al., 1981; Schnell and Tan-

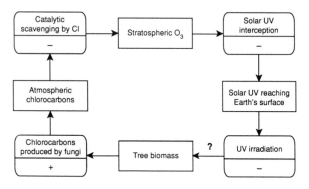

Figure 4.4 Major features of a feedback loop involving the stimulation of stratospheric ozone destruction by fungi. UV; ultraviolet light. (See figure 4.1 for conventions used.)

Schnell, 1982; Lindemann et al., 1982) have been studying the ice-nucleation properties, behavior, and distribution of bacteria that are very effective ice-nucleating agents and that have been implicated in the initiation of precipitation.

In particular, *Pseudomonas syringae*, closely related *P. fluorescens,* and *Erwinia herbicola* have been identified as the bacteria involved at least in terrestrially generated ice nucleation. Inorganic soil particles and extraterrestrial dust have generally been considered to be common ice-nucleating agents. But these bacteria were found to be 100 to 1,000 times more active ice nucleators than are dust particles, as determined by the ratio of active nuclei resulting in the condensation of water into ice to the total number of nuclei in the cloud. Evidence points to the fact that for *P. syringae,* the bacterial cells themselves are the nucleators and, more precisely, that the lipoproteins contained in the coats of the bacteria are the active agents. These lipoproteins can be shed from the bacteria to produce stable but less active nuclei when the bacteria die. Ecologically, these bacteria assist the decay of plant material and leave on litter lipoprotein products that in turn can be dispersed into the atmosphere where they serve as ice nucleators. However, entire bacteria have been recovered from air samples including two types, only one of which was partially identified as *Pseudomonas* sp., taken from the Arctic atmosphere where they were found to be 10 times more abundant in clouds than outside clouds (Jayaweera and Flanagan, 1982). The ice nuclei appear to be more abundant where vegetation and thus leaf litter are denser. Some observations indicate that a large proportion of active ice nuclei occurring in the atmosphere over land may be derived from decayed vegetation.

Tropical forests with high densities of vegetation appear to provide an ideal environment for supporting large populations of the bacteria. Thus it can be envisaged, as outlined in figure 4.5, that tropical forests could harbor vast populations of these bacteria, which stimulate the extraction of rain from passing clouds. The rain then promotes vegetation growth, which results in more leaf litter and more ice-nucleating bacteria. The positive feedback loop connecting these processes is probably limited by the moisture available in the clouds. As a local biogenic influence, the mechanism could be useful in reforestation projects where the climates are satisfactory.

In addition, it can be concluded from other scien-

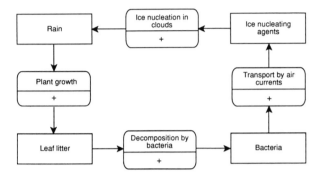

Figure 4.5 Main elements of a possible feedback loop for the stimulation of rainfall by bacteria. (See figure 4.1 for conventions used.)

tific work that air-borne bacterial and phytoplankton species are involved in stimulating rain in coastal marine environments where the sea supports an abundance of life forms (Bigg, 1973; Schnell, 1975b; Schnell and Vali, 1975 and 1976; Schnell, 1977; Nagamoto et al., 1984; Fall and Schnell, 1985). However, it is interesting to contemplate the prospect that a single of the multitude of interacting species in a tropical rain forest may be charged with the critical responsibility of bringing the rain on which the survival of the entire ecosystem depends.

Biogenic Weathering

Recent studies have identified a number of roles the biota can play in weathering, particularly of silicates. In fact, there are strong arguments that the rate of silicate weathering is biologically determined (Lovelock and Whitfield, 1982; Schwartzman and Volk, 1989).

In a study of the effect of weathering of silicate rocks on atmospheric carbon dioxide and temperature, Schwartzman and Volk (1989) considered several biological weathering-enhancing roles. A very important role involves the interaction of the biota and soil. Not only is the biota an active producer of soil, but the soil microbial and plant life (from algae to vascular plants) are also essential to stabilizing soil and inhibiting its erosion. The accumulated soil enhances chemical reactions by providing large surface areas and retaining water that can act as a medium for acid attack.

Although Schwartzman and Volk also considered the role of the biota in the microfracturing of mineral grains and the elevation of carbon dioxide partial pressures in the soil by soil biota and root respiration (see also Volk, 1987), another important

biotic role involves the production of acids and chelating agents by microorganisms (Duff et al., 1963; Silverman and Ehrlich, 1964; Aristovska et al., 1969; and Ehrlich, 1981), lichens (Schwartzman and Volk, 1989), plant roots, and root mycorrhizae (primarily fungi) (Knoll and James, 1987). These acids are very effective in weathering silicates and converting them to carbonates, a process that requires the incorporation of carbon dioxide from the atmosphere. With all these effects taken together, Schwartzman and Volk concluded that, in comparison to an abiotic world, the biota could be enhancing silicate weathering by a factor of at least 100 and thereby lowering the global mean surface temperature by about 30°C.

Volk (1989) has further demonstrated that among the vascular terrestrial plants, it is the angiosperms (and associated root mycorrhizae) that should be most effective in reducing atmospheric carbon dioxide and temperature.

Callot et al. (1987) have reported that two species of siderofungi corrode amorphous and crystalline silicate much faster than is expected from organic-acid excretions alone. They conclude from laboratory studies that the fungi synthesize very efficient siderophores in the cell membranes. They suggest that this process may act in the natural environment.

However, Shachak et al. (1987) have found that not all active faunal weathering agents are microbial. They have identified two species of snail, *Euchondrus albulus* and *E. desertorum,* that consume endolithic lichens by ingesting the limestone rock substrate. The annual weathering rate attributed to these snails is 0.7 to 1.1 tonnes per hectare in the Negev desert. Furthermore, a density of twenty-one snails per square meter can generate soil at a rate similar to the deposition of wind-borne dust. Thus the biogenic influence of some macroscopic fauna on weathering can be significant.

Plant-to-Plant Communication

Also interesting and important to Gaia are the modes of transmitting signals for coordinated response by the active components of the biota. Organisms can respond to climatic signals en masse through their individual instinctive reactions to the stimulus, and thus do not need to be organized with a communication system to produce the major impacts they are suspected of having. However, the process of direct communication between plants has been demonstrated. Chemicals appear to provide the medium for transmitting signals between plants, probably of the same species. Although several examples of this phenomenon have been identified, they consist largely of signals warning of pest attack on the "sender" plant that triggers an increase of defensive chemicals in the "receiver" plant (Baldwin and Schultz, 1983). It was found possible to transmit a signal to fifteen saplings by damaging only two leaves on each of fifteen other saplings. Perhaps this system of communication is responsible for a number of synchronous phenomena including some of those important to biogenic influence on the environment.

Conclusion

From this sampling of proposed, suspected, and identified biogenic influences on the environment, it is obvious that a number of different components of the biosphere could be working in concert to control a particularly critical climatic variable. For example, it is possible that several mechanisms have evolved that contribute to achieving planetary temperature control.

In the course of preparing this review, I found the number of biogenic influences on the environment to be much greater than originally anticipated. It remains to be seen whether this indicates a natural trend toward diversification similar to the continuous branching process of biological organisms, or merely a further step in revealing a system of unexpected complexity. In contemplating the origin of this complexity, I found particularly thought-provoking the notion of Barlow and Volk (1990) that "prokaryote evolution can be looked upon as the stepwise development of the total of open-system life forms working within the parameters of a [materially] closed [but energetically open] global system. One shortage after another drove the evolution of metabolic pathways, with [others] driven by the other face of closure—the fact that there is no external environment into which Gaia can eject wastes."

The prospects of finding other biogenic influences on the environment are very great, for so far the surface has just been scratched in the egophysiological examination of the functioning of Gaia. Much more new research and reexamination of available but seemingly irrelevant or unconnected data are needed before the details of the vast system that constitutes life on Earth can be worked out.

Acknowledgments

The author thanks the reviewer, T. Volk, for his critiques and assistance, J. Lovelock for general discussions and encouragement, R.C. Schnell for discussions on the stimulation of precipitation by bacteria, R.J. Charlson for discussions on the effects of dimethylsulfide from marine plankton and A. Watson for assistance. The support of the United Nations University and the United Nations Centre for Science and Technology for Development during the preparation of the manuscript is also gratefully acknowledged.

References

Anon. 1987. *Discover* 8, 8.

Aristovska, T.V., Daragan, A. Yu., Zykina L.V., and Kutuzova, R.S. 1969. *Soviet Soil Sci,* 5, 538–546.

Baldwin, I.T., and Schultz, J. C. 1983. *Science,* 221, 277–278.

Barlow, C., and Volk, T. 1990. *BioSystems,* 23, 371–384.

Bates, T.S., Charlson, R.J., and Gammon, R.H. 1987. *Nature,* 329, 319–321.

Benson, A.A., and Muscatine, L. 1974. *Limnol Oceanogr,* 19, 810–814.

Bigg, E.K. 1973. *J Atmospher Sci,* 30, 1153–1157.

Callot, G., Maurette, M., Pottier, L., and Dubois, A. 1987. *Science,* 328, 147–149.

Charlson, R.J., Lovelock J.E., Andreae, M.O., and Warren, S.G. 1987. *Nature,* 326, 655–661.

Deacon, E.L. 1979. *Boundary-Layer Meteorol,* 17, 517–521.

Duff, R.B., Webbley, D.M., and Scott, R.O. 1963. *Soil Sci,* 95, 105–114.

Ehrlich, H.L. 1981. In Ehrlich, H., ed. *Geomicrobiology.* New York: Dekker, 125–135.

Fall, R., and Schnell, R.C. 1985. *J Marine Res,* 43, 257–265.

Franken, W., Leopoldo, P.R., Matsui, E., and Goēs Ribeiro, M.N. 1982. *Acta Amazonica,* 12, 327–331.

Graedel, T., and Eisner, T. 1988. *Tellus,* 40B, 335–339.

Harper, O. 1986. *J Gen Microbiol,* 132, 1231.

Hicks, B.B., Drinkow, R.L., and Grauze, G. 1974. *Boundary-Layer Meteorol,* 6, 287–297.

Idso, S.B., Kimball, B.A., Anderson, M.G., and Mauney, J.R. 1987. *Agriculture, Ecosystems, Environment,* 20, 1–10.

Jayaweera, K., and Flanagan, P. 1982. *Geophys Res Lett,* 9, 94–97.

Knoll, M.A., and James, W.C. 1987. *Geology,* 15, 1099–1102.

Leopoldo, P.R., Franken, W., and Matsui, E. 1984. In *Change in the Amazon, Proceedings of the 44th International Congress of Americanists.* Manchester, UK: Manchester University Press.

Lindemann, J., Constantinidou, A., Barchett, E.R., and Upper, C.D. 1982. *Appl Environmental Microbiol,* 44, 1059–1063.

Lindow, S.E., Arny, D.C., Upper, C.P., 1978. *Appl Environmental Microbiol,* 36, 831–838.

Lovelock, J.E. 1979. *Gaia: A New Look at Life on Earth.* Oxford: Oxford University Press.

Lovelock, J.E. 1988. *The Ages of Gaia.* Oxford: Oxford University Press.

Lovelock, J.E., and Margulis, L. 1974. *Tellus, 26, 1–10.*

Lovelock, J.E., and Watson, A.J. 1982. *Planetary Space Sci,* 30, 795–802.

Lovelock, J.E., and Whitfield, M. 1982. *Nature,* 296, 561–563.

Maki, L.R., and Willoughby, K.J. 1978. *J Appl Meteorol,* 17, 1049–1053.

Mooney, H.A., Vitousek, P.M., and Matson, P.A. 1987. *Science* 238, 926–932.

Nagamoto, C.T., Rosinski, J., Haagensen, P.L., Michalowska-Smak, A., and Parungo, F. 1984. *J Aerosol Sci,* 15, 147–166.

Salati, E., and Vose, P.B. 1984. *Science* 225, 129.

Schnell, R.C. 1975a. *Biogenic ice nucleus removal by overgrazing: A factor in the Sahelian drought?* (final report). New York: Rockefeller Foundation.

Schnell, R.C. 1975b. *Geophys Res Lett,* 2, 500–502.

Schnell. R.C. 1977. *J Atmospher Sci,* 34, 1299–1305.

Schnell, R.C., Miller, S.W., and Allee, P.A. 1981. *Extended Abstracts of the 15th Conference on Agriculture and Forest Meteorology and Fifth Conference on Biometeorology.* Boston: American Meteorological Society, 22–24.

Schnell, R.C., and Tan-Schnell, S.N. 1982. *Tellus,* 34, 92–95.

Schnell, R.C., and Vali, G. 1975. *Tellus,* 27, 321–323.

Schnell, R.C., and Vali, G. 1976. *J Atmospher Sci,* 33, 1554–1564.

Schwartzman, D.W., and Volk, T. 1989. *Nature,* 340, 457–460.

Shachak, M., Jones, C.G., and Granot, Y. 1987. *Science,* 236, 1098–1099.

Silverman, M.P., and Ehrlich, H.L. 1964. *Adv Appl Microbiol,* 6, 153–206.

Vali, G., Christensen, M., Fresh, R.W., Galyan, E.L., Maki, L.R., and Schnell, R.C. 1976. *J Atmospher Sci,* 33, 1565–1570.

Volk, T., 1987. *Am J Sci,* 287, 763–779.

Volk, T., 1989. *Geology,* 17, 107–110.

Yankofsky, S.A., Levin, Z., Bertold, T., and Sandlerman, N. 1981. *J Appl Meteorol,* 20, 1013–1019.

II
Philosophical Foundations of Gaia

Gaia and the Myths of Harmony: An Exploration of Ethical and Practical Implications

In Stephen Schneider's draft of an article on the Gaia hypothesis for the *Encyclopedia Britannica,* he makes the interesting observation that while the hypothesis "was virtually ignored by the scientific community," it was "embraced by what one might call, for want of a better description the 'eco-freaks'" and that it "was also appealing to the polluting industries" (Schneider, 1986). This is interesting because the same set of ideas appears to have radically different practical and ethical implications. Some, hearing about a possible mechanism allowing living organisms to regulate their global environment, suggested greater caution in our dealings with the natural world, while others thought that the existence of such a mechanism implied that we could actually afford to exercise less caution.

The hypothesis seems to have revived some long-standing disputes in our culture concerning the nature of our world and our responsibilities for our actions. That a scientific hypothesis should have such extrascientific implications is not surprising, for science is never done in a vacuum and its models and metaphors are often drawn upon, whether rightly or wrongly, to cast light on issues of cultural concern. That a scientific hypothesis should be drawn upon to justify such apparently different sets of extrascientific implications should also not be surprising for, as I shall try to show, the model is subject to a common metaphysical interpretation that is essential to both Schneider's "ecofreaks" and his "polluters."

While the term *Gaia hypothesis* is new and the particular content of that hypothesis as spelled out in the various versions suggested by James Lovelock and Lynn Margulis will not be found by examining the history of ideas, the term *Gaia* can be used to indicate a whole set of conceptions bearing a close family resemblance to one another—conceptions that have been important in the formation of the intellectual perspective of the modern world.

If we understand the Gaia hypothesis most generally as a series of ideas that attempt to explain the apparent harmony between living beings and their environment, we can distinguish two different kinds of Gaia hypotheses in accordance with the kinds of factors that determine and regulate the apparent harmony. In the first case we find theories that depict the relationship between organisms and their environment in terms of an organic unity that displays some kind of intelligence and purposiveness. The concept of a world-soul (*anima mundi*), or the image of a superorganism, commonly plays an important role in this conception. For want of a better term let us refer to this version of the Gaia hypothesis as the *organic model*. In the second case we find theories that regard the apparent harmony in the natural world as being caused by various kinds of mechanical and automatic feedback processes governed without the immediate participation of intelligent or purposive factors.

Both of these versions of the Gaia hypothesis are found in many contemporary discussions concerning Gaia, and we can generally find our "ecofreaks" upholding one side and our "polluters" the other. What unites these disparate views and justifies my classifying them as different versions of the Gaia hypothesis is their common employment of the concept of harmony. It is this concept that I am most concerned with in what follows, and after a brief examination of the traditions that gave rise to these different models of Gaia, I consider the appropriateness of the concept of harmony in the current debate.

The organic model of the earth has a long tradition that goes back to the early Greek philosopher and mathematician Pythagoras. Rocks and minerals were thought of as elemental forms of life which, like simple vegetables and plants, grow from metallic seeds planted deep within the earth. Veins of metal rise toward the surface of the earth like the roots and branches of large trees. It was thought that miners "found by experience that the vein of gold is a living tree and that by all ways that it spreadeth and springeth from the root by the soft pores and that passages of the earth putting forth branches even unto the uppermost part of the earth and ceaseth not until it discover itself unto the open air: at which time it showeth forth certain beautiful colors instead of flowers, round stones of golden earth instead of fruits and thin plates instead of leaves" (Merchant, 1983). Once mined and allowed to lay fallow like the meadows on the surface of the earth, the metals would grow again and replenish themselves. In this sense mining was like agriculture and the same kinds of care had to be taken through good husbandry.

The Stoic philosophers of Greek and Roman times regarded the earth as a living and intelligent organism and they discouraged mining of all kinds for fear of injuring Mother Earth and producing all sorts of disastrous consequences such as earthquakes and raging storms. The necessities of mining were hotly disputed and even down to the fifteenth century "metallurgy was intentionally compared with obstetrics: ores were seen to grow in the womb of the earth like embryos . . . and the sinking of a new mine was accompanied by religious ceremonies, in which miners fasted, prayed, and observed a particular series of rites" (Berman, 1981).

The organic model of the living earth was used to explain the kind of harmonies that were observed in nature, and the importance of such a model to the subsequent development of science lay in the fact that it regarded the harmony and apparent intelligence of the earth-system in natural rather than supernatural terms. For the bulk of the period that we have come to regard as the Middle Ages earthly harmonies were understood for the most part as the direct result of the actions of a creator god. During the twelfth century there was revival of interest in Greek naturalism and the search for natural causes became a general cultural enterprise. Many scholars regard this period as the intellectual beginning of the modern period. Though from our point of view naturalistic organicism was an improvement on animism (which is another hypothesis accounting for harmony) and what might be called *creatorism,* the same moral and ethical injunctions seem to be implied. For if the natural world was governed by living beings or life-like principles, our interactions with nature must be based upon the concept of care to avoid possible insult or injury.

The earth, particularly as viewed as a living organism, was delicate and any injuries that we produced as a result of our actions and activities would have serious ethical and prudential consequences.

To upset the natural harmonies of the world would evoke the simple principle of cosmic justice, and we would deserve our just desserts. I have found that some of our contemporary organicists evoking their version of the Gaia hypothesis have appealed to similar principles of cosmic justice to explain disastrous earthquakes and devastating storms.

There was a tremendous revival of organicism during the period of the Renaissance. Many eclectic philosophies were developed which drew upon the ideas of many cultures and many periods. Concepts from Christianity and neo-Platonism were combined with various elements from Jewish mysticism, Arabic philosophy, gnosticism, alchemy, and Egyptian religion and mixed liberally with Stoic concepts of nature and the natural order in an attempt to explain the kinds of forces that governed both the human and natural worlds. The earth was again seen as a living being but the belief in the neo-Platonic conception of the soul produced a slightly different organic model with important implications for the future of naturalism. The soul was essentially seen as an intelligent moving force that animated the various objects in the natural world and was responsible for their actions and interactions. As matter was essentially passive the soul served as an intelligible principle that could produce movement, growth, and development. There were different levels of soul and the possession of a soul conferred a unity to the object that possessed it. Thus the soul of the world (the *anima mundi*) conferred a unity on the world, helped to orchestrate its many actions and interactions, and was responsible for various forms of natural harmony. This view was different from the one that saw the earth as a kind of living superorganism, for in the latter view life force was for the most part seen as permeating matter and inseparable from it, while for the former it animated and guided matter.

This belief was of great conceptual importance to many of those individuals whom we regard as the earliest of modern scientists. William Gilbert, for example, in his *De Magnete* expresses the following opinion: "As for us, we deem the whole world animate, and all globes, all stars and this glorious earth too, we hold to be from the beginning by their own destinate souls governed and from them to have the impulse of self-preservation . . ." (Kearney, 1969, p 110). Copernicus and Kepler both expressed similar beliefs. Here is a brief quotation—one among many possible on the subject—from the writings of Kepler:

It is the custom of some physicians to cure their patients by pleasing music. How can music work in the body of a person? Namely in such a way that the soul of the person, just as some animals do also, understands the harmony, is happy about it, is refreshed and becomes accordingly stronger in its body. Similarly the earth is affected by harmony and quiet music. Therefore there is in the earth not only dumb, unintelligent humidity, but also an intelligent soul which begins to dance when the aspects pipe for it. If strong aspects last, it carries in its function more violently by pushing the vapors upwards, and thus causes all sorts of thunderstorms; while otherwise when no aspects are present, it is still and develops no more exhalation than is necessary for the rivers (Kearney, 1969, p 139).

There were two aspects of the neo-Platonic soul that made it important for these early scientists. In the first place the soul was intelligent and therefore intelligible, that is, as an intelligent force its workings were capable of being understood by intelligent beings such as ourselves. In the second place, its intelligence was expressible and hence understandable in mathematical terms. This concept of intelligibility runs back through Plato to Pythagoras. Thus Kepler attempts to understand the harmonies of planetary motion by means of a mathematical investigation of the actions of the soul.

These neo-Platonic conceptions were closely associated with other organic conceptions of the earth and generally inspired the same sort of cautious behavior that discouraged large-scale interference with natural systems. Yet of course this kind of attitude and philosophy was not in spirit with the increasing commercial and industrial expansion of the times and it is not surprising to find that by the middle of the seventeenth century organicism had been replaced by mechanism as the official philosophy of the new science movement. The shift from neo-Platonic organicism to mechanism was not as discontinuous as might be supposed. The neo-Platonists had already made matter passive and subject to the manipulation of outside forces. It was a simple step to substitute mechanical forces for the movements of the soul. Mechanists, such as Galileo, also accepted the idea that the world was intelligible in mathematical terms and governed by mathematical principles: "Philosophy is written in this grand book, the universe, which stands continually open to our gaze. But the book cannot be understood unless one first learns to comprehend the language and read the letters in which it is composed. It is written in the language of mathematics, and its characters are triangles, circles, and other geometric figures, without which it is humanly impossible to under-

stand a single word of it; without these, one wanders about in a dark labyrinth" (Dijksterhuis, 1969).

By the time that the great synthesis of Newton was absorbed into society in the eighteenth century the universe was seen—at least by the educated public—as a grand and harmonious machine working in accordance with natural laws and mathematical principles. Such a machine cannot be hurt or injured and it is not likely to break down. The manner in which we describe the world can have important effects on our attitudes and actions towards that world. The shift in metaphors—from soul to machine—helped to shift sensibilities as well. What was impermissible before now becomes permissible; a prohibition becomes a sanction with a change in the terms or representation.

The important thing to be noted from our point of view, however, is that though the image of nature changed, the belief in harmony persisted. Though the world could not be injured by our actions, we ourselves could be injured if we ignored the workings of the grand machine of nature. Like ants inhabiting a giant grandfather clock we constantly risked getting ground up in the gears. If we could discover how the laws of nature applied to human society, and acted in such a way as not to interfere with them, then we might be able to employ the harmonizing forces of nature to the benefit of humankind. Thus an overwhelming concern of the eighteenth century became the search for nature and the natural. In an effort to share in the kinds of harmonies that nature is constantly producing, countless philosophers tried to give sense to terms like *the state of nature, balance of nature, natural rights, natural government,* and so on. Frederick the Great even performed experiments on children in which he kept them from all human contact in order to see which of the many possible languages they would come to speak "naturally."

It is the economists of the eighteenth century who were the first to believe that they had discovered the natural law that applied to human society. Noticing that prices were determined fairly by the interactions of supply and demand in an unregulated market, the physiocrats spoke of the "magic of a well-ordered society" in which each man works for others while believing that he is working for himself. This magic was displayed in "the principles of economic harmony" which derived from God and nature. Adam Smith spoke of the "invisible hand" which leads an individual "to promote an end which was no part of his intention . . . By pursuing his own interest he frequently promotes that of the society more effectually than when he really intends to promote it" (Gay, 1969).

Here nature helps us to invert the normal understandings of vice and virtue. Self-interest, if pursued in a natural manner, can produce more virtuous results than can deliberate altruism. This kind of understanding of the natural harmonious mechanism that governs human affairs found its way in various forms to Malthus and his arguments against the poor laws. From Malthus it filtered into biology in the form of the virtues of natural competition and inspired the theories of Wallace and Darwin. The so-called social Darwinists borrowed their favorite terms from biology and applied them to the marketplace to proclaim the virtues of "survival of the fittest" and "the improvement of the species." These ideas in turn found their way into some of the darkest recesses of the twentieth century.

The champions of industry need not worry about actions taken for the sake of progress. Nature is resilient and creative; change always tilts with favor toward the future. Such may be the philosophy that inspires Schneider's polluters.

The Gaia hypothesis, in its rich association with earth goddesses and telic forces that guide the workings of nature, seems to give new support to the concept of harmony at a time when the life sciences are becoming increasingly mechanical and probabalistic in their interpretation of living systems. When the notions of harmony are thus reinforced, the major explanations of harmony rise to new prominence along with their readings of the signposts of nature. Though the organicists as eco-fundamentalists and the mechanists as laissez-faire industrialists read the signposts differently, I have suggested that they arise out of the same roots and that, at least in metaphysical terms, they are more similar than different.

But of course the concept of harmony has no place on the current maps of biology or of science in general. It is a term of evaluation concerning the appropriateness or goodness of a state of affairs, characteristics more appropriate to prescriptive rather than descriptive language. Take away the idea of harmony and you take away the moral and ethical implications. It is easy to see that equilibrium or homeostatic states are not synonymous with preferred states, and it would be considered naive to think that any particular state of nature had only winners and no losers. Whose preferences are to predominate?

Many of the concepts that provided the biological underpinnings for the idea of harmony are currently being called into question. The ideas of the balance of nature and the fragile interdependence of all the elements of an ecosystem are regarded in many quarters as being more fiction than fact. Natural systems seldom display the long-term tendencies toward stasis that would justify such notions of balance, nor are they so fragile that any change will throw the whole system into convulsions.

Repeatedly these days, one hears conservationists using the dogma that each species fills a function in a holistically organized community whose sum creates a circumstance that guarantees the needs of all the component parts. If one pulls at one part they argue, one affects all other parts, so if we do not know what the function of a part is, we should not tamper for fear that we may do irreparable damage. However, recent research indicating lack of stability of numbers, lack of coupling among subsystems, redundancy of systems, and opportunistic use of several systems by many elements of what we might like to call one ecosystem, indicates that this concern is unfounded and based on outmoded ecological models. In fact experience indicates that one can seldom prepare an ecological model that will allow a priori predictions of the effects of manipulations of parts of a natural system. This is because most of the elements of a system operate largely independently of most other elements (Drury, 1974).

Even the much-used concept of succession, which holds that there is a general order in terms of which species of plants will succeed themselves in a particular habitat and move toward a climax mixture, has been largely criticized as being too teleological and not in accord with observation. Various homeostatic concepts used to explain population fluctuations have also come under strong criticism in an atmosphere of increasing scepticism concerning the belief in long-term direction or stability in nature (Egerton, 1973).

In such an atmosphere the claims about Gaia are bound to become very modest and lack the inspiration desired by those who wish to look beneath the surface of nature. The conditions described by Gaia theories will be seen as arising from fortuitous happenstance and indicating at best a relatively enduring homeostatic system of uncertain future, with neither more nor less teleology than shown in the Darwinian formation of the forms of flowers. A weakened form of the Gaia hypothesis would certainly settle for this much.

But what else can we expect? What else can we hope for? The world is less fragile than the organicists would have us believe, and is less resilient than the pollutors would have us believe. The nature we have come to know plays no favorites and there is no reason to think that nature is either designed to produce us or to preserve us. To think that nature is moving by its own forces to produce our preferred states is to smuggle our ethical concepts into our description of nature. It is no great feat once we have put them there to pull them out again and pretend that nature has told us how to act.

The Gaia hypothesis, just by the connotation of its name alone, dredges up all the images of harmony that we have courted for so long and that we have only recently begun to put into perspective. There are enough interesting scientific questions to be raised and answered concerning the relationship between living organisms and the atmosphere. Why describe that relationship in such a way that seems to determine our practical and ethical choices? Nature cannot tell us what harmony is; we have to discover this on our own. Once we decide that question, individually or collectively, then we have to look at nature to see how we can achieve what we have envisioned. In this sense the only harmony that we will find in nature is one that we will have brought about through our own actions and the applications of our own values.

References

Berman, M. 1981. *The Reinchantment of the World*. Ithaca, N.Y.: Cornell University Press, 88.

Dijksterhuis, E.J. 1969. *The Mechanization of the World Picture*. Oxford: Oxford University Press, 362.

Drury, W.H. 1974. Quantity, quality, and the recognition of values. *Rare Species Biol Conserv*, 6, 18.

Egerton, F.N. 1973. Changing concepts of the balance of nature. *Quart Rev Biol*, 48, 322–350.

Gay, P. 1969. *The Enlightenment: The Science of Freedom* (Volume 2). New York: W.W. Norton & Co., 364–365.

Kearney, H. 1969. *Science and Change: 1500–1700*. New York: W.W. Norton & Co., 110.

Merchant, C. 1983. *The Death of Nature: Women, Ecology and the Scientific Revolution*. San Francisco: Harper and Row, 29.

Schneider, S.H. 1987. Editorial. *A goddess of the earth? The debate over the Gaia hypothesis*. 1988 *Yearbook of Science and the Future*, Chicago, Encyclopedia Britannica, Inc. 30–43.

James W. Kirchner

6
The Gaia Hypotheses: Are They Testable? Are They Useful?

The reader may wonder why, in my title, I refer to the Gaia hypotheses in the plural. I do it because I think that many logically different theories have been put forth under the single banner of "the Gaia hypothesis." Perhaps the Gaia hypothesis is all things to all people, but the differences between these theories are both subtle and crucial. I suspect that a lot of debate has resulted from a simple misunderstanding of which of the multiple hypotheses is on the table at any one time. In the interests of clarity and precision, I propose the following taxonomy of the Gaia hypotheses:

A Taxonomy of the Gaia Hypotheses

Influential Gaia. The weakest of the hypotheses (here I use "weak" and "strong" in reference to the extremity, not the plausibility, of the hypotheses), the influential Gaia theory asserts simply that the biota has a substantial influence over certain aspects of the abiotic world, such as the temperature and composition of the atmosphere.

The Gaia hypothesis . . . states that the temperature and composition of the Earth's atmosphere are actively regulated by the sum of life on the planet (Sagan and Margulis, 1983).

Coevolutionary Gaia. The coevolutionary Gaia hypothesis asserts that the biota influences the abiotic environment, and that the environment in turn influences the evolution of the biota by Darwinian processes.

The biota have effected profound changes on the environment of the surface of the earth. At the same time, that environment has imposed constraints on the biota, so that

life and the environment may be considered as two parts of a coupled system (Watson and Lovelock, 1983).

Homeostatic Gaia. The homeostatic Gaia hypothesis asserts that the biota influences the abiotic world, and does so in a way that is stabilizing. In the language of systems analysis, the major linkages between the biota and the abiotic world are negative feedback loops.

The notion of the biosphere as an active adaptive control system able to maintain the earth in homeostasis we are calling the 'Gaia' hypothesis (Lovelock and Margulis, 1974a).

Teleological Gaia. The teleological Gaia hypothesis holds that the atmosphere is kept in homeostasis, not just by the biosphere, but by and for (in some sense) the biosphere.

. . . the Earth's atmosphere is more than merely anomalous; it appears to be a contrivance specifically constituted for a set of purposes (Lovelock and Margulis 1974a).

Optimizing Gaia. The optimizing Gaia hypothesis holds that the biota manipulates its physical environment for the purpose of creating biologically favorable, or even optimal, conditions for itself.

"We argue that it is unlikely that chance alone accounts for the fact that temperature, pH and the presence of compounds of nutrient elements have been, for immense periods of time, just those optimal for surface life. Rather we present the 'Gaia hypothesis,' the idea that energy is expended by the biota to actively maintain these optima" (Lovelock and Margulis, 1974b).

This is just one taxonomy of the Gaia hypotheses. One can take issue with my way of classifying them. It can be done many other ways, but I think most will agree that it must be done somehow, because (as the examples above make clear) different people mean different things when they use the same words. Sometimes even the *same* people appear to mean different things when they use the same words. Some of these claims are relatively weak (as

(Author's note: A substantially refined and expanded version of this contribution appeared in the May, 1989 *Reviews of Geophysics* (Kirchner, 1989). That paper makes some points more carefully and precisely than this one, and addresses geophysiology, Daisyworld, and Lovelock's newest book, which was in press at the time of the conference. The version presented here, by contrast, has the advantage of saying things more plainly, and better revealing one practicing scientist's difficulties with Gaia.)

39

The Gaia Hypotheses: Are They Testable? Are They Useful?

in the influential or coevolutionary Gaia theories, which seem to state just that the biota and the physical environment have something to do with one another), and others are, of course, quite strong stuff. If we all talk about "the Gaia hypothesis," without specifying *which* Gaia hypothesis, we can create a lot of confusion.

This confusion can appear in different guises. One of the most serious lies in claiming that evidence for one of the weaker versions of the hypothesis somehow proves the much stronger versions of the hypothesis as well. Some believe, as I do, that the biota affects the physical environment. Some also think, as I do, that the physical environment shapes biotic evolution. Those holding these views are in good company, because scientists have thought these things for over a hundred years. So if I were asked whether I believed in the Gaia hypothesis, referring to *that* Gaia hypothesis, I would say that I do. But does that mean that I believe that the biota is part of a global cybernetic control system, the purpose of which is to create biologically optimal conditions—that is another matter entirely.

Weak Gaia Is Not New

Some might be surprised at my statement that scientists have believed in Gaia—believed in "weak" Gaia, believed that life shapes the physical environment—for over a hundred years. We have all become accustomed to reading that the Gaia hypothesis is a radical departure from the earlier view that the biota simply responds to a fixed physical environment. If that is a radical departure, then some people have been radically departing for a very long time. Consider T.H. Huxley. In 1877 he wrote what could be considered to be the very first textbook in physical geography. In it he wrote, "Since the atmosphere is constantly receiving vast volumes of carbonic acid from various sources, it might not unnaturally be assumed that this gas would unduly accumulate, and at length vitiate the entire bulk of the atmosphere. Such accumulation is, however, prevented by the action of living plants" (Huxley, 1877).

So a century ago Huxley thought the biota was responsible for the chemical disequilibrium of the atmosphere. He not only thought this, but he also thought it was elementary enough, and obvious enough, to put it into a textbook.

Thirty years earlier, Huxley's compatriot Herbert Spencer wrote about the same phenomenon. He not

only thought that the biota had shaped the earth's atmosphere; he also thought that changes in the atmosphere had charted the course of evolution (which Spencer called "progressive development," Darwin's *Origin of Species* being still in the future). Spencer called his theory

. . . an entirely new and very beautiful explanation of the proximate causes of progressive development . . . not only do the organisms of the vegetable kingdom decompose the carbonic acid which has been thrown into the atmosphere by animals, but they likewise serve for the removal of those extraneous supplies of the same gas that are continually poured into it through volcanos, calcareous springs, fissures, and other such channels . . . Assuming then that the present theory, supported as it is by the fact that the constituents of the atmosphere are not in atomic proportions, and borne out likewise by the foregoing arguments, is correct, let us mark the inferences that may be drawn respecting the effects produced upon the organic creation. . . .

"If rapid oxidation of the blood is accompanied by a higher heat and a more perfect mental and bodily development, and if in consequence of an alteration in the composition of the air greater facilities for such oxidation are afforded, it may be reasonably inferred that there has been a corresponding advancement in the temperature and organization of the world's inhabitants" (Spencer, 1844).

In other words, Spencer held that the emergence of green plants produced our present abundance of oxygen, and that oxygen made the evolution of higher animals possible. The biota, in other words, shaped the physical world in a way that seems fortuitous for the course of evolution.

My contention is not that Spencer was correct (his view is simultaneously grandiose and simplistic), but that he was, in a sense, *Gaian*. His theory has the key elements: the biota alters the physical environment, which in turn shapes biotic evolution. Indeed, his theory sounds surprisingly similar to contemporary Gaian treatments that portray the creation of earth's oxidizing atmosphere as a cathartic event, necessary for the further progress of evolution.

I certainly do not claim familiarity with the whole history of the evolution of such ideas. The fact that I could find these two "Gaian" references in an afternoon of library browsing, however, suggests to me that such passages may be relatively common. Indeed, the whole field of biogeochemistry, although more cautious in its speculations, is centrally concerned with the same biotic interactions that Gaia alludes to.

So the first two statements of the Gaia hypothesis—what I have labeled *influential* and *coevolutionary* Gaia, respectively—have a long history. This weak hypothesis has such a long history, indeed, and seems so intuitively plausible, that it seems odd to call it a hypothesis at all. Rather than a theory, it seems to be simply an observation that the physical and biotic worlds have something to do with one another. We can, of course, argue about the relative importance of these interactions.

Thus those who believe in the weak forms of the Gaia hypothesis are carrying on a long and honorable scientific tradition, but one so long, and so honorable, that it may deprive them of the pleasure of being part of a revolution in scientific thought. But what about the stronger versions of the hypothesis? Are they testable, and are they useful? Before I address that question, I must briefly review a bit of basic epistemology.

Criteria for Testability

Much of the debate surrounding any scientific theory, including the Gaia theories, consists of finding and weighing the evidence, for and against. This is the day-to-day business of scientists, and of scientific conferences like the San Diego meeting. We call it testing a theory.

But not every theory can be tested. Now, as a matter of strict logic, a theory that is untestable is far worse than one that is merely false. A false theory, once known to be false, at least helps restrict the sphere of possibilities. It teaches us something, namely that the truth lies elsewhere. Testing an untestable theory, on the other hand, is simply a waste of time. So true, false, and untestable theories are, respectively, "the good, the bad, and the ugly." What must a theory be, to be testable?

First, it must be well defined. Its meaning must be clear and its terms must be unambiguous. Second, it must be intelligible in terms of observable phenomena of the real world. Finally, it must not be tautological. That is, it must not be true simply by definition. Equivalently, it must not encompass all logical possibilities. It must be logically possible for the theory to be false, and there must be some conceivable fact that, if it were in fact the case, would prove the theory false. This is what separates empirical hypotheses from pure logical deductions.

A tautology is a theory that is true no matter what the facts are. A theory should be logically consis-

tent, but it should not be completely airtight; it has to let a little empirical truth in at some point.

Metaphors

Metaphors constitute a whole class of untestable theories. If Shakespeare tells you that "all the world's a stage," could you test his hypothesis? I doubt it. What would you measure or observe to tell whether the world is a stage? What would a world that is *not* a stage look like? If you could complain to Shakespeare about the ambiguity of his metaphor, he might reply, "OK. The entire world is made of wooden flooring, and at the edge of the earth you'll find a few footlights." Now you have a hypothesis. You can now go out and very quickly verify that the world is not a stage, at least in that sense. But of course, in some more poetic sense, the world is indeed a stage. That is what makes metaphors so inviting; at the same time that they are literally false, they are figuratively true.

A metaphor makes a poor hypothesis because it does not specify *in what sense* the metaphor is true. Showing that the world is a stage in one sense does not prove it is a stage in any other sense. Now, "All the world's a stage" sounds a lot like "All the world is a global organism," and some have indeed claimed that the Gaia hypothesis is just a metaphor. My point is not that metaphors are useless—they inspire fruitful speculation—but that they are untestable. Treating a metaphor as a scientific proposition that is factually true or false is simply a waste of time.

Now, some may think that I'm being a terrible spoil sport, that I am far too serious about what should be considered just a metaphor, and that I take the whole Gaia hypothesis far too literally. Perhaps I do. But if Gaia is just a metaphor, why do we keep referring to the Gaia *hypothesis?* Why to we keep talking about *evidence for* or *proof of* the Gaia hypothesis? If it is a metaphor, why do we talk about it as if it were a scientific proposition, as if it were either true or false?

Criteria of Usefulness

Besides testability, another fundamental issue to consider is usefulness. Some theories, although coherent and perhaps even true, are simply not useful in furthering scientific progress. Theories are useful to the degree that they are distinct from related theories. If a hypothesis simply restates other tried-

and-true theories, or can be logically derived from them, why bother testing it?

The second major criterion of usefulness is predictive or explanatory power. Theories are useful in proportion to the phenomena they can predict or explain, and—perhaps more importantly—in inverse proportion to what they force you to assume. This is simply Ockham's Razor: *all else equal,* choose the theory that burdens you with the least baggage of unverifiable assumptions. If two theories explain the same data, reject the one that forces you to assume the most. Note that Ockham's Razor does not say that all simple theories are better than all complex ones. It simply says that one should not invoke extraordinary assumptions to explain phenomena that can be understood more straightforwardly.

If I have any quibble with weak Gaia, it is on these grounds. It is not clear that Influential Gaia or Coevolutionary Gaia say anything that was not already said by Huxley, Darwin, and others of their age. Does Gaia say anything new? If not, is there any advantage to restating tried-and-true theories in Gaian language?

The same point can be raised with respect to the strong versions of the Gaia hypotheses, to the extent that they claim to explain why the physical environment and the biota are well matched. Darwin said a long time ago that the biota fits the physical environment well. Gaia reverses the statement, and says that the physical environment suits the biota well. Is there any advantage in standing poor old Darwin on his head? And is that advantage great enough to justify the assumptions we have to make? Natural selection—without any of the embellishments that Gaia offers—explains why the environment and the biota are well matched. Organisms suited to a different environment, having been wiped out long ago, are no longer part of the biota, to which the current environment seems so well suited. Why invoke a global cybernetic control system to explain the good fit of biota to environment, if you can invoke simple natural selection instead?

Homeostatic Gaia

I shall now turn for a moment to homeostatic Gaia, which claims, in essence, that the biota is vital in maintaining the long-term stability of the physical environment. What is stability? Does it mean resistance to change, resilience under change, or bounds

on the magnitude of change? The experience of ecologists in the debate over complexity and stability shows that it is hard enough to pin down the meaning of stability or homeostasis in the case of a neatly bounded ecosystem; it is harder still when the bounds are the entire biosphere. One could precisely define homeostasis, but it has never been done. So the first problem is one of definition.

There are many interrelationships between the biota and the physical environment (that is, many feedback loops). Given that any feedback loop must be either stabilizing or destabilizing, it should come as no surprise that some of them are stabilizing. The Gaia hypothesis has prompted a lot of efforts to look for biological mechanisms of homeostasis, and there are some outwardly plausible candidates.

But we should not just look for confirmatory evidence. We should be cautious in characterizing the putative stability of a paleoclimatic record that is sketchy and ambiguous, one whose error bounds could hide quite a bit of instability. More to the point, without knowing what destabilizing biological mechanisms may also be at work to undermine homeostasis—and there is every reason to believe that there are some, and that some are potent—it is impossible to make a balanced assessment of the role of the biota.

Even the most passionate advocates of Gaia will admit that the biota was once one of the most destabilizing forces on earth. The biota was responsible for the drastic shift in the earth's redox potential in the Precambrian period (a shift that made most of the earth uninhabitable for the anaerobic organisms that precipitated it). Indeed, some accounts claim that this event is evidence of the power of the biotic world and the resilience of Gaia.

But there is a fundamental problem here. If the most destabilizing period in earth's history can be cited as evidence for Gaia, and the apparent stability since can also be cited as evidence for Gaia, I'm left wondering what conceivable events could not be used as evidence for Gaia. If Gaia stabilizes, and Gaia destabilizes—those are the only two possibilities—then is there any possible behavior that is not Gaian? Is Gaia, then, simply a theory so flexible (and, by implication, free of specific empirical content) that it can be wrapped around any conceivable paleoclimatic record?

Anyone attempting a Gaian interpretation of earth's history must think hard about this. And it won't do to say that the Precambrian blue-green algae were not Gaian because they were so violently destabilizing. Such a statement is blatantly tautological. It defines Gaia as stabilizing interactions and then asserts that Gaia has a stabilizing effect. Anything defined to be homeostatic has to be stabilizing . . . there would be no other possibility, so there would be no testable hypothesis.

Teleological Gaia

Teleological Gaia asserts that the biota controls the environment, and does so for a purpose. There is a definitional problem here; the purpose of the putative biological control mechanism has never been defined.

A claim that the atmosphere is a "contrivance specifically constituted for a set of purposes" (Lovelock and Margulis, 1974a) is ill defined without a statement of what the purposes are. This criticism may seem silly, and the purposes may seem perfectly obvious. Clearly, the atmosphere has a number of biologically important functions. Surely the function of the atmosphere is the purpose it was contrived for.

There is a subtle, but serious, error in such a line of reasoning. It is this: if all you know is that the atmosphere functions in some way, how can you say it was contrived? How do you know what its intended purpose was? If you say its intended purpose is the function it serves, then how would you ever know if anything was *not* contrived? Everything has some function, after all. Purpose and function coincide only in contrivances that work well; whether the atmosphere works well, or is contrived at all, is precisely the question at hand. Without an independently defined purpose, teleological Gaia simply says that the atmosphere serves the purpose of doing whatever the atmosphere does.

Optimizing Gaia

The theory I have termed "optimizing Gaia" tries to solve the problem of definition by stating what Gaia's purpose is: Gaia's purpose is maintaining a biologically optimal physical environment. In solving that definitional problem, it creates another. What is optimal for the whole biosphere? We can define an optimal environment for an individual organism in many ways, but what would be optimal for a blue-green anaerobe, a chimpanzee, a pine tree, and a penguin, taken together? Nor does

dismissing the notion of optimality, and simply claiming that Gaia creates biologically favorable conditions, solve the problem. What would be favorable, let alone optimal, for the biota, a vast collection of diverse organisms with different, and even conflicting, requirements?

Would it be "better" for the whole biosphere to have more species, more biomass, or more productivity? No matter what the answer, the next question is unanswerable: Why should that be better?

One might respond that what we have now is optimal. But if what is optimal is simply defined by what exists, what content is left in the idea of optimality? The theory boils down to "Gaia created and maintains the world we have now, which is, of course, optimal." (Nor does the simple fact of life's persistence on Earth—great extinctions and all—prove that Gaia maintains biologically favorable conditions. Gaia must mean not just that life did persist, but that it could not fail to persist. Would the environment of a nongaian earth have been "unfavorable" enough to sterilize the planet?)

Thus it is hard to define what we mean by optimality. But we must define it, for as long as the criterion of optimality remains unspecified, optimizing Gaia is clearly a tautological theory, in the rigorous sense that it includes all logical possibilities and does not exclude any possible data. It is a basic theorem of operations research that for any behavior of a system, there is some objective function which that behavior optimizes. For any given behavior, I can write a function that the behavior maximizes. Every conceivable environment is optimal for something, as long as one has complete freedom to specify what the "something" is.

So the concept of Gaian optimization needs a lot of work to save it from tautology. But there is another serious problem. Gaian optimization is internally contradictory. Stability and optimality (for the agent supplying the regulatory mechanism) are mutually exclusive. If an organism is keeping a system stable, the stable point cannot be optimal for the organism. We can see why by looking at the Daisyworld model, in which plants regulate the temperature of a theoretical planet by changing its reflectance.

Consider a world with only white daisies. The daisies keep the temperature stable because if the temperature or solar flux rises above the stable point, more daisies grow, the surface becomes whiter, and the albedo increases. But that means

43

The Gaia Hypotheses: Are They Testable? Are They Useful?

that at a higher temperature, there would be more daisies. A higher temperature would be "better" for white daisies, and the daisies' response *prevents* a temperature increase that would be favorable for them. At the temperature that is optimal for the daisies, there is no stability. At the optimal point, any change in temperature decreases the number of daisies. So if the temperature increases, daisies die, and the temperature increases still further. More daisies die, and the temperature increases still further. And so on. The optimum will be reached only in an unstable transition between the stable suboptimum and total extinction.

What I have described is true of both colors of daisies, and indeed is not specific to the Daisyworld model. You can demonstrate it as a purely mathematical proposition. It is completely general. It is a straightforward theorem of systems analysis that no homeostatic system can be stable at a point that is optimal for the component supplying the homeostasis. If the biota regulates the atmosphere, the atmosphere cannot be optimal for the biota.

Besides, what do we gain by assuming that Gaia has a purpose, or that Gaia optimizes? What more can we predict or explain? If we make such extreme assumptions, but do not gain any explanatory power, Ockham's Razor will slice us to ribbons.

Summary

Some may be either baffled or irritated by the discussion I have presented. Some may be thinking, "Oh come on. I'm just interested in exploring the connections between the biotic and abiotic worlds, and there's nothing wrong with that. My hypothesis is just that the organisms of the biota influence their local environments, that the sum of these influences can be globally significant, and that organisms evolve by chance and are selected by Darwinian processes, in terms of where they survive, whether they survive, and what their characteristics are."

I think that is a great starting point for illuminating research. It probably explains all that the more extreme Gaia hypotheses do, without invoking global entities, imputing teleological intentionality, or assuming optimal control. It is testable at many scales, from the laboratory to the globe. And in its basic outline it is almost certainly correct. Those holding that view are in good company, and are carrying on an honorable scientific tradition that is at least a century old.

On the other hand, those who think that the idea of a global organism is an intellectually appealing metaphor, but not a rigorous scientific theory, will only distract their colleagues by talking about it as if it were a hypothesis that could be tested or proved.

Some think that Gaia is the stabilizing interaction of the biotic and abiotic worlds. That is an interesting possibility. Given that stabilizing and destabilizing interactions are the only two choices, in any particular case there is at least a 50% chance that this theory is correct. Indeed, if Gaia were violently destabilizing throughout the earth's history, we probably would not be here to carry on this debate. In any event, we should explore all the links between the biotic and abiotic worlds . . . not just those that agree with a particular theory. The destabilizing feedbacks are important too.

Does Gaia have a purpose? Does Gaia maintain optimal conditions for life? I do not think these theories are testable. Nobody will be able to test such theories until Gaia's purpose is defined and the meaning of optimality is specified. And nobody will be able to test such theories until it is clearly stated what conceivable result of an experiment could possibly prove them false.

Addenda and Errata

After presenting this paper, I received a number of thought-provoking questions that have made it clear that some issues I addressed needed to be discussed further, and more precisely.

My Central Concern with Gaia

A number of people suggested that I was expecting far too much, that the nature of the hypothesis and the system itself make it unrealistic to expect that the question be answered after only a decade of work. I am not complaining that the question has not been answered, but that it has not yet been asked in a scientifically meaningful way. The central problem is not a lack of information (though good data are by no means abundant here) but a lack of something to do with the information. Until we can frame a scientifically coherent and significant question, we will not know what the answer means, or even whether we have found it.

Why Untestable Hypotheses Are Ugly

Steve Schneider asked why untestable hypotheses are "ugly." He suggested that the nuclear winter theory, although not testable, was useful in molding our approach to international security.

There are two types of untestability. Theories about nuclear winter are untestable in practice; "ugly" theories are untestable in principle. (In fact, the nuclear winter theory is eminently testable. We are all at risk of becoming involuntary participants in a full-scale, uncontrolled, irreproducible experiment . . .)

Hypotheses that are untestable in principle are those for which every conceivable experiment can be shown, on logic alone, to have only one possible result. Consider the hypothesis, "Once perturbed out of steady state, the system will exhibit transient behavior until it again settles down into steady state." That will always be true of any behavior of any system. Showing that it is true in a particular case, in a particular system, cannot give you any information about the object of study.

"Always true?" one might ask. Yes indeed. The system is only perturbed out of steady state if it begins some sort of transient behavior (if there were no transient behavior, it would still, by definition, be in steady state). Similarly, when transient behavior ends, the steady state begins, by definition. Note that the hypothesis does not say a new steady state must be reached, but only that if it is, it will occur at the end of transience.

What is "ugly" about that hypothesis is that it claims to be revealing aspects of the system under study, when in fact it is just defining the words *steady state* and *transient*. Because the result of the experiment was obvious strictly as a matter of logic, the experiment and the hypothesis have no empirical content. What is truly "ugly" about these sorts of hypotheses is that they are misleading, and in the minds of the unwary they are entrancing; one believes one understands the system very, very well, because one's predictions are always confirmed.

Other "ugly" theories violate the criterion of intelligibility. Most of the pseudoscientific blather currently clogging the media is untestable because the proponents will never say exactly what they mean in terms of empirically observable things (I speak here with the prejudices of a practicing scientist). One hears a lot about "essences" and "vital forces," but never anything independently detectable. At best, such theories do not explain observable phenomena, they just give them new names. At worst, they give one a very idiosyncratic view, which nobody else can verify or falsify, of personal experience. They let us paper over our ignorance by explaining away puzzling phenomena with unobservable spirits and vapors that are assumed, but cannot be proven, to be responsible for the otherwise inexplicable facts. (It is precisely on this point that science and religion part company, in deference to their fundamentally different precepts and purposes.)

Why Newton's Laws and Natural Selection Are Not Tautologies

I received many comments such as, "All of science is built on tautologies. Newton's law, $F = ma$, is a tautology. Survival of the fittest is a tautology. You're holding Lovelock to a standard that you wouldn't apply to Newton or Darwin." The common wisdom behind this objection is so pervasive, so persuasive, and so subtly (but seriously) fallacious, that I must spill a little ink here to straighten things out.

All definitions and purely logical deductions are tautologically true. Science is built on a system of definitions and deductions, so science is built on tautologies, but science has to consist of more than tautologies if it is to say anything about the real world, instead of about our words and how we define them. Mathematics is a very structured, elegant, and powerful system of definitions and deductions, and it is the workhorse of modern science, largely because it helps us to deduce consequences (e.g., experimental predictions) from assumptions without error. But even the best mathematics, all by itself, will tell you absolutely nothing about the real world. We also need a set of assertions about what the mathematics means in real-world terms. Mathematics is the language of science, but we still must have something to say.

Newton's $F = ma$ is just a definition. The left hand side could be called "gzork" rather than "force" and it would make no difference. With only $F = ma$, Newton can only play the engrossing game of restatement. "You give me a measurement of mass and acceleration, and I tell you what the 'force' is." $F = ma$ is—according to some of our educators—what Newton is famous for. But if Newton had stopped at $F = ma$ he would have been just as forgettable as all the non-Newtons in scientific history. What made Newton famous is that he came up with an independent measure of force. He not only asserted $F = ma$; he simultaneously asserted $F = Gm_1m_2/r^2$, and then (here was the brilliant part) he asserted that G is a universal constant, the two forces are equal, and mass is an intrinsic property of matter that means the same thing in both equations.

Those latter assertions are not definitions; they are a statement about what Newton believed to be true about the real world. They should have been warranted for three centuries or twelve orders of magnitude, whichever comes first. (Scale, not time, caught up with Newton, but that's another story).

With only definitions, Newton could only have pinned new labels on old facts. But because he understood both what force was (that which accelerates mass), and what controlled the gravitational force between planetary bodies (mass and separation), Newton could make a new statement about how the world works (the motion of planets is controlled, in a very specific way, by their relative positions and masses). And so he could explain Kepler's descriptions of planetary orbits, and the rest is history.

(As an aside, consider the difference between Newton's approach and the heuristic reasoning of the ancients about things consisting of "earth" "wanting" to return to their "proper" home. This bit of teleology can be restated in nonteleological fashion as things acting *as if* they wanted to return to their proper home, but note how much farther Newton was able to go by not thinking teleologically at all. Newton, having what can only be termed a considerable capacity for generalization, saw that if apples fell out of trees, the moon must be "falling" too (despite the obvious difference in their apparent trajectories) and the earth must be "falling" the opposite way to meet them (despite the complete lack of apparent motion on its part). The success of ignoring teleology and appearances entirely makes me skeptical of the usefulness of simply trying to recast Gaia as the biotic world acting *as if* it wanted to create a nice home for itself . . . but perhaps this says more about my background in physics than about Gaia or the methods of science.)

The point is that science contains definitions—but not *only* definitions. Equivalently, the definitions must be reciprocal.

Which brings me to natural selection. Is "the survival of the fittest" a tautology? First of all, natural selection concerns dominance of the next generation's gene pool by the fittest, rather than merely survival of the fittest, but the tautology could exist in either case, so I will indulge in the man-on-the-street parlance. One often hears the claim that "the survival of the fittest means just the survival of

those who survive." But evolutionary biology does not have to be done that way, and that is not the way competent scientists do it nor the way Darwin meant it to be done.

If one seeks to prove that the fittest survive, but assumes that the fittest survive in defining or measuring fitness (in terms of who survived), a tautology is created, one that an unwary scientist could find very seductive. Some evolutionary biologists do measure so-called fitness coefficients by measuring chances of survival. They must assume that natural selection works, and so cannot—and do not—use those measurements to prove that natural selection works. (Measuring fitness coefficients or selection coefficients is really an attempt to pin down what contributes to fitness; thus these researchers assume that Darwin got the basic scheme right—but those who forgot that they were assuming this could get themselves into trouble.) To prove (without tautology) that natural selection works, an independent definition of fitness is necessary.

For example, the survival advantages of black moths on sooty trees are intuitively obvious, so one can predict (without needing the results of the experiment itself to define fitness) that blacker moths will dominate the gene pool when trees become sootier, as happened in Britain as industrialization spread. When blacker moths do in fact become dominant (remember, it did not have to come out this way; if Darwin were wrong, bright yellow moths could have become common instead), one has begun to collect evidence that natural selection (in admittedly unnatural conditions) really works.

Why Models Cannot Prove the Gaia Hypothesis
Some think that Gaia can be proven with models (e.g., Lovelock, 1983).

A model, like any other statement in mathematical language, can only derive conclusions from assumptions. It cannot show that either the assumptions or the conclusions are empirically realistic. Gaia is an assertion about the real world, not about models. The fact that Gaian mechanisms stabilize a model implies nothing about whether Gaian mechanisms are in fact stabilizing the real world. A model and the real world can give the same behavior for different reasons.

Now, that last statement is not quite fair; any testable prediction made from a hypothesis can be right for the wrong reason. That is why the logical positivists (who, I think, carried the whole thing way too far) stressed the importance of disconfirmatory evidence.

The point here is that in most cases the results from Gaian models are not the kind that can be tested against the behavior of the real world. Consequently, success for the theory is often measured, not by a good match between the model behavior and the real world, but by a good match between the model behavior and the behavior predicted by the theory. That kind of success is guaranteed (barring math or logic errors) because rather than comparing theory and data, this "test" instead compares a theory (in words) with itself (in math).

My point is not that models are useless (I use them all the time myself), but that we must do more than build models. Models can be used to deduce the consequences of Gaian thinking, but not to test the empirical realism of the Gaia hypothesis.

Why I Mention Teleological Gaia and Optimizing Gaia

I understand that Jim Lovelock's thinking has evolved considerably since 1974. I addressed at length the more far-out versions of strong Gaia, not because I thought he was still stuck in 1974, but because I think some of his followers and some of the media are still stuck in 1974, because I don't think we're doing a very good job of getting them unstuck from 1974, and because I think 1974 is (at least in this sense) a bad place to be stuck.

The common perception is that Gaia means that "the earth is alive" or that the biosphere is trying to make itself a nice home here. Because many people do not understand the risks of treating poetic statements as scientific propositions, the public at large thinks that scientists are busy trying to figure out whether the earth *really is* "alive." I don't think that perception helps any of us.

Acknowledgments

J. Harte first introduced me to this topic, suggested that a taxonomy of Gaia hypotheses was needed, and offered many valuable comments and suggestions. I am grateful to M.E. Power, B.A. Roy, S.H. Schneider, H.D. Holland, J.E. Lovelock, and the conference participants for their comments, and I thank the University of California and the William and Flora Hewlett Foundation for financial support. I particularly want to acknowledge Jim Lovelock's gracious response to this paper at the conference. I wish that all scientific debates could be as free of acrimony.

References

Huxley, T.H. 1877. *Physiography.* London: MacMillan & Co.

Kirchner, J.W. 1989. The Gaia hypothesis: can it be tested? *Rev Geophys,* 27, 223–235.

Lovelock, J.E. 1983. Daisy World: A cybernetic proof of the Gaia hypothesis. *Coevolution Quart,* 38, 66–72.

Lovelock, J.E., and Margulis, L. 1974a. Atmospheric homeostasis by and for the biosphere: The gaia hypothesis. *Tellus,* 26, 2–9.

Lovelock, J.E., and Margulis, L. 1974b. Homeostatic tendencies of the Earth's atmosphere. *Orig Life,* 5, 93–103.

Sagan, D., and Margulis, L. 1983. The Gaia perspective of ecology. *The Ecologist,* 13, 160–167.

Spencer, H. 1844. Remarks upon the theory of reciprocal dependence in the animal and vegetable creations, as regards its bearing upon paleontology. *The London, Edinburgh, and Dublin Philosophical Magazine and Journal of Science,* 24, 90–94. Reprinted in Cloud, P. ed. 1970. *Adventures in Earth History,* New York: W.H. Freeman,

Watson, A.J., and Lovelock, J.E. 1983. Biological homeostasis of the global environment: The parable of daisyworld. *Tellus,* 35B, 284–289.

Ideas of interconnectedness and harmony in nature have existed since earliest recorded times (Visvader, 1988, and chapter 5, this volume). Such ideas are represented today in the concept of Gaia (Abram, 1985). Like the historical views, many modern notions of Gaia have been only metaphorically or phenomenalistically defined, and are therefore difficult to analyze scientifically (Kirchner, 1988, and chapter 6, this volume). Yet some of the difficulty may also stem from narrow interpretations of the nature of science and overly simplistic assumptions in biological theory (Goldsmith, 1990). This situation has motivated intense debate but few attempts to integrate differing theoretical perspectives that are inseparably linked to our basic view of life. In this chapter I investigate epistemological issues raised by the concept of Gaia and develop a model for evaluating the foundations of new theory in order to explore the possibility of a scientific basis for a strong theory of Gaia.

Two forms of James Lovelock's Gaia hypothesis were identified during the Chapman conference. These have been termed *weak Gaia* and *strong Gaia,* referring to the degree of supposed influence of biota on the environment at microscopic to global levels. The degree of influence that has been variously proposed has included, on the one hand, the influential, stabilizing, and coevolutionary taxonomies proposed by Kirchner (1988, and chapter 6, this volume); and on the other hand, various superorganism concepts, which include teleological or even conscious control on the part of the biota as a whole. Even within the more conservative weak Gaia views that have emerged, there remains a persistent concept that is not part of the way traditional science has been formalized or the way traditional biology is formalized; one in which life itself is seen as a causal agent both in ecology and evolution (see Lovelock, 1979, 1988; Margulis and Lovelock, 1989; Jantsch, 1980; Plotkin, 1988; Wheeler, 1981; Wigner, 1981; Bohr, 1958, 1961, 1963; Odling-Smee, 1988).

In this chapter I define *weak Gaia* as a class of phenomena that represents an attempt to understand global and interactive systems phenomena in terms of present theoretical concepts (including control theory). It is thus bound by current theoretical structures (including the modern synthetic theory of evolution and adaptation, and theoretical ecology) and is confined to current scientific assumptions and definitions of life. The main epistemological concern for this class of hypotheses is testability within established scientific disciplines and within the traditional empirical methods of science. Weak Gaia theories would thus be judged in regard to how well they conform to current paradigms and concepts of science. Examples in this category might be the hypothesis that land cover tends to have a regulating effect on global climate (e.g., Lovelock's Daisyworld model), or that atmospheric compositions have coevolved with life. Certainly, the initial steps toward a "science of the earth" must begin in this manner (e.g., Rambler et al., 1989).

Strong Gaia must then refer to interpretations of Gaia that require modification to existing theoretical assumptions about nature or our methods of science. For example, a literal concept of a superorganism would probably fall into this category because it violates traditional ways of defining life in reproductive terms. A strictly theological approach to Gaia would also fall into this category because it rejects science as a method of discovery. Thus it is not the degree of biotic influence or specific phenomena that distinguishes a strong Gaia theory from existing theories, but rather the kind and origin of influence that is assumed. Accepting this distinction between the two forms of Gaia, the focus of this chapter is on possibilities within this second category, that is, on acceptable interpretations of strong Gaia that nevertheless challenge current assumptions and epistemology.

It should be made clear that no complete strong Gaia theory currently exists in scientific terms, nor do I pretend to develop one (although a number of serious efforts are evidently being developed). However, I do try to uncover a common root for strong Gaia concepts in terms of fundamental principles on which a theory might legitimately be based. This necessarily exposes critical epistemological issues for which we must establish guidelines for evaluation. After a brief background discussion, I address the problem in three stages. First, I propose a definition of strong Gaia as a worldview. Second, I develop an epistemological model that shows how various methods of science can interact and become integrated and that provides a means by which new theoretical approaches (such as strong Gaia) can be evaluated. Finally, I discuss some likely implications of a strong Gaia worldview in terms of epistemology and the relationship between this worldview and more traditional theories.

Background

It was suggested during the Chapman conference that strong Gaia can only be taken seriously as a metaphor. For example, one version of the Gaia hypothesis (Lovelock, 1979) states metaphorically that 'The entire range of living matter on Earth, from whales to viruses, from oaks to algae, could be regarded as constituting a single living entity capable of manipulating the Earth's atmosphere to suit its overall needs and endowed with faculties and powers far beyond those of its constituent parts.' The problem with a metaphor is that, at most, it describes phenomena—it cannot be used to construct theory. Lovelock's statement is not a scientific hypothesis, but rather a metaphorical description of phenomena, and it is not prescriptive in that form. On the other hand, it should be no more bothersome than Darwin's references to "struggle for survival," which he himself called metaphor, but then continued to employ in describing his theory (Todes, 1989; Richards, 1987). The ability of each of these metaphors to produce popular misconceptions has been similar, and perhaps their ability to stimulate genuine scientific thought may not be so different either.

First, we must recognize that all theories are based on founding assumptions, often metaphysical, that are not themselves subject to experimental confirmation. Such foundations often involve circular (i.e., tautological) definitions and arbitrary

views of nature that provide the starting point and structure for theory. For example, the Euclidean geometry assumed by Newton was consistent with all tests at the time and was therefore accepted as an accurate model. The fact that it was eventually found to be inaccurate on relativistic scales does not damage Newtonian theory itself, but rather establishes the limits of its worldview. Such definitions and underlying assumptions represent the way we choose to perceive reality, that is, from what perspective (paradigm or worldview)[1] we will develop theories, all of which are limited and many of which have taken dramatic turns historically. The value of theory thus cannot be judged on the testability of its assumptions and definitions, but rather on its performance as a structure for scientific thought. It is, in contrast, individual processes or mechanisms[2] proposed within theory that can be tested empirically. This distinction between assumptions and causal processes of theory is critical to evaluating new concepts such as strong Gaia.

Second, a nonmetaphorical theory of strong Gaia must involve explanations in terms of both ecological and evolutionary processes. Evolution is as fundamental to the way we see the universe as are space and time. As Peter Medawar once said regarding creationism, "For a biologist, the alternative to thinking in evolutionary terms is not to think at all" (Little, 1980). In other words, if we hypothesize novel emergent properties of living systems, we must be able to explain how they might have come about, perhaps using new theory, but without contradicting known processes. This is true for Lovelock's obviously metaphorical and phenomenalistic description of a self-organizing Gaia, just as it was for the Darwinian (metaphorical and phenomenalistic) struggle for survival. Current models of evolution incorporate many confirmed causal processes (such as genetic variation and expression, heritability, and differential survival), but are also composed of definitions (such as for life, and fitness) and starting assumptions (such as genetic novelty and the role of environmental selection). It is the limitations of these definitions and assumptions that new theory must rigorously explore, and if current theory cannot explain observable Gaian phenomena, it may be as reasonable to examine our theoretical assumptions about life and evolution as it is to challenge such enigmatic observations.

Finally, it is apparent that any strong Gaia theory emerging from such efforts must be truly interdisciplinary, and thus will require a commonly accepted epistemology. It is likely that a unified view of global systems will require both new scientific perspectives and epistemological synthesis to fully accommodate interdisciplinary issues (Roederer, 1985; Goldberg, 1989). Yet there has been little work on interdisciplinary synthesis, and even our models of science tend to be divided along disciplinary lines, perhaps most sharply between the physical and biological sciences, but also within biological disciplines. This engages two philosophical debates that have been active during the past quarter century; one concerning the applicability of scientific methods across disciplines (particularly the applicability of the methods of physics to the fields of evolution and ecology), and the other concerning the relative merits of instrumentalism versus realism (see section on epistemology). A brief history illustrates the problem.

Physics envy was especially common among biologists in the early 1960s. This was epitomized by an article calling for the use of "strong inference" (Platt, 1964), which emphasized the tradition of testing and exclusion of "multiple alternative hypotheses" (after the traditions of Bacon, Popper, Chamberlin, etc.), citing this as "a surer method to produce more rapid results." A greater emphasis on this hypothetico-deductive (H-D) methodology, or strong inference (the same process emphasized by Kirchner, 1988, and chapter 6, this volume), did indeed take place, but with less robust theoretical results than in physics. This prompted Paine (1977), for example, to translate Platt's appeal for hard science into an appeal for greater emphasis on experimental approaches in building theory, and less reliance on theoretical dogma—particularly the "dogmatic predictions of steady-state competition theory." While the experimental ecologists have apparently fared well with the method, disenchantment seems to surround the development of theory. Simberloff (1981) perhaps symbolized this exasperation by suggesting (somewhat facetiously) that only the results of field or laboratory experiments should be recognized as "valid contributions" to the scientific literature. In contrast to blaming the ecologists, Hall (1985), for example, asserted that Platt's strong inference may be inapplicable to ecology due to the many "system-dependent results" and the "multi-factorial world of ecology." Another claim defensively asserts that physics is in trouble, having advanced rapidly to the point where, as Bohr (1961) declared in 1929, it is impossible to uphold the concept of a purely objective reality.

Others (e.g., Thompson, 1989) have used this development in physics to justify the pursuit of instrumentalist methods in evolution theory and theoretical ecology.

Regardless of where we attempt to point the finger, the concern in linking evolution and ecology seems to be over an apparent lack of vitality in theory development and the lack of correspondence between this and other disciplines. This has created a situation described by Ehrlich (1988) in which ecological theory cannot be based on physical or even universal laws, because each ecological system seems unique. This condition should raise serious concern. For one thing, it is hard to accept that physics has not had to deal with similar epistemological problems, yet its tradition of seeking consistent and universal theory has resulted in great advances. Perhaps more to the point, and where Hall (1985) is probably right, is that we do not understand all of the epistemological processes that have, in some areas of physics, permitted success in integrating theory and eliminating theoretical system dependencies.

Instrumental theories (which are accorded meaning by virtue of their behavior in relation to nature, as opposed to being based on supposedly "real" quantities or principles, such as mass, force, etc.), by their design tend to develop as distinct paradigms. This can result in diverse theories and models that are incommensurable (i.e., they cannot be merged). However, it is important to remember that instrumentalism emerged in physics not because of the failure of attempts to describe nature in real terms, but because of the limits of perception itself. In fact it was a form of Platonic realism (strictly speaking, the notion of a primary unitary reality that scientific theory attempts to describe and predict, but which may never be fully known) that allowed physics to discover the limits of classical reality. Faced with the situation that beyond this point concepts of "real" in the classical sense necessarily became blurred, it then became a philosophical question whether or not the constructs of theory in the quantum world could be called "real" at all. In regard to ecological and evolutionary theories, however, we have yet to consider seriously nonclassical views, having not defined limits to the concept of a single reality. Yet there is little effort in ecology and evolution to integrate theories or combine their assumptions, as was characteristic in the realism of physicists, even for classical mechanistic models. Furthermore, the instrumentalist view has not been fully accepted even in quantum physics, which may instead be leaning toward a "scientific quantum realism" that maintains the pursuit of a parsimonious reality (Rohrlich and Hardin, 1983; Rohrlich, 1989). Finally, a truly interdisciplinary science cannot develop if we pursue epistemologies that cannot be integrated between theories and disciplines.

Thus it is not surprising that an emphasis on H-D methodology (or strong inference) in ecology has worked well for experimentalists and not so well for theoreticians. The vitality of theory development that has characterized physics is not primarily attributable to H-D methods, but to rigorously questioning the basis of theory through attempts to understand the ultimate nature of reality (i.e., what I refer to simply as realism), a process that can challenge one's basic perspective and lead to necessary transitions to new assumptions. Perhaps the problem of vagueness attributed to Gaian concepts results from trying to force them into current biological theory (which lends little mechanistic support and has numerous controversies of its own) without identifying the new assumptions that strong Gaia may require.

Strong Gaia

In this section I try to define strong Gaia in terms that permit its evaluation. To do this, it is necessary to uncover fundamental principles on which the overall paradigm appears to be based. This means examining basic assumptions and underlying metaphysics. Given the distinction between hypothesis and worldview described above, it is clear that strong Gaia must first be defined as a worldview (within which specific causal theories may then be possible).[3]

While Gaia may be most often described phenomenalistically and metaphorically, we may still be able to infer both new assumptions and useful hypotheses from these descriptions, as did the neo-Darwinists in defining natural selection and the mechanism of inheritance from more general concepts of evolution. Certainly strong Gaia, if anything, is a view of life as a creative and active agent. From this beginning alone it is challenging to current theory; but it must itself be challenged to propose an acceptable modification to present assumptions and a viable process for its operation, that is, to allow theory development and confirmation.

What seems most characteristic about the stronger versions of Gaia is the notion of an emergent property of living systems, not predicted by current theory, whereby an ecosystem, or the biosphere as a whole, may seem to act in a coordinated manner and tend to maintain itself through its effect on resources. Our current theories, including coevolution, do not easily extend such organismic behavior to the system level, where evolution cannot proceed by the same means as for reproductive organisms. The mechanism for deriving large-scale organization from currently known processes is problematic, mostly because of present assumptions about life, and the limitations of theory mentioned earlier. Traditional theory treats biological organization as an epiphenomenon, that is, as a result of other causal processes, but concepts of Gaia unanimously describe life itself as an organizing causal process.

The Gaian view (so far described only in terms of phenomenon) implies a general principle that life is fundamentally self-organizing; and, in the strongest sense, that life is fundamentally self-determining (Jantsch, 1980). It also implies that living structures have the ability to manifest this property to various degrees, at various levels of biological organization. (That the process is exhibited significantly on a planetary scale would then be a subsidiary hypothesis.) Many examples of organization, self-regulation, and environmental manipulation clearly exist in the weak sense (i.e., treated by current theory as epiphenomena), but as a theoretical construct the idea implies a radically new principle in the definition of life. This is a big step that will be hard for many theoreticians to accept unless the proposed principle can be based on causal processes that are consistent with our most fundamental concepts of reality and natural law.

Ironically, at the most fundamental level of physics, there is a direct analogy and possible basis for the strong Gaia principle stated above in terms of "the quantum postulate" of Niels Bohr (Bohr, 1958, 1961, 1963).[4] This postulate introduced a worldview in which a newly discovered property of nature, which seems to be related to life, may be the primary causative agent in determining physical conditions at the quantum level. Wheeler summarized, writing that "useful as it is under everyday circumstances to say that the world exists 'out there' independent of us, that view can no longer be upheld. There is a strange sense in which *this is a 'participatory universe'*" (italics added). This phenomenon has been termed *observer participancy*.

While the findings of elementary particle physics

have completely changed the way we view the universe, classical descriptions of nature are unchallenged at material dimensions significantly larger than the "quantum of action" (systems with large quantum numbers). Yet the manifestation of quantum phenomena is not restricted to the scale of elementary particles, as is most often assumed. Bohr wrote extensively on the implications for life and "analogies with some fundamental features of the quantum theory exhibited by the laws of psychology," particularly the "difficulty of distinguishing between subject and object."[5] As with others who followed, Bohr thought that "free will" might be linked with quantum uncertainty and that the connection might go beyond analogy: "Yet it may well be that behind these analogies there lies not only a kinship with regard to the epistemological aspects, but [also] that a more profound relationship is hidden behind the fundamental biological problems which are connected to both sides . . . there is much which indicates that we are concerned here with questions which closely approach the circle of ideas of the quantum theory" (Bohr, 1961). Wigner (1981) wrote: "a being with consciousness must have a different role in quantum mechanics than the inanimate measuring device" and that "it will remain remarkable . . . that the very study of the external world led to the conclusion that the content of the consciousness is an ultimate reality."[6]

The discussion did not end with psychology, however. Bohr was of the opinion that "some amplifying mechanism" exists in living organisms that magnifies the effects of quantum processes, noting that the human brain and sensory system is developed "to the utmost limit permitted by physics." He wrote that "Indeed, the essential characteristics of living beings must be sought in a peculiar organization in which *features that may be analyzed by usual mechanics are interwoven with typically atomistic features to an extent unparalleled in inanimate matter*" (Bohr, 1985; italics added). There has been recent confirmation that sensory receptor cells, in a variety of sensory systems and in a wide range of organisms, operate as quantum mechanical amplifiers by maintaining a quantum "non-equilibrium state" (Bialek and Schweitzer, 1985). This supports Bohr's amplification hypothesis, wherein life forms are capable of retaining sensitivity to quantum indeterminism. Wheeler (1981) asked: "If the elementary quantum process is an act of creation, is an act of creation of any other kind required to bring into being all that is?" Within this view, it

would not be a great leap for strong Gaia to suggest, as did Bohr, that the phenomenon of observer participancy (which we may interpret as a fundamental decision event) may be amplified and expressed to various degrees within all living organisms. An acceptable explanation of how such a phenomenon can become manifest in macroscopic (e.g., organismic) systems through evolution would seem to involve, as a minimum, a combination of the currently accepted elements of evolution theory (e.g., heredity, variation, and natural selection) with cumulative effects of observer participancy.

This approach has been considered in the study of "dissipative structures," which seem to exhibit properties that can be expressed by "only a few quantum numbers" (Jantsch, 1980). From this view, the innovative, adaptive, and self-sustaining properties of organisms are almost axiomatic, and it becomes reasonable that living systems should exhibit self-regulation, self-organization, and various degrees of control over the environment, as a predictable result of nonequilibrium processes characteristic of living forms. Jantsch, in fact, does take the view that life is fundamentally "self-determining" and further suggests that the decision-making ability of nonequilibrium systems may be related to quantum indeterminacy, which dissipative structures are capable of magnifying into "macroscopic indeterminacy." He points out that such indeterminacy should not be confused with random uncertainty; that it is fundamentally nonrandom and nondeterministic (thus agreeing with Bohr). The theory of dissipative structures seems to model many salient characteristics in the holistic nature of living systems (autopoiesis, self-reference, high malleability, system maintenance and evolution, etc.).

Such theories suggest that there are grounds for serious consideration of a strong Gaia worldview based on a universal concept of life as a causal agent. This view appears more to violate traditions of disciplinary compartmentalization than acceptable views of the nature of reality. Thus while theories that could form a basis for strong Gaia are developing rapidly on their own, the reluctance to integrate them with current theories, coupled with the lack of a commonly accepted epistemology, leaves us with no objective tools for evaluation. This lack of interdisciplinary synthesis or development of correspondences between fields, including evolution and ecology, may forestall potentially important revolutions in thought.

New approaches in holistic science inevitably deal with concepts of mind or psyche, an issue which post-Darwinian biology has traditionally tried to exclude from causative processes. The roots of this are mostly cultural and historical: One could argue that confusion between psychological and material theories has been so damaging to both that it has been the more prudent course to keep them apart. For many reasons such arbitrary separations are now crumbling (Roederer, 1985), and we must find the means for scientific integration, including an understanding of science as a process applying equally across disciplines, even if those disciplines cannot yet be integrated themselves. An examination of epistemology is therefore provided as a conceptual framework before proceeding with further discussion of the implications of a strong Gaia worldview,

Epistemology

The following discussion offers guidelines for evaluating the foundations of new theory, and presents a simplified attempt at epistemological synthesis. The epistemological model presented here (figure 7.1) does not pretend to describe the intricacies of science, but rather is constructed to model the relationship between theory development, transitions to new founding assumptions (in either the gradualist sense of Toulmin or the revolutionary sense of Kuhn as described by Suppe, 1977), and processes of integration. The model attempts to combine the postpositivist tradition represented by logical empiricism, the instrumentalist view of independent theories, the realist view of seeking fundamental laws of nature, and the historicist tradition, which deals with the context for science in terms of paradigms of scientific theory, or worldviews. The dominant view in recent years has been historical realism, which "recognizes an historically shifting yet relatively theory-neutral empirical basis for theory confirmation" (Goldberg, 1990). What is most important, however, is how the various epistemic processes interrelate and the results they produce.[7]

The model presented here recognizes the existence and value of instrumental theories, but views the search for "real" elements of theory as a more robust pursuit. This form of realism (i.e., Platonic, as opposed to existential) maintains that there is a hidden reality "out there," and is intent on representing it from basic principles. Theory then becomes a parsimonious attempt to represent natural law that is assumed to be universal, consistent, and

unique (qualities that are also sought for the foundations of worldviews). Even though it is recognized that theory is never perfect, this philosophy maintains that closer approximations to reality are always possible, and that a unique, ultimate reality exists (e.g., Rohrlich, 1989). Thompson (1989), in contrast, argues for adopting a formal instrumentalist epistemology that accepts current (separated) ecological and evolutionary theory structures as part of a "family of interacting theories." This "semantic" construction of theory abandons the idea of constructing theory in terms of elements with "real" meaning, and instead constructs abstract models, according reality only to what can be observed or measured.

Thus instrumentalism represents a practical view of how theory exists today, and the realism described represents an ideal of where theory development should be aimed.[8] Each of these views actually contains elements of the other, and therefore they are not so much opposing views, as different aspects of the growth of knowledge (this relationship is represented in the model). The view presented here is that the goal of realism forces basic assumptions and theory structures to be questioned and modified (by increasing their predictive scope and thereby uncovering contradictions), and thus advances science through revolutions generating new and more inclusive paradigms. Theoretical pluralities inherent in instrumentalism, on the other hand, may be balanced by attempts at theory integration or the development of interdisciplinary approaches. Such integration may reveal important contradictions in the foundations of theory, thus opening the way for new ideas, in a similar manner as revolutions in theory.

Figure 7.1 shows a model of the growth and evolution of knowledge facilitated by the identification of theoretical crises. In this figure, scientific investigation (phase A) considers theory development within established paradigms as a combination of phenomenal and causal studies which ultimately result in paradox due to limited assumptions (phase B). The transition phase (phase C) shows a process of crisis resolution, which necessitates a move from one theoretical basis to another (hopefully more inclusive) view. Finally, the figure shows theoretical pluralities (phase D), which may become linked or unified (phase E).

Phase A depicts a relationship between two methodological extremes, shown as the study and description of phenomena (on the left), and the search

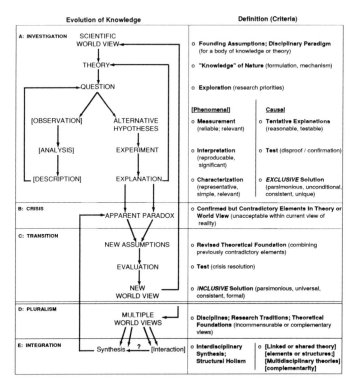

Figure 7.1 Model for knowledge growth, facilitated by crises.

for explanations in terms of causal processes (on the right). This relationship includes the more restrictive positivist ideal of logical empiricism (i.e., hypothetico-deductive or strong inference methodology). In practice these methods often interrelate, giving a variety of operational approaches.[9] On the one extreme, the essence of logical empiricism (Popper, 1959 and 1965) can be described as disproof of reasonable alternatives (hypotheses) in relation to observation and existing knowledge (i.e., which must necessarily be used when designing experiments and interpreting data). Within the established paradigm, new ideas that are contradicted by experiment (or prior knowledge) are rejected, and those that cannot be rejected (or as some philosophers argue, are confirmed) are added to the body of knowledge, which thus grows by accumulating consistent concepts. This quest for theory that is logically self-consistent and consistent with both observation and experiment is shown as the operating procedure or routine of science.

Yet philosophers have discovered the impossibility of defining an absolute set of knowledge. Historicism therefore recognizes that a body of knowledge that is built upon previous learning must

be relative to a particular set of assumptions. These assumptions form a worldview that is defined by historical scientific development, cultural influences, and current philosophy. Furthermore, as described by Kuhn (1970) and his followers, there have repeatedly been scientific revolutions. This is shown in figure 7.1, where the emphasis on empirical and theoretical studies in the primary cycle (phase A) leads to paradigm shifts in phase C. In this view, theory growth can become punctuated when contradictions in theory are seen as representing a philosophical and scientific crisis. This assumes, of course, a strong epistemological motivation to resolve apparent paradoxes, as is most prevalent in the (Platonic) concept of realism described here. Whereas apparent paradoxes (for example, resulting from causal explanations that are accorded some sense of reality) are crisis inducing within the old theoretical context (phase A), they are the fuel for new worldviews in phase C. This combines philosophical traditions into a simple model of punctuated equilibrium, where opposite criteria are employed in the testing process at these two levels. The epistemology in phase A operates on the assumption that two alternative explanations cannot both be correct. Phase C, however, operates on the assumption that two apparently paradoxical elements of theory that have otherwise been confirmed must both be correct.

Empirical methods of science thus operate within established thought structures (i.e., paradigms and worldviews), testing well-posed hypotheses to build a theory, but not testing the structure itself. As an example, empirical science does not test the idea of force directly: under appropriate circumstances, it is equally valid to view gravity as a force or as an artifact of curved space, and the merits of each view is an independent issue from how they are formalized. Empirical testing is concerned with how forces act (e.g., $f = ma$) or interrelate (e.g., the equivalence of acceleration and gravitational force). The paradigm itself is judged first on whether or not it can be formalized, and then on its overall predictive value and applicability to new phenomena. Therefore, the means for evaluating the foundations of theory are quite different from the means for testing hypotheses about its operation. Both can be scientific if they are not confused with each other; but confusion between these two levels of thought is common and characteristic of statements (and criticisms) about Gaia.

Still, the above synthesis is an incomplete picture, especially in terms of the debate between realism and instrumentalism (the idea that theory need not be based on a common reality) and the obvious existence of theoretical pluralism. The realist view works well in classical physics, which is easily referenced to basic axioms; however, other branches of science have not been so blessed. Instrumentalism is thus represented in several places in the model. In the form of purely phenomenal or descriptive theories (such as Ptolemy's model of a geocentric Solar System, as described, for example, by Rohrlich, 1989) it might be seen as a hybrid of the two extremes in phase A (i.e., a theory that does not seek basic laws, but yet has predictive value based on the regularity of phenomena). Although logical contradictions can be identified within such theories, it is undetermined whether they will become crisis inducing or remain unchallenged. A more formal instrumentalism appears in phase E (right side), where theoretical pluralities are treated as a "family of interacting theories" (Thompson, 1989). As shown, it is questionable whether this approach will similarly preserve theoretical contradictions or will eventually resolve them through some form of synthesis.

The immediate concern, in regard to strong Gaia, is to determine by what means the worldview portion of this model (i.e., new founding assumptions) can be evaluated. As mentioned earlier, the basis for theory cannot be evaluated in the same way as the content of theory (i.e., by logical empiricism and hypothesis testing). There are, however, specific criteria that can be employed for evaluating worldview assumptions. Five such criteria are discussed here.

Criterion 1: Parsimony

Parsimony, or "Ockham's razor," is an appeal to concepts that improve our understanding of nature through the use of simplifying assumptions. If we find a more parsimonious view of nature, operating from that view will make description and explanation of phenomena simpler (once the new idea is understood well enough to be used). Explanations should then lead to more revealing questions and useful applications to other phenomena.

Various forms of parsimony can apply to descriptive models (e.g., characterizations should be as simple as possible in regard to their intended use), to theory development (explanations), and to critical assumptions that might make up a worldview. In the latter case, the goal is to provide a more useful thought system, recognizing that a simplifying assumption rarely seems simple when first perceived from a different worldview. As Bohr (1961) stated: "Only by experience itself do we come to recognize those laws which grant us a comprehensive view of the diversity of phenomena. As our knowledge becomes wider, we must always be prepared, therefore, to expect alterations in the points of view best suited for the ordering of our experience. In this connection we must remember, above all, that, as a matter of course, all new experience makes its appearance within the frame of our customary points of view and forms of perception" (which, we might add, may be deceiving). *A correct use of parsimony requires that one judge by results, not by appearance.* Parsimony, in evaluating a new worldview, must be established by experience with the new view itself, a process that may involve long periods of development. An often cited example in the history of physics is the parsimonious nature of Newton's laws of motion (based on the concept of force) in contrast to Ptolemy's increasingly elaborate mathematical description of a geocentric Solar System. In regard to building theory, it should thus be considered parsimonious to seek deeper levels of causality.

Historically, natural science became simplified by avoiding problematic fields such as psychology. This simplified the job by reducing its scope; however, it did not simplify our explanation of nature. Similarly, scientific disciplines are sometimes described as complementary, but this does not mean that their separation is parsimonious. The principle of complementarity that has been found to be parsimonious in physics is proposed as a fundamental and necessary property of nature (the uncertainty principle); whereas the complementary separation between two theories or disciplines (say between psychology and biology), or among Thompson's family of interacting theories in evolution and ecology, is not a requirement of nature, but has to do with our lack of knowledge and with different assumptions or theory elements.[10] The "family of theories" concept is not chosen out of consideration of parsimony, but rather expedience, to accommodate a multiplicity of perspectives. The realist perspective favored here implies that integration of theories or worldviews (when achievable) involves a more parsimonious and fundamental understanding of nature.

Criterion 2: Universality
The search for universal principles as the basis for explanation is essential to the development of a general theory in the realist tradition. Within a given worldview, the search for ever deeper levels of explanation (i.e., causation),and thus the successive formalization of more universal principles, extends theory to new situations by making it less conditional on presupposed limits. If one seeks universal and causal explanations *within* a world view, rigorous development must ultimately challenge the universality of the worldview itself. On the other hand, solutions that are designed to be system dependent tend to reinforce their own theoretical foundations and provide less pressure to modify original assumptions. Strong Gaia, as defined earlier, is universal in that it rests on a principle that is assumed to be present in all life.

Criterion 3: Crisis Resolution
As history implies, the relentless pursuit of a consistent and complete body of theoretical knowledge (phase A of figure 7.1) can eventually lead to a crisis in scientific thought (Kuhn, 1970). Such crises can be defined by one or more apparent or specific par-

adoxes (i.e., a paradox that is specific to the given worldview). A specific paradox, as defined here, consists of at least two inescapable theoretical conclusions that are mutually exclusive, given our original assumptions about nature. Paradoxes in thought or theory, whether consciously identified or not, can thus form the psychological basis for reevaluating assumptions both in everyday thought and during major scientific revolutions. As an example, paradoxes develop from Euclidean geometry when it is applied over large distances, due to the curvature of space (or in geodesy, due to the curvature of the Earth). Such crises are perceived when theory becomes incompatible with our concept of a unitary reality (as with two logically contradictory conclusions). However, if we do not actively challenge the foundations of theory, we may not discover their paradoxical elements. For example, paradoxical views mentioned earlier between biological theories are often ignored. Wave-particle complementarity, on the other hand, is no longer paradoxical because we have accepted duality as our idea of nature. Paradoxes are thus a result of present theoretical contradictions and an epistemological realism that claims such contradictions should not exist.

Paradox was a particular interest of Niels Bohr (1961) and was prominent in the many discussions between Bohr and Einstein. In fact, it is safe to say that the identification and resolution of paradox became an intentional characteristic in the progress of physics beginning with Einstein (e.g., the EPR Paradox, Schrödinger's Cat Paradox, Twin Paradox, etc.). The exercise of analyzing paradox was essential in clarifying one's theory (or worldview), or overthrowing it by proving a logical inconsistency.

An excellent description of the purposeful use of paradox as part of the scientific method was presented by Einstein (1916) in his layperson's explanation of special and general relativity. Einstein introduced the reasoning that led to his formulation of special relativity theory—a new worldview—by pointing out "the apparent incompatibility of the law of propagation of light" (constant speed in a vacuum) "with the principle of relativity" (that the laws of nature are unchanged at constant velocities). Physics had reached this inconsistency after a painstaking pursuit of traditional scientific experimentation and hypothesis testing, with agreement among the scientific community that the resulting paradox was logically unresolvable within the classical worldview. At this point, the essence of solving the dilemma was not to reject one of the alternatives, as in testing hypotheses, but to accept both and revise our assumptions about the nature of the universe. In Einstein's own words, "As the result of an analysis of the physical conceptions of time and space" [i.e., the formulation of his new worldview] "it became evident that in reality there is not the least incompatibility between the principle of relativity and the law of propagation of light, and that *by systematically holding fast to both these laws, a logically rigid theory could be arrived at*" (italics added). This was the theory of special relativity, and it required changing our assumptions about the geometry of space and time. The process, so beautifully understood and illustrated by Einstein, is an essential process for every architect of new scientific thought, whether it is done consciously or by intuition.

This implies that developing a new worldview is a very different process from building consistent theory. In building causally related theory, reasonable alternatives within a given framework can be established and selectively excluded based on evidence. Successional and more advancing worldviews, however, require altering the assumptions; and advances to a more inclusive view are made most reliably by unifying empirically confirmed but logically contradictory conclusions (paradox) that appear within the former world view. Thus this latter process is one of inclusion, because the new view is now able to explain how both sides of the apparent paradox can be seen as true. In forming a new worldview, we are considering a change in basic assumptions brought on by a logical failure of the previous view.

The value of demonstrating paradox is illustrated by the noticeable lack of such demonstrations in pseudoscientific theories. With two opposite processes within the scientific method (selection and unification) and no clear way of deciding when to apply each, science easily degenerates into chaos because revolutions are no longer asked to address a genuine issue (i.e., they are solutions without a demonstrated problem). The criterion of crisis resolution establishes both the need for new directions and the likelihood that the line of reasoning to which one is led will be useful. The search for theoretical paradoxes should be relentless.

As the model indicates, paradox can also appear when previously separate theories, worldview, or disciplines are combined. The process of disciplinary or worldview integration can identify logical conflicts between interacting theories, which can stimulate unification. I mentioned this earlier in regard to opposite perspectives within current views of behavioral ecology and evolution. As long as these perspectives are considered separate or complementary, no crisis will be perceived; but if they are combined (in a realist context), one must resolve the issue of interdependence between organism and environment. This is what strong Gaia must attempt to do, if it is going to be a useful approach.

Criterion 4: Consistency
A fourth criterion can also be stated, that an acceptable new worldview must be consistent not only with itself but with previous knowledge (previous observations and the principles they confirmed). This idea is similar to Bohr's principle of "correspondence" between quantum theory and classical physics, except that consistency is less demanding than Bohr's concept, which may not always be achievable.[11]

The idea of consistency is implied in identifying and resolving paradox. The argument goes like this: To demonstrate that a paradox exists in the first place, we rely on previous observations. In doing so, we implicitly accept previous forms of evidence and methods of confirmation; otherwise the paradox, and thus the justification for seeking a new theory, has itself been invalidated. Therefore, a new, more explanatory worldview cannot reject results of the old, even though it may provide radically new ways of explaining them. For example, relativity does not reject results obtained by scientists working within the thought paradigms defined by Newtonian mechanics and Cartesian geometry, at the level of precision that was obtainable from them (in this case, they were shown to be derivable from relativity theory). A view that rejects previous experience in its opening assumptions would suffer from being out of context, and would be less likely to be useful scientifically.

Like the quantum theory, strong Gaia based on observer participancy would not be able to dispense with the classical objective view (an observer separated from nature). This is because, as Bohr put it: "We must not forget that, in spite of their limitation, we can by no means dispense with those forms of perception which colour our whole language and in terms of which all experience must ultimately be expressed." As individual organisms with sense perception, the objective view will always be important to us as our means of conceptualizing the world. Thus while nonmaterialist formalism may be included within theory, it is necessary to maintain consistency (and correspondence when possible) with the classical, objective, and materialistic view of nature. There seems to be nothing inherent in the assumption that living structures have magnified observer participancy that would a priori contradict current knowledge of nature. It would, however, extend the range of explainable phenomena beyond the domain of pure materialism, which would then be treated as a limited case of a more general theory. This would satisfy consistency, just as the theory of relativity is consistent with Newtonian mechanics.

Criterion 5: Formalization of Theory and Testable Hypotheses

The fifth requirement is that an acceptable worldview must allow theory to be formalized in a way that allows testable hypotheses about its causal processes. In practice, a revolutionary theory will not be taken seriously unless it can include acceptable causalities in its formalization. This requirement rules out, for example, cosmically theistic world views (as a basis for scientific theory) that attribute final cause to one or more external gods, who or which transcend our ability to investigate. Within such views, experiments to determine cause, and thus to develop causal theory, are meaningless, and theory itself is unnecessary (note that I do not reject such views, but only claim that they cannot be used as a basis for scientific theory).

It is essential to the scientific method (as modeled earlier) to be able to create an objective viewpoint for testing hypotheses, in order to produce unambiguous results. Strong Gaia as described here is no exception and is not subjective science. It is participatory in the sense that it is holistic, and the effects of participation are theoretically limited. It allows theory to include a fundamentally subjective process (observer participancy), but retains the use of objectivity as the means for confirming results. As with the quantum theory itself, it is still possible to study objectively the results of a fundamentally subjective and nondeterministic process that has quantifiable limits.

Discussion

In the preceding sections I have attempted to establish both a worldview context for strong Gaia, and an epistemological basis for dealing with such new paradigms. In this section I consider some of the more problematic implications and potential conflicts with existing theory. The discussion is meant only to be indicative of the basic issues that must be dealt with.

Teleology and the Origin of Novelty

The view of life as a causal process introduces a major issue in epistemology: This is the issue of teleology (purpose or goal directedness). When studying physics, it is easy to define a quantity called "observer participancy," or "registration" (Wheeler, 1981) and treat it as a random factor. Because this quantity takes on the role of decision maker in the physical experiments, the physics itself (aside from hidden variables theories) does not have to deal with how or why decisions are made (e.g., what causes the observer to measure a quantum system, or correspondingly, what causes individual registration events?). However, in a formal theory about the decision maker (i.e., life as defined by strong Gaia) the question of purpose seems inescapable. Bohr (1958), for example, stated flatly that teleology (although perhaps not the cosmic teleology of Kant) must, because of the quantum discoveries, be a part of biology.

There are recent formal treatments of teleology (George and Johnson, 1985); and while the debate continues, teleological explanations are no longer considered "automatic evidence of sloppy thinking." Specific theories are emerging on how it can be treated scientifically (e.g., in cybernetics). Mayr (1988) distinguishes between "teleomatic" processes, defined as progression toward an end state through physical processes (i.e., inevitable change in a predictable direction, such as the Hubble expansion of the universe or the second law of thermodynamics), and "teleonomic" processes, which are those that are guided by a "program" (defined by Mayr as coded information controlling an end-directed process). Teleonomic processes, including those adapted through natural selection, can incorporate new information to alter the outcome, but apparently not the program itself, which is the result of natural selection. Mayr excludes "cosmic" teleology, that is, a "causally effective end result," from acceptable science, stating boldly that: "Indeed, I do not know of a single modern scientist who believes in it."

Although, in Mayr's words, teleonomy is "perhaps the most characteristic feature of the world of living organisms," it seems to be viewed strictly as a system-dependent process, not a general principle. This allows its application in ecology and organismic biology (e.g., migration, courtship, ontogeny, and numerous other goal-directed processes) but prevents its consideration in evolution theory (which would generalize it to cosmic dimensions). Mayr, reflecting the traditional worldview, states: "It is illegitimate to describe evolutionary progress or trends as goal directed (teleological). Selection rewards past phenomena . . . but does not plan for the future." Biologists thus generally deny any form of evolutionary "progress" that might be motivated by a goal, or imply "final cause" (Futuyma, 1979). Trends in evolution, then, must be due to either chance occurrences (e.g., disturbance, migration, environmental change, and so forth) or teleomatic end results (e.g., adaptation, niche segregation, optimization, and others).

However, within ecology and organismic biology organisms are treated as if they were active agents, responding to and modifying their environment during the course of their life spans, in ways that "promote survival." Here, the distinction between "survival" as a goal (cosmic teleology) and "survival" as an existential (and thus teleomatic) result of natural selection is somewhat obscure; but it is nevertheless maintained by the circular argument that good survival strategies (coded in the genes of fit survivors) have been selected for, but cannot include a plan or vision for an ultimate state (such as long-term survival) because a future state could not have been a selective factor in ecological time. Thus evolution theory has been used to establish survival as the paradigm for ecology, while excluding it as an actual goal within organismic behavior. It follows that teleonomic behavior should only evolve to benefit survival of kin and reproductive offspring in ecological time (thus implying great importance for competition, because only the survival "programs" represented in related genes can reinforce themselves).

These traditional theories also exclude consideration of true novelty at the phenotypic or ecological level, for if behavioral novelties (i.e., not the result of selection) could also promote survival, then it would be impossible to distinguish this from final cause. Furthermore, the concepts of behavioral novelty and a teleonomy that can include a vision or goal of abstract states approach the concept of mind or psyche (although not necessarily in the human sense), and the comparison is unavoidable.

Thus in order to deny final cause, the tendency is also to exclude concepts of mind.

This attempt to avoid the problem of final cause, by the selective exclusion from evolution theory of principles that might introduce teleology, has resulted in an unrealistic separation of disciplines and timescales and, not surprisingly, some controversy. Odling-Smee (1988) citing B.C. Patten, for example, claims that the modern synthesis "leads us directly to the separation of organisms from their environments." He further states that "[the modern synthesis] cannot model environmental changes in terms of anything at all . . . the synthetic theory lacks any medium of inheritance that could allow it to describe environmental changes as an integral part of the evolutionary process. Instead it is forced to assume that the environment is autonomous and that environmental change is a separate matter from changing organisms. The result is two disciplines: ecology, which handles environmental change, and evolutionary biology, which deals with changing organisms . . . Hence the modern synthesis has to rule out the possibility that the outputs of active organisms are capable of modifying their own subsequent inputs in evolutionarily significant ways." According to Odling-Smee, this paradox was first pointed out by the physicist Schrödinger (famous for the Schrödinger wave equation of quantum physics).

The common view in adaptation and evolution theories is that novelty (including survival strategy) originates in genetic variation, which is then selected by an independent environment. Because genes are the medium of inheritance, not phenotypes, all the phenotypic processes intervening between generations (i.e., everything the organism does) tend to be treated as merely the mechanism of interaction between the genotype and natural selection, but not itself a source of novelty. This view may owe much of its basis to the rejection of Lamarckism (which held, incorrectly, that such a process could operate through direct heredity); but it seems to be untenable if one considers that novel behavior can alter the evolutionary pathway in indirect ways. Yet behavior is typically reduced to a sophistication of genetic programming, and therefore a preselected result that cannot introduce true novelty in ecological time.

It then follows that the organism is viewed as a passive agent acted upon by the total environment (which is virtually undefinable, yet assumed to include the physical influence of living organisms), ignoring autogenic effects (i.e., influences from the one organism that is always present). This is directly analogous to the Newtonian or atomistic worldview in which passive objects are "forced" externally. The opportunity for organisms to influence their own selection through behavioral novelty (Plotkin, 1988), and subsequently influence evolutionary pathways (Jantsch, 1980), is thus excluded from current evolution theory by the way it has been formalized.

The division of disciplines thus preserves the contradiction of, on the one hand, a passive or random biological model for evolutionary novelty, and on the other, evidence of creativity in life strategies, decision-making, and our own (human) experience of choice. Perhaps by this division we are able to formulate useful first order theories that describe certain aspects of living organisms; however, the arbitrary separation also ensures that some second-order system properties will be ignored. For example, if such unrealistic limitations of traditional theory are relaxed, the concept of internal causal processes influencing behavior and life strategies may be integrated with models for external environmental effects and interactions with other species, including feedbacks over both ecological and evolutionary time scales.

Strong Gaia

The strong Gaia view would be forced to treat purpose as a real quantity that is determined at the organismic level through the amplification of observership, which thus provides the theoretical basis for creativity at the organismic level. The presence of sophisticated biological examples for the magnification of this phenomena, as noted earlier, implies that this capability has evolved from rudimentary beginnings. Innovation at the organismic level may then exhibit original effects on the environment and, therefore, selection. This implies a complementarity between form and function over the course of generations, where (as in physics) observation of one aspect results in change in the other. It would thus be impossible for living organisms to determine exactly both form and function, because functional definitions would imply morphological uncertainty over evolutionary time, and vice versa. This property of functional indeterminacy, from its simplest beginnings, might be assumed to exist in anything we call life. In contrast to the

mechanistic view that function is determined solely by the relationship between morphology and the environment (thus allowing for no inputs from the present), strong Gaia would formally assume that function, though largely determined by phylogeny, is partly self-defined or modified (i.e., independently of prior selective factors). This self-definition could then lead to future evolutionary forms that are not strict derivatives of environmental factors, but may in fact have, and be partly the result of, a creative influence on their environment. The acceptability of a truly interdisciplinary strong Gaia view rests on the reasonableness of such assumptions.[12]

A further criterion is whether the question of teleology can be resolved by identifying the source of novelty as observer participancy. Certainly any biological purpose of exclusively external origin violates the ability to form testable causal hypotheses in the same way that theistic views do, as there can be no process by which external purpose (final cause) can drive behavior, development, or evolution, unless it is reflected as an internal drive. The question that must be considered here is if the appearance of purposeful goals can be treated scientifically if they are of internal definition within the system (or organism) under study.

Of course, as a general principle that can apply equally to the simplest and most complex of organisms, the concept of purpose must not be equated with consciously and knowingly planning for future events, as in the human sense, which is clearly a recent evolutionary complexity (Crook, 1980; Wilber, 1986). Still, the ability, expressed according to the complexity of the organism, to define function, expressed through novel behavior, would be an unrecognized case in Mayr's definitions, falling short of cosmic teleology but going beyond teleonomy (programmed direction where the program is strictly a result of prior selection). The case would rather be that such functional definitions could alter teleonomic programs and provide them with an implied goal. To the extent that a future state can be represented by present function, this comes perhaps uncomfortably close to the notion that an envisioned end can be causally effective.

It is thus critical to this strong Gaia worldview to formally decouple behavior from genetic determinism by providing an alternative causal process: Yet this point is missed in many recent accounts. Augros and Stanciu (1988), in a popular account, for example, miss this point entirely by arguing that the

"new biology" cannot be derived from physical principles; whereas, presumably, the point is that it cannot be derived from classical principles. Even Plotkin's (1988) account does not provide a causal basis for "novelties" expressed as behavior. There are, meanwhile, a number of deterministic theories that relate function (and behavior) solely to genetics or other physical determinants, as in mechanical response to stimuli. It is by no means accepted among biologists that even human psychological experiences such as "free will" are other than deterministic or genetic manifestations. Honderich (1988), for example, attempts to defend a deterministic approach for explaining psychological phenomena associated with life (free will, life hopes, etc.), but sidesteps the obvious problem of quantum theory by claiming that it will one day be replaced by determinism (apparently ignoring evidence to the contrary). Such claims can be used to defend anything, and thus are useless—we must work with the evidence at hand.

Although everyone is in doubt about the full implications of observer participancy, the principle is being linked to biological phenomena. A formal treatment of the relationship between observership and perception (observer mechanics), for example, has recently been published (Bennett et al., 1989). Since there would be little reason to doubt a connection between perception and behavior, a causal chain may be possible. Incorporating observership into models of how organisms translate form into function (and vice versa) introduces a process that may also help explain evolutionary novelty at a system level. As a possible scenario, behavioral innovations may create a positive selective feedback, through the effect of environmental modification on the development and behavior of future generations, including other species. As natural selection is assumed to favor characteristics that are adaptive to the new environment, behavioral and functional innovations could, in this way, influence the phylogeny of even unrelated organisms and thus become registered in the course of evolution.

This view poses problems for optimization theories, stating that optimization would be impossible beyond limits set by the fundamental uncertainties in the system (which, as yet, we have no way to quantify). It also implies that we could not assume that a theoretical "optimal" actually exists, as a given state would be the combined effect of adaptation and unpredictable functional definitions that ensure nonequilibrium.

Under such a view, even the simplest abilities to stimulate positive selective feedback could be self-reinforcing, giving rise to seemingly purposeful trends that actually reflect functional decisions made at the individual level. This means that we would have to view the course of evolution as partially determined by the organism, although not in the Lamarckian sense, but over the course of many generations through the combined effect of behavioral choices, their effect on the environment, and reciprocal selection. In a very real sense, selective forces would be seen as partly cocreated by the organism; increasingly so, in accordance with organismic complexity (e.g., Corning, 1983). It could also be suggested that the ability to affect evolution in this way has itself been selected for, thus creating a teleomatic process in evolution that may partly explain the emergence of the extreme capabilities of humans in this regard, with the further complexification of self-awareness, or consciousness (Crook, 1980; Wilber, 1986).

The possibility for natural selection to reward (and register) innovative behavioral interactions and environmental modifications would likely have coevolutionary implications in terms of interactive complexities (Corning, 1983; Goldberg, 1989). In a highly simplified example, Axelrod (1984) has proposed a model of strategic interactions in terms of game theory ("the prisoner's dilemma") to explain the evolution of cooperation. In this model, cooperative strategies emerge naturally from rudimentary organismic abilities that are all included in the strong Gaia view considered here. These abilities are (1) a motivation for gain (self-defined purpose); (2) ability to recognize the presence or absence of benefits (sensory perception and self-reference); and (3) ability to modify behavior in innovative ways, based on current experience (observership or decision making). Given these basic psychobiological abilities (which in actual life would operate entirely in the present, not presupposing conscious awareness, memory, or intellectual reasoning; and given an environmental context that favors long-term interactions; the emergence of coevolutionary and cooperative systems is predicted at many levels of complexity.

Similarly, strong Gaia, as described, may bear a close resemblance to information theory, since by accepting organismic life as a causative agent (i.e., source of novelty), information and self-determination can become driving forces for system phenomena. Current theory relates life form with information by identifying DNA as the primary agent for defining organismic structure. But the evolutionary complementarity between form and function proposed here suggests a continuous interchange of information between organism and environment over generations, where the evolution of form only partly determines function, which may then modify and direct the evolution of form. It is interesting to speculate that, given this process, the basic model presented in figure 7.1 for the growth of intellectual knowledge may also be a model for the evolution of species, complex organisms, communities, and ecosystems.

The Cultural Paradigm of Global Science

Holistic concepts of the earth, including its environment and biota, have been increasing in prominence (e.g., deep ecology, Gaia). Most recently (circa 1986), there has been a major shift in the goals of geoscience towards an interdisciplinary earth systems view (Earth System Science Committee, 1988; International Geosphere-Biosphere Program, 1988). This is a commitment that will require major changes in the way we do science, as well as in theory development itself.

It is interesting to look at these recent events in terms of a social and historical perspective (an approach that Thomas Kuhn increasingly favored in his philosophy of scientific revolutions). This view claims that both current and new scientific worldviews involve not just scientists, but all of society and historical developments. If we are nearing a paradigm shift requiring a radically new view of life and systems, then it should be evident in all walks of society.

Figure 7.2 depicts this Kuhnian perspective for global geoscience, showing a trend toward integration and globalization in three critical areas, represented as science, technology, and society. From this perspective, advancement from one stage to the next depends on a sufficient level of development in all three areas of the preceding stage. We may now be witnessing the maturation of stage II and the beginnings of stage III, where interdisciplinary global science will spawn new theory. From this perspective, the conditions seem right for profound change at all levels of our worldwide society, and one must wonder what changes in scientific thinking are in store, or indeed, required.

Thought Problem

A characteristic notion in statements about Gaia is that it is impossible even for humans to separate ourselves from the system of study, as reflected in the concept of participatory science (Abram, 1985). The increasing global impact of human activity appears to be developing in a way that will not allow us to avoid this issue much longer. A thought problem can illustrate this in regard to human psychology and the study of global climate:

Hypothesis 1: Scientific beliefs significantly affect cultural values and beliefs (Kuhn, 1970).

Hypothesis 2: Cultural beliefs about humanity's relation to nature significantly affect (through industry and policy) the amount and kind of impact we have on nature. Specifically, societies with strong cultural beliefs that humans are an integral part of nature tend to have less overall impact, and vice versa (Posey, 1989).

Hypothesis 3: Human activity significantly affects the global climate system (e.g. Schneider, 1989).

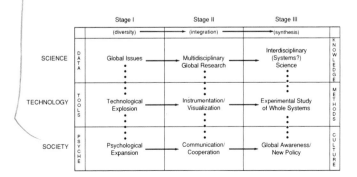

Figure 7.2 The growth of a new paradigm (scientific, technological, and cultural synthesis).

If we accept each of these above hypotheses (all reasonable and testable), then it follows that a dominant scientific paradigm wherein science must be purely objective (necessarily equating knowledge with separation from nature) will result, paradoxically, in participatory effects on the climate system.

The worldview of life as a fundamentally creative and interactive force, and corresponding adjustments in our theory of knowledge, are quite different from the idea that separation from nature is possible for scientific or other purposes. The above scenario thus claims that it is not possible to retain a belief in separation within our theory about knowledge (i.e., pure objectivity), without having it also reflected in our theory and practice as a society. Ultimately, then, the denial of ourselves as participants will have a destructive effect on the environment (and, epistemologically, a contradictory effect on the original premise). Treating strong Gaia as metaphor may not be a strong enough position to alter the scenario. Western traditions, for example, recognize metaphor for cultural enrichment, but believe it is science that leads to progress. The kind of progress we will have as a society may then be strongly influenced by epistemology (i.e. how we choose to pursue science).

Conclusion

In this chapter I have examined the roots of a strong Gaia worldview by drawing inferences from currently phenomenalistic concepts of Gaia, outlining epistemological arguments, and making interdisciplinary comparisons. Whether this view will prove to be fruitful scientifically, however, is yet to be determined. Toward this end, some reasonable avenues for thought seem to exist.

Theory resulting from a strong Gaia view should pose no threat to science in general, or to prior theories except to propose that those theories have limits (which any sound epistemology should expect). It is clear that strong Gaia would be a theoretical pursuit that must develop its own formalism and remain interdisciplinary. Furthermore, any such attempt to develop a truly interdisciplinary worldview will require epistemological synthesis. In presenting both a descriptive and normative model for epistemology, it is implied that science as a means of acquiring knowledge may be a natural process itself, and thus may have parallels in the natural world (Roederer, 1978; Jantsch, 1980; Goldberg, 1989). In such a view, living organisms are not so much struggling for survival as they are modifying and fulfilling function and in so doing, acquiring knowledge, which is incorporated into their very structure–a truly participatory process that is analogous to science.

Theories within strong Gaia, like other macroevolution theories, may describe very different processes than traditional biology and geoscience. Because it attempts to be holistic in its consideration of ecological and evolutionary time, and because of the critical, causal role that observer participancy could have in forming a strong Gaia theory, it would place great importance on theories of perception and psychology (e.g., Abram 1985 and chapter 8, this volume), the role of behavior in directing evolution (Plotkin, 1988), an epistemology that allows theory formally to include fundamental (ontic) uncertainties instead of only experimental unknowns (Rohrlich, 1989), and certain kinds of teleology (George and Johnson, 1985). It would incorporate a new assumption into evolution theory that might have significant implications for coevolution and cooperation theory at all levels by allowing novelty in ecological time to influence selection (Corning, 1983; Axelrod, 1984; Odling-Smee, 1988; Lovelock, 1988).

It is implied by the opinions expressed here that we must pursue classical views of ecology and evolution (i.e., the present norm); however, not as a dogmatic limit to biological investigation, but rather as a useful first-order approximation to reality, which we know is more complex. Quantum physical processes (observer participancy) expressed macroscopically and magnified over time by the operation of classical evolutionary processes, may account for the emergence of self-determination as a significant second-order factor in evolution and ecology. In this view, self-determination (resulting from an indeterminacy of organismic function) cannot be uniquely isolated to the human example, but must rather be recognized as a property of living organisms expressed variably at all levels of complexity. This view might imply evolutionary tendencies toward large-scale coevolution and cooperation as a function of the degree of expression and interdependence of teleonomic indeterminism originating with the phenotype. This may present intriguing possibilities for the development of interdisciplinary ecological and evolutionary models that take into account the evolutionary feedback of functional modifications and their collective effect on environmental selection (i.e., complementarity of form and function through evolutionary time). It seems possible that some of the emergent properties of living systems attributed to Gaia may be derivable from such an approach. At the very least, we might suspect that the human equation, including our relationship with earth systems and our own evolution, may be an important example.

Notes

1. Use of the term *paradigm* tends to vary, but here refers to the set of operating assumptions for a given thought exercise at any level. The term *worldview* refers to the grand paradigm for a scientific theory or discipline. At still another level, one can speak of the *paradigm of science,* which has to do with science methodology, or epistemology (the subject of this chapter).

2. Many branches of science use the term *mechanism* to refer to the inner workings or processes proposed by theory, disregarding the term's restrictive mechanical, materialistic, and deterministic connotations (a distinction that is unnecessary in fields that study only classical phenomena). To avoid confusion, the term *process* or *causal process* is used except when *classical mechanism* is the intended meaning.

3. This does not presume to usurp the task from researchers active in developing Gaia-like theories. It does, however, undertake to isolate fundamental principles as characteristics of these attempts in general.

4. In Bohr's words the quantum postulate states that "the finite magnitude of the quantum of action prevents altogether a sharp distinction being made between a phenomenon and the agency by which it is observed" (Bohr, 1958). Or, as Wheeler puts it: "No elementary phenomenon is a phenomenon until it is a registered (i.e. observed) phenomenon. . . . We are all inescapably involved in bringing about that which appears to be happening" (Wheeler, 1981).

5. These analogies between physics and the mind have had a profound effect on modern thinking, which indirectly shapes our scientific, technological, and cultural paradigms. The reader may note Capra (1975) and a whole genre of other popular books.

6. Note, however, that both Bohr and Wheeler avoid using the term consciousness because of its human connotations, preferring the term "registration" for the most rudimentary observation event. Bohr also referred to the "psyche" in this context, which he argued must, in its most basic nature, be a part of all living forms, and have its basis in inanimate nature. He thus saw living systems as magnifying this registration ability, which is already evident in inanimate matter, although in seemingly random events.

7. It is not feasible or appropriate here to attempt a review of the literature on the philosophy of science. Donovan et al. (1988) have provided a recent review of the field and Rohrlich (1989) provides a simplified account of the central idea presented here (paradox). Most of what is presented recognizes the philosophies of Popper (1959 and 1965) and Kuhn (1970). Except for retaining a place for traditional H-D methodology, the model presented should be compatible with Suppe's (1977) account of "historical realism," which provides a balance of philosophical views.

8. The question of what is "real" has no unequivocal answer. The current trend (Suppe, 1977) is to define "real" as our present concept of reality, our belief in that concept, having

evidence for it, our belief in our evidence, and so forth (sometimes called the "K-K thesis"). Implicit in this philosophy is that there is, in fact, something to know, that is, an ultimate reality that theory approximates. The term *realism* as used here is thus somewhat relative to current beliefs, although the important point is that it *seeks* to base theory on real constructs.

9. Many philosophers today claim that rigorously positivistic models do not reflect what really takes place in most disciplines. Elements of positivism are retained here as an idealized process, operating within definable limits (i.e., the worldview). Even as a theoretical process, its manifestation in practice may be obscured by other factors, such as the linkage with observational analysis that is depicted in the diagram.

10. Complementary views are views or theories that are each necessary for a complete description of a system or phenomenon, but that cannot be combined (for example, inspecting the weave of a Persian rug versus evaluating the artistry of its pattern—Rohrlich, 1989). Such inability to obtain all the information simultaneously is "epistemic uncertainty." In the case of complementarity in quantum physics, not only is it impossible to merge the different views (e.g., elementary particle states), but choosing one actually alters states within the other, because of the uncertainty principle. This is "ontic uncertainty," a property of nature (as best we know).

11. Consistency means lack of conflict at the level of knowledge, not necessarily that one theory is derivable from another as in strict reductionism, even though derivability is the most powerful demonstration of consistency. The fact that Newtonian dynamics and Cartesian geometry represent a special, derivable case of the theory of relativity was a very satisfying result. Nevertheless, mathematical consistency or correspondence may be difficult or impossible to demonstrate, as Bohr discovered in his attempt to express quantum theory in classical terms. It is not the mathematics that must be treated consistently between theories (or worldviews), but rather the predictions of theory or specific phenomena that have been experimentally verified.

12. This does not imply that we can study the source of self-definition, just as the Heisenberg uncertainty principle does not imply a study of uncertainty itself, but rather formulates theory around the limits to uncertainty.

References

Abram, D. 1985. The perceptual implications of Gaia. *Ecologist,* 15, 96–103.

Augros, R., and Stanciu, G. 1988. *The New Biology: Discovering the Wisdom in Nature.* Boston: Shambhala Publications.

Axelrod, R. 1984. *The Evolution of Cooperation.* New York: Basic Books.

Bennett, B.M., Hoffman, D.D., and Prakash, C. 1989. *Observer Mechanics: A Formal Theory of Perception.* San Diego: Academic Press.

Bialek, W. and Schweitzer, A. 1985. Quantum noise and the threshold of hearing. *Physical Rev Lett,* 54, 725–728.

Bohr, N. 1958. *Atomic Physics and Human Knowledge.* New York: John Wiley & Sons.

Bohr, N. 1961. *Atomic Theory and the Description of Nature. Four Essays With an Introductory Survey.* London: Cambridge University Press.

Bohr, N. 1963. *Essays 1958–1962 on Atomic Physics and Human Knowledge*. New York: Interscience Publishers.

Capra, F. 1975. *The Tao of Physics: An Exploration of the Parallels Between Modern Physics and Eastern Mysticism*. Boston: Shambhala Publications.

Corning, P.A. 1983. *The Synergism Hypothesis: A Theory of Progressive Evolution*. New York: McGraw-Hill.

Crook, J.H. 1980. *The Evolution of Human Consciousness*. Oxford: Clarendon Press.

Donovan, A., Laudan, L., and Laudan, R., eds. 1988. *Scrutinizing Science*. Boston: Kluwer Academic Publishers.

Earth System Science Committee (ESSC). 1988. *Earth System Science: A Closer View*. Report of the ESCC, NASA Advisory Council. Boulder, Co.: University Corporation for Atmospheric Research, Office of Interdisciplinary Earth Studies.

Einstein, A. 1916. *Relativity: The Special and General Theory*. Authorized translation by R. W. Lawson. Reprinted in 1961 by the Estate of Albert Einstein. New York: Crown Publishers.

Ehrlich, P. 1988. Personal comments in the epistemology panel discussion during the Chapman Conference on the Gaia Hypothesis. March 7–11, 1988, San Diego.

Futuyma, D.J. 1979. *Evolutionary Biology*. Sunderland, Mass.: Sinauer Associates.

George, F., and Johnson, L. 1985. *Purposive Behavior and Teleological Explanations*. New York: Gordon and Breach Science Publishers.

Goldberg, L.P. 1989. *Interconnectedness in Nature and in Science: The Case of Climate and Climate Modeling*. NCAR Cooperative Thesis No. 121. Boulder, Co.: University of Colorado and National Center for Atmospheric Research.

Goldberg, L.P. 1990. Personal communication.

Goldsmith, E. 1990. Evolution, neo-Darwinism and the paradigm of science. *Ecologist*, 20, 67–73

Hall, C.A.S. 1985. Models in ecology: Paradigms found or paradigms lost? *Bull Ecol Soc Am*, 66, 339–346.

Honderich, T. 1988. *A Theory of Determinism*. Oxford: Clarendon Press.

International Geosphere-Biosphere Program (IGBP). 1988. *Global Change Report No. 4. A Plan for Action*. A report prepared by the Special Committee for the IGBP for discussion at the First Meeting of the Scientific Advisory Council for the IGBP, October 24–28, 1988, Stockholm. Stockholm: IGBP.

Jantsch, E. 1980. *The Self-Organizing Universe: Scientific and Human Implications of the Emerging Paradigm of Evolution*. Oxford: Pergamon Press.

Kirchner, J. 1988. Presentation for the epistemology panel discussion during the Chapman Conference on the Gaia Hypothesis. March 7–11, 1988, San Diego.

Kuhn, T. S. 1970). *The Structure of Scientific Revolutions*, 2nd. ed. Chicago: University of Chicago Press.

Little, J. 1980. Evolution: Myth, metaphysics, or science? *New Scientist*, 87, 708–709.

Lovelock, J. 1979. *Gaia: A New Look at Life on Earth*. Oxford: Oxford University Press.

Lovelock, J. 1988. *The Ages of Gaia: A Biography of Our Living Earth*. New York: W.W. Norton, Co.

Margulis, L., and Lovelock, J., 1989. Gaia and geognosy. In: *Global Ecology: Towards a Science of the Biosphere*. New York: Academic Press.

Mayr, E. 1988. *Toward a New Philosophy of Biology: Observations of an Evolutionist*. Cambridge, UK: The Belknap Press of Harvard University Press.

Odling-Smee, F.J. 1988. Niche-constructing phenotypes. In: *The Role of Behavior in Evolution*. Cambridge, Mass.: MIT Press.

Paine, R.T. 1977. Controlled manipulations in the marine intertidal zone, and their contributions to ecological theory. In: *The Changing Scenes in Natural Sciences, 1776–1976*, Special Publication 12. Philadelphia: Academy of Natural Sciences.

Platt, J.R. 1964. Strong inference. *Science*, 146, 347–353.

Plotkin, H.C., ed. 1988. *The Role of Behavior in Evolution*. Cambridge, Mass.: MIT Press.

Popper, K. 1959. *The Logic of Scientific Discovery*. London: Hutchinson & Co.

Popper, K. 1965. *Conjectures and Refutations: The Growth of Scientific Knowledge*, 2nd ed. New York: Basic Books.

Posey, P.A. 1989. Alternatives to forest destruction: Lessons from the Mebengokre Indians. *Ecologist*, 19, 241–244.

Rambler, M.B., Margulis, L., and Fester. R. 1989. *Global Ecology: Towards a Science of the Biosphere*. New York: Academic Press.

Richards, R.J. 1987. *Darwin and the Emergence of Evolution Theories of Mind and Behavior*. Chicago: University of Chicago Press.

Roederer, J.G. 1978. On the relationship between human brain functions and the foundations of physics, science, and technology. *Foundations Physics*, 8, 423–438. Bruges, Belgium: Plenum Publishing.

Roederer, J.G. 1985. Tearing down disciplinary barriers. *EOS*, 66, 681, 684–685.

Rohrlich, F. 1989. *From Paradox to Reality: Our Basic Concepts of the Physical World*. Cambridge, UK: Press Syndicate of the University of Cambridge.

Rohrlich, F., and Hardin, L. 1983. Established theories. *Phil Sci*, 50, 603–617.

Schneider, S.H. 1989. *Global Warming: Are We Entering the Greenhouse Century?* San Francisco: Sierra Club Books.

Simberloff, D. 1981. The sick science of ecology. *Eidema* 1.

Suppe, F. 1977. *The Structure of Scientific Theories*. Chicago: University of Illinois Press.

Thompson, P. 1989. *The Structure of Biological Theories*. New York: State University of New York Press.

Todes, D. P. 1989. *Darwin Without Malthus: The Struggle for Existence in Russian Evolutionary Thought*. New York: Oxford University Press.

Visvader, J. 1988. Presentation for the epistemology panel discussion during the Chapman Conference on the Gaia Hypothesis. March 7–11, 1988, San Diego.

Wheeler, J.A. 1981. Law without law. In: Wheeler, J.A., and Zurek, W.H., eds. *Quantum Theory and Measurement*. Princeton, N.J.: Princeton University Press.

Wigner, E. P. 1981. Remarks on the mind-body question. In: Wheeler, J.A., and Zurek, W.H., eds. *Quantum Theory and Measurement*. Princeton, N.J.: Princeton University Press.

Wilber, K. 1986. *Up from Eden: A Transpersonal View of Human Evolution*. Boston: Shambhala Publications.

Acknowledgment

I wish to thank Jesse R. Kineman, who helped greatly with many concepts; Dr. Larry Goldberg and Dr. Jim Lodge for their kind suggestions and comments on several drafts of this paper; Joy Ikelman for editing and creating the graphs; Patty Kineman, who lent moral support and tolerated (almost) my seemingly endless revisions and discussions; and the external reviewers who provided valuable criticism on the earlier drafts and forced me to consider a wider range of views. This acknowledgment does not imply agreement or endorsement on the part of these individuals for the final form of the document or the views expressed.

Many scientists and theorists claim that the Gaia hypothesis is merely a fancy name for a set of interactions, between organisms and their presumably inorganic environment, that have long been known to science. Every high school student is familiar with the fact that the oxygen content of our atmospheric environment is dependent on the photosynthetic activity of plants. The Gaia hypothesis, according to such researchers, offers nothing substantive. It is simply a new—and unnecessarily obfuscating—way of speaking of old facts. In the words of biologist Stephen Jay Gould: "The Gaia Hypothesis says nothing new—it offers no new mechanisms. It just changes the metaphor. But metaphor is not mechanism!"[1]

What Gould failed to state is that "mechanism," itself, is nothing more than a metaphor. It is an important one, to be sure. Indeed the whole process of modern science seems to get underway with this metaphor. In 1644 the brilliant philosopher Rene Descartes wrote, "I have described the earth, and all the visible world, as if it were a machine."[2] In his various writings, Descartes, developing a notion already suggested by other philosophers, effectively inaugurated that tradition of thought we call "mechanism," or, as it was known at that time, the "mechanical philosophy." And his metaphor is still with us today.[3]

But let us explore how this metaphor operates upon us. What are the assumptions, explicit and implicit, that we wittingly or unwittingly buy into when we accept the premise that "the visible world" and, most specifically, the earth, is best understood as a very intricate and complex machine?

The Mind of a Metaphor

First, the mechanical philosophy suggests that matter, itself, is ultimately inert, without any life or creativity of its own. The great worth of the machine metaphor is that it implies that the material world is, at least in principle, entirely predictable.

According to this metaphor, the material world operates, like any machine, according to fixed and unvarying rules; laws that have been built into the machine from the start. It has no creativity, no spontaneity of its own. As a watch or a clock ticks away with complete uniformity until it runs down, so the material world cannot itself alter or vary the laws that are built into it. The laws of a mechanical world are preset and constant; if we can discover those laws, we will be able to predict with utter certainty the events of the world. Or so the mechanical philosophers thought in the seventeenth century.

The second assumption implicit in the mechanical metaphor is rather more hidden than the first. A machine always implies someone who invented the machine—a builder, a maker. A machine does not, in the manner of an embryo, generate itself. Clocks, carriages, or steam engines do not take form of themselves—if they did, they would be very wild and magical entities indeed, and we could not ascribe to them the fixity, uniformity, and predictability that we associate with any strictly mechanical object. If we view nature as a machine, then we tacitly view it as something that has been built, something that has been made *from outside*. This is still evident in much of the language that we use in our science today: we speak of behavior that has been "programmed" into an animal's genes, of information that is "hardwired" into the brain. But who wrote the program? Who wired the brain? As mechanists we borrow these metaphors from our own experience of built things—things that have been invented and constructed by humans—and then we pretend that the inventor or the builder (or the programmer) does not come along with the metaphor. But, of course, it does. If the material world is like a machine, then this world must have been constructed from outside.

This implication, I would claim, is precisely why the mechanical philosophy triumphed in the seventeenth and eighteenth centuries, to become part of the very fabric of conventional science. Mechanism gained ascendancy not because it was a necessary adjunct of scientific practice, but because it disarmed the objections of the Church, the dominant social and political institution of the time. The mechanical philosophy became a central facet of the scientific worldview precisely because it implied the existence of a maker (a divine interpreter) and thus made possible an alliance between science and the Church. But in order to make sense of this claim (and to better understand the power of the mechanical metaphor today) we must look briefly at the cultural forces and tensions that set the stage for the historical ascendency of the mechanical philosophy in seventeenth- and eighteenth-century Europe.

A Brief Historical Excursus

We moderns tend to assume that the adoption of the mechanical metaphor was a necessary precondition for the growth and flourishing of experimental science. Yet an attentive study of the various conflicts and debates that gave rise to the scientific revolution quickly calls such assumptions into question.[4] Until the latter half of the seventeenth century, the tradition of experimentation was *not* associated with the mechanical philosophy. On the contrary, the method of careful experimentation was associated with those who practiced it, those who developed and refined it to the level of an art, individuals who had a very different perspective from that of the mechanists. For these were the people who called themselves "natural magicians" and "alchemists." They viewed the material world, and indeed *matter itself,* as a locus of subtle powers and immanent forces, a dynamic network of invisible sympathies and antipathies. For the Renaissance natural magician Marsilio Ficino (1433–1499, founder of the Florentine Academy, and the first translator of Plato's works into Latin), for the Hermetic natural magicians Giordano Bruno (1548–1600) and Tommaso Campanella (1568–1639), for the brilliant physician and alchemist Paracelsus (1493–1541) and, indeed, for the entire alchemical tradition, material nature was perceived as alive, as a complex, living organism with which the investigator—the natural magician, or scientist—was in relation. ("It is an error," wrote Campanella, "to think that the world does not feel just because it does not have legs, eyes, and hands.") The experimental method was developed and honed as the medium of this relation, as a practice of dialogue between oneself and

animate nature. Experimentation was here a form of participation, a technique of communication or communion which, when successful, effected a transformation not just in the structure of the material experimented upon, but in the structure of the experimenter himself.[5]

Many of the great discoveries that we associate with the scientific revolution and, indeed, many of the scientists themselves, took their inspiration from this participatory tradition of natural magic—one need only mention Nicholas Copernicus, who wrote of the sun as the visible God, quoting the legendary Egyptian magician Hermes Trismegistus; Johannes Kepler, whose mother was imprisoned and nearly executed for practicing witchcraft—on the evidence of Kepler's own writings; William Gilbert, the great student of magnetism, which he termed "coition" as if it were a type of sexual intercourse that matter has with itself, and who, in his book *De Magnete,* published in 1600 (the year that Bruno was burned at the stake), wrote of the whole earth as a living body with its own impulse for self-preservation! And, of course, we must mention Francis Bacon, the "father" of experimental science, who saw his scientific method as a refinement of the tradition of natural magic and who wrote that through his work the term "magic," which "has long been used in a bad sense, will again be restored to its ancient and honorable meaning."[6]

How is it that we have forgotten this intimate link between experimental science and natural magic? How or why was this link with magic so obscured by the subsequent tradition of natural science? Why, for instance, did Isaac Newton, arguably one of the greatest of all natural magicians, find it necessary to hide and very publicly deny the vast alchemical researches that occupied him throughout his life?

Clearly, the Church in the sixteenth and seventeenth centuries felt itself threatened by this powerful tradition which held that the material world was a source of itself, this tradition—with roots in the high culture of Renaissance Neoplatonism as well as in the diverse folk knowledge of the peasant countryside—which spoke of the enveloping earth as a living being, a living matrix of spiritual powers and receptivities. Such a way of speaking threatened the theological doctrine that matter itself is passive and barren, and that the corporeal realm of nature was a fallen, sinful realm, necessarily separated from its divine source. (I do not refer here to

Christian doctrine in general, but to the institution-alized Church of the sixteenth and seventeenth centuries—a period, let us remember, that saw hundreds of thousands of persons, most of them women, tortured and executed as "witches" by the ecclesiastical and lay authorities.)

The *true* source, according to the Church, was radically external to nature, outside of the earthly domain in which we are bodily immersed. The teachings of natural magic, however, with their constant reference to immanent powers, implied that the divine miracles reported in the Old and the New Testaments might be explained by subtle principles entirely *internal* to material nature. This was her-esy—heresy of the first order!—because it enabled one to doubt the very agency and existence of the God outside nature. Clearly then, if natural experi-mentation was to become a respectable or even a permissible practice, it would have to find a new rhetoric for itself. It would have to shed its origins in the magical and participatory worldview and take on a new way of speaking more in line with Church doctrine.

It was mechanism, or the mechanical philosophy, that provided this new and much safer way of speaking. For again, a metaphorical machine entails a metaphorical builder, a creator. Like the Church, the mechanical philosophy necessitated belief in a creative source entirely outside of the material or sensible world. And, like the Church, the mechani-cal philosophy involved a denigration of corporeal matter, not exactly as fallen, sinful and demonic, but as barren, inert, and ultimately dead.

Here, then, was a perfect cosmology for the ex-perimental scientists to adopt—one that would al-low them to continue to investigate nature without fear of being persecuted, or even executed, for her-esy. The mechanical metaphor made possible an al-liance between seventeenth-century science and the Church. And thus mechanism became a central tenet of the scientific world view.[7]

Mechanism and Human Privilege

We are now in a position to discern the third and most powerful assumption implicit in the mechani-cal metaphor. The only true machines of which we have direct experience are those that have been in-vented by humans. Hence, if the world really func-tions as a complex machine, then the one who built that machine must be very much like us. There is,

in other words, an implied correspondence between humans and the one who built or programmed the complicated, vast machine of the world. We are, af-ter all, made in his or her image. If the material Earth is a created machine, it falls to us—because we are not just created, but *creators* in our own right—to figure out how the machine works.

The mechanical metaphor, then, not only makes it rather simple for us to operationalize the world, by presenting nature as an assemblage of working parts that have no internal relation to each other—a set of parts, that is, that can be readily taken apart or put back together without undo damage; it also provides us with a neat justification for any and all such manipulations. The correspondence between the creative human mind and that which created the mechanical universe (between humans and God) en-sures that the human researcher has a divine man-date to experiment upon, to operate upon, to manipulate earthly nature in any manner that he or she sees fit. The inertness of matter, the clear lack of sentience in all that is not human, absolves the researcher of any guilt regarding the apparent pain he or she may happen to inflict upon animals or eco-systems (such pain, as Descartes taught us, is en-tirely an illusion, for automatons cannot really *feel* anything).[8]

The mechanical worldview thus implicates us in a relation to the world which is that of an inventor, an operator, or an engineer to his or her machine (the very notion of "genetic *engineering*" can have sense only for a culture that maintains a mechanical view of nature). When the natural world is con-ceived as a machine, the human mind necessarily retains a godlike position *outside* of that world. It is this privileged position, the license it gives us for the possession, mastery, and control of nature, that makes us so reluctant to drop the mechanical met-aphor today. If mechanism rose to prominence in the seventeenth century due to its compatibility with the belief in a divine creator, it remains in prominence today largely due to the deification of human powers that it promotes.

The Phenomenology of Perception

But this deification, this human privilege, comes at the expense of our perceptual experience. If, at any moment, we suspend our theoretical awareness in order to attend to our sensory experience of the world around us (to our experience not as disembodied intellects but as intelligent, sensing animals), we find that we are not outside of the world, but entirely *within* it. We are thoroughly encompassed by the physical world, immersed in its depths. Hence our sensory relation to the world is hardly that of a spectator to an object. As sensing animals, we are never disinterested onlookers but participants in a dynamic, shifting, and ambiguous field.

Maurice Merleau-Ponty, the French phenomenologist and philosopher who has perhaps most carefully analyzed the experience of perception, underscored the participatory nature of this experience by calling attention to the obvious but easily overlooked fact that our hand, with which we touch the world, is itself a touchable thing, and thus is itself entirely a part of the tactile field that it explores. Likewise the eyes, with which we see the world, are themselves visible. They are themselves entirely included *within* the visible world that they see—they are one of the visible things, like the bark of a tree, or a stone, or the sky. For Merleau-Ponty, to *see* is also, at one and the same time, to feel oneself *seen*, and to touch the world is also to be touched by the world! Clearly a wholly immaterial mind could neither see nor touch things, could not experience anything at all. *We* can experience things, can touch, hear, and taste things, only because, as bodies, we are ourselves a part of the sensible field, and have *our own* textures, sounds, and tastes. We can perceive things at all only because we are entirely a part of the sensible world that we perceive. We might just as well say that we are organs of that world, and that the world is perceiving itself through us.[9]

But here the main point to get from Merleau-Ponty is that, from the perspective of our embodied, animal awareness, perception is always experienced as an interactive, reciprocal participation. The event of perception is never instantaneous—it has always a duration, and in that duration there is always movement, a questioning and responding, a subtle attuning of the eyes to that which they see, or of the ears to what is heard, and thus we enter into a relationship with the things we perceive.

When, for instance, a particular stone on the beach catches my eye, I may respond to this solicitation by bending to pick it up. I thereby discover that the stone is larger than I had at first thought—I now see that much of its bulk had been hidden beneath the sand. In order to heft it my body shifts

its stance, legs and feet planting themselves a bit more solidly in the sand as I raise the stone to eye level. Now, as one hand moves over its surface, my fingers must adjust themselves to the particular texture of that surface; they must find the right rhythm, the right way to touch it if the stone is to disclose its subtle furrows and patterns. Likewise, only as my eyes find the right way to focus and question its surface will the stone begin to reveal to me the secrets of its mineral composition. As my body adjusts itself to the stone, the stone begins to speak its mute language, to subtly instruct and inform my senses. And the more I linger with this stone, the more I will learn. My experience, then, is of a reciprocal interaction, a mutual engagement of the stone by my body and of my body by the stone. And so it is with everything that we perceive, constantly, continually—the paved streets we walk upon, the trees that surround our home, the clouds that catch our gaze. Perception is always an active engagement with what one perceives, a reciprocal participation with things. As such, our direct perception always discloses things and the world as uncertain, animate presences with which we find ourselves in a sort of communication. That this is our native, human experience of things is attested by the discourse of virtually all indigenous, oral, tribal peoples, whose languages simply refuse any designation of things, or of the sensible world, as ultimately inanimate. If a thing has the power to "call my attention" or to "capture my gaze," it can hardly be thought of as inert. "If the moon was not in some sense alive, you would no longer see it," I was told by an old tribal shaman in the Mexican desert. By which he meant to say, I think, that simply to see or to perceive a phenomenon is already to be in an active relation with that phenomenon, and yet how could one be in a dynamic relationship with something if it was entirely inanimate, without any potency or spontaneity of its own? How indeed? By implying that matter is utterly passive and inert, mechanism denies our perceptual experience. It denies our sensory involvement in the world.

The scientist who holds a fundamentally mechanical view of the natural world must suspend his or her sensory participation with things. He strives to picture the world from the viewpoint of an external spectator. He conceives of the earth as a system of objective relations laid out before his gaze, but he does not include the gaze, his own seeing, within the system. Denying his sensory involvement in that which he seeks to understand, he is left with a purely mental relation to what is only an abstract image.

Likewise with any *particular* object or organism that the mechanist studies. There as well, she must assume the position of a disinterested onlooker. She must suppress all personal involvement in the object; any trace of subjectivity must be purged from her account. But this is an impossible ideal, for there is always some interest or circumstance that leads us to study one phenomenon rather than another, and this necessarily conditions what we look for, and what we discover. We are always in, and of, the world that we seek to describe from outside. We can deny, but we cannot escape being involved in whatever we perceive. Hence, we may claim that the sensible world is ultimately inert or inanimate, *but we can never wholly experience it as such.* The most that we can do is attempt to render the sensible world inanimate, either by killing that which we study, or by deadening our sensory experience. Thus our denial of participation ultimately manifests as a particular *form* of participation, but one that does violence to our bodies and to the earth.

Mechanism, then, is a way of speaking that denies the inherently reciprocal and participatory nature of perceptual experience. Thus it constricts and stifles the senses; they are no longer free to openly engage things like oak trees, bird song, and the movement of waves. We grow more and more oblivious to the animate earth as our body becomes closed in upon itself; our direct intercourse with the sensible world is inhibited. Mechanism sublimates our carnal relationship with the earth into a strictly mental relation, not to the world, but to the abstract image of a finished blueprint, the abstract ideal of a finished truth.

This mentalistic epistemology, with its fear of direct relationship and its intolerance of ambiguity, is the mark, I suggest, of an immature or adolescent science, a science that has not yet come into its own. Although it sporadically fosters grandiose feelings of power and godlike mastery over nature, science as mechanism is inherently unstable, because it is founded upon a denial of the very conditions that make science possible at all. Such a science cannot last—it must either obliterate the world in a final apotheosis of denial, or else give way to another mode of science: one that can affirm, rather than deny, our living bond with the world that surrounds us.

Toward an Ecological Epistemology

The Gaia hypothesis may well signal the emergence of just such a mature science—a science that seeks not to control the world but to participate with the world, not to *operate upon* nature, but to *co-operate with* nature. If the chemical composition of the air that we are breathing is, at this very moment, being actively monitored and maintained by all of the earth's organisms acting in concert, as a single, coherent, living metabolism, then the material world that surrounds us is not, in any sense, inert or inanimate. Nor are these insects, these trees, or even these boulders entirely passive and inert. For material nature can no longer be perceived as a collection of detachable working parts. It is not a created machine but rather a vast, self-generative, living physiology, open and responsive to changing circumstances. In short, it is an entity.

Of course, we may still attempt to speak of Gaia in purely mechanical terms, or try to conceive of Gaia as a strictly objective set of processes, straining thus to hold our science within the old mechanical paradigm to which we have become accustomed. We may be reluctant to give up the dream of a finished objectivity, and of the fixed reality to which it would correspond. Nevertheless, Gaia will never fit very neatly within the discourse of mechanism. A mechanism is entirely determined; it acts, as we have seen, according to a set of predictable and fixed rules and structures that it itself did not generate. Yet it is precisely such a formulation that Gaia, as an autopoietic or self-generating system, resists. Of course, we may say that Gaia is a machine, or a set of mechanisms, that is building itself. But then we will have given up, perhaps without realizing it, that part of the metaphor that makes mechanism so compelling. That is, a machine that generates itself could never be wholly predictable. For it must improvise itself as it goes, creatively. (We have no guarantee, for instance, that the so-called mechanisms that Gaia employs to regulate the salinity of the oceans, or to limit the influx of ultraviolet radiation into the atmosphere, are precisely the same that Gaia will be employing two centuries from now.) Gaia, as a self-organizing entity, is no more and no less predictable than a living organism, and we might as well simply acknowledge the fact, and cease pretending that it is anything like a machine that we could build. The Gaia hypothesis suggests that the world we inhabit is rather more like a living physiology than it is like a watch, or a spaceship, or even a computer.

And we are entirely inside of, circumscribed by this organic entity. For the Gaia hypothesis indicates that the atmosphere in which we live and think is itself a dynamic extension of the planetary surface, a functioning organ of the animate earth. As I have written elsewhere:

It may be that the new emphasis it places on the atmosphere of this world is the most radical aspect of the Gaia Hypothesis. For it carries the implication that before we as individuals can begin to recognize the Earth as a self-sustaining organic presence, we must remember and reacquaint ourselves with the very medium within which we move. The air can no longer be confused with mere negative presence or the absence of solid things; henceforth the air is itself a density—mysterious indeed for its invisibility—but a thick and tactile presence nonetheless. We are immersed in its depths as surely as fish are immersed in the sea. It is the medium, the silent interlocutor of all our musings and moods. We simply cannot exist without its support and nourishment, with its active participation in whatever we are up to at any moment.

In concert with the other animals, with the plants, and with the microbes themselves, we are an active part of the Earth's atmosphere, constantly circulating the breath of this planet through our bodies and brains, exchanging certain vital gases for others, and thus monitoring and maintaining the delicate makeup of the medium.[10]

So simply by breathing we are participating in the life of the biosphere. But not just by breathing! When we consider the biosphere not as a machine, but as an animate, self-sustaining entity, then it becomes apparent that everything we see, everything we hear, every experience of smelling and tasting and touching is informing our bodies regarding the internal state of this other, vaster physiology—the biosphere itself. Sensory perception, then, discloses itself as a form of communication between an organism and the animate earth. (And this can be the case even when we are observing ourselves, noticing a headache that we feel or the commotion in our stomach caused by some contaminated water. For we ourselves are a part of Gaia. If the biosphere that encompasses us is itself a coherent entity, then introspection, listening to our own bodies, can become a way of listening and attuning to the earth.) Perception is a communication, or even a communion—a sensuous participation between ourselves and the living world that encompasses us. Yet we have seen that, phenomenologically, this is precisely the way that we commonly experience

perception—as an interaction, a participation or intertwining between ourselves and that which we perceive. Perception is never experienced as strictly objective, because to perceive anything at all is to be engaged by that thing, and to feel oneself influenced, however minimally, by the encounter. We have seen that mechanism denies this dialectic by assuming that the material world is ultimately a determinate object, incapable of open reciprocity and response. The Gaia hypothesis, on the other hand, ultimately affirms our perceptual experience, because it describes the sensible environment as open-ended and alive, which is precisely the way that our sensing bodies spontaneously experience the things around us. Thus the Gaia hypothesis enables, quite literally, *a return to our senses*. We become aware once again of our breathing bodies, and of the bodily world that surrounds us. We are drawn out of that ideal, Platonic domain of thoughts and theories back into this realm that we corporeally inhabit, this land that we share with the other animals, and the plants, and the microbial entities who vibrate and spin within our cells and the cells of the spider. Our senses loosen themselves from the mechanical constraints imposed by an outmoded language. They begin to participate, once again, in the ongoing life of the land around us.

Conclusion

We are now in a position to contrast succinctly the epistemology of mechanism with the epistemological implications of Gaia. The mechanical model of the world entails a mentalistic epistemology, the assumption that the most precise knowledge of things is a detached, intellectual apprehension purged of all subjective, situated, or bodily involvement. It is an abstract, disembodied knowledge. Meanwhile, the Gaian understanding of the world—that which speaks of the encompassing earth not as a machine but as an autopoietic, living physiology—entails an embodied, participatory epistemology. As the earth is no longer viewed as a machine, so the human body is no longer a mechanical object housing an immaterial mind, but is rather a sensitive, expressive, thinking physiology, a microcosm of the autopoietic Earth. It is henceforth not as a detached mind, but as a thoughtful body that I can come to know the world, participating in its processes, feeling my life resonate with its life, becoming more a part of the world. Knowledge, ecologically considered, is always, in this sense, carnal knowledge—a wisdom born of the body's own attunement to that which it studies, and to the earth.

This view is entirely akin to that of Ludwig Fleck, the great epistemologist and sociologist of science, who wrote in 1929 that "Cognition is neither passive contemplation nor acquisition of the only possible insight into something given. It is an active, live interrelationship, a shaping and being reshaped, in short, an act of creation [or, we might add, cocreation]."[11]

Finally, we may wonder what science would come to look like if such an epistemology were to take hold and spread throughout the human community. It is likely, I believe, that scientists would soon lose interest in the pursuit of a finished blueprint of nature, in favor of discovering ways to better the relationship between humankind and the rest of the biosphere, and ways to rectify current problems caused by the neglect of that relationship. I have written of a science that seeks not to control nature but to communicate with nature. Experimentation might come to be recognized, once again, as a discipline or art of communication between the scientist and that which he or she studies.

Indeed, many scientists are already familiar with the experience of a deep communication or communion with that which they study, although current scientific rhetoric makes it rather difficult to admit, much less articulate, such experience. Moreover, the taboos against participation are much harsher in some scientific disciplines than in others. Physicists, from Heisenberg to Bohm, have generally been much freer to openly affirm such experiences than have biologists, and many have done so. Yet the freedom many physicists enjoy to speak of participatory or even mystical modes of awareness rests upon the fact that their objects remain transcendent to the world of our immediate experience. In other words, to mystically "participate" with subatomic quanta (in the manner of Heisenberg's recent interpreters), or to feel oneself fuse and participate with the ultimate origin of the universe (as do adherents of the strong version of the "anthropic principle") need not in any way move science, or society, to alter its assumptions regarding the determinate, mechanical character of the world accessible to our unaided senses (i.e., the surrounding landscape),and so does not directly threaten our assumed human right to control and to manipulate the natural world of our everyday experience. How-

ever, biologists and ecologists, geologists and climatologists, study this very world—the world that we can directly perceive—and they are for this reason in a much more precarious position politically. They cannot so readily acknowledge, much less discuss scientifically, their felt participation or rapport with the entities they study, whether insects or forests, for this would directly jeopardize our assumed human privilege and the many cultural practices currently justified by that assumption.

However, in a genuinely Gaian science, or in a genuinely ecological community of scientists, it would be manifestly evident that one is always already involved, or participant, in that which one studies. The effort then, would no longer be made to avoid or to repress this involvement, but rather to clarify and to refine it. Scientists, in other words, might begin openly to develop and cultivate their personal rapport with that which they study as a means of deepening their scientific insight.

The work of biologist Barbara McClintok, who was awarded the Nobel Prize for her discovery of genetic transposition, exemplifies the epistemology implied by a Gaian science. She insists that a genuine scientist must have "a feeling for the organism"—and not only for "living" organisms but "for any object that fully claims our attention."[12] McClintok describes a rather magical shift in her orientation that enabled her to identify chromosomes that she had previously been unable to distinguish. It is the shift to a participatory epistemology: "I found that the more I worked with them, the bigger and bigger the chromosomes got, and when I was really working with them, I wasn't outside, I was down there. I was part of the system. I was right down there with them and everything got big. I even was able to see the internal parts of the chromosomes—actually everything was there. It surprised me because I actually felt as if I was right down there and these were my friends. As you look at these things, they become a part of you. And you forget yourself."[13]

As Barbara McClintok came to perceive herself inside of the living system she was studying, so the Gaia hypothesis situates all of us *inside of* this world that we share with the plants and the animals and the stones. The things around us are no longer inert. They are our coparticipants in the evolution of a knowledge and a science that belongs to humankind no more, and no less, than it belongs to the earth.

Notes

1. Gould's comments on Gaia were made during a lecture on evolution at the State University of New York at Stony Brook, in the spring of 1987.

2. Rene Descartes, *Principles of Philosophy,* part IV, principle CLXXXVIII; in *The Philosophical Works of Descartes,* translated by Haldane and Ross (Cambridge University Press, 1931).

3. Maintaining a position similar to Gould's, J.W. Kirchner in Chapter 6, this volume states that "If you try to treat a metaphor as a scientific principle, you will waste your time." Metaphors, he asserts, "are not testable." Kirchner provides, as an example, Shakespeare's phrase, "all the world's a stage," and he suggests that such an assertion can never be tested. It would be testable, he writes, only if Shakespeare provided an independent definition of "stage," such as, for instance, "a raised wooden platform with footlights at the edge."

But let us resist taking Shakespeare's assertion in such an absurdly literal fashion. His metaphor for the world, *as a metaphor,* is eminently testable just as it is. Indeed, it has already stood "the test of time." The value or validity of a metaphor is readily tested according to the ability that it has to articulate our experience, to express succinctly a previously mute or unexpressed sensation (or complex of sensations). Kirchner might well reply that this is hardly the sort of test to which he is referring. Assessing the validity of a metaphor *as a metaphor* is clearly a somewhat subjective and imprecise affair; only by reducing the suggestive metaphor to a literal assertion can one attain a statement amenable to the precise criteria which, he assumes, is required by scientific analysis.

Yet Kirchner neglects to acknowledge that these very criteria by which he would judge all scientific propositions are themselves supported by a metaphor, and it is one which is no less suggestive and ambiguous than Shakespeare's. This is the claim that "the world is a machine"—the potent metaphor that, for three centuries, has provided the framework within which most scientific research has been conducted. This metaphor of a world-machine, certainly no more falsifiable than Shakespeare's theater of the world, has nevertheless proved itself by its immense heuristic value—its suggestion, for instance, that every aspect of reality should be susceptible of mathematical analysis, its tendency to render natural phenomena in a manner that opened them to technological intervention, and its concomitant ability to inspire and catalyze numerous research programs, many of them astonishingly fruitful. Still, this metaphor has also had its shadow side; it has deflected our attention away from many aspects of nature as well as of our own experience. Indeed, it may be that our mechanical view of the natural world has dangerously outlived its usefulness.

Kirchner makes the mistake of assessing Gaia according to the criteria of a science still structured by the metaphor of the machine. Condemning Gaia as "just a metaphor," he fails to recognize his own allegiance to a set of metaphors. Thus he is unable to discern the real level at which the hypothesis operates. He assumes that Gaia must be a hypothesis regarding some aspect of the determinate, mechanical nature he takes for granted, while in truth the Gaia hypothesis postulates an entirely alternative view of nature (and of our relationship to nature), and hence an alternative way of doing science.

The organismic metaphor of the world must be assessed, like any metaphor, according to the sense that it is able to make of our experience, its ability to articulate the previously inexpressable and in this case its power to catalyze new insights, and new research. Kirchner may maintain that this is a very fuzzy and unscientific way to "test" a theory. Yet such is the manner in which the metaphor of the machine was *itself* tested, by countless scientists, in the course of three centuries.

Originally illuminating for our experience and catalytic for our science, today the mechanical metaphor, taken alone, obfuscates our experience and, I believe, precludes an adequate response, by scientists and laypersons alike, to the ecological predicament in which we find ourselves. In this chapter I discuss some of the reasons for our reluctance to recognize, much less set aside, the mechanical metaphors that now limit our vision, and I propose some first thoughts regarding the value of Gaia as an alternative way of speaking, and hence of seeing.

4. For an excellent and finely documented historical overview of these controversies, see Brian Easlea's *Witch-hunting, Magic and the New Philosophy: An Introduction to Debates of the Scientific Revolution, 1450–1750* (Humanities Press, New Jersey 1980).

5. Campenella is quoted in Easlea, p. 105. A fine discussion of alchemy may be found in Frances Yates, *Giordano Bruno and the Hermetic Tradition* (Vintage Press, 1969). See also discussions of alchemy in relation to early modern science in Evelyn Fox Keller, *Reflections on Gender and Science* (New Haven: Yale University Press, 1985), and Carolyn Merchant, *The Death of Nature: Women, Ecology, and the Scientific Revolution.* (San Francisco: Harper and Row, 1983)

6. From *Of the Dignity and Advancement of Learning,* cited in Easlea, p. 128. See also P. Rossi, Francis Bacon: *From Magic to Science,* translated by S. Rabinovitch (Routledge, 1968).

7. On this reading mechanistic science went hand in hand with a Christian metaphysics. The schism that we have come to assume today between the scientists and the theologians, or between science and religion, only really got underway with the publication and dissemination of the *Origin of Species.* For Darwin was beginning to speak of a sort of creative power inherent in nature itself; he wrote of a "natural" selection—a selective power not outside of nature but internal to nature. Of course, by using the metaphor of selection he was still propagating a metaphysics somewhat similar to that of the Church (in which he had been steeped as a young man): "Selecting" is the kind of thing that an anthropomorphic divinity does; and we can see from newspaper articles of that time that many readers interpreted Darwin's use of the term "selection" as a sort of indirect argument for the existence of God. His correspondence indicates that Darwin himself remained somewhat attached to the idea of a transcendental divinity; it may well be that his use of the term "selection," with all its associations of humanlike *will* or *choice,* helped him to reconcile his revolutionary theory with his religious beliefs. (See Robert M. Young, *Darwin's Metaphor.* 1985, Cambridge University Press, pp. 79–125.) Nevertheless, Darwin's work was the first in the modern era to imply a creativity inherent in nature itself, and this was a blow to the church . . . We now are beginning to discern that if the so-called environment selects the organisms that inhabit it, so those organisms also selectively influence that environment; perhaps, then, given this more open, circular causality, "selection" is not such a useful term. The interaction is a much more reciprocal phenomenon than that suggested by the metaphor of selection—it is more of a sort of dialogue wherein the environment puts questions to the organism and the organism, in answering those questions, poses new questions to the environment—which that environment, in turn, answers with further questions. It is precisely this sort of open dialectic, this mutual participation between the organism and the earth, that the Gaia hypothesis is beginning to thematize and articulate.

8. Descartes' major follower, Nicholas Malebranche, wrote succinctly that (nonhuman) animals "eat without pleasure, they cry without pain, they grow without knowing it; they desire nothing, they fear nothing, they know nothing" (cited in Easlea, p. 128). The mechanical philosophy was the principle and oft-cited justification for the vivisection experiments that began to proliferate in the seventeenth century (and that continue, in one form or another, in numerous laboratories today).

9. Maurice Merleau-Ponty, *The Visible and the Invisible,* edited by Claude Lefort, translated by Alphonso Lingis (Evanston: Northwestern University Press, 1968). See also Merleau-Ponty's seminal text, *The Phenomenology of Perception,* translated by Colin Smith (Routledge and Kegan Paul, 1962).

10. David Abram. "The Perceptual Implications of Gaia." *The Ecologist,* Vol. 15, No. 3, 1985.

11. Ludwik Fleck. "On the Crisis of 'Reality.'" In *Cognition and Fact: Materials on Ludwik Fleck,* edited by Robert Cohen and Thomas Schnelle (D. Reidel Publishing Co., 1986), pp. 47–57. Fleck's brilliant writings on the genesis of scientific "facts" were a major (and at first, unacknowledged) source for Thomas Kuhn's later work on the structure of scientific revolutions.

12. Evelyn Fox Keller. *Reflections on Gender and Science* (New Haven: Yale University Press 1985), p. 166.

13. Cited in Keller, p. 165.

III
Theoretical Foundations of Gaia

John Harte

9

Ecosystem Stability and Diversity

In terms of conventional physics, the grouse represents only a millionth of either the mass or the energy of an acre. Yet subtract the grouse and the whole thing is dead.
Aldo Leopold

It is the mark of an instructed mind to rest satisfied with the degree of precision which the nature of the subject permits and not to seek an exactness where only an approximation of the truth is possible.
Aristotle

Most discussions about Gaia lead eventually to the notion of stability. Ecologists, particularly the modelers, have given considerable thought to the subject of stability and the characteristics of systems that possess this property. I have been asked to summarize here how models are used in ecology and what models teach us about ecosystem stability. I am mainly concerned here with the internal dynamics among the plants and animals in ecosystems, as opposed to the couplings between life and the geosphere, but I will inject comments along the way about biota-geosphere interactions.

The models used by ecologists to learn about stability are highly simplified cartoons of the real world. Although consistent with the fundamental laws of physics, they are not derivable from these laws (in contrast, for example, with the way that models of satellite orbits are). Many ecologists like to think of their models as toys to play with, to use in an exploratory fashion rather than to provide detailed predictions. Because of the complexity of ecosystems, it is widely considered to be more valuable to explore the consequences of a wide variety of simple models rather than to get locked into one cumbersome and putatively realistic model. If a question such as, "Is stability linked to diversity?" is explored with a wide variety of plausible ecological models, and if all or nearly all the models provide a common answer, then ecologists tend to place some stock in that answer. They trust not the results of any one model as much as the overlapping results of many models.

The two quotes opening this chapter illuminate

the plight of ecosystem modelers. All of us who study ecosystems in the field share Leopold's insight, yet all who attempt to learn from models about ecosystems know that Aristotle also wrote the bitter truth. Caught in this bind, modelers usually do ignore Leopold's "grouse," leaving us with the grim awareness that perhaps the whole thing *is* dead. It is mainly for this reason, I believe, that no one model should ever be taken very seriously in ecology. But we still have to take on faith that by accepting the common insights of many different types of models, we have somehow restored the "grouse."

The most widely used toys of the ecosystem modeler are the generalized Lotka-Volterra models in which birth and death, predation, competition, mutualism, and saturation of carrying capacity are represented by simple differential equations for the rates of change of each population of concern in the system. There are numerous variations on this model, for one can include stochastic effects, time lags, prey-switching when the prey population is low, satiation of food supply when the prey population is high, and many more complexities. The geosphere enters into the model through interaction coefficients such as the environmental carrying capacities for each population, which may, for example, be temperature dependent, stochastic, or both.

What do these models tell us about stability? There are many different notions of stability, and unfortunately what models say about one such notion is not necessarily true of others. Practically all concepts of stability have something to do with recovery following a disturbance. If an ecosystem is perturbed (say by the removal of half the individuals in a particular population), the system may or may not eventually return to the configuration it was in, or the trajectory it was on, before the disturbance. One notion of stability is simply that it does return eventually. Another involves the rate it returns. Another involves how far the system becomes temporarily displaced from its original state as a result of the initial disturbance. And there are many more. So when we look for characteristics of ecosystems that correlate with stability, we have to be careful and ask what we mean by stability.

Several decades ago it was widely believed that ecological diversity (or complexity) correlated with any reasonable notion of stability. *Diversity* referred to the variety of species in the system or to the richness of the pattern of linkages among the species. But here, too, there are many measures of diversity. Often the famous Shannon index of diversity from information theory is used, but even then there is ambiguity. If, for a particular system, we describe species in terms of numbers of individuals we get one value for diversity; if we describe species in terms of the their biomass, we get another. Thus, elephants make a larger contribution to diversity if you use biomass per species, while microorganisms make a much larger contribution if you count numbers of individuals.

Nevertheless, a number of modeling studies of the putative connection between diversity and stability converge on the result that there is nothing intrinsically stabilizing about diversity, whatever the definition of stability and whatever the definition of diversity. The converse hypothesis, that stability is associated with low diversity, also does not stand up except for the case of certain randomly assembled ecosystems (which are studied numerically by a Monte Carlo procedure). In other words, there is no robust (true in a wide variety of models) theoretical relation between stability and diversity. The old dogma has been shattered. Indeed, the terms of the question have now shifted from "does diversity induce stability" to "what permits diversity and what types of disturbance might reduce it?" This of course still leaves open the question of whether there are some other ecosystem characteristics that do induce stability or instability. In fact, there are some that seem to be robust in the sense that it does not much matter which model or which notion of stability you use. Generally, time lags create instability. Stochastic phenomena also have that effect. Competitive or mutualistic interactions tend to destabilize ecosystems whereas predator-prey interactions tend to stabilize them. And a variety of density-dependent processes such as the self-shading of trees at high density or the switching of a predator from its normally favored prey to a different one when the former becomes sparse are stabilizing. Just as common sense suggests, however, other density-dependent phenomena, such as the

difficulty an individual has finding a mate when the population is sparse, tend to destabilize.

An important caveat applies to these generalities. In the real world, ecosystem response to disturbance is highly dependent on the nature of the disturbance. In the model analyses that have led to the results mentioned above, the initial disturbance is nearly always the removal from, or addition to, the initial populations. But in fact the kinds of stresses that occur in nature are of bewildering variety. The Everglades mangroves would likely be destroyed if we were ever successful at preventing hurricanes because those mangroves require periodic high seas to resist invasion from inland vegetation. However, modest changes in the temperature of the coastal waters would be less likely to affect this plant community. Tundra ecosystems, on the other hand, could be affected considerably by the same modest temperature change and yet be relatively unaffected by a change in storm frequency. The models that have been used to study ecosystem stability are generally poor at exploring responses to the variety of stresses that occur in nature. To say that one ecosystem is more stable than another, without specifying the type of disturbance against which it is stable, is like saying that one person is more attentive than another without mentioning the stimulus.

There has been a lot of effort by ecosystem modelers to find some ecosystem characteristic that is optimized in the course of evolution or succession, in the same way that Gibbs free energy is minimized in physical systems. Of course, ecosystems do not violate the laws of thermodynamics, but the search is for so-called emergent properties—ones that are uniquely properties of the whole system and not the sum of the parts. Productivity per unit of biomass, and diversity, have been suggested as candidates, but as yet theorists have not made a convincing case that such a variable exists. Maybe when one looks at the larger system, with geosphere and biota coupled, some emergent optimized quantity will be found, but at the moment it looks like a fruitless search.

I have talked mainly about the internal couplings among the species in ecosystems. All the various formulations of the Gaia notion, however, refer to stability of a wider set of linkages. My favorite and unabashedly simpleminded view of Gaia is that it hypothesizes a preponderance of stabilizing feedbacks in the linkages that couples the biota to the hydrosphere-atmosphere-lithosphere. Combined biota-geosphere models can be used to explore whether the processes that dampen stress predominate over those that amplify it and whether the biota plays a major role in the dampening processes. The evidence I have seen does not suggest such a predominance; a list of the various ways in which the biota might amplify the greenhouse effect, for example, is as impressive looking as a list of the ways in which the biota might dampen the effect. Clearly more investigation of this is needed.

Of course, it is easy to concoct a model (like Daisyworld) in which the biota dampens disturbance. Unfortunately for Gaia it is equally easy to concoct models in which the biota enhances disturbance. Indeed, it took me a few minutes to concoct a model (I call it Lupineworld) in which soil microorganisms and lupines grow in a world that is subject to a climate-warming stress. The response of the model is to enhance the warming (destabilize) because microorganisms digest soil carbon more effectively under warmer conditions. Lupineworld is no less real than Daisyworld, and no more evidence for anything at all.

The lesson to be drawn from many person-years of ecological investigation into ecosystem stability is that you should never trust one particular model, nor should you draw broad system-level conclusions from a variety of models that examine only one particular stress or one particular system linkage. The field of mathematics is rich and mathematical modelers often have fertile imaginations. In consequence, many splendid creations sprout forth. Only observation and experimentation can sort out which predictions are valid and which are fanciful. The most constructive application of ecosystem modeling is to highlight plausible and robust options; it is futile to attempt to demonstrate that a view of the world is correct, or even plausible, merely by constructing a model that incorporates that view.

B. Henderson-Sellers, A. Henderson-Sellers, S. M. P. Benbow, and K. McGuffie

10
Earth—The Water Planet: A Lucky Coincidence?

The two most fundamental characteristics of the planet Earth are the existence of a wide variety of life forms and the domination of not only the physical but also the biochemical environment by water in one of its three phase states: liquid and solid water on the surface and (largely) water vapor and liquid water in its atmosphere. Water played a vital role in the genesis of life itself (Lovelock, 1979; Schwartz and Henderson-Sellers, 1983; Cairns-Smith, 1985) and plays a part in its continuing existence. Over 60% of the present-day planetary surface is water covered and, for about two thousand million years before the emergence of continents, was almost completely ocean covered (Hargraves, 1976; Cogley and Henderson-Sellers, 1984).

For almost the first half of earth's history (about two thousand million years), the Archean period (figure 10.1), the climate appears to have been remarkably stable, as demonstrated by geological evidence for liquid water on the surface (Lowe, 1980). The Gaia hypothesis (Lovelock, 1979) suggests that in the planetary environment following the establishment of bacterial cells about 3.5 Ga ago, the mutual interactions between life and the abiotic environment maintained this stability such that the earth's climate has remained equable for the continuing development of life.

Two questions can be raised regarding this planetary stability: (1) Can the stability over the evolutionary timescale of the Sun of a planet dominated by the hydrological cycle be explained without invoking the Gaia hypothesis? (2) In the prelife era (and consequently before the "birth of Gaia" [Lovelock, 1988]) could a water-dominated planet have retained an "abiotic homeostasis" long enough to maintain conditions appropriate for the origin of life? It is this latter question that we consider in this chapter.

The immediate, and intuitive, problem is that in the early Archean period, the solar luminosity was approximately 70% that of the present day (Newman and Rood, 1977; Gough, 1977), suggesting that surface temperatures must have been too cool for biotic synthesis: an argument supported by climate models in the late 1960s and early 1970s (Budyko, 1969; Sellers, 1969; Sagan and Mullen, 1972) that predicted a total planetary glaciation. Because geological evidence refutes the possibility of such a widespread glaciation, the "enhanced surface temperature, reduced solar luminosity paradox" has been the subject of much speculation (e.g., Sagan and Mullen, 1972; Hart, 1978; Kuhn and Atreya, 1979; Owen et al., 1979; Walker et al., 1981; Levine, 1982; Kuhn and Kasting, 1983; Kasting et al., 1983; Kasting and Ackerman, 1986; Walker, 1986; Kiehl and Dickinson, 1987).

Clearly the components of the planetary radiation balance in the Archean period must have been different from those of the present day. Either more outgoing infrared radiation must have been trapped (an enhanced greenhouse effect) (Hart, 1978: Owen et al., 1979; Kiehl and Dickinson, 1987) or the planetary albedo must have been lower such that less incoming solar flux was reflected away back to deep space. This could have occurred as a result of the larger percentage area of the planet covered by ocean and/or as a result of there being less cloud cover. Indeed these two features may have been interlinked. On an ocean-dominated planet the very small areas of tropical land would give rise to reduced formation of convective clouds, and the absence of continents would provide few areas where cold water upwelling could occur. (On the earth today, banks of marine stratus cloud are associated with areas of coastal upwelling). Within these constraints, it is thus possible to hypothesize a value of the order of 0.1 for the planetary albedo in the Archean period. At a global scale this results in the effective planetary temperature being decreased by a factor of $0.9^{0.25}$. Furthermore, we choose to assume here a constant globally averaged greenhouse effect for the Archean period equal to that for the present day of 33K. Based on geochemical considerations, Walker (1986) suggests that the very pres-

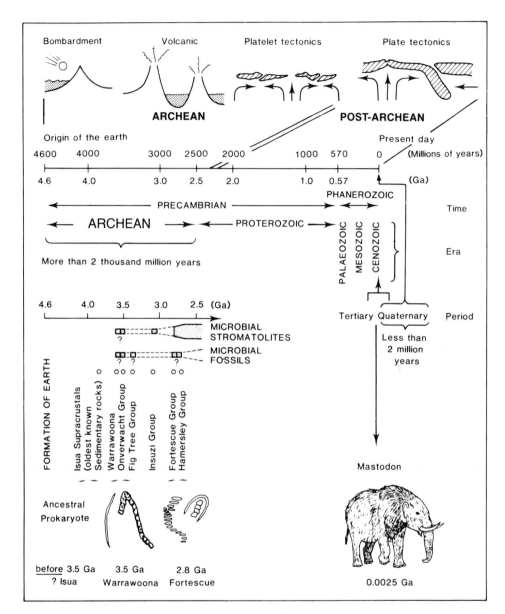

Figure 10.1 The Archean period represents almost half of earth's history from the formation of the earth around 4.6 Ga to the Archean–Proterozoic transition at 2.5 Ga. Geophysically the Archean differed from the post-Archean because plate tectonics had not become established. Instead the surface was first bombarded by cometary and meteoritic material as the debris from the planetesimals was "swept up." This was followed by a period of surface vulcanism and then by a platelet tectonic regime. Life must have become established around or before 3.5 Ga because rocks from that era contain fossil evidence of viable and diverse microbial communities. The oldest known rocks, the Isua supercrustal, are dated at 3.83 Ga and show evidence of a climatological regime not grossly different from that of the present. In particular they contain sedimentary material that was waterborne.

ence of a global ocean could cause considerably enhanced atmospheric carbon dioxide levels. This might counterbalance, to some degree, the decreased greenhouse effect likely from decreased cloud cover and possibly decreased water vapor in the atmosphere and thus justifies, to a first approximation, our assumption of a constant (present-day) greenhouse effect. Interestingly, a similar conclusion regarding the equivalence of the Archean and present-day greenhouse effects can be derived from the Gaian model of the Archean period (Lovelock, 1988).

Numerical Models of the Archean Ocean

In order to examine the climate of the ocean-dominated early-Archean earth, three models, two developed originally for present-day climate simulations, have been modified for the Archean period and interlinked. First, a long-term integration of the global version of the Bryan-Cox-Semtner (BCS) (e.g., Cox, 1984) primitive equation model has been undertaken. Second, both this model and the Multiple Advection-Diffusion for the Archean (MADA) box model, based on but extending the approach of, for instance, Harvey and Schneider (1985), has been run for a full annual cycle with atmospheric temperature data provided by the third model: an energy balance model (EBM). In addition, the upwelling velocity required for the MADA model has been supplied by the BCS model simulation (figure 10.2).

The BCS primitive equation model has been used by many groups in studies of both present-day ocean circulation and the impact of, for example, increasing atmospheric carbon dioxide (Meehl et al., 1982; Bryan et al., 1984; Foreman, personal communication, 1988; Washington and Meehl, 1989). The model simulates the three velocity components (and associated mass fluxes) and includes temperature and salinity as tracers. The basic model (as used here) has no explicit prognostic mixed layer.

In order to simulate the Archean ocean, the present-day model was adapted as follows:

1. Land masses were redefined: an arbitrary hypothesized land configuration consistent with the lack of continental areas as described above (figure 10.3).

2. A horizontal resolution of 6° was chosen (both latitude and longitude): this is the resolution of the standard global BCS model offering relative speed of integration and compatibility with coarser-resolution present-day atmospheric general circulation climate models (e.g., Goddard Institute for Space Studies, Community Climate Model Version 1).

3. Sixteen (staggered) layers in the vertical were chosen to give higher resolution near the surface and less resolution at depth.

4. The effect of 70% of present-day solar luminosity was reflected in the surface boundary condition prespecified—Newtonian cooling with constants appropriately modified for the Archean period.

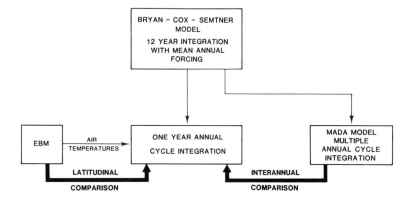

Figure 10.2 Links between the various models used. The BCS model was integrated for twelve years with mean annual forcing. Subsequently a SEB parameterization was added to the BCS model and a one-year annual cycle integration performed using air temperatures (in the SEB calculation) prespecified from the EBM. In parallel an extended advection-diffusion model (MADA) was used for an annual cycle integration using upwelling velocities provided by the BCS twelve-year integration. Comparisons are made between the two annual cycle experiments and the BCS annual cycle simulation.

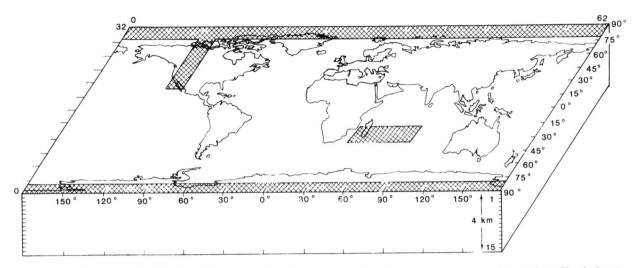

Figure 10.3 The hypothesized land configuration is also shown (cross-hatched); we assume a peninsula (Northern Hemisphere) and an island (Southern Hemisphere) only. The small polar land areas are required by the OGCM to avoid numerical singularities.

As noted previously, it has been postulated that the Archean ocean had a near global coverage. Consequently the land mass chosen for the Archean (figure 10.3) is a single peninsula in the northern hemisphere and a small island in the southern hemisphere (land masses were necessarily at the poles to avoid singularities in the computation). It must be emphasized that this land distribution is purely hypothetical but the areal cover ($< 5\%$) is consistent with volcanoes and impact crater rims being the only features creating positive topographic anomalies in the era before continental crust formation and plate tectonics. However, this land mass configuration has the further advantage of providing three essentially different dynamic regimes: (1) a latitude band in which the zonal flow is disrupted by the peninsula wherein large-scale gyre formation may be anticipated; (2) an island disrupting zonal flow; and (3) an (equatorial) latitude region where there are no obstructions and where planetary-scale Rossby waves may develop.

Mean Annual Spin-up Integration In the version of the BCS model used for the initial twelve-year "spin-up" integration, mean annual forcing was utilized with differential timesteps for velocities and tracers. Although this spin-up method distorts the physics insofar as velocities and tracers are not calculated synchronously, it is the standard way of achieving equilibrium within a feasible computational period (e.g., the initial twelve-year integration required about 100 hours of Cyber 205 supercomputer time). In this model a relaxation method is used for the temperature and salinity

fields such that an additional term of the form $k_l(T - T_{obs})$, where T is the current, calculated sea surface temperature (SST), T_{obs} a prescribed surface temperature field, and k_l a proportionality constant, is added to the temperature rate-of-change equation. This method is frequently referred to as Newtonian cooling. The method requires specification of observed temperature, T_{obs}, as a function of latitude and ensures that the calculated temperatures do not drift too far away from the observed (and therefore "correct") values (Sarmiento and Bryan, 1982). For the Archean simulation, the present-day equator-to-pole surface water temperature gradient of 298K to 274.4K was replaced by a postulated Archean gradient of 291K to 268K. This modified profile was derived by assuming a reduction of solar luminosity to 0.7 of the present-day value and a reduction in the global planetary albedo from 0.3 to 0.1. (This lower albedo value is consistent with a near-global ocean and fewer clouds; see introductory section). The specification of a latitudinal temperature profile to be used in the Newtonian cooling term is consistent with our intention to explore the plausibility of one of the two radiative solutions to the "enhanced early surface temperature, lowered solar luminosity" paradox of the Archean period: that the planetary albedo was lower. In order to explore this proposal, cloud amount has been assumed to be approximately 10% and the effects of sea ice initially ignored. It is important to recognize that the Newtonian cooling term is used *only* in the spin-up integration. Later (in the section, "Annual Cycle Experiment"), a full surface energy budget replaces this arbitrary specification.

Because the main concern here is establishing whether an equable ocean climate is sustainable in the early Archean forced by solar luminosity only 70% of that of the present day, the ocean model was run to quasi-equilibrium for the surface temperature. This was accomplished in twelve years of integration; while acknowledging that deep water temperatures are unlikely to equilibrate within about 100 to 1000 years (Bryan, 1984).

The annually integrated ocean climate shows a strong equatorial jet (consistent with planetary-scale Rossby waves around the equator) with gyres in the northern hemisphere under the influence of the peninsula (Henderson-Sellers and Henderson-Sellers, 1988). Specific values are dependent on the assumptions made about the surface wind stress. Here, in the absence of any other information, we have used the present-day distribution. However, sensitivity tests for $\pm$ 10% stress globally show no qualitative change in the oceanic stream function, which is primarily determined by the lack of land. SSTs from this annual-mean-forced experiment are about 298K at the equator with a less steep latitudinal temperature gradient than that of the present

day (figure 10.4) (279K at about 42°N and S). The zonal pattern of temperatures also reflects the chosen land positions. The isolated island in the Southern Hemisphere has little effect on SSTs, whereas the Northern Hemisphere peninsula has a marked effect, especially on the eastern coast.

The global nature of the Archean ocean also has strong repercussions for the northward heat transport—an important parameter for modifying equator-pole temperature gradients in both ocean and atmosphere (e.g., Covey and Thompson, 1989). Figure 10.5 contrasts the calculated Archean total northward heat transport values with present-day values calculated with the same global ocean model (but for present-day land configuration) by Meehl and colleagues (1982). Similarity is evident with Archean poleward transport attaining a maximum at about 60° and 20°. (The comparison should probably be made with the diffusive transport of the modern ocean because the total is influenced strongly by the intense transport of the land-locked boundary currents that cannot be present in the Archean ocean as postulated). Differences exist, however, in the magnitude of the terms. The Archean total (largely

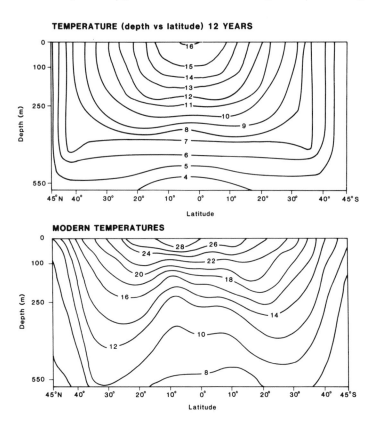

Figure 10.4 Comparison of the depth-latitude structure of temperature for the Archean twelve-year integration and for present day for approximately the upper 550 m of the ocean. (Redrawn from Levitus, 1982.)

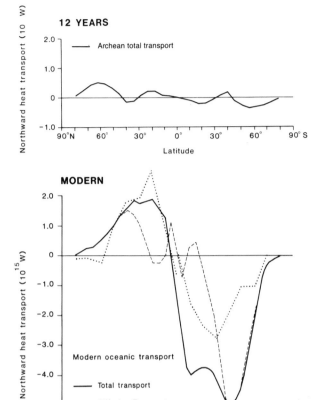

Figure 10.5 The Archean total northward heat transport simulated by the BCS model (Cos, 1984) (upper) can be compared with present-day values calculated by Meehl and colleagues (1982) with the same ocean general circulation model (lower). The observed values for present-day are from Oort and Vonder Haar (1976) for the Northern Hemisphere and from Trenberth (1979) for the Southern Hemisphere.

diffusive) transport has maximum values of approximately 0.5×10^{15} watts in comparison with the maximum diffusive transport in the modern ocean of approximately 1.4×10^{15} W (northern hemisphere) and approximately -5.0×10^{15} W (southern hemisphere). It is this much reduced poleward transport of heat that is partially responsible for oceanic equatorial temperatures not too different from today's. Indeed this is supported by Covey and Thompson's (1989) recent analysis in which they showed that, with present-day fluxes, a halving of the ocean heat transport could be associated with a 5K increase in equatorial SSTs.

Annual Cycle Experiment The results, using mean annual forcing, show that the average temperatures,

especially in equatorial latitudes, are equable. However, annual mean temperature values do not have the same influence on habitability as temperatures that take into account the annual cycle. Consequently, it was considered desirable to undertake a simulation in which the annual forcing of the BCS model was replaced by values more accurately reflecting the annual cycle of variability.

The SSTs calculated in the mean annual case used the Newtonian cooling term and are hence, to some extent, constrained by the latitudinal variation of T_{obs}, which is prescribed. In the annual cycle simulation, the values of T_{obs} were replaced by a full calculation of the surface energy budget (SEB) and a consequent calculation of SST at each grid point. The SEB gives the net energy available to the ocean, ϕ_N, as a sum of the air-water fluxes:

$$\phi_N = \phi_s(1 - A_s) + \phi_{ri}(1 - A_L) - \phi_{ro} - (\phi_c + \phi_e) \quad (1)$$

where $\phi_N, \phi_s, \phi_{ri}, \phi_{ro}, \phi_c, \phi_e$ are the net, incoming shortwave, incoming longwave, outgoing longwave, convective (or sensible), and evaporative fluxes, respectively; and A_s, A_L are the shortwave and longwave reflectivities (albedos). The parametrizations are those used in the numerical thermal stratification model EDD1 (= Eddy Diffusion Dimension 1) (Henderson-Sellers, 1987).* This net energy is then used to calculate the temperature increment ΔT over a timestep Δt by

$$\Delta T = \frac{\phi_N}{p c_p} \Delta t \quad (2)$$

where ρ is the density and c_p the specific heat of water. This (SEB) calculation is implemented at each grid square and therefore it is possible to include latitudinal and longitudinal variation of solar radiation, cloud cover (which affects both longwave and shortwave fluxes), and so forth. Consequently, the calculated surface temperatures are also location dependent. In addition, the latent heat flux, sensible heat flux, and downwelling longwave flux all depend on air temperature. The values for the Archean air temperatures are thus a necessary input to simulation of SST. Consequently a further, stand-alone, numerical model was used for this calculation.

A simple atmospheric Energy Balance Model (EBM) was constructed and forced with Archean solar luminosity (solar constant of approximately

*The SEB code for the BCS model has been made available for distribution through Geophysical Fluid Dynamics Laboratory, Princeton University.

959 W m^{-2}) to illustrate the effects on the atmospheric climate of reducing meridional heat transport and using various cloud cover scenarios and to provide air temperatures as a function of latitude.

The Archean atmospheric climate thus computed has hospitable (13° to 18°C) equatorial temperatures, midlatitudes around freezing, and very low polar temperatures. The global atmospheric climate predicted is not in conflict with the mean annual ocean climate generated using the BCS model. It is not our intention, however, to justify the ocean simulation by appeal to the results from this EBM because the prescribed parameters (e.g., cloud cover) are so poorly known that the results provide order-of-magnitude best guesses only. However, plausible values give rise to results not incompatible with the ocean circulation experiment and we require air temperatures for the more complete annual cycle integration described below.

Because the SEB can be calculated on a daily basis from equation (1) using prespecified air temperatures and including changes in both shortwave and longwave radiation as a function of cloud cover changes, this permits an annual cycle experiment to be undertaken. We have taken the air temperatures computed by the EBM for the case of Archean solar luminosity, ocean albedo, no clouds, and 67% of the present-day meridional transport. This annual cycle experiment was undertaken for a simulation period of one year commencing at the Northern Hemisphere spring equinox.

At the end of a one-year simulation, SST has decreased by no more than 2K at the equator; at mid-depths the cooling is approximately 1K, while deep ocean temperatures are little changed. There is also midlatitude ($\sim 40°$ to 50°) cooling, bringing the isothermal region several degrees of latitude equatorward, although near the poles the SSTs actually increase marginally. Also of interest is the shallowing of the thermocline at the equator in comparison with the tropics. This nonlinearity in the thermocline depth is also typical of present-day observed temperature values, consistent with the annual variation in the maximum solar altitude. This strongly supports the contention that it is necessary to include a full annual cycle parametrization in any ocean general circulation climate model (OGCM) study. The meridional mass transport at the end of the twelve-month period also shows marked changes. In the stream function field, the largest changes are in the Southern Hemisphere at the latitude of the "island." "Summer minus winter" val-

ues of SST in terms of the July minus January difference are of the order of 0.8K at the equator. The corresponding difference field for the stream function has maximum differences of 50 Sverdrups ($= 50 \times 10^6$ m^3 s^{-1}). Small changes in circulation pattern that occur are likely to be due to the strong influence of the near-global sea.

Because both the initial impact to the SST field caused by the introduction of the SEB parameterization (a decrease of ~ 1.5K) and the range associated with the seasonal variability are both less than 2K, it seems not unreasonable to conclude that the twelve-year mean annual temperatures discussed above are likely to be in error by less than this amount.

Extended Box Models

It is important to recognize that neither the twelve-year annually forced integration nor the one-year diurnally forced integration are equilibrium simulations. Much longer times are required to achieve equilibrium in ocean models. An alternative to very long three-dimensional simulations is the use of simpler "box" ocean models (e.g., Harvey and Schneider, 1985; Wigley and Schlesinger, 1985) in order to examine the equilibrium ocean climate. Harvey and Schneider (1985) describe a global box model in which three sections are identified. In figure 10.6A are identified a polar downwelling "pipe" that recirculates surface water to the deep ocean; a surface fixed-depth mixed layer (ML); and a deeper advective-diffusive model. In this deep ocean, advection is simulated with a constant upwelling, with

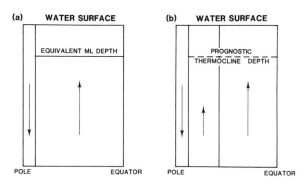

Figure 10.6 **A,** BAD model (after Harvey and Schneider, 1985) in which there is a polar downwelling "pipe" (left) and a deep advective-diffusive box overlain by an (equivalent) fixed-depth ML (right) representing the majority of the latitude range of the ocean. **B,** MADA model in which the almost-pole-to-equator advective-diffusive ocean is divided into two upwelling boxes, both of which contain an embedded prognostic thermocline (ML) model.

a velocity, w, of 4 m yr^{-1}, and a constant value for the eddy diffusion coefficient, K. The equation for the temperature, T, in this box is

$$\frac{\delta T}{\delta t} + w \frac{\delta T}{\delta z} = K \frac{\delta^2 T}{\delta z^2} \qquad (3)$$

In this model an overlying atmospheric box is added to the system that supplies a value of air temperature, T_a, for the ML temperature calculation.

Two modifications have been made to the Harvey and Schneider (1985) box-advection-diffusion (BAD) model described above: (1) the single upwelling box has been divided into two upwelling boxes in which there is a larger upwelling velocity in the low-latitude box than in the midlatitude box; (2) a prognostic ML has replaced the fixed ML depth (figure 10.6B): the model EDD1 (Henderson-Sellers, 1987), which describes the upwelling and thermal diffusion processes. For each box, equation (3) is replaced by

$$\frac{\delta T}{\delta t} + w \frac{\delta T}{\delta z} = \frac{\delta}{\delta z}\left(K \frac{\delta T}{\delta z}\right) - \frac{\frac{\delta \phi}{\delta}}{\rho\, c_p} \qquad (4)$$

in which both w and K can be functions of space (i.e., box location) and time. The functional form for K (Henderson-Sellers, 1987) for wind-induced turbulence is

$$K = k\, \mathring{w}_s\, z\, exp(-k^* z)\, (1 + 37\, R_i^2)^{-1} \qquad (5)$$

where k is von Kármán's constant, $\mathring{w}_s$ is the surface friction velocity, z is the depth, the parameter k^* (Smith, 1979) is inversely proportional to the Ekman depth, and R_i is the Richardson number.

In this experiment, the value of the vertical velocity, w, was retained as a constant, but its value

was derived from the BCS model (end of the twelve-year "spin-up"). The air temperatures used in the SEB were calculated interactively by an overlying single-layer atmospheric model and the solar constant was 70% of the present-day value. The resulting model is referred to as the Multibox Advection Diffusion (MAD) model or, when applied to the Archean period, the MADA model.

Model Interrelationships
Sea surface temperatures for January and July are given in table 10.1, remembering that the MADA model is a gross simplification insofar as there is significantly lower latitudinal resolution than in the BCS model. The results are taken from a 1000-year run, although stability was achieved in less than 200 years. These equilibrium values strongly support those from the BCS model integration. (The surface air temperatures are given in parentheses for the equilibrium state of the box model calculations.)

The two ocean models described (BCS and MADA) are of contrasting spatial resolution, and the low-resolution MADA model contains no dynamics. Despite these differences, a cross-validation (figure 10.2, right) highlights several similarities. As discussed previously, the low-resolution MADA model is less intensive of computer time (by a factor of about 1:10,000) such that an equilibrium state is more rapidly attained. On the other hand, although the deep waters of the BCS model are unlikely to attain equilibrium within any reasonable computer cost limit (using 1988 and 1989 supercomputer hardware), for many (but not all) ocean-atmosphere climatic studies, the attainment of a quasi-equilibrium, at least in the surface layers (as discussed

Table 10.1 Ocean surface temperatures (K) calculated from the extended box diffusion model (MADA) compared with ocean surface temperatures at similar latitudes calculated using the BCS (Cox, 1984) ocean general circulation model.

| | Ocean SST, K | |
	January	July
MADA box model		
Low latitude (0°–30°)	288.5 (288.5)	289.0 (289.3)
Midlatitude (30°–60°)	280.3 (280.2)	281.0 (282.0)
BCS model		
Low latitude (15°S)	286.4	286.5
Midlatitude (40°S)	279.0	279.5

*Values are for the low and midlatitude boxes, which represent latitude ranges of approximately 0°–30° and 30°–60°, respectively, and air temperatures given in parentheses. Typical values are selected from the ocean general circulation model for the central latitudes of each of these boxes. SSTs from the ocean general circulation model are from an annual cycle simulation following a twelve-year mean annual "spin-up" integration.

here) is largely validated by the results of the complementary MADA model. It thus seems reasonable to interpret the results of the BCS model as a first-order approximation to the ocean climate of the early Archean period even though strictly speaking the "equilibrium" attained by the global model pertains only to the surface layers.

Discussion

We have explored one aspect of one of the two radiative solutions to the paradox of early Archean temperatures: whether lowered planetary albedo resulting from a near-global ocean (and the anticipated decreased cloud amounts) can itself give rise to temperatures consistent with geological evidence. We find that the majority of the ocean does not freeze despite incident solar radiation of only around 70% that of the present day. On the contrary, low-latitude temperatures lie between 16°C (equator) and 13°C (15°); temperatures at around 40° latitude being about 6°C.

It must be emphasized, however, that there are many guesses and approximations inherent in these calculations. The ice model is very simple and does not permit us to calculate high-latitude ocean temperatures below the ice, and the atmospheric calculation (including clouds) in all three models is highly simplified. Although present-day wind fields, humidities, and other factors have been used, a sensitivity analysis of the BCS model suggests that this causes no significant errors. We do not know that the atmospheric meridional transport would be reduced in line with the reduction in oceanic meridional transport. Finally, changes in the planetary rotation rate have not been considered here (the Archean rotation rate being about six hours), but could be considered in future, more sophisticated numerical experiments. None of these may be fundamental flaws because it is very hard to see how the early Archean ocean in the region of the very rapid equatorial jet could freeze. Exploration of most of these limitations must await coupled atmosphere-ocean models substantially more robust than those presently available.

In a future project, experiments could be conducted to embed a prognostic stratification model in the BCS model; but this may be either computationally expensive (e.g., using the model EDD1 discussed above) or, using an ML model, conceptually incompatible (Adamec et al., 1981).

Conclusions

The use of a suite of ocean models in the investigation of the ocean climate of the water-dominated, prelife Archean earth suggests that a radiative solution to the paradox of enhanced surface temperature and reduced solar luminosity can be found not only in an increased greenhouse effect but also in a lower planetary albedo (although, of course, it is likely that both effects operated together, possibly synergistically: Cogley and Henderson-Sellers, 1984; Walker, 1986). Climatic conditions resulting from this near-global ocean appear to have been conducive to the origin of life and to the "birth of Gaia" at around 3.5 Ga.

Acknowledgments

We wish to acknowledge the provision of Cyber 205 time at the University of Manchester Regional Computer Centre by the Natural Environment Research Council of the U.K. We also wish to thank Dr Ivan Kühnel for undertaking the 1000-year simulations using MADA. Some of this work has been funded by Australian Research Council awards to B.H-S. and A.H-S.

References

Adamec, D., Elsberry, R. L., Garwood, R.W., Jr., and Haney, R. L. 1981. An embedded mixed layer-ocean circulation model. *Dyn Atmos Oceans*, 5, 69–96.

Bryan, K. 1984. Accelerating the convergence of ocean-climate models. *J Phys Oceanogr*, 14, 666–673.

Bryan, K., Komro, F.G., and Rooth, C. 1984. The ocean's transient response to global surface temperature anomalies. In: Hansen, J.E., and Takahashi, T., eds. *Climate Processes and Climate Sensitivity*. Geophysics Monograph 29, Maurice Ewing Vol. 5. Washington, D.C.: American Geophysical Union, 29–38.

Budyko, M.I. 1969. The effect of solar radiation variations on the climate of the earth. *Tellus*, 21, 611–619.

Cairns-Smith, A.G. 1985. *Seven Clues to the Origin of Life*. Cambridge: Cambridge University Press.

Cogley, J.G., and Henderson-Sellers, A. 1984. The origin and earliest state of the earth's hydrosphere. *Rev Geophys*, 22, 131–175.

Covey, C., and Thompson, S.L. 1989. Testing the effects of ocean heat transport on climate. *Palaeogeogr, Palaeoclimatol, Palaeoecol*. (Global and Planetary Change Section), 75, 331–341.

Cox, M.D. 1984. A primitive equation, 3-dimensional model of the ocean. GFDL Ocean Group Technical Report No. 1. Princeton, N.J.: Geophysical Fluid Dynamics Laboratory.

Gough, D.O. 1977. Theoretical predictions of variations of the solar output. In: White, O.R., and Newkirk, G., eds. *The Solar Output and Its Variations*. Boulder, CO: University of Colorado Press, 451–473

Hargraves, R.B. 1976. Precambrian geologic history. *Science*, 193, 363–371.

Hart, M.H. 1978. The evolution of the atmosphere of the earth. *Icarus*, 33, 23–39.

Harvey, L.D.D., and Schneider, S.H. 1985. Transient climate response to external forcing on 10^0–10^4 year time scales. Part 1: Experiment with globally averaged, coupled, atmosphere and ocean energy balance climate models. *J Geophys Res*, 990, 2191–2205.

Henderson-Sellers, B. 1987. Modelling sea surface temperature rise resulting from increasing atmospheric carbon dioxide concentrations. *Climatic Changer*, 11, 349–359.

Henderson-Sellers, A., and Henderson-Sellers, B. 1988. Equable climate in the early Archaean. *Nature*, 336, 117–118.

Kasting, J.F., and Ackerman, T.P. 1986. Climatic consequences of very high carbon dioxide levels in the Earth's early atmosphere. *Science*, 234, 1383–1385.

Kasting, J.F., Zahnle, K.J., and Walker, J.C.G. 1983. Photochemistry of methane in the earth's early atmosphere. *Precambrian Res*, 20, 121–148.

Kiehl, J.T., and Dickinson, R.E. 1987. A study of the radiative effects of enhanced atmospheric CO_2 and CH_4 on early Earth surface temperatures. *J Geophys Res*, 92, 2991–2998.

Kuhn, W.R., and Atreya, S.K. 1979. Ammonia photolysis and the greenhouse effect in the primordial atmosphere of the earth. *Icarus*, 37, 207–213.

Kuhn, W.R., and Kasting, J.F. 1983, Effects of increased CO_2 concentrations on surface temperature of the early earth. *Nature*, 301, 53–55.

Levine, J.S. 1982. The photochemistry of the paleoatmosphere. *J Mol Evol*, 18, 161–172.

Levitus, S. 1982. *Climatological Atlas of the World Ocean*. National Oceanic and Atmospheric Administration Professional Paper 13, Washington, D.C.: Government Printing Office.

Lovelock, J.E. 1979. *Gaia: A New Look at Life on Earth*. New York: Oxford University Press.

Lovelock, J.E. 1988. *The Ages of Gaia*. New York: W.W. Norton & Co.

Lowe, D.R. 1980. Archean sedimentation. *Ann Rev Earth Planetary Sci*, 8, 145–167.

Meehl, G.A., Washington, W.M., and Semtner, A.J., Jr. 1982. Experiments with a global ocean model driven by observed atmospheric forcing. *J Phys Oceanogr*, 12, 301–312.

Newman, M. J., and Rood, R.T. 1977. Implications of solar evolution for the Earth's early atmosphere. *Science*, 198, 1035–1037.

Oort, A.H., and Vonder Haar, T.H. 1976. On the observed annual cycle in the ocean-atmosphere heat balance over the Northern Hemisphere. *J Phys Oceanogr*, 6, 781–800.

Owen, T., Cess, R.D., and Ramanathan, V. 1979. Early earth: An enhanced carbon dioxide greenhouse to compensate for reduced solar luminosity. *Nature*, 277, 640–642.

Sagan, C., and Mullen, G. 1972. Earth and Mars: Evolution of atmospheres and surface temperatures. *Science*, 177, 52–56.

Sarmiento, J.L., and Bryan, K. 1982. An ocean transport model for the North Atlantic. *J Geophys Res*, 87, 394–408.

Schwartz, A.W., and Henderson-Sellers, A. 1983. Glaciers, volcanic islands and the origin of life. *Precamb Res*, 22, 167–174.

Sellers, W.D. 1969. A climate model based on the energy balance of the earth-atmosphere system. *J Appl Meteorol*, 8, 392–400.

Smith, I.R. 1979. Hydraulic conditions in isothermal lakes. *Freshwater Biol*, 9, 119–145.

Trenberth, K.E. 1979. Mean annual poleward energy transports by the oceans in the southern hemisphere. *Dyn Atmos Oceans*, 4, 57–64.

Walker, J.C.G. 1986. Carbon dioxide on the early Earth. *Origins of Life*, 16, 117–127.

Walker, J.C.G., Hays, P.B., and Kasting, J.F. 1981. A negative feedback mechanism for the long-term stabilization of Earth's surface temperature. *J Geophys Res*, 86, 9776–9782.

Washington, W.M., and Meehl, G.A. 1989. Climate sensitivity due to increased CO_2: Experiments with a coupled atmosphere and ocean general circulation model. *Climate Dynamics*, 4, 1–38.

Wigley, T.M.L., and Schlesinger, M.E. 1985. Analytical solution for the effect of increasing CO_2 on global mean temperature. *Nature*, 315, 649–652.

Jeffrey T. Kiehl

11

The Climate System and Its Regulation by Atmospheric Radiative Processes

The Gaia hypothesis is based on the idea of a self-regulating climate system (Lovelock and Margulis, 1974). In this chapter I review how such regulation can occur in the most general of climate systems. The specific mechanisms considered for climatic regulation are of a radiative nature (the transfer of solar and longwave radiation through the earth's atmosphere).

Over the past twenty years a hierarchy of climate models has been developed to study the earth's climate system (Schneider and Dickinson, 1974). These models range from the simplest nondimensional climate models, like Daisyworld (Watson and Lovelock, 1983), to the most sophisticated three-dimensional general circulation models. The climate state in any of these models is governed by the amount of solar energy available to drive the climate system. For an equilibrium state to exist the energy going into the system must be equal to that leaving the system. The efficiency with which the climate system can emit this energy back to space is governed to a large extent by the greenhouse effect of the atmosphere. The study described here is concerned with how the climate system's equilibrium depends on various components of the atmosphere that determine its greenhouse efficiency. First, I review the way climate modelers have come to look at the climate system. This view is based on systems control theory and uses concepts like positive and negative feedback. I then consider a number of radiative feedbacks that affect the climate system. I use the evolution of the climate system through the Archean period as an example of climate regulation. Then I discuss the more general question of climate stability, with particular emphasis on the runaway greenhouse problem. Finally, I consider how the more complex three-dimensional climate models can be used to study possible examples of self-regulation of the global system.

Climate Regulation through Feedback

Climate regulation can occur in a number of ways. In this section I consider how changes in the radiative balance of the earth can be offset by changes within the climate system. I consider the surface and atmosphere as a coupled system (figure 11.1). The climate of this system is determined by a balance of energy going into and out of the system. The reference level for this energy balance is taken to be the tropopause. The tropopause is used as the reference level because the surface and troposphere are in general strongly coupled to one another through convective heat transfer, unlike the stratosphere, which is in a state of radiative equilibrium. The net balance, N, is defined as

$$N = S^{\downarrow} - S^{\uparrow} - (F^{\uparrow} - F^{\downarrow}) \qquad (1)$$

where we let

$$S^N = S^{\downarrow} - S^{\uparrow} \text{ and } F^N = F^{\uparrow} - F^{\downarrow} \qquad (2)$$

S^N is the net input of solar radiation, that is, the incident solar radiation minus the outgoing reflected solar radiation. F^N is the net outgoing longwave radiation, that is, the upward longwave flux from the troposphere minus the downward longwave flux from the stratosphere. By using existing concepts from control theory (Schlesinger, 1985; Hansen et

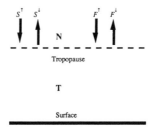

Figure 11.1 The coupled surface-atmosphere climate system.

al., 1984), we can relate changes in N to changes in the temperature of the surface-atmosphere system.

We assume that some change takes place either internally or externally to the climate system. The resultant change in the energy balance of the surface-troposphere system is given by the following equation:

$$\Delta N = \frac{\partial N}{\partial T}\Delta T + \sum_j \frac{\partial N}{\partial E_j}\Delta E_j + \sum_k \frac{\partial N}{\partial I_k}\frac{dI_k}{dT}\Delta T \qquad (3)$$

where E_j represents all external forcing agents (e.g., changes in the solar flux), and I_k represents all internal processes (e.g., cloud amount, water vapor, cloud thickness). The first term in equation (3) represents the change in the radiation balance due to the dependence of this energy on temperature alone. This process is dominated by the longwave cooling of the system (i.e., F^N). Obviously this initial imbalance in the climate system cannot exist for long, for the system must come into equilibrium again, thus ensuring that

$$\Delta N = 0 \qquad (4)$$

Using this relation in (3) and solving for the temperature change ΔT, we find that

$$\Delta T = \frac{\frac{\partial N}{\partial E_j}\Delta E_j}{-\frac{\partial N}{\partial T} - \sum_k \frac{\partial N}{\partial I_k}\frac{dI_k}{dT}} \qquad (5)$$

where we have limited ourselves to one external forcing change labeled j. If there are no changes to the internal system, then there are no feedbacks operating in the system. We thus define the *no-feedback gain* of the system as

$$G_0 = -\left(\frac{\partial N}{\partial T}\right)^{-1} \qquad (6)$$

We also define the initial radiative forcing as

$$\Delta Q = \frac{\partial N}{\partial E_j}\Delta E_j \qquad (7)$$

Equation (5) can now be simplified to

$$\Delta T = \frac{G_0 \Delta Q}{1 - G_0 \sum_k \frac{\partial N}{\partial I_k}\frac{dI_k}{dT}} \qquad (8)$$

The *climate feedback factor* is defined as

$$f = G_0 \sum_k \frac{\partial N}{\partial I_k}\frac{dI_k}{dT} \qquad (9)$$

where $-\infty < f < 1$. From equation (9), f is composed of three separate terms, the no-feedback gain, the dependence of the energy balance on any individual internal climate variable, such as clouds, and finally the dependence of the internal climate variables on the temperature of the system. Of these three factors the last is the most difficult to understand. The variable f can be thought of as a measure of how efficient the internal climate processes are at responding to the initial radiative forcing, ΔQ. Finally, we can define the *climate sensitivity factor* as

$$\lambda = \frac{G_0}{1 - f} \qquad (10)$$

which in conjunction with equations (8) and (9) leads to the following simple relation between the equilibrium change in temperature and the initial radiative forcing:

$$\Delta T = \lambda \Delta Q \qquad (11)$$

Thus, if the climate sensitivity factor is known, the surface temperature change due to a given initial radiative forcing can be obtained from equation (11). For example, the sensitivity factor of most one-dimensional radiative convective models is close to $0.5 \, K°(Wm^{-2})^{-1}$. A doubling of carbon dioxide produces a 4-Wm^{-2} initial radiative forcing. Therefore one would expect a surface temperature change of $2°K$ for a doubling of carbon dioxide from these models, which is what is found from these models. There are very few types of feedback in the one-dimensional radiative convective models, the largest being the water vapor feedback mechanism resulting from the warming of the atmosphere under the assumption of fixed relative humidity (Manabe and Wetherald, 1967). More sophisticated models such as three-dimensional general circulation models contain sea-ice albedo feedbacks and cloud feedbacks that can enhance the magnitude of the climate sensitivity.

If there are no feedbacks present in the system, then $f = 0$ and we have

$$\Delta T_0 = G_0 \Delta Q \qquad (12)$$

where now the no-feedback surface temperature change, ΔT_0, is solely determined by G_0. The no-feedback system contains only one process for maintaining stability: infrared cooling to space. Assuming this process alone, then the net flux is determined by

$$N = F = \sigma T^4$$

which from equation (6) implies that

$$G_0 = (4\sigma T^3)^{-1}$$

and assuming a globally averaged effective temperature of 252 °K yields

$$G_0 \approx 0.3 \; K°(Wm^{-2})^{-1}$$

Thus without the water vapor feedback the surface temperature change from a one-dimensional model due to a doubling of carbon dioxide would be only 1.2 °K. If $f < 0$, then from equations (10), (11), and (12) we see that $\Delta T < \Delta T_0$ and we have a negative feedback system, because the final equilibrium temperature change is less than the no-feedback temperature change. If $f > 0$, then we would find that $\Delta T > \Delta T_0$, and we would have a positive feedback system.

It is important to remember that estimating the initial radiative forcing, ΔQ, from radiative transfer models is fairly easy. It is much more difficult to estimate either the sign or magnitude of f for the real climate system. This is mainly due to our ignorance regarding the dependence of the internal processes, I_k, on temperature. How do these concepts relate to the Gaia hypothesis? If we consider the earth at 4.25 Ga, then we know from stellar evolution theory that the Sun was roughly 24% less luminous than it is at present. We also know with less certainty that the surface temperature was close to the existing range of present-day temperatures, thus $\Delta T \approx 0$ (Walker, 1982). A 24% reduction in the solar constant implies that $\Delta Q = \Delta S^N = -53 \; Wm^{-2}$. Given this initial radiative forcing and equation (11), how can we maintain the condition of $\Delta T \approx 0$?

The Nongaian View
One way of solving this problem is to consider the other component of the initial radiative forcing, ΔF^N. Kiehl and Dickinson (1987) have used a sophisticated one-dimensional radiative transfer model to calculate the change in F^N due to increases in carbon dioxide and methane. The dependence of ΔF^N for these two gases is shown in figure 11.2. The changes in flux are relative to the present amounts of these gases. Thus where ΔF^N is equal to 0 represents present-day mixing ratios of these gases. Knowing this dependence of ΔF^N on the mixing ratio μ, we can calculate the required greenhouse

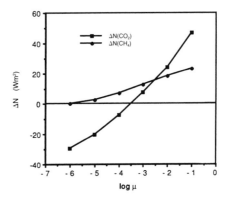

Figure 11.2 Radiative effect of carbon dioxide and methane as a function of gas amount.

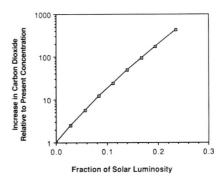

Figure 11.3 Amount of carbon dioxide needed to keep surface temperature fixed for given solar flux reduction.

warming from carbon dioxide to offset a given solar luminosity reduction. This yields a curve of constant $\Delta T \approx 0$, as shown in figure 11.3. Thus for a 24% reduction in solar luminosity a 428-fold increase in carbon dioxide would be sufficient to offset the reduction in solar luminosity at 4.25 Ga. We call this the nongaian view because no biospheric influences have been used to keep the surface temperature unchanged. High carbon dioxide levels resulted from geochemical processes that were independent of the biosphere. These carbon dioxide levels were fortuitously sufficient to keep $\Delta T \approx 0$.

The Gaian View
Another way of ensuring that $\Delta T \approx 0$ for the reduced solar luminosity case is to have a climate system where $\lambda \approx 0$, which implies from equations (9) and (10) that f is large and negative. This would be analogous to a system that is extremely resilient to any external forcings. By definition this is what the Gaia hypothesis is stating. Furthermore, Gaia relies

on the biosphere to keep f large. For example, consider the following feedback term:

$$\sum_k \frac{\partial N}{\partial I_k} \frac{dI_k}{dT} = \frac{\partial N}{\partial \mu_{co_2}} \frac{d\mu_{co_2}}{dT} \qquad (13)$$

The first partial derivative on the right-hand side is just the slope of the curve shown in figure 11.2. This term depends solely on the greenhouse efficiency of carbon dioxide and is easily obtained from radiation models. The second factor on the right-hand side is more problematic and can further be broken down into

$$\frac{d\mu_{co_2}}{dT} = \frac{\partial \mu_{co_2}}{\partial T} + \frac{\partial \mu_{co_2}}{\partial b} \frac{db}{dT} + \frac{\partial \mu_{co_2}}{\partial g} \frac{dg}{dT} \qquad (14)$$

For the present problem the first term on the right hand side would be negligible. The second term refers to the direct effect of the biosphere on the atmospheric carbon dioxide mixing ratio, and the effects of temperature on the biosphere. The last term represents the effects of geochemistry on the carbon dioxide content of the atmosphere, and the link between geochemistry and climate (i.e., temperature). According to the Gaian view the second term would be important in creating sufficient negative feedback in the system to keep f large. An example of this type of mechanism would be the biota's effect on the rate of weathering; which in turn, would alter the carbon dioxide concentration in the atmosphere. The discovery and understanding of importance of the feedback processes embedded within equation (13) is one of the great challenges of present-day interdisciplinary research.

It is important to remember that equation (11) is based on the assumption that the system has come into equilibrium. Obviously the physical processes are associated with certain timescales. In fact, this is one way the Gaian and nongaian interpretations can be compared. If the process for putting carbon dioxide into the atmosphere is much *faster* than any other physical process, it may be viewed as part of the external forcing. However, if the timescales of the various physical processes are of the same magnitude, then distinguishing cause and effect can be difficult. The present analysis has addressed the role of feedback processes for the equilibrium climate system and has not explored the dependence of the timescales of these feedbacks. This is an important aspect of the Gaia hypothesis that certainly needs more attention.

Three Radiative Feedbacks

I now consider three potential feedbacks to the climate system that are based on atmospheric radiative processes. In terms of equation (9), these are represented by

$$f_{A_c} = G_0 \frac{\partial N}{\partial A_c} \frac{dA_c}{dT}$$

$$f_\tau = G_0 \frac{\partial N}{\partial \tau} \frac{d\tau}{dT}$$

$$f_q = G_0 \frac{\partial N}{\partial q} \frac{dq}{dT}$$

where A_c is the amount of cloudiness, τ denotes the cloud optical depth, and q is the amount of water vapor in the atmosphere. The evaluation of the partial derivatives of the net radiative balance, N, with respect to these variables can be obtained from a radiation model. The total derivatives of the atmospheric variables with respect to temperature are more difficult to quantify. In fact even the signs of these quantities are in general unknown. Just how the amount of cloudiness depends on the surface temperature is mired in the complexity of cloud formation processes. It has been suggested that an increase in surface temperature will lead to an increase in available moisture within the atmosphere, which in turn could increase the total cloud cover of the planet. Thus the sign of the term from this argument would be positive. However, it can be argued that more moisture availability does not necessarily imply that cloudiness will increase. Other factors such as the availability of cloud condensation nuclei also effect the outcome of an increase in cloud amount. For this reason I concentrate on the behavior of the first set of partial derivatives that contain the sensitivity of the radiative balance to atmospheric variables.

We first consider the dependence of the net balance of energy at the tropopause on the amount of the cloud cover. Rather than consider the absolute net balance, N, we subtract off the contribution of the clear sky radiative energy. Thus we consider ΔN, where the Δ refers to the difference between the total N and the clear sky N. We use the radiation model of Ramaswamy and Kiehl (1985) because this model includes a detailed method of calculating the solar energy balance from clouds. We focus on the high cirrus type clouds. We also use a tropical profile to study the radiative balance

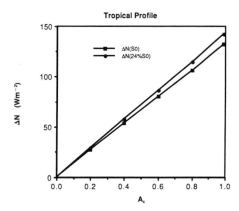

Figure 11.4 Effect of cirrus cloud cover on the net radiative balance at the tropopause.

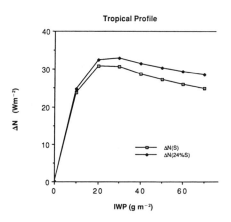

Figure 11.5 Effect of IWP on net radiative balance at the tropopause.

problem. The tropical profile is chosen for the following reason. The tropopause is highest in the tropics and thus allows for the existence of high cirrus clouds. This implies that the temperature difference between the earth's surface and the cloud top is maximized for the following calculations. This large temperature difference in turn leads to a larger impact on F^N. Figure 11.4 shows the effect of cloud cover on the net balance at the tropopause. The ice water path (IWP) of this particular cloud is 30 g m^{-2}, and cloud top is at an altitude of 15 km. The two curves are for present solar constant and for a 24% reduced solar constant, respectively. The linear form of the curve suggests that $\partial N/\partial A_c$ is a positive constant. An increase of cirrus cloudiness from 20% to 30% cloud cover can increase the net flux by nearly 15 Wm^{-2}. This is a substantial change in the net radiative balance of the tropopause considering that a doubling of carbon dioxide changes N by 4 Wm^{-2}.

The second quantity to be considered is the optical depth of cirrus, τ. The optical depth is a measure of how thick the cloud appears to solar radiation. The optical depth is in turn related to the IWP of the cirrus cloud. We shall use the IWP as a more physical measure of the clouds optical thickness. The IWP also affects how thick the clouds appear to longwave radiation. With sufficiently large liquid water contents, clouds appear black to longwave radiation. This means that they absorb all incident longwave radiation and reemit it at the temperature of the cloud. If the water path becomes sufficiently low the clouds are no longer completely absorbing or black, and they can transmit some of the longwave radiation incident on them, and this leads to a less efficient greenhouse trapping of the outgoing

longwave radiation emitted from the earth's surface. The water path of cirrus clouds can be quite variable and for this reason it is worth considering the sensitivity of N to changes in cirrus optical depth. This quantity also reveals the competing effects of solar and longwave radiative processes in determining N. Once again we consider ΔN where the Δ refers to the difference between the total N and the clear sky N. Figure 11.5 shows the change in the net balance as function of IWP.

The interesting feature of this figure is that ΔN increases with IWP up to approximately 25 g m^{-2}, and then decreases with IWP for larger water path amounts. Whether the optical depth leads to a positive or negative feedback mechanism depends on the slope of N. Thus for IWPs less than 25 g m^{-2} this part of f_τ implies a positive feedback. For IWPs greater than 25 g m^{-2} figure 11.5 implies that this part of f_τ leads to a negative feedback. The reason for this behavior is that for IWPs less than 25 g m^{-2} the cirrus clouds are optically thin to longwave radiation and any increase in IWP will lead to a substantial increase in the effective blackness of the cloud. Thus the greenhouse trapping efficiency of the cloud increases rapidly with increased IWP. For solar radiation, as the IWP is increased the reflective efficiency of the cloud also increases; however, this increase in cirrus albedo is being overwhelmed by the increase in greenhouse trapping efficiency.

Once the IWP reaches 25 g m^{-2}, the clouds have become black to longwave radiation. They can no longer increase their greenhouse trapping efficiency. But the solar reflective efficiency can still increase with increases in IWP; this property is not near its saturation point. Thus with further increases in IWP beyond 25 g m^{-2} the albedo effectively overtakes the greenhouse effect, and we actually see a decrease in N with increased IWP. The implications of this result for climate sensitivity are enormous. If we start with a climate whose cirrus clouds have IWPs less than 25 g m^{-2} and an increase in carbon dioxide leads to an increase in IWP of these clouds, then the positive feedback from these clouds would enhance the initial carbon dioxide warming. However, if the cirrus clouds of the initial climate had IWPs greater than 25 g m^{-2}, then an increase in IWP would lead to a negative feedback and the final equilibrium temperature increase would be smaller than the no-feedback change. This argument obviously assumes that $d\tau/dT > 0$, which has generally been accepted as true for cirrus clouds. We also point out that the threshold value of 25 g m^{-2} is dependent on modeling assumptions, and thus a different model could predict a different threshold value.

The change in N shown in figure 11.5 is relative to the case of no clouds, that is, clear sky conditions. Recently, this flux change has become recognized as an interesting climate diagnostic. It is called the *cloud radiative forcing*. Note that for larger IWPs the curve continues to decrease until the solar properties exactly cancel the longwave greenhouse effect, and at this point $\Delta N \approx 0$. Thus an exact cancellation occurs between the solar and longwave effects of the cloud. Such cancellations have been observed recently in the Earth Radiation Budget Experiment satellite data by Ramanathan and colleagues (1989). It is intriguing to hypothesize that this cancellation is not fortuitous, and that some physical mechanism is forcing this cancellation to occur. If so this would be an example of regional-scale climate regulation by the cirrus cloud formation processes.

The question now arises whether a combination of changes in cloud amount, A_c, and cloud ice water path, IWP, can offset the effects of a solar flux reduction of the magnitude experienced during the Archean? Remember that in order to keep the Archean surface temperature unchanged from the present value we must offset a 53-Wm^{-2} reduction in N. Using the radiation model employed for the previous sensitivity studies, we find that if the high cloud amount is increased to 100% and at the same time the IWP is increased above 25 g m^{-2}, while keeping the cloud albedo fixed, N increases by 63 Wm^{-2}. The suggestion that global coverage of cirrus clouds kept surface temperatures close to its present value during the Archean was first dis-

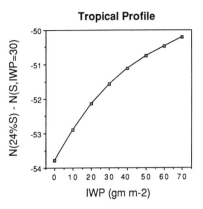

Figure 11.6 Effect of IWP on the net radiative balance for the Archean climate.

cussed by Rossow and colleagues (1982). This analysis has shown that the net radiative balance is quite sensitive to the amount of high cirrus clouds. This large sensitivity arises from the longwave warming effect of the cirrus clouds. These clouds may act as an efficient greenhouse agent due to the large temperature difference between the earth's surface and the cloud top.

With relation to the Archean problem, we can ask whether variations in the cloud optical thickness could offset the -53-Wm^{-2} reduction due to the reduced luminosity. This sensitivity is shown in figure 11.6.

This figure indicates that for a fixed cirrus cloud amount of 20%, no amount of IWP will offset the solar flux reduction. Thus the only solution to the faint sun problem that depends on high clouds is for the existence of 100% black cirrus cloud. Physically this is difficult to justify because cirrus clouds are associated with deep convective updrafts in the troposphere. Simple conservation of mass suggests that this requires regions of downward motion that are cloud free. Thus 100% cirrus coverage seems difficult to achieve in the atmosphere.

The final climate variable we consider is the amount of moisture within the atmosphere, q. Related to the issue of the sensitivity of the climate to q, is the question of the overall stability of the climate system. Initial interest in this problem concentrated on understanding the "runaway" greenhouse effect of Venus (Ingersoll, 1969). More recently, a number of investigations concerning the stability of earth's atmosphere have used one-dimensional radiative convective models (Lindzen et al., 1982; Lal and Ramanathan, 1984; Kasting et al., 1984). To study this question these investigators used the solar constant as a means of increasing the moisture content of the atmosphere. Under the assumption of fixed atmospheric relative humidity, increases in temperature lead to increases in the amount of moisture in the atmosphere. Increasing the solar flux leads to increased atmospheric temperatures, which in turn lead to increased moisture within the atmosphere. The parameter that is commonly used to study the climate stability is defined by Schneider and Mass (1975) as

$$\beta = S_0 \frac{dT}{dS} \tag{15}$$

where S_0 is the solar constant value about which the change dS is performed. This parameter relates the absolute change in temperature to a given fractional change in S. Results from several models are shown in figure 11.7.

For present-day solar flux B ≈ 110°K, for all these models. This implies that for a 1% change in the solar constant the surface temperature will change by 1.1 K. Figure 11.7 shows the value of B for increases in S by up to 30%. The L and R curve are results taken from the Lal and Ramanathan (1984) study. For this model B increases for solar fluxes up to 10% of the current value and then monotonically decreases for large solar fluxes. This model thus remains stable for all increases in S, or in turn for all increases in water vapor amount. The straight line at the bottom of figure 11.7 marked BB is the value of B assuming a simple black body (BB) behavior for the earth's atmosphere. If this curve

included the changes in solar flux the value of BB and L and R would be equal for the 30% increase case. Thus the L and R atmosphere has approached the asymptote of a black body atmosphere. This can occur only if the emissivity of the atmosphere has reached a value of 1, which would imply that the water vapor emissivity scheme used in this model has become opaque to longwave radiation.

The curve marked CCM1 is based on a radiative convective model that employs the same radiation model as used in the latest version of the National Center for Atmospheric Research Community Climate Model. The value of B from this model shows a modest increase with increased solar flux or water vapor. Thus this model suggests that the climate system is unstable to increases in solar flux or water vapor increases. Finally, the curve marked NBRCM (Narrow Band Radiative Convective Model) is the radiative convective model used by Kiehl and Dickinson (1987). This model is radiatively the most sophisticated of the three models shown in figure 11.7. For this model β increases rapidly as the solar flux is increased. Thus this result suggests that the climate system is quite unstable to increases in solar flux or water vapor content.

The most important difference among these three models is the treatment of the transmission of longwave radiation by water vapor. Kasting and colleagues (1984) have shown the importance of the treatment of the water vapor continuum in the case of climate stability. Figure 11.7 suggests that even the treatment of transmission due to water vapor lines has a substantial impact on the estimated stability of the climate system. The interpretation of these results should not be that the climate system is unstable to increases in water vapor amount. All of the models presently used to study this problem are very simple one-dimensional radiative convective models. The conclusion from this study, however, is that more understanding of the transmission of longwave radiation by water vapor is needed before substantial progress can be made on this aspect of the climate system.

Beyond the One-Dimensional View

The model results discussed so far have come from one-dimensional radiative convective models. Traditionally these models have been used to study paleoclimate problems and issues related to climate stability. One of the significant problems with these

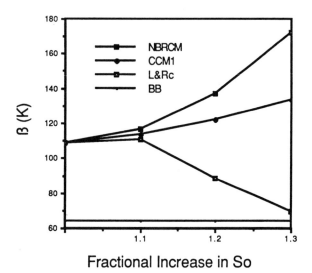

Figure 11.7 Sensitivity of the surface temperature to increases in the solar flux for three radiative models CCM1—NCAR Community Climate Model I. BB—black body behavior.

types of models is that they are highly constrained with respect to their moisture processes. As I have pointed out, changes in cloud amount and optical properties can act as important feedback processes to the climate system. Another facet of the climate system that is ignored in the one-dimensional models is of a dynamic nature. An example of this can be seen in figure 11.8A and B and 11.9 A and B. Shown are the zonally averaged wind and temperature from a general circulation model (Kiehl and Boville, 1988) for the present climate and for a climate state in which all ozone has been removed. From figure 11.9 A and B, we can see that large changes have occurred in the zonal wind structure. Figure 11.8 A and B indicate considerable variation with latitude in the temperature change to removing the ozone. This result suggests that more complex models could be used to study climate regulation issues. Of course the three-dimensional models also suffer from the fact that physical processes are

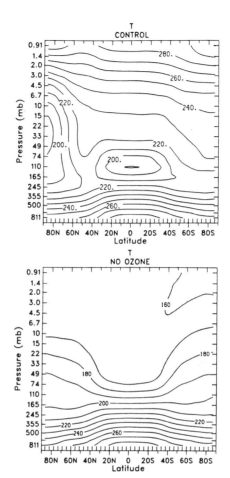

Figure 11.9 **A**, Control, and **B**, no-ozone zonally averaged temperature. (From Kiehl and Boville, 1988.)

poorly understood, but they are less restricted in their feedbacks than simple one-dimensional models.

Conclusions

The present study has concentrated on the way climate modelers have come to look at the climate system. We have considered three particular physical mechanisms for climate regulation. These mechanisms have all been of a radiative nature. Obviously, there are a large number of other feedback processes present in the climate system. The sign and magnitude of some of these are explored by Schlesinger (1985). Perhaps the most important aspect of studying climate regulation is that it allows us to further our knowledge of how the internal physical processes depend on the state of the climate. Until the sign and magnitude of these mechanisms are understood, we have little hope of

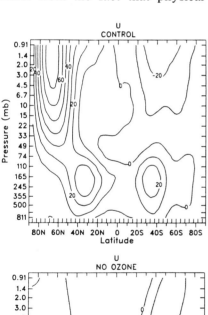

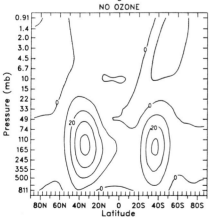

Figure 11.8 **A**, Control, and **B**, no-ozone zonally averaged winds. (From Kiehl and Boville, 1988.)

answering the more important question of whether Gaia is regulating the climate system. The furthering of our understanding will depend to a large degree on how closely scientists of many disciplines interact with one another. More importantly scientists within given disciplines but whose interests are concerned with various spatial and temporal scales must begin to communicate with one another. This is especially true of efforts to understand the hydrological cycle, which is perhaps the most important component of the climate system. Finally, it has been suggested that we should devote more effort in applying three-dimensional models to climate regulation problems. Although nondimensional and one-dimensional models have traditionally been the work horses of climate regulation studies, they are severely limited in their ability to model the robustness of our complex climate system.

References

Hansen, J.E., Lacis, A., Rind, D., Russell, G., Stone, P., Fung, I., Ruedy, R., and Lerner, J. 1984. Climate sensitivity: Analysis of feedback mechanisms, In: Hansen, J.E., and Takahashi, T., eds. Climate Processes and Climate Sensitivity. *Geophys Mon*, 29, 130–163,

Ingersoll, A.P. 1969 The runaway greenhouse: A history of water on Venus. *J Atmos Sci*, 26, 1191–1198.

Kasting, J.F., Pollack, J.B., and Ackerman, T.P. 1984. Response of earth's atmosphere to increases in solar flux and implications for loss of water from Venus. *Icarus*, 57, 335–355.

Kiehl, J.T., and Boville, B.A. 1988. The radiative-dynamical response of a stratospheric-tropospheric general circulation model to changes in ozone. *J Atmos Sci*, 45, 1798–1817.

Kiehl, J.T., and Dickinson, R.E. 1987. A study of the radiative effects of enhanced atmospheric CO_2 and CH_4 on early earth surface temperatures. *J Geophys Res*, 92, 2991–2998.

Lal, M., and Ramanathan, V. 1984. The effects of moist convective and water vapor radiative processes on climate sensitivity. *J Atmos Sci*, 41, 2238–2249.

Lindzen, R.S., Hou, A.Y., and Farrell, B.F. 1982. The role of convective model choice in calculating the climate impact of doubling CO_2. *J Atmos Sci*, 39, 1189–1205.

Lovelock, J.E., and Margulis, L. 1974. Atmospheric homeostasis by and for the biosphere: The Gaia hypothesis. *Tellus*, 26, 1–9.

Manabe, S., and Wetherald, R.T. 1967. Thermal equilibrium of the atmosphere with a given distribution of relative humidity. *J Atmos Sci*, 24, 241–259.

Ramanathan, V., Cess, R.D., Harrison, E.F., Minnis, P., Barkstrom, B.R., Ahmad, E., and Hartmann, D. 1989. Cloud-radiative forcing and climate: Results from the Earth Radiation Budget Experiment. *Science*, 243, 57–63.

Ramaswamy, V., and Kiehl, J.T. 1985. Sensitivity of the radiative forcing due to large loadings of smoke and dust aerosols. *J Geophys Res*, 90, 5597–5613.

Rossow, W.B., Henderson-Sellers, A., and Weinreich, S.K. 1982. Cloud feedback: A stabilizing effect for the early earth? *Science*, 217, 1245–1247.

Schlesinger, M.E. 1985. Feedback analysis of results from energy balance and radiative-convective models. In: MacCracken, M.C., and Luther, F.M., eds. *Projecting the Climatic Effects of Increasing Carbon Dioxide*. Washington, D.C.: U.S. Department of Energy, 280–319.

Schneider, S.H., and Dickinson, R.E. 1974. Climate modeling. *Rev Geophys Space Phys*, 12, 447–493.

Schneider, S.H., and Mass, C. 1975. Volcanic dust, sunspots and temperature trends. *Science*, 190, 741–746.

Walker, J.C.G., Climatic factors on the Archean earth. *Paleogeo, Paleoclim, Paleoeco*, 40, 1–11.

Watson, A.J. and Lovelock, J.E. 1983. Biological homeostasis of the global environment: The parable of Daisyworld. *Tellus*, 35B, 284–289.

Penelope J. Boston
Starley L. Thompson
12
Theoretical Microbial and Vegetation Control of Planetary Environments

The Gaia hypothesis (Lovelock and Margulis, 1973; Lovelock 1988, 1979) has come to mean many different things to many people (see chapters 1 and 6, this volume). The idea of a biosphere that controls features of the physical environment for its overall benefit is difficult to reconcile with existing theories that pit organisms against one another as adversaries in an evolutionary competition (see chapters 3 and 9, this volume).

However one defines Gaia, it can be a slippery set of concepts to apply operationally to real-world cases. Complex, nonlinear, realistic feedback processes are tractable only when viewed as simplified abstractions of reality. Computer models of Gaian feedback systems can extend the simulation of reality beyond that which is perceivable by the unaided human mind. However, having a fundamental demonstration of the plausability of a given simplified scenario is an essential precursor to incorporating it into a human-intractable computer model. In an attempt to help ourselves think about Gaian feedback processes, we have devised a model which we call the *Gaia machine*. This is simply a looping flow diagram through which various candidate Gaian mechanisms can be run to see if they meet the specific criteria that we use to define Gaia. Stripping it down to its essentials, we have attempted to accommodate the apparently disparate features of homeostatic Gaian processes and the forces of change and evolution.

Gaian Worlds

In this chapter we adopt a streamlined definition of Gaia that entails the notion of one or more *negative feedback* cycles. *Gaian* processes act to maintain the system in its present state. In addition, we distinguish such negative feedback cycles from positive feedback cycles; the latter we call antigaian cycles. Antigaian cycles force evolutionary changes in the physical and biological components of the environment that, when finally constrained by some process outside of the antigaian loop, result in a new

equilibrium state. Thus for our purposes, the maintenance of the status quo is the essence of Gaian processes and the forces of change are the essence of antigaian processes.

The simplest of all Gaian machines includes only two components: the biota and the physical environment (figure 12.1). It can respond to either internal or external forcing factors. There are subtle differences between internal and external perturbations.

In the case of internal forcing, the perturbation comes from within the system either from the biota itself or from geochemical or geological changes. In response to either physical forcing or the activities of some organisms, some other species or class of organisms acts on a property or properties of the environment. The resulting *damping* of change

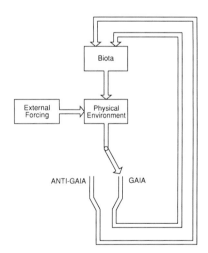

Figure 12.1 Simple "two-box" flow diagram of a biologically controlled world. In this description, an externally forced global environmental perturbation causes organisms to act in such a way as to modify the global environment in a direction opposite to that caused by the external perturbation (negative feedback, or the Gaian response) or in the same direction as the initial perturbation (positive feedback, or the antigaian response). We define a world having a planetary-scale, actively biologically mediated, negative feedback system as a *classical* Gaian world.

(negative feedback) in the environment then modulates either the population numbers, activity, or distribution of the same organisms. The crucial Gaian link is that the perturbed organisms act in a way to partially counter the initial forcing, thus keeping the environment within some relatively narrow bounds. Alternatively, if the feedback is positive (that is, the activity of the organisms *amplifies* a change in the environment) then change continues until some other effect slows the process and a new environmental state is reached. The organisms in question (and presumably other organisms) must respond to this state change evolutionarily by either speciating, adapting in some other way, or suffering extinction. We call this *antigaia* and define it as synonymous with the concept of *coevolution* (chapter 3, this volume; Schneider and Londer, 1984).

In the case of external forcing, some extraplanetary factor is the source of the perturbation (e.g., changes in luminosity or radiation spectrum of the primary star, impacts from extraterrestrial bodies, loss of tidal heating or slowing of rotation, or invasion by the Klingon Empire). Here again, some portion of the planetary biota can respond to alleviate the effects of the perturbation, attempting to return the planet to pre-event status (the Gaian response) or it can simply respond to the change adaptationally (the antigaian response). Obviously the choices open to the biota depend on the magnitude of the event or its progressive inevitability. One can easily imagine external forcing factors that would be likely to overwhelm any conceivable biotic response, for instance, major stellar changes.

Classical Gaia To meet our strict definition of the classical Gaian condition, a system must be able to exert planet-wide control of some critical environmental parameter (e.g., temperature). Merely local control, including the enhancement or persistence of some variety of habitat due to the activities of organisms, does not qualify. Secondly, the organisms involved must be active in the cycle, that is, they must respond to environmental changes (e.g., by growth, reproductive rate, exudation of materials) rather than simply affecting the environment by their passive existence.

Variant Gaia Variations on the classical theme include sub-planetary-scale changes in the environment as a result of biological activity. One suggested terrestrial example of this kind of habitat-scale control is the notion that the wetness of the

Amazonian rain forest is self-perpetuating (Salati and Vose, 1984). Below a critical mass of forest, the local hydrological cycle might collapse and be unable to reestablish itself within the present overall planetary climatic milieu. Variants also include passive participation by organisms in a feedback loop where the mere presence of the organisms controls some environmental change but the environmental forcing does not bear directly on the physiology or abundance of the organisms in question.

Gaian Maintenance of Habitability
By definition, Gaian processes must maintain the habitability, or suitability for life, of a planet. Because different forms of terrestrial life can exist under a wide variety of environmental conditions, the Gaian imperative of maintaining habitability is rather arbitrary. A plausible subset of minimum conditions for life as we know it is (1) temperatures suitable for liquid water somewhere; (2) not too much ionizing electromagnetic or particle radiation to disrupt aqueous carbon-based chemistry; and (3) not too high a concentration of toxic materials. The first condition, which is essentially a global temperature restriction, is by far the best studied habitability condition, both in Gaian (Lovelock, 1979) and nongaian contexts (Sagan and Mullen, 1972; Hart, 1979; Schneider and Thompson, 1980) It is not difficult to speculate on biosphere-climate feedback systems that can affect surface temperatures on a global scale and satisfy the first condition.

The second condition would require the control of harmful radiation from the planet's primary star (in the case of the Earth this means solar ultraviolet [UV] and solar flare particle radiation) or from radiation belts in which the planet travels (e.g., the intense particle radiation belts encountered by the large Jovian moons). Earth's abiologically controlled magnetic field shields terrestrial life from particle radiation, but harmful UV radiation is absorbed by free oxygen and ozone derived from biological sources.

The third condition, the constraint on toxic materials, is the most problematical because toxic substances would most likely be a planetary product rather than being externally supplied. Moreover, one organism's toxin can be another organism's main course. The classic example of planetary "toxic shock" is the rise of oxygen in the earth's atmosphere that must have created a habitability catastrophe for virtually all the organisms in existence at the time, but which also created excellent opportunities for the few organisms that developed defenses. In our discussion here of example Gaian worlds we concentrate on the temperature habitability condition, except for one case in which UV is biologically controlled. We do not consider further the toxic materials condition, although we invite imaginative readers to ponder this topic.

Biological Operatives: The Microbiocentric Point of View

We postulate that even on real planets where Gaian and antigaian processes operate, only a relatively small number of species serve as *biological operatives,* that is, make the major contributions to either global homeostasis or change. This leaves most of the biota in the category of freeloaders, irritants, and reactionaries. If one accepts this idea, then clearly feedback cycles (either negative or positive) must be robust enough to be able to stand the drag on the system from myriad supernumerary organisms. The first and still primary biological operatives on earth are various groups of microorganisms.

Organisms that function as biological operatives cannot be expected to violate self-interest by their participation in a global Gaian cycle. The notion of altruism that applies to kinship selection within a species (Wilson, 1971) is clearly inappropriate in a multispecies context. Any such cross-species altruism, if expressed, would jeopardize the survival of the operative organisms and quickly diminish or terminate a Gaian cycle. One must view two separate levels of possible cost and benefit to organisms that participate in a Gaian cycle. The first requirement is immediate short-term benefit to the organisms from the property or activity that is salient to the Gaian cycle. Second, as a by-product the property or activity must enter into a cycle with nonbiological components and processes of the environment that regulate that property or activity. This may not be of direct benefit to the organisms, but it must not have negative selective value only for the organisms involved. If the cycle works to inhibit many organisms, including the Gaian organisms, then they are not at a unique disadvantage and will not be disproportionately evolutionarily taxed for their participation in the Gaian cycle.

By and large, with the possible exception of worthy species like earthworms, which turn over tremendous quantities of nutrients and contribute to weathering (Ghilarov, 1970; Evans, 1948), various reef-building animals that have been spectacularly active at different geological times (Gall, 1983), and the technological human (whose worthiness is currently unclear, e.g., Catton, 1985), most macroscopic animals fall into the freeloader category. Biogeochemically speaking, they are largely window dressing. Of course, we realize that they play roles in governing the rates of transfer of materials and of residence times of materials in various states, serve as additional habitat for worker organisms like microbes, and reduce the biomass of both microbes and plants by grazing. However, on the whole, planets could—and Earth did for about two billion years or more (Glaesner and Wade, 1966; Cloud, 1976)—do quite well without animals.

Large plants made their major contributions on earth by venturing out onto land sometime probably during the early Silurian period (Lowry et al., 1980; Banks, 1975) and figuring out how to remain upright by producing lignin (Niklas and Pratt, 1980; Delwiche et al., 1989). This has increased the amount of standing biomass possible, and increased the recycling rate of carbon dioxide and oxygen (Volk, 1987). In addition, of course, they have also increased the diversity of possible microbial habitats (Starkey, 1958; Katznelson, 1965; Preece and Dickinson, 1971), as have animals, and provided greater quantities of biomass for microbes to break down and metabolize. Plants can also tie up carbon by leaving buried remains as geological structures (Dunbar, 1949; Daugherty, 1941). Their roots are a dominant force in soil development (Jenny, 1958; Crocker, 1952) and their appearance has enhanced terrestrial weathering (Knoll and James, 1987).

Microbes are the key organisms in global interactive processes. They possess many properties that uniquely suit them for this role. They were not only the first organisms to evolve at least 3.5 to 3.8 billion years ago, but they were the *only* organisms until 0.8 to 1.0 billion years ago (Schopf and Walter, 1983). About 75% of the history of life on our planet so far has been exclusively microbial.

The microbial menu of biochemical talents is legion. They produce compounds as disparate as methane, oxygen, and dimethylsulfide (DMS) (e.g., Atlas and Bartha, 1971). They can metabolize compounds ranging from glucose, that most friendly of life's substrates, to jet fuel, plastics, pesticides deadly to most other forms of life, iron and other metals, sulfur compounds, crude oil, organic solvents, and carbon monoxide (Beveridge, 1989; Schlegel and Bowien, 1989; Reineke and Knackmuss, 1988; Dagley, 1987 and 1975; Meyer and Schlegel, 1983; Fox, 1983; Stafford et al., 1982; Ehrlich, 1978).

Microbes of many kinds have evolved to inhabit an amazing array of hostile conditions on earth. Microorganisms live in boiling hot springs (Brock, 1978; Madigan, 1976; Madigan and Brock, 1975, 1977a and b), on the flanks of active terrestrial volcanoes (Wissmar et al., 1982; Staley et al., 1982; Baross et al., 1982; Ivanov and Karavaiko, 1966), within the crater and plumes of an erupting submarine volcano (Huber et al., 1990), in hot brine lakes (Imhoff and Truper, 1977; Volcani, 1944; Smith and ZoBell, 1937), in hydrogen sulfide–rich geothermal springs (Cohen, 1984; Castenholz, 1973), in extremely acid mine-tailing pools (Langworthy, 1978; Dugan et al., 1970), *within* rocks in the polar deserts (Friedmann and Ocampo, 1972; Friedmann, 1980), at the bottoms of ice-covered lakes and sea ice in the Antarctic (Wharton et al., 1983; Wharton, 1982), in deep aquifers from one to over three km below the surface of the earth (Daumas et al., 1986; Olson et al., 1981; Willis et al., 1975; McNabb and Dunlap, 1975; Rozanova and Khudyakova, 1974; ZoBell, 1958), and in the depths of the oceans around hot vents (Corliss et al., 1979; Jannasch and Wirsen, 1979; Karl et al., 1980; Fischer et al., 1983).

Because microorganisms are so tiny and can be so incredibly numerous, they behave almost as chemical compounds in many important ways. They can be dealt with on the basis of large-number statistics in the same way as chemical reactions. On top of this, they also possess life's talents for self-perpetuation and rapid increase or decrease in population numbers, allowing them to respond to or initiate biogeochemical processes on very short timescales. On the other end of the time spectrum, they can assist in the process of removing various materials from the earth's surface for geologically significant periods of time. For example, causing large amounts of sulfurous and metalliferous materials to be deposited for subsequent burial (Ehrlich, 1990; Beveridge, 1989) or creating large chalk deposits from their secreted tests (Schopf, 1980; Ramsay, 1977).

Physical Environmental Leverage Points

Biogeochemically significant organisms can function on several levels (fig. 12.2). Their direct physical presence can alter properties such as the albedo

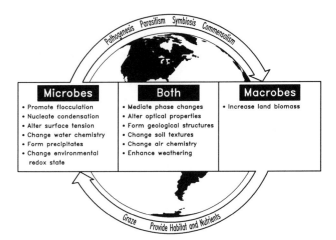

Figure 12.2 Activities and interactions of biological operatives.

of clouds, water surfaces, and land surfaces, or act as nucleating agents for condensation. They can significantly change the chemistry of water, soil, and air. They can affect the distribution and transport of materials and they can affect other biota and change its behavior and evolution.

Biological process can affect the physical environment in myriad ways, but the magnitude, not the sheer number, of the induced effects is crucial for determining the potential strength of a Gaian system. It is conceivable that a Gaian system could operate through a rather direct brute-force biological influence on the global environment. The Daisyworld educational model of Watson and Lovelock (1983), wherein a hypothetical planet's climate is controlled by the relative abundance of solar-absorbing black plants and reflective white plants, is an example of such a direct global control. However, in real life it is likely that considerations of efficiency would select for indirect biological influences on environmental *leverage points*—points in the physical system where small changes can produce large environmental effects analogous to the way in which hormones operate in multicellular creatures. Four such leverage points in earth's present climate system are greenhouse trace gas species, water clouds, surface-atmosphere transfer conditions, and catalytic atmospheric chemical cycles.

The lower atmospheric and surface temperatures of an Earth-like planet are determined by a balance between stellar (i.e., solar) energy absorbed at the surface and a surface-atmosphere mix of outgoing infrared energy to space (Schneider and Dickinson, 1974). Thus the atmosphere tends to be heated from below, carries heat upward by convection or latent heat transport, then radiates to space from an effective radiating level. The effective radiating temperature depends only on the amount of stellar energy absorbed, because by definition it is the temperature a black body would need to balance the absorbed stellar energy. The thermal infrared opacity of the atmosphere determines the difference between the surface temperature and the effective radiating temperature. In the absence of the infrared opacity of water vapor, carbon dioxide, and clouds, the global mean surface temperature of earth would be about $-18°C$, or $33°C$ colder than at present. Trace amounts of infrared absorbing gases (so-called greenhouse gases) can exert a powerful influence on surface temperatures, for example, a doubling of earth's present carbon dioxide concentration of 350 ppmv would produce roughly a $3°C$ global warming (Dickinson and Cicerone, 1986).

Water clouds play a major role in earth's radiation budget by both reflecting solar radiation (causing a cooling effect) and trapping infrared radiation (causing a warming effect because most clouds are virtually opaque to thermal infrared radiation). On average, the solar effect is the larger of the two influences and clouds tend to cool Earth on the whole (Ramanathan et al., 1989). However, there is a large variability in the balance of the two effects depending on season, latitude, and cloud height and type. The most interesting climatic leverage points regarding clouds are cloud height, because this changes the cloud infrared radiating temperature without necessarily affecting solar energy, and cloud droplet size, because this changes the cloud albedo (hence solar absorption) with little effect on the cloud infrared opacity.

Important transfers of energy, materials, and momentum between the atmosphere and underlying surface depend in part on surface properties that can be determined by biological processes. The surface-atmosphere interface can be an effective leverage point by virtue of proximity to biological processes and by the efficient use of a quasi-two-dimensional boundary to control a three-dimensional volume. The Daisyworld model (Watson and Lovelock, 1983) relies on a surface albedo change, that is, control of energy transfer, to determine planetary temperatures. There are many important surface-atmosphere material transfers on earth, one of the most obvious being the water evaporation and precipitation of the global hydrological cycle. On the other hand, the global cycle of angular momentum transfer between the atmosphere and surface is not obvious, but is a fundamental factor in determining the general circulation of the atmosphere and global climate (Lorenz, 1967).

Biologically controlled chemical catalysts that could act on important atmospheric trace gases could create powerful effects on the physical environment. A significant terrestrial example is the biological production of N_2O, its subsequent oxidation to NO_x in the stratosphere, and the catalytic destruction of stratospheric ozone by NO_x (Crutzen, 1970). However, in this case the Gaian "switch" (figure 12.1) is not closed, given that there is no obvious direct feedback between the enhanced UV radiation accompanying the loss of ozone and the actions of the soil microbes that produce N_2O.

The General-Purpose Gaia Machine

Our general-purpose Gaia machine is illustrated in figure 12.3. Elements of the top row of our machine, namely microbes, higher organisms, and biological products, are expected to act on the physical environment through a variety of processes. From the wide range of possible processes we are constrained by our previous discussion to choose those that can be effective in maintaining habitability; those that biological entities can produce; and those entities that can act on physical environmental leverage points. For the second row in our Gaia machine we have chosen radiative transfer, material phase changes, and momentum transfer as the three phys-

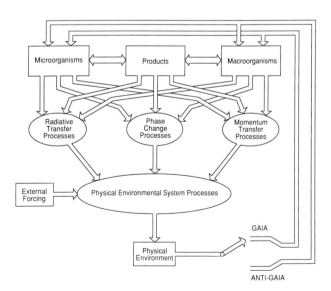

Figure 12.3 The general-purpose Gaia machine used to test various idealized Gaian worlds.

ical process elements we will consider further. (For example, greenhouse trace gas changes would act through the radiative transfer process. On the other hand, an effect that would change the ice nucleation point of cloud droplets would act through the phase change process, and then secondarily through the radiative transfer process.) Our choices are not meant to imply that other processes do not exist or could not be important, merely that these processes meet our particular set of conditions and are worth examining.

The general-purpose Gaia machine is sufficiently comprehensive to describe the possible interactions in dissected individual feedback cycles on hypothetical planets of many kinds. For the human mind to evaluate any complex nonlinear interactions must be simplified to the point where individual pathways are perceivable. Of course, on the real planet Earth many side-branches of main pathways and more complex interactions no doubt exist. For example, a more complex network can be imagined in which one type of organism initiates a process that affects another type of organism in an ongoing chain reaction that continues until the environment is affected. The chain could be said to be Gaian if the net result of all this furious activity was negative feedback on the environmental condition that modulated the behavior of the first level of organisms. Such chains (whether Gaian or antigaian) are probably more common in nature than more simple relationships, yet they are presently opaque to human scientific techniques.

The Gaia switch operates in our general purpose model (figure 12.3) just as it does in the simpler two-box model (figure 12.1). When the switch is in the "Gaia" position, the biological component exerts control over the environment that remains relatively constant over some timescale and in turn inhibits biological change and evolution. When the switch is in the "anti-Gaia" position, positive feedback forces the environment to move to a new steady state, which in turn promotes biological selection resulting in evolution and speciation.

Example Worlds

The value of our Gaia machine lies in its ability to serve as a quick test for assessing the viability of various hypothetical feedback ideas before one wastes serious effort on a scheme that would have little or no impact on a planet. It serves as an initial screening mechanism for hare-brained ideas that

seem brilliant when first conceived but may not be worth pursuing upon the application of more sober thought. In this spirit, we have devised our own selection of hare-brained ideas that we have translated into hypothetical planets (à la Daisyworld) for the purpose of grinding them through our Gaia machine to see if they survive the test of plausibility.

The Taxonomy of Gaian Worlds

In keeping with our previous classification of negative feedback cycles as *classical* or *variant Gaian*, we extend this to *classical* and *variant antigaian* cycles. Two examples of Gaian mechanisms that have been proposed and investigated for earth are the dimethylsulfide (DMS) temperature cycle (Charlson et al., 1987) and the biotic weathering-CO_2-temperature cycle suggested by Schwartzman and Volk (1989) and Lovelock and Whitfield (1982). Let us see how these examples fare in our Gaia machine.

In the first example, which we will call *DMS World*, the planet is reasonably mature with a well-developed biota and oxygen-containing atmosphere, but otherwise its stage of development is not important. A large fraction of DMS World must be covered by oceans. The nature of the biota is relatively unconstrained, except that some marine plankton produce DMS as a byproduct of their daily metabolic activities. We assume that overall DMS production increases as temperature increases. DMS produced by the microorganisms is converted in the atmosphere to form atmospheric sulfate aerosol, which acts as effective cloud condensation nuclei (CCN) for marine clouds. In the absence of other sources of CCN, owing to the limited land source, the DMS-generated CCN dominates. Under the assumption of fixed cloud liquid-water content, an increase of CCN will act to decrease the mean cloud droplet size and, as a result, increase the cloud solar reflectivity and cool the planet.

The Gaia machine pathway (figure 12.3) for DMS World is: Microorganisms (plankton) → products (DMS) → phase change processes (more CCN) → physical environmental system processes (smaller cloud droplets) → physical environment (greater cloud albedo, lower temperature) → "Gaia" switch setting (negative feedback) → microorganisms (less DMS production). This fits our definition of a classical Gaian cycle.

Although this Gaian feedback system could be effective on DMS World, the weakness of applying it to earth lies in the currently unverified assumption that increased temperatures act to increase DMS production. There is as yet no reliable evidence that this is the case for present-day earth and, in general, the factors controlling DMS production are not well understood (Caldiera, 1989; Vairavamurthy et al., 1985) So, while the concept is plausible by our Gaia machine test, the particulars are as yet unproven for earth. We refer the reader to Charlson et al. (1987) for a more detailed discussion of the real-world situation.

The second example, which we will call *Weathering World,* involves the notion that biologically enhanced weathering rates could be factors of 10 to 1000 higher than abiological weathering alone (Schwartzman and Volk, 1989). The planet must be relatively Earth-like with respect to land surface and possessing a multifaceted biota. The weathering of silicate minerals forms the principal long-term sink for atmospheric carbon dioxide. As the weathering rate is increased by increased biological activity, the drawdown on atmospheric carbon dioxide results in lower temperatures. This depresses biological activity, which allows the carbon dioxide to stabilize at some level.

The Gaia machine pathway for Weathering World is: Micro- and macroorganisms (bacteria, lichens, and land plants) → products (enhanced soil CO_2 and weathering) → radiative transfer processes (less atmospheric CO_2) → physical environmental system processes (climate system processes) → physical environment (decreased temperature) → "Gaia" switch setting (negative feedback) → micro- and macroorganisms (reduced biological activity). Again, a classical Gaian cycle.

Weathering World passes the Gaia Machine test for plausibility but for application to the case of earth, confirmation of biological enhancement of weathering rates must be sought empirically. If weathering is not significantly biologically enhanced, then the Walker et al. (1981) abiological version of silicate weathering control would more accurately describe the situation and this example would fail the Gaia machine test.

Classical Gaian Worlds

In keeping with our definitions above, the first set of worlds we consider conforms to the strict negative feedback criteria that we have postulated. The effects must be global and directly affect some facet of the organisms' biology.

Prestone World   *Type of planet.* Terrestrial.

Stage of development. This world has some characteristics of earth at approximately 2 to 3 Ga.

Special physical characteristics of planet. The planet is mostly ocean covered, and relatively cold. Sea ice covers about 20% to 30% of the planet. This planet would be vulnerable to the "ice-catastrophe" positive ice-albedo feedback (Schneider and Dickinson, 1974) in the event of a sufficiently large external cooling perturbation.

Salient Biology. The dominant cold-region marine organism is a type of photosynthetic alga. These algae produce an internal antifreeze compound that allows them to stay active in subfreezing conditions. Even so, low light levels in winter or under thick sea ice decrease the living algal biomass. The dying algae release their antifreeze compounds as they decompose, and the compounds act to depress the freezing point of the ambient water.

Physical system affected. Antifreeze compounds build up in the water as winter sets in. This acts to reduce the maximum sea-ice thickness reached during the winter, and thus to increase the ice-free area created during the summer. The antifreeze algae would not only suppress seasonal ice growth, but would also act to hold back the equatorward advance of the ice edge in the event of a global cooling.

Gaia machine pathway. Microorganisms (photosynthetic algae) → products (antifreeze) → phase change processes (less sea-ice growth) → physical environmental system processes (climate system processes) → physical environment (higher temperature) → "Gaia" switch setting (negative feedback) → microorganisms (reduced mortality, hence less antifreeze).

Discussion. Reducing the growth rate of sea ice during the cold season would result in an overall warmer climate because the increased open ocean area in the summer would absorb much more solar energy than would sea ice. However, the amount of antifreeze required might be too large to be supplied by any plausible organism. Rather than depressing the freezing point of seawater, a more effective way to slow sea-ice growth would be to decrease its thermal conductivity. Sea-ice growth, which occurs at the bottom of the ice, is controlled by heat conduction through the ice to the cold atmosphere above (Makyut and Untersteiner, 1971). Small trapped air bubbles could reduce the thermal conductivity (like insulating foam), but it is unclear how an organism could accomplish this, or what selective advantage would accrue to individual organisms having this trait.

Exxon-Valdez World *Type of planet.* A largely ocean-covered, terrestrial, earthsized planet that orbits a strongly UV-emitting star (probably an A-type star on the main sequence[1]).

Stage of development. The atmosphere contains free oxygen of biological origin.

Special physical characteristics of planet. The near-absence of land sources results in very low atmospheric concentrations of N_2O and CH_4. Limited N_2O implies that stratospheric ozone concentrations are controlled by stratospheric water vapor concentrations via the formation of hydroxyl radicals that catalytically destroy ozone. Limited CH_4 implies that the source of stratospheric water vapor is dominated by transport from below rather than by in situ production.

Salient Biology. To protect themselves from the high UV fluxes while still maintaining access to visible light, planktonic organisms contain UV-absorbing substances that protect their sensitive interior compounds from denaturation, for instance, flavanoid pigments like anthocyanins and carotenoids as in modern plants (Caldwell, 1971), or as in high-altitude yeasts and algae (Stein and Amundsen, 1967; Caldwell, 1964). Even so, UV damage is a dominant factor in determining mortality rates and biological turnover. When the organisms die, the cells are lysed and a mixture of oils and pigments is released. This allows a thin *oil slick* of UV absorber to be present on the water surface that blocks UV wavelengths while allowing penetration by photosynthetically active wavelengths (~400 to 700 nm).

Physical system affected. Because the planet is all water, the thin layer of oily UV-absorbing material on the ocean surface can exercise a strong control on global evaporation rates. A reduction in the rate of global evaporation will decrease moist convective activity which, in turn, will decrease the water vapor transport into the stratosphere and lower the tropopause. Both effects will act to increase the thickness and UV shielding ability of the stratospheric ozone layer. Increased stratospheric UV shielding will act to reduce mortality rates and thus reduce the replenishment of the UV-absorbing oil slick.

Gaia machine pathway. Microorganisms (plankton) → products (oil slick) → phase change processes (less evaporation) → physical environmental system processes (less moist convection) → physi-

cal environment (less stratospheric water vapor, more ozone, less surface UV) → "Gaia" switch setting (negative feedback) → microorganisms (lower mortality rate, less oil slick).

Discussion. The success of this cycle lies in the postmortem release of materials as a waterborne ultraviolet shield. Such a shield is composed of the byproducts of organism activity. In this case, organism death or leakage produces the shield. In the case of earth's ozone layer, the airborne shield is also composed of the byproduct of organism activity, that is, oxygen and hence ozone. Water alone is a very poor attenuator of UV (Smith and Tyler, 1976). The advantage of having a floating shield created by the lysis of predecessors and not the leakage of living cells is the reduction in the metabolic costs of producing UV-absorbing pigments by living cells. It is known that in many organisms on earth photosynthetic pigments are produced in different proportions over very short timescales to accommodate the cells to varying amounts of available light (known as shade adaptation; Darley, 1982). Another conjecture might be that in a very high UV environment, organisms would evolve with genetic material less sensitive to UV wavelengths than earth life. Such an alternative adaptation would render the UV protection described here unnecessary.

Taiga World *Type of planet.* Terrestrial.

Stage of development. Mature, with highly evolved plant life.

Special physical characteristics of planet. This world is assumed to be rather small and somewhat similar to Mars in terms of initial volatile endowment and presumed outgassing history. (Klein, 1978; Levin and Straat 1977; Magur et al., 1978; Horowitz 1977, Horowitz and Hobby 1977, Oyama and Berdahl, 1977, Oyama and Berdahl 1978; Clark and Van Hart, 1981; Toulmin et al., 1977.) However, unlike Mars, Taiga World is close enough to its primary star to be habitable without the need for very high atmospheric CO_2 concentrations. This world is almost completely land covered, except for some small water bodies on the scale of large lakes or small seas, and global tectonic processes do not exist. These assumptions preclude a long-timescale carbon cycle and eliminate the possibility of a vast sedimentary reservoir of carbon as carbonates. On this world, carbon resides in the biosphere, soil, and atmosphere, with roughly equal amounts in each reservoir.

Salient Biology. Taiga World gets its name from

its relatively cool climate, the dense vegetation that covers the land, and the role the plants play in the global carbon cycle.

Physical system affected. The similarity in size of surface and atmospheric carbon reservoirs implies that variations in the biosphere will have a large influence on the concentration of atmospheric CO_2 and on climate. The balance between plant photosynthesis and respiration controls the atmospheric CO_2 concentration. We speculate that net carbon storage in the plants and soil increases as temperature increases. (There is some evidence that this is now happening in Earth's boreal forests; Tans et al., 1990). In this case, a global warming perturbation would increase global carbon storage, decrease atmospheric CO_2, and decrease the global temperature, thus providing a negative feedback on the warming forcing.

Gaia machine pathway. Macroorganisms (plants) → products (sequestered carbon) → radiative transfer processes (less atmospheric CO_2) → physical environmental system processes (climate processes) → physical environment (reduced temperature) → "Gaia" switch setting (negative feedback) → macroorganisms (decreased plant growth).

Discussion. This world could work only if there are no significant long-term sources or sinks of CO_2 (unlike Earth, which has both), and only if the biosphere and soil reservoir of carbon is large enough so that its variations will strongly perturb the atmospheric CO_2 concentration. If Mars had developed life, could it have taken this path? Probably not, because of Mars' distance from the Sun, the amount of CO_2 needed for Earth-like warmth (10^3 to 10^4 kg C m^{-2}) is large compared to the amount that could plausibly be stored as accessible living or dead biomass ($\sim 10^2$ kg C m^{-2} by analogy to high-storage Earth ecosystems). In this case, photosynthesis and respiration changes could not control atmospheric CO_2 concentrations to any climatically significant extent.

The implied dense, global forest on Taiga World is contradictory given the absence of large oceans. It may be more likely that the global vegetation cover would be large, water-conserving succulents. In this Saguarro World, the limiting factor on biomass would likely be water, although temperature would still play a role. If the planet tended to be cool (more Mars-like), then a warm perturbation would stimulate biomass growth both through temperature and by increasing the global cycling rate of water.

Root World *Type of planet.* This planet is smaller than Earth and conditions resemble those suggested for Mars several billion years ago (McKay and Stoker, 1989).

Stage of development. The planet is about three billion years old. It is past the golden age of warmer, wetter climate, but not yet devoid of atmosphere.

Special physical characteristics. This planet has no plate tectonics as in the case of Mars. Geological cycling of materials is thus not possible. Net burial of materials is lowering the available pool of carbon and other nutrients. The planet is becoming arid and colder. Surficial bodies of water are small, shallow, and scarce. There is a proportionately large concentration of carbon dioxide in the atmosphere. There is no large geochemical sink for CO_2 as carbonates because of the scarcity of water bodies.

Salient Biology. In response to water limitation, large treelike plants evolve with massive interconnected root systems extending to levels deep enough to tap underground brines and allow the plants also to tap the small surficial bodies of water while growing considerable distances from them. There is a large subterranean community of consumer organisms and detrital organisms that graze on the root material and break down remains, forming a super rhizosphere community. The living and dead biomass is a significant sink for carbon compared with the carbon dioxide still in the tenuous atmosphere.

Physical system affected. This Gaian system is plant dominated, acting to draw down or increase the CO_2 levels in the atmosphere in response to temperature. As with earth plants, the trees on Root World photosynthesize faster at higher temperatures within their optimum window. This draws down CO_2, cooling the planet slightly, which in turn depresses photosynthesis. The massive root system serves the needs of the organisms, that is, permits the search for water, while also serving as a large reservoir of carbon comparable to the reservoir in the atmosphere as CO_2. Earth's atmospheric carbon content is 0.7×10^{18} g, while the amount of carbon in living biomass and soil is 2.0×10^{18} g. It is quite plausible therefore to imagine that the Root World ecosystem could contain a great deal of carbon as biomass.

Gaia machine pathway. Macroorganisms (plants) → products (sequestered carbon) → radiative transfer processes (less atmospheric CO_2) → physical environmental system processes (climate system processes) → physical environment (lower temperature) → "Gaia" switch setting (negative feedback) → macroorganisms (lower plant growth rate).

Discussion. The CO_2 respiration in the soil by the microbes and animals that graze upon the roots remains far more constant than the rate of photosynthesis because they are buffered from short-term changes in temperature. Because of this their participation in the CO_2 and climate-control cycle is minimal except over long timescales, when they act to prevent the permanent sequestering of carbon.

Root World is a description of the waning stages of life on a Mars-like planet that had given rise to life at a warmer, wetter period in its history and evolved to the point of advanced multicellular organisms. Before long, geologically speaking, the Root World ecosystem will begin to lose out to the inevitable aging of the planet. As the planet experiences increased solar luminosity from its aging sun, it will be able to maintain relatively constant climate with less CO_2. However, there will be a lower limit at which the root trees can no longer photosynthetically maintain large standing root biomass. This will impair their ability to construct the massive roots necessary for the transport of water on the arid world. The plants will gradually diminish in areal extent and their impact on global climate will dwindle.

Variant Gaian Worlds
The worlds described in this section depart from the classical scheme either by exercising only local habitat control, or by the passive nature of the role played by the biological operative organisms.

Stromatolite World *Type of planet.* Terrestrial.
Stage of development. Not specific, but probably similar to Earth of about 2 to 3 Ga.

Special physical characteristics. This world is virtually completely ocean covered with mostly shallow seas. The planet on the whole has a relatively high surface temperature. Ocean tides are of several meters' amplitude, implying either a nearby large moon or that the planet is fairly close to its primary star.

Salient Biology. The dominant life forms (at least physically) are stromatolites distributed in huge numbers throughout the midlatitude shallow seas. The closely spaced stromatolites extend a couple of meters above the water line at low tide. Stromatolite growth is prevented in higher latitudes by winter light restrictions, and in lower latitudes by high water temperatures.

Physical system affected. The stromatolites act to increase the effective surface roughness for turbulent air-sea transfers of momentum. Assuming the magnitude of the global angular momentum transport cycle remains constant (i.e., the net transfer of westerly momentum from low to midlatitudes), an increase in surface roughness requires a decrease in surface wind speed. However, decreasing surface winds act to decrease evaporation by two mechanisms: reduction of evaporation from a given amount of water surface, and decreasing the amount of water surface area by reduction of waves and, especially, whitecaps. The reduction of evaporation, the primary means by which ocean surfaces lose heat, acts to keep the surface temperatures in the stromatolite zone higher than they would be otherwise. A positive global temperature excursion would cause a dieback of stromatolites at the lower latitude edge of the life zone. This would cause local surface wind speeds to increase, acting to cool the surface. The local cooling would prevent further dieback of the stromatolites.

Gaia machine pathway. Microorganisms → products (stromatolites) → momentum transfer processes (reduced surface winds) → physical environmental system processes (reduced evaporation) → physical environment (increased temperature) → "Gaia" switch setting (negative feedback) → microorganisms (reduced stromatolite coverage).

Discussion. It is doubtful whether evaporation would be sufficiently controlled by the wind speed to create a substantial effect on surface temperatures, or whether such temperature effects would control the stromatolite growth. This is an example of failure to pass the Gaia machine test. The plausibility of this mechanism is low.

Gas Giant World *Type of planet.* This world is a gas giant planet similar to Jupiter. It is close enough to its primary star to receive some light energy in the outer cloud layers, but far enough away that low temperatures are a consideration in a microorganism-habitable cloud zone. As on Jupiter, planetary heating drives large convection cells that circulate materials vertically over characteristic timescales. These act as major transport pathways for organisms.

Stage of development. A mature aerosol ecosystem similar to conjectures advanced by Sagan and Salpeter (1976) has become established in the water cloud layers of the outer atmosphere.

Special physical characteristics. The planet possesses a water cloud between the 4- and 9-bar pressure level in the atmosphere depending on assumptions of water abundance ranging from solar to ten times solar (Stoker and Boston, 1984; Thompson et al., unpublished calculations).

Salient Biology. A mature cloud-droplet biota has evolved that is photosynthetically driven and resides in the water cloud layer. The primary producer microorganisms that live in the cloud droplets of the water cloud layer rely on photons from above to conduct photosynthesis. The environmental temperatures are maintained by internal planetary heating. The organisms move through the atmosphere by means of large-scale convection driven by energy from below. Loss of organisms occurs when they are swept downward out of the habitable zone to pyrolytic depths. Limitation on metabolic activities occurs when the organisms are cooled as they are transported by convection to the upper cold layers of the water cloud. A useful adaptation of the organisms is to maintain warmer interior temperatures by growing darker as they become colder, perhaps by means of a photochromic pigment (Shropshire, 1977; Precht et al., 1973). This would allow them to remain at metabolically feasible temperatures longer while they are in the upper zones of the water cloud. Such an adaptation would not only allow them to avoid shutting down but would enable maximum use to be made of available photons for photosynthesis at the best-lighted outer layers of the atmosphere. If the pigments employed for heat gain were also photosynthetically light trapping as is common in many phototrophs (Fork, 1977) then both warming and energy-producing tasks could be performed by a common substance, a savings in metabolic energy.

Physical system affected. The darkening of the organisms will not only allow the organisms to function better and throughout a greater portion of their ecological range but will also retard or eliminate the period during which the cloud droplets will become icy on their convection-driven trip through the upper cloud layers. This property will act to maintain the local habitat (i.e., the cloud droplets themselves) for the organisms as long as possible.

Gaia machine pathway. Microorganisms → products (dark pigments) → phase change processes (reduced cloud droplet freezing) → physical environment (larger habitable zone) → "Gaia" switch setting (negative feedback) → microorganisms (faster growth, more pigment).

Discussion. Obviously, this is a relatively local effect. However, in a relatively homogeneous environment like the atmosphere of a gas giant planet, this "local" effect will occur on a virtually planet-wide basis. The organisms derive direct immediate short-term benefits from this adaptation while globally affecting the temperature of the upper water cloud droplets. We make no assumptions about the mode of reproduction of these organisms other than to invoke the idea of division within a water droplet. The daughter cells then acquire their own additional protective water for their surrounding droplets by simple coalescence onto their hydrophilic surfaces.

Europa World "All these worlds are yours except Europa. Attempt no landing there. Use them in peace for all mankind."—Clark (1982)

Type of planet. This world is modeled after Europa, the fourth moon of Jupiter. It is a small icy body orbiting a large planet. It receives some light from the primary star (Jupiter receives approximately 3.7% the light of Earth). Heating from the interior is provided by the tidal action of the large planet and outer moons.

Stage of development. The tidal heating and internal radioactive heating of the moon have diminished as the various moons gradually become tidally locked and earlier radiogenic and interior heating has cooled.

Special physical characteristics of planet. The outer surface of the planet is entirely ice covered. It has no atmosphere to speak of. The inner core is solid (rocky silicate) overlain by a liquid water ocean heated from below as has been suggested for Europa (Cassen et al., 1979; Cassen et al., 1980; Squyres et al., 1983). Recycling of nutrient elements is accomplished by upwelling convective cells driven by bottom heating. The ocean is well mixed as has also been suggested for Europa (Reynolds et al., 1983).

Salient Biology. Photosynthetic life forms have evolved, possibly from primordial chemosynthetic organisms sustained by higher geothermal energy available when the planet was younger. They receive light through the many cracks that form in the ice crust in response to tidal flexure (suggested for Europa by Cassen et al., 1980 and Helfenstein and Parmentier, 1980) or stresses from a tidal bulge (Reynolds et al., 1983). As a crack forms, the water boils out immediately forming a bubbly ice crust of minimal thickness (~ 50 cm). For Europa, Reynolds et al. (1983) have calculated that 5 km^2 of cracks are created on the planet per year. They estimate that each crack will persist with ice thicknesses allowing adequate light to sustain algae with the same re-

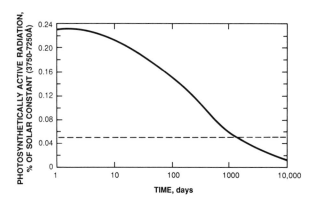

Figure 12.4 Amount of photosynthetically active radiation that could penetrate a crack in the ice cover of Europa versus time from crack formation. (Redrafted with permission from Reynolds et al., 1983).

quirements of Antarctic lake algae for about 4.5 years (figure 12.4). The photosynthetic organisms possess several dark photosynthetic pigments allowing them to let few photons go to waste in this light-limited environment. In addition, they produce antifreeze substances to increase their freeze resistance. On earth, various organisms use electrolytes and osmotic substances, or change various aspects of their biochemistry to reduce the freezing temperatures of their cellular constituents and protect their enzymes and nucleic acids from inhibition at low temperatures (Innis and Ingraham, 1978; Baross and Morita, 1978; Precht et al., 1973). It is obviously to the immediate advantage of the Europa World photosynthesizers to remain active at the ocean and ice crack interface to make maximum use of light.

Physical system affected. The photosynthesizing organisms both would benefit from enduring the circum-crack environment for the sake of light and could affect the region around each crack, thus prolonging the photosynthetically useful lifetime of a crack. The absorption maxima of photosynthetic pigments could be divided between different Europa species, each specialized for a particular wavelength. As is the case on Earth, water column photosynthesizers will array themselves in different positions in the subcrack fluid so that very little light is not absorbed by some eager phototroph. This local absorption by dark pigmented organisms helps to retard the thickening of the bubbly ice that forms in a crack. The longer this ice "wound" can be kept thin, the more photosynthetic activity it can sustain. Algae and mineral grains act to maintain liquid water similarly in cryoconite holes on earth

(Wharton et al., 1985; Gerdel and Drouet, 1960). A small percentage (~ 10%) of heating may also come from the metabolic activities of algae themselves (McIntyre, 1984). In addition, the antifreeze products produced are released by both living and dead cells. The lifetime of a crack as a habitat can be greatly prolonged by these means. More light is available from wide, shallow cracks than from narrow, deep cracks (Reynolds et al., 1983), which also contributes to the benefit derived by maintaining a crack with minimum ice cover. However, the ice cannot become too thin because if it were excessively melted from below the crack might rerupture, losing additional water vapor, or be redeposited until the 50-cm layer of ice needed on a Europa-like body to equal the vapor pressure of water at freezing (Reynolds et al., 1983) was achieved.

Gaia machine pathway. Microorganisms → products (dark pigments) → phase change processes (reduced freezing rates) → physical environment (larger time/space habitable zone) → "Gaia" switch setting (negative feedback) → microorganisms (more growth, more pigment).

Discussion. The presence of life on Europa has been suggested (Hoagland, 1980; Clark, 1982). In our Europa World, the organisms can prolong the availability of photosynthetic habitat. As Europa World ages further, the organisms will eventually lose. As tidal forces of the primary gas giant planet wane, there will be a reduction in the number of new cracks produced. Assuming that the lifetime of a crack is finite even when prolonged by organism-induced heating, the overall habitat available for photosynthesizers will gradually diminish. A possible counterbalancing increase in luminosity of the primary star would probably be too slow and too far away to do this planet much good at its distance from its sun (similar to the distance of Jupiter from the Sun). In addition to heating effects on cracks, there will undoubtedly be nutrient limitations no matter what mode of ocean mixing is imagined. Under such conditions, light might not be the dominant limiting factor.

Classical Antigaian Worlds

The worlds in this category include those with a specifically positive feedback cycle. Again, the effects are global, but here the net result is change in the environment resulting presumably in evolutionary changes in the biota.

Respiration World *Type of planet.* This world is an easy one to consider. It is Earth.

Stage of development. Its stage of development is similar to that of Earth now. Carbon dioxide is increasing in the atmosphere because of the release of previously buried carbon.

Salient Biology. The biota is fully mature having spread through both the ocean and terrestrial environments. Much carbon has been fixed photosynthetically over the eons and buried. Due to the activities of tool-using life forms on the planet, large proportions of this previously buried carbon is being released over very short timescales, geologically speaking.

Physical system affected. Increased atmospheric concentrations of carbon dioxide begin to warm the planet. The warmer climate stimulates microbes and other decomposer organisms to respire at an increased rate. This releases even more carbon dioxide from the stored organic carbon pool and contributes even more warming. The stimulatory effect on respiration continues until either the upper temperature tolerances of the respirers is reached and they begin to decline in population from the effects, or until some other limiting factor comes into play, such as the depletion of stored organic carbon.

Gaia machine pathway. Microorganisms (CO_2 respirers) $\rightarrow$ products (CO_2) $\rightarrow$ radiative transfer processes (more atmospheric CO_2) $\rightarrow$ physical environmental system processes (climate system processes) $\rightarrow$ physical environment (higher temperature) $\rightarrow$ "Gaia" switch setting (positive feedback) $\rightarrow$ microorganisms (greater microbial growth rates).

Discussion. Obviously, this world is the exaggerated extreme case possibly to be faced here on earth as a consequence of anthropogenic changes in the global carbon cycle (Lashof, 1989; Dickinson and Cicerone, 1986). Many counterbalancing effects have been suggested including greater uptake of carbon dioxide by the land and oceanic vegetation and nonbiological uptake of increased carbon dioxide by the carbonate cycle in the ocean. Such arguments depend on the relative magnitudes of these various effects. The Gaia machine cannot, of course, address these more quantitative issues. However, it does show that the worst-case scenario is not implausible if the counterbalancing processes are too weak or slow to alleviate the primary effects.

Wally World   *Type of planet*. This world is an earthlike planet.

Stage of development. The planet has evolved to the point where atmospheric CO_2 is significantly affected by oceanic calcareous plankton productivity.

Special physical characteristics of planet. This world has ocean and land in roughly earthlike proportions, with extensive continental shelves. Wally World is also fairly cold, with the potential for substantial land glaciation.

Salient Biology. The oceans have a substantial biomass of calcareous plankton, the activities of which act to draw down the atmospheric CO_2 concentration. The marine biotic productivity is strongly limited by phosphate nutrient availability.

Physical system affected. On Wally World, the atmospheric concentration of CO_2 is controlled by the productivity of ocean calcareous microorganisms, just as it is, in part, on Earth today. On this world a global-cooling perturbation acts to increase global land ice volume, decrease sea level, and expose phosphate-rich continental shelf sediments, which then erode and fertilize the calcareous microorganisms that draw down the atmospheric CO_2 and further cool the planet.

Gaia machine pathway. Microorganisms (calcareous plankton) $\rightarrow$ products (calcium carbonate tests) $\rightarrow$ radiative transfer processes (less atmospheric CO_2) $\rightarrow$ physical environment system processes (climate system processes) $\rightarrow$ physical environment (lower temperature, more glaciation, more phosphate fertilization) $\rightarrow$ "anti-Gaia" switch setting (positive feedback) $\rightarrow$ microorganisms (more plankton growth).

Discussion and caveats. The essence of this world was first described by Broecker (1981, 1982) as a model for atmospheric CO_2 excursions during interglacial-glacial transitions. Although largely abandoned as an explanation for short-term CO_2 excursions (Broecker, 1984), the model remains instructive as an example of antigaian feedback. The role of the oceans and ice sheets in this world prevents rapid changes of CO_2 from being possible (which is why the model was abandoned as an explanation for paleoclimatic observations). Long-term behavior (over millions of years) is also ruled out because the mechanism requires the continental shelf sediments to be replenished and eroded in a continuing cycle. Thus the Wally World phosphate extraction mechanism can act to amplify global climate changes but is not a candidate to drive the global climate system to a permanently different equilibrium state.

Variant Antigaian Worlds

The worlds described here still involve positive feedbacks, but exert only local control over habitats or involve only passive participation on the part of the relevant organisms.

Amazonia World   *Type of planet.* This is an earth-like world.

Stage of development. Mature biosphere.

Special physical characteristics of planet. This world is mostly land covered, except for some small seas, and is fairly warm.

Salient Biology. A large fraction of the tropical land area is covered by dense vegetation.

Physical system affected. The large areas of tropical forest control their regional hydrological environment by precipitation recycling; that is, most of the evapo-transpiration from the forest falls back on the forested area as precipitation instead of running off into the seas. The recycling efficiency would have to be high in order to maintain the forest on a planet having small ocean area. In principle, this could be achieved by having a large forest area so that the loss of water to nonforested areas is minimized. The edge of the forested area would occur at the point where just enough precipitation fell to maintain the forest. A negative perturbation on the forested area (e.g., from a global precipitation reduction or deforestation) would decrease the precipitation recycling efficiency, increase the water loss to runoff, and act to further decrease the forested area.

Gaia machine pathway. Macroorganisms (trees) → phase change processes (increased evapotranspiration) → physical environment system processes (increased precipitation) → physical environment (increased soil moisture) → "anti-Gaia" switch setting (positive feedback) → macroorganisms (increased tree habitat).

Discussion. This world is an antigaian variant because regional habitat-scale perturbations are amplified. Although our world is highly idealized, there is some indication that the tropical forests of the Amazon have some of the characteristics of this world (Salati and Vose, 1984), hence our chosen name.

Whitecap World   *Type of planet.* This is an earth-like world.

Stage of development. No special stage.

Special physical characteristics of planet. This is an ocean-covered world.

Salient Biology. On Whitecap World there is a substantial marine biomass of planktonic ice-nucleating bacteria (INB) (Vali et al., 1976).

Physical system affected. INB from the ocean are the dominant source of ice nuclei for cirrus clouds. More INB in the atmosphere would act to increase the number, while decreasing the size, of cirrus cloud particles. This would increase the optical opacity of the cirrus clouds, but more for visible than for infrared radiation. A greater atmospheric concentration of INB would, therefore, cool the planet. The interesting thing about this world is the way in which the atmospheric concentration of INB are controlled. We expect that the ocean-atmosphere transfer of INB is controlled by surface wind speeds. It is well known that the surface air concentration of large aerosol particles over the oceans (including INB) increases exponentially with increasing wind speed (Roll, 1965) as a result of particles injected by whitecap activity. On this world, an external forcing towards global cooling would increase the equator-pole temperature gradient, increase the vigor of the atmospheric general circulation, and increase surface wind speeds, which would increase the atmospheric INB concentration and, through the effect of cirrus clouds, further cool the planet.

Gaia machine pathway. Microorganisms (INB) → phase change processes (increased cirrus cloud particles) → physical environment system processes (radiative transfer) → physical environment (lower temperature, stronger winds) → "anti-Gaia" switch setting (positive feedback) → microorganisms (more ice nuclei injected).

Discussion. This is a variant antigaian world because the atmospheric concentration of the relevant organism (INB) does not depend on the biology of the organism. Nor is anything about the organism, except its presence, necessarily dependent on environmental conditions.

Ambiguous Worlds

These are worlds where both Gaian and antigaian feedbacks are possible. An example where a single biological effect can produce either positive or negative feedback follows.

Smoke World   *Type of planet.* This is an earthlike planet with significant land mass and large oceans.

Stage of development. There is a mature land plant biota with fully developed oxygenic photosynthesis.

Special physical characteristics of planet. Atmospheric oxygen concentration is suitable for sustained combustion, as is the case on earth. The land flora possesses combustible materials that accumulate until buried, mineralized, or burned.

Salient Biology. The biological operatives on this world are INB. These organisms live on the surfaces of plants as they do on Earth (Schnell, 1976; Vali et al., 1976). When temperatures drop seasonally or diurnally, the INB promote ice crystal formation in plant tissues at higher than usual temperatures, thus causing greater plant damage and death than would be the case without them (Maki et al., 1974). In addition to their effects on plants, INB also are transported in the atmosphere, often to very high altitudes (Jayaweera and Flanagan, 1982). Here they serve as condensation nuclei and may promote precipitation.

Physical system affected. Fire is a normal ecological phenomenon on a planet with significant atmospheric oxygen and large amounts of driable land biomass. Biomass burning produces a great deal of smoke (Small and Bush, 1985). Smoke has been shown to depress the activities of ice-nucleating bacteria (Zagory et al., 1983). Two possible feedback loops involving INB and fire on Smoke World are illustrated in figure 12.5. The Gaian loop tends to maintain populations of bacteria and levels of burning. The antigaian loop escalates the burning, depressing the bacteria, until some other limiting factors come into play.

In the Gaian case, the depression of INBs by smoke will result in less frost damage, less dead fuel, and fewer (or less intense) fires. Less smoke then favors the rebuilding of INB populations once again. In the antigaian case, INB suppression results in a depression of local cloud seeding. Rainfall is diminished, more fires occur (both because of

drying out of fuel and from greater plant mortality), and the resulting smoke depresses the INB populations even further.

Gaia machine pathway. Microorganisms (INB) → products (ice crystals) → macroorganisms (frost-damaged plants) → products (more smoke) → "Gaia" switch setting (negative feedback) → microorganisms (fewer INB).

Alternate Gaia machine pathway. Microorganisms (INB) → phase change processes (cloud seeding) → physical environmental system processes (increased rainfall, suppressed fires) → physical environment (less smoke) → "ANTI-GAIA" switch setting (positive feedback) → microorganisms (more INB).

Discussion. Will this world be dominated by Gaian or antigaian forces? Clearly, no answer to this question can be derived from the Gaia machine that we use here. Quantitative information on all the various steps in the cycles would be necessary to predict the behavior of this system as a whole. Employing the Gaia machine has merely enabled us to think through the various possibilities that this scenario suggests. Undoubtedly, even though this case is still a vast oversimplification of Real Life, the analysis of real gaian or antigaian mechanisms will resemble this compound case much more than they are likely to resemble the idealized single-loop scenarios painted in the other worlds.

Summary

An important evolutionary implication of having Gaian and antigaian feedbacks available to the biosphere is related to recent ideas of punctuated equilibrium. Eldredge and Gould (1972) state that drastic environmental change causes an evolutionary bottleneck that promotes rapid corresponding evolutionary changes in the biota. With the idea of the Gaia switch in mind, one could conceive of interesting nonequilibrium, time-dependent effects. An initial internal or external forcing would cause an immediate antigaian response, that is, rapid evolution to a new physical and biological state. This could be followed by a more slowly acting Gaian response that would return the physical state to something similar to its prior form even though the biota itself had undergone radical evolutionary change. This double-timescale, force-restore notion could help explain biotic catastrophes and subsequent recovery following severe environmental ex-

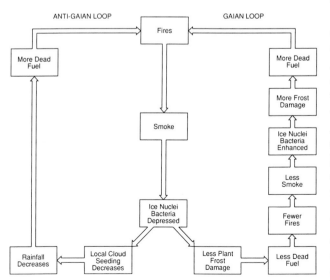

Figure 12.5 Gaian and antigaian cycles for Smoke World.

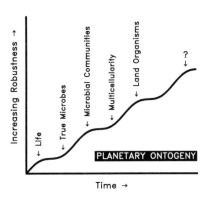

Figure 12.6 An ontogenetical view of the development of planets and life. On some planets, life arises and goes through a series of major changes interspersed with long periods of relatively little change.

cursions over geological time, such as those caused by asteroid or comet impacts (Pollack et al., 1983).

What we have described is an ontogenetical rather than strictly homeostatic view of the development of planets and life (figure 12.6). On some planets, life arises and goes through a series of major changes interspersed with long periods of relatively little change. This could be thought of as corresponding to the childhood of the planet-biota system. It is perhaps more vulnerable to both external perturbations and internal changes during this phase. At some point, the presence of life becomes the dominant feature of the planet. This could be viewed as the adulthood, or main sequence (speaking in stellar terms), of the planet. The biota is mature, most theoretical niche space is filled, and the system is most resistant to change. At some point, the planetary biota must begin to succumb to the inevitable senescence of the plant occasioned by nonreversible processes. These include gradual loss of light elements in the atmosphere, loss of internal heating, and the inevitable aging of the parent star. In a few billion years, Earth will be enveloped and incinerated by the expanding shell of the Sun as it enters its Red Giant phase. Probably, the Earth will not be entirely devoid of microbial life until it reaches this point and can be said to be truly a dead planet. Such, too, is the inevitable fate of microbes, humans, planets, stars, and perhaps even universes.

Acknowledgment

The National Center for Atmospheric Research is sponsored by the National Science Foundation.

Note

1. Our Sun's radiated spectrum peaks in the visible wavelengths at about 500 nm, corresponding to a radiating temperature of 5800 K. An A-type star has a spectral peak at about 300 nm (long UV), corresponding to a radiating temperature of about 10,000 K (Aller, 1963). Vega is an example of such a star (Massey, personal communication).

References

Aller, L.H. 1963. *The Atmosphere of the Sun and Stars,* 2nd ed. New York: The Ronald Press.

Atlas, R.M., and Bartha, R. 1981. *Microbial Ecology: Fundamentals and Applications.* Manilla, Philippines: Addison-Wesley.

Banks, H.P. 1975. Early vascular land plants: Proof and conjecture. *BioSci,* 25, 730–737.

Baross, J.A., Dahm, C.N., Ward, A.K., Lilley, M.D., and Sedell, J.R. 1982. Initial microbiological response in lakes to the Mt. St. Helens eruption. *Nature,* 296, 49–52.

Baross, J.A., and Morita, R.Y. 1978. Microbial life at low temperatures: Ecological aspects. In: Kushner, D.J., ed. *Microbial Life in Extreme Environments.* New York: Academic Press.

Beveridge, T.J. 1989. Role of cellular design in bacterial metal accumulation and mineralization. *Ann Rev Microbiol* 43, 147–171.

Brock, T.D. 1978. Life in boiling water. In: *Thermophilic Microorganisms and Life at High Temperatures.* New York: Springer-Verlag, 303–336.

Broecker, W.S. 1981. Glacial to interglacial changes in ocean and atmosphere chemistry. In: Berger, A., ed. *Climatic Variations and Variability: Facts and Theories.* Boston: D. Reidel, 111–121.

Broecker, W.S. 1982. Glacial to interglacial changes in ocean chemistry. *Prog Oceanog,* 11, 151–197.

Broecker, W.S. 1984. Carbon dioxide circulation through ocean and atmosphere. *Nature,* 308, 602.

Caldeira, K. 1989. Evolutionary pressures on planktonic production of atmospheric sulphur. *Nature,* 337, 732–734.

Caldwell, M.M. 1964. Solar ultraviolet radiation as an ecological factor for alpine plants. *Ecol Monogr,* 38, 243–268.

Caldwell, M.M. 1971. Solar UV irradiation and the growth and development of higher plants. In: Giese, A.C., ed. *Photophysiology,* Vol. 6. New York: Academic Press, 131–177.

Cassen, P.M., Peale, S.J., and Reynolds, R.T. 1980. Tidal dissipation in Europa: A correction. *Geophys Res Lett,* 7, 987–988.

Cassen, P.M., Reynolds, R.T., and Peale, S.J. 1979. Is there liquid water on Europa? *Geophys Res Lett,* 6, 731–734.

Castenholz, R.W. 1973. The possible photosynthetic rise of sulfide by the filamentous phototrophic bacteria of hot springs. *Limnol Oceanogr,* 18, 863–876.

Catton, W.R. 1985. On the dire destiny of human lemmings. In: Tobias, M., ed. *Deep Ecology.* San Diego: Avant Books.

Charlson, R., Lovelock, J.M., Andreae, M., and Warren, S. 1987. Oceanic phytoplankton, atmospheric sulphur, cloud albedo, and climate. *Nature,* 326, 655–661.

Clark, A.C. 1982. *2010: Odyssey Two.* New York: Ballantine Books.

Clark, B.C. 1979. Solar-driven chemical energy source for a Martian biota. *Origins of Life,* 9, 241–249.

Clark, B.C., and Van Hart, D.C. 1981. The salts of Mars. *Icarus,* 45, 370–387.

Cloud, P.E. 1976. Beginnings of biospheric evolution and their biogeochemical consequences. *Paleobiology,* 2, 351–387.

Cohen, Y. 1984. Photosynthetic life under sulfide. In: Cohen, Y., Castenholz, R.W., and Halvorsen, H.O., eds. *Microbial Mats: Stromatolites.* MBL Lectures in Biology, Vol. 3. New York: Alan R. Liss, 133–148.

Corliss, J.B., Dymond, J., Gordon, L.I., Edmond, J.M., von Herzen, R.P., Ballard, R.D., Green, J., Williams, D., Bainbridge, A., Crane, K., and van Andel, T.H. 1979. Submarine thermal springs on the Galapagos Rift. *Science,* 203, 1073–1083.

Crocker, R.L. 1952. Soil genesis and the pedogenic factors. *Q Rev Biol,* 27, 139–168.

Crutzen, P.J., 1970. The influence of nitrogen oxides on the atmospheric ozone content. *Q J Roy Meteorol Soc,* 96, 320–325.

Dagley, S. 1975. Microbial degradation of organic compounds in the biosphere. *Am Sci,* 63, 681–689.

Dagley, S. 1987. Lessons from biodegradation. *Ann Rev Microbiol,* 41, 1–23.

Darley, W.M. 1982. *Algal Biology: A Physiological Approach.* Oxford: Blackwell Science Publishers.

Daugherty, L.H. 1941. *Upper Triassic Flora of Arizona.* Pub. 526. Washington, D.C.: Carnegie Institute of Washington.

Daumas, S., Lombart, R., and Bianchi, A. 1986. A bacteriological study of geothermal spring waters dating from the Dogger and Trias period in the Paris Basin. *Geomicrobiol J,* 4, 423–433.

Delwiche, C.F., Graham, L.E., and Thomson, N. 1989. Lignin-like compounds and sporopollenin in *Coleochaete,* an algal model for land plant ancestry. *Science,* 245, 399–401.

Dickinson, R.E., and Cicerone, R.J. 1986. Future global warming from atmospheric trace gases. *Nature,* 319, 109–115.

Dugan, P.R., MacMillan, C.D., and Pfister, R.M. 1970. Aerobic heterotrophic bacteria indigenous to pH 2.8 acid mine water: Microscopic enumeration of acid streams. *J Bacteriol,* 101, 973–981.

Dunbar, C.O. 1949. *Historical Geology.* New York: John Wiley and Sons.

Ehrlich, H.L. 1978. How microbes cope with heavy metals, arsenic and antimony in their environment. In Kushner, D.J., ed. *Microbial Life in Extreme Environments.* London: Academic Press.

Ehrlich, H.L., 1990. *Geomicrobiology,* 2nd ed. New York: Marcel Dekker.

Eldredge, N., and Gould, S.J. 1972. Punctuated equilibria: An alternative to phyletic gradualism. In: Schopf, T.J.M., ed.

Models in Paleobiology. San Francisco: Freeman, Cooper and Co., 82–115.

Evans, A.C. 1948. Studies on the relationships between earthworms and soil fertility: II. Some effects of earthworms on soil structure. *Ann Appl Biol,* 35, 1–13.

Fischer, F., Zillig, W., Stetter, K.O., and Schreiber, G. 1983. Chemolithoautotrophic metabolism of anaerobic extremely thermophilic archaebacteria. *Nature,* 301, 511–513.

Fork, D.C. 1977. Photosynthesis. In: Smith, K.C., ed. *Photobiology.* New York: Plenum Press.

Fox, J.L. 1983. Soil microbes pose problems for pesticides. *Science,* 221, 1029–1031.

Friedmann, E.I. 1980. Endolithic microbial life in hot and cold deserts. *Origins of Life,* 10, 223–235.

Friedmann, E.I., and Ocampo, R. 1972. Endolithic blue-green algae in the dry valleys: Primary producers in the Antarctic cold desert ecosystem. *Science,* 193, 1247–1249.

Gall, J-C. 1983. *Ancient Sedimentary Environments and the Habitats of Living Organisms.* Berlin: Springer-Verlag.

Gerdel, R.W., and Drouet, F. 1960. The cryoconite of the Thule area, Greenland. *Trans Am Microscop Soc,* 79, 256–272.

Ghilarov, M.S. 1970. Soil biocoenosis. In Phillipson, J., ed. *Methods of Study in Soil Ecology.* Paris: UNESCO.

Glaesner, M.F., and Wade, M. 1966. The late Precambrian fossils from Ediacara, South Australia. *Palaeontology,* 9, 599–628.

Hart, M.H. 1979. Habitable zones about main sequence stars. *Icarus,* 37, 351–357.

Helfenstein, P., and Parmentier, E.M. 1980. Fractures on Europa: Possible responses of an ice crust to tidal deformation. *Lunar Planet Sci Conf Proc,* 11, 1987–1998.

Hoagland, R.C. 1980. The Europa enigma. *Star and Sky,* 2, 16–31.

Horowitz, N.H. 1977. The search for life on Mars. *Sci Am,* 237, 52–61.

Horowitz, N.H., and Hobby, G.L. 1977. Viking on Mars: The carbon assimilation experiments. *J Geophys Res,* 4659–4662.

Huber, R., Stoffers, P., Cheminee, J.L., Richnow, H.H., and Stetter, K.O. 1990. Hyperthermophilic archaebacteria within the crater and open-sea plume of erupting Macdonald Seamount. *Nature,* 345, 179–181.

Imhoff, J.F., and Truper, H.G. 1977. Ectothiorhodospira halochloris, sp. nov., a new extremely halophilic phototrophic bacterium containing bacteriochlorophyll b. *Arch Microbiol,* 114, 115–121.

Innis, W.E., and Ingraham, J.L. 1978. Microbial life at low temperatures: Mechanisms and molecular aspects. In: Kushner, D.J., ed. *Microbial Life in Extreme Environments.* New York: Academic Press.

Ivanov, M.V., and Karavaiko, G.I. 1966. The role of microorganisms in the sulfur cycle in crater lakes of the Golovnin crater. *Zeitschr Allg Mikrobiol,* 6, 10–22.

Jannasch, H.W., and Wirsen, C.O. 1979. Chemosynthetic primary production at East Pacific sea floor spreading centers. *Bioscience,* 29, 592–598.

Jayaweera, K., and Flanagan, P. 1982. Investigations on biogenic ice nuclei in the arctic atmosphere. *Geophys Res Lett*, 9, 94–97.

Jenny, H. 1958. Role of the plant factor in pedogenic function. *Ecology*, 39, 5–16.

Karl, D.M., Wirsen, C.O., and Jannasch, H.W. 1980. Deepsea primary production at the Galapagos hydrothermal vents. *Science*, 207, 1345–1347.

Katznelson, H. 1965. Nature and importance of the rhizosphere. In: Baker, K.F., and Snyder, W.C., eds. *Ecology of Soil-borne Plant Pathogens*. Berkeley: University of California Press.

Klein, H.P. 1978. The Viking biological experiments on Mars. *Icarus*, 34, 666–674.

Knoll, M.A., and James, W.C. 1987. Effect of the advent and diversification of vascular land plants on mineral weathering through geologic time. *Geology*, 15, 1099–1102.

Langworthy, T.A. 1978. Microbial life in extreme pH values. In: Kushner, D.J., ed. *Microbial Life in Extreme Environments*. London and New York: Academic Press.

Lashof, D.A. 1989. The dynamic greenhouse: Feedback processes that may influence future concentrations of atmospheric trace gases and climatic change. *Climatic Change*, 14, 213–242.

Levin, G.V., and Straat, P.A. 1977. Recent results from the Viking labeled release experiment on Mars. *J Geophys Res*, 82, 4663–4667.

Lorenz, E.N. 1967. *The Nature and Theory of the General Circulation of the Atmosphere*. World Meteorological Organization Pub. No. 218, T.P. 115. Geneva, Switzerland

Lovelock, J.M. 1979. *Gaia: A New Look at Life on Earth*. Oxford: Oxford University Press.

Lovelock, J.M. 1988. *The Ages of Gaia: A Biography of Our Living Earth*. New York: W.W. Norton and Co.

Lovelock, J.M., and Margulis, L. 1973. Atmospheric homeostasis by and for the biosphere: the Gaia hypothesis. *Tellus*, 26, 2–6.

Lovelock, J.M., and Whitfield, M. 1982: Life span of the biosphere. *Nature*, 296, 561–563.

Lowry, B., Lee, D., and Hebant, C. 1980. The origin of land plants: A new look at an old problem. *Taxon*, 29, 183–197.

Madigan, M. 1976. *Studies on the physiological ecology of Chloroflexus aurantiacus, a filamentous photosynthetic bacterium*. PhD. dissertation, University of Wisconsin at Madison.

Madigan, M.T., and Brock, T.D. 1975. Photosynthetic sulfide oxidation by *Chloroflexus aurantiacus*, a filamentous, photosynthetic, gliding bacterium. *J Bacteriol*, 122, 782–784.

Madigan, M.T., and Brock, T.D. 1977a. Adaptation by hot spring phototrophs to reduced light intensities. *Arch Microbiol*, 113, 111–120.

Madigan: M.T., and Brock, T.D. 1977b. CO_2 fixation in photosynthetically-grown *Chloroflexus aurantiacus*. FEMS Microbiology Letters, 1, 301–304.

Maki, L.R., Galyan, E.L., Chang-Chien, M.-M., and Caldwell, D.R. 1974. Ice nucleation induced by *Pseudomonas syringae*. *Appl Microbiol*, 28, 456–459.

Maykut, G.A., and Untersteiner, N. 1971. Some results from a time-dependent thermodynamic model of sea ice. *J Geophys Res*, 76, 1550–1575.

Mazur, P., Barghoorn, E.S., Halvorson, H.O., Jukes, T.H., Kaplan, I.R., and Margulis, L. 1978. Biological implications of the Viking mission to Mars. *Space Sci Rev*, 22, 3–34.

McIntyre, N.F. 1984. Cryoconite hole thermodynamics. *Can J Earth Sci*, 21, 152–156.

McKay, C.P., and Stoker, C.R. 1989. The early environment and its evolution on Mars. *Reviews of Geophysics*, 27, 189–214.

McNabb, J.F., and Dunlap, W.J. 1975. Subsurface biological activity in relation to ground-water pollution. *Groundwater*, 13, 33–44.

Meyer, O., and Schlegel, H.G. 1983. Biology of aerobic carbon monoxide-oxidizing bacteria. *Ann Rev Microbiol*, 37, 277–310.

Niklas, K.J., and Pratt, L.M. 1980. Evidence for lignin-like constituents in early Silurian (Llandoverian) plant fossils. *Science*, 209, 396–397.

Olson, G.J., Dockins, W.S., McFeters, G.A., and Iverson, W.P. 1981. Sulfate-reducing and methanogenic bacteria from deep aquifers in Montana. *Geomicrobiol J*, 2, 327–340.

Oyama, V.I., and Berdahl, B.J. 1977. The Viking gas exchange experiment results from Chryse and Utopia surface samples. *J Geophys Res*, 82, 4669–4676.

Pollack, J.B., Toon, O.B., Ackerman, T.P., McKay, C.P., and Turco, R.P. 1983, Environmental effects of an impact-generated dust cloud: Implications for the Cretaceous-Tertiary extinctions. *Science*, 219, 287–289.

Precht, H., Christophersen, J., Hensel, H., and Larcher, W. 1973. *Temperature and Life*. New York: Springer-Verlag.

Preece, T.F., and Dickinson, D.H. 1971. *Ecology of Leaf-surface Microorganisms*. London: Academic Press.

Ramanathan, V., Barkstrom, B.R., and Harrison, E.F. 1989. Climate and the Earth's radiation budget. *Physics Today, May*, 22–32.

Ramsay, A.T.S. 1977. *Oceanic Micropaleontology*. New York: Academic Press.

Reineke, W., and Knackmuss, H-J. 1988. Microbial degradation of haloaromatics. *Ann Rev Microbiol*, 42, 263–287.

Reynolds, R.T., Squyres, S.W., Colburn, D.S., and McKay, C.P. 1983. On the habitability of Europa. *Icarus*, 56, 246–254.

Roll, H.U. 1965. *Physics of the Marine Atmosphere*. New York: Academic Press.

Rozanova, E.P., and Khudyakova, A.I. 1974. A new nonspore-forming thermophilic sulfate-reducing organism, *Desulfovibrio thermophilis* nov. sp. *Microbiology (English transl.)*, 48, 807–911.

Sagan, C., and Mullen, G. 1972. Earth and Mars: Evolution of atmospheres and surface temperatures. *Science*, 177, 52–56.

Sagan, C., and Salpeter, E.E. 1976. Particles, environments, and possible ecologies in the Jovian atmosphere. *Astrophys J Suppl Ser*, 32, 737–755.

Salati, E., and Vose, P.B. 1984. Amazon basins: A system in equilibrium. *Science*, 225, 129–138.

Schlegel, H.G., and Bowien, B. 1989. *Autotrophic Bacteria.* Berlin: Springer-Verlag, and Madison, Wi.: Science Tech. Publishers.

Schneider, S.H., and Dickinson, R.E. 1974. Climate modeling. *Rev Geophys Space Phys,* 12, 447–493.

Schneider, S.H., and Londer, R. 1984. *The Coevolution of Climate and Life.* San Francisco: Sierra Club Books.

Schneider, S.H., and Thompson, S.L. 1980. Cosmic conclusions from climatic models: Can they be justified? *Icarus,* 41, 456–469.

Schnell, R.C., 1976. Naturally occurring biological ice nucleants: A review. Preprint Volume, International Conference on Cloud Physics. July 26–30, 1976. Boulder, Colorado. Boston: American Meteorological Society, 57–60.

Schopf, T.J.M. 1980. *Paleoceanography.* Cambridge, Mass.: Harvard University Press, 239–240.

Schopf, J.W., and Walter, M.R. 1983. Archean microfossils: New evidence of ancient microbes. In: Schopf, J.W., ed. *Earth's Earliest Biosphere: Its Origin and Evolution.* Princeton, N.J.: Princeton University Press.

Schwartzman, D.W., and Volk, T. 1989. Biotic enhancement of weathering and the habitability of Earth. *Nature,* 340, 457–460.

Shropshire, W. 1977. Photomorphogenesis. In: Smith, K.C., ed. *Photobiology.* New York: Plenum Press.

Small, R.D., and Bush, B.W. 1985. Smoke production from multiple nuclear explosions in nonurban areas. *Science,* 229, 465–469.

Smith, R.C., and Tyler, J.E. 1976. Transmission of solar radiation into natural waters. In: Smith, K.C., ed. *Photochemical and Photobiological Reviews.* Vol. 1. New York: Plenum Press, 117–155.

Smith, W.W., and ZoBell, C.E. 1937. Direct microscopic evidence of an autochthonous bacterial flora in Great Salt Lake. *Ecology,* 18, 453–458.

Squyres, S.W., Reynolds, R.T., Cassen, P.M., and Peale, S.J. 1983. Liquid water and active resurfacing on Europa. *Nature,* 301, 225–226.

Stafford, S., Berwick, P., Hughes, D.E., and Stafford, D.A. 1982. Oil degradation in hydrocarbon- and oil-stressed environments. In: Burns, R.G., and Slater, J.H., eds. *Experimental Microbial Ecology.* Oxford and London: Blackwell Science Publishers.

Staley, J.T., Lehmicke, L.G., Palmer, F.E., Peet, R.W., and Wissmar, R.C. 1982. Impact of Mount St. Helen's eruption on bacteriology of lakes in the blast zone. *Appl Environ Microbiol,* 43, 664–670.

Starkey, R.L. 1958. Interrelations between microorganisms and plant roots in the rhizosphere. *Bacteriol Rev,* 22, 154–172.

Stein, J.R., and Amundsen, C.C. 1967. Studies on snow algae and fungi from the front range of Colorado. *Can J Bot,* 45, 2033–2045.

Stoker, C.R., and Boston, P.J. 1984. Energy sources, nutrients, and environmental limits to growth of contaminating terrestrial microorganisms on Jupiter. *Bull Am Astron Soc,* 16, 649.

Tans, P.P., Fung, I.Y., and Takahashi, T. 1990. Observational constraints on the global atmospheric CO_2 budget. *Science,* 247, 1431–1438.

Toulmin, P., III, Baird, A.K., Clark, B.C., Keil, K., Rose, H.J., Jr., Christan, R.P., Evans, P.H., and Kelliher, W.C. 1977. Geochemical and mineralogical interpretations of the Viking inorganic chemical results. *J Geophys Res,* 82, 4625–4634.

Vairavamurthy, E., Andreae, M.O., and Ivarson, R.L. 1985. DMS production in plankton. *Limnol Oceanog,* 30, 59–70.

Vali, G., Christensen, M., Fresh, R.W., Galyan, E.L., Maki, L.R., and Schnell, R.C. 1976. Biogenic ice nuclei. Part II: Bacterial sources. *J Atmos Sci,* 33, 1565–1570.

Volcani, B.E. 1944. The microorganisms of the Dead Sea. In: *Papers Collected to Commemorate the 70th Anniversary of Dr. Chaim Weizman.* Collective volume. Rehovot, Israel: Daniel Sieff Research Institute, 71–85.

Volk, T. 1987. Feedbacks between weathering and atmospheric CO_2 over the last 100 million years. *Am J Sci,* 287, 763–779.

Walker, J.C.G., Hays, P.B., and Kasting, J.F. 1981. A negative feedback mechanism for the long-term stabilization of Earth's surface temperature. *J Geophys Res,* 86, 9776–9782.

Watson, A.J., and Lovelock, J.E. 1983. Biological homeostasis of the global environment: The parable of Daisyworld. *Tellus,* 35, 284–289.

Wharton, R.A., Jr. 1982. *Ecology of algal mats and their role in the formation of stromatolites in Antarctic dry valley lakes.* PhD. Dissertation, Virginia Tech., Blacksburg, Va.

Wharton, R.A., Jr., Parker, B.C., and Simmons, G.M., Jr. 1983. Distribution, species composition and morphology of algal mats in Antarctic dry valley lakes. *Phycologia,* 22, 355–365.

Wharton, R.A., McKay, C.P., Simmons, G.M., and Parker, B.C. 1985. Cryoconite holes on glaciers. *Bioscience,* 35, 499–503.

Willis, C.J., Elkan, G.H., Horvath, E., and Dail, K.R. 1975. Bacterial flora of saline aquifers. *Groundwater,* 13, 406–409.

Wilson, E.O. 1971. *The Insect Societies.* Cambridge, Mass.: Harvard University Press.

Wissmar, R.C., Devol, A.H., Staley, J.T., and Sedell, J.R. 1982. Biological responses of lakes in the Mt. St. Helens blast zone. *Science,* 216, 178–181.

Zagory, D., Lindow, S.E., and Parmeter, J.R. 1983. Toxicity of smoke to epiphytic ice nucleation-active bacteria. *Appl Environ Microbiol,* 46, 114–119.

ZoBell, C.E. 1958. Ecology of sulfate reducing bacteria. *Producers Monthly,* 22, 12–29.

Ralph Keeling

13

Mechanisms for Stabilization and Destabilization of a Simple Biosphere: Catastrophe on Daisyworld

The Daisyworld model of Watson and Lovelock (1983) illustrates a mechanism by which a simple biosphere, consisting of black and white daisies, regulates the planetary temperature. Recently, Kirchner (1989) has shown that a modified Daisyworld model can exhibit "pathological" behavior in the presence of climate changes. My purpose here is similar, and I will show that a modified Daisyworld can lead to a global catastrophe in the presence of evolutionary changes.

For these calculations, I used the original model with only one modification: in addition to black and white daisies, I introduced a third species, kudzu. Like black daisies, kudzu has an albedo of 0.25, and its growth curve is the same amplitude and shape as that of the daisies; however, its optimum growth temperature is 33°C. The optimum growth temperature of white daisies and black daisies remains at 22.5°C. For all the other model parameters, I used values from figure 1 in Watson and Lovelock (1983).

Let us consider a particular scenario for the succession of life on Daisyworld. This scenario uses a solar luminosity corresponding to L = 0.75 (i.e., 75% of the present luminosity on earth). We start by introducing a 1% coverage of black daisies onto a barren planetary surface. The daisies spread, thereby warming the planet, until a steady state is reached (figure 13.1A). Next, we add a 1% coverage of kudzu. The kudzu slowly replaces the black daisies, eventually driving them to extinction (figure 13.1B). Finally, after the black daisies are totally extinct, we add a 1% coverage of white daisies. Because they cool the planet, the white daisies initially compete well against the kudzu. However, once the planet cools beyond a certain point, the kudzu dies off catastrophically. The temperature plunges, eventually cooling to below the tolerance limits of both species. In the end, all that remains is a barren planet (figure 13.1C).

In order to understand the mechanism of this catastrophe it is helpful to introduce a few simple concepts. First, we define the *generation range* of a species as that range of external conditions (e.g., solar luminosity) over which an arbitrarily small population of the species will propagate. Second, we define the *survival range* of a species as that range of external conditions over which some finite population is capable of surviving. Because a species at least must be able to survive where it can propagate, it follows that the generation range is a subset of the survival range. Finally, we define that part of the survival range which lies outside of the generation range as the *marginal-stability range*.

Figure 13.2 shows the steady-state solutions to the equations for (1) area covered and (2) effective temperature as a function of luminosity for each species growing without any other species. From the area-versus-luminosity curves, the generation range can be identified as the range where the solution with zero area is unstable (i.e., where the zero solution is represented by a dashed line). The marginal-stability range corresponds to the range spanned by the overhang in the area-versus-luminosity curves. For white daisies, for example, the generation range extends from L = 0.833 to 1.208, and the survival range extends from L = 1.208 to 1.559. Note that the existence of a marginal-stability range depends on strong feedback between the area of surface covered and the temperature. For example, if the albedo of the daisies is sufficiently close to that of bare ground, a marginal-stability range will not exist.

The key to understanding the catastrophe described above is to note that a solar luminosity of L = 0.75 lies within the generation range for black daisies, within the marginal-stability range for kudzu, and outside both the generation and marginal-stability ranges (i.e., outside the survival range) for white daisies. Whereas the black daisies could have survived any perturbation that left a finite population remaining, the kudzu is eliminated by any perturbation that reduces their area to below the dashed line in figure 13.2C. The introduction of white daisies is sufficient to trigger this instability.

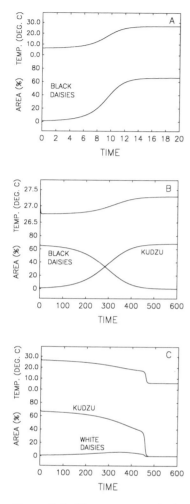

Figure 13.1 Three sequences in the scenario for the succession of life on Daisyworld. **A,** Black daisies propagate on a barren planet. **B,** Kudzu replaces black daisies. **C,** White daisies and kudzu annihilate each other. Time is in model units.

The scenario demonstrates (1) that it is possible for a species in its marginal-stability range to drive a species in its generation range to extinction, and (2) that it is possible for a species outside its survival range to drive a species in its marginal-stability range to extinction. In either case the more fit species is actually categorically less robust than the eliminated species in the sense that it is one step further removed from its generation range. In the latter case the more fit species is left outside its survival limits, so it also dies out.

It is worth considering the question of whether the presence of daisies stabilizes the temperature with respect to luminosity changes. This idea, which is the principal conclusion of Watson and Lovelock (1983), is true if we define net stabiliza-

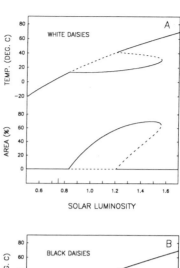

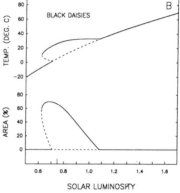

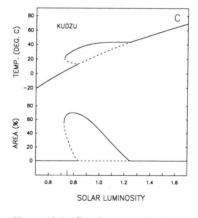

Figure 13.2 Steady-state solutions to the Daisyworld model for effective temperature and area covered. Stable steady-state solutions are represented by a solid line, unstable solutions by a dashed line. **A,** Solutions for white daisies. **B,** Solutions for black daisies. **C,** Solutions for kudzu. Stable solutions were found by numerically integrating the equations forward in time. Unstable solutions were found by integrating the equations backwards in time. The extra tick mark at L = 0.75 indicates the luminosity used in the catastrophe scenario.

tion in terms of the extension of the survival range beyond the generation range. From figure 13.2 it is clear that this definition is equivalent to requiring that the average slope of the temperature-versus-luminosity curve over the survival range is less with daisies than without daisies. The above scenario suggests, however, that the same feedback mechanism that extends a species' survival limits with respect to the external environment (e.g., luminosity) can reduce its survival limits with respect to competing species.

One possible objection to this catastrophe scenario is that the evolutionary sequence is imposed a priori, so that it is not clear if such a sequence is probable, or even possible, in a biosphere whose evolution is under the control of variation and natural selection. It should be noted, however, that the original Daisyworld model can be criticized on the same grounds. The regulation of planetary temperature on Daisyworld also requires a specific evolutionary sequence, namely, once the two species of daisies have formed, no further evolutionary changes are allowed. In this sense the original and modified Daisyworld models are both teleological in that they require manipulation of the evolutionary process to produce a desired effect. It might be possible to overcome this objection by constructing a Daisyworld model that allowed for realistic natural variations. This suggests a direction for further work.

Another possible objection to the catastrophe scenario is that it depends on the assumption that the earliest life forms, black daisies, are driven to complete extinction. In contrast, anaerobic bacteria, among the earliest life forms on earth, are still abundant today. Here it should be pointed out that the succession of black daisies by kudzu is not essential to the catastrophe: any process that drives the biosphere into a marginally stable state would suffice. For example, the catastrophe scenario could have started with a solar luminosity of L = 1.0, with kudzu populating a barren planet. A cooling of the sun to a luminosity of L = 0.75 would then put the biosphere in the same state as existed prior to the introduction of white daisies. Neither catastrophe scenario has any obvious relevance to the earth. It is conceivable, nevertheless, that the increase in the solar luminosity over geological time could drive (or could already have driven) the earth's biosphere towards a marginally stable state. This is an issue that, perhaps, deserves closer examination.

In summary, a scenario for evolution on a modified Daisyworld illustrates how a simple biosphere can destroy itself if the wrong sequence of evolutionary changes takes place. The self-destruction occurs after a stable environmental feedback loop has been established. The catastrophe is possible because, by modifying the physical environment, a species accomplishes two distinct ends: (1) an extension of its survival limits and (2) the elimination of competing species. Furthermore, the same modification that succeeds at eliminating competing species may fail at maintaining the environment within critical tolerance limits. Perhaps there is a lesson for humans here.

Acknowledgments

I thank Mark Schitzer, who provided competent programming assistance and useful insights during the exploratory phase of this work. I also thank Justin Lancaster, Bob Chatfield, and Andrew Watson for their helpful comments.

References

Kirchner, J.W. 1989. The Gaia hypothesis—Can it be tested? *Rev Geophys,* 27, 223–235.

Watson, A.J., and Lovelock, J.E. 1983. Biological homeostasis of the global environment: The parable of daisyworld. *Tellus,* 35B, 284–289.

Glen B. Lesins

14
Radiative Entropy as a Measure of Complexity

Although the total biospheric mass is negligible compared with the mass of the Earth, life has strategically flourished at the critical interfaces between the atmosphere, hydrosphere, and lithosphere of the earth system. In this position life is able to exploit the possibilities offered by both the radiant energy of the Sun, which drives the atmospheric, and oceanic circulations including the hydrological cycle, as well as the geothermal energy that drives the mantle convection including the resupply of material from volcanoes.

When all the rich activity of the biota, oceans, atmosphere, and lithosphere are taken together it is very tempting to make the subjective conclusion that the Earth is a highly dynamic entity that in some grander sense has a life of its own (Lovelock, 1987). However, this type of intuition does not prove whether or not there is some encompassing principle called Gaia that can explain the regulatory processes that apparently are needed to understand the relative stability of the earth system during geological time.

One of the difficulties in searching for tests of the Gaia hypothesis is the sheer complexity of the system. When numerical models, consisting of a few biological feedback loops, predict stability, it is not clear that we have some hint of a proof or disproof for Gaia. Present-day computers do not have the capability of simulating the effect that life may have on the stability of the climate system. Even the most sophisticated general circulation models suffer from inadequate resolution, poor physical parameterizations (including the clouds), and a lack of realistic biological and chemical couplings. Is there some way of addressing the issue of the complexity and interrelationships that exists in the Earth without resorting to oversimplified differential equations or highly truncated models?

Irreversible thermodynamics does provide one objective technique to analyze the earth system. A case will be made for utilizing the entropy flux leaving the Earth by the radiative stream in order to address some of the issues of stability and complexity.

Entropy

Entropy is a concept that arises when statistical mechanics is applied to the detailed microscopic description of a system in order to derive a macroscopic or averaged description of the same system. The objective is to reduce the number of degrees of freedom required to specify adequately the macroscopic state of the system. An indication of the success of this theory is the reduction of the number of variables from 6N to 2 for an ideal gas of a given mass in equilibrium, where N is the number of simple molecules. The entropy of a given macroscopic state is simply proportional to the logarithm of the number of microstates compatible with that particular macroscopic state (Lifshitz and Pitaevskii, 1980, is one of many texts on this subject).

When a system is completely isolated its entropy will increase until the system has achieved thermodynamic equilibrium, at which point the entropy has attained its maximum value in accordance with the second law of thermodynamics. At thermodynamic equilibrium the isolated system's state variables are all steady. In particular at thermal equilibrium the temperature of the system is uniform throughout and the system lacks macroscopic dynamics. Most real systems, however, have open boundaries and hence can exchange energy and entropy with their environments. This allows systems to move further from equilibrium by exporting entropy into its environment. Schrodinger (1944) discussed the maintenance of life using similar arguments.

For a fixed amount of energy, the entropy of a system is a measure of its proximity to equilibrium. As the entropy is lowered the system moves further from equilibrium with the accompanying increase in magnitude of the thermodynamic gradients and fluxes. It is these fluxes that attempt to bring the system back into equilibrium and provide a fundamental stability. Even when local instabilities develop, during which energy is flowing from the background to the evolving structure, nature's quest for equilibrium always provides a global limit to the growth of the instability and the complexity of the structure. Nicolis and Prigogine (1977) noted that as a system moves further from equilibrium greater complexity, patterns, correlations, and symmetry breaking are observed. In the limit of zero entropy there is only one allowed microstate, meaning that a complete molecular configuration is required to describe the system.

In applying the ideas of entropy to the Earth, fortunately one can invoke the concept of local thermodynamic equilibrium (LTE) without introducing a significant error. In LTE the molecular collision relaxation time is small enough that the macroscopic state variables such as temperature, pressure, and chemical potential can be defined locally using equilibrium concepts. An example of where LTE breaks down is the upper atmosphere where the air density is so low that collisional relaxation is unable to thermalize the absorbed solar radiation and prevents definition of a unique local temperature. The contribution of non-LTE regions to the total energy and entropy flux will be neglected. As a system moves further from equilibrium larger temperature gradients appear resulting in a larger variance of the temperature distribution. The entropy of this nonequilibrium state can still be calculated using local equilibrium measurements allowing a temperature distribution to be defined. The second law of thermodynamics can now be written as

$$dS \geq \frac{\delta Q}{T} \tag{1}$$

where Q is the heat added to the system. This succinct form of the second law expresses (1) LTE through a locally defined temperature, T; (2) the status of entropy (S) as a state function through its exact differential; and (3) irreversible and reversible processes through the inequality and equality sign, respectively. In general the temperature field will be a function of position and hence the second law has to be integrated over the volume of the system.

The entropy production of a system can be written as the sum of the net entropy flux flowing into the system through its boundary plus the entropy produced internally.

$$\frac{dS}{dt} = \frac{dS}{dt_{ext}} + \frac{dS}{dt_{int}} \tag{2}$$

It should be noted that the internal generation term that expresses the irreversible processes must be positive from the second law. Also, for steady-state systems in which the left hand side of equation (2) is zero, the net flux of entropy leaving the system must equal its internal production.

In applying these ideas to the Earth it is important to distinguish between radiative entropy and mass entropy. The mass flux leaving (hydrogen escape) or entering (meteors, solar particles, etc.) the Earth can be neglected so that the only significant boundary flux of entropy for the earth is carried by the radiation field. In this approach the mass exchanges between the biosphere and the Earth (e.g., outgassing and subduction) are not considered. Another reason for separating the radiation component from the mass component was pointed out by Essex (1984a), who showed that the Gibbsian bilinear formalism for entropy production cannot in general be extended to radiative processes. Hence for the Earth, equation (2) can be rewritten as the change of the entropy of the Earth over some time interval:

$$\Delta S = \Delta S_{r,incoming} - \Delta S_{r,outgoing} + \Delta S_{r,generation} + \Delta S_{m,generation} \tag{3}$$
$$(1) \qquad (2) \qquad\qquad (3) \qquad\qquad (4) \qquad\qquad (5)$$

Term 1 is the change in the total entropy of the Earth. A positive (negative) value means the Earth is gaining (losing) energy or moving closer to (further from) thermal equilibrium. Term 2 is the solar entropy flux intercepted by the Earth. It is relatively small (Essex, 1984b) because the solar disk subtends a small solid angle in the sky that gives solar radiation a high directional organization. Term 3 is the outgoing terrestrial entropy flux, which is relatively large because the terrestrial radiation is much more isotropic than the incoming solar flux. Term 4 is the internal entropy production due to radiative scattering, absorption, and emission with the material component of the Earth system. The net result is the conversion of directional visible photons from the Sun into nearly isotropic infrared and visible photons that leave the Earth. Finally, term 5 is the internal entropy production due to irreversible material processes such as thermal conduction, chemical reactions, and viscous processes that provide the dissipation for atmospheric and oceanic circulations and biological activity.

Equation (3) is written so that the terms on the

right-hand side are all positive. Hence the only way for the Earth to remain in a state away from equilibrium, so that its entropy is nearly constant, is for the outgoing radiative entropy flux to nearly balance the sum of the other three terms. Essex (1984b) showed that the ratio of the outgoing to incoming entropy flux is about 100 and hence the magnitude of term 2 is about 1% of term 3. Most of this entropy production comes from term 4, the irreversible conversion of solar to terrestrial radiation. One obtains nearly the same radiative entropy result for a dead, black solid planet with no atmosphere or oceans and without dynamic, chemical, or biological processes. It is term 5 that arises from the dynamic organization that exists on the Earth. Although it is difficult to measure the global value for the internal material entropy production, it will be seen below that it is not likely to be more than a couple of percents of the total outgoing entropy flux. Furthermore most of this material entropy production is due to the atmospheric and oceanic circulations, since dissipation due to photosynthesis is roughly an order of magnitude less.

Ebeling (1985) has described this situation as a photon mill in which short-wavelength 5800°K photons from the sun are converted into longer-wavelength 255°K photons that escape to the 3°K background radiation of the universe. It is the fact that the stars are compact localized source regions of low entropic energy that allow the Earth to rid itself of its internally generated entropy. This permits the Earth to maintain itself far enough from equilibrium that the highly organized structures of fluid circulations and life processes can be maintained.

Stability

Most of the dynamics of the Earth's atmosphere, oceans, and biota are not steady state but are characterized by fluctuations on many timescales. Some of the fluctuations, such as diurnal and seasonal changes, are responses to external forcing whereas others, such as turbulence, are internally generated.

A simple way to see global stability in spite of fluctuations is to reexamine equation (3). Assume that term 2 is constant, so that the fluctuations are generated internally. Now assume that the fluctuation causes the system to move to a lower entropy state without changing its total energy and hence to move further from equilibrium. The system nor-

mally responds by increasing its internal fluxes in an attempt to move back towards equilibrium according to the second law. This results in an increase in the internal material entropy production, which would increase the entropy of the system, unless the radiative contributions also adjust and allow the extra entropy produced to escape to space. Hence it is the interplay between the internal entropy production due to irreversible processes and the radiative removal of entropy that determines the stability of any fluctuations.

Consider the following simple example. A fluctuation occurs in which the equator-to-pole heat transport is reduced. This will increase the global meridional temperature gradient and hence lower the entropy of the Earth. The increase in the thermal gradient may increase the meridional fluxes to bring the system back to its original state. If, however, the Earth's configuration with the stronger meridional gradient allowed a greater flux of radiative entropy to space, then the Earth may have found a new state in which the new energy and entropy balances allow stability.

It is clearly impossible to calculate the various terms of the entropy balance equation for the whole Earth. Determining the actual entropy requires a complete thermodynamic inventory of the constituents of the Earth system. Such a task is overwhelming even if we were to restrict ourselves to the atmosphere, which is probably the best measured subsystem of the Earth. Although an internal measurement of entropy is unlikely, the possibility of examining the flux term at the boundary should be considered.

Recently, I demonstrated (Lesins, 1990a and b) that satellite remote sensing provides us with a tool for measuring the net entropy flux leaving the Earth. Monitoring this flux may aid our understanding of the global entropy budget because it is created by all the internal contributions.

Measuring Radiative Entropy

Planck's distribution function for radiant energy in equilibrium is given by the familiar form

$$E(v, T_v) = \frac{2hv^3}{c^2 \left[\exp\left(\frac{hv}{kT}\right) - 1 \right]} \tag{4}$$

where h is the Planck's constant, k is the Stefan-Boltzmann constant, c is the speed of light, v is the frequency of radiation, and T_ν is the radiant temperature at frequency ν. The derivation of Planck's function (see Kittel and Kroemer, 1980, for example) is valid for each individual mode or frequency of radiation and hence the temperature in equation (4) can be made a function of the photon frequency. This is a consequence of the linearity of the theory of electromagnetism in which light beams pass through one another without interacting. The blackbody distribution of radiation, in which the radiative temperature is the same for all light frequencies, occurs for radiation within a cavity whose walls are in thermal equilibrium.

Using the second and third laws of thermodynamics, it is straightforward to derive an analogous expression for the entropy distribution function for radiation (Planck, 1913; Rosen, 1954; Ore, 1955):

$$S(\nu,T_\nu) = \frac{2h\nu^3}{c^2 T_\nu} \left\{ \frac{1}{\left[\exp\left(\dfrac{h\nu}{kT} \right) - 1 \right]} - \frac{kT_\nu}{h\nu} \, ln \left[1 - \exp\left(\frac{-h\nu}{kT} \right) \right] \right\}$$

(5)

The first term can be written as the radiant energy divided by the temperature. This would be the result for the entropy using classical thermodynamics without regard to photon statistics. However, when the quantum nature of radiation is correctly accounted for, one also obtains the second term in equation (5), which shifts the maximum in the entropy function to a slightly lower frequency compared with the maximum in the energy function. This is because lower-frequency light has less energy per photon, which increases the photon number for a fixed energy. Higher photon numbers represent a more random state and hence higher entropy.

Once a radiative stream of energy has left the Earth and is traveling in the near vacuum of space, its entropy content is essentially constant. The outgoing entropy flux, which could in principle be measured by satellites orbiting the Earth, would measure the excess entropy production of the planet due to interactions with matter. Some of this measured entropy would be the result of photons interacting with matter, some the result of material interactions (which eventually influences the outgoing terrestrial radiation), and some may be due to the release of stored entropy and energy.

The total radiative entropy flux can be measured by integrating equation (5) over a spherical shell surrounding the Earth, over all directions from which planetary radiation is being received, over all wavelengths of planetary radiation and over the two possible polarizations of light. Note that planetary radiation in this context refers to both the terrestrial and scattered or reflected solar radiation streams.

If it is assumed, for demonstration purposes only, that the total energy flux leaving the Earth is a constant in time, equation (5) can be used to see how the various distributions of this fixed total energy will affect the total entropy flux. The entropy flux is maximized when the energy is distributed in such a way that the radiative temperature as measured from space is homogeneous over the entire Earth, isotropic over all directions pointing toward the Earth, uniform over all wavelengths resulting in black-body radiation, and finally, identical for the two polarizations (unpolarized radiation).

Conversely, the entropy flux becomes progressively lower for the same total energy flux as radiative temperature gradients increase, as the radiation becomes more anisotropic, as stronger line and band structures appear in wavelength space, and as the radiation becomes more polarized. It is possible to estimate the effect of these various energy distributions on the total outgoing entropy flux from highly simplified models that isolate the influence of meridional temperature gradients, anisotropy due to a gray atmosphere, and artificial line structure in a non–black body distribution of radiant energy. I have provided additional details elsewhere (Lesins, 1990).

Meridional Gradients

The effect of meridional (north-south) radiative temperature gradients can be estimated by calculating the outgoing entropy flux for two extreme and unrealizable cases: (1) an isothermal Earth in which the internal heat transfer has eliminated all temperature gradients and (2) an Earth with no meridional heat transport, resulting in much larger equator-pole temperature differences than observed. Essex (1984b) calculated the isothermal radiative entropy production to be about 6×10^{14} W K^{-1}. For case 2, a local radiative equilibrium temperature can be computed as a function of latitude assuming the Sun is over the equator, the Earth is a black body, and the albedo is uniform. The radiative entropy production is 0.9903 of the isothermal case. In other words the difference in the entropy production due to meridional transport between these two extremes is only about 1%. The actual Earth is clearly between these two extremes with global monthly means ranging from 0.998 to 0.999 of the isothermal case. Although the difference appears small such meridional gradients and their corresponding radiative entropy fluxes can be detected easily by satellites, which can detect changes in monthly averaged entropy fluxes of less than 0.01%.

Anisotropy

The effect of directional radiative temperature gradients due to anisotropic radiation can be crudely estimated by solving the nonscattering Schwarzschild radiative transfer equation for two layers consisting of an isothermal, gray atmosphere and a different isothermal, black-body Earth. Figure 14.1 shows that the entropy flux ratio is minimized for an atmospheric infrared emissivity of 0.58. When the emissivity is zero the radiation is isotropic at the surface temperature whereas an emissivity of 1

results in isotropic radiation at the atmospheric temperature. This same crude model predicts an atmospheric emissivity of 0.77 if a surface temperature of 288°K is used. This corresponds to an entropy flux of 0.981 times the isotropic value. Hence for current greenhouse conditions the entropy flux reduction due to directional radiative temperature is larger than the meridional effect. Clearly more elaborate models are needed to verify these results since the Earth's atmosphere is neither gray nor single layered.

Line Structure

The effect of wavelength radiative temperature gradients was estimated by superimposing an artificial line structure of constant temperature amplitude upon the Planck black-body curve. Figure 14.2 shows how the radiative entropy flux decreases as the temperature amplitude increases. The Earth's infrared emission exhibits more complex structure but if we assume that the typical difference in radiative temperature between the window and opaque regions of the spectrum is roughly 30°K then from figure 14.2 the entropy flux is 0.994 times the black-body value or about a 0.6% reduction.

For each of the three effects examined here using highly simplified calculations the entropy flux for

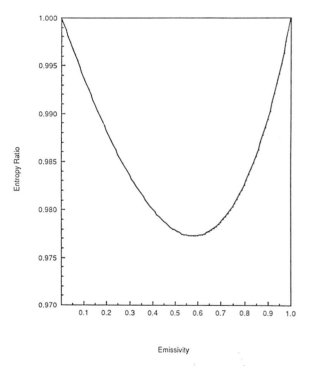

Figure 14.1 The entropy flux ratio, defined as the actual entropy flux divided by the maximum entropy flux, as a function of the effective infrared emissivity of the atmosphere. Note that the entropy flux is a maximum when the atmosphere is completely transparent, for which the radiation is isotropic at the ground temperature, or when the atmosphere is completely opaque, for which the radiation is isotropic at the atmosphere temperature. For intermediate emissivities the radiation is nonisotropic because the atmosphere and ground are at effective black-body temperatures that are colder and warmer, respectively, than the planetary effective temperature. As a result of this anisotropy the entropy flux lowers.

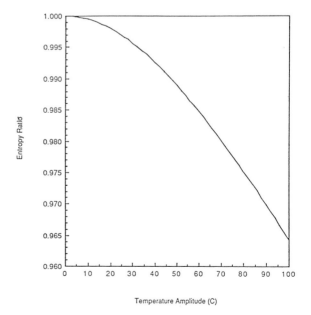

Figure 14.2 The entropy flux ratio defined as the entropy flux divided by its black-body value, which occurs with zero temperature amplitude. The radiative entropy decreases by about 1% of its equilibrium value for a peak-to-peak temperature amplitude of 50°K.

typical Earth conditions was lowered by 1% to 2% compared with equilibrium values. There is no clearly dominant process that can be isolated as carrying most of the entropic structure of the outgoing flux. This may serve as a warning that more precise calculations using real Earth radiance data and more sophisticated models including all the possible ways of distributing radiative temperature are needed. It may be insufficient to isolate only one process, such as the meridional heat flux, in understanding the entropy production of the planet.

Summary

The outgoing radiative entropy is an important term in the entropy balance equation for the Earth. This outward flux carries with it information from all the forms of internal entropy production that occur on the Earth including the activity of the biosphere. Furthermore entropy production is linked to a system's distance from equilibrium and the appearance of complex structures.

Photographs of the Earth taken from space reveal some of this structure in the form of cloud patterns organized into rotating midlatitude cyclones, long frontal bands, bright thunderstorm complexes, and cellular shallow convection. However, the full extent of the complexity can be quantified only if the radiative temperature is determined as a function of its four distribution spaces: position, direction, wavelength, and polarization. Simple calculations indicate that important modulation of the outgoing entropy flux may be carried by all the forms of the radiative temperature distributions. Clearly more precise calculations are necessary before any definite conclusions can be made.

Although a prescription exists for the determination of the net entropy flux leaving the Earth it must be asked how this information can be used. Currently satellites are capable of determining the meteorological fluctuations in the radiative entropy flux on a timescale from a day to a decade and with a spatial resolution of several tens of kilometers. The entropy signal is due to the horizontal variations in the radiative temperature and do not yet include directional or frequency dependencies. With current measurements there is an excellent potential of relating the outgoing entropy flux to the dynamical state of the atmosphere, a calculation that may prove useful in climate monitoring and perhaps even climate prediction.

If the biosphere is indeed responsible for shaping the evolutionary as well as transitory trends of the Earth system in some Gaian way, then it seems reasonable to expect that this impact can be measured in global entropy and energy budgets. At this point the arguments are still qualitative and lacking in empirical evidence. Clearly one problem is the fact that the energy in global photosynthesis is only about 10% of the energy that is dissipated by atmospheric circulations, which in turn is only about 1% of the average solar energy absorbed by the Earth. The biosphere's impact on the entropy is not likely to be observed with current satellite technology as a direct signal in the entropic radiation leaving the planet; however, if the biosphere indirectly influences the atmospheric circulation then perhaps some of the meteorological signal in the entropy flux can be attributed to Gaia. Unfortunately, this sounds too much like the tail-wagging-the-dog difficulty that plagues some of the Gaian hypotheses.

The thermodynamic distinctiveness of life is its ability to maintain a persistent highly structured, low-entropy state in the presence of continuous dissipation. The atmosphere also creates low-entropy structures, but they undergo a complete cycle of formation and dissipation without leaving any memory of their existence. Hence biological structures were able to evolve while other nonliving structures are transients forced by the surroundings. Nevertheless both living and nonliving entities are alike in that they must export the entropy produced by internal irreversible processes to their surroundings. In spite of over a billion years of evolution, life is able to utilize less than 0.1 W m^{-2} of solar energy to do work, compared with over 1 W m^{-2} for atmospheric circulations, and hence life does not make a significant impact on the total energy dissipated. The total living biomass is simply too small to make a significant energy contribution. Furthermore, the dissipated energy that contributes to internal entropy production and hence must eventually be exhausted to space through the radiation field is very small compared with the contributions to the entropy flux from the conversion of sunlight to infrared radiation and from the radiative temperature distribution.

A possible counter to the above argument is that over the past billion years life has gradually changed the chemical composition of the atmosphere, which through radiative feedbacks has resulted in a climate much different from what would have existed in the absence of life. In other words, perhaps the correct thermodynamic test of Gaia is to compare the outgoing entropy fluxes between the current Earth and one devoid of life. Another criticism that can be raised is that horizontal radiative temperature distributions may not be the best test for Gaian influences; instead the frequency dependence of the radiative temperature should be considered. Using spectral information we would be measuring the influence of the composition of the atmosphere on the outgoing entropy flux. This may be a more fruitful test because we know that life has created an atmosphere that is far from chemical equilibrium and that this nonequilibrium mixture may produce a significant entropy signal.

This chapter has concentrated on the question of whether the current satellite-measured data sets can be used to identify a Gaian signal in the outgoing radiation stream. The answer appears to be no, given that the meteorological and nonliving physical conversions dominate the entropy signal. It was already known that life does not utilize a significant amount of the average incoming solar energy, but life's effect on radiative entropy has not been considered before and also appears to be insignificant. However, the more general question of remotely determining the influence of living processes is still open and requires further work.

A technique has been proposed to help us understand the stability and complexity of systems from the point of view of global radiation thermodynamics. One of the great difficulties in dealing with the Gaia hypothesis is the sheer complexity of the total Earth system. Lovelock (1987) has speculated that the Earth may act as some vastly complex cybernetic control system that at some higher hierarchical level takes on properties that may be interpreted as lifelike. Although such statements are alluring, one needs some physical insights and analytical tools to assess the likelihood of this. The special and defying role that life has when cast in terms of entropy has been recognized for some time; however, quantifying this ability in sufficient detail has proven difficult.

Radiative entropy is a particularly easy form of entropy to quantify. Furthermore, the total Earth system can be viewed as interacting with the rest of the universe primarily through the radiative field. Hence irreversible thermodynamics and the use of radiative entropy are particularly suitable in understanding the Earth system. The problem with the more traditional methods of identifying and analyzing the stability properties of individual feedback cycles is that one is usually neglecting all of the other cycles. Because there are so many degrees of freedom in the Earth's system, and because there is such fantastic complexity and coupling, the reductionist approach of explicit modeling will likely never approach the true complexity of the Earth system in the near future. It is for this reason that the concepts of radiative entropy may have a role to play in explaining how the Earth maintains its stability. Once we attain a physical understanding of the nature of the stability characteristics of the Earth we may then be better poised to address the validity of Gaia.

References

Ebeling, W. 1985. Thermodynamics of selforganization and evolution. *Biomed Biochim Acta*, 44, 831–838.

Essex, C. 1984a. Radiation and the violation of bilinearity in the thermodynamics of irreversible processes. *Planet Space Sci*, 32, 1035–1043.

Essex C. 1984b. Radiation and the irreversible thermodynamics of climate. *J Atmos Sci*, 41, 1985–1991.

Kittel, C., and Kroemer, H. 1980. *Thermal Physics*, 2nd ed. San Francisco: W.H. Freeman.

Lesins, G.B. 1990a. On the relationship between radiative entropy and temperature distributions. *J Atmos Sci*, 47, 795–803.

Lesins, G.B., 1990b: Climate Monitoring using Radiative Entropy from ERB Observations. In proceedings of Seventh Conference on Atmospheric Radiation, San Francisco, July 23–27, pp. 149–152. Boston: American Meteorological Society.

Lifshitz, E.M., and Pitaevskii, L.P. 1980. *Statistical Physics*, part 1, 3rd ed. New York: Pergamon Press.

Lovelock, J.E. 1987. Geophysiology: A new look at Earth science. In: Dickinson, R.E., ed. *The Geophysiology of Amazonia: Vegetation and Climate Interactions*. New York: Wiley-Interscience, 11–23.

Nicolis, G., and Prigogine, I. 1977. Self-organization in nonequilibrium systems. New York: Wiley-Interscience.

Ore, A. 1955. Entropy of radiation. *Phys Rev*, 98, 887–888.

Planck, M. 1913. The theory of heat radiation. Authorized Translation by Morton Masius, 1959. New York: Dover Publications.

Rosen, P. 1954. Entropy of radiation. *Phys Rev*, 96, 555.

Schrodinger, E. 1944. *What is Life?* Cambridge: Cambridge University Press.

IV
Mechanisms: Sulfur

M. O. Andreae

15

Geophysiological Interactions in the Global Sulfur Cycle

In this chapter I provide a basic picture of the biogeochemical sulfur cycle and discuss some of the frustrations we have experienced in trying to understand feedback loops within this system. Figure 15.1 represents a conceptual view of the sulfur cycle, in which the world is broken down into a set of spheres or reservoirs. There are two almost completely uncoupled sulfur cycles: one operates in the anoxic environment, in the absence of oxygen, and is largely characterized by the formation of hydrogen sulfide (H_2S) from sulfate, followed by the incorporation of some of this sulfide into rocks and sediments, and eventually by the recycling of sulfide to sulfate during the weathering process. Another cycle takes place in the oxic environment, where the biota reduces sulfate to a variety of compounds. In the marine hydrosphere the most important of these is dimethylsulfide (DMS); in terrestrial environments the volatile reduction products emitted from plants and soils include DMS, H_2S, carbon disulfide (CS_2), and carbonyl sulfide (COS).

Biological Sulfate Reduction and Assimilation

The reason for the existence of two almost uncoupled sulfur cycles is that sulfate reduction has an entirely different purpose in each system (for a review, see Andreae, 1986). In the anoxic system, the main purpose of sulfate reduction is for sulfate to act as a terminal electron acceptor in an anaerobic respiration chain, a process that occurs because oxygen is absent. It is absent from this system because there is typically a barrier to the transport of oxygen into the system, either because diffusion is too slow (e.g., in sediments), or because of a density gradient that prevents turbulent mixing and thus blocks the rapid transport of oxygen into the system (e.g., in a stratified pond). The same barrier that prevents oxygen from coming in also prevents H_2S from going out. In addition to the physical barrier there is usually also a microbial barrier that consumes H_2S as it tries to escape from the anoxic re-

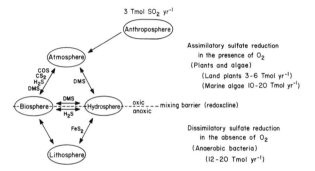

Figure 15.1 Schematic representation of interactions in the global biogeochemical sulfur cycle.

gion into the oxic system. Therefore, the H_2S that is produced in very large amounts in anoxic systems has almost no access to the atmosphere.

Conversely, the purpose of sulfate reduction in the oxic regime is predominantly the assimilation of nutrient sulfur into the reduced form in which it exists in amino acids and proteins. This process, assimilatory sulfate reduction, takes place in the presence of oxygen, and volatile products are therefore easily able to escape into the atmosphere.

Figure 15.2 gives an overview of the biochemistry of this process. Sulfate is attached to an organic carrier molecule (represented by R in the figure) via a sulfur-sulfur bond, essentially as an organic thiosulfate. This carrier-bound sulfate is reduced stepwise to the sulfide level. Then, depending on the need of the organism to produce sulfur-containing amino acids, the carrier-bound sulfide either follows one of the paths shown in figure 15.2, or it is cleaved off and thrown back as H_2S into the atmosphere. In the latter case, we have a production pathway for H_2S that is independent of dissimilatory sulfate reduction, that is, from anaerobic respiration: an overflow valve by which excess reduced sulfur is vented by organisms, predominantly plants.

In cases where sulfur is needed by the organism, the sulfide first becomes incorporated into cysteine and can then be transferred to proteins, gluta-

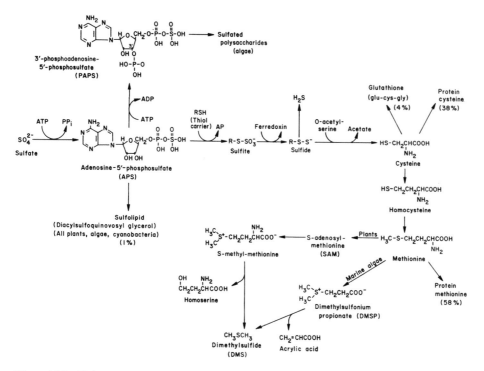

Figure 15.2 Major metabolic pathways of sulfur in algae and plants. The percentages represent the approximate distribution of the major organosulfur compounds in *Chlorella*.

thione, or other compounds, or into methionine, another sulfur-containing amino acid. From methionine there are two pathways (figure 15.2). In marine algae the path leads to dimethylsulfonium propionate (DMSP), where the sulfur is in an onium structure with two methyl groups that can be easily cleaved to form acrylic acid and dimethylsulfide. In plants, sulfur in methionine can also be methylated to form a sulfonium compound, *S*-methyl-methionine, which can then be cleaved again to give homoserine and DMS. This is the pathway whereby plants make DMS, in contrast to the algal pathway, which goes through DMSP.

Production of Dimethylsulfide by Marine Plankton

Why is all this of any interest to a consideration of global feedbacks and Gaia? Figure 15.3 depicts a feedback loop proposed by Charlson and colleagues (1987). In this feedback cycle DMS is produced in the ocean by phytoplankton; being a volatile compound it escapes into the atmosphere; in the atmosphere it is oxidized to sulfate, which provides the predominant number of cloud condensation nuclei (CCN) in the remote marine atmosphere (Nguyen et al., 1983). The abundance of CCN influences cloud albedo, and cloud albedo influences the radia-

tion budget, feeds back into climate, and then somehow feeds back into marine ecology and into the processes. that regulate the production of DMS by phytoplankton.

The first indications that DMS might be produced by phytoplankton came from the type of vertical profile in the ocean shown in figure 15.4. We found that DMS, dissolved DMSP, and particulate (intracellular) DMSP, were all present at elevated concentrations in the upper levels of the ocean, where phytoplankton is abundant and active (Andreae and Barnard, 1984; Iverson et al., 1989). Observations such as these suggested a relationship between DMS and primary producers (phytoplankton). We verified this by looking at pure algal cultures, and found that DMSP was both present in the algae and excreted, and also that DMS was excreted (Vairavamurthy et al., 1985).

We had discovered, then, that the source of DMS in the oceans is marine phytoplankton. This led to the supposedly straightforward working hypothesis that if DMS is produced by marine phytoplankton, we could parameterize its concentration simply by obtaining a variable representing phytoplankton abundance or activity, such as chlorophyll *a* concentration or carbonate uptake. We would thereby have a predictor variable that would enable us to

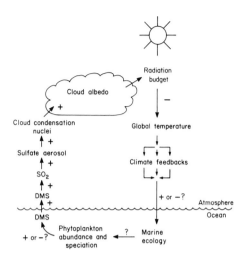

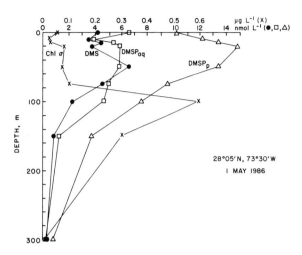

Figure 15.3 Proposed feedback cycle between climate and marine DMS production. The pluses and minuses indicate if an increase in the value of the preceding parameter in the cycle is expected to lead to an increase (+) or decrease (−) in the value of the subsequent parameter.

Figure 15.4 Typical vertical distribution of particulate DMSP (DMSP$_p$), dissolved DMSP (DMSP$_{aq}$) and DMS, and chlorophyll a during the April/May 1986 cruise of the R/V Columbus Iselin in the northwestern Atlantic Ocean.

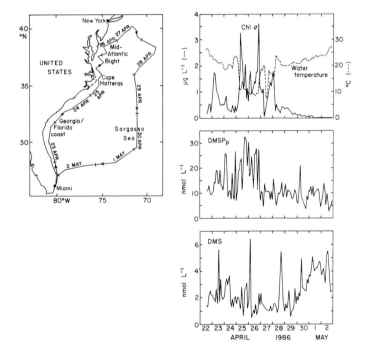

Figure 15.5 Cruise track of the R/V Columbus Iselin, 22 April–3 May 1986, with surface water temperatures and concentrations of chlorophyll a, particulate DMSP, and DMS measured during this cruise.

estimate DMS abundance and flux into the atmosphere throughout the oceans, given, for example, a map of the distribution of phytoplankton. Thus we started with a simple linear working hypothesis that there should be a correlation between phytoplankton abundance and DMS concentrations.

In order to look for this relationship, we conducted oceanographic cruises covering a wide range of biogeographic regimes, and attempted to see how the abundance of phytoplankton related to that of DMS. In some instances, the hypothesis seemed to work (e.g., Barnard et al., 1984), but figure 15.5 illustrates a case where it did not work so well. This cruise started in Miami, passed through coastal waters along the Florida-Georgia coast, then the frontal area near Cape Hatteras, a cold water coastal regime in the mid-Atlantic Bight, and then a classic oceanic desert, the Sargasso Sea.

The water mass characteristics are most easily seen in the temperature-versus-time plot of figure 15.5. First we enter the warm waters of the Gulf Stream and Florida-Georgia coast, and then pass through the fronts near Cape Hatteras and cold coastal waters in the mid-Atlantic Bight. There are some eddies and fronts during the most northerly part of the cruise, then we return to the warm waters of the Sargasso Sea. These water mass characteristics relate to biogeographical regimes, which can be seen in the phytoplankton distribution as represented by the chlorophyll *a* plot in figure 15.5. In the warm coastal waters we find a moderate amount of phytoplankton; in the frontal regimes, big peaks in phytoplankton abundance, with relatively high levels typically present in the colder coastal waters, and then a drop to very low levels in the oligotrophic Sargasso Sea waters.

If we compare this with the distribution of DMSP, which is known to be an algal metabolite, we see that although there are some fluctuations that seem to agree with some of the fronts, basically the two signals do not seem to cohere at all. Looking at DMS, it is actually worse, in particular in the Sargasso Sea, where chlorophyll *a* is at very low levels yet DMS reaches its highest average concentrations.

Processes Controlling Dimethylsulfide Abundance in the Ocean

We must remember here that we should not have expected a simple linear relationship between phytoplankton abundance and DMS, even under ideal circumstances. That is because the processes that regulate DMS concentration are rather complex (figure 15.6). There is direct algal excretion of DMS, and there is algal excretion of DMSP followed by hydrolysis of DMSP in seawater, which both feed into the pool of DMS dissolved in seawater. There is the escape of DMS into the atmosphere, which supplies our atmospheric feedback loop, but there is also downward mixing into the deep ocean. There is photochemical oxidation of DMS in seawater (Brimblecombe and Shooter, 1986), and finally, there is the most problematic process, microbial consumption. Why is microbial consumption such a problem? Algal blooms, or algal successions, are a time-dependent variable, and typically if a group of algae grows up and exists in a system, there will also be a group of microbial consumers growing up in that system that uses up the exudate (excretion products) of the phytoplankton. The relationship

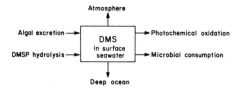

Figure 15.6 Schematic view of processes which regulate DMS concentration in surface seawater.

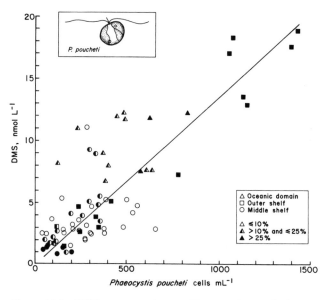

Figure 15.7 DMS concentration vs. *Phaeocystis poucheti* cell density in the southeastern Bering Sea during spring 1981. Open, half-full, and full symbols represent the percentage of *P. poucheti* cells relative to total phytoplankton cell density. The regression line is calculated from the data with a percentage of *P. poucheti* > 25%.

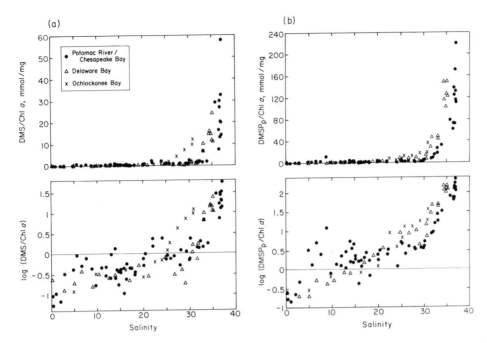

Figure 15.8 Concentrations of (a) DMS and (b) particulate DMSP vs. salinity in three estuaries during September 1986.

between these producers and consumers is nonlinear and time-variant rather than constant and linear. Thus the microbial consumption term for DMS will certainly not be first order with respect to DMS concentration and will show a complex time dependency. Therefore, we cannot hope for a simple linear relationship between DMS levels and algal biomass, even in the best of worlds.

But I think a worse problem is this: if we look at individual algal cultures, we find differences of some four orders of magnitude in the specific excretion rate of DMS (that is, the rate of excretion of DMS per unit algal biomass). We have seen, for instance, that DMS concentration in the Bering Sea (figure 15.7) was controlled by essentially one species, *Phaeocystis poucheti,* even in the presence of diatom concentrations that were many times higher than the abundance of this one organism, and yet there was no relationship between DMS and these diatom concentrations. The relatively small amount of *Phaeocystis* explained all the variability in DMS. There seems to be a tendency for the algal group known as prymnesiophytes to be relatively prolific producers: *Phaeocystis* is one member of this group; the coccolithophorids also belong to it. Keller and colleagues (1989) examined a large number of algal cultures for their DMSP content and also found the prymnesiophytes and dinoflagellates

contain the highest average concentration of this substance.

In all this disorder, we have nevertheless found a good amount of order. For example, we looked at the distribution of biomass-normalized DMS in estuaries (figure 15.8). This normalization is necessary, because otherwise we would obtain a very complex profile simply because the distribution of algae in estuaries is extremely patchy. In figure 15.8, we see that concentrations of both DMS and intracellular DMSP are strongly dependent on salinity. The data are shown on both a logarithmic and a linear scale so that the variation at lower salinities is visible. The reason for the relationship between DMSP and salinity is quite straightforward. In previous work (Vairavamurthy et al., 1985), we have shown that DMSP acts to maintain internal osmotic pressure in some algae. In a pure culture, the DMSP content of the cell and the rate of DMS excretion into the environment are linear functions of salinity, at least within the salinity range at which the particular phytoplankton species can grow without serious problems (figure 15.9). The relationship that we see in the estuary, however, is extremely nonlinear, and in fact seems to be represented reasonably well by an exponential function (figure 15.8). This was observed consistently in a number of different estuaries: Delaware Bay, the Chesapeake-Potomac

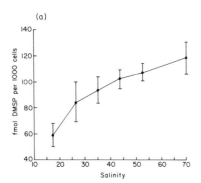
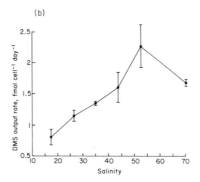

Figure 15.9 (a) DMSP levels in cells of *Hymenomonas carterae* and (b) output of DMS by this phytoplankton species as a function of salinity in an artificial seawater medium at a constant sulfate concentration of 28 mmol L^{-1}.

system, and Ochlockonee Bay in northern Florida (Iverson et al., 1989). The data points from all these estuaries fall more or less on the same line, which is rather surprising considering the variability that we have seen typically in DMS concentrations.

Because the DMSP-salinity relationship in a culture is a simple linear function, we must look for another reason for the high nonlinearity that we see in these estuaries. Once again the explanation we arrive at is the community structure of the phytoplankton: in the relatively low salinity part of the estuary, the system was dominated by diatoms, which tend to have very low DMSP content and produce little DMS, whereas in the higher-salinity regions of the estuary, there was a transition toward prymnesiophyte-dominated communities. So the salinity response that we see in these estuaries is predominantly again a community effect rather than a simple physical-chemical effect. The importance of community and trophic action has been further pointed out by Leck and colleagues (1990) in the Baltic Sea.

So we come away with the frustrating conclusion that at this point there is no good predictor variable for DMS concentrations in seawater. Sometimes it seemed as if temperature would be a useful predictor variable (Bates et al., 1987), but this is probably only because temperature reflects seasonality effects (Turner et al., 1988) and differences between communities existing in cold water bodies and those in the very oligotrophic warm water bodies that again tend to be high in prymnesiophytes. Salinity works as a predictor variable for DMS in estuaries, but again only indirectly, because it reflects community structure; the salinity range that is actually present in the open ocean will have little effect, because sensitivity to salinity at the high end of the

range becomes rather small. Finally we must conclude that we cannot use anything like phytoplankton biomass to predict DMS, because it is overshadowed by the speciation effect.

Sea-to-Air Flux of Dimethylsulfide and Its Fate in the Atmosphere

Let us return now to the discussion of the next step in our feedback loop (figure 15.3): DMS escapes from the ocean across a thin layer at the sea surface, where its rate of escape is controlled by comparatively slow molecular diffusion, rather than by the much faster process of eddy diffusion, which moves it about in the euphotic zone. The rate of DMS emission from the ocean surface can therefore be predicted on the basis of a model of its diffusion across this thin, so-called stagnant layer (Liss and Merlivat, 1986). After reaching the atmosphere, DMS is oxidized by a number of pathways (represented in figure 15.10) to products including sulfur dioxide (which eventually becomes sulfate aerosol), and methanesulfonic acid (MSA) (Yin et al., 1986; Plane, 1989). This scheme seems to be consistent with what we see when we measure these species in the atmosphere. For instance, figure 15.11 shows the vertical profiles obtained off the coast of Tasmania. In the boundary layer, the lowest kilometer, over the ocean, we see a concentration of something like 30 ppt of DMS, and coexisting with this about 25 ppt of non–seasalt sulfate. Considering the residence times of the two components, this is in reasonable agreement with the hypothesis that the oxidation of DMS in this layer can explain the amount of non–seasalt sulfate and MSA observed in the atmosphere over the ocean (Andreae et al., 1988, Berresheim et al., 1990).

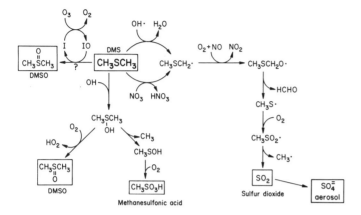

Figure 15.10 Reaction pathways for the oxidation of DMS by OH, NO_3, and IO radicals.

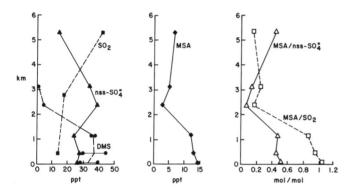

Figure 15.11 Vertical distributions of DMS, SO_2, MSA, non–seasalt sulfate (nss–$SO_4^=$), and the ratios of MSA to nss–$SO_4^=$ and SO_2 over the Southern Ocean near Tasmania during December 1986.

Conclusions

Coming back to the feedback loop again (figure 15.3), we now have a clear indication that DMS is produced by marine phytoplankton and is released to the atmosphere by sea-to-air transport, and where a chain of oxidation produces sulfate aerosol and CCN. But we must conclude that at this time we do not know how climate may feed back into phytoplankton speciation, or how phytoplankton speciation then feeds back into DMS production. We see that obviously there is an important phenomenon here, but the quantification of the relationships involved and the transfer functions between feedback steps are very difficult to investigate. There are only a few clues: we do see a seasonal variability of DMS (Bates et al., 1987; Turner et al., 1988; Berresheim and Andreae, unpublished data) that seems to correlate with the seasonal variability in CCN (Bigg et al., 1984). This would tend to decrease the effect of seasonality, because the lower concentration of CCN in winter would let more en-

ergy reach the surface. We do not know what long-term variability of DMS flux there is, but it is clear that there could indeed be significant long-term variability, because we know of nothing that would keep it constant. Another cue relating the emission of DMS to climate is that the warmest parts of the oceans, even though they have relatively low primary production, seem to have the highest DMS fluxes (Andreae, 1986). It thus appears that phytoplankton, especially in the warm equatorial and tropical parts of the ocean, are in a way shading themselves by the emission of DMS. It is quite clear, however, that we still have a long way to go from the observations of these clues to a complete solution of the puzzle of the relationship of DMS and climate.

References

Andreae, M.O. 1986. The ocean as a source of atmospheric sulfur compounds. In: Buat-Ménard, P., ed. *The Role of Air-Sea Exchange in Geochemical Cycling*. Dordrecht: Reidel, 331–362.

Andreae, M.O., and Barnard, W.R. 1984. The marine chemistry of dimethylsulfide. *Marine Chem,* 14, 267–279.

Andreae, M.O., Berresheim, H., Andreae, T.W., Kritz, M.A., Bates, T.S., and Merrill, J.T. 1988. Vertical distribution of dimethylsulfide, sulfur dioxide, aerosol ions, and radon over the northeast Pacific Ocean. *J Atmos Chem,* 6, 149–173.

Barnard, W.R., Andreae, M.O., and Iverson, R.L. 1984. Dimethylsulfide and *Phaeocystis poucheti* in the southeastern Bering Sea. *Cont Shelf Res,* 3, 103–113.

Bates, T.S., Cline, J.D., Gammon, R.H., and Kelly-Hansen, S.R. 1987. Regional and seasonal variations in the flux of oceanic dimethylsulfide to the atmosphere. *J Geophys Res,* 92, 2930–2938.

Berresheim, H., Andreae, M.O., Ayers, G.P., Gillett, R.W., Merrill, J.T., Harris, V.J., and Chameides, W.L. 1990. Airborne measurements of dimethylsulfide, sulfur dioxide, and aerosol ions over the Southern Ocean south of Australia. *J Atmos Chem,* 10, 341–370.

Bigg, E.K., Gras, J.L., and Evans, C. 1984. Origin of Aitken particles in remote regions of the Southern Hemisphere. *J Atmos Chem,* 1, 203–214.

Brimblecombe, P., and Shooter, D. 1986. Photo-oxidation of dimethylsulphide in aqueous solution. *Marine Chem,* 19, 343–353.

Charlson, R.J., Lovelock, J.E., Andreae, M.O., and Warren, S.G. 1987. Oceanic phytoplankton, atmospheric sulphur, cloud albedo, and climate. *Nature,* 326, 655–661.

Iverson, R.L., Nearhoof, F.L., and Andreae, M.O. 1989. Production of dimethylsulfonium propionate and dimethylsulfide by phytoplankton in estuarine and coastal waters. *Limnol Oceanogr,* 34, 53–67.

Keller, M.D., Bellows, W.K., and Guillard, R.R.L. 1989. Dimethyl sulfide production in marine phytoplankton. In: Saltzman, E.S., and Cooper W.J., eds. *Biogenic Sulfur in the Environment.* ACS Symposium Series 393. Washington, D.C.: American Chemistry Society, 167–182.

Leck, C., Larsson, U., Bågander, L.E., Johansson, S., and Hajdu, S. 1990. DMS in the Baltic Sea—Annual variability in relation to biological activity. *J Geophys Res,* 95, 3353–3363.

Liss, P.S., and Merlivat, L. 1986. Air-sea gas exchange rates: Introduction and synthesis. In: Buat-Ménard, P., ed. *The Role of Air-Sea Exchange in Geochemical Cycling.* Dordrecht: Reidel, 113–127.

Nguyen, B.C., Bonsang, B., and Gaudry, A. 1983. The role of the ocean in the global atmospheric sulfur cycle. *J Geophys Res,* 88, 10,903–10,914.

Plane, J.M.C. 1989. Gas-phase atmospheric oxidation of biogenic sulfur compounds: A review. In: Saltzman, E.S., and Cooper, W.J., eds. *Biogenic Sulfur in the Environment.* ACS Symposium Series 393. Washington, D.C.: American Chemistry Society, 404–423.

Turner, S.M., Malin, G., Liss, P.S., Harbour, D.S., and Holligan, P.M. 1988. The seasonal variation of dimethyl sulfide and dimethylsulfoniopropionate concentrations in nearshore waters. *Limnol Oceanogr,* 33, 364–375.

Vairavamurthy, A., Andreae, M.O., and Iverson, R.L. 1985. Biosynthesis of dimethylsulfide and dimethylpropiothetin by *Hymenomonas carterae* in relation to sulfur source and salinity variations. *Limnol Oceanogr,* 30, 59–70.

Yin, F., Grosjean, D., and Seinfeld, J.H. 1986. Analysis of atmospheric photooxidation mechanisms for organic sulfur compounds. *J Geophys Res,* 91, 14,417–14,438.

Glenn E. Shaw

16
Planetary Homeostasis Through the Sulfur Cycle

The Gaia hypothesis (Lovelock and Margulis, 1974) assumes the existence of an unspecified biological mechanism for stabilizing climate. It can be supposed that the Gaian climate-regulating machinery has been in existence a large fraction of the time since the emergence of life, 3 to 5×10^9 years ago, and has been the active agent responsible for the remarkable stability of the planet's climate in spite of the fact that the Sun's radiant energy has increased by about 25%. The rising solar luminosity is a feature common to all Main Sequence stars, a consequence of continual depletion of hydrogen in the Sun's core by nuclear fusion.

In order better to specify the control system's mechanism, Lovelock and Whitfield (1982) suggested that the climate stabilization feedback loop might involve the abundance of the atmospheric greenhouse gas, CO_2. A feedback loop using CO_2 would have had to gain active control of the carbon cycle soon after the emergence of life and would systematically lead to the depletion of the CO_2, and therefore to a limited life span of the biosphere compared with the interval the Sun spends on the Main Sequence.

An alternative proposal was put forward for a biocontrol mechanism (Shaw, 1983); it involves the natural sulfur cycle and would work by altering the planetary albedo, hence causing cooling because of light-scattering sulfate particles. The rationale for introducing this admittedly rather speculatory hypothesis was that its operation would involve very small quantities of material cycling through the biosphere (Shaw, 1986a). Furthermore, one could cite circumstantial evidence for its possible operation, because submicron sulfate aerosols are ubiquitous throughout the atmosphere, even at remote locations like the polar regions or over the central oceans.

Charlson et al. (1987) (and also Mesazaros, 1988) extended Shaw's light-scattering sulfur aerosol hypothesis by pointing out the considerable amplification or leverage that could be introduced by

imagining the biogenic sulfur aerosol to serve as cloud condensation nuclei (CCN) and to modulate the albedo of clouds. This is tantamount to introducing an amplifier into the feedback climatic control system; the amplification arises from the huge amount of water condensing out during cloud formation (figure 16.1). A relatively small mass of CCN, according to the hypothesis, would strongly perturb the radiation balance.

The mechanism proposed by Charlson and colleagues assumed a proportionality between cloud droplet concentration, N_c, and atmospheric particle concentration. In fact a more usual situation is that only some (variable) fraction of atmospheric particles are activated as nuclei during cloud growth. It is erroneous, in general, to assume a linear relationship between C, the aerosol concentration, and N_c, except under specific conditions (which may or may not be realized for marine aerosols at unpolluted ocean locations). In the following sections, I explore the component parts of a feed-

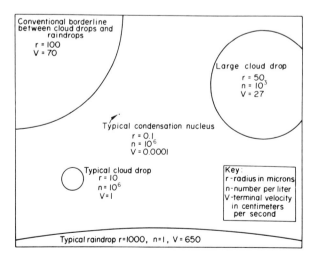

Figure 16.1 Relative sizes of raindrops, cloud droplets, and the progenitor nucleus of condensation. r—radius in microns. n—number per liter. V—terminal velocity in centimeters per second. (After McDonald, 1958.)

back control system of the type proposed by Charlson and colleagues.

The Nuclei of Cloudy Condensation

Aitken conducted experiments indicating that "when there is dust in the air the (water) vapor condenses out in a visible form, but when no dust is present, the fog particles are . . . few." He drew the following pertinent conclusions: "1. that when water vapor condenses in the atmosphere, it always does so on some solid nucleus; 2. that the dust particles in the air form the nuclei on which it condenses; 3. if there was no dust in the air there would be no fogs, no clouds, no mists, and probably no rain" (Aitken, 1888). Wilson (1897) later performed experiments demonstrating that without nuclei (dust), the atmosphere could be raised to hundreds of percent relative humidity before condensation would occur.

After Aitken's work, it became abundantly clear that the troposphere is always charged with more than sufficient numbers of particles to yield the observed cloud droplet concentrations (Landsberg, 1938; Jaenicke, 1980; Bodhaine, 1983). Of course this supposes that an airmass is brought to a supersaturated state, say by mixing two parcels of humid air or by adiabatic lifting, radiative cooling, or a similar mechanism. Though cloud droplets do condense on atmospheric particles, not all of the particles are necessarily involved and it is not a priori obvious that altering the particle concentration will alter the cloud droplet concentration proportionally. I explore the relationship existing between particle concentration and cloud droplet concentration in the next two sections.

Cloud Activation: Preliminary Considerations

During cloud formation, a certain fraction—not all—of the atmospheric particles serve as nuclei for water condensation. When the water droplets first condense and grow, the growing surface area of the population of water droplets represents an increasing sink for water vapor and prevents the supersaturations from rising high enough to activate small and insoluble particles. For example, particles of sodium chloride larger than radius r will be nucleated by applying supersaturation S, where

$$r = 1.16 \times 10^{-6} S^{-2/3} \tag{1}$$

and S is in percent. According to equation (1), 1% supersaturation (typical of that occurring in natural cloud formation) would only nucleate particles larger than 0.024 μ in diameter; smaller salt crystals would remain unactivated in such a condition.

The fraction of available particles activated in a cloud depends not only on the size but also on the particle's solubility. Because particles are distributed with a variety of sizes and solubilities in the atmosphere, the cloud activation process is quite complicated and turns out to be nonlinear. The nonlinear behavior of the cloud activation has so far not received attention in the sulfur-aerosol-cloud-climate feedback loop scenario. Insight into the process can be obtained through considering the theory of cloud activation developed by Twomey.

Illustration of the Nonlinear Behavior from Twomey Activation Theory

Particles in the atmosphere occur over a range of sizes and chemical compositions; all require slight supersaturation to nucleate cloud droplets. The smaller and less soluble particles to varying supersaturations require higher supersaturations to nucleate than larger, soluble particles. The behavior of the population of particles is conveniently conveyed with a CCN spectrum, $N(S)$, where N is the number concentration of particles nucleated upon exposure to water supersaturation S. The CCN spectrum may be determined by experiment, for instance by using thermal diffusion chamber methods (Twomey, 1963).

The Twomey theory makes the assumption that the cloud condensation nucleus spectrum can be approximated with a power law form,

$$N = CS^k \tag{2}$$

where C and k are constants. Measurements of N versus S at a large number of locations have confirmed that the power law expression is frequently reasonable (Twomey, 1959, 1977a), though we show later that it may be invalid at very low supersaturations.

The Twomey theory provides the following approximate expression for the maximum supersaturation, S_{max}, reached during cloud activation:

$$S_{max} a C^{-1/(k + 2)} V^{3/(2(k + 2))} \tag{3}$$

where the cooling that brings about the increasing water supersaturation is caused by ascent of an air parcel with uniform updraft speed V (Twomey, 1977a). Figure 16.2 illustrates the way in which different-sized nuclei activate and grow in air forced

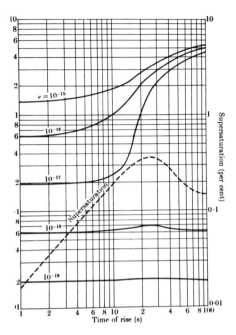

Figure 16.2 Calculated growth of cloud droplets in an ascending air mass undergoing uniform cooling. The ordinate corresponds to particle diameter in micrometers. Nuclei with dry mass larger than 10^{-17}g (corresponding to a dry particle of NaCl 0.014 μm in diameter) activate and go on to become cloud droplets. Smaller nuclei remain as instital, unactivated haze particles. Notice that the supersaturation of the ascending air parcel undergoes a maximum, approximately 0.35%, during the cloud formation process. This S_{max} sets the number concentration of cloud droplets—see equation (3). (After Howell, 1949).

into supersaturation by cooling. The maximum supersaturation occurs at the point where the rate of excess vapor supply equals the rate of its removal by condensation on the growing surface area of water droplets. The number of cloud droplets which then finally form, N_c, is dictated by the CCN spectrum equation (1) using a value of S_{max} for S.

When the slope of the CCN supersaturation spectrum, k, is $>>2$, equations (2) and (3) provide a relationship of the approximate form

$$N_c a V^{3/2} C^2 \text{ for } k >> 2 \qquad (4)$$

and the cloud drop concentration approaches independence on k. If, however, $k << 2$, the Twomey activation theory indicates that

$$N_c = C V^{3k/4} \approx C \text{ for } k << 2 \qquad (5)$$

and the cloud droplet concentration, N_c, is approximately proportional to the nucleus concentration C.

Under the approximations of the Twomey activation theory (assumption given in equation 2), we see that the parameter k is the key to determining

whether the cloud microphysical parameters, hence albedo, will be sensitive or insensitive to number concentration of atmospheric particles. The nonlinear behavior of the cloud activation process may explain why the cloud albedo differs only slightly, if at all, (Schwartz, 1988) in the two hemispheres, even though anthropogenic sulfur emissions are predominantly in the northern hemisphere.

Pervasiveness of Biogenic Sulfur Cloud Nuclei

It is reasonable to inquire whether biogenic sulfur is sufficiently pervasive to generate the required numbers of cloud nuclei to alter cloud properties on the global scale. Prior to the discovery of biogenic dimethylsulfide (DMS), it was known that the sulfur budget was approximately 60 Tg yr^{-1} out of balance (Junge, 1960). The deficit was attributed to H$_2$S sources in estuaries and tidal flats and in the oceans. Lovelock and colleagues (1972) pointed out that the oceans are too oxidizing to support large productions of H$_2$S. Lovelock and colleagues (1972) and Rasmussen (1974) suggested that in source strength of organic sulfides may dominate over H$_2$S and put forward the suggestion that DMS and dimethyldisulfide (DMDS) might be important players in the sulfur budget. This bold suggestion was followed by a series of attempts to quantify the source strength in the global sulfur budget; Maroulis and Bandy (1977) verified an oceanic source, but estimated that DMS might account for at most a small percent of the total sulfur cycling through the biosphere, while Nguyen and colleagues (1978) estimated that DMS sulfur represented a substantial fraction. Throughout the late 1970s and early 1980s the situation was confused, but a consensus emerged that DMS is probably the dominant source term in the natural sulfur budget (Andreae and Raemdonck, 1983; Bates et al., 1987); its source strength is estimated to be 30 Tg/yr and its mean residence time before being converted to methane sulfonic acid and sulfate is approximately one day (Charlson et al., 1987).

The existence of an oceanic source of sulfur has also been inferred from the composition of aerosols at unpolluted locations. On the basis of the way that condensation nuclei disappear following passage through heated tubes, Twomey (1971) deduced that many of the CCN may be sulfates. Sulfate dominates by mass in the submicron aerosol at the South Pole (Cunningham and Zoller, 1981) and at locations in the central oceans.

Dimethylsulfide emission tends to increase in

warm, saline, sunlit upper layers of the oceans (Charlson et al., 1987). One factor to consider in the proposed feedback mechanism is whether the observed flux of biogenic sulfur is sufficient to supply CCN. Consider:

DMS sulfur flux: 30×10^{12} g yr^{-1}

Volume of the troposphere: 3×10^{24} cm^{-3}

Residence time of a nucleus: 5 days

Mass of a CCN: 3×10^{-17} g (r = 1.6×10^{-6} cm) (Twomey, 1977b).

Nuclei that can be sustained: 10^{28}

Number concentration available for cloud growth: 2000 cm^{-3}

Mean CCN concentration at Cape Grim: 250 cm^{-3}

We conclude that there is enough sulfur available from the biogenic release of DMS to supply the observed concentration of CCN; this, of course, is a necessary but not sufficient condition for the operation of the cloud modulation feedback system.

Modeled Cloud Activation

Twomey (1963) reported extensively on CCN spectra measurements carried out with thermal diffusion chambers; the largest fraction of measurements indicated that $k << 2$, which suggests that one can indeed expect an approximate proportionality between cloud droplet concentration and aerosols, as was assumed by Charlson and colleagues (1987). Thermal diffusion chambers, however, cannot measure accurately below about 0.2% supersaturation, so Twomey's measurements pertain to values of S larger than this. One can raise the question, "what would happen if the CCN spectrum was steeper (higher value of the parameter k) in the very low supersaturation regions that are inaccessible to thermal diffusion chamber technique?"

To estimate the behavior of the CCN spectrum at the very low supersaturations, the spectrum was calculated from measurements made of the particle-size probability distribution, assuming the particles to be soluble salts. Calculated CCN spectra in air samples that had been over the Pacific Ocean for many days are shown in figure 16.3. The underlying assumption of a power law relationship for $N(S)$ holds over regions, but is inadequate over a large range of supersaturations. The slope is relatively large at the lower supersaturations.

The cloud activation equations were solved with numerical techniques, using spectra like those illustrated in figure 16.3. The results (table 16.1) are geometric means of air samples taken in northern Pacific marine airmasses and for Arctic-derived airmasses in Alaska, and for urban pollution (Tucson, Arizona), where the condensation nuclei (CN) concentration was two to three orders of magnitude higher than in the clean airmass systems.

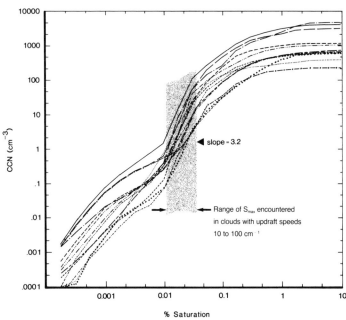

Figure 16.3 Cloud condensation spectra computed from aerosol size probability spectra in clean air samples. It was assumed that the particles are soluble salts.

Table 16.1 Maximum Supersaturations Experienced During Cloud Growth, Numbers of Cloud Droplets Nucleated, and Fraction of Aerosols Nucleated During Adiabatic Cooling of Moist Air at Updrafts of 10 and 100 cm s^{-1}

Aerosol Type	Updraft Speed (cm s^{-1})	S_{max} (%)	N_c (cm^{-3})	Fraction Nucleated (%)
Arctic haze	10	0.059	59	17.0
	100	0.34	197	56.0
Pacific marine	10	0.12	27	3.0
	100	0.46	160	16.0
Urban pollution	10	0.042	93	0.7
	100	0.14	690	5.0

In the case of the Pacific marine CCN spectra, only 3% to 16% of the particles nucleate (the two numbers pertain to an updraft of 10 cm/sec, representative of strataform cloud formation, and 100 cm/sec, which would be more characteristic of marine cumuli). The predicted cloud droplet number concentration, N_c, is 30 to 200 cm^{-3}, typical for marine clouds. Though the Arctic-derived air samples possessed smaller numbers of CN (350 cm^{-3} versus 1000 cm^{-3} for Pacific marine airmasses), the cloud droplet concentration ended up comparable (60 to 210 cm^{-3}).

In the case of urban pollution, even though the particle number concentrations were increased by a factor of 100, the simulated cloud droplet concentration underwent only modest increases (90 to 600 cm^{-3}). The Twomey activation theory provides insight as to how this may happen; evidently it is a result of the nonlinear behavior of the activation process.

Notice that in the range from 0.01% to about 0.1% supersaturation the slope of the CCN spectra in figure 16.3 is fairly steep. The numerical calculations indicate that for low updraft speeds (several centimeters per second) the maximum supersatsurations encountered during cloud formation rarely rise above a few tenths of 1%. Thus to an approximation, the cloud activation process would be controlled by the steep portion of the CCN spectrum where, from the Twomey activation theory, we showed that the cloud becomes only weakly dependent on aerosol concentration, according to equation (4). The CCN spectra in figure 16.3 were calculated under the assumption that all the particles are soluble salts, and this may be incorrect; if it is correct, the implication of the Twomey theory is that cloud number concentrations over clean locations like oceans may not be very sensitive to number changes in the aerosol particles. This deduction is highly provisional, however, because there are many possible sources of error in the calculated spectra shown in figure 16.3. This points out the importance of performing more experimental work in this area, however.

Cloud Albedo Modulation

The optical depth of a cloud, τ, varies with cloud droplet concentration as

$$\tau \alpha N_c^{1/3} \qquad (6)$$

(invariance of liquid water content of the cloud is assumed). If the slope of the CCN spectrum remains low enough over the supersaturation range encountered during the cloud formation, then cloud number concentration, N_c, and aerosol concentration would be approximately proportional to one another. If, in addition, we assume that aerosol particle concentration is proportional to the mass flux of emitted DMS, then the differential changes in cloud albedo can readily be related to differential changes in cloud optical depth (e.g., Twomey et al., 1984; Twomey, 1974). The approximate relation, fitting Twomey et al.'s curves and employing equation (6) is

$$\Delta \alpha_c = 0.07 \Delta F/F \qquad (7)$$

where α is the cloud albedo, and F is biogenic sulfur emission flux.

According to equation (7), a 10% change in DMS might modulate cloud albedo by 0.7%. This would be an upper limit in the albedo forcing, for as we have seen there is some evidence that the dependency of N_c on CCN may be relatively weak (high k).

Climate Forcing by Cloud Albedo Changes

Increasing cloud amount, reckoned in terms of cloud coverage or cloud optical thickness, has two opposing influences on climate: a cooling, forcing term arising from the increased albedo, and a heating term arising from the reduction in outgoing thermal-band radiation. The latter is similar to a greenhouse effect, in that the outgoing thermal infrared radiation is impeded; however, clouds differ from greenhouse gas by turning back visible-band photons near the top of the atmosphere.

Schneider (1972) evaluated the outgoing infrared flux emitted to space with a numerical radiation code to handle the equations of transfer, keeping relative humidity constant. The model employed an ensemble average of many cloud layers of various albedos. The salient features of this type of simple model (which elicits most of the necessary physics) are illustrated in figure 16.4, where the variation of outgoing infrared flux to space is shown as a function of global cloud cover fraction. Schneider drew curves for a selection of mean global cloud top heights as a free parameter. The outstreaming thermal infrared emanates from an effective radiating layer near the cloud tops. All the graphs are computed for a constant surface temperature of 288° K. The broken line is the solar radiation absorbed by the earth-cloud system (the shortwave term: SW). The present cloud cover fraction of the planet is approximately 0.5 and for this, the SW and (longwave) LW fluxes balance at an effective cloud top height of approximately 5.5 km.

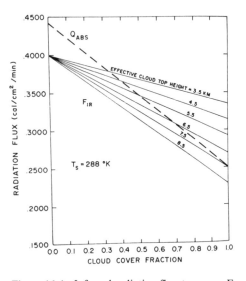

Figure 16.4 Infrared radiation flux to space, F_{IR}, emitted by the earth-atmosphere system and the absorbed solar energy, Q_{ABS}, (dotted line), as a function of fractional cloud cover and for several values of effective cloud height. (After Schneider, 1972). T_s is the surface temperature.

Figure 16.4 illustrates that the rate of decrease of solar absorption (SW) with increased cloud fraction is faster than rate of decrease of infrared flux (LW); therefore the net effect on the radiation balance of increasing cloud cover is an imbalance that causes LW to exceed SW. The radiative equilibrium temperature of the planet would therefore reduce, assuming that convection maintains the lapse rate constant and that the cloud albedo does not change and that the cloud tops do not change altitude. It appears likely, therefore, that the planet is cooled by clouds. Ramanathan and colleagues (1989) have also deduced, from satellite measurements, that the global-averaged cloud forcing is a cooling, and they estimate it to be 13 w m^{-2}.

Though it is now fairly clear that clouds refrigerate the planet (by an amount approximately five times that of a doubling of carbon dioxide greenhouse gas) there still remains much uncertainty about the strength of several cloud-climate feedback loops, that is, the effects on the clouds caused by a change in climate. Schneider's model, illustrated in figure 16.4, indicates that the effect of a sustained global increase in the effective cloud top height, hc, would be an increase in the global surface temperature, provided that the amount of cloud cover, fc, and cloud albedo remain unchanged. In practice, we can expect both the mean height of clouds, hc, and cloudiness fraction, fc, to alter in a complex manner in response to an impressed climatic change.

The sensitivity, $\Delta T^s/\Delta\alpha$ of Ts to a change in cloud albedo, α, is $-50°K$ per fraction change of α for a climate system with no atmospheric feedback, but about double (to $-108°K$) if one uses Budyko's empirical expression for LW emission to space. It was evaluated to be $-145°K$ with a zonal energy balance model (Jenssen, 1988) that incorporated advective heat transport and ice-albedo feedback (North et al., 1981, have reviewed such models). Adopting the latter value of cloud albedo-Ts dependency, we have, by combining with equation (7)

$$F\frac{\Delta T}{\Delta F} \approx 10.2 \qquad (8)$$

Thus according to this simple model, a 10% increase in biogenic sulfur production flux ($\Delta F/F = 0.1$) might lead to a surface cooling of 1°K. I know of no data giving the temperature dependence of DMS in the mixing layer of oceans, but Adams and colleagues (1981) provide evidence for temperature

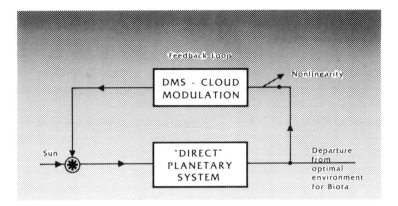

Figure 16.5 The proposed nonlinear, homeostatic feedback control system.

sensitivity of very nearly this magnitude for reduced sulfur compounds from soils and wet marshlands.

Conclusions

The essential feature of the cloud activation process is its lack of linearity. The key factor is the slope of the cloud condensation spectrum on logarithmic plots. Extensive measurements of k, the slope of the CCN spectrum, by Twomey suggest that the slopes are modest, which would mean that there would be high sensitivity in the feedback climatic control mechanism proposed by Charlson and colleagues. I have uncovered provisional information indicating that the slope, k, may be higher at very low supersaturations. Should the slope of the CCN spectrum steepen, as it might well do if global sulfur emissions were to increase substantially, the climate-stabilizing control system would tend to lose sensitivity and become ineffectual as a temperature-regulating mechanism. This may explain the relatively small differences in cloud reflectivity between the (polluted) northern and southern hemispheres (Schwartz, 1988). One might pose the question, "what, if any, role does this tendency for the feedback system to switch off (figure 16.5), or saturate, in the evolution of the proposed climate stabilization control system?"

The successful operation of the phytoplankton DMS-CCN-cloud-temperature control system depends on the sensitivity of changes of DMS emissions to alterations in planetary temperature. These are not known for the ocean environment, but are of the correct magnitude for marshes and wetlands.

Acknowledgment

This research was supported by grants from the National Science Foundation (DPP 86-20395) and from the Office of Naval Research (N00014-86-K-0055).

References

Aitken, J. 1888. On the numbered dust particles in the atmosphere. Reprinted in Knott, C.G., ed. *Collected Scientific Papers of John Aitken*. Cambridge: Cambridge University Press, 39.

Andreae, M.O., and Raemdonck, H. 1983. Dimethyl sulfide in the surface ocean and the marine atmosphere: A general view. *Science*, 221, 744–747.

Bates, T.S., Cline, J.D., Gammon, R.H., and Kelly-Hansen, S.R. 1987. Regional and seasonal variation in the flux of oceanic dimethyl sulfide to the atmosphere. *J Geophys Res*, 92, 2930–2938.

Bigg, E.K. 1986a. Discrepancy between observation and prediction of concentrations of cloud condensation nuclei. *Atmos Res*, 20, 82–86.

Bigg, E.K. 1986b. Technique for studying the chemistry of cloud condensation nuclei. *Atmos Res*, 20, 75–80.

Bodhaine, B. 1983. Aerosol measurements at four background sites. *J Geophys Res*, 88, 10,753–10,768.

Charlson, R.J., Lovelock, J.E., Andreae, M.O., and Warren, S.G. 1987. Oceanic phytoplankton, atmospheric sulfur, cloud albedo and climate; a geophysiological feedback. *Nature*, 326, 655–661.

Cunningham, W.C., and Zoller, W.H. 1981. The chemical composition of remote area aerosols. *J Aerosol Sci*, 12, 367–384.

Jenssen, D. 1988. A simple energy-balance model. Parkville, Victoria 3052, Australia; Meteorology Department, University of Melbourne.

Howell, W.E. 1949. The growth of cloud droplets in uniformly cooled air. *J Meteorol*, 6, 127–132.

Jaenicke, R. 1980. Natural aerosols. *Ann N Y Acad Sci*, 338, 317–329.

Junge, G.E. 1960. Sulfur in the atmosphere. *J Geophys Res*, 65, 227.

Landsberg, H. 1938. Atmospheric condensation nuclei. *Ergebn Kosm Phys*, 3, 155.

Lovelock, J.E., Maggs, J., and Rasmussen, R.A. 1972. Atmospheric dimethyl-sulphide and the natural sulfur cycle. *Nature*, 237, 452–453.

Lovelock, J.E., and Margulis, L. 1974. Atmospheric homeostasis by and for the biosphere: The Gaia hypothesis. *Tellus*, 26, 1–10.

Lovelock, J.E., and Whitfield, M. 1982. Life span of the biosphere. *Nature*, 296, 561–563.

Maroulis, P.J., and Bandy, A.R. 1977. Estimate of the contribution of biologically produced dimethyl sulfide to the global sulfur cycle. *Science*, 96, 647–648.

McDonald, J.E. 1958. The physics of cloud modification. *Adv Geophys*, 5, New York: Academic Press, 223–303.

Mesazaros, E. 1988. On the possible role of the biosphere in the control of atmospheric clouds and precipitation. *Atmos Env*, 22, 423–424.

North, G.R., Cahalan, R.F., and Coakley, J.A. 1981. Energy balance climate models. *Rev Geophys Space Physics*, 19, 91–121.

Nguyen, B.C., Gaudry, A., Bonsang, B., and Lambert, G. 1978. Re-evaluation of the role of dimethyl sulphide in the sulfur budget. *Nature*, 275, 637–639.

Ramanathan, V., Cess, R.D., Harrison, E.F., Minnis, P., Barkstrom, B.R., Ahmad, E., and Hartmann, D. 1989. Cloud-radiative forcing and climate: Results from the earth radiation budget experiment. *Science*, 243, 57–63.

Rasmussen, R.A. 1974. Emission of biogenic hydrogen sulfide. *Tellus*, 26, 254–260.

Schneider, S.H. 1972. Cloudiness as a global climatic feedback mechanism: The effects on the radiation balance and surface temperature variations in cloudiness. *J Atmos Sci*, 29, 1413–1422.

Schwartz, S.E. 1988. Are global cloud albedo and climate controlled by marine phytoplankton? *Nature*, 336, 441–445.

Shaw, G.E. 1983. Bio-controlled thermostasis involving the sulfur cycle. *Climatic Change*, 5, 297–303.

Shaw, G.E. 1986a. Aerosols as climate regulators: A climate-biosphere linkage? *Atmos Env*, 20, 985–986.

Twomey, S. 1959. The nuclei of natural cloud formation. *Geofis Pura Appl*, 43, 227–249.

Twomey, S. 1963. Measurements of natural cloud nuclei. *J Rech Atmos*, 1, 101–105.

Twomey, S. 1965. Size measurements of natural cloud nuclei. *J Rech Atmos*, 4, 113–119.

Twomey, S. 1971. The composition of cloud nuclei. *J Atmos Sci*, 28, 377–381.

Twomey, S. 1974. Pollution and the planetary albedo. *Atmos Env*, 8, 1251–1256.

Twomey, S. 1977a. *Atmospheric Aerosols*. Amsterdam: Elsevier Scientific Pub. Co.

Twomey, S. 1977b. On the minimum size of particles for nucleation in clouds. *J Atmos Sci*, 34, 1832–1835.

Twomey, S., Piegrass, M., and Wolfe, T.L. 1984. An assessment of the impact of pollution on global cloud albedo. *Tellus*, 36b, 356–366.

Wilson, C.T.R. 1897. Condensation of water vapour in the presence of dust-free air and other gases. *Phil Trans Roy Soc*, A191, 311–353.

Appendix A: On the Assumption of Soluble Salts for the Cloud Condensation Nuclei

Bigg (1986a) found in comparing measured CCN spectra with those calculated, like we did, from the measured aerosol distribution that the proportion of CCN in the total is often less than unity, except when the air is very clean. Because fewer than 1% of the particles were wholly insoluble, Bigg suggested that the discrepancies between predicted and observed CCN might be due to adsorbed surface-active organic compounds associated with the nuclei; diffusion chamber experiments, using cyclohexane vapor (Bigg, 1986b) were confirmatory. When the particle concentration was low, however, less than a few hundred per cubic centimeter as it is likely to be over the central oceans, the calculated and directly observed CCN spectra were in substantial agreement. Thus there is at least some reason to believe that the CCN spectra that we calculated from measured aerosol size distributions in clean air (e.g., figure 16.4) are reasonably accurate, but those calculated for dirtier conditions may be in error.

Robert J. Charlson

17

Atmospheric Sulfur from Oceanic Phytoplankton Versus Sulfur from Industry: Which Dominates Cloud Condensation Nuclei?

Historical Notes

The substance of the arguments proposing a hypothetical feedback system appear in Charlson and colleagues' 1987 study in *Nature*. To give proper credits, I should say that this article came about when Jim Lovelock was at the University of Washington giving a series of lectures in 1984. He came to me and said, "The faculty of your institution are giving me a very hard time because I don't have any specific mechanisms for the Gaia hypothesis. You work on aerosols, what do you have? Do you believe this work by Glenn Shaw (1983)?" I said, "Yes, Glenn Shaw's numbers on radiative effect are correct. The only problem is that we need an amplifier. There is just not quite enough sulfate aerosol presently up there in the unpolluted atmosphere to have an effect itself on the albedo of the earth." Jim asked what kind of amplifier I might have in mind. I replied that Twomey (1977) proposed via theoretical calculations that clouds might do that, at which point we dug into this line of thinking. Later we asked Andi Andreae, "How do we know that the natural, marine non–sea salt sulfate aerosol comes almost exclusively from phytoplankton?" His reply (summarized in the preceding chapter) was convincing and we invited him to be a coauthor. Still later, Steve Warren came up to me after a seminar and said I could make a lot stronger case if I would use a real cloud distribution. My reply was "Steve, do it!" and he also became a coauthor. So this is very much an interdisciplinary, team project.

Atmospheric Aerosol and Cloud Condensation Nuclei

The atmospheric aerosol is depicted as a multimodal distribution in figure 17.1. This plot of the distribution of the number, surface, and volume on their three ordinates against the log of size on the abscissa is such that the areas under the curves are proportional to the total number population, surface, and volume concentrations, respectively.

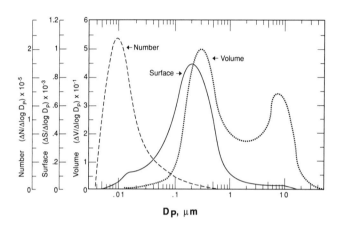

Figure 17.1 Normalized plots of number, surface, and volume distributions for a tropospheric aerosol. D_P is the particle diameter in μm.

What we see first is that the number populations of these systems (whether they are marine or continental) is dominated by very different sizes than either surface or volume. When we examine the volume concentration, we see in almost all situations (both continental and marine) a bimodal distribution with one mode that is submicrometer in size and another mode that is supermicrometer. We also now know that these two modes are composed of chemically different species. In the marine atmosphere, which I focus on here, the larger mode is mainly sea salt, and some very small amounts of continental soil dust and some non–sea salt sulfate (nss–$SO_4^=$). The submicrometer mode is composed primarily of acidic nss–$SO_4^=$ and some methanesulfonic acid (CH_3SO_3H).

Although the bimodal mass or volume distribution was first proposed for urban pollution (Whitby et al., 1972), this distribution actually is seen in unpolluted, remote marine settings. This is demonstrated by a variety of data showing a mass peak of approximately 400 nm in particle diameter, a minimum at approximately 1.0 μm, and then an increasing mass or volume of material above that size. The mass concentration inferred from the volume distri-

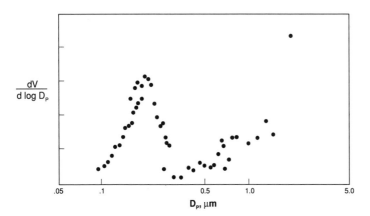

Figure 17.2 Volume distribution of aerosol observed aboard the Soviet research vessel *Korolev*, 24 November 1983. Location 10°S, 135°W. Diameter in micrometers, vertical axis in arbitrary units. Total submicrometer mass concentration is approximately 1 μg/m³. (From Clarke, 1983.) D_p is particle diameter in μm.

bution taken on the Soviet vessel *Korolev* at 10°S,135°W by Clarke (1983) (figure 17.2) could not be explained by pollution from a continental area because it is too far from industrial sources in the Northern Hemisphere. The total sub-μm mass concentration of nss–$SO_4^=$ in figure 17.2 is about 1 μg/m³.

Another important variable is the cloud condensation nuclei (CCN). If pure water were to condense in the atmosphere, it would effectively require a very large supersaturation. Figure 17.3 is a plot of the relative humidity against the droplet size (on a log scale) in which pure water exhibits the so-called Kelvin effect, that is, the increase of vapor pressure of water due to radius of curvature. Water-soluble CCN such as the sulfates that we find in the atmosphere or sodium chloride from sea salt provide the needed solute mass to depress vapor pressure and provide curves as in the rest of figure 17.3. This represents the condensation nucleus theory proposed by Swedish scientist Koehler (1936). I refer to a CCN as a particle of water-soluble material that allows the formation of droplets with typical water supersaturations of a very small fraction of a percent.

Marine Cloud Condensation Nuclei and Cloud Albedo

It is necessary to present a few facts to counter some of the ancient lore in the meteorological literature. First, in marine air, which is most of the atmosphere, there are not enough sea salt particles to explain the measured population of the aerosol itself or of the cloud droplets, typically by a factor of

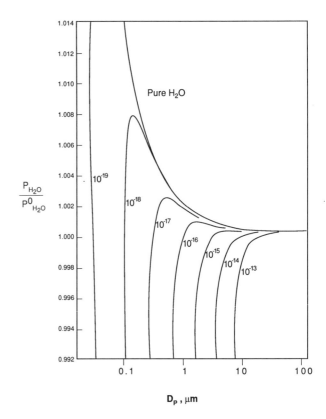

Figure 17.3 The Koehler curves describing relative humidity, $P_{H_2O}/P_{H_2O}°$ over a water droplet as a function of radius, *r*. *im/M* is given as the parameter, where *i* is the van't Hoff factor, *m* is soluble mass, and *M* is molecular weight of solute. D_p is the droplet diameter in μm.

149

Atmospheric Sulfur from Oceanic Phytoplankton Versus Sulfur from Industry: Which Dominates Cloud Condensation Nuclei?

100 or so. In clean marine clouds like the ones we have today, we find something of the order of 100 droplets per cubic centimeter with considerable variability. Typically, the sodium chloride particle concentration is 1 cm^{-3}, such that there must be some other particles present to nucleate the formation of droplets.

The second point is one which Steve Warren and I have traced to the excellent old book *Physics of Rain Clouds* by Fletcher (1966). It is the likely source of the generalization around meteorological circles that there is always an overabundance of particles to act as CCN. That is true in polluted continental air (e.g., Los Angeles or San Diego) but it is not true in the most remote places in the marine atmosphere. There, the total number population often is close to 100 cm^{-3}, a significant fraction of which are observed to be CCN. This point I must attribute to Keith Bigg (1986), who is among the few people who have made a significant number of measurements of CCN in remote marine locations.

The next point (which definitely is not archaic) is that climatologically important properties of clouds, particularly their albedo, are calculated to be strongly influenced by CCN populations. The sense of this is given thoroughly in the last chapter of Twomey's (1977) book on atmospheric aerosols. We see a set of sigmoid curves (to a chemist, shapes like titration curves) in which the albedo curves increase to unity and flatten out for very thick clouds and decrease and flatten out to zero for thin clouds, as in figure 17.4. The parameter here separating the three curves is the droplet population, which is calculated at factors of eight apart (that is, factors of

two in mean droplet size). These numerical calculations that Twomey (1977) did thus present rather large changes in droplet populations; but the sense of the result is that for a given physical depth of clouds, if we increase the particle population, we increase the albedo. What struck Jim Lovelock and me the day we looked this up was that, for clouds like marine stratus in the range of thicknesses of 0.1 to 1 km, even a small change in the droplet number population could produce a large change in the albedo of the cloud. It appears to be very sensitive indeed. Because this idea for the sensitivity of albedo to CCN was largely explored by Twomey, we suggest it should be known as the *Twomey cloud brightening effect*.

Finally, the point Andreae made in chapter 16 is that the marine non–sea salt sulfate for the CCN appears to be produced almost exclusively from a biological source in the ocean and particularly from some species of phytoplankton. There are a number of lines of evidence to support the notion that the marine CCN are sulfates, although some of this evidence is circumstantial. Certainly more data are needed, and they are not easy data to acquire. I think there are, for example, only four or five working CCN instruments in the United States and not many more in the entire world. The community of people who do these measurements is very small. But we know that in the cleanest marine locations the number concentration of particles is comparable to the number of CCN observed, for example, with a cloud chamber, and most of the submicrometer mass is $SO_4^=$ (Bigg, 1986). The chemical composition of rain in remote locations is not that of car-

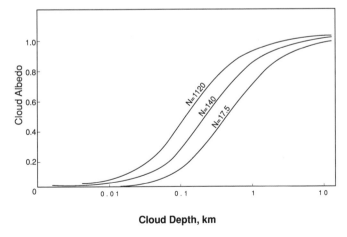

Figure 17.4 The Twomey cloud brightening effect. Cloud albedo is plotted versus cloud depth (log axis) with cloud droplet population N as a parameter. Liquid water content is 0.3 g/m^3. (From Twomey, 1977.)

bonic acid with a little salt thrown in, but precipitation in remote locations has sulfuric acid in it. The amount of sulfuric acid, typically about 10 μm, is about the amount one would get from nucleation scavenging of the submicrometer acidic sulfate aerosol that I mentioned previously.

Another line of evidence, also from Twomey (1971), is that most marine CCN are heat labile and lose the property of being able to produce droplets above about 300°C. This also implies that the CCN cannot be sea salt because sodium chloride is not heat labile at 300°C. And finally, the sulfate concentration from chemical analyses is a large fraction (half or so) of the submicrometer mass.

A Possible Feedback Loop

This leads us again to follow around the feedback loop that Andreae proposed in the previous chapter (figure 17.5) starting with marine phytoplankton, which are ubiquitous, excreting dimethylsulfide (DMS). This escapes to the air, makes sulfate and some methane sulfonate (with a typical mass concentration of non–sea salt sulfate of a fraction of a microgram per cubic meter and a number popula-

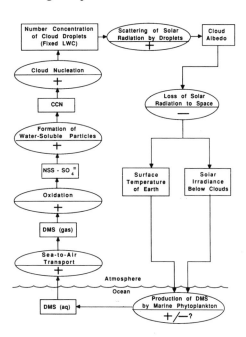

Figure 17.5 Hypothetical feedback loop. The rectangles are measurable quantities and the ovals are processes linking the boxes. The sign (+/−) in the oval indicates the effect of a positive change of the quantity in the preceding box on that in the succeeding one. The most uncertain link is the effect of cloud albedo on DMS emission; its sign would have to be positive in order to provide a degree of thermostasis. Of course, the +/− could be zero as well.

tion of a few hundred cm^{-3} or perhaps even less). This is found everywhere in the marine atmosphere and, as far as we know, DMS is the only source. The same excess or non–sea salt sulfate is the main component of the CCN. The next most abundant materials apparently are condensed organics that during some other climatological epoch might very well have been another biological source of CCN. Cloud condensation nuclei are necessary for clouds as we know them and are important in determining cloud albedo. The most important type of clouds that we have today are marine stratus, stratocumulus, altostratus, and altocumulus, which altogether cover about 20% to 25% of the earth's surface. Taking that fraction of the earth, if we take Twomey's calculation and increase the particle population only over the ocean by a factor of 8 it would cool the entire globe by 6° (Charlson et al., 1987). A change of the CCN population of ± 30%, again only over the ocean, was calculated by Warren to yield a change in the surface temperature of the whole globe of ±1°K, so that even very small changes in the particle population (if they cause a change in the marine cloud droplet population) are calculated to be a very major feature of terrestrial climate. This leads then to the notion of a feedback system that Andreae has presented.

Proposal of an Hypothesis

This also leads to some conclusions. First of all, if DMS emissions stopped (e.g., if we killed off the DMS-producing phytoplankton), the earth would become several degrees warmer. This might happen, for example, if the cocoliths and dinoflagellates were replaced by diatoms (i.e., if species of phytoplankton changed). The sensitivity of the CCN control of cloud albedo appears to be strong enough, for example, to have mediated climate in the past. There is so much sulfate in seawater that it is never limiting. Thus in principle there could be large swings in the production of DMS and the population of CCN that could force substantial changes in climate. We must not assume that the sulfur cycle has been constant for all time. This allows us, then, to pose a hypothesis that is the goal that Jim Lovelock wanted us to provide 5 years ago. The hypothesis is that non–sea salt sulfate in particles derived from biologically generated DMS are the primary CCN in the remote unpolluted atmosphere and that they are climatologically significant.

151

Atmospheric Sulfur from Oceanic Phytoplankton Versus Sulfur from Industry: Which Dominates Cloud Condensation Nuclei?

Tests of the Hypothesis

This is a testable hypothesis; or rather, these are testable hypotheses. A number of tests can be proposed for which simultaneous observations of cloud albedo, aerosol particles, DMS, and so forth are needed. Characterizing the system both physically and chemically will help us understand it more fully. We must examine seasonal variations because seasonal variations are in fact a regular climate change that can help us understand the dynamic behavior of the system. We must track isotopically the sulfur atoms in the sulfur cycle to make sure that indeed it is the sulfur from DMS that we find in the CCN. We believe that is the case, but we must verify it with a tracer.

Finally, a very exciting experiment that I hope we will be able to do is to add an aerosolgenic gas (Lovelock suggested that SO_3 could be used) to add particles to the planetary boundary and look for albedo changes in the stratus clouds. Coakley and colleagues (1987) performed an uncontrolled version of this experiment by observing the influence of ship-stack effluents on the radiative properties of marine stratus clouds. They compared the enhancement of albedo in visible wavelengths with Twomey's calculations and found there is indeed a sensitivity to the addition of particles. While to some degree this was an uncontrolled experiment, it is possible to perform a controlled experiment, including a full characterization of the aerosol particles acting as CCN.

There are some important gaps in our understanding, and Andreae has already mentioned the biological ones in the preceding chapter. We need clearer proof that water-soluble organics presently are not also important as a component of CCN. Even if they are, they are still from a biological source and might very well be involved in another kind of feedback system. We need an understanding of the relationship of DMS to changes in climate. We need an understanding of the relationship of CCN population to the DMS concentration and flux. We need to understand more about the relationship to cloud albedo because it is a very important quantity in the overall climate equation. We would like to know if CCN influence cloud cover or cloud droplet lifetime, and we need to know if albedo is the only effect that these particles have or whether there are effects, for example, on the hydrological cycle. We need to understand the sensitivity of CCN populations to changes in the aerosol

concentration, both with mass and number. Finally, we need to know how the marine sulfur cycle has changed, both over climatological time and due to the addition of pollution sulfur, which is my last point.

Industrial Sulfur Dioxide as a Source of Cloud Condensation Nuclei

Figure 17.6 plots the emission of industrial SO_2 sulfur in teragrams of sulfur per year from 1860 to the present. The quantity is now about 100 teragrams (100 Tg = 100 megatons) of sulfur annually. I have made some estimates to compare with figure 17.6 of the natural source strength—these are presented as wide stripes to indicate uncertainty ranges. Presently, the global total emission of DMS sulfur plus volcanic sulfur and biologically produced sulfur is approximately 60 Tg, such that (on a global basis), the anthropogenic sulfur is roughly of the same magnitude as the natural sulfur. In a given year, of course, this could be radically different if we had another volcano like El Chichon, which was estimated to itself have produced about 10 Tg of sulfur, demonstrating that these are highly variable quantities. But it is not entirely relevant to consider these global figures because virtually all of the 100 Tg of SO_2-S emission is in the Northern Hemisphere. This emission can be assumed to have little or no influence on the Southern Hemisphere be-

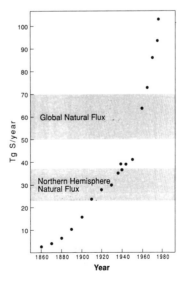

Figure 17.6 Change over time of the global emission of SO_2-S from anthropogenic sources. (From Ryaposhapko, 1983.)

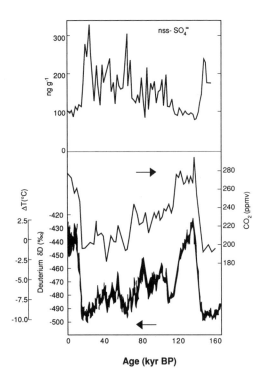

Figure 17.7 Variations with time of nss–SO$_4^=$ (top), CO$_2$ (middle), and deuterium inferred temperature (bottom) through the Wisconsin age. (From Legrand et al., 1988, and Barnola et al., 1987). kyrBP is age in kiloyears before present time.

cause the lifetime of these sulfur compounds in air is only days and the time to mix hemispheres is a year or more. I also estimate, for comparison with figure 17.6, that the Northern Hemispheric natural sulfur flux is around 30 Tg, such that at present, roughly three-quarters of the Northern Hemisphere sulfur budget is man-made. I think it is valid to ask what has this done to the aerosol particle concentrations and the CCN populations and, especially, what it has done to cloud albedo. Is there already a climatic forcing that we have not yet discovered?

Turning from changes produced by this anthropogenic sulfur to the natural variability of the system, figure 17.7 shows variation of nss–SO$_4^=$, CO$_2$ and temperature over approximately the last 160,000 years. First, the sulfur cycle seems to have been relatively constant through our present interglacial time, such that the anthropogenic change does not represent the usual magnitude of variability. Second, these sulfur compounds varied in synchrony with both temperature and CO$_2$, suggesting either a common cause or linked response or both. Third, sulfate was enhanced during the ice age, such that

if the DMS-CCN-albedo system had any effect it was not thermostatic (Legrand et al., 1988).

References

Barnola, J.M., Raynaud, D., Korutkevich, Y.S., and Lorius, C. 1987. Vostok ice-core provides a 160,000 year record of atmospheric CO$_2$. *Nature*, 329, 408–414.

Bigg, E.K. 1986. Discrepancies between observation and prediction of concentrations of cloud condensation nuclei. *Atmos Res*, 20, 82–86.

Charlson, R.J., Lovelock, J.E., Andreae, M.O. and Warren, S.G. 1987. Oceanic phytoplankton, atmospheric sulphur, cloud albedo and climate. *Nature*, 326, 655–661.

Clarke, A.D. 1983. Personal communication. Also in Charlson, R.J., Chameides, W.L., and Kley, D. The transformation of sulfur and nitrogen in the remote atmosphere: Background paper. In: Galloway, J.N., Charlson, R.J., Andreae, M.O., and Rodke, H.,eds. 1985. *The Biogeochemical Cycling of Sulphur and Nitrogen in the Remote Atmosphere*. Dordrecht: Reidel, 67–82.

Coakley, J.A., Jr., Bernstein, R.L., and Durkee, P.A. 1987. Effect of ship-stack effluents on cloud reflectivity. *Science*, 237, 1020–1022.

Fletcher, N.H. 1966. *The Physics of Rainclouds*. Cambridge: Cambridge University Press.

Koehler, H. 1936. The nucleus in and growth of hygroscopic droplets. *Trans Faraday Soc*, 32, 1152.

Legrand, M.R., Delmas, R.J., and Charlson, R.J. 1988. Climate forcing implications from Vostok ice-core sulphate data. *Nature*, 334, 418–419.

Ryaposhapko, A.G. 1983. The atmospheric sulphur cycle, SCOPE 19. In: Ivanov, M.W., and Fressey, J.R., eds. *The Global Biogeochemical Sulphur Cycle*. Chichester: John Wiley.

Shaw, G.E. 1983. Bio-controlled thermostasis involving the sulfur cycle. *Climatic Change*, 5, 297–303.

Twomey, S.A. 1971. The composition of cloud nuclei. *J Atmos Sci*, 28, 377–381.

Twomey, S.A. 1977. *Atmospheric Aerosols*. Amsterdam: Elsevier.

Whitby, K.T., Husar, R.B., and Liu, B.Y.H. 1972. The aerosol size distribution of Los Angeles smog. *J Colloid Interface Sci*, 39, 177–204.

Ken Caldeira
18
Evolutionary Pressures on Planktonic Dimethylsulfide Production

The term *Gaia hypothesis* has been used to refer to a wide variety of hypotheses, ranging from an optimizing global homeostasis by and for the biosphere (Lovelock and Margulis, 1974) to the idea that life has been important in the evolution of the earth's atmosphere and climate. To the question, "Is the Gaia Hypothesis true?" the appropriate response has been, "What do you mean by *Gaia hypothesis?*" The central metaphor of the Gaia hypothesis is the statement: The earth is alive. All of us would be willing to say that trees are alive. Many would be willing to say that a forest is alive, even if the definition of *forest* includes air and soil, arguing that even the human body contains noncellular material. Some would say "The earth is alive" is literally true, others would say that there are sufficient parallels between archetypical living things (bacteria, clams, humans) and the planet Earth to give the statement metaphoric truth, and others would say the statement is false, literally and metaphorically. Questions about the truth of this statement fall into at least two categories: questions about the planet Earth and questions about the meaning of the word *alive*.

In an effort to shift the discussion from semantics to matters of fact, Charlson and colleagues (1987) proposed a specific feedback loop involving cloud albedo and the planktonic emission of dimethylsulfide (DMS). Although it has been proposed that DMS-producing plankton produce DMS as a byproduct of some metabolic process that they carry out for reasons other than climate modification (Andreae, 1986), Charlson and colleagues (1987) suggested that climate modification and altruism (sacrificing individual benefits for the greater good) may have played a significant role in the evolution of planktonic DMS production. This suggestion is relevant to some of the stronger versions of the Gaia hypothesis, in which altruism or purposeful intent is expected to play a role. I here present several models representing the world of phytoplankton in evolutionary time in order to examine questions

such as: What are the trade-offs available to phytoplankton regarding DMS emission? How strong are the direct climatic benefits of emitting DMS? How do those benefits compare with the cost of producing DMS? What about altruism—might a plankter sacrifice some of its own well-being so that other plankton, or even elephants and giraffes, might enjoy a better life or reproduce more successfully? As with all models, these models are simplifications of reality and have implications for the real world only insofar as they capture the salient features of the modeled processes.

Osmoregulation: A Plausible Explanation for Planktonic Dimethylsulfide Production

A known mechanism could explain all or part of the observed phytoplankton DMS emission. To balance the high osmotic pressure of seawater, phytoplankton produce osmostatic and osmoregulatory substances. Andreae (1986) suggests that dimethylsulfonium propionate (DMSP), a DMS-precursor, has the properties of good osmolyte, and might be selected for use as an osmolyte in regions where nitrogen may be limiting phytoplankton growth. The use of a sulfur-based osmolyte would make bound nitrogen available for other purposes such as making amino acids. Intracellular DMSP varies with the salinity of the ambient seawater in a way that is consistent with its hypothesized role as an osmoregulator (Vairavamurthy et al., 1985). Further evidence that DMS release is a byproduct of DMSP production can be found in the fact that the rate of DMS release increases greatly during the senescence phase of phytoplankton blooms (Nguyen et al., 1988), and when phytoplankton are subjected to grazing by zooplankton (Dacey and Wakeham, 1986), indicating that much DMS release is a consequence of loss of cellular integrity.

I am primarily concerned here with a question suggested by Charlson and colleagues (1987): Could climate feedbacks or altruism have been significant factors in the evolution of DMS emission? There-fore, I set aside for the moment internal metabolic reasons (e.g., osmoregulation) for producing DMS, in order to examine possible evolutionary roles of climate feedbacks and altruism. In this chapter, un-less I am specifically referring to osmoregulation, discussion of DMS production refers to DMS pro-duction for climate modification, that is, DMS production in excess of that which is needed for osmoregulation or other internal metabolic processes.

A Sense of the Word *Cost*
That Makes Sense for Phytoplankton

Conceptual problems are associated with assessing the costs or benefits of something whose value is nonmonetary, whether it is the cost to society of a fouled environment or the benefit to an individual of a good novel. The problem is that there is no common unit of exchange, no measure which non-arbitrarily applies to all things we may value. So how can we sensibly apply a quantitative measure of costs and benefits to plankton? I assume, for the purposes of this chapter, that we may think of plankton primarily in evolutionary terms, and that by *cost* we mean *cost to Darwinian fitness*, that is, cost to the planker's reproductive success. Modi-fying the definition of Uyenoyama and Feldman (1980) to include the time dimension, *Darwinian fit-ness* may be defined for a set of individuals as the average number of offspring surviving to reproduce per individual in that set per unit time, which may be measured in units of doublings per day. Under this definition, anything that enhances a planker's ability to reproduce is considered a benefit. The concept of *fitness* provides a nonarbitrary measure allowing us to compare the possible climatic bene-fits of increased cloud condensation nuclei (CCN) number with the metabolic costs of producing DMS. Note that Darwinian fitness is far easier to define than it is to measure in practice, and that myriad factors control the fitness of an organism. Note also that the notion of Darwinian fitness ig-nores any possible esthetic or moral benefits that plankton may enjoy. Whereas such considerations should be important in a human calculus, we are concerned here with evolutionary paths that may have led to mid-ocean DMS production, therefore fitness, and not moral or esthetic well-being, is the measure of interest.

The Cost to Phytoplankton of
Producing Dimethylsulfide

How do we estimate the cost of producing DMS? A first approach might be to measure the cell's DMS carbon output relative to the amount of carbon needed to produce a new cell. Unfortunately, car-bon certainly is not the appropriate unit of measure, because the availability of light (in high latitudes), phosphate, nitrate (Broecker and Peng, 1982), or iron (Martin and Fitzwater, 1988) limits phytoplank-ton growth, and carbon is ubiquitous in the surface waters of the ocean, as are the other elements in DMS, hydrogen and sulfur (Broecker and Peng, 1982). Given that the materials in DMS may be vir-tually "free" in the world's oceans, the cost of mak-ing DMS may be largely the cost of constructing the cellular machinery that makes DMS. Because the details of that machinery are largely unknown at this time (Andreae, 1986), it is difficult to estimate the cost of its production. In addition, some of the biochemical pathways that lead to DMS production are also used to produce other biochemically im-portant compounds (Andreae, 1986), further com-plicating any cost assessment effort.

With these considerable caveats in mind, I pro-ceed. Based on the examination of two species of phytoplankton, about one part in 3700 (2.7×10^{-4}) of the cell's carbon is emitted, on average, in the form of DMS each day (Caldeira, 1989). For the sake of further discussion, I take the cost of DMS production to be at least one part in 10^7 of the cell's total metabolic effort, that is, I assume that if a cell could reap all the benefits of producing DMS with-out bearing the costs, the cell would experience 10^{-7} additional doublings per day. My argument is relatively insensitive to the exact value chosen for this parameter, as long as this estimate is within several orders of magnitude of the actual cost of DMS production.

The Direct Climatic Benefits to Groups and
Individuals of Producing Dimethylsulfide

It is as difficult to assess the climatic benefits of DMS production as it is the metabolic costs. The relationship between DMS emission and cloudiness remains unclear (Bates et al., 1987; Schwartz, 1988; Savoie and Prospero, 1989). Charlson and col-leagues (1987) suggest several possible climatic ben-efits of DMS emission, including shielding from solar ultraviolet radiation and increased nitrogen flux to the surface waters through increased rainfall. However, the question is still open whether the proposed DMS-climatic feedback loop is a positive factor in phytoplankton growth (Charlson et al., 1987; Caldeira, 1989). Because we are unable to quantify the climatic feedback from DMS emission to phytoplankton growth rates, as an upper bound for the climatic benefits of DMS production I take the maximum observed oceanic growth rate for phytoplankton—about one doubling per day (Eppley, 1972).

If we accept the above numbers, 10^{-7} doublings day^{-1} as the cost, and 1 doubling day^{-1} as the benefit of DMS production, it seems that DMS production might be strongly selected for on evolutionary timescales, given that the benefit strongly outweighs the cost. However, this is not the case, because the cost of DMS production is borne by the individual phytoplankter, whereas most of the climate benefits of DMS production stem from being part of a group of DMS producers. What are the benefits to the individual plankter of the individual plankter's DMS production?

The relatively constant DMS concentration in the deep ocean suggests that DMS loss in seawater is a relatively slow process (Andreae, 1986). When DMS diffuses out of the sea surface into the atmosphere it is usually oxidized by OH or NO_3, with an estimated time constant from 14 hours (Hewitt and Davison, 1988) to 36 hours (Andreae, 1986). Some of the SO_2 produced by these processes is further oxidized into $SO_4^=$, with a time constant of about 17 hours (Andreae, 1986). It is the $SO_4^=$ particle that acts as the CCN, so there is on average at least 31 to 53 hours of diffusion and advection in the troposphere prior to the generation of a DMS-derived CCN. If we take the horizontal eddy diffusion coefficient for the troposphere, D, to be on the order of 10^6 m^2 s^{-1} (Bolin and Keeling, 1963) and a diffusion time, t, of about 30 hours, we have a scale area for the diffusion of DMS-derived CCN precursors of Dt, or about 10^{11} m^2. This suggests that plankton within a scale distance of 300 km would experience essentially the same cloudiness conditions with respect to biogenic releases of DMS. Because typical phytoplankton densities are on the order of 10^6 m^{-3} (Hulbert, 1962), and 100 m is a characteristic depth for the photic zone (Broecker and Peng, 1982), we have 10^{18} phytoplankton as the minimum group size that could consistently experience cloud-cover differentiation due to biogenic DMS releases. There-

fore, one plankter's emission or nonemission of DMS would, on average, change the overhead biogenic CCN number density on the order of one part in 10^{18}. If the benefits of CCN scale linearly with CCN number (or the benefits begin to saturate at high CCN numbers), and using our upper bound of one additional doubling day^{-1} due to the entire group's DMS emission, the benefit to an individual phytoplankter due to its own DMS emission is less than 10^{-18} doublings day^{-1}.

Based on the ideas of Maynard Smith (1982) we can state that at evolutionary equilibrium, the partial derivative of the cost of DMS production with respect to the individual DMS production rate ($\delta c/\delta r$) will equal the partial derivative of the benefits relative to the rate of production ($\delta b/\delta r$). To understand this, suppose that the differential cost is less than the differential benefit, that $\delta c/\delta r < \delta b/\delta r$. If this were the case, a mutant plankter that produced slightly more DMS would experience higher growth rate as a result of the higher production rate. Therefore this mutant would dominate the ecosystem on ecological time. The argument is similar for the mutant that produces less DMS in the case where $\delta c/\delta r > \delta b/\delta r$. Because in both of these situations the system is unstable with respect to mutants with slight variation in DMS production rate, the system is not in evolutionary equilibrium. Thus if planktonic DMS production were maintained by climatic feedbacks through individual selection, we would have, at evolutionary equilibrium, $\delta c/\delta r = \delta b/\delta r$. Given the above cost estimate and assuming that the costs of DMS production, to first order, scale linearly with DMS production, we can estimate that $\delta c/\delta r$ is on the order of 10^{-7} per mean daily DMS emission. If we make similar assumptions with respect to the benefits of biogenic CCN, we have $\delta c/\delta r$ on the order of 10^{-18} per mean daily DMS emission. The fact that $\delta c/\delta r$ differs from $\delta b/\delta r$ by approximately 10 orders of magnitude strongly suggests that DMS production for climate modification is not an evolutionarily stable strategy (Smith, 1982). The problem is that phytoplankton that do not produce DMS for the purpose of climate modification will experience essentially the same conditions as nearby DMS producers. While experiencing the same conditions, the non–DMS producers could apply more of the available resources to growth and reproduction than climate-modifying DMS producers and would therefore have a higher reproductive rate. Because the non–DMS producers would reproduce more rapidly, the non–DMS producers would dominate the DMS producers' ecological niches on ecological timescales.

Can Altruism or Group Selection Explain Planktonic Dimethylsulfide Emission?

Altruism, the giving up of fitness by an individual in order to increase the fitness of others (Hamilton, 1975), has evolved. We have all heard tales of someone giving up his or her life in order to save the lives of others (for reviews, see Grafen, 1984, and Nunney 1985). Could not altruism have evolved in the case of midocean DMS production for climate modification? Could not groups of DMS producers replicate so much more rapidly than groups of non–DMS producers that the non–DMS producers would be overwhelmed? Could not the group advantage of producing DMS for climate modulation be more evolutionarily significant than the within-group ecological disadvantage? Charlson and colleagues (1987) suggest that excess DMS production (i.e., DMS production for climate modification) may have evolved during periods of higher salt stress, such as glacial epochs, and that present levels of DMS emission may be maintained because groups that emit DMS are at a selective advantage. The problem with this strategy is that DMS-producing groups would be subject to invasion by non–DMS producers, which would then dominate the group of DMS producers on ecological timescales. Three possible resolutions to this "selfish-invader problem" are: (1) the DMS-producers could police themselves against invasion by non–DMS producers; (2) the groups could intermix and reform on a timescale shorter than the timescale of ecological succession; or (3) groups of DMS producers might send out migrants to groups containing non–DMS producers, so that the immigration rate plus internal growth rate for DMS producers exceeds that for non–DMS producers. Examination of these strategies suggests that the conditions necessary for the evolution of altruistic DMS production have not existed on earth.

First, if the DMS producers had some way of policing themselves, of destroying non–DMS producers, then DMS production would confer a higher probability of survival and reproductive success, and therefore increase individual fitness and not be an altruistic trait (Nunney, 1985).

Regarding the second possibility, assume that the growth rate of any group is a function of the number of altruists in each group. If we randomly divide the population of phytoplankton into groups, the groups with more altruists will grow more rapidly. However, given a nonzero initial nonaltruist population, the nonaltruists would dominate any group on the timescale of ecological succession. One possible resolution to this problem is to have the groups intermix and reform on a timescale shorter than that of ecological succession, so that before the nonaltruists can dominate any group, there is a new set of groups. A number of workers have investigated models based on this mechanism (Charnov and Krebs, 1975; Hamilton, 1975; Wilson, 1975; Nunney, 1985) (figure 18.1). If a_i is the growth rate of altruistic DMS producers and s_i is the growth rate of the selfish non–DMS producers in group i in doublings day^{-1}, then $a_i < s_i$ for all i. If S_i and A_i are the number of nonaltruists and altruists, respectively, in group i, then the growth rate of altruists over all groups is

$$(\frac{1}{\sum_i A_i})\sum_i A_i a_i$$

and for nonaltruists,

$$(\frac{1}{\sum_i S_i})\sum_i S_i s_i$$

If altruists are to be selected for on evolutionary time scales we need

$$(\frac{1}{\sum_i A_i})\sum_i A_i a_i > (\frac{1}{\sum_i S_i})\sum_i S_i s_i$$

even though for all i, $a_i < s_i$. Given the high number density of phytoplankton in the ocean, random division of phytoplankton into groups will not generate the suprabinomial distributions necessary for this mechanism to work. For this process to function consistently and repeatedly, we need an assortive mechanism, a trait that results in altruists being grouped with altruists. But this trait itself would confer a selective advantage and therefore not be altruistic. If DMS production for climate modulation results in getting grouped with other climate-modifying DMS producers, then this trait would confer higher reproductive success, increase individual fitness, and therefore not be altruistic (Nunney, 1985).

Regarding the third possibility, Wright (1945) sug-

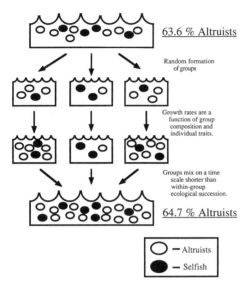

63.6 % Altruists

Random formation
of groups

Growth rates are a
function of group
composition and
individual traits.

Groups mix on a time
scale shorter than
within-group
ecological succession.

64.7 % Altruists

○ — Altruists

● — Selfish

Figure 18.1 A possible way that altruists might experience a higher growth rate than nonaltruists overall even though altruists never experience a higher growth rate than neighboring non-altruists. Note that in the groups composed of three-fourths altruists the altruist population increases by 60%, whereas the nonaltruists increase by 100%. In order for this process to function, the groups must consistently remix before the nonaltruists ecologically succeed the altruists, and the initial partitioning into groups must repeatedly and consistently produce suprabinomial distributions of altruists and nonaltruists (Nunney, 1985). Therefore this mechanism does not function in the case of midocean DMS production.

gested that groups containing many altruists may emit more migrants than groups of nonaltruists, so that groups may tend to get more altruist migrants than nonaltruist migrants. Even though in any group, $a_i < s_i$, perhaps the altruist growth rate, a_i, plus the altruist net immigration rate exceeds the selfish growth rate, s_i, plus the selfish net immigration rate. In an effort to criticize Dawkins' (1976) theory based on genic selfishness, Harpending and Rogers (1987) examined a discrete-time model based on Wright's ideas, and concluded that altruism is favored by weak local selection, c, against altruism, strong group beneficial effect, g, and small local size, n. Their results suggest that altruists can achieve nonzero frequency when $n + 1 < g/c$. But, above, we estimated n to be on the order of 10^{18} and c to be on the order of 10^{-7}. This suggests that for altruistic DMS production to be selected by this process, the group beneficial effect would have to be on the order of 10^{11}, that is, groups composed entirely of altruists would have to emit 10^{11} times as many migrants as groups composed of nonaltruists. This is an implausibly high differential.

Conclusions and Discussion

In this I have examined the suggestion that climate feedbacks and altruism may have been significant factors in the evolution of DMS emission by marine phytoplankton, and conclude that neither climate feedbacks nor altruism could have been significant factors in the evolution of midocean DMS production. The need of plankton to regulate internal osmotic pressure provides a sufficient explanation for the planktonic production of DMS precursors.

The problem of osmoregulation supplies us with a possible analogue of the proposed temperature regulation by phytoplankton. Faced with the high osmolarity of seawater ($\sim$1.1 mol L^{-1}) and the need for osmotic balance across the cell membrane, evolution proceeded in such a way as to maintain this balance through the development of mechanisms for maintaining internal osmotic homeostasis. But perhaps evolution could have gone the other way. Maybe the plankton could have adopted the strategy of trying to excrete substances to reduce the osmolarity of the surrounding seawater. But, because of the diffusive properties of seawater and the small size of phytoplankton relative to the size of the ocean, any individual phytoplankter would little feel the effects of its own effort. And, because of diffusion, any "cheats" that did not expend resources on this venture would also experience the benefits of this lower osmolarity without paying the costs, and thus would experience a higher growth rate and eventually dominate the ecosystem.

Similarly, it is possible that phytoplankton could find themselves in too warm an environment. In evolutionary time, phytoplankton could respond to this challenge in a number of ways. The population could migrate poleward—in an ocean characterized by eddies on all scales, unobstructed by physical barriers, the more poleward segments of the population would experience cooler temperatures and higher growth rates, thus encouraging this poleward expansion. Or the phytoplankton could evolve mechanisms to alleviate the thermal stress. The costs of such an effort would be borne by the individual plankter, but unlike DMS production for temperature regulation, the benefits would accrue to the individual undertaking the effort. But the idea that the plankton would respond to a thermal challenge through an effort to modify global climate is an idea wanting in mechanisms. If plankton play a role in global thermal homeostasis through the proposed DMS-cloud-albedo feedback (Schwartz,

1988; Savoie and Prospero, 1989), it is probably a consequence of plankton's need for internal osmolar homeostasis.

It may be that we find ourselves in a world replete with stabilizing feedbacks, many of them involving biological mechanisms. If this is the case, the evolution of those biological mechanisms need not be explained in terms of those stabilizing feedbacks, even though their persistence might be explained in those terms. As Prigogine and Stengers (1984) suggest, unstable systems do not persist for long periods of time, whereas stable systems do. If we rank all systems ever evolved in terms of stability, the ones in existence at any given time will more than likely, almost tautologically, be the more stable ones, which would be systems more likely to have stabilizing feedbacks. Thus if the DMS-cloud-albedo feedback loop does modulate climatic fluctuations and climatic fluctuations increase the probability of species extinction, then the existence of such a stabilizing feedback might increase the longevity of the DMS-emitting species without explaining the evolution of planktonic DMS emission. Thus while the proposed feedback loop may not explain why DMS emitters evolved, it may help explain why they have not become extinct.

Acknowledgments

I thank Michael Rampino for essential criticisms and Tyler Volk, Steve Schwartz, Alan Grafen, and Vijay Narayanan for helpful comments.

References

Andreae, M.O. 1986. The ocean as a source of sulfur compounds. In: Menard-Buat, P., ed. *The Role of Air-Sea Exchange in Geochemical Cycling*. Dordrecht: Reidel, 331–362.

Bates, T.S., Charlson, R.J., and Gammon, R.H. 1987. Evidence for the climatic role of marine biogenic sulphur. *Nature*, 329, 319–321.

Bolin, B., and Keeling, C.D. 1963. Large-scale atmospheric mixing as deduced from seasonal and meridional variations of carbon dioxide. *J Geophys Res*, 68, 3899–3920.

Broecker, W.S., and Peng, T.H. 1982. *Tracers in the Sea*. Palisades, N.Y.: Eldigio Press.

Caldeira, K. 1989. Evolutionary pressures on planktonic production of atmospheric sulphur. *Nature*, 337, 732–734.

Charlson, R.J., Lovelock, J.E., Andreae, M.O., and Warren, S.G. 1987. Oceanic phytoplankton, atmospheric sulphur, cloud albedo and climate. *Nature*, 326, 655–661.

Charnov, E.L., and Krebs, J.R. 1975. The evolution of alarm calls: Altruism or manipulation? *Am Natur*, 109, 107–112.

Dacey, J.W.H., and Wakeham, S.G. 1986. Oceanic dimethylsulfide: Production during zooplankton grazing on phytoplankton. *Science*, 233, 1314–1316.

Dawkins, R. 1976. *The Selfish Gene*. Oxford: Oxford University Press.

Eppley, R.W. 1972. Temperature and phytoplankton growth in the sea. *Fish Bull*, 70, 1063–1085.

Grafen, A. 1984. Natural selection, kin selection and group selection. In: Krebs, J.R., and Davies, N.B., eds. *Behavioural Ecology*. Oxford: Blackwell Scientific, 62–84.

Harpending, H., and Rogers, A. 1987. On Wright's mechanism for intergroup selection. *J Theor Biol*, 127, 51–61.

Hewitt, C.N., and Davison, B.M. 1988. The lifetimes of organosulphur compounds in the troposphere. *Appl Organometallic Chem*, 2, 407–415.

Hamilton, W.D. 1975. Innate social aptitudes of man: An approach from evolutionary genetics. In: Fox, R., ed. *Biosocial Anthropology*. New York: Wiley, 133–155.

Hulbert, E.M. 1962. Phytoplankton in the Southwestern Sargasso Sea and North Equatorial Current, February, 1961. *Limnol Oceanogr*, 7, 307–315.

Lovelock, J.E. and Margulis, L. 1974. Atmospheric homeostasis by and for the biosphere: The gaia hypothesis, *Tellus*, 26, 2–9.

Martin, J.H., and Fitzwater, S.E. 1988. Iron deficiency limits phytoplankton growth in the north-east Pacific subarctic. *Nature*, 331, 341–343.

Maynard Smith, J. 1982. *Evolution and the Theory of Games*. Cambridge: Cambridge University Press.

Nguyen, B.C., Belviso, S., Mihalopoulos, N., Gaston, J., and Nival, P., 1988. Dimethyl sulfide production during natural phytoplankton blooms. *Mar Chem*, 24, 133–141.

Nunney, L. 1985. Group selection, altruism, and structured-deme models. *Am Natur*, 126, 212–230.

Prigogine, I., and Stengers, I. 1984. *Order Out of Chaos*. New York: Bantam Books.

Savoie, D.L., and Prospero, J.M. 1989. Comparison of oceanic and continental sources of non-sea-salt sulphate over the Pacific Ocean. *Nature*, 339, 685–687.

Schwartz, S.E. 1988. Are global cloud albedo and climate controlled by marine phytoplankton? *Nature*, 336, 441–445.

Uyenoyama, M., and Feldman, M.W. 1980. Theories of kin and group selection: A population genetics perspective. *Theor Pop Biol*, 17, 380–414.

Vairavamurthy, E., Andreae, M.O., and Iverson, R.L. 1985. Biosynthesis of dimethylsulfide and dimethylpropiothetin by *Hymenomonas carterae* in relation to sulfur source and salinity variations. *Limnol Oceanogr*, 30, 59–70.

Wilson, D.S. 1975. A theory of group selection. *Proc Natl Acad Sci USA*, 72, 143–146.

Wright, S. 1945. Letter. *Ecology*, 26, 415–419.

V
Mechanisms: Oxygen

One might think that the most obvious atmospheric gas affected by life processes would be O_2. After all, the major reason that there is so much O_2 in the atmosphere, and the reason that it rose to such a high concentration in the first place, is photosynthesis. In fact, the presence of abundant oxygen in the atmosphere of the Earth, as compared with the other planets, is an indirect indication of the presence of life (Lovelock, 1988). Nevertheless, there are major controls on the level of atmospheric oxygen that are geological in origin and not dependent on life processes. In this chapter I examine these processes and discuss how they work.

The Geochemical Cycles of Carbon and Sulfur

The long-term production and consumption of atmospheric oxygen are intimately tied to the biogeochemical cycles of carbon and sulfur (Garrels and Perry, 1976; Holland, 1978, 1984; Walker, 1986; Kump and Garrels, 1986; Berner, 1989). In general, about 60% of O_2 production and consumption are brought about by the carbon cycle, 30% by the sulfur cycle, and only about 10% by other cycles involving iron, manganese, and other elements (Holland, 1978).

The pertinent overall reactions are:

$$CO_2 + H_2O \rightleftarrows CH_2O + O_2$$
$$2Fe_2O_3 + 16Ca^{2+} + 16\ HCO_3^- + 8SO_4^{2-} \rightleftarrows 4FeS_2 + 16CaCO_3 + 8H_2O + 15O_2$$

The carbon reaction, going from left to right, represents the net production of oxygen due to the burial in sediments of organic matter whose stoichiometry is summarized by the formula CH_2O. The same reaction, going from right to left, represents the oxidation of old organic matter in sedimentary rocks as a result of weathering on the continents. Note that this carbon reaction is the same as that normally used to represent the biological processes of photosynthesis and respiration. However, photosynthesis and respiration are much faster and on

a worldwide basis almost exactly balance one another. Only an extremely small fraction of photosynthetically produced organic matter escapes respiration and is buried in sediments, and it is this burial that results in the *net* production of atmospheric O_2. Likewise it is the reaction of O_2 with old organic matter in sedimentary rocks, by uplift, erosion, and weathering on the continents, that results in net oxygen consumption. Estimates of organic burial and weathering rates indicate that the replacement time for O_2 in the atmosphere is about 5 to 10 million years.

The sulfur reaction above is analogous to the carbon reaction and represents the formation and burial of sedimentary pyrite (FeS_2) in sediments, going from left to right, and the oxidative weathering of pyrite in old sedimentary rocks, going from right to left. A number of reactions of geochemical interest are combined in order to produce this simple overall reaction. The most important process is bacterial sulfate reduction (Berner, 1989):

$$2CH_2O + SO_4^{2-} \rightarrow H_2S + 2HCO_3^-$$

This reaction takes place only under anoxic conditions and results in the oxidation of organic matter, originally produced by photosynthesis, without the consumption of O_2. In other words, the oxidizing agent is sulfate and not O_2. Thus the net effect of combined photosynthesis, sulfate reduction, and burial of the reduced sulfur as pyrite is to produce oxygen as shown in the reaction above. Reaction of H_2S with iron minerals and formation of pyrite is necessary to produce the O_2; otherwise the H_2S passes out of the sediment into the overlying seawater where it is oxidized by O_2 back to sulfate.

Besides the sedimentary processes, there are other processes, such as basalt-seawater reaction and the oxidation of reduced volcanic gases, that could exert an influence on atmospheric oxygen, but these can be shown to be minor compared to the sedimentary ones. There is too little dissolved O_2 in seawater for direct reduction by basalt minerals to constitute a major removal process. Similarly permanent removal of seawater sulfate (and its included O_2) by reaction with basalt is not as important as weathering and sedimentary pyrite formation (Kump and Garrels, 1986; Berner and Berner, 1987). Much reduced volcanic gas arises from the thermal breakdown at great depth of buried organic matter and pyrite; thus oxidation of these gases by atmospheric O_2, when combined with the breakdown, is equivalent to weathering and need not be considered separately.

In sum, the major processes affecting the level of atmospheric O_2 are the weathering and burial of organic matter and pyrite in sediments. These processes have a definite biological component including the synthesis of organic matter by green plants, the destruction of the organic matter mainly by bacteria, the reduction of sulfate by bacteria, and the enhancement of weathering on land by vascular plants. However, the amount of organic matter that is buried is also affected by tectonics, and weathering is controlled to a large extent by tectonics. Thus it is imperative to include tectonics in any discussion of what controls atmospheric oxygen over geological time. (*Tectonics* refers to geological processes such as mountain building, sea floor spreading, continental drift, and volcanism that are driven by the internal energy of the earth).

Tectonics and Oxygen

Most organic matter by far is deposited in siliciclastic sediments along the margins of the continents (Berner, 1989), and in the marine environment a major control on its rate of burial is the rate of deposition of total sediment (Berner and Canfield, 1989). On a worldwide basis total sedimentation must be equivalent to total erosion of the continents. Thus greater erosion means greater deposition, more organic carbon burial, and greater O_2 production. Oxidative weathering of the sedimentary rocks that contain most of the pyrite and organic matter (black and gray shales) is controlled mainly by erosion. This is because the shales weather so fast that further weathering is inhibited until the cap of oxidized weathered material is stripped by erosion and fresh rock can come into contact with atmospheric O_2. Erosive stripping, in turn, is controlled by relief; in other words, higher slopes lead to greater erosion of the shales. (This latter idea has been forcefully illustrated by the recent work of Pinet and Souriau, 1988, on the major drainage basins of the world.)

The relief of the continents is a function of tectonic uplift; with greater uplift, there is more relief. Thus more uplift leads to higher relief, greater erosion, greater weathering, and greater consumption of O_2. However, at the same time greater erosion, as we have noted, means greater worldwide sediment deposition, greater burial of organic matter, and more rapid O_2 production. Here we have a natural geological feedback system *that is independent of biological phenomena*. An increase in weathering and O_2 consumption is matched by an increase in sediment burial and O_2 production, and the overall controlling factor is tectonics, not life.

In addition to the effects of bulk erosion and sedimentation, there is an additional geological feedback mechanism. Accompanying a greater worldwide erosion rate there would be greater liberation of the nutrient element phosphorus to solution by weathering. Given that phosphorus is thought to be the ultimate limiting element for organic production (Holland, 1978), an increased supply of phosphorus to the environment should result in an increase in the worldwide supply of organic matter to sediments. If the extra organic matter were successfully buried along with additional pyrite, this would result in increased O_2 production that would offset the increased O_2 consumption accompanying the faster weathering rate that provided the extra phosphate.

Because the transport of eroded material to the sea by rivers is so fast, one might expect that the O_2 erosion-deposition feedback is practically instantaneous on a geological timescale and thus serves as a rigid O_2 control mechanism. However, the story is more complicated. Control of O_2 depends also on where the sediment is deposited. If all sediment is deposited in the sea, then the simple argument developed thus far applies. But sediment is also deposited on the continents. If the site of deposition is well drained, such as occurs in upland areas, then any organic matter deposited with the sediment is eventually destroyed by air oxidation. This is why ancient paleosols are organic free and why most continental sedimentary deposits are colored red. The red color is due to ferric oxide, which would be reduced if any organic matter were present. None is present in red beds and that is why they are red (see Van Houten, 1973, for a discussion of red bed deposition).

In contrast to the formation of red beds in well-drained areas, the deposition of eroded material on the continents in low-lying swamps and lakes results in the preservation of organic matter because of the limited access of O_2 to the organic matter as a result of waterlogging. This results in the burial of high concentrations of organic matter, some of which over geological time is converted to coal. On the average, coal basin sediments contain a greater concentration of total organic carbon (economic coal plus disseminated organic matter) than do marine sediments (Berner and Canfield, 1989).

It can now be seen why the location of sediment deposition is so important. If there were a shift of deposition of eroded material from marine to continental red bed environments, for the same amount of total sediment burial there would be much less organic matter burial (remember that redbeds are organic free) and thus much less oxygen production. Likewise if there were a shift from marine burial to deposition in coal basins, the rate of organic matter burial and oxygen production would go up. In this way the simple erosion-deposition control mechanism can undergo perturbations that otherwise would not take place.

What has been said here about organic matter applies also, for the most part, to the burial and weathering of pyrite. Because of the dependence of bacterial sulfate reduction on organic matter, in most marine sediments (of Devonian age or younger) there is a good correlation between pyrite and organic matter (Raiswell and Berner, 1986; Berner, 1989). In red beds there is no pyrite (or organic matter), whereas in coal basin sediments there is some pyrite but much less, relative to organic matter, than in marine sediments. The burial of pyrite, although coupled to organic burial in normal marine sediments, can be uncoupled when there is a shift of organic burial from the marine environment to coal swamps or to burial in euxenic marine basins (Berner, 1989). Overall, however, because pyrite generally tracks organic matter and because it exerts a quantitatively less important influence on O_2 than does organic matter, fluctuations in the worldwide burial rate of pyrite are of secondary importance.

Atmospheric Oxygen over Phanerozoic Time

A model has been constructed (Berner and Canfield, 1989) for calculating rates of burial and weathering of organic matter and pyrite over Phanerozoic time, that is, the past 570 million years. It is based on the relative abundance of (1) marine sandstones and shales, (2) coal basin sediments, and (3) other continental sediments (mainly red beds) (table 19.1), and the average organic carbon and pyrite sulfur

Table 19.1 Distribution of Clastic Sediments Among Three Major Groups*

Period	Time Span (my BP)	Marine Clastics (%)	Coal Basin Sediments (%)	Red Beds (%)
Pliocene	2–9	74	2	24
Miocene	9–25	85	1	14
Oligocene	25–37	87	2	11
Eocene	37–58	89	3	8
Paleocene	58–66	80	3	17
Upper Cretaceous	66–100	81	5	14
Lower Cretaceous	100–132	78	3	19
Jurassic	132–185	75	4	21
Upper Triassic	185–210	50	1	49
Middle Triassic	210–220	77	1	22
Lower Triassic	220–235	55	0.5	44
Upper Permian	235–255	47	6	47
Lower Permian	255–280	61	10	29
Upper and Middle Carboniferous	280–320	58	22	20
Lower Carboniferous	320–345	74	8	18
Upper Devonian	345–360	74	0	26
Middle Devonian	360–376	82	0	18
Lower Devonian	376–400	76	0	24
Silurian	400–435	91	0	9
Ordovician	435–490	93	0	7
Upper Cambrian	490–515	95	0	5
Middle Cambrian	515–545	95	0	5
Lower Cambrian	545–570	93	0	7

*Based on data of Ronov (1976) and Budyko et al. (1989). Time scale of Ronov (1976) used for consistency. (After Berner and Canfield, 1989.)

Rapid Recycling Model

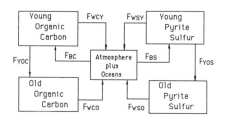

Figure 19.1 The rapid recycling model used to calculate values of atmospheric O_2 concentration over Phanerozoic time. (After Berner and Canfield, 1989).

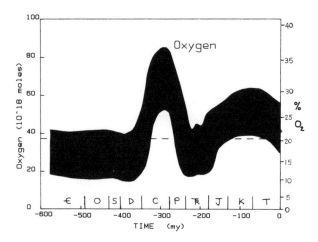

Figure 19.2 "Best estimate" of atmospheric oxygen level versus time from Berner and Canfield (1989). The shading represents the range of values from sensitivity analysis. Note the large increase during the Carboniferous and the sharp drop during the Permian periods due to major shifts in the site of clastic deposition (see Table 1).

contents of each of the three rock types. Included in the model is the important geological observation that younger sedimentary rocks weather faster than older rocks. The model is represented in figure 19.1. From results for rates of burial and weathering, curves of atmospheric O_2 versus time have been constructed based on different choices of such critical parameters as the average content of organic carbon in coal basins and the rate by which organic matter and pyrite are recycled by weathering. Rates of burial of organic carbon, calculated from this model for reasonable values for the critical parameters, agree well with those based on the independent modeling of carbon isotopes, giving credence to both approaches.

Because of the erosion-deposition O_2-feedback mechanism, results for O_2 versus time calculated via the model were found to be more or less the same for constant and time-variable total worldwide sedimentation. Thus most of the modeling was done using a constant worldwide sedimentation rate over time. Results for an average simulation are shown in figure 19.2. Note the rather large variations of O_2 concentration. The primary cause for these variations are changes with time in the relative importance of deposition of siliciclastic material as marine sediments versus red beds versus coal basin sediments. However, the high values of O_2 in the Carboniferous and early Permian periods are also partly a biological phenomenon. A major cause is the evolution and spread of vascular plants on the continents at this time. Such plants provided a new source of organic matter for deposition in sediments, both on the continents in swamps and lakes and in the sea after transport there by rivers. Greater burial of terrestrial, as opposed to marine-derived, organic matter, given the same supply of nutrients, would be expected because the lignin-rich terrestrial material is more resistant to bacterial

destruction (Lyons and Gaudette, 1979) and it exhibits a higher ratio of carbon to nutrient elements than does marine material such as plankton and algae (Kump, 1989).

Increased organic burial during the Carboniferous and Permian periods was not due solely to the rise of vascular land plants. The other factor is that the organic matter had to be buried in suitable locations in order to be preserved. This was provided by vast swamps that were present on the continents during this time as evidenced today by widespread coal deposits from the Carboniferous and Permian ages. Extensive swamps result where there is a lot of low-lying land above sea level, in addition to abundant rainfall. During the Carboniferous and Permian periods the continents were joined to form the supercontinent of Pangea and were largely emergent due to very low sea level. Low-lying flat continental areas that would normally be submerged at higher sea level were emergent and available for swamp formation. Thus large swampy areas resulted, thereby raising the rate of worldwide organic matter burial and O_2 production. The presence of vast stretches of water-logged emergent land is a tectonic factor related to the size and hypsometry of the continents and the level of the sea. In this way tectonic factors, in addition to biology, affected organic matter burial and brought about higher levels of atmospheric O_2 during the Carboniferous and Permian ages.

During the late Permian, according to the model

calculations (figure 19.2) the level of atmospheric O_2 dropped sharply. This drop was due mainly to a large rise in red bed deposition. The coal swamps dried up, and due to the emergent nature of Pangea, much deposition of sediment on land occurred at the expense of deposition in the sea. Organic-rich swamp and oceanic sediments were replaced by organic-free and pyrite-free red beds. Thus rates of O_2 production plummeted and, assuming that the mix of sediments being weathered did not change greatly, the value of atmospheric O_2 concentration also dropped sharply.

The shift of depositional environments during the late Permian (and continuing on into the Triassic) was most likely due to climatic change and the drying of the continents (Frakes, 1979). Such conditions would be favorable to the deposition of less worldwide organic matter because there would be decreased productivity on land and a lack of sufficient rainfall for coal swamp formation. Why there was increased aridity is not clear, but it likely had to do with the existence of such a large supercontinent (Kutzbach and Gallimore, 1989) to the presence of vast stretches of land in subtropical latitudes where high rates of evaporation occurred (Tardy et al., 1989) and to the rain-shadowing effect of major mountain ranges. The existence of a large supercontinent, its latitudinal position, and the presence of extensive mountains are all tectonic phenomena resulting from continental drift, and in this way tectonics again can be called upon to explain the drop of O_2 level at the end of the Permian.

An alternative explanation, more in keeping with the Gaia hypothesis, for the drop in O_2 level at the end of the Permian period is provided by Kump's hypothesis (1988). According to Kump if the level of O_2 becomes too high, then the continental biomass is decimated by oxygen-enhanced forest fires. This leads to greater transfer of the nutrient phosphorus from the land to the sea and more ocean productivity and less terrestrial productivity. Given that the carbon-to-phosphorus ratio of marine organic matter is considerably less than that of terrestrial plants, for a given supply of P there is less burial of carbon, and therefore less O_2 production, when the organic matter is marine in origin. Thus if there were a major shift in organic source for burial in sediments from terrestrial plants to marine organic matter, then there would be less O_2 production and a lowering in atmospheric O_2 level. In this way a negative feedback against excessive O_2 fluctuations is provided based on forest fires, not tec-

tonics. Such a forest fire explanation can be applied to the late Permian period, but there is still the evidence of less coal basin deposition and greater red bed deposition. Perhaps both phenomena were important because of the greater aridity at this time. (Dryness accelerates burning, lowers productivity, and inhibits coal swamp formation).

Summary

Atmospheric O_2 is a biologically produced gas that is necessary for all higher forms of life. However, as I have shown many nonbiological processes also exert a significant control on the level of O_2. If a major portion of sediment deposition were to shift from the oceans to the continents, a situation that occurred during the Carboniferous and Permian periods 350 to 250 million years ago, then the level of O_2 would be expected to either rise or drop depending on where the sediment was deposited. If worldwide climate were to change due to a shift in the position of the continents, then this could also result in changes in atmospheric O_2. If increased erosion of the continents resulted in increased weathering and a rise in the rate of delivery of the nutrient element phosphorus to the oceans, then more organic matter could be provided to marine sediments for burial, resulting in greater O_2 production. All of these scenarios are ultimately tectonic in nature. Thus the level of atmospheric O_2, which must be a major factor in the evolution of life, has been affected over geological time to a significant extent by tectonic processes.

References

Berner, E.K., and Berner, R.A. 1987. *The Global Water Cycle: Geochemistry and Environment.* Englewood Cliffs, N.J.: Prentice-Hall.

Berner, R.A. 1989. Biogeochemical cycles of carbon and sulfur and their effect on atmospheric oxygen over Phanerozoic time. *Paleogeogr Paleoclimatol Paleoecol (Global Planet Change Section)*, 75, 97–122.

Berner, R.A., and Canfield, R.A. 1989. A new model for atmospheric oxygen over Phanerozoic time. *Am J Sci*, 289, 333–361.

Budyko, M.I., Ronov, A.B., and Yanshin, A.L. 1987. *History of the Earth's Atmosphere.* Berlin: Springer-Verlag.

Frakes, L.A. 1979. *Climates Throughout Geologic Time.* Amsterdam: Elsevier.

Garrels, R.M., and Perry, E.A. 1974. Cycling of carbon, sulfur, and oxygen through geologic time. In: Goldberg: E.D., ed. *The Sea, Vol. 5.* New York: Wiley, 303–316.

Holland, H.D., 1978. *The Chemistry of the Atmosphere and Oceans*. New York: Wiley.

Holland, H.D. 1984. *The Chemical Evolution of the Atmosphere and Oceans*. Princeton, N.J.: Princeton University Press.

Kump, L.R. 1988. Terrestrial feedback in atmospheric oxygen. Regulation by fire and phosphorus. *Nature*, 335, 152–154.

Kump, L.R. 1989. Chemical stability of the atmosphere and ocean. *Paleogeogr Paleoclimatol Paleoecol (Global and Planet Change Section)*, 75, 123–136.

Kump, L.R., and Garrels, R.M. 1986. Modeling atmospheric O_2 in the global sedimentary redox cycle. *Am J Sci*, 286, 337–360.

Kutzbach, J.E., and Gallimore, R.G. 1989. Pangean climates: Megamonsoons of the megacontinent. *J Geophys Res*, 94, 3341–3357.

Lovelock, J. 1988. *The Ages of Gaia*. New York: W.W. Norton.

Lyons, W.B., and Gaudette, M.E. 1979. Sulfate reduction and the nature of organic matter in estuarine sediments. *Organic Geochem*, 1, 151–155.

Pinet, P., and Souriau, M. 1988. Continental erosion and large-scale relief. *Tectonics*, 7, 563–582.

Raiswell, R., and Berner, R.A. 1986. Pyrite and organic matter in Phanerozoic normal marine shales. *Geochim Cosmochim Acta*, 50, 1967–1976.

Ronov, A.B. 1976. Global carbon geochemistry, volcanism, carbonate accumulation, and life. *Geochem Int* (translation of *Geokhimiya*), 13, 172–195.

Tardy, Y., N'Kounkou, R., and Probst, J.-L. 1989. The global water cycle and continental erosion during Phanerozoic time (570 my). *Am J Sci*, 289, 455–483.

Van Houten, F.B. 1973. Origin of red beds: A review—1961–1972. *Ann Rev Earth Planet Sci*, 1, 39–61.

Walker, J.C.G. 1986. Global geochemical cycles of carbon, sulfur, and oxygen. *Marine Geol*, 70, 159–174.

G. R. Williams

20
Gaian and Nongaian Explanations
for the Contemporary Level of Atmospheric Oxygen

The question of the stability and steady-state level of atmospheric O_2 must play an important part in any discussion of the Gaia hypothesis. Historically, the concept of Gaia was first drawn to the attention of the wider scientific community by the publication of two papers in *Atmospheric Environment* in 1972. It was the second of these (Lovelock, 1972) that formally stated the hypothesis but it was adumbrated in the paper published first (Lovelock and Lodge, 1972) entitled (significantly for the following discussion) "Oxygen in the contemporary atmosphere." Apart from this historical point, the question clearly illustrates one of the more controversial aspects of the concept, for it is on the topic of O_2 that the Gaia hypothesis is boldest in asserting optimalization for the biosphere.

An atmosphere containing 20% O_2 is far from optimal for many organisms and Margulis and Lovelock (1974) correctly emphasize that atmospheric O_2 is optimized only in relation to a biosphere in which "the dominant species on the present Earth are obligate aerobes" (Lovelock and Margulis, 1974). But the dominance of obligate aerobes is conventionally thought of as the endpoint of a Darwinian selection between anaerobes carrying out fermentative or chemoheterotrophic processes and species capable of carrying out more energetically efficient modes of metabolism that use molecular O_2 as a terminal electron acceptor. The Gaia hypothesis, by suggesting that the high level of O_2 in the environment is set by the requirements of a biosphere dominated by aerobes as well as being a cause of that dominance, risks turning Darwinian evolution into a circular argument. The only obvious escape from such circularity is to define optimalization in such a way that it implies maximal exploitation of earth's surface by living organisms (and, therefore, maximization of oxygenated zones) but such a definition may introduce teleological assumptions.

The willingness of the scientific community to give serious consideration to a radically new hypothesis is influenced by the success, or lack thereof, of existing models in answering the question under discussion. Therefore, in what follows, three nongaian explanations for the level of O_2 in the atmosphere are considered. It will be argued that two of these three explanations carry implications that turn out to be equivalent to explicit assertions within a Gaian frame of reference.

Sources and Sinks for Atmospheric Oxygen

Scientists generally agree that atmospheric O_2 is of biological origin. The primary reaction responsible for the production of O_2 is the photosynthetic cleavage of water and, as noted below, this reaction is responsible not only for the production of free O_2 but also for the global inventory of oxidized sulfur and iron (Garrels and Lerman, 1981). Most of the annual photosynthetic production of O_2 is consumed in the oxidation of reduced carbon compounds but in the oceans a small proportion of the global net primary production ($< 0.2\%$) escapes oxidation and is buried in marine sediments and a stoichiometrically equivalent amount of O_2 remains in the atmosphere. This net production of O_2 is opposed by O_2 consumption in weathering processes (oxidation of C^0, S^{2-}, and Fe^{2+}). Presumably there is some dependence on the partial pressure of oxygen (pO_2) in the atmosphere of both the net rate of production of O_2 by photosynthesis and of the rate of consumption by weathering.

The details of these relationships are not known. Both Holland (1973, 1978) and Walker (1974) assume that the weathering consumption rate will plateau at high levels of pO_2. It is reasonable to assume also that an increased O_2 content of seawater will bring about a decrease in the rate of burial of organic matter and therefore that high values of pO_2 will result in a decrease in net photosynthetic production of O_2. The effect of atmospheric O_2 below 0.2 atm is less obvious and the argument for a plateau (Holland, 1978, figure 6-12) or even a decrease (Holland, 1973, figure 3) in net photosynthetic O_2

production depends on the limitation of total photosynthesis by the nutrient content of seawater. Burial of a significant proportion of the organic production of the surface ocean would carry with it phosphorus and combined nitrogen and thus interrupt the efficient recycling of these nutrients.

The precise shape of these curves is not particularly important in the context of the Gaia hypothesis. Margulis and Lovelock (1974) pointed out that the persistence of a continuous record of a flourishing metazoan fauna since the Cambrian period suggests that atmospheric O_2 has been relatively constant from that period to the present. This stability has been remarked upon by others (e.g., Holland, 1973; Walker, 1974). With respect to the issue of stability, the Gaia hypothesis may be thought of as an entertaining simile in which the regulation of atmospheric composition is likened to organismic homeostasis. Lovelock and Watson (1982) write ". . . we are postulating no more than a large control system which includes the biosphere as a component." However, for O_2, not dissimilar suggestions have been made outside the Gaian framework. Broecker (1970) suggested that "the oxygen content of the atmosphere is self-regulating." Holland (1973) states, "The modesty of the excursions in atmospheric oxygen even after more than twenty turnover times virtually demands a control mechanism which couples the rate of oxygen production during sedimentation to the rate of oxygen use during weathering . . ." and Walker (1974), after acknowledging the suggestions of Broecker and Holland, asks, "Where, in the geochemical cycle . . . does this feedback mechanism operate?" This question is clearly an example of the general question posed by Lovelock and Margulis (1974), "What are the sensors, amplifiers and control mechanisms operating to maintain constant the steady state chemical composition of the gases of the atmosphere?"

Both Gaian and nongaian analysis of this stability problem can be presented as attempts to understand the angle of intersection of the O_2 consumption and net production rate curves and satisfactory analyses from either point of view might be difficult to distinguish. A clearer demarcation between Gaian and nongaian points of view presents itself if one asks not about the angle of intersection of the two curves but rather about the level of atmospheric O_2 at which the net rate of change of O_2 is zero. The question is, "How come the level of O_2 in the atmosphere is 21%?" (Using the colloquialism "How come?" permits an answer in causal terms whereas "Why?" seems to open the door to teleological answers.) The question of the stability of atmospheric O_2 can be answered by the weak form of the Gaia hypothesis (homeostasis *by* the biosphere); if there is a Gaian answer to the question of how the level of atmospheric O_2 is set, it must be derived from a stronger version (homeostasis *for* the biosphere) in which the steady-state value is at least partially determined by characteristics of the global biota.

Nongaian Explanations

Geochemical

Most explanations of the level of atmospheric O_2 assume that it is maintained far from thermodynamic equilibrium by the free energy input from solar radiation. Sillen (1965) did point out that the atmospheric pO_2 might be determined by the equilibrium between geothite and magnetite:

$$12FeOOH(s) \rightleftharpoons 4Fe_3O_4(s) + 6H_2O + O_2(g)$$

Indeed, some determinations of the equilibrium constant of this reaction do yield approximately correct values of pO_2 but there is considerable uncertainty about the value of the equilibrium constant and Sillen was forced to conclude that although "It would have been pleasing to an equilibrium chemist if $p(O_2)$ were maintained by some chemical equilibrium . . . ," the alternative of a steady state involving biological processes had to be considered. In a geochemical explanation such biological processes would merely catalyze the establishment of a solar energy–driven steady state, at a level that would be completely determined by geochemical considerations.

From a geochemical point of view the molecular O_2 of the atmosphere constitutes only a small fraction of the global inventory of the oxidized products of photosynthesis (table 20.1). Much of the O_2 lib-

Table 20.1 Global Inventory of Oxidized Products of Photosynthesis

	Oxygen Equivalents (10^{20} Moles)
Molecular oxygen	0.4
Sulfate	4.4
Ferric iron	1.6–3.2

erated in the Precambrian period would be recaptured by inorganic sinks such as ferrous iron and sulfides (Broecker, 1970; Schidlowski et al., 1975). The stoichiometry of the liberation and recapture during the transition to the O_2-rich atmosphere of the Phanerozoic period is problematic (Van Valen, 1971). Garrels and Perry (1974) pointed out that the oxidation of inorganic sinks such as FeS_2 and FeO in the form of ferrous silicate would remove oxygen from the atmosphere without a compensatory release of CO_2. In contradistinction, the oxidation of ferrous carbonate (siderite) liberates, on a molar basis, four times as much CO_2 as it consumes O_2. It is thus possible to write a balanced chemical equation in which reducing equivalents are transferred from a mixture of FeS_2, $FeSiO_3$, and $FeCO_3$ to CO_2, producing organic carbon. The ferrous iron is oxidized to Fe_2O_3 and the pyrite sulfide to sulfate but the mixture of products also includes free O_2. The amount of O_2 produced is dependent on the amount of $FeCO_3$ in the original mix (table 20.2). "The level of free oxygen in the present steady-state atmosphere would seem to be fortuitous, in that it apparently was controlled by the relative amount of siderite in the preoxygen rocks. If there had been more siderite, the Phanerozoic steady state might have operated at a somewhat higher level" (Garrels and Perry, 1974).

The role of the biota in models such as this is merely to provide the necessary phototransducers to effect the change from the chemical composition of the primitive Earth to the approximate steady state that has persisted throughout the last 500 to 800 My. Although Garrels and Perry do suggest that the low CO_2 content of the recent atmosphere is determined by the affinity of the photosynthetic apparatus for CO_2, there is nothing about the characteristics of the biological catalysis that determines the end result so far as O_2 is concerned. On the other hand, a remarkable feature of such models is that the massive transfers between sulfur reservoirs and carbon reservoirs that are indicated by the isotopic composition of sulfates and carbonates (Garrels and Lerman, 1981) appear to have taken place without major excursions in atmospheric O_2.

Schidlowski and colleagues (1977), on the basis of similar evidence, conclude that one "cannot exclude severe repercussions on atmospheric pO_2 during the Phanerozoic" and that during this period "atmospheric oxygen can be expected to have fluctuated within some 20% of its present level." The recent reports at the 1987 meeting of the Geological Society of America of analyses of air bubbles in amber suggest that fluctuations of this order of magnitude may have occurred with O_2 levels as high as 30% in the Cretaceous period (Berner and Landis (1988) but cf. Cerling (1989)). If these reports are confirmed, it will be important to note that such changes, significant though they may be in biological terms, are relatively small in relation to the pools of oxidized and reduced carbon and sulfur (table 20.1) and that they are certainly well within the range of uncertainty associated with current estimates of the relevant geochemical parameters.

Geophysical

The concept of the control of atmospheric O_2 at a "kinetic maximum" (Broecker, 1970) arises from the observation that there are large areas of the world ocean in which O_2 is substantially depleted. Such depletion would be expected if burial of organic matter is to occur, and the observation of hypoxic zones within the deep ocean provides evidence for the model. In such a model the steady-state level of atmospheric O_2 is just sufficient to permit marginal ventilation of the deep ocean. If the deep ocean were better oxygenated burial of organic carbon would be decreased, and if the deep ocean were less well oxygenated burial of organic carbon would be increased. The effects on atmo-

Table 20.2 Oxygen Content of the Atmosphere As a Function of the Composition of Ferrous Minerals Prior to Photosynthetic Production of Oxygen*

Reactants	Products	Stoichiometric Coefficient	
$FeSiO_3$		x	
	SiO_2		x
FeS_2		y	
	Fe_2O_3		0.5 (x + y + z)
$FeCO_3$		z	
$CaCO_3$	$CaSO_4$	2y	2y
H_2O	CH_2O	2y + z	2y + z
	O_2		$0.75z - (1.75y + 0.25x)$

*From Garrels and Perry, 1974.

spheric O_2 would be reciprocal and self-adjusting. The level of oxygen at which stabilization takes place, however, depends on the details of the supply of oxygen to deep waters, that is, on the geophysics of ocean circulation. The point is most easily illustrated by considering the situation on a planet similar to Earth but with oceans of different volume.

In an ocean of area A_m, depth D, mean respiration rate (on a volume basis) R, mean photosynthetic productivity (on an areal basis) P; then

$$\text{burial rate} = A_m \times (P - R \times D) \quad (1)$$

If the weathering rate is proportional to the partial pressure of oxygen, and the planetary area is A_t, then

$$\text{weathering rate} = k_w \times (A_t - A_m) \times O_2$$

In the steady state, the burial rate and weathering rate are equal. Therefore:

$$O_2 = \frac{(P - R \times D) \times A_m}{k_w \times (A_t - A_m)}$$

For hypothetical oceans of the same depth, the O_2 content of the corresponding atmospheres would be related to oceanic volume. For instance, in an ocean of smaller area (A_m) the hypoxic conditions that permit the burial of organic materials would be prevented by a lower atmospheric pO_2 than is necessary to prevent such hypoxia in a world ocean of larger volume. For hypothetical oceans of the same area, lower values of D result in increased values of pO_2. This latter conclusion accords well with the greater burial rates of organic carbon in coastal areas (cf. figure 3 of Walker, 1974). Clearly, this reasoning is greatly oversimplified but it does perhaps permit the conclusion that the atmospheric content of O_2 may be strongly determined by geophysical considerations. However, there are biological assumptions built into even such a simple model. As written here, it is assumed that, while weathering is proportional to pO_2, the mean oceanic respiration rate is independent of the dissolved O_2 content. It is probable that neither of these assumptions represents the actual state of affairs; both weathering and respiration are likely to have some fractional order dependence on O_2, that is, rate $\propto O_2^n$, where $n < 1$. The conclusions of this argument concerning the influence of ocean depth and area on atmospheric pO_2 will be valid provided that the value of n applicable to the weathering process is greater than that applicable to oceanic respiration.

Oceanographers have in fact found that "in most aquatic organisms, respiratory consumption of oxygen is essentially independent of the oxygen tension down to some lower limit of the latter" (Richards, 1957). Nonetheless, it is germane to any discussion of the Gaia hypothesis that in distinction to the geochemical explanation of the level of atmospheric O_2, the argument for a geophysical determination does depend on a particular characteristic of the biological processes involved, namely, the high affinity of the respiratory enzymes for O_2. A higher value for the apparent Michaelis constant for oxygen of the respiratory enzymes of the marine heterotrophs would imply that the balance of weathering rate by burial rate would occur at a higher level of atmospheric O_2; that is, the descending limb of the plot of net O_2 production as a function of pO_2 would be shifted to the right. Complexities arising from the nutrient requirements of the photosynthetic phytoplankton make this argument unamenable to simple quantification. The purpose of raising it is simply to point out that the geophysical explanation is, in the spectrum of Gaian and nongaian answers, not so clearly nongaian as the geochemical accounts. Even closer to the Gaian viewpoint are the biogeochemical explanations discussed in the next section.

Biogeochemical

The classic biogeochemical explanation for the level of atmospheric O_2 is presented in the well-known paper of Redfield (1958) on "The biological control of chemical factors in the environment." As in all discussions of the stability and level of atmospheric O_2, emphasis is laid on the burial of products of oceanic photosynthesis. Such burial also sequesters marine nutrients that have been incorporated into biomass. It is for this reason that Holland (1973, 1978) considered that oceanic productivity would be markedly limited at low pO_2. Redfield assumes that in anaerobic situations sulfate-reducing bacteria would be sufficiently active to decompose buried organic material, simultaneously regenerating nutrients in the stoichiometric ratio in which they occur in that buried material. "If, however, in the past the oxygen of the atmosphere were lower than at present, anaerobic conditions may have been much more prevalent. The reduction of sulfates may then have served to bring the oxygen content of the atmosphere and sea into correspondence with the requirements set by the quantities of phosphorus available." It seems possible that such a feedback mechanism might provide an explanation for the maintenance of a relatively constant atmospheric pO_2 despite the large movements between sulfur and carbon reservoirs alluded to in the previous section on geochemical explanations.

Such regeneration of nutrients by microbiological activity is clearly consistent with the Gaian hypothesis of homeostasis *by* the biosphere. Redfield's explanation of how it comes about that the pO_2 in the atmosphere is about 0.2 atm is not so obviously consistent with the Gaian answer of optimalization *for* the biosphere. He suggested that "the partial pressure of oxygen in the atmosphere [is] determined through the requirements of the biochemical cycle, by the solubility of phosphate in the ocean." The removal of phosphate from the ocean is now understood to depend on more complex processes than the simple precipitation of apatites (Froelich et al., 1977; Moody et al., 1981), and recent discussions of glacial and interglacial variability in the distribution of phosphate in the ocean also suggest a more complex situation. It is important to note, in the context of the latter discussions, that although the proposed changes in phosphorus content at various depths of the ocean may be important for understanding atmospheric CO_2 variability and may bring about marked vertical changes in dissolved O_2 (Boyle, 1988), the long half-life of atmospheric oxygen (4×10^6 years) precludes significant change of pO_2 on the timescale of glacial episodes (Broecker, 1983). Such a physicochemical determination (related to the solubility product of calcium phosphate) would, in any case, indicate only an upper bound to atmospheric O_2. The propensity of pO_2 to remain at or near this limit throughout the Phanerozoic must, on Redfield's argument, be attributed to the biological regeneration of phosphate in anaerobic situations by chemoheterotrophs.

There is also a Gaian aspect to this theory in that the level of atmospheric O_2 achieved by this process depends on the kinetic capability of marine phytoplankton to photosynthesize at the low concentrations of phosphate found in surface seawater. This capability is attributable to active phosphate transport mechanisms in the cell surface. Such phosphate transporters operating at a high affinity for phosphate ions play a key role in the overall process and provide a link between the genome of the phytoplankton species involved and the dynamics of the global biogeochemical cycle of O_2. It is much

easier to call attention to this linkage than to assert any corelationship between the evolution of phosphate carriers in phytoplankton and the rise of metazoa with a requirement for a relatively high atmospheric O_2 content.

Gaian Explanations

The Gaia hypothesis first surfaced in the scientific literature in connection with the explanation of the contemporary O_2 content of the atmosphere (Lovelock and Lodge, 1972). Lovelock (1975) used the anomalous pE of Earth (as seen against the background of the other terrestrial planets of the solar system, presumed to be lifeless) as part of the evidence for the reality of Gaia. However, Margulis and Lovelock (1974) suggested that the problem of control of redox potential is perhaps "the least serious of all for life." Oxygen thus may be distinguished from temperature, acidity, and nutrient distribution, for which levels must be maintained that are "tolerable to the earth's biota." Gaia's role with respect to O_2 is not one of ensuring tolerable levels but of maintaining pO_2 at or close to an optimal level. This optimization "can be considered the outcome of greater fitness, in the neo-Darwinian sense, of the aerobes in relation to the anaerobes." The concept of optimization as one of the distinguishing features of Gaia is reiterated in Lovelock's writing until about 1982, and, although it is not raised explicitly in the Daisyworld model, it is clearly present in the equations relating the growth rate of the daisies to temperature (Watson and Lovelock, 1983).

What would it mean to speak of a pO_2 of about 0.2 atm as optimal for Gaia? An O_2 content of about 20% seems to ensure a balance between almost complete ventilation of the oceans without incurring greater risks of toxicity or increased combustibility of organic material. However, the fact that most complex metazoa (including man) are able to function adequately at heights up to 4000 m, at altitudes where the pO_2 is only about 60% of that at sea level, and that others can adapt to long periods of hypoxia or anoxia (Hochachka, 1980), taken together with the reports of a high O_2 content in the Cretacean atmosphere, suggest a wide zone of tolerability. The case for optimality seems to rest on the thesis that "life tends to grow until the supply of energy or raw materials set a limit" (Margulis and Lovelock, 1974). To reach such limits of maximal exploitation by aerobic organisms, a pO_2 of 0.2 atm might be essential. It is unclear, however, even if one accepts this thesis, why "life" should be identified with the current composition of the global biota. When one considers the case of O_2 it is not surprising that critics of Gaia have detected teleological assumptions underlying the hypothesis.

It is perhaps worth noting in passing that many theoretical evolutionists would have difficulty with the concept of optimization even within the framework of Darwinism (e.g., Lewontin, 1978). It is interesting that Lovelock has illustrated the Gaia hypothesis by invoking an imaginary planetary engineer whereas Levins and Lewontin (1985) have given cogent reasons for doubting whether "design analysis . . . makes it possible to determine fitness a priori." Thus the claim of optimality for a diagnostic feature of the planetary organism Gaia may be a nonessential part of the metaphor. If it is unnecessary to view all traits of organisms as adaptive then there may be no particular utility in trying to defend a pO_2 of 0.2 atm as optimal for Gaia.

Conclusion

Within the gaian simile two hypotheses are embedded concerning atmospheric O_2. The first is that biochemical processes, catalyzed by the global biota, constitute essential components of the feedback loops, which have achieved a relatively stable level of atmospheric O_2 over a period of at least twenty times and possibly over 100 times as long as the half-time that characterizes the processes of O_2 removal by present-day inorganic and organic sinks of reducing equivalents in rocks exposed to weathering. Such an expansion of the gaian slogan, "homeostasis *by* the biosphere," is probably not controversial. All current discussions of the question of the stability of atmospheric O_2 levels on a geological timescale postulate significant roles for the biota.

The second hypothesis is that the current level of atmospheric O_2 of about 20% is set by characteristics of the contemporary biosphere, much as in Daisyworld the mean planetary temperature is set by the numerical constants of the equation relating the growth rate of daisies to local temperature. Such an expansion of the gaian slogan, "homeostasis *for* the biosphere," is much more controversial. Of the three nongaian explanations for the contemporary level of atmospheric O_2 presented here, two do in fact suggest that the level would be different in a world in which one or other of the parameters that

characterize the biochemical processes in the feedback loops had different values. These values, however, are genetically determined characteristics of marine microorganisms and it is not clear that a credible scenario can be constructed for the co-evolution of these characteristics to achieve a level of O_2 appropriate for the land-based metazoan fauna and other obligate aerobes that dominate the current global biota.

Indeed, the coexistence within the biosphere of complex aerobes and obligate anaerobes makes it clear that, at least so far as O_2 is concerned, the concept of optimality is not well formed. The case of atmospheric O_2 is particularly useful for demonstrating the existence of two forms of the Gaia hypothesis. A realization that the weak hypothesis of homeostasis *by* the biosphere does not entail the strong hypothesis of homeostasis *for* the biosphere and that support for the former does not necessarily constitute support for the latter would do much to clarify the debate over Gaia.

References

Berner, R.A., and Landis, G.P. 1988. Gas bubbles in fossil amber as possible indicators of the major gas composition of ancient air. *Science,* 239, 1406–1409.

Boyle, E.A..1988. Vertical oceanic nutrient fractionation and glacial/interglacial CO_2 cycles. *Nature,* 331, 55–65.

Broecker, W.S. 1970. A boundary condition on the evolution of atmospheric oxygen. *J Geophys Res,* 75, 3553–3557.

Broecker, W.S. 1983. The ocean. *Scientific American,* 249, 146–160.

Cerling, T.E. 1989. Does the gas content of amber reveal the composition of palaeoatmospheres? *Nature,* 339, 695–696.

Froelich, P.N., Bender, M.L., and Heath, G.R. 1977. Phosphorus accumulation rates in metalliferous sediments on the East Pacific rise. *Earth Planet Sci Lett,* 34, 351–359.

Garrels, R.M., and Lerman, A. 1981. Phanerozoic cycles of sedimentary carbon and sulfur. *Proc Natl Acad Sci USA,* 78, 4652–4656.

Garrels, R.M., and Perry, Jr., E.A. 1974. Cycling of carbon, sulfur, and oxygen through geologic time. In: Goldberg, G.E., ed. *The Sea,* 5, 303–336.

Hochachka, P.W. 1980. *Living without Oxygen.* Cambridge, Mass.: Harvard University Press.

Holland, H.D. 1973. Ocean water, nutrients and atmospheric oxygen. *Proc Symp Hydrogeochem Biogeochem,* 1, 68–81.

Holland, H.D. 1978. *The Chemistry of the Atmosphere and Oceans.* New York: Wiley-Interscience.

Levins, R., and Lewontin, R.C. 1985. *The Dialectical Biologist.* Cambridge, Mass.: Harvard University Press.

Lewontin, R.C. 1972. Adaptation. *Scientific American,* 239, 156–169.

Lovelock, J.E. 1972. Gaia as seen through the atmosphere. *Atmospher Environ*, 6, 579–580.

Lovelock, J.E. 1975. Thermodynamics and the recognition of alien biospheres. *Proc Soc Lond B*, 189, 167–181.

Lovelock, J.E., and Lodge, Jr., J.P. 1972. Oxygen in the contemporary atmosphere. *Atmospher Environ*, 6, 575–578.

Lovelock, J.E., and Margulis, L. 1974. Homeostatic tendencies of the Earth's atmosphere. *Origins of Life*, 5, 93–103.

Lovelock, J.E., and Watson, A.J. 1982. The regulation of carbon dioxide and climate: Gaia or geochemistry. *Planet Space Sci*, 8, 795–802.

Margulis, L., and Lovelock, J.E. 1974. Biological modulation of the Earth's atmosphere. *Icarus*, 21, 471–489.

Moody, J.B., Worsley, T.R., and Manoogian, P.R. 1981. Long-term phosphorus flux to deep-sea sediments. *J Sediment Petrol*, 51, 307–312.

Redfield, A.C. 1958. The biological control of chemical factors in the environment. *Am Scientist*, 46, 205–222.

Richards, F.A. 1957. Oxygen in the ocean. *Mem Geol Soc Am*, 67, 185–238.

Schidlowski, M., Eichmann, R., and Junge, C.E. 1975. Precambrian sedimentary carbonates: Carbon and oxygen isotope geochemistry and implications for the terrestrial oxygen budget. *Precambrian Res*, 2, 1–69.

Schidlowski, M., Junge, C.E., and Pietrek, H. 1977. Sulfur isotope variations in marine sulfate evaporites and the Phanerozoic oxygen budget. *J Geophys Res*, 82, 2557–2565.

Sillen, L.G. 1965. Oxidation state of Earth's ocean and atmosphere II. The behavior of Fe, S and Mn in earlier states. Regulating mechanisms for O_2 and N_2. *Arkiv Kemi*, 25, 159–176.

Van Valen, L. 1971. The history and stability of atmospheric oxygen. *Science*, 171, 439–443.

Walker, J.C.G. 1974. Stability of atmospheric oxygen. *Am J Sci*, 274, 193–214.

Watson, A.J., and Lovelock, J.E. 1983. Biological homeostasis of the global environment: The parable of Daisyworld. *Tellus*, 35B, 284–289.

Heinrich D. Holland

21

The Mechanisms That Control the Carbon Dioxide and the Oxygen Content of the Atmosphere

The nature of the atmosphere has been and continues to be central to the Gaia hypothesis. Lovelock (1988) proposed that "the atmosphere, the oceans, the climate, and the crust of the Earth are regulated at a state comfortable for life because of the behavior of living organisms." This is a testable hypothesis. We know a good deal about the processes that influence the composition of the atmosphere, and we can inquire to what extent these processes are dominated by living organisms. In this paper I will deal only with the CO_2 and the O_2 content of the atmosphere. Both gases are heavily involved in biological cycling. I try to show that the mechanisms that control the CO_2 content of the atmosphere are quite different from those that control the O_2 content of the atmosphere today, and that living organisms affect but do not control the partial pressure of these gases in the atmosphere.

The Mechanisms That Control the Carbon Dioxide Content of the Atmosphere

The apparent behavior of CO_2 depends somewhat on the timescale over which it is observed. On timescales longer than several hundred thousand years we can regard the atmosphere, the biosphere, and the oceans as being reasonably well mixed. It has been shown repeatedly (e.g., Holland, 1978; Sundquist, 1985) that the residence time of CO_2 in this system is approximately 100,000 years. Carbon dioxide is added to the atmosphere by degassing of the Earth, partly via volcanoes, partly via hydrothermal systems. Carbon cycles rapidly through the biosphere, spends a good deal of time in the oceans, largely as a constituent of HCO_3^-, and is finally removed from the atmosphere-biosphere-ocean system in part as a constituent of $CaCO_3$, in part as a constituent of organic matter.

The residence time of CO_2 in this system is very short compared with the age of the Earth. The quantity of CO_2 that has passed through the atmosphere-biosphere-ocean system is very large compared with the quantity that is presently in this system and that has been present in the system at any given time during much, if not all, of Earth's history. The CO_2 content of such a system is determined by the requirement that the output of CO_2 averaged over several residence times is nearly equal to the input. At steady state, the rate of output equals the rate of input. A representation of the behavior of the system during the preindustrial era is shown in figure 21.1. Inputs are plotted on the positive side of the vertical axis, outputs on the negative side. Prior to 1800 AD, the CO_2 content of the atmosphere was approximately 280 ppm (2.8×10^{-4} atm) (Oeschger and Siegenthaler, 1988). The rate of CO_2 output from the system was approximately 4×10^{14} g/year (Holland, 1978). The system was probably close to steady state at that time; the input rate of CO_2 was therefore also approximately 4×10^{14} g/year. There is no functional connection between the CO_2 content of the atmosphere and the rate of CO_2 emission from volcanoes and geothermal systems. Hence the input rate has been drawn as a horizontal line in figure 21.1.

Because the input of CO_2 to the atmosphere is independent of the CO_2 content of the atmosphere,

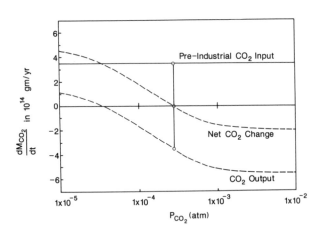

Figure 21.1 Input, output, and net rate of change of atmospheric CO_2 in the preindustrial era as a function of the CO_2 content of the atmosphere.

there is no direct feedback, and to this extent the CO_2 system is a nonfeedback system. The input of CO_2 does depend on the long-term history of the carbon cycle, especially on the availability of carbon in the sedimentary rocks that are undergoing metamorphic degassing at any given time. However, the rate of CO_2 degassing at any given time is not related in any direct way to the CO_2 content of the atmosphere at that time.

The output rate is clearly a complicated function of pCO_2. The functional relationship between the two is still rather poorly defined, as indicated by the dashed curve in figure 21.1. The output rate must increase with increasing pCO_2, because the rate of weathering and hence the rate of carbonate deposition both increase with increasing pCO_2. Decreasing pCO_2 has the opposite effect, and at very low values of pCO_2 the output curve crosses the zero line, because CO_2 is made available by the conversion of dolomite to calcite plus one or more magnesium silicates during weathering followed by sedimentation (Holland, 1978).

The output curve depends on a host of parameters other than pCO_2 (e.g., Lasaga et al., 1985; Volk, 1987). Among these, climate and tectonism are particularly important. Climate is almost certainly influenced by pCO_2 via the greenhouse effect of this gas, but other parameters are at least equally important. The connection between pCO_2, climate, and the output rate of CO_2 from the atmosphere-oceans system creates an important negative feedback mechanism for earth surface temperatures (Walker et al., 1981); this has probably served to mitigate the climatic effects of increasing solar luminosity during the past 4.5 billion years (Gilliland, 1989; Kasting, 1989). The shape and the position of the CO_2 output curve have therefore almost certainly changed during earth's history. The input rate of CO_2 has almost certainly varied as well. The curve representing the net CO_2 change has therefore also varied with time, as has the steady-state value of pCO_2 (e.g., Barron and Washington, 1985; Kasting, 1987).

Although the CO_2 output curve is still poorly defined, we can inquire to what extent the biosphere might be expected to counteract and to have counteracted the effects of processes that increase and decrease the CO_2 content of the atmosphere. If the representation in figure 21.1 is roughly correct, a doubling of the rate of volcanic CO_2 emission would require a very significant increase in the steady-state pCO_2 in the atmosphere, all other factors re-

maining constant. Other factors would, of course, change as well, including the biosphere. It could be argued that an increase in pCO_2 would increase the rate of photosynthesis, hence the mass of the biosphere, and thus the rate of burial of organic matter. This chain of events would tend to lower pCO_2, and to this extent the biosphere might serve to reduce excursions in atmospheric pCO_2.

Some indication of the magnitude of this regulatory effect can be gained from the events of the last century. Fossil fuel burning has added CO_2 to the atmosphere at a progressively greater rate. At present, the CO_2 flux from fossil fuel burning is about forty times the nonanthropogenic flux. The CO_2 content of the atmosphere has increased rapidly in response to the inputs from fossil fuel burning and from land clearance, which is adding CO_2 to the atmosphere at a rate that is probably approximately 20% of the CO_2 flux from fossil fuel burning (e.g., Oeschger and Siegenthaler, 1988). The observed increase in pCO_2 is only about half of what might be expected if all of the CO_2 from fossil fuel burning and land clearance were accumulating in the atmosphere. A good deal of the missing half has probably disappeared from the atmosphere by dissolving in the oceans. Some of the missing half is probably entering the biosphere, in part due to the effect of increasing pCO_2, in part due to the progressively increasing use of fertilizers in agriculture.

The effect of the biosphere as a regulator of pCO_2 during the past century has been minor. This is not surprising. The rate of photosynthesis in deserts is limited by the availability of water, in jungles it is limited by the availability of light and nutrients. In the oceans, the rate of photosynthesis is limited largely by the availability of phosphates and nitrate, and increases in pCO_2 are apt to influence the rate of photosynthesis only slightly. If the last 100 years are at all representative, the biosphere per se does not exert a strong control on atmospheric pCO_2. The major biospheric agent has been humankind; fossil fuel burning and land clearance have shocked the system considerably.

Schwartzman and Volk (1989) have proposed that the development of a land cover of primitive organisms during the Precambrian period had a major effect on pCO_2 and surface temperatures. However, the evidence in support of this proposition is still weak, and it seems more likely that in the distant geological past the effects of the biota as a regulator of pCO_2 were smaller than they are today. Vascular land plants developed about 450 million years ago.

Prior to that time, the land cover was probably restricted to algal mats, whose ability to influence pCO_2 was almost certainly much smaller than that of the present biota. It is not clear when terrestrial algal mats developed. They might be quite ancient, perhaps more than 2000 million years old. Before their development, the land surface was probably bare, and weathering was largely, if not entirely, dominated by inorganic processes.

It seems likely, then, that the CO_2 content of the atmosphere is influenced by the biosphere, but that the biosphere is a poor regulator of pCO_2. To that extent CO_2 is not a good Gaian gas. We cannot, for instance, expect the biosphere to counteract to a major extent the effects of rapid fossil fuel burning and land clearance during the next century.

The Mechanisms That Control the Oxygen Content of the Atmosphere

The mechanisms that control pO_2 are shown schematically in figure 21.2 In the absence of anthropogenic effects, the major outputs of atmospheric O_2 are the oxidation of volcanic gases and the oxidation of organic carbon, sulfide, and ferrous iron during weathering. The oxidation of volcanic gases probably accounts for about one quarter of the total preindustrial O_2 use rate (Holland 1978). Today, both outputs are overshadowed by O_2 use in fossil fuel burning. The effect of O_2 loss on pO_2 by this process is much less noticeable than the effect of CO_2 gain on pCO_2, because O_2 is so much more

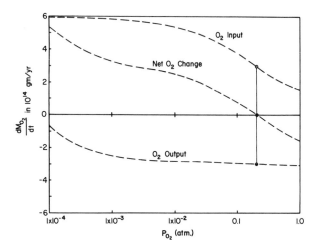

Figure 21.2 Input, output, and net rate of change of atmospheric O_2 in the preindustrial era as a function of the O_2 content of the atmosphere.

abundant that CO_2 ($pO_2/pCO_2 \approx 600$) in the atmosphere today.

Oxygen is produced almost entirely by green plant photosynthesis. Nearly all of the O_2 produced in this fashion is consumed on a short timescale by the oxidative destruction of organic matter. Only about 0.3% of the organic matter produced by the biosphere today is sequestered by burial with sediments. Hence the quantity of O_2 that is available for the oxidation of volcanic gases and of rocks undergoing weathering is only 0.3% of the total quantity that is generated annually by green plant photosynthesis.

The relationship between pO_2 and the output of O_2 by these two processes is reasonably well understood (figure 21.2). Volcanic gases are oxidized rapidly, even in the presence of very small amounts of atmospheric O_2. The rate of oxidation of C^0, S^{-2}, and FeO in rocks undergoing weathering is a complex function of their mineralogy and chemistry, of pO_2, pCO_2, climate, rainfall, and plant cover (e.g., Holland and Zbinden, 1988; Pinto and Holland, 1988). However, even at O_2 levels much lower than 0.2 atm the oxidation of rocks undergoing weathering is nearly complete. Hence O_2 output is nearly insensitive to minor changes in pO_2 today, and the output portion of the O_2 cycle cannot exert an effective control on pO_2.

The processes that determine the rate of O_2 generation are less well understood. Most of the organic matter that grows on land is destroyed on land, but the organic matter that passes down rivers to the oceans is probably greater than the quantity of organic matter that is buried as a constituent of marine sediments (Meybeck, 1982). Kump (1988) has discussed the implications of this for pO_2 regulation. Much of the river-borne organic matter apparently becomes part of the marine food chain. The rate of photosynthesis in the oceans is limited largely by the availability of phosphate and nitrate. These nutrients are recycled very efficiently in the oceans (e.g., Broecker and Peng, 1982). Ultimately, approximately one third of the input of dissolved phosphate leaves the oceans as a constituent of organic matter that is buried with marine sediments (Mach et al., 1987). The remaining phosphate is removed with iron and manganese oxide-hydroxides (Berner, 1973; Froelich et al., 1977; Palmer, 1985; Sherwood et al., 1987), with apatite, and probably with several other mineral phases (Froelich et al., 1982).

The quantity of organic matter buried with marine sediments is equal to the product of the total quantity of organic matter generated in and brought to the oceans times the fraction of the organic matter that is preserved. Most of the organic matter preserved in marine sediments is incorporated in sediments fairly near shore (Berner, 1982). Most of these sediments are deposited in well-oxygenated seawater. The fraction of organic matter preserved in this setting is probably only a weak function of the O_2 content of the water column, except possibly in areas where the concentration of dissolved O_2 is less than approximately 50 μmol/kg, about one fifth of the O_2 concentration in equilibrium with an O_2 pressure of 0.2 atm (Emerson, 1985). The rate of sedimentation is a much more important parameter (Müller and Suess, 1979; Henrichs and Reeburgh, 1987).

It has been suggested that in low-O_2 environments like the Black Sea and anoxic fjords, the fraction of organic matter preserved in sediments is significantly greater than in well-oxygenated environments (Glenn and Arthur, 1985; Canfield, 1989). The evidence for this, has however, been questioned (e.g., Calvert, 1987; Calvert et al., 1987), and a recent analysis of all the available data (Betts and Holland, 1991) has shown that the effect of the oxidation state of the water column on the burial efficiency of organic carbon is slight.

The effects of changes in atmospheric oxygen on nutrients and on the trace metals that are critical for photosynthesis are not well known. The concentration of NO_3^- in the oceans is probably most sensitive to changes in pO_2. A sudden increase in pO_2 of 10% would increase the concentration of dissolved O_2 in seawater sufficiently to eliminate denitrification in the O_2-minimum zone (e.g., Codispoti, 1989). The NO_3^- content of seawater would therefore increase. As a consequence, the productivity of the oceans would increase until the rate of denitrification in the O_2-minimum zone had increased to the point that dynamic equilibrium in the marine nitrogen cycle is reestablished.

At this new steady state more organic carbon would arrive at the sea floor and be buried than under present-day conditions. The operation of the nitrogen cycle therefore acts as a positive rather than as a negative feedback on O_2 production. Other factors, presumably involving PO_4^{3-} and/or the trace metals, must be important in establishing the negative feedback that stabilizes pO_2. Upward excursions of pO_2 to approximately $\leq$ 0.35 atm and downward excursions to approximately $\geq$ 0.13 atm during the past 300 million years are apparently allowed by the evidence for well-developed forests and by the presence of charcoal in coal deposits (Watson et al., 1978). The rather narrow limits to pO_2 during this rather long period of time suggests that the mechanism that has controlled pO_2 has been quite effective (see for instance Berner and Canfield, 1989, and Kump, 1989)

To what extent, then, has the O_2 content of the atmosphere been "regulated by living organisms at a state comfortable for life"? If we take the long view geologically speaking, the answer is surely "not very well," The first living organisms almost certainly used H_2 and other reduced gases to convert CO_2 to organic matter by reactions such as

$$CO_2 + 2H_2 \rightarrow CH_2O + H_2O \qquad (1)$$

No molecular O_2 is produced in such reactions. During this period of Earth's history, the O_2 content of the atmosphere was therefore almost certainly very low. The rise of pO_2 to its present level is still poorly documented. The evidence from paleosols (Holland et al., 1989) and from the weathering of iron formations (Holland and Beukes, 1990) suggests that pO_2 was approximately 1% of the present atmospheric level until about 1.9 b.y.b.p., and rose to values $\geq$ 15% of the present atmospheric level at or about that time. The evolution of metazoans at the end of the Precambrian period has been related to an increase in atmospheric O_2 (Rhodes and Morse, 1971), but the evidence for this hypothesis is still rather weak. Although the evolution of atmospheric O_2 is still poorly defined, it is virtually certain that the major change early in Earth's history was related to the development of green plant photosynthesis. The term *regulated at a state comfortable for life* applies to the history of atmospheric O_2 only if the term *life* is used in the sense of *life adapted to particular atmospheric* conditions. But if the phrase is used in that fashion, the distinction between a gaian and a Darwinian view of Earth's history becomes very small.

The relatively narrow limits that we now seem to be able to set on excursions of pO_2 during the past 300 million years have been interpreted in terms of a Gaian control on pO_2 (Lovelock, 1988). If the fragments of the control mechanism that I have described above turn out to be correct, then the relative constancy of pO_2 during the past 300 million years owes as much to inorganic chemical processes and to physical oceanography as it does to the biosphere. A much more quantitative understanding of this complex control mechanism is needed, before we can be sure of the role that living organisms have played in stabilizing the O_2 content of the atmosphere during the past 300 million years.

Conclusions

The nature of the CO_2 control mechanism, and the behavior of pCO_2 during the past century suggest that the behavior of pCO_2 is largely nongaian. The mechanisms that probably control pO_2 depend heavily on biological processes. Evolutionary changes in these processes seem to be responsible for major changes in pO_2 during geological history. In this sense the factors that control pO_2 are also not Gaian. However, a good deal of evidence suggests that the level of atmospheric O_2 has varied rather little during the past 300 million years; it is too early to say how much of this stability is due to the influence of nonbiological and how much to that of biological processes.

Acknowledgments

I wish to acknowledge my indebtedness to Andrew Knoll for many illuminating discussions, to Lee Kump for his thoughtful review of the manuscript, and to the National Aeronautics and Space Administration for support under Grant No. NAGW-599 to Harvard University.

References

Barron, E.J., and Washington, W.M. 1985. Warm Cretaceous climates: High atmospheric CO_2 as a plausible mechanism. In: Sundquist, E.T., and Broecker, W.S., eds. *The Carbon Cycle and Atmospheric CO_2: Natural Variations Archean to Present.* Geophysical Monograph 32. Washington, D.C.: American Geophysical Union, 546–553.

Berner, R.A. 1973. Phosphate removal from seawater by adsorption on volcanogenic ferric oxides. *Earth Planet Sci Lett,* 18, 77–86.

Berner, R.A. 1982. Burial of organic carbon and pyrite sulfur in the modern ocean: Its geochemical and environmental significance. *Am J Sci,* 282, 451–473.

Berner, R.A., and Canfield, D.E. 1989. A new model for atmospheric oxygen over Phanerozoic time. *Am J Sci,* 289, 333–361.

Betts, J.N., and Holland, H.D. 1991. The oxygen content of ocean bottom waters, the burial efficiency of organic carbon, and regulation of atmospheric oxygen. Paleogeogr, Paleoclim, Paleoecol, in press.

Broecker, W.S., and Peng, T.-H. 1982. *Tracers in the Sea.* Palisades, N.Y.: Lamont-Doherty Geological Observatory.

Calvert, S.E. 1987. Oceanographic controls on the accumulation of organic matter in marine sediments. In: Brooks, J., and Fleet, A.J., eds. *Marine Petroleum Source Rocks.* London: Blackwell Scientific, 137–151.

Calvert, S.E., Vogel, J.S., and Southon, J.R. 1987, Carbon accumulation rates and the origin of the Holocene sapropel in the Black Sea. *Geology,* 15, 918–921.

Canfield, D.E. 1989. Sulfate reduction and oxic respiration in marine sediments: Implications for organic carbon preservation in euxinic environments. *Deep Sea Res,* 36, 121–138.

Codispoti, L.A. 1989. Phosphorus vs. nitrogen limitations of new and export production. In: Berger, W.H., Smetacek, V.S., and Wefer, G., eds. *Productivity of the Ocean: Present and Past.* Dahlem Workshop Reports, Life Sciences Research Report 44. New York: Wiley, 377–394

Emerson, S. 1985. Organic carbon preservation in marine sediments. In: Sundquist, E.T., and Broecker, W.S., eds. *The Carbon Cycle and Atmospheric CO_2: Natural Variations Archean to Present.* Geophysical Monograph 32. Washington, D.C.: American Geophysical Union, 78–87.

Froelich, P.N., Bender, M.L., and Heath, G.R. 1977. Phosphorus accumulation in metalliferous sediments on the East Pacific Rise. *Earth Planet Sci Lett,* 34, 351–359.

Froelich, P.N., Bender, M.L., Luedtke, N.A., Heath, G.R., and De Vries, T. 1982. The marine phosphorus cycle. *Am J Sci,* 282, 474–511.

Gilliland, R.L. 1989. Solar evolution. *Palaeogeogr, Palaeoclim, Palaeoecol (Global and Planetary Change Section),* 75, 35–55.

Glenn, C.R., and Arthur, M.A. 1985. Sedimentary and geochemical indicators of productivity and oxygen contents in modern and ancient basins: The Holocene Black Sea as the "type" anoxic basin. *Chem Geol,* 48, 325–354.

Henrichs, S.M., and Reeburgh, W.S. 1987. Anaerobic mineralization of marine sediment organic matter: Rates and the role of anaerobic processes in the oceanic carbon economy. *Geomicrobiol J,* 5, 191–237.

Holland, H.D. 1978. *The Chemistry of the Atmosphere and Oceans.* New York: Wiley-Interscience.

Holland, H.D., Beukes, N.J. 1990. A paleoweathering profile from Griqualand West, South Africa: Evidence for a dramatic rise in atmospheric oxygen between 2.2 and 1.9 B.Y.B.P. *Am J Sci,* 290A, 1–34.

Holland, H.D., Feakes, C.R., and Zbinden, E.A. 1989. The Flin Flon paleosol and the composition of the atmosphere 1.8 b.y.b.p. *Am J Sci,* 289, 362–389.

Holland, H.D., and Zbinden, E.A. 1988. Paleosols and the evolution of the Precambrian atmosphere, Part I. In: Lerman, A., and Meybeck, M., eds. *Physical and Chemical Weathering in Geochemical Cycles.* NATO ASI series. Dordrecht: Kluwer Academic Publishers, 61–82.

Kasting, J.F. 1987. Theoretical constraints on oxygen and carbon dioxide concentrations in the Precambrian atmosphere. *Precambrian Res,* 34, 205–229.

Kasting, J.F. 1989. Long-term stability of the Earth's climate. *Palaeogeogr, Palaeoclim, Palaeoecol (Global and Planetary Change Section),* 75, 83–95.

Kump, L.R. 1988. Terrestrial feedback in atmospheric oxygen regulation by fire and phosphorus. *Nature*, 335, 152–154.

Kump, L.R. 1989. Chemical stability of the atmosphere and ocean. *Palaeogeogr, Palaeoclim, Palaeoecol (Global and Planetary Change Section)*, 75, 123–136.

Lasaga, A.C., Berner, R.A., and Garrels, R.M. 1985. An improved geochemical model of atmospheric CO_2 fluctuations over the past 100 million years. In: Sundquist, E.T., and Broecker, W.S., eds. *The Carbon Cycle and Atmospheric CO_2: Natural Variations Archean to Present*. Geophysical Monograph 32. Washington, D.C.: American Geophysical Union, 397–411.

Lovelock, J. 1988. *The Ages of Gaia*. New York: W.W. Norton and Co.

Mach, D.L. Ramirez, A., and Holland, H.D. 1987. Organic phosphorus and carbon in marine sediments. *Am J Sci*, 287, 429–441.

Meybeck, M. 1982. Carbon, nitrogen and phosphorus transport by world rivers. *Am J Sci*, 282, 401–450.

Müller, P.J., and Suess, E. 1979. Productivity, sedimentation, and sedimentary organic carbon in the oceans. I. Organic carbon preservation. *Deep Sea Res*, 26, 1347–1362.

Oeschger, H., and Siegenthaler, U. 1988. How has the atmospheric concentration of CO_2 changed? In: Rowland, F.S., and Isaksen, I.S.A., eds. *The Changing Atmosphere*. New York: Wiley, 5–23.

Palmer, M.R. 1985. Rare earth elements in foraminifera tests. *Earth Planet Sci Lett*, 73, 285–298.

Pinto, J.P., and Holland, H.D. 1988. Paleosols and the evolution of the atmosphere, Part II. In: Reinhardt, J., and Sigleo, W.R., eds. *Paleosols and Weathering Through Geologic Time: Principles and Applications*. Special Paper 216. Boulder, CO: Geologic Society of America, 21–34.

Rhodes, D.C., and Morse, J.W. 1971. Evolutionary and ecologic significance of oxygen-deficient marine basins. *Lethaia*, 4, 413–428.

Schwartzman, D.W., and Volk T. 1989. Biotic enhancement of weathering and the habitability of Earth. *Nature*, 340, 457–460.

Sherwood, B.A., Sager, S.L., and Holland, H.D. 1987. Phosphorus in foraminiferal sediments from North Atlantic Ridge cores and in pure limestones. *Geochim Cosmochim Acta*, 51, 1861–1866.

Sundquist, E.T. 1985. Geological perspectives on carbon dioxide and the carbon cycle. In: Sundquist, E.T., and Broecker, W.S., eds. *The Carbon Cycle and Atmospheric CO_2: Natural Variations Archean to Present*. Geophysical Monograph 32. Washington, D.C.: American Geophysical Union, 5–59.

Volk, T. 1987. Feedback between weathering and atmospheric CO_2 over the last 100 million years. *Am J Sci*, 287, 763–779.

Walker, J.C.G., Hays, P.B., and Kasting, J.F. 1981. A negative feedback mechanism for the long-term stabilization of Earth's surface temperature. *J Geophys Res*, 86, 9776–9782.

Watson, A., Lovelock, J.E., and Margulis, L. 1978. Methanogenesis, fires and regulation of atmospheric oxygen. *Biosystems*, 10, 293–298.

VI
Mechanisms: Carbon and Biomass

James C. G. Walker

22

Feedback Processes in the Biogeochemical Cycles of Carbon

In this chapter I discuss my favorite greenhouse gas—carbon dioxide—and how life affects its abundance. For this purpose, I use a theoretical model of the global biogeochemical system. Both John Harte (chapter 9) and Steve Schneider (Schneider 1987) have described models and their uses and limitations; I endorse entirely what they have said. In the model that yielded the results I am going to describe, there is nothing that I did not put in. The model can yield no brilliant new discoveries. On the other hand, the model is good at helping us remember details and features of complex systems that I am good at forgetting.

The equations I use are just like those that Harte described except that in my calculations the amount of a chemical replaces the population of a biological species. I use a specific set of equations for the time rate of change of the amount of one chemical or another in one reservoir or another. At present there are twenty-four equations in the model for such species as oxygen in the atmosphere, carbon in the shallow oceans, carbon in the deep oceans, strontium isotopes, and carbon isotopes. The equations most directly involved with the carbon cycle are presented in the Appendix to this chapter. Within the system there are many close links and feedbacks. I propose to use this model first to explore a possible impact of human activities on the biogeochemical cycles of carbon.

Doomsday

The first hypothetical situation I am going to describe serves to remind us that carbon responds very differently on different timescales. Imagine that some catastrophe wipes out all of the photosynthetic organisms on earth and consider how the system responds to this sudden destruction of plant life. According to the model, the response of two interesting atmospheric gases is as shown in figure 22.1. Over a period of some five to ten million years atmospheric O_2 disappears while CO_2 increases,

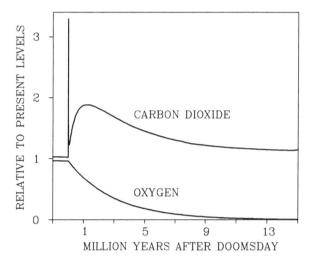

Figure 22.1 Calculated response of atmospheric CO_2 and O_2 to the sudden and complete cessation of photosynthesis.

then decreases, then increases again, before finally decreasing to almost its original value.

The behavior of O_2 is not surprising; indeed, it is well understood. The factors that control atmospheric oxygen have been explored by Holland (1973, 1978) and by me (Walker, 1974, 1977, 1980). A very simple version of the oxygen budget is depicted in figure 22.2. The experiment that I describe here eliminates photosynthesis, which is the source of O_2. Without a source, atmospheric O_2 disappears over a period of five to ten million years as a result of weathering, particularly of kerogen, the reduced carbon in sedimentary rocks.

Why CO_2 behaves as shown in figure 22.1 is not nearly as obvious. The major surface short-term reservoirs of carbon are shown in figure 22.3. The figure reveals that there is much more carbon in the biota, which includes recently dead organisms, than there is in the atmosphere. In my doomsday experiment, photosynthesis stops suddenly, but respiration does not. On a timescale of about twenty years, respiration releases carbon from the biota. This re-

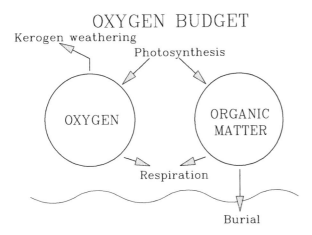

Figure 22.2 The source of atmospheric O_2 is photosynthesis followed by burial of organic carbon. The main sink is weathering of organic carbon in sedimentary rocks.

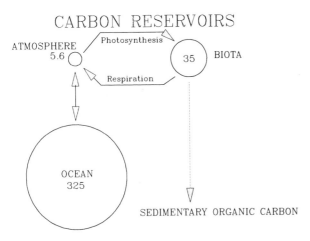

Figure 22.3 There is much more carbon in the ocean than in the biota and much more in the biota than in the atmosphere. The units are 10^{16} moles.

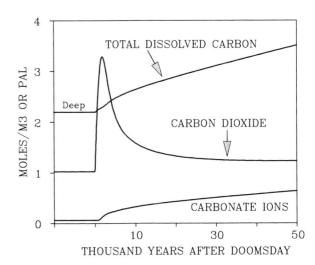

Figure 22.4 Response of the carbon system in the first fifty thousand years after doomsday.

lease contributes to the increase in atmospheric CO_2 shown in figure 22.1, but it is not the main factor. More important is the cessation of the biological pump that transfers carbon and alkalinity from the surface ocean into the deep ocean (Broecker and Peng, 1982). The CO_2 spike disappears on a timescale of a thousand years or so as the enhanced CO_2 pressure causes rapid dissolution of shallow water and terrestrial carbonate sediments. Carbonate dissolution releases alkalinity that neutralizes excess carbonic acid. In this calculation, the concentration of carbonate ions in the deep-sea increases from the beginning of the perturbation, because the rain of particulate organic carbon stops, so deep sea carbonate sediments do not dissolve.

One of the nice things about a computational model is that it allows us to zoom in for a closer look at interesting phenomena. In figure 22.4 I show a closer look at the carbon system in the first fifty thousand years after doomsday. Look first at the curves for total dissolved carbon in deep and shallow oceanic reservoirs. Before doomsday, the settling of biogenic particles into the deep sea maintains a gradient, with more dissolved carbon in the deep ocean than in the shallow. This biological pumping stops when photosynthesis stops; the concentration of dissolved carbon in the shallow ocean rapidly approaches that in the deep ocean. At the same time, the elevated pCO_2 results in more rapid dissolution of calcium carbonate minerals on land and on the continental shelves and thus in an increased flux of dissolved carbon into the ocean. But the cessation of photosynthesis has brought to a halt the precipitation of biogenic carbonate minerals. The steady and continuing increase in total dissolved carbon that appears in figure 22.4 is a consequence of imbalance between the rate of supply of carbon to the ocean by rivers and the rate of removal by precipitation of new carbonate minerals.

The long-term response of the system can be understood in terms of the flow of total carbon and alkalinity through the ocean. The relationships are illustrated in figure 22.5. Carbon is supplied by volcanic and metamorphic emissions, by oxidative weathering of kerogen, and by dissolution of carbonate minerals. It is removed by the burial of organic carbon, photosynthetically produced, and by the precipitation of carbonate minerals, today also

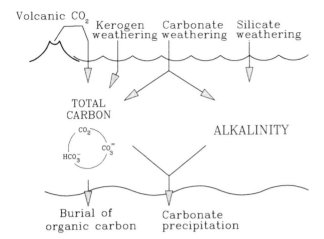

Figure 22.5 Partitioning of total carbon between dissolved ions and atmospheric gas depends on the balance between alkalinity and total carbon.

largely biogenic. Dissolution of carbonates is a source also of alkalinity, which is removed only by precipitation of carbonates (at least in the simplest system; in fact, imbalances in the sulfur budget can also affect alkalinity). Dissolution of silicate minerals supplies alkalinity but not carbon to the system of ocean and atmosphere. The partitioning of total dissolved carbon between CO_2, bicarbonate ions, and carbonate ions depends on the concentrations of total dissolved carbon and of alkalinity (Broecker and Peng, 1982). It is necessary to calculate both concentrations in order to calculate pCO_2 or the degree of saturation of seawater with respect to calcium carbonate, which depends on the concentration of carbonate ions.

Dissolution of a mole of calcium carbonate results in the addition of a mole of total dissolved carbon to the ocean and two equivalent moles of alkalinity, because the calcium ion carries two charges. The excess of carbonate dissolution over precipitation therefore causes alkalinity to increase more rapidly than total dissolved carbon. Seawater therefore becomes less acidic and the concentration of carbonate ions increases, as shown in figure 22.4.

Increasing concentrations of dissolved carbonate ions result in increasing levels of supersaturation of seawater with respect to calcium carbonate and an increasing rate of precipitation of abiogenic carbonate minerals. After about a million years, the saturation of seawater has increased to the point where abiogenic carbonate precipitation has more than compensated for the loss of biogenic carbonate precipitation. Until abiogenic precipitation catches up with the rate of weathering of carbonate minerals,

total dissolved carbon, alkalinity, and atmospheric CO_2 all continue to increase. It is this adjustment to the loss of biogenic carbonate precipitation that causes the second increase in CO_2 shown in figure 22.1. The final decrease to nearly the original CO_2 amount is a response of the system to imbalances between the rate of volcanic and metamorphic release of CO_2 and the rate at which this CO_2 is neutralized by the dissolution of silicate minerals and release of calcium ions.

It is significant that the CO_2 pressure on the lifeless Earth is very nearly the same as on the inhabited Earth, in spite of the substantial change in the composition of seawater that results from the elimination of biogenic carbonate precipitation. This result can be understood in terms of the cartoon representation in figure 22.6 of the processes that control atmospheric CO_2 on a geological timescale. For simplicity, assume that the oxidation budget of ocean and atmosphere is balanced so that the rate of burial of organic carbon equals the rate of oxidation of sedimentary organic carbon. Under these conditions, the biological processes indicated on the right in figure 22.6 do not influence CO_2. The controlling processes on the ten-million-year timescale are the release of CO_2 from the solid earth by volcanic and metamorphic processes and the return of CO_2 to the solid phase by the precipitation of carbonate minerals. The calcium and magnesium in these minerals is supplied by weathering reactions at a rate that depends on the amount of CO_2 in the atmosphere. The system achieves a balance when the weathering rate is equal to the volcanic release rate.

In my model, the weathering rate does not depend on life and the volcanic release rate is constant, so long-term equilibrium is possible only with the CO_2 pressure at its original, steady-state value.

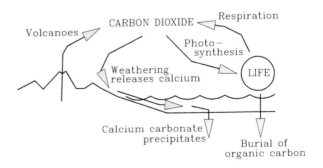

Figure 22.6 On a geological timescale, atmospheric CO_2 depends on the balance between volcanism and weathering and on the net rate of burial of organic carbon.

There is every reason to suppose that terrestrial vegetation does influence the weathering rate (Lovelock and Whitfield, 1982). My calculations therefore have demonstrated only that the amount of CO_2 in the atmosphere does not depend on calcium carbonate precipitation processes. On a geological timescale, CO_2 depends on the balance between volcanism and weathering, not on the presence or absence of carbonate-precipitating organisms.

Origin of Carbonate-Secreting Plankton

I want to turn now to the question of how we can test the workings of the earth system, of Gaia. I agree with Lovelock about the importance of testing, but I do not think we will get to conduct any controlled experiments on a global scale. I agree with Schneider that we should look at the record of what has changed in the past, particularly at Earth's history. We can test the system by looking at historical changes. Here is an illustration of this process.

In figure 22.7, look first at the bottom curve, which shows the rate of accumulation of calcium carbonate sediments on shallow-water platforms during the Phanerozoic period. This is the apparent rate, uncorrected for possible destruction of ancient carbonates by weathering or tectonism. The data are from Budyko and colleagues (1987). Observational uncertainties are fewest during the last 100 million years or so; during this time there has been a pronounced decline in the rate of accumulation of

carbonate sediments on continental platforms. Kuenen (1950) suggested some years ago that this decline is a consequence of the origin of calcareous plankton, which occurred 150 to 200 million years ago. The idea is that calcareous plankton have transferred carbonate from the shelves into the deep ocean.

The proposed mechanism can be understood in terms of the budget of marine calcium shown in figure 22.8 (Wilkinson and Walker, 1989). The calcium in the ocean comes largely from carbonate weathering, partly from silicate weathering, and partly from sea floor hydrothermal systems. The largest removal process is the precipitation of calcium carbonate minerals, today partly in the deep ocean and partly on the continental shelves. The deep ocean is undersaturated with respect to calcium carbonate. Carbonates accumulate there today because they rain down from above; they are precipitated downward by calcareous plankton. By precipitating carbonates on the sea floor these plankton today are diverting calcium and carbon that would otherwise have precipitated on the shelves. The idea is that the biological event, the origin of calcareous plankton, may, in this way, have caused the decline in the rate of accumulation of shelf carbonates that is observed during the last 100 million years of Earth's history.

Unfortunately, there is another explanation of the observations (Milliman, 1974; Berger and Winterer, 1974; Hay, 1988), forcefully developed by my colleague, Bruce Wilkinson (Wilkinson and Walker, 1989). Wilkinson calls attention to the close correlation between the carbonate accumulation rate and the area of shallow seas plotted at the top of figure 22.7. Shelf carbonates accumulate in shallow seas; perhaps the decline in the rate of carbonate accu-

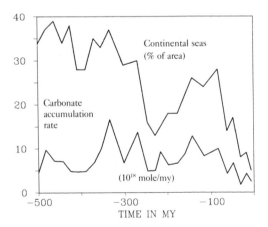

Figure 22.7 Observed rate of accumulation of carbonate sediments on the continental shelves and the fraction of total continental area covered by shallow seas. (From Budyko, et al., 1987).

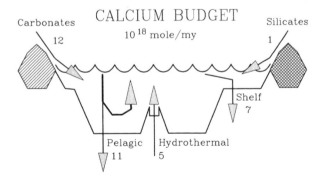

Figure 22.8 The calcium budget of the modern ocean. (From Wilkinson and Walker, 1989).

mulation is simply a consequence of a decline in the area in which shelf carbonates can accumulate. The area of shallow seas has declined precipitously over the past 100 million years.

I can use my simulation to explore this situation, comparing results of a calculation in which calcareous plankton do not change during the course of the Phanerozoic period with results of a calculation in which they evolve. Figure 22.9 shows the rate of accumulation of shelf carbonates. The points are Ronov's data (Budyko, et al., 1987), now corrected for erosion by multiplication by a function that increases exponentially with age. The dashed line shows the carbonate precipitation rate calculated with diversification of calcareous plankton between 100 and 150 million years ago. The results reveal the expected transfer of precipitation from the shelves to the deep ocean. The solid line in the middle represents the results of the calculation with no change in plankton behavior. The decrease at the end, during the past 100 million years, is a consequence simply of the decrease in shelf area. Neither calculation yields a particularly good fit to the data, and neither reproduces the amplitude of the decrease observed in the past 100 million years. I do not believe that this analysis enables us yet to discriminate between the two explanations for the observed decrease in the rate of accumulation of shelf carbonate.

As a side issue, note that the two calculations yield essentially identical CO_2 histories. Carbon dioxide histories are shown by the solid and dotted

lines right on top of each other in the middle of figure 22.10. The solid line shows results of the calculation with no change in the plankton; the dotted line shows results of the calculation in which plankton originate 150 million years ago. The CO_2 histories are essentially the same. Just for illustration, the top panel of figure 22.10 shows how carbonate precipitation is being transferred from shelf to deep sea in the calculation with plankton evolution. The calculation with no evolution of plankton shows much less change in the relative rates of pelagic and shelf carbonate precipitation during the course of Phanerozoic history.

The results in figure 22.10 show a close inverse correlation between CO_2 and land area, plotted relative to the present as a solid line at the bottom of the figure (Budyko, et al., 1987). This correlation arises because CO_2 depends on the weathering rate, and the weathering rate presumably depends on how much land is exposed to weathering. In the absence of variation in the rate of volcanic emission, the weathering rate alone is what controls the amount of CO_2 in the atmosphere on a geological timescale. This is not a new result—it has been described before by Berner and colleagues (1984) and by Lasaga and colleagues (1985).

Turning to the question of how can we test the Gaia hypothesis, I suggest that one potentially very fruitful approach is to study the earth's history. Earth history offers a good geological record of evolving life and the evolving environment of ocean, atmosphere, and rocks. The rock record

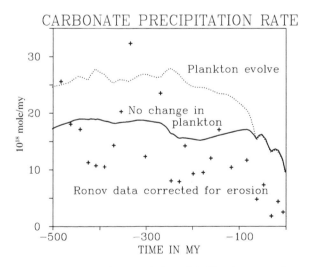

Figure 22.9 Rate of accumulation of shelf carbonates calculated with plankton evolution (dashed line) and without (solid line) compared with observations (pluses).

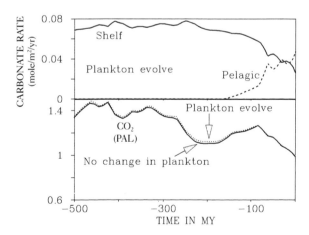

Figure 22.10 Results of calculations of the Phanerozoic history of CO_2 with and without allowance for the evolution of calcareous plankton relative to present atmospheric levels (PAL). Data on the land area exposed to weathering are from Budyko and colleagues (1987).

includes evidence of change in isotope ratios, sediment volumes, trace element composition, sedimentological setting, and climate. The rock record also offers good evidence of biological changes of potential importance to the global environment such as the origin of oxygenic photosynthesis, the first eukaryota, the origin of Metazoa, and the origin of land plants. I have discussed the origin of calcareous plankton and their impact on the environment as an illustration of what might be done. Perhaps we can learn how the earth system works by observing and interpreting the geological record, particularly with the help of theoretical analyses.

Acknowledgment

I am grateful to Bruce Wilkinson and Jim Kasting for many useful ideas. An anonymous referee helped me to understand the results of my own calculation. This research was supported in part by the National Science Foundation under Grant ATM-8209760.

References

Berger, W.H., and Winterer, E.L., 1974. Plate stratigraphy and the fluctuating carbonate line. In: Hsu, K.J., and Jenkyns, H.C., eds., *Pelagic Sediments on Land and Under the Sea,* International Association of Sedimentologists, Spec Pub. 1, pp. 11–48.

Berner, R.A., Lasaga, A.C., and Garrels, R.M. 1984. The carbonate-silicate geochemical cycle and its effect on atmospheric carbon dioxide over the past 100 million years, *American J Sci,* 283, 641–683.

Broecker, W.S., and Peng, T.H., *Tracers in the Sea,* 1982. Palisades, New York, Lamont-Doherty Geological Observatory.

Budyko, M.I., Ronov, A.B., and Yanshin, A.L., 1987. *History of the Earth's Atmosphere,* Berlin: Springer-Verlag.

Hay, W.W. 1988. Paleoceanography: A review for the GSA Centennial, *Geological Soc America Bull,* 100, 1934–1956.

Holland, H.D. 1973. Ocean water, nutrients, and atmospheric oxygen, in *Proceedings of Symposium on Hydrogeochemistry and Biogeochemistry,* Vol. 1, Washington: The Clarke Co., 68–81.

Holland, H.D. 1978. *The Chemistry of the Atmosphere and Oceans,* New York: Wiley-Interscience.

Kuenen, P.H. 1950. *Marine Geology,* New York: John Wiley and Sons, 568 pp.

Lasaga, A.C., Berner, R.A., and Garrels, R.M. 1985. An improved model of atmospheric CO_2 fluctuations over the past 100 million years, in *The Carbon Cycle and Atmospheric CO_2: Natural Variations Archean to Present,* Washington, D.C. American Geophysical Union, 397–411.

Lovelock, J.E., and Whitfield, M. 1982. Life span of the biosphere. *Nature,* 296, 561–563.

Milliman, J.D. 1974. Marine carbonates. In: Milliman, J.D., Mueller, G., and Foerster, U., eds. *Recent Sedimentary Carbonates,* Part 1. Heidelberg: Springer-Verlag.

Schneider, S.H., 1987. Climate modeling. *Sci. Amer. 256,* No. 5, 72–80.

Walker, J.C.G. 1974. Stability of atmospheric oxygen. *Am J Sci,* 274, 193–214.

Walker, J.C.G. 1977. *Evolution of the Atmosphere.* New York: Macmillan Publishing Co.

Walker, J.C.G. 1980. The oxygen cycle. In: Hutzinger, O., ed. *The Natural Environment and the Biogeochemical Cycles.* Berlin: Springer-Verlag, 87–104.

Wilkinson, B.H., and Walker, J.C.G. 1989. Phanerozoic cycling of sedimentary carbonate. *Am J Sci,* 289, 525–548.

Appendix

The program used for these illustrative calculations solves for the time histories of twenty-four dependent variables, not all of which are directly relevant to this discussion. I list here the equations for the thirteen variables that bear most directly on the carbon cycle. The dependent variables are called y(i); their time derivatives are yp(i). Time is measured in years. This documentation is not complete, but it indicates the most important assumptions that enter into the calculations. The solution is by the inverse Euler method.

y(1) = bwoxy = dissolved O_2 in deep sea

y(2) = bwcorg = reactive organic carbon in deep sea

y(3) = shcorg = reactive organic carbon in shelf sediments

y(4) = pco2 = atmospheric CO_2 relative to present

y(5) = sigcs = total dissolved carbon in shallow sea

y(6) = sigcd = total dissolved carbon in deep sea

y(7) = calc = sea floor carbonates susceptible to dissolution

y(8) = alks = alkalinity in shallow sea

y(9) = mg = magnesium in seawater

y(10) = ca = calcium in seawater

y(11) = sulf = sulfate in seawater

y(12) = tphos = total phosphorus, both dissolved and particulate

y(13) = po2 = atmospheric oxygen relative to present

Redox Balance

yp(1) = (so − bwoxy) / vtime − (corgox + bsulfred) * 1.3

yp(1) = yp(1) + 2 * (bpyrp − hydrof * frox)

yp(2) = pprod − bkerp − corgox − bsulfred

yp(3) = shprod − shkerp − shkoc * po2 ∧ 2 * shcorg − shsulfred

Carbon Cycle
yp(4) = (pco2s − pco2) / distime + (volc + kerox − tkerp) / matmco2

yp(5) = −(pco2s − pco2) * matmco2 / distime − (1 + corat) * pprod

yp(5) = yp(5) + (sigcd − depth * sigcs / thicks) / vtime'continuation statement

yp(5) = yp(5) − shcarb − cement + carbw − dolprc − shprod + shsulfred

yp(5) = yp(5) + shkoc * po2 ∧ 2 * shcorg

yp(6) = (depth * sigcs / thicks − sigcd) / vtime

yp(6) = yp(6) + corgox + bsulfred + calcdis

yp(7) = corat * pprod − calprc − calcdis

Cations
yp(8) = (alkd − alks * depth / thicks) / vtime − (2 * corat) * pprod

yp(8) = yp(8) + 2 * (silw + carbw − shcarb − cement − pyrox + shpyrp − dolprc)

yp(9) = fmsil * silw + fmcarb * carbw − dolprc − mg * hydrof / (tmg * hydrofz)

yp(10) = (1 − fmsil) * silw + (1 − fmcarb) * carbw − cement

yp(10) = yp(10) − shcarb + mg * hydrof / (tmg * hydrofz) * (1 − sfhk * co3d)

yp(10) = yp(10) + evdis − evap + calcdis − corat * pprod

Anions
yp(11) = evdis + hydrof * frox + pyrox − evap − bpyrp − shpyrp

yp(12) = (calprc + shcarb + cement) / caprat + (bkerp + shkerp) / kphos

yp(12) = phosw − phos * (yp(12) + psed)

Oxygen
yp(13) = bkerp + shkerp + 2 * (bpyrp + shpyrp) + tkerp − kerox

yp(13) = (yp(13) − 2 * (hydrof * frox + pyrox)) / matmo

so = .48 * po2 'Concentration of dissolved O_2

vtime = 1140 'Ventilation time of deep sea

corgox = bwoxy * bwcorg * koc 'Respiration in the deep sea

bsulfred = bwcorg * sulf * ksc 'Sulfate reduction in deep sea sediments

bpyrp = bpytsred * bsulfred 'Pyrite deposition in deep sea sediments

frox = 10 * po2 / (1 + 9 * po2) 'Oxidation probability for hydrothermal

phos = tphos − (bwcorg + shcorg) / kphos − calc / caprat 'Dissolved phosphorus

phos = phos / (1 + pfp * thicks / depth) 'Continuation

pprod = phos * (1 − pfp) * 105 / (vtime * (1 + 105 * corat / caprat))

Plankton Productivity
bkerp = bwcorg / bwbt 'Kerogen deposition in deep sea

caprat = 1060 'Calcium-to-phosphorus ratio in carbonate tests

pfp = .05 'Preformed phosphorus

depth = 3420 'Thickness of the deep sea reservoir in meters

thicks = 380 'Thickness of the shallow sea reservoir

corat = .25 'Calcium carbonate to organic ratio in particulates

sharea = aream − area 'Shelf area = continental area − land area

shprod = SQR(sharea) * phos * kshprod 'Productivity on shelves

shkerp = shcorg / shbt 'Shelf kerogen precipitation rate

shsulfred = shksc * sulf * shcorg 'Shelf sulfate reduction rate

Carbon Cycle
hco3s = 2 * sigcs − alks 'Bicarbonate in shallow sea

co3s = alks − sigcs 'Carbonate ions in shallow sea

pco2s = kco2 * hco3s ∧ 2 / co3s 'Equilibrium pressure of CO_2

distime = 8.64 'Time for atmospheric CO_2 to dissolve

arfre = area * frsed 'Area of sedimentary rock exposed to weathering

frafre = arfre * frox 'Sedimentary area times oxidation probability

kerox = kocst * frafre 'Rate of oxidation of sedimentary kerogen

matmco2 = .056 'Mass of CO_2 in atmosphere, $10 \wedge^{18}$ moles

shcarb = shprod * kshcp * ((co3s * ca − ssat) + ABS(co3s * ca − ssat))

Rate of Deposition of Shelf Carbonates
calprc = calc / sedt 'Rate of deposition of deep sea carbonates

dolprc = kdol * ((mg * co3s − msat) + ABS(mg * co3s − msat)) * sharea

Rate of Precipitation of Dolomite

cement = kcem * ((co3s * ca − ssat) + ABS(co3s
  * ca − ssat)) * sharea

**Rate of Precipitation of Abiotic Shallow Marine
Carbonate Cement**

calcdis = calc * cd1 * ((csat − co3d * ca) +
  ABS(csat − co3d * ca))

**Rate of Dissolution of Deep Sea Carbonate
Sediments**

carbw = cwconst * frsed * area * pco2

Dissolution of Terrestrial Carbonates

alkd = kalkd + 2 * (ca + mg − sulf) 'Alkalinity of
  deep sea

shpyrp = spytsred * shsulfred 'Pyrite deposition on
  shelves

silw = (fryi * yiwcst + froi) * siwcst * area * pco2
  $\wedge$2 ' Silicate weathering

pyrox = pocst * arfre * po2 'Pyrite oxidation rate

evdis = edcst * arfre 'Evaporite dissolution rate

evap = kevap * sulf * ca * sharea * interpol(6)
  'Evaporite formation rate

phosw = pwcst * carbw * interpol(8) 'Phosphorus
  weathering rate

psed = kpsed * hydrof 'Phosphorus removal in
  metal-rich deposits

froi = 1 − frsed − fryi 'Fractional exposure of old
  igneous rocks

Lee R. Kump and Tyler Volk

23
Gaia's Garden and BLAG's Greenhouse:
Global Biogeochemical Climate Regulation

Among earth scientists the idea is readily accepted that the biota plays a major role in surficial processes. Bacteria catalyze virtually every chemical reaction important in the weathering and precipitation of minerals. Vascular land plants accelerate chemical denudation rates on the continents (e.g., Knoll and James, 1987). Burrowing organisms reconstitute the fabric and chemical composition of surface sediments. Life processes are responsible for the oxygen in the atmosphere. The entire mass of carbon dioxide in the oceans and atmosphere passes through the biosphere's cycle of respiration and decay in less than 500 years. In short, the biota has a significant impact on the environment for life.

Surprisingly few accept, however, the hypothesis that the biota regulates the global surface environment (the "Gaia hypothesis" of Lovelock and Margulis, 1974). Surprising, because the regulation of the environment may require only one additional influence, that is, the influence of the environment on the biosphere. Where strong feedback exists, the possibility of regulation arises (Tregonning and Roberts, 1979). When the overall feedback is negative, perturbations are damped, and the regulated factor is continually drawn toward a stable state.

This chapter discusses the role of the biota in long-term climate regulation. The prevailing ideas concerning the physical (abiotic) controls on global temperatures are considered first. Our purpose in this chapter is to show that these "abiotic" controls both involve the biosphere as an integral component and behave as a Gaian regulator. We also present some evidence for the role of the biota in climate regulation.

Physical Controls on Weathering

A widely cited feedback mechanism for the control of Earth's temperature on long timescales, proposed by Walker and colleagues (1981) and referred to here as the *WHAK* model, requires no role by the biosphere. Walker and colleagues suggest that as our Sun has evolved, the CO_2 concentration of the atmosphere has decreased. Carbon dioxide is a greenhouse gas, so a decline in its partial pressure would tend to offset the increase in solar luminosity.

The feedback involves the role of CO_2 in climate and in chemical weathering of the Earth's crust. Higher CO_2 contents of the atmosphere, at fixed solar luminosities, should stimulate chemical weathering rates both directly, because of increased carbonic acidity in soils, and indirectly, as a result of the increases in global temperature and hydrologic cycling. Chemical weathering consumes CO_2 during the carbonation of silicate rocks, so this feedback is negative. Walker and colleagues argue that this mechanism should have been sufficient to keep surface temperatures in the range of liquid water during a time in Earth's evolution in which the black body temperature was below or near freezing. If the temperature were to fall below freezing, chemical weathering rates would diminish dramatically, and thus there would be a large excess of CO_2 production, during volcanism, over CO_2 consumption during weathering. Carbon dioxide pressures would rapidly increase, as would the global temperature via the greenhouse effect (Marshall, et al., 1988).

Biological Controls on Weathering

A slight modification of this feedback mechanism was used in the global geochemical cycling model developed by Berner and colleagues (1983) and referred to here as the BLAG model. The most important difference in BLAG was the inclusion of the important role of soil systems, and especially of root and bacterial respiration, in the regulation of climate. As a result of soil respiration, the CO_2 pressure in soils is on the order of 10 to 100 times atmospheric pressure (Cawley, et al., 1969; Holland, et al., 1986). BLAG's feedback is thus indirect. An increase in CO_2 pressure causes an increase in global temperature, which stimulates soil respiration and leads to higher soil CO_2 pressures. These high soil pressures enhance the chemical weathering rates of silicate rocks and hence the CO_2 consumption rates during weathering. Although BLAG does not have WHAK's direct dependency of the weathering rate on CO_2 pressure, the net effect is the same: an increase in CO_2 level is countered by an increase in CO_2 consumption.

Several studies have explored even more explicit forms of biological controls on weathering. Volk (1987) linked the pressure dependency term in the WHAK weathering relation to soil pCO_2, which in turn was linked to terrestrial primary productivity as a function of atmospheric CO_2. The climatic consequences of the evolution of ecosystems with inherently higher rates of weathering was computed for angiosperm–deciduous ecosystems by Volk (1989). Finally, Schwartzman and Volk (1989) looked at the influence on climate of a system of biological weathering effects including the maintenance of soil itself. In this chapter we concentrate on and extend the system of feedbacks used in Volk's analysis (1987) of BLAG and WHAK.

Case A: Living Soil with Asymptotic Productivity
Walker and colleagues derived an expression for the weathering rate, relative to today's rate, as a function of temperature and CO_2 pressure:

$$f_{wr} = \left(\frac{P_{atm}}{P_{atm,0}}\right)^{0.3} \exp\left(\frac{T - T_0}{13.7}\right) \tag{1}$$

where:

f_{wr} = ratio of the weathering rate to today's value

P_{atm} = the atmospheric CO_2

$P_{atm,0}$ = today's P_{atm}

T = the mean global surface temperature

T_0 = today's T

Walker and colleagues derived this empirical relation from mineral weathering studies at higher P and T and from runoff data from climate models. Global temperature was calculated from a greenhouse relation between P_{atm} and global temperature:

$$T - T_0 = 4.6\left(\frac{P_{atm}}{P_{atm,0}}\right)^{0.364} - 4.6 \tag{2}$$

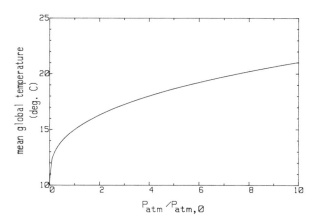

Figure 23.1 The greenhouse effect of CO_2 on global temperature, from equation (2) in the text (Walker, et al., 1981). Carbon dioxide pressures are relative to today's atmospheric pressure; mean global temperature today is assumed to be 15°C.

as shown in figure 23.1. A combination of equations (1) and (2) yields an expression for the weathering rate as a function of P_{atm} only:

$$f_{wr} = \left(\frac{P_{atm}}{P_{atm,0}}\right)^{0.3} \exp\left[\frac{4.6\left(\frac{P_{atm}}{P_{atm,0}}\right)^{0.364} - 4.6}{13.7}\right] \tag{3}$$

In WHAK, P_{atm} represents the actual atmospheric CO_2 pressure. Volk (1987) raised the possibility that the important CO_2 pressure is actually the soil CO_2 pressure. In that case equation (1) becomes

$$f_{wr} = \left(\frac{P_{soil}}{P_{soil,0}}\right)^{0.3} \exp\left[\frac{4.6\left(\frac{P_{atm}}{P_{atm,0}}\right)^{0.364} - 4.6}{13.7}\right] \tag{4}$$

Two assumptions were made to remove the P_{soil} term from equation (4). The first was an assumption of a balance between CO_2 gain during soil respiration and CO_2 loss by diffusion from the soil:

$$K_{soil}(P_{soil} - P_{atm}) = f_{root} \tag{5}$$

where:

K_{soil} = diffusive exchange coefficient

f_{root} = fraction of π respired below ground

π = global terrestrial primary productivity

The second was that f_{root} and K_{soil} are constant. With these two additional assumptions, Volk formulated a weathering expression that was a function only of atmospheric CO_2 and global productivity:

$$f_{wr} = \left[\frac{\pi}{\pi_0} \left(1 - \frac{P_{atm,0}}{P_{soil,0}} \right) \right.$$

$$\left. + \frac{P_{atm}}{P_{soil,0}} \right]^{0.3} \exp\left[\frac{4.6 \left(\frac{P_{atm}}{P_{atm,0}} \right)^{0.364} - 4.6}{13.7} \right] \quad (6)$$

Volk considered two cases: one in which productivity was held constant, $\pi = \pi_0$, and another in which it was assumed to be functionally related to P_{atm} according to Michaelis-Menten kinetics:

$$\pi = \pi_{max} \left(\frac{P_{atm} - P_{min}}{P_{1/2} + (P_{atm} - P_{min})} \right) \quad (7)$$

where:

π_{max} = maximum supportable π

P_{min} = P_{atm} at which photosynthesis equals respiration by the plant (i.e., no net photosynthesis)

$P_{1/2}$ = P_{atm} at which $\pi = 1/2\ \pi_{max}$

Since $\pi = \pi_0$ when $P_{atm} = P_{atm,0}$:

$$P_{1/2} = \left(\frac{\pi_{max}}{\pi_0} - 1 \right) (P_{atm,0} - P_{min}) \quad (8)$$

Reasonable values for maximum productivity and minimum CO_2 pressures for photosynthesis are (Volk, 1987):

$$\pi_{max} = 2\pi_0 \quad (9)$$

$$P_{min} = 0.2\ P_{atm,0} \quad (10)$$

Using these values, we can write one biogeochemical weathering rate expression as:

$$f_{wr} = \left[2 \left(\frac{\frac{P_{atm}}{P_{atm,0}} - 0.2}{\frac{P_{atm}}{P_{atm,0}} + 0.6} \right) \left(1 - \frac{P_{atm,0}}{P_{soil,0}} \right) + \right.$$

$$\left. \left(\frac{P_{atm}}{P_{atm,0}} \cdot \frac{P_{atm,0}}{P_{soil,0}} \right) \right]^{0.3} \cdot \exp\left[\frac{4.6 \left(\frac{P_{atm}}{P_{atm,0}} \right)^{0.364} - 4.6}{13.7} \right] \quad (11)$$

Case B: Abiotic Soil
If this expression describes the weathering rate in the presence of an active soil biota, then one may wonder what the weathering rate would be in the absence of the elevated soil pCO_2 due to life. We will call weathering in this absence the *abiotic soil case*. Note this is not the same as weathering in a completely abiotic Earth, where soil itself may be

largely absent. Because soil is a reservoir of tiny particles with a large total surface area and retains ground moisture necessary for carbonic acid formation, the total effect of the biota is substantially more than enhancing the pCO_2 of the soils (Schwartzman and Volk, 1989). However, of all these biological effects, that of enhanced soil pCO_2 can be individually quantified in most detail. For example, soil pCO_2 can be accurately measured and can easily be placed as a separate component into the weathering equations.

We can ask, therefore, what the weathering rate and the global temperature would be without soil respiration. If we assume a conservative value of 10 for the ratio of $P_{soil,0}/P_{atm,0}$ today, then we can rewrite equation (3) as

$$f_{wr} = \left(\frac{P_{atm}}{10P_{atm,0}} \right)^{0.3} \exp\left[\frac{4.6 \left(\frac{P_{atm}}{P_{atm,0}} \right)^{0.364} - 4.6}{13.7} \right] \quad (12)$$

Below we calculate what the global temperature and $P_{atm,0}$ would be today if there were no soil biota.

Case C: Living Soil with Parabolic Productivity
Experiments of plant growth under elevated pCO_2 show increased yields up to a maximum pCO_2, above which yields start to decline. Wheat yields, for example, begin to decline when pCO_2 rises above about 1000 ppm (Bugbee and Salisbury, 1986).

To make an analogy to Watson and Lovelock's (1983) Daisyworld* let us assume that global productivity is a parabolic function of P_{atm}. Then:

$$\frac{\pi}{\pi_0} = \frac{\pi_{max}}{\pi_0} - a \left(\frac{P_{atm,opt}}{P_{atm,0}} - \frac{P_{atm}}{P_{atm,0}} \right)^2 \quad (13)$$

where

$P_{atm,opt}$ = the optimum CO_2 pressure for photosynthesis

In addition, we will retain the assumptions that

$$\frac{\pi}{\pi_0} = 0 \text{ when } P_{atm} = 0.2\ P_{atm,0};$$

$$\frac{\pi}{\pi_0} = 1 \text{ when } P_{atm} = P_{atm,0};$$

$$\pi_{max} = 2\pi_0;$$

*A system of planetary temperature regulation based on feedback loops involving albedo effects of daisies and parabolic growth rates of daisy populations.

then we can solve for a and $\left(\dfrac{P_{atm,opt}}{P_{atm,0}}\right)$:

$$a = 0.268$$

$$\frac{P_{atm,opt}}{P_{atm,0}} = 2.93$$

and the full weathering expression becomes:

$$f_{wr} = \left\{ \left[2 - a \left(\frac{P_{atm,opt}}{P_{atm,0}} - \frac{P_{atm}}{P_{atm,0}} \right)^2 \right] \right.$$
$$\left. \left(1 - \frac{P_{atm,0}}{P_{soil,0}} \right) + \left(\frac{P_{atm}}{P_{atm,0}} \cdot \frac{P_{atm,0}}{P_{soil,0}} \right) \right\}^{0.3}$$
$$\cdot \exp\left[\frac{4.6 \left(\frac{P_{atm}}{P_{atm,0}} \right)^{0.364} - 4.6}{13.7} \right] \qquad (14)$$

Summary of Three Cases

Thus, we have three relationships between atmospheric CO_2 and global chemical weathering rates. The first, represented by equation (12), is the expression for weathering without elevated soil pCO_2 from the biota. The second, represented by equation (11), is the expression for an Earth with an active biotic soil system, one whose photosynthetic rate is asymptotically related to P_{atm}. The third, represented by equation (14), is the expression for an Earth with an active biotic soil system whose respiration rate is parabolically related to P_{atm}.

The solutions to these equations are shown in figure 23.2. Note first that in all three cases, the feedback is in the correct sense: an increase in P_{atm} is countered by an increase in CO_2 consumptive weathering. In addition, the effect of soil respiration is clear. At all CO_2 pressures the weathering rate is higher in the presence of a living soil. Finally, there is an interesting difference between the weathering rates calculated for asymptotic and parabolic productivity and respiration. At lower P_{atm}, weathering rates are higher for the parabolic case. As P_{atm} increases, CO_2 toxic effects wax in importance, and productivity falls below the asymptotic case. Eventually the flora become extinct, and the soil system reverts to its lifeless state.

Feedbacks in the Carbon Dioxide–Climate System

Having established three functional relationships between P_{atm} and chemical weathering rates, we are now in a position to investigate feedbacks in the full CO_2-climate system. On long timescales pCO_2 changes are believed to be primarily driven by changes in the rate of volcanic and metamorphic degassing, although changes in global land area and in the types of rocks being weathered and metamorphosed also affect pCO_2 on these timescales. Our interest is in long-term steady states for CO_2 that result from a required balance between CO_2 production via volcanism and CO_2 consumption during weathering. Thus, we shall consider P_{atm} to be in, steady state, and shall calculate these steady states for a range of production values.

The Steady-State Balance

Berner and colleagues (1983), Kasting (1984), and Volk (1987) have demonstrated that a simple equation defines this steady-state situation:

$$f_{wr} f_A = f_{SR} f_{DC} \qquad (15)$$

where

f_{SR} = global sea floor spreading rate, relative to today

f_A = exposed continental area, relative to today

f_{DC} = ratio of susceptibility of dolomite versus calcite to metamorphic decarbonation

For simplicity's sake we will assume that $f_{DC} = 1$; Berner and colleagues showed that over the last 100 million years this has been a factor of secondary importance. We shall also adopt the convenience proposed by Volk (1987) of defining the geophysical forcing ratio (GFR) as f_{SR}/f_A. Therefore,

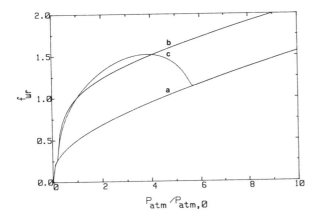

Figure 23.2 Global weathering rates relative to today (f_{wr}), calculated as a function of atmospheric CO_2 pressure according to three models: (a) an Earth without biotic enhancement of soil pCO_2; (b) an Earth with a biotic soil system whose respiration rate is asymptotically related to atmospheric CO_2 pressure; (c) same as b, but assuming a parabolic relationship between respiration and P.

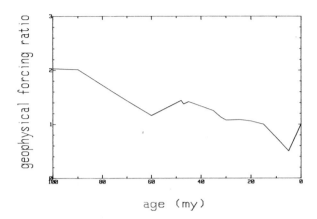

Figure 23.3 The geophysical forcing ratio (the ratio of the global mean sea floor spreading rate to the global land area, both relative to today) over the last 100 my. (From Berner, et al., 1983).

$$f_{wr} = GRF \qquad (16)$$

Recognize that increases in GFR can signify either increased volcanicity (assumed proportional to spreading rate, per the BLAG model) or decreased exposed land area for weathering (f_A can change via eustatic sea level fluctuation, continental collision, etc; see Pitman, 1978). Figure 23.3 shows the variation in the GFR over the last 100 million years, using the corrected Southam and Hay (1977) spreading rate curve and the land area curve calculation used by Barron and colleagues (1980), as in BLAG.

Results with Three Cases

Steady-state P_{atm} values are shown in Figure 23.4 for this range in the GFR. P_{atm} is always highest for a given GFR in the abiotic soil case. Thus, one result of this analysis, as also shown by Volk (1987), is that P_{atm} would be significantly higher today in the absence of soil respiration. Steady-state P_{atm} on an Earth with an abiotic soil system may be on the order of five times today's value.

In the GFR range of 1.0 to 1.6 there is a divergence in the two cases incorporating soil respiration. In the asymptotic case, P_{atm} monotonically increases with GFR, paralleling the abiotic soil case at lower P_{atm}. In contrast, the parabolic formulation reverses the trend of P_{atm} with GFR in this range. An interesting consequence of this reversal is the appearance of three steady states for P_{atm} in the parabolic system. The basins of attraction for these steady states are shown in figure 23.5. Two of the steady states are stable (one is the abiotic soil condition) and one is unstable. Perturbations in P_{atm} are

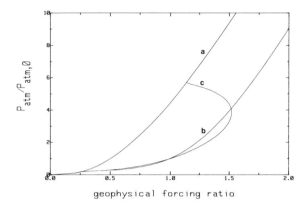

Figure 23.4 Steady-state atmospheric CO_2 pressures, relative to today, as a function of the geophysical forcing ratio. Calculated from the same three models as in figure 23.2.

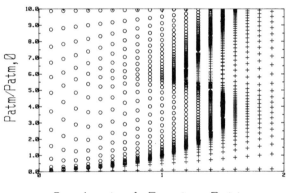

Figure 23.5 Same as figure 23.4, but showing the response to perturbation from steady state. The basins of attraction of a steady state are shown by the symbols. Circles indicate a trajectory towards lower P_{atm}, crosses towards higher P_{atm}. Stable steady states are indicated by convergence of crosses (from below) and circles. For example, if the system is perturbed from the stable steady state (1.0, 1.0) to a new GFR between 1 and about 1.5, $P_{atm}/P_{atm,0}$ will increase (rapidly at first and then more slowly) to the new, stable steady state (between 1.0 and about 3.5).

followed by a return to the stable steady state indicated by the trajectories in this figure.

Global mean temperatures can also be calculated from the steady-state P_{atm} for the range in GFR using equation (2). The results are shown in figure 23.6. The highest temperatures for a given GFR are calculated for the abiotic soil case. A lifeless Earth today would be 3°C warmer at a minimum. Eliminating all additional biological effects on weathering would increase this warming by about an order of magnitude (Schwartzman and Volk, 1989). The temperatures calculated for the two cases of an active, biotic soil system are similar, and confirm the con-

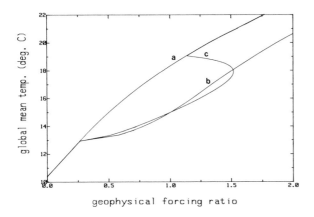

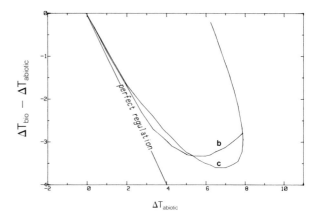

Figure 23.6 The global temperatures calculated for the steady states of figure 23.4.

Figure 23.7 The extent of regulation provided by the feedbacks in two biotic cases. Perfect regulation occurs when $\Delta T_{bio} = 0$ (the feedbacks perfectly compensate for changes in the forcing). The line $\Delta T_{bio} = \Delta T_{abiotic}$ indicates no regulation. Line b represents the case with $\Delta T_{bio} = \Delta T_{asym}$; line c represents case with $\Delta T_{bio} = \Delta T_{para}$.

clusion of Lovelock and Whitfield (1982) that in the presence of land vegetation and soils, the Earth system can operate at lower temperatures.

Degree of Regulation

One way to examine quantitatively the strength of the negative feedback given by the change in global productivity as a function of P_{atm} (either asymptotic or parabolic) is to compare these cases (equations 11 and 14) with the same cases were π not affected by P_{atm}, in other words, if it were constant. The case of $\pi = $ constant is obtained by using the abiotic soil case. As before, we use equation (16) to solve for P_{atm} as a function of GFR for equations (11), (12), and (14) and for T in each case using equation (2). In the absence of biotic feedbacks (equation 12), we define a $\Delta T_{abiotic} = T - T_o$. We can also similarly define ΔT_{bio} values for the two feedback cases: ΔT_{asym} for equation (11) with asymptotic feedback and ΔT_{para} for equation (14) with parabolic feedback. As GFR changes, a system with ideal regulation would maintain T constant. Because ΔT values for all three cases vary with changing GFR, plotting the two cases of ΔT_{bio} (ΔT_{asym} and ΔT_{para}) against $\Delta T_{abiotic}$ can show how much regulation is provided in each case. Figure 23.7 graphs these values, comparing them to the line of perfect regulation ($\Delta T_{bio} = 0$) and the line of no regulation ($\Delta T_{bio} = \Delta T_{abiotic}$).

Note that in figure 23.7, the regulation is closest to perfect in the region closest to today's state and becomes less and less perfect as the ΔT_{ref} increases with higher GFR. This is because the slope of P_{atm} is greatest near today's conditions, which is generally true in plant growth experiments (Acock and

Allen, 1985). If Gaia could evolve, one might expect just such a situation: greatest regulatory capability in the vicinity of the properties of any given "present" environment. Here we point this out as intriguing circumstantial evidence for Gaian feedback and as an issue to be considered further.

Lifeless Earth After the Parabolic Maximum

There is a marked similarity between the Daisyworld (Watson and Lovelock, 1983) and parabolic productivity-temperature plots (figure 23.6). In both cases, the response of temperature to the forcing factor is damped compared with other responses. Also, in both cases, there is an upper limit to this regulatory ability, beyond which the system reverts to its lifeless state. One can only conclude that if productivity is related to P_{atm}, with minimum, optimum, and perhaps maximum conditions, the earth system, that is, Gaia, has the ability to moderate climate, even though the regulation may not be perfect. An increase in GFR, due perhaps to an episode of enhanced volcanicity or a transgression of the ocean, would cause an initial rise in P_{atm}, but the stimulation of productivity, root respiration, and thus silicate weathering rates would damp the response. A new, higher, steady-state P_{atm} would be achieved, but this P_{atm} would be less than that on a lifeless Earth. In fact, there is an additional, parabolic relationship between temperature and productivity that has not been incorporated into these calculations. Its appropriateness may be even less controversial, because the growth of all organisms is known to exhibit such behavior as a function of temperature.

Note that the present model for productivity as a parabolic function of atmospheric CO_2 produces a dead Earth when GFR is greater than about 1.5. This presents a problem, because according to available data (see figure 23.3), GFR had a value of about 2 at a time 100 million years ago. Clearly the Earth had abundant life then. We emphasize again that although plant growth reaches a maximum at an optimal value of P_{atm}, and then begins declining at higher values of P_{atm}, the details of this phenomenon have not been a research priority and therefore have been virtually unexplored in experiments. We could change the parabolic formulation of equation (13) to be able to accommodate life at higher values of GFR by increasing the optimal value of P_{atm}.

However, the important point is that an optimum exists. For example, we might consider only the plant growth response to temperature, and link temperature to P_{atm} (see equation 2). Although the optimal temperature for the parabolic case shown in figure 23.6 is about 18°C, higher optimal temperatures are clearly likely. But the dynamics of the model would remain qualitatively the same, and our point concerns these dynamics. In other words, if the physical forcing pushes the P_{atm} or T beyond their optimal values, and the feedbacks operate in the manner proposed here, then the system would quickly revert to the lifeless state. To avoid this catastrophe, the system should operate below the optimum. This is the case today: P_{atm} is about 30% of the value at which plant growth is maximum. Here we have not considered metabolic evolution as a factor. These issues are fundamental and should be explored further.

Geological Evidence for Biogeochemical Climate Regulation

Evidence that the Earth system has operated at lower temperatures since the establishment of terrestrial vegetation and soils is all but absent. There is one possible indication of this in the isotopic composition of carbonate minerals in Phanerozoic rocks (Kump, 1989). A permanent shift in the mean isotopic composition apparently occurred in the middle to late Paleozoic period (figure 23.8). An argument exists whether this recorded a change in the ocean oxygen isotopic composition as a result

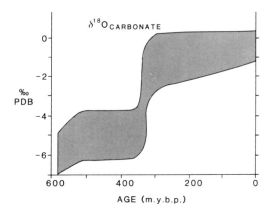

Figure 23.8 The range of oxygen isotopic compositions of Phanerozoic marine carbonates, showing an apparent shift in the mean value (relative to the Pee Dee Belemnite standard) in the late Paleozoic period. (After Veizer, et al., 1986).

of geologic processes (Veizer, et al., 1986; Lohmann and Walker, 1989), or a global cooling of the mean surface temperature (Karhu and Epstein, 1986). Walker and Lohmann (1989) apparently prefer a geological explanation but suggest that the isotopic shift was too rapid for geological processes alone to have been the cause. They conclude that "perhaps the change represents a combination of marked change in climate combined with the fastest possible change in the isotopic composition of seawater." It is interesting to speculate that the possible cooling was due to the establishment of terrestrial ecosystems. There may, for example, be a connection between the rise and spread of angiosperm ecosystems (acting in the same direction as the geophysical forcing from plate tectonics as described in the BLAG model) and the cooling of the last 100 million years (Volk, 1989).

Here we have shown that the enhancement of soil pCO_2 presently maintains the Earth about 3°C cooler than it would be without such enhancement. Other biological factors in weathering may augment this figure substantially (Schwartzman and Volk, 1989). It is not yet clear, however, where in the geological record one should look for evidence of cooling as a result of life's evolution and diversification on land. For example, in the national parks of Utah, there are soils that are stabilized by microbes. The living component of these so-called cryptogamic or microphytic soils is typically 98% cyanobacteria (J. Belnap, personal communication). Without the cryptogamic life, the soil is not stable and is quickly blown away to expose rock.

The photosynthetic bacteria of the cryptogamic soils can tolerate heat and drought, conditions uninhabitable by higher plants. The cryptogamic soils might be a model for soils billions of years earlier than the evolution of vascular land plants about 400 million years ago. Therefore, evidence of cooling due to biological effects on weathering may have to be sought in the early Earth.

Conclusions

This chapter arose out of a curious combination of perspectives. Some proponents of the Gaia hypothesis have argued that box models such as BLAG are inadequate for describing Earth's chemical evolution. On the other hand, geochemical modelers have tended to reject the concept that the biosphere can play a regulatory role in climate and surficial processes (e.g., Veizer, 1988). Yet by including a biological component in the geochemical model, one that cannot be disputed to have a significant effect on chemical weathering rates, we have found that neither of these criticisms is valid. Gaia's garden, the soils, enhances the negative feedback in the greenhouse of BLAG and WHAK in a way that contributes to the stability of Earth's surface temperatures.

An Earth with an active terrestrial biota, one that maintains soil CO_2 pressures at order-of-magnitude higher levels than that of the atmosphere, operates at a lower temperature than a lifeless Earth. That conclusion seems virtually incontrovertible. The true, functional relationships among terrestrial productivity, climate, and weathering rates are probably not any of those discussed in this chapter. In particular, the parabolic relationship proposed for productivity as a function of P_{atm} is most likely in error, for many plants may not begin to show the toxic effects of CO_2 until much higher pressures are achieved (and, in general, the response of the biosphere to higher pCO$_2$ in terms of global productivity is a major uncertainty; B. Strain, personal communication). The true relationship also involves a feedback with temperature. It is interesting that the optimum temperature for C3 photosynthesis is a function of P_{atm} (Acock and Allen, 1985); as P_{atm} increases the optimum temperature shifts to warmer values. Given that P_{atm} and T have presumably coevolved through geological history, this adaptation of the plants may have proven beneficial.

References

Acock, B., and Allen, L.H., Jr 1985. Crop responses to elevated carbon dioxide concentrations. In Strain, B.R., and Cure, J.D., eds. *Direct Effects of Increasing Carbon Dioxide on Vegetation*. Washington, D.C.: United States Department of Energy, 53–98.

Barron, E.J., Sloan, J.L., II, and Harrison, C.G.A. 1980. Potential significance of land-sea distribution and surface albedo variations as a climatic forcing factor: 180 m.y. to the present. *Palaeogr Palaeoclim Palaeoecol*, 30, 17–40.

Berner, R.A., Lasaga, A.C., and Garrels, R.M. 1983. The carbonate-silicate geochemical cycle and its effect on atmospheric carbon dioxide over the past 100 million years. *Am J Sci*, 283, 641–683.

Bugbee, B.G., and Salisbury, F.B. 1986. Studies on maximum yield of wheat for the controlled environments of space. In: MacElroy, R.D., Martello, N.Y., and Smernoff, D.T., eds. *Controlled Ecological Life Support Systems: CELSS 1985 Workshop*. NASA-TM-88215. Washington, D.C.: National Aeronautics and Space Administration, 447–486.

Cawley, J.L., Burruss, R.C., and Holland, H.D. 1969. Chemical weathering in central Iceland: An analog of pre-Silurian weathering. *Science*, 165, 391–392.

Holland, H.D., Lazar, B., and McCaffrey, M. 1986. Evolution of atmosphere and oceans. *Nature*, 320, 27–33.

Karhu, J., and Epstein, S. 1986. The implication of the oxygen isotope records in coexisting cherts and phosphates. *Geochim Cosmochim Acta*, 50, 1745–1756.

Kasting, J.F. 1984. Comments on the BLAG model: The carbonate-silicate cycle and its effect on atmospheric carbon dioxide over the past 100 million years. *Am J Sci*, 284, 1175–1182.

Knoll, M.A., and James, W.C. 1987. Effect of the advent and diversification of vascular land plants on mineral weathering through geologic time. *Geology*, 15, 1099–1102.

Kump, L.R. 1989. Chemical stability of the atmosphere and ocean. *Palaeogeogr Palaeoclim Palaeoecol*, 75, 123–136.

Lohmann, K.C., and Walker, J.C.G. 1989. The ^{18}O record of Phanerozoic abiotic marine cements. *Geophys Res Lett*, 16, 319–322.

Lovelock, J.E., and Margulis, L. 1974. Atmospheric homeostasis by and for the biosphere: The Gaia hypothesis. *Tellus*, 26, 2–9.

Lovelock, J.E., and Whitfield, M. 1982. Lifespan of the biosphere. *Nature*, 296, 561–563.

Marshall, H.G., Walker, J.C.G., and Kuhn, W.R. 1988. Long-term climate change and the geochemical cycle of carbon. *J Geophys Res*, 93, 791–802.

Pitman, W.C. 1978. Relationship between eustacy and stratigraphic sequences of passive margins. *Geol Soc Am Bull*, 89, 1289–1403.

Schwartzman, D., and Volk, T. 1989. Biotic enhancement of weathering and the habitability of Earth. *Nature*, 340, 457–460.

Southam, J.R., and Hay, W.W. 1977. Time scales and dynamic models of deep-sea sedimentation. *J Geophys Res*, 82, 3285–3842.

Tregonning, K., and Roberts, A. 1979. Complex systems which evolve towards homeostasis. *Nature*, 281, 563–564.

Veizer, J. 1988. The Earth and its life: Systems perspective. *Origins Life Evolution Biosphere*, 18, 13–39.

Veizer, J., Fritz, P., and Jones, B. 1986. Geochemistry of brachiopods: Oxygen and carbon isotopic records of Paleozoic oceans. *Geochim Cosmochim Acta*, 50, 1679–1696.

Volk, T. 1987. Feedbacks between weathering and atmospheric CO_2 over the last 100 million years. *Am J Sci*, 287, 763–779.

Volk, T. 1989. Rise of angiosperms as a factor in long-term climatic cooling. *Geology*, 17, 107–110.

Walker, J.C.G., Hays, P.B., and Kasting, J.F. 1981. A negative feedback mechanism for the long-term stabilization of Earth's surface temperature. *J Geophys Res*, 86, 9776–9782.

Walker, J.C.G., and Lohmann, K.C. 1989. Why the oxygen isotopic composition of sea water changes with time. *Geophys Res Lett*, 16, 323–326.

Watson, A.J., and Lovelock, J.E. 1983. Biological homeostasis of the global environment: The parable of Daisyworld. *Tellus*, 358, 284–289.

Thomas R. Worsley, R. Damian Nance, and Judith B. Moody

24

Tectonics, Carbon, Life, and Climate for the Last Three Billion Years: A Unified System?

The Earth, with its convecting mantle, liquid surface water, atmospheric carbon dioxide, exposed silicate rocks, and life, possesses two powerful built-in systems for buffering surface temperature (Walker et al., 1981; Lovelock and Whitfield, 1982; Worsley et al., 1986; Worsley and Nance, 1989; Schwartzman and Volk, 1989). These systems prevented the planet from freezing over early in its history when the Sun was approximately 70% of its current luminosity and have since then strongly counteracted the tendency of the planet's surface temperature to rise as the Sun has continually brightened. Both systems have kept the planet cool by progressively drawing down the atmospheric greenhouse gas CO_2. The first and far stronger of the two is a silicate-carbonate buffering system (figure 24.1A), which is presently responsible for burying 80% of the Earth's outgassed CO_2 by reacting it with silicate rocks to form carbonate. Biotic enhancement of silicate weathering rates (Schwartzman and Volk, 1989) serves to further lower atmospheric CO_2, and hence, surface temperatures. The second system is a totally life-mediated buffering system (figure 24.1B) that currently buries the remaining 20% as organic matter.

The silicate-carbonate buffering system operates because gaseous CO_2, when dissolved in water, produces a natural form of acid rain that reacts with calcium and magnesium-containing silicate rocks to produce two solids; $(Ca,Mg)CO_3$, or limestone/dolomite plus SiO_2, or quartz. In this way, 80% of the CO_2 added by volcanism to the earth's atmosphere from its actively convecting and degassing mantle is removed and buried as $CaCO_3$. Tectonic cycling guarantees the continued availability of these silicate rocks. In a similar manner, the organic (C-org) buffering system operates by converting gaseous CO_2 to solid organic matter. Hence, when CO_2 gas plus liquid H_2O photosynthetically combine to form solid organic matter (CH_2O or C-org) plus gaseous O_2, the result is transfer of carbon from the atmosphere to organisms. That fraction of the organisms

not reoxidized after death is then buried in the Earth's crust as C-org.

As a first-order approximation, the rates of chemical reaction increase exponentially with increasing temperature. We suggest that they roughly double with every 10°C rise in temperature in the range of zero to 50°C. Hence, should surface temperatures rise, a strong tendency would exist for the increased acid rainout of CO_2, and therefore, a decreased greenhouse effect because warm air holds more moisture and because the resulting acid rain is more reactive. Conversely, the acid rain rate would drop sharply should temperatures approach the freezing point. This decrease would greatly curtail CO_2 removal from the atmosphere, thereby allowing its continued buildup from volcanic sources, thus

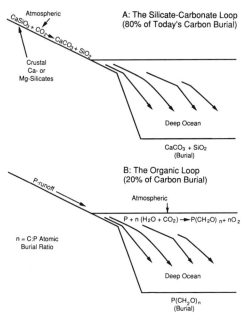

Figure 24.1 The earth's two carbon burial loops. In the silicate-carbonate loop (A), One atom of calcium liberated from silicate rocks always buries one atom of carbon. In the organic loop (B), one atom of phosphorus liberated from crustal silicate rocks can bury anywhere from 100 to 1000 or more atoms of carbon depending on the burial pathway.

warming the planet's surface via the greenhouse effect. Similar reasoning would apply to C-org burial rates to the extent that metabolic rates in organisms are also controlled by temperature (i.e., free of enzymatic catalytic control). Higher temperatures would increase metabolic rates, and thereby increase C-org production, whereas lower temperatures would do the opposite. However, C-org production is weakly coupled to C-org burial or temperature (Worsley et al., 1986; Worsley and Nance, 1989; Berner, 1989; Kump, 1989). This weak coupling results because C-org burial is dependent on phosphorus availability, which in turn depends on the temperature-related chemical erosion rate of the continents (Kump, 1989; Worsley and Nance, 1989). We can therefore conclude that in the presence of the silicate-carbonate and the C-org buffers, the calculated continuous rise in solar luminosity throughout Earth's 4.5 billion-year history (Owen et al., 1979; Kasting et al., 1988; Gilliland, 1989) would entail a much smaller increase in the Earth's surface temperature.

However, if the two temperature buffers operated solely as outlined above, they would be no more than negative feedback systems and the Earth's surface should have heated slightly during its 4.6-Ga history. The rise need not be large; perhaps no more than 10° to 20°C (Schwartzman and Volk 1989, and Worsley and Nance, 1989 for a discussion). Contrary to these theoretical predictions, the Earth's long-term average surface temperature for the past three Ga has apparently, despite significant climatic oscillations caused by tectonic cycles, remained constant or has decreased slightly to today's average value of approximately 15°C (Worsley and Nance, 1989). Maintenance of constant or declining surface temperatures requires temperature buffers that are more than passive negative feedback systems. Therefore, we see no way that the silicate-carbonate system (even if silicate weathering is biotically accelerated) (Schwartzman and Volk, 1989) can operate other than by negative feedback. Hence, the record of constant or slightly dropping surface temperatures must involve C-org burial and the coupling between the silicate-carbonate and the C-org burial loops cannot be linear (Worsley et al., 1986). Instead, the coupling must involve an amplifier that progressively increases the fraction of carbon buried as C-org in order to maintain constant or declining surface temperatures (Worsley and Nance, 1989). We therefore think that the Earth's long-term paleoclimatic record is best explained by

a continuous increase in the ratio of reduced carbon (organic carbon or C-org) to oxidized carbon (carbonate or C-carb) burial through time from some past lower value to today's 20% (but see Schidlowski, 1987 for the more conventional interpretation).

Organic Carbon and Phosphorus

Because there has always been a surfeit of water, CO_2, and sunlight on Earth's surface, the rate of carbon fixation by marine organisms via the photosynthetic reaction $CO_2 + H_2O \rightarrow CH_2O + O_2$ has never been limited by their availability. Rather, it is the toxicity of life's waste products (e.g., O_2) or the limited supply of other dissolved nutrients (most notably phosphorus) that has probably controlled the rate of photosynthesis, and hence the rate of C-org burial, throughout geological time (e.g., Broecker, 1985). However, the phosphorus (P) incorporated into organic matter is known to be selectively recycled prior to and during C-org burial (Holland, 1984; Moody et al., 1988) and reused to produce yet more organic matter (Worsley et al., 1986; Worsley and Nance, 1989). The intensity of this recycling is a function of the environment of deposition which, in turn, is largely a function of the availability of the O_2 required by C-org scavengers. Furthermore, for the inorganic burial loop, one atom of buried calcium or magnesium is always associated with one atom of carbon as carbonate whereas burial of one atom of phosphorus in the organic loop can be associated with the burial of between 100 to 1000 atoms of carbon, depending on environmental conditions (Kump, 1989). Hence, possible differences in global C-carb:C-org burial ratios through time must be the result of phosphorus-mediated changes in the C-org burial rate rather than the immutable C-carb rate (Worsley et al., 1986; Worsley and Nance, 1989). Unfortunately, the measured value of the global carbon-to-phosphorus burial ratio in organic matter through geological time is very poorly known. Even today's ratio is poorly constrained but is thought by Kump (1989) to be approximately 250 and by us (Worsley and Nance, 1989) to be on the order of 300.

As regards the ultimate availability of phosphorus, it would appear to be directly and linearly related to the availability of carbonate produced by silicate weathering (Worsley and Nance, 1989). This relationship would hold regardless of whether the biota were capable of enhancing chemical weathering rates, as proposed by Schwartzman and Volk (1989). It would then seem that organisms are at the mercy of inorganic processes. Hence the burial rate of organic matter on Earth should have been controlled by the availability of this limiting nutrient. If so, the silicate-carbonate and the C-org burial loops are coupled in that they are both ultimately dependent on chemical denudation of the continents to supply the reactants (calcium, magnesium, and phosphorus) required to remove CO_2 from the atmosphere. As we now show, however, the two loops differ significantly in the way in which they accomplish the carbon burial once the reactants are dissolved from the continents.

Figure 24.2 illustrates three possible stages in the continuous evolution of C-org burial over geological history. The metabolic requirements of modern organisms mandate a carbon-to-phosphorus atomic ratio of about 100 (the so-called Redfield ratio of Redfield et al., 1969), which is not likely to have changed significantly over time. If C-org is fixed and buried at the Redfield ratio (figure 24.2A), one Redfield unit of phosphorus (i.e., one atom) will bury one Redfield unit of carbon (i.e., 100 atoms). Such a scenario is unlikely because organisms selectively concentrate phosphorus in their protoplasm rather than in their structural components (Liebau and Koritnig, 1978) because its main use is in metabolism. When the organism dies, the phosphorus-rich protoplasm decays first and the phosphorus it contains is selectively returned to the water column and recycled. The buried C-org, in contrast, is enriched in phosphorus-poor structural components (figure 24.2B) having a carbon-to-phosphorus ratio of perhaps 2:1 relative to the Redfield ratio (i.e., 200 carbon atoms to one phosphorus atom). This results in a doubling of the C-org burial rate using the same amount of phosphorus. If the C-org is subject to bioturbation (overturn by burrowing scavengers) before burial (figure 24.2C), the scavengers will again selectively attack and recycle the more labile, phosphorus-enriched fraction and leave behind a more refractory phosphorus-depleted residue with an even higher carbon-to-phosphorus ratio relative to the Redfield ratio (4:1 in our example).

Today, carbon-to-phosphorus burial ratios can exceed 1000:1 in slowly sedimenting, highly oxygenated marine environments (Sandstrom, 1982) where only the most refractory phosphorus-poor portion of the C-org is preserved. However, the

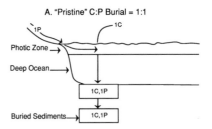

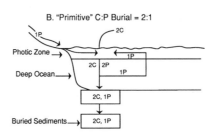

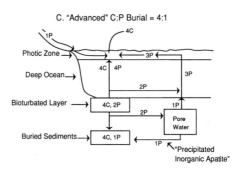

Figure 24.2 Hypothetical stages in the evolution of marine organic carbon burial (after Worsley and Nance, 1989). The atomic ratio of carbon to phosphorus in living material is approximately 100:1 and likely has not changed through time. In a "pristine" world (A) with no postmortem recycling, one unit of phosphorus (i.e., 1 atom) would bury one unit of carbon (i.e., 100 atoms). In a "primitive" world where recycling of phosphorus is limited to the water column and sea floor, one unit of phosphorus could bury two units of carbon. In an "advanced" world (C) where scavengers are able to burrow below the sediment-water interface, one unit of phosphorus could bury perhaps four units of carbon as shown. In today's world, there are instances where one unit of phosphorus buries more than ten units of carbon.

global marine average is approximately 250 or 300:1. Burial ratios of 1000:1 also occur in some terrestrial aqueous environments where vascular plant remains (which have very low phosphorus contents in their nonliving cell walls) and woody tissue (Kump, 1988, 1989) are buried as peat, lignite, and coal. However, we suggest that the terrestrial average is probably closer to 400:1. If, as an illustrative first approximation, we assume that two thirds of today's C-org burial occurs in the marine realm (Berner, 1989) at an approximately 250:1 ratio, and the remainder on land with an approximately 400:1 ratio, the global average of carbon-to-phosphorus burial ratios would be approximately 300:1. As life evolved, the ratio of C-org to phosphorus burial is likely to have increased; escalating from perhaps 150:1 early in Earth's history to today's value of approximately 300:1. Such an increase could well be expected for two reasons: Firstly, because marine organisms have become more complex and better able to differentially recycle phosphorus in the bioturbated layer as O_2 levels have risen (Worsley et al., 1986; Worsley and Nance, 1989); and secondly, because the relatively recent vascular plants have evolved intrinsically high carbon-to-phosphorus ratios (Berner, 1989; Kump, 1989). Hence, the rate of C-org burial could have increased by a factor of approximately 2 without significantly affecting the phosphorus burial rate. Furthermore, it is this life-mediated acceleration in the rate of C burial (and hence a temperature-independent tendency toward CO_2 drawdown) that is likely to have maintained or slightly lowered Earth's surface temperature over approximately the last 3 Ga despite an increase of solar luminosity from 80% of its present value during the same time interval.

Figure 24.3 summarizes the relationship between a nearly linearly increasing solar luminosity and the roughly hundredfold decrease of atmospheric CO_2

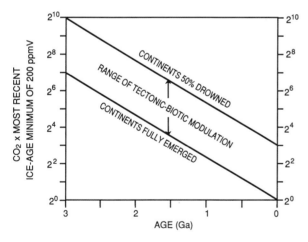

Figure 24.3 The history of atmospheric CO_2 drawdown required to keep Earth's surface temperature constant in the face of linearly increasing solar luminosity. We assume that a halving of CO_2 levels corresponds to a loss of approximately 3°C in greenhouse warming and that the halving time of CO_2 levels in the atmosphere is approximately 0.4 Ga. Half-drowned continents yield CO_2 levels 2^3 higher than totally emergent ones at any given instant and produce surface temperatures approximately 10°C warmer.

levels required to maintain Earth's surface temperature at approximately 20° for approximately the past 3 Ga (Kasting, 1987). We find it convenient to use halving times because each halving of the CO_2 level lowers surface temperature by approximately 3°C (Kasting, 1987; Barron and Washington, 1985) regardless of the quantity in question. This figure is similar to midrange estimates of general circulation models attempting to predict the magnitude of the forthcoming anthropogenic greenhouse effect that would result from a doubling of CO_2 (Ramanathan et al., 1989), and therefore facilitates comparisons between these models and the geological record. We suggest that approximately seven halvings of the atmospheric CO_2 content are required to offset a rise in surface temperature of approximately 20°C that would result from a continuous increase in solar luminosity from 80% of its current value (Kasting, 1987). Dividing the total time interval by the total number of halvings yields a nominal CO_2 halving time of approximately 0.4 Ga. The potential 2^3 range of CO_2 values of figure 24.3 for any given instant results from tectonic and biotic influences (Worsley et al., 1986; Worsley and Nance, 1989) that we discuss later.

As the silicate-carbonate carbon burial loop releases no free O_2 and in fact consumes it (Kump, 1989), the presence of O_2 in the atmosphere is solely due to the life-mediated C-org burial loop. In fact, the accumulation of O_2 in the atmosphere testifies to a continual increase in C-org burial through time. Figure 24.4 summarizes the somewhat sketchy history of atmospheric O_2 based on the measurements and calculations of Holland (1984), Berner (1987, 1989), and Kasting (1987). Again, we use doublings to facilitate comparison with figure 24.3. Oxygen (figure 24.4) shows the expected reciprocal relationship between CO_2 and O_2 although the trends are not quite mirror images of each other. This offset occurs because some of the photosynthetically liberated O_2 combines with other reduced substances besides C-org (mainly iron and sulfur) and is buried as oxides of these substances. Figure 24.4 suggests that O_2 has undergone approximately 10 doublings to produce a roughly thousandfold increase at a time between approximately 2.75 Ga ago and approximately 0.25 Ga ago when modern levels were reached (Berner, 1987). It might have undergone another doubling in the past 0.25 Ga but limitation by fire has likely suppressed further buildup (Lovelock and Whitfield, 1982). Dividing the total time inter-

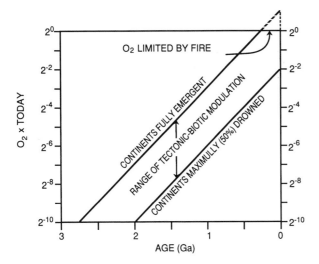

Figure 24.4 The history of rising atmospheric O_2 levels resulting from the increasing rate of carbon burial through time. The O_2 doubling time is approximately 0.25 Ga. We speculate that prior to 0.25 Ga ago, emergent continents corresponded to O_2 levels approximately 2^3 higher than drowned ones at any given instant. Oxygen reached modern levels approximately 0.25 Ga ago and can go no higher because they are limited by wildfire. The range of tectonic-biotic modulation of O_2 levels has become progressively more damped since then.

val it took to reach modern levels by the total number of doublings yields a nominal O_2 doubling time of approximately 0.25 Ga; a rate of increase in broad agreement with that obtained by geochemical modeling (Kasting, 1987; Holland, 1984). Again, the potential range in values at any given time reflects tectonic and biotic influences that form the next topic of discussion.

Tectonic Modulation of Climate and Life

To this point, we have emphasized that the Earth's climate maintenance system has continually lowered atmospheric CO_2 to keep surface temperature nearly constant as the Sun brightened, and that O_2 liberation is a byproduct of the process. We do not mean to imply, however, that the system has operated smoothly. We have already alluded to the fact that tectonic modulation can greatly alter the operation of the climate maintenance system at any given instant. We now illustrate how the alternating assembly and breakup of supercontinents (the supercontinent cycle), which is the main mechanism of tectonic modulation, influences continental emergence and drowning (Worsley et al. 1984; Nance et al. 1988). We then show how changes in

continental emergence and drowning propagate corresponding adjustments in the CO_2 and O_2 levels of the Earth's atmosphere that, in turn, instigate biotic innovations that amplify the environmental effects of the tectonically caused changes.

Figure 24.5 illustrates the main phases and environmental consequences of the supercontinent cycle proposed by Worsley and colleagues (1984). The mechanism of this cycle depends on the influence of the earth's crust on the dissipation of mantle-generated heat. Total mantle heat dissipated through oceanic crust is approximately 6 times that dissipated through continents. Therefore, during periods when the continents are assembled to form a supercontinent, the superoceanic hemisphere should tend to remain an area of general mantle upwelling, the net effect of which would be to maintain an antipodal supercontinent in a near-stationary position. However, the heat shielding effect of a stationary supercontinent should result in its thermal doming (position "a" of figure 24.5) and, ultimately, in hot spot–induced rifting of the supercontinent followed by a radial dispersal of continental fragments off the thermal dome. This dispersal allows for thermal subsidence of the continents via growth of new heat-dissipating interior oceans in the continental hemisphere (position "b" of figure 24.5). The final result (position "c" of figure 24.5) is relaxation of the thermal dome itself. Upon complete thermal relaxation, the hemispherical heat production asymmetry reasserts itself (position "d" of figure 24.5), closing the interior oceans and resulting in a new stationary supercontinent (position

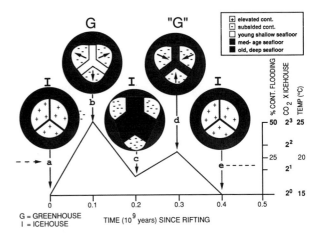

Figure 24.5 Stages of the supercontinent cycle and their effect on continental emergence and drowning, atmospheric CO_2 levels, and surface temperature. See text for explanation.

"a" of figure 24.5). The heat shielding properties of a supercontinent are therefore reestablished and the cycle repeats.

Because the elevations of both continents and ocean floors are positively correlated with their respective thermal structures (i.e., hot = high), it is possible to estimate the amount of drowning of the continents at any given phase of the cycle. The lower portion of figure 24.5 shows the effects of the supercontinent cycle upon sea level. While the supercontinent is assembled (position "a" of figure 24.5), it will attain maximum thermal doming and will be surrounded by an exterior ocean of continuously recycling sea floor that should maintain an intermediate age and depth. Hence, the continents should be fully emergent. During supercontinent breakup and dispersal, growth of young and shallow interior oceans between the supercontinental fragments is offset by removal of an equivalent area of intermediate age exterior ocean. Hence, the world ocean floor should shoal while the cooling continental fragments thermally subside. Both effects will combine to cause continental drowning. However, drowning can only continue until the continents are completely subsided and the age and depth of the world sea floor reach a minimum (position "b" of figure 24.5). Maximum drowning will occur approximately 0.1 Ga after rifting when the continents are approximately 50% flooded. After this point, the nonrecycling and hence continually aging, cooling, and subsiding sea floor of the interior oceans will cause the average age of the world sea floor to increase again, and sea level will fall. However, this process can continue only until the margins of the aging interior oceans become sufficiently old, cold, and dense that their subduction and recycling becomes inevitable. As subduction must occur within approximately 0.2 Ga of rifting, growth of these oceans at today's spreading rates can reduce the size of the exterior ocean by only one third. At this point, the continental fragments are fully subsided and the world ocean floor has reached maximum age and depth (position "c" of figure 24.5). Sea level will once again be very low, like that of today. Following the onset of subduction in the aged interior oceans, and their closure by mantle upwelling beneath the larger exterior ocean, the age of the world sea floor decreases once again to cause a secondary rise in sea level (position "d" of figure 24.5) approximately 0.3 Ga after initial rifting. Final closure of the interior oceans reestablishes initial conditions approximately 0.4 Ga after rifting by

reassembling a highly emergent supercontinent surrounded by an exterior ocean of constant and intermediate age. The thermally domed supercontinent is estimated to persist for another approximately 0.1 Ga prior to breakup, so that the entire supercontinent cycle takes approximately 0.5 Ga.

The tectonically mediated variations in sea level, which are a consequence of the supercontinent cycle, in turn influence the rate of C-burial and hence modulate atmospheric CO_2, O_2, and surface temperature by way of the silicate-carbonate and the C-org carbon burial loops. In addition to the effects of increasing solar luminosity, changes in the area of emergent continent exposed to chemical weathering can also shift C-burial rates by modifying the amount of calcium and phosphorus available to mediate carbon burial. Organisms themselves can increase the rate of C-org burial by developing innovations that selectively recycle phosphorus prior to burial (figure 24.2). As we will show later, such biotic innovations tend to occur in step with the tectonic controls that produce emergent continents. If we begin with the simplest assumption that the supply of calcium and phosphorus is proportional to continental area and temperature (Worsley et al., 1986; Worsley and Nance, 1989; Berner, 1989), emergent continents will increase calcium and phosphorus supplies that result in greater rates of CO_2 burial, O_2 liberation and hence lower surface temperature. Higher O_2 levels in turn allow for biotic innovation and invasion of new niches. Such innovations tend to increase selective phosphorus scavenging (Worsley et. al., 1986; Worsley and Nance, 1989) and hence amplify the initial response to produce an even colder, more CO_2-poor and O_2-rich world. Such conditions are conducive to icecap growth if an emergent continent is in polar position. Sequestration of water on an icecap will further emerge the continents, produce more calcium and phosphorus runoff, and further lower CO_2 levels, resulting in a still colder world that contains yet more ice. Fischer (1984) refers to such a world as an "icehouse" and notes that we are currently living in one. Drowning of the continents will cause the opposite conditions, which Fischer refers to as a "greenhouse." Such conditions characterized the warm, moist, half-drowned Cretaceous world of 0.1 Ga ago. Since the geological record marking the change from maximum 50% continental drowning 0.1 Ga ago to the total emergence of today's most recent ice age is relatively well measured, we can use it to calibrate the effect of the supercontinent cycle on climate.

During the Cretaceous period, when the continents were approximately 50% drowned (position "b" of figure 24.5), CO_2 levels were approximately 2^3 higher and surface temperature was approximately 10°C warmer than those of the total emergence of the most recent ice age of the current icehouse (Barron and Washington, 1985; Barnola et al., 1987) (position "c" of Figure 24.5). In other words, the area of continent available to supply calcium and phosphorus to remove CO_2 from the atmosphere was halved, but the resulting 10° temperature rise doubled chemical weathering rates. Hence CO_2 drawdown rates remained unchanged but CO_2 levels were an order of magnitude higher. These figures are consistent with the calculations of Kasting (1987), which suggest that an order of magnitude increase of CO_2 would yield an approximately 10°C rise for any arbitrarily selected CO_2 level. Information for O_2 is much more sketchy so that our proposed 2^3 difference between icehouse and greenhouse worlds for times prior to approximately 0.3 Ga ago is highly speculative. The calculations and measurements of Holland (1984) and Kasting (1987) are permissive for such changes but do not predict them. The calculations of Berner (1987, 1989) for the past 0.6 Ga suggest high O_2 levels during emergence and low levels during drowning. However, quantifying these estimates is very difficult for two reasons. Firstly, O_2 is not a strong greenhouse gas and hence leaves no clear climatic signal like that of CO_2. Secondly, the atmosphere became saturated with O_2 (subject to O_2 removal by fire) about 0.3 Ga ago (figure 24.4) so that subsequent icehouse-greenhouse shifts in atmospheric O_2 content are likely to have been greatly damped compared with the more pronounced effects of earlier shifts. Since approximately 0.25 Ga ago, biotic "attempts" to achieve atmospheric O_2 levels above today's 21% have resulted in fires (Lovelock and Whitfield, 1982; Kump, 1988, 1989). In any case, we can speculate (figure 24.5) that drowning of the continents of approximately 50% will yield lower O_2 levels, a CO_2 level 2^3 higher, and a temperature approximately 10°C higher than fully emergent continents. We therefore conclude that over the last three Ga, the supercontinent cycle has predictably modulated CO_2 levels, O_2 levels, and surface temperature from the monotonically changing values predicted by the smoothly running silicate-carbonate and C-org carbon burial loops alone. We further

believe that the geological record of tectonics, climate, and life corroborates this conclusion, as we now attempt to demonstrate.

Tectonics, Life, and Climate for the Last Three Billion Years

Figure 24.6 illustrates the history of solar luminosity, atmospheric CO_2 and O_2 levels, episodes of biotic innovation, and icehouse intervals for the last three Ga, and relates these to the supercontinent cycle. Prior to approximately 2.75 Ga, photosynthesis was likely to have been accomplished by oxyphobic types of blue-green algae that relied on

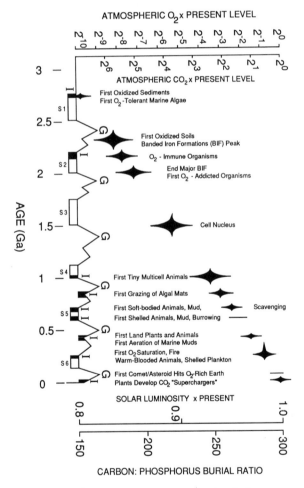

Figure 24.6 Summary of Earth's surface evolution expressed in terms of exponentially declining atmospheric CO_2, exponentially increasing O_2, approximately linearly increasing solar luminosity, and approximately linearly increasing organic carbon-to-phosphorus burial ratios. S1, S2 (etc.) refer to the phases of the supercontinent cycle and sea level change as a function of geologic time (Worsley et al., 1986). G represents the greenhouse interval and I is the icehouse interval. See text for explanation.

reduced inorganic material to neutralize their toxic waste O_2 (Schopf et al., 1983). At this time, carbon and phosphorus were presumably buried at or slightly above today's Redfield carbon-to-phosphorus ratio of approximately 100:1 (i.e., somewhere between stages A and B of figure 24.2) as suggested by the lack of any indication of appreciable phosphorus scavenging and reflux in the totally unbioturbated sediments. The first evidence of supercontinent assembly (S1) occurs at approximately 2.75 Ga (Windley, 1984), which corresponds to the first recorded icehouse (Harland, 1983) and the first tenuous indication of terrestrial redbeds (Shegelski, 1980) that record the buildup of very minor amounts of O_2 in the atmosphere. It is possible that a biotic innovation at this time led to the first O_2-tolerant organisms near the top of the photic zone (Schopf et al., 1983). If so, it would have further lowered the depressed atmospheric CO_2 levels that resulted in glaciation of portions of the emergent part of S1.

The icehouse conditions at approximately 2.1 to 2.2 Ga (Harland, 1983) may correspond to the lowered sea levels at maximum dispersal of S1. This icehouse correlates with the first clear indication of iron-oxidation in paleosols (Gay and Grandstaff, 1980) and with the peak in banded iron formation deposits. These deposits contain insoluble oxidized iron that was presumably precipitated from seawater when soluble reduced iron encounters free O_2. It is possible that algal O_2-mediating enzymes originated at this time. These catalysts eliminate molecular O_2, which is lethal to nitrogen fixation, from the nitrogen-fixing sites of a green plant. Oxygen-mediating enzymes therefore permit green plants to live in aerobic environments. The enzymes' first recorded presence as fossil heterocysts (specialized organelles in which nitrogen fixation occurs) is at approximately 2 Ga (Cloud, 1983), by which time the photic zone and atmosphere would have been weakly oxic, whereas the aphotic zone would have remained anoxic.

The geological record between 2.2 and 1.0 Ga (S3 and S4) is devoid of evidence for icehouses (Harland, 1983) although the continents seem to have remained highly emergent. The emergence is likely to have been at least a partial consequence of supercontinental stasis. An abortive attempt at supercontinental breakup at approximately 1.5 Ga may have produced sufficient lateral separation to dissipate some of the subcrustal heat but apparently failed to produce a major interior ocean, and hence, failed to completely remove the thermal bulge. Furthermore, the persistent bulge may have been maintained on the equator due to centrifugal forces and, therefore, may have inhibited icehouse conditions by denying the system a polar continent. Instead, the continually increasing solar luminosity could have produced a trend of warming surface conditions. Interestingly, the development at approximately 1.5 Ga of the cell nucleus, which is certainly one of the greatest biotic innovations in the history of the planet, left no clear geochemical signal. Perhaps the advent of the nucleated cell was not a single event but rather consisted of a gradual and protracted series of steps.

Our putative interval of severe hyperthermal stress came to an abrupt end with the breakup of the long-lived and elevated S3 and S4 approximately 1 Ga ago. This breakup ushered in a series of alternating icehouse-greenhouse episodes that continues today. On the basis of the oldest preserved traces of multicellular animals at approximately 1 Ga (Schopf et al., 1983), we infer that O_2 at concentrations sufficient to support tiny multicellular animals first became widely available on the sea floor of agitated (sandy-bottomed) platforms and shelves at this time. The high organic content of quiet-water shelves would still have suppressed O_2 buildup there. The invasion of agitated and aerated shelves by these multicellular animals greatly enhanced the potential for differential scavenging of phosphorus from the sediment-water interface before burial. To our thinking, multicellular animals induced a sharp increase in C-org burial rates that lowered atmospheric CO_2 and helped to trigger the icehouse at approximately 1 Ga. Global carbon-to-phosphorus burial ratios may have correspondingly risen to perhaps 200.

The next icehouse episode, at approximately 0.85 Ga (Harland, 1983; Knoll et al., 1986) may indirectly record the first intense grazing of stromatolites (Awramik, 1971). These are quiet-water, bottom-dwelling, reef-building algae and hence their grazing by animals heralds sea floor oxygenation under all but the most productive and organic-rich marine shelves where C-org was still able to suppress O_2 buildup. The episode probably occurred during the lowered sea level accompanying maximum dispersal of S4.

Ediacarians, which are small, soft-bodied, lenticular-shaped animals that presumably made a living by grazing and scavenging (Schopf et al., 1983), appeared during the icehouse accompanying the initial emergence of S5 at approximately 0.68 Ga. We suggest that the explosion of these nonburrowing sheetlike organisms was the consequence of the aeration of the world's more productive quiet-water shelves. Such aeration would have finally permitted the intense grazing of stromatolites that led to their decline (Awramik, 1971). It would also have permitted another step-function increase in the differential recycling of phosphorus and consequent lowering of atmospheric CO_2 that guaranteed icehouse conditions. The advent of shelled animals approximately 0.6 Ga ago again corresponds to a major icehouse episode (Harland, 1983) just prior to the breakup of S5. This icehouse features the first of the modern marine shelled animals (Conway-Morris, 1987) and the first intense burrowing of quiet-water muds by these animals. Hence O_2 quantities sufficient to support benthic aerobic metabolism were available even under C-org-rich productivity belts. Scavenger exploitation of this rich food source greatly enhanced the differential recycling of phosphorus and thereby permitted a further increase in global marine carbon-to-phosphorus burial ratios to perhaps 250:1.

The first vascular plants (and their grazers) appeared approximately 0.44 Ga ago (Gensel and Andrews, 1987) during the continental emergence accompanying maximum dispersal of S5. Intense terrestrial photosynthesis resulted in a major new C-org burial mechanism that allows for very high carbon-to-phosphorus burial ratios, perhaps approaching 400:1. The resulting sharp increase in C-org burial rate must have had a profound influence on surface O_2-CO_2 budgets, permitting aeration of even the bioturbated layer of subbottom sediments. Aeration of these sediments opened them up to increased scavenging by organisms which, in turn, resulted in higher marine carbon-to-phosphorus burial ratios. The resulting icehouse (Crowell, 1983) was intense. Evidence exists for combustion at this time (Cope and Chaloner, 1980). However, it remains questionable whether the earliest preserved specimens of fossil charcoal are the result of open fires or volcanic sintering in an environment still too weakly aerobic to support open fires (G. Mapes, personal communication, 1988). We prefer to believe, but cannot prove, that open fires became a major sink for O_2 approximately 0.3 Ga ago, based on fusain associated with coal deposits. If so, the following scenario is plausible.

Fire, which requires at least 75% of present atmospheric O_2 levels (Lovelock and Whitfield, 1982) first appears during initial assembly of S6 at approximately 0.3 Ga. By approximately 0.25 Ga, during the S6 emergence and just prior to its breakup, flowering plants and calcareous plankton developed. Flowering plants increased terrestrial C-org production and calcareous plankton increased pelagic sedimentation rate and hence C-org burial rate. As some marine-buried C-org has a terrestrial origin, the advent of the flowering plants probably raised global carbon-to-phosphorus burial ratios to near-modern values, resulting in major CO_2 drawdown and O_2 increase. Severe icehouse conditions (Crowell, 1983) confirm low CO_2 levels while the advent of warm-blooded animals and powered flight indicate O_2 saturation (figure 24.4) at modern levels. The levels can go no higher because the highly unstable separation of carbon and O_2 that life attempts to maintain is buffered by fire (Lovelock and Whitfield, 1982; Kump, 1989). Besides directly lowering O_2 levels by combustion, wildfire also increases CO_2 both by combustion and, more subtly, by the transfer of phosphorus from the terrestrial realm, where carbon-to-phosphorus burial ratios are approximately 400:1, to the marine realm where they are approximately 250:1 (Kump, 1988). We therefore suggest that fire poses a long-term threat to Earth's surface thermostasis because it prevents the CO_2 drawdown necessary to counteract continual solar brightening. The confirming greenhouse warming experiment, of course, is now being conducted. We are rapidly exhuming and burning the fossil carbon that previous life has invested so much effort burying in order to maintain a stable climate for the past four Ga (e.g., Broecker, 1985).

Interestingly, the unique, spectacular, and catastrophic terminal Cretaceous extinction event at 0.065 Ga, which lists the dinosaurs as the most prominent of its long list of victims, also provides strong evidence of the long-term instability that extreme separation of the carbon and O_2 reservoirs can produce. The event is widely attributed to the impact of one of a number of large comets and asteroids (Alvarez et al., 1980) that have collided with the Earth at intervals that roughly average 0.1 Ga (Wetherill, 1979). Hence, bodies at least as large as the terminal Cretaceous impactor must have collided with the Earth before. If so, however, they seem to have been far less devastating in terms of instantaneous mass extinction. We therefore suggest that the uniquely catastrophic terminal Cretaceous event highlights the susceptibility of the Earth to conflagration now that a large quantity of terrestrial organic matter is available to burn and the O_2 is available to burn it. We note sadly, however, that nuclear war, rather than a comet or asteroid, could accomplish the same result.

About 0.2 Ga have elapsed since the breakup of Pangea (S6). The resulting greenhouse flooding of the continents peaked approximately 0.1 Ga ago. We are now experiencing the maximum emergence of the continents that accompanies supercontinent dispersal as well as an icehouse that commenced 0.03 Ga ago. This current icehouse has witnessed the first prominence of herbs and grasses (Thommasson et al., 1986) and an explosion of marine diatom burial (Barron, 1986). According to supercontinent cycle timing, the temporal coincidence of these events is not fortuitous. Atmospheric CO_2 first dropped low enough (i.e., ≈ 200 ppmv) (Barnola et al., 1987) to initiate widespread C-4 photosynthesis approximately 0.04 Ga ago (Lovelock and Whitfield, 1982). This form of photosynthesis (Bidwell, 1983) is characterized by a greater net photosynthetic rate, a much lower CO_2 compensation point (2 to 5 ppm) that allows growth at very low CO_2 levels, and minimal photorespiration (thereby conserving water). C-4 photosynthesis is therefore favored under the dry, CO_2-poor conditions that must have characterized the development of the herbs and grasses. The evolution of the grasses must, in turn, have greatly increased the dissolved silica flux to the oceans because they incorporate opaline silica in their structural portions. As opal is much more soluble than clay minerals or quartz, decay of grasses and herbs enriches the soil layer in opaline silica and hence increases delivery of dissolved silica to the oceans by rivers. Thus the advent of savannas might have ushered in the prolific bloom (Barron, 1986) of the photosynthetically efficient diatoms that continues today.

As the biotically controlled atmospheric CO_2 reservoir dwindles to the point where C-4 photosynthesis itself becomes taxed, the Earth may undergo a rise in surface temperature as plants become starved for CO_2 (Lovelock and Whitfield, 1982). Unless another, previously unsuspected thermoregulatory feedback mechanism takes over, perhaps to produce yet another icehouse, the life of the biosphere will end (Lovelock and Whitfield, 1982). If a future icehouse is possible, we speculate that it will correspond to assemby of "S7" approximately 0.2 Ga from now. This future icehouse should be char-

acterized by a total dominance of C-4 photosynthesis on a cloud-covered Earth that is kept so by cloud condensation nuclei provided either by technology or marine plankton (Charlson et al., 1987). However, this future icehouse may be the last one possible before the Earth begins evolving toward a Venus-like thermodynamic equilibrium as the Sun continues its inevitable increase in luminosity.

Acknowledgments

We thank Steve Schneider for the invitation to participate in the 1988 Gaia conference in San Diego and for his efforts in helping to secure travel funds for the participants. Many of the ideas expressed in this paper are the result of the fruitful discussions we had with those participants. We also thank Lee Kump, whose thoughtful and thorough review of the original manuscript greatly improved it.

References

Alvarez, L.W., Alvarez, W., Asaro, F., and Michael, W.V., 1980. Extraterrestrial cause of the Cretaceous-Tertiary extinctions. *Sci*, 208, 1095–1108.

Awramik, S.M. 1971. Precambrian columnar stromatolite diversity: Reflection of metazoan appearance. *Science*, 174, 825–826.

Barnola, J.M., Raynaud, D., Korotkevich, Y.S., and Lorius, C. 1987. Vostok ice core provides 160,000-year record of atmospheric CO_2. *Nature*, 329, 408–414.

Barron, E.J., and Washington, W.M. 1985. Warm Cretaceous climates: High atmospheric CO_2 as a plausible mechanism. In: Sundquist, E.T., and Broecker, W.S., eds. *The Carbon Cycle and Atmospheric CO_2: Natural Variations Archean to Present. Geophysical Monograph Series*. Vol. 32. Washington, D.C.: American Geophysical Union, 546–555.

Barron, J. 1986. Paleoceanographic and tectonic controls on deposition of the Monterey Formation and related siliceous rocks in California. *Paleogeog, Paleoclim, Paleoecol*, 53, 27–46.

Berner, R.A. 1987. Models for carbon and sulfur cycles and atmospheric oxygen: Application to Paleozoic geologic history. *Am J Sci*, 287, 177–196.

Berner, R.A. 1989. Biogeochemical cycles of carbon and sulfur and their effect on atmospheric oxygen over Phanerozoic time. *Paleogeog, Paleoclim, Paleoecol*, 75, 97–122.

Bidwell, R.G.S. 1983. Carbon nutrition of plants: Photosynthesis and respiration. In: Steward, F.C., ed. *Plant Physiology: A Treatise*. New York: Academic Press, 287–457.

Broecker, W.S. 1985. *How To Build a Habitable Planet*. Palisades, N.Y.: Eldigio Press.

Charlson, R.J., Lovelock, J.E., Andreae, M.O., and Warren, S.G. 1987. Oceanic phytoplankton, atmospheric sulphur, cloud albedo and climate. *Nature*, 326, 655–661.

Cloud, P.E. 1983. The biosphere. *Sci Am*, 249, 176–189.

Conway-Morris, S. 1987. The search for the Precambrian-Cambrian boundary. *Am Scientist*, 75, 157–167.

Cope, M.J., and Chaloner, W.G. 1980. Fossil charcoal as evidence of past atmospheric composition. *Nature*, 283, 647–649.

Crowell, J.C. 1983. Ice ages recorded on Gondwanan continents. *Trans Geol Soc S Africa*, 86, 237–262.

Fischer, A.G. 1984. Climatic oscillations in the biosphere. In: Berggren, W.A., and Van Couvering, J., eds. *Catastrophies and Earth History*. Princeton, N.J.: Princeton University Press, 129–150.

Gay, A.L., and Grandstaff, D.E. 1980. Chemistry and mineralogy of Precambrian paleosols at Elliot Lake, Ontario, Canada. *Precambrian Res*, 12, 349–373.

Gensel, P.G., and Andrews, H.N. 1987. The evolution of early land plants. *Am Scientist*, 75, 478–489.

Gilliland, R.L. 1989. Solar evolution. *Paleogeog, Paleoclim, Paleoecol*, 75, 35–55.

Harland, W.B. 1983. *The Proterozoic Glacial Record*. Geological Society of America Memoir 161. Boulder, Geological Society of America, 279–288,

Hoffman, P.F. 1988. United plates of America, the birth of a craton: Early Proterozoic assembly and growth of Laurentia. *Ann Rev Earth Planet Sci*, 16, 543–603.

Holland, H.D. 1984. *The Chemical Evolution of the Atmosphere and Oceans*. Princeton, N.J.: Princeton University Press.

James, H.L., and Trendall, A.F. 1985. Banded iron-formation: Distribution in time and paleoenvironmental significance. In: Holland, H.D., and Schidlowski, M., eds. *Mineral Deposits and the Evolution of the Biosphere*. New York: Springer-Verlag, 199–218.

Kasting, J.F. 1987. Theoretical constraints on oxygen and carbon dioxide concentrations in the Precambrian atmosphere. *Precambrian Res*, 34, 205–229.

Kasting, J.F. 1989. Long-term stability of the Earth's climate. *Palaeogeog, Palaeoclim, Palaeoecol*, 75, 83–95.

Kasting. J.F., Toon, O.B., and Pollack, J.B. 1988. How climate evolved on the terrestrial planets. *Sci Am*, 258, 90–97.

Knoll, A.H., Hayes, J.M., Kaufman, A.K., Swett, K., and Lambert, I.B. 1986. Secular variation in carbon isotope ratios from Upper Proterozoic successions of Svalbard and East Greenland. *Nature*, 321, 832–838.

Kump, L.R. 1988. Terrestrial feedback in atmospheric oxygen regulation by fire and phosphorus. *Nature*, 335, 152–154.

Kump, L.R. 1989. Chemical stability of the atmosphere and ocean. *Palaeogeog, Palaeoclim, Palaeoecol*, 75, 123–136.

Liebau, F., and Koritnig, S. 1978. Phosphorus. In: Wedepohl, ed. *Handbook of Geochemistry, II-2*. New York: Elsevier, 15-A-1 to 19.

Lovelock, J.E., and Whitfield, M. 1982. Life span of the biosphere. *Nature*, 296, 561–563.

Moody, J.B., Chaboudy, L.K., and Worsley, T.R. 1988. Pacific pelagic phosphorus accumulation during the last 10 M.Y. *Paleoceanog*, 3, 113–136.

Nance, R.D., Worsley, T.R., and Moody, J.B. 1988. The supercontinent cycle. *Sci Am*, 259, 72–79.

Owen, T, Cess, R.D., and Ramanathan, V. 1979. Enhanced CO_2 greenhouse to compensate for reduced solar luminosity on early earth. *Nature*, 277, 640–642.

Ramanathan, V, Barkstrom, B.R., and Harrison, E.F. 1989. Climate and the Earth's radiation budget. *Physics Today*, 42, 22–32.

Redfield, A.C., Ketchum, B.H., and Richards, F.A. 1969. The influence of organisms on the compositions of seawater. In Hill, M.N., ed. *The Sea*, Vol. 2. New York: Interscience, 26–77.

Sandstrom, M.W. 1982. Diagenesis of organic phosphorus in marine sediments. In: Freney, J.R. and Gallally, I.E., eds, *Cycling of Carbon, Nitrogen, Sulfur, and Phosphorus*, New York: Springer-Verlag, 133–141.

Schidlowski, M. 1987. Application of stable carbon isotopes to early biochemical evolution on Earth. *Annu Rev Earth Planet Sci*, 15, 47–72.

Schopf, J.W., Hayes, J.M., and Walter, M.R. 1983. Evolution of Earth's earliest ecosystems: Recent progress and unsolved problems. In: Schopf, J.W., ed. *Earth's Earliest Biosphere: Its Origin and Evolution*. Princeton, N.J.: Princeton University Press, 361–384.

Schwartzman, D.W., and Volk, T. 1989. Biotic enhancement of weathering and the habitability of Earth. *Nature*, 340, 457–460.

Shegelski, R.J. 1980. Archean cratonization, emergence and red bed development, Lake Shebandowan area, Canada. *Precambrian Res*, 9, 331–347.

Thommasson, J.R., Nelson, M.E., and Zakrzewski, R.J. 1986. A fossil grass with Kranz anatomy. *Science* 233, 876–878.

Walker, J.C.G., Hays, P.B., and Kasting, J.K. 1981. A negative feedback mechanism for the long-term stabilization of Earth's surface temperature. *J Geophys Res*, 86, 9776–9782.

Wetherill, G. 1979. Apollo objects. *Sci Am*, 240, 54–65.

Windley, B.F. 1984. *The Evolving Continents*. 2nd ed. New York: Wiley.

Worsley, T.R., and Nance, R.D. 1989. Carbon redox and climate control through Earth history: A speculative reconstruction. *Palaeogeog, Palaeoclim, Palaeoecol*, 75, 259–282.

Worsley, T.R., Nance, D., and Moody, J.B. 1984. Global tectonics and eustacy for the past 2 billion years. *Marine Geol*, 58, 373–400.

Worsley, T.R., Nance, R.D., and Moody, J.B. 1986. Tectonic cycles and the history of the Earth's biogeochemical and paleoceanographic record. *Paleoceanog*, 1, 233–263.

Manfred Schidlowski

25

Quantitative Evolution of Global Biomass Through Time: Biological and Geochemical Constraints

Extrapolating from currently available paleontological and biogeochemical evidence (see Schopf, 1983, and Schidlowski, 1987, for recent overviews), we may reasonably infer that the Earth had continuously supported a veneer of life (or biosphere that comprises the totality of living and dead surficial biomass) over almost 4 Gyr of its history. Specifically, a good case can be made that photoautotrophy as the quantitatively most important process of biological carbon fixation had been extant as both a biochemical process and as a geochemical agent since 3.8 Gyr ago (Schidlowski et al., 1979, 1983; Schidlowski, 1987). With this established, the problem of the quantitative evolution of the terrestrial biomass through time poses a question of considerable scientific and practical concern, notably in view of the fact that fossil organic carbon has come to figure as the prime energy source of modern industrial societies. Given that the geochemical cycles of a large number of elements are biologically modulated, information on the quantity of biogenic substances involved in the turnover of the exogenic cycle (which channels transformations of matter in the atmosphere-ocean-crust system) might provide crucial insight into the potential steering function of the biosphere in global geochemical processes.

The following discourse briefly addresses the principal determinants controlling the quantity of biomass on this planet and the evidence that might potentially permit a semiquantitative assessment of the organic carbon content of both the surficial and sedimentary compartments of the exogenic cycle during the geological past. The argument is based on a blend of plausible theoretical approaches and empirical evidence (in the form of biological and geochemical data) that together could furnish a set of constraints for the problem under consideration.

Global Biomass: Limits to Growth?

Primarily, all forms of organic matter are produced by, and tied up to, living organisms (microorganisms, plants, animals). Accordingly, any attempt to determine an upper limit for average biomass production per unit space on the Earth's surface should commence with an assessment of maximum possible biomass densities of standing crops and populations.

It is well established that living systems possess an intrinsic property of being able to proliferate until they encounter externally imposed limits, striving to occupy all empty spaces available and thereby straining the spatial and nutritional carrying capacity of the supporting environment to virtual exhaustion. Ultimately, this phenomenon is germane to an innate drive of protein chemistry towards boundless self-expression, that is, the drive to establish itself at the expense of the inorganic world with a concomitant reckless exploitation of all environmental resources. With such tendency intrinsic to life, the proliferation pressure exercised by organisms on their habitats is—according to a pointed dictum by J.B.S. Haldane—"not a problem, but rather an axiom" (cf. Vernadsky, 1930, p. 179). As a result of their adaptive faculties, organisms have successfully populated a wide range of environments inclusive of extremely harsh and seemingly inhospitable reaches (such as brines, glaciers, endolithic pores, and intestinal milieus). The trend towards unrestricted proliferation usually culminates in the establishment of a steady state termed *biotic plenitude* (i.e., fullness) in which the components of a given ecosystem have completely occupied the available space and sequestered its nutritional resources to virtual exhaustion, and where new mouths can be fed only after a corresponding number of old ones have been eliminated.

It is worth noting in this context that early students of these phenomena were stunned by the prodigious reproduction rates notably of microorganisms. For instance, as early as 1854 Ehrenberg (one of the founders of micropaleontology) came to realize that a single diatom was potentially capable of creating a progeny equivalent to the mass of the Earth within eight days, provided all obstacles to

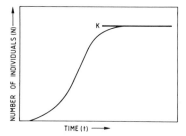

Figure 25.1 Growth of biological populations according to the logistic curve. Note exponential increase in number of individuals N when reproduction rates are not resource limited (i.e., at values of N well below K). With the exhaustion of life-supporting supplies (notably critical nutrients), the population is tethered to a near-stationary upper level K defining the biotic saturation or plenitude of the ecosystem.

unretarded proliferation were eliminated. Similar and even more impressive examples were subsequently furnished by many other investigators working, inter alia, on *Paramecium* species and notably on bacteria whose reproduction rates are among the largest in the living world. Striking illustrations of unretarded reproduction are also provided by algal blooms in locally eutrophicated environments where a temporal abundance of otherwise critical nutrients gives testimony to an ultimate trophic control of these outbursts (and similar ones) of productivity.

First attempts to assess quantitatively the reproduction process and the resulting population dynamics date back to the work of Verhulst (1845), who is to be credited for drafting the first version of what he had termed the "logistic curve" (figure 25.1). This function describes the growth of a population within a finite system and is the integral of the differential equation

$$\frac{dN}{dt} = rN\frac{(K - N)}{K} \tag{1}$$

According to this relationship, the increase of a population N is proportional to N, to a factor r expressing the potential average increase of this population with no intrinsic or external coercion imposed, and a negative feedback term $(K - N)/K$ reflecting the proportion of vacant spaces (or "life opportunities") to the total number of spaces K available within the system (K giving a numerical expression for the upper ceiling, i.e., the limit to growth). In the context of equation (1), the term *space* does not necessarily have a territorial connotation but rather refers to the chance of the single

individual to share in the life-supporting resources primarily secured by the logistics of nutrient supply.

Although important details of the growth and stabilization process are not addressed by the logistic curve, the function provides a plausible model for the observation that living populations tend to proliferate exponentially until they hit a ceiling that precludes a further increase of the community, and thereby terminates biomass production. Hence, by implication, the saturation level K in figure 25.1 also stands for an upper limit of the standing biomass, which is consequently fixed at a quasistationary level as a result of a dynamic equilibrium between the buildup and decay of organic matter.

With the obvious existence of boundary conditions for the production of biogenic matter, a brief review of the principal agents apt to constrain standing crops, notably of primary producers, is in order. Crucial factors that have limited biomass growth ever since water and CO_2 became abundant on the Earth's surface, and the oldest microbial ecosystems had established themselves in appropriate habitats, were (1) the availability of biologically utilizable reducing power for the reduction of CO_2 to the carbohydrate level; (2) the exhaustion of critical nutrients (notably phosphorus and nitrogen); and (3) autotoxic effects induced by an excessive release of metabolic wastes in high-density ecosystems. There is reason to believe that these limits appear to be universal, applying, with appropriate adaptions, to microbial communities as well as to populations of a seemingly unrestricted biological superdominant such as *Homo sapiens*. Apart from these cardinal constraints, second-order limits on biomass densities, notably on the continents, are imposed by temperature (as in arctic and boreal regions) and water supply (deserts and semi-arid areas).

As has been detailed elsewhere (Broda, 1975; Schidlowski, 1978, 1984), any major proliferation of biomass was primarily contingent upon a sufficient supply of electrons for the reduction of CO_2. A quantitative assessment of the principal reductants available (H_2O, H_2S, H_2, Fe^{2+}) leaves little doubt that water constitutes the geochemically most abundant electron donor, which, however, is difficult to utilize because of the high-activation energy required for splitting the H—O bonds of the water molecule. This increased energy demand was, however, subsequently met by water-splitting photosynthesis as an evolutionary adaption of the photosynthetic pathway. Capitalizing on this innovation, the oldest cyanobacterial (prokaryotic) communities were bound to overwhelm this particular constraint when starting to exploit the virtually inexhaustible electron pool of the terrestrial hydrosphere as a convenient source of reducing power. As the advent of water-splitting photosynthesis apparently dates back to at least 3.5 Gyr (cf. Schidlowski, 1978; Awramik et al., 1983; Schopf and Packer, 1987), a good case can be made for a basically trophic (nutritional) biomass control over the last 3.5 Gyr of Earth's history, with critical nutrients such as phosphorus and nitrogen functioning as prime determinants for the size of the biosphere.

Phosphorus figures as an essential constituent of living matter (Todd, 1981) and is present in different groups of organisms in specific and usually well-defined carbon-to-phosphorus ratios. Being preferentially utilized in the biosynthesis of nucleic acids and proteins (apart from its function in the energy-transducing systems of all organisms), protein-rich biomass such as marine phytoplankton is characterized by low carbon-to-phosphorus values of about 106:1 (Redfield ratio; cf. Redfield, 1958), whereas this ratio may soar up to about 500 or more in the case of carbohydrate-rich biomass such as represented by the bulk of land plants (cf. Lerman, 1979, p. 23). In contrast to the amount of biologically utilizable nitrate that can be augmented by increased frequencies of atmospheric lightning discharges or by certain groups of plants such as the *Leguminosae,* the quantity of phosphate available to the biosphere is basically fixed because the stationary phosphate burden of the surficial environment is ultimately supplied by the weathering cycle that liberates phosphorus from the exposed parts of the lithosphere. Assuming globally quasi-uniform average denudation rates through the ages, phosphate could have been flushed through the surficial compartment so as to maintain near-constant PO_4^{3-}-levels, which in turn might have tethered the maximum size of the surficial biomass (living and dead) to a long-term mean permitting only limited oscillations. This basic scenario is, however, almost always gravely upset by the *internal* cycling of phosphate within the surficial exchange reservoir, where sizeable quantities of the element may be temporarily trapped in the anoxic layer of a stratified ocean and episodically released along with upwelling waters, with consequent fluctuations of fertility and biomass densities imposed on the world ocean. If, on

the other hand, these disturbances and similar ones were basically leveled out on mid-term ($\approx 10^7$-yr) geological timescales, an acceptance of the role of phosphorus as the ultimate determinant for the quantity of biologically fixed carbon on earth (cf. Broecker, 1971, 1973; Junge et al., 1975; Holland, 1978, 1984) might imply the existence of a quasi-stationary biosphere as from the time the oldest prokaryotic ecosystems had established dominion on the juvenile planet. In the following section, the potential implications of the sedimentary carbon record for the quantitative evolution of biomass through time is briefly discussed.

Sedimentary Record of Organic Carbon: A Four-Billion-Year Perspective on the Earth's Biosphere

The last two decades have witnessed an impressive accumulation of data on the content and isotopic composition of organic (reduced) carbon in sedimentary rocks. Because this data pool holds crucial qualitative and potentially quantitative information with regard to biomass evolution through geological time, a brief review of the relevant findings seems appropriate at this stage.

The *record of organic carbon* (C-org) in the form of kerogen (the ultimate product of the diagenetic alteration of biogenic substances buried alteration in sediments) and its graphitic derivatives can be traced back to the Earth's oldest sediments represented by the 3.8-Gyr-old metasedimentary Isua suite of West Greenland (Schidlowski et al., 1979, 1983; Hayes et al., 1983). Systematic assays for C-org carried out on Phanerozoic rocks (Trask and Patnode, 1942; Ronov, 1958) as well as the markedly sparser data hitherto available for Precambrian sediments seem to indicate that the C-org content of the average sediment has oscillated moderately around a mean of perhaps 0.5% over almost 4-Gyr of Earth history (figure 25.2). Although both the preserved rock record and available analytical data are becoming progressively attenuated as we go back into the geological past, there is no indication that the scatter of organic carbon in Precambrian (time > 0.6 Gyr) rocks differs basically from that in the Phanerozoic (time < 0.6 Gyr). Hence there is no clear-cut evidence arguing for a substantial decline of the organic carbon content of geologically older formations. It seems worth noting in this context that the extensively graphitized kerogen fraction of the 3.8-Gyr-old Isua metasediments at the

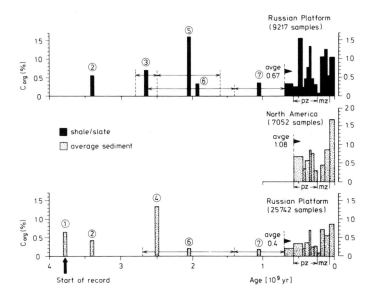

Figure 25.2 Organic carbon content of shales and average sediments over 3.8 Gyr of Earth history (1 Gyr = 10^9 yr). Note that the data base for the Precambrian (Archean and Proterozoic, $t > 0.6$ Gyr) record is scant as compared with the younger (Phanerozoic) one, but the scatter of C-org is apparently of the same order. (Phanerozoic data from Trask and Patnode, 1942; and Ronov 1958, 1980). Numbered Precambrian occurrences: (1) Mean of 69 metasediments from Early Archean Isua suite, West Greenland (Schidlowski, unpublished data); (2) means of three shales and 81 various sediments, Swaziland Supergroup, South Africa (Reimer et al., 1979); (3) mean of 406 Archean shales, Canadian Shield (Cameron and Garrels, 1980); (4) mean of 29 different sediments, Hamersley Group, Australia (Hayes, unpublished data); (5) mean of 326 Proterozoic shales, Canadian Shield (Cameron and Garrels, 1980); (6) means of 460 paragneisses and meta-argillites and of 1408 various sediments from Proterozoic 1–2 of Russian Platform (Ronov, 1980); (7) means of 34 composites from 1226 shales and of 83 composites from 2694 different sediments from Proterozoic 3, Russian Platform (Ronov, 1980). (From Schidlowski, 1982.)

beginning of the record may account for more than 0.6% of the total rock in the case of carbon-rich members of the suite (cf. figure 25.2). In spite of the patchiness of the evidence summarized in figure 25.2, a reasonable case can be made for a basically uniform C-org content of the average sedimentary rock from Archean to recent time, with a mean somewhere between 0.4% and 0.7%. This range comfortably accommodates previous estimates of 0.62% (Ronov, 1980) and 0.54 (Schidlowski, 1982), based on background data from Hunt, 1972 for the organic carbon burden of the Earth's sedimentary cover. Incidentally, with the mass of terrestrial sediments totaling about 2.4 × 10^{24} g (Garrels and Mackenzie, 1971), 0.5% to 0.6% C-org would translate into a sedimentary organic carbon reservoir between 1.2 and 1.4 × 10^{22} g exceeding the amount of carbon fixed in the surficial biomass ($\approx 10^{18}$ g) by about four orders of magnitude.

A second parameter that is particularly important for an assessment of the organic carbon-to-carbonate (C-org:C-carb) ratio in the exogenic system is provided by the *isotopic composition of organic carbon and carbonate* through Earth's history (figure 25.3). It is well established that both biogenic matter and marine bicarbonate as the principal carbon species in the surficial exchange reservoir have entered the sedimentary record continuously in the form of organic carbon (kerogen) or carbonate (limestone, dolomite), with their original isotopic compositions basically retained except for a minor diagenetic overprint. Consequently, isotopic fractionations between organic (reduced) and inorganic (oxidized) carbon have become encoded in sedimentary rocks with relatively little change, propagating the kinetic isotope effect inherent in autotrophic carbon fixation right back to the beginning of the sedimentary record (cf. Schidlowski et al., 1979, 1983; Schidlowski, 1987). As is obvious from figure 25.3, the isotope age functions of carbonate carbon and organic carbon both represent fair transcriptions into the geological past of the isotopic compositions of their respective progenitor materials in the surficial compartment of the exogenic cycle. δ ^{13}C-carb roughly reflects the isotopic composition of the marine bicarbonate pool through time and appears to be tethered to a long-term mean close to zero permil, whereas δ^{13}C-org integrates

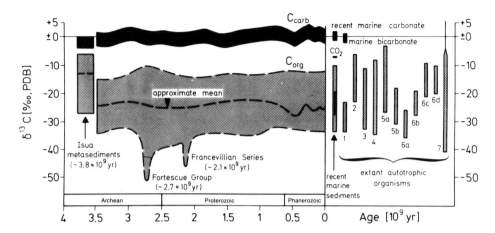

Figure 25.3 Isotope age curves of organic carbon (C-org) and carbonate carbon (C-carb) over the hitherto known sedimentary record, compared with the isotopic compositions of their progenitor substances in the contemporary environment (i.e., biogenic matter of various parentage and marine bicarbonate, see right box). Isotopic compositions are given as $\delta^{13}C$ values indicating either an increase (+) or decrease (−) in the $^{13}C{:}^{12}C$ ratio of the respective substance (in permil difference) relative to the $^{13}C{:}^{12}C$ ratio of the Peedee belemnite (PDB) standard that defines zero permil on the δ-scale (i.e., $\delta^{13}C = [(^{13}C/^{12}C)_{sa}/(^{13}C/^{12}C)_{st} - 1] \times 1000$, where sa = sample and st = standard). The pronounced enrichment of light carbon (^{12}C) in biogenic matter as reflected by the negative $\delta^{13}C$-org values is due to a kinetic isotope effect that favors higher reaction rates of ^{12}C as compared to ^{13}C in all pathways of autotrophic (specifically photosynthetic) carbon fixation. Note that the $\delta^{13}C$-org spread of the extant biomass is virtually transcribed into recent marine sediments and further into the older record back to 3.8 Gyr (the Isua values have been moderately reset by amphibolite-grade metamorphism). The envelope shown for fossil organic carbon (kerogen) is an update of the database originally presented by Schidlowski and colleagues (1983) that covers the means of some 150 Precambrian kerogen provinces and the currently available Phanerozoic record (Phanerozoic data after Degens, 1969; Veizer et al., 1980; and others). The negative offshoots at 2.7 and 2.1 Gyr indicate a large-scale involvement of methylotrophic pathways in the formation of the respective kerogen precursors. Extant autotrophs with $\delta^{13}C$-org spreads listed are (1) C3 plants; (2) C4 plants; (3) CAM plants; (4) eukaryotic algae; (5a and b) natural and cultured cyanobacteria; (6a through d) anoxygenic photosynthetic bacteria (Chromatiaceae, Rhodospirillaceae, Chlorobiaceae, Chloroflexaceae), (7) methanogens. $\delta^{13}C$-org range in recent marine sediments according to Deines (1980), based on some 1600 analyzed samples (black insert in bar covers > 90% of the database).

over a wide range of primary biological values that scatter around an average somewhere between −24‰ and −27‰.

Because the characteristic enrichment of light carbon (^{12}C) in fossil organic matter (reflected by distinctly negative $\delta^{13}C$-org values mainly in the range −20‰ to −30‰) is largely identical to that observed in the biological precursor materials, there is little doubt that the isotopic record of ancient kerogens gives a remarkably consistent signal of autotrophy, and specifically photoautotrophy, over almost 4 Gyr of Earth's history. In fact, the mainstream of the envelope for $\delta^{13}C$-org depicted on figure 25.3 can be most readily explained as the geochemical manifestation of the isotope-discriminating properties of ribulose-1,5-bisphosphate (RuBP) carboxylase, the key enzyme of the Calvin cycle that channels most of the carbon transfer from the nonliving to the living realm. The uniformity through time of this isotopic signal is likely to reflect an extreme degree of evolutionary conservatism in the biochemistry of autotrophic carbon fixation. As for the isotope shifts shown by the 3.8-

Gyr-old Isua sediments, these are due to an isotopic reequilibration between C-org and C-carb in response to the amphibolite-grade metamorphism suffered by the rocks during their postdepositional history. A detailed discussion of this and other questions related to the interpretation of the $\delta^{13}C$-org age function as an index line of photosynthetic carbon fixation has been recently given elsewhere (Schidlowski, 1987).

Although on the 10^4- to 10^8-year scale both isotope age curves display distinct (though limited) oscillations that are particularly well documented for carbonates and constitute important stores of geochemical and paleoceanographic information, such variations are largely smoothed out as we approach the 10^9-year (Gyr) perspective (cf. figure 25.3). The near-time-invariance on the Gyr-scale is an intriguing feature of the carbon isotope record that has straightforward implications for the relative proportions of both sedimentary carbon species (C-org and C-carb) within the exogenic compartment. Because all crustal carbon was originally derived from the mantle, its bulk isotopic composition is constrained by an isotope mass balance that governs the carbon transfer from the mantle to the crust. Accepting δ^{13}C-prim $= -5‰$ as a reasonable approximation for the isotopic composition of primordial mantle carbon (Des Marais and Moore, 1984; Mattey et al., 1984), the isotope mass balance

$$\delta^{13}\text{C-prim} = R\delta^{13}\text{C-org} + (1 - R)\delta^{13}\text{C-carb} \qquad (2)$$

would yield R = C-org/(C-org + C-carb) = 0.2 when substituting the long-term averages of δ^{13}C-org and δ^{13}C-carb from figure 25.3 (i.e., $-25‰$ and $\pm 0‰$) into the above equation. $R = 0.2$ indicates, by implication, a C-org:C-carb ratio of 0.2:0.8 or 1:4, respectively. Hence, within the constraints of the above mass balance, organic carbon accounts for approximately 25% and carbonate carbon for 80% of total sedimentary carbon. The fact that the δ^{13}C-org and δ^{13}C-carb values fed into equation (2) hold as from the very beginning of the record (if allowing for a metamorphic overprint of the Isua suite) would imply that the 20% to 80% partitioning between organic carbon and carbonate carbon had been established very early and was subsequently stabilized over 3.8 Gyr of recorded Earth history.

Since the isotope values conveying this information were originally established in the terrestrial near-surface environment before being propagated to the rock record, they primarily indicate the above C-org:C-carb ratio of 20% to 80% for the surficial compartment of the cycle. In other words, they tell us that about 20% of total carbon residing at the Earth's surface was always tied up to organic mat- (living and dead), the rest being retained in the surficial reservoir as oxidized carbon (carbon dioxide and marine bicarbonate). With bicarbonate ion (HCO_3^-) as the most abundant carbon species in this surficial carbon reservoir, having a residence time in seawater on the order of 10^5 year (Holland, 1978), there is good evidence that this compartment is currently being flushed at a geologically fairly rapid rate. Even with this residence time increased by an order of magnitude or so, a steady state complying with the above mass balance equation would still be attained in a geologically short time span. Because of the wide scatter of biological isotope fractionations (cf. figure 25.3), the overall partitioning of surficial carbon between the reduced (organic) and the oxidized (HCO_3^-, CO_3^{2-}, CO_2) moiety is best reflected by the narrow δ^{13}C mean of dissolved oceanic bicarbonate that subsequently comes to be encoded in marine carbonate rocks

with a minor change of about $+1‰$. In view of the short mixing time of the world ocean (10^3 year), the marine bicarbonate mean is apt to integrate most faithfully over the surficial compartment as a whole, conveying a reliable signal of the state of the system at any given time. Thus summing up the mass balance argument, it can be stated that the long-term constancy of δ^{13}C-carb $\approx \pm 0‰$ and δ^{13}C-org $\approx -25‰$ (figure 25.3) reflects a correspondingly constant partitioning through time of exogenic carbon between C-org and C-carb in the approximate proportion 20% to 80%.

Content and Isotopic Composition of Organic Carbon in Sediments: Implications for Biomass Evolution?

With the currently available sedimentary age functions of carbon content and isotopic composition at hand, the possible significance of these two parameters for the evolution of both life and biomass over 3.8 Gyr of recorded Earth history would be of considerable interest. Apart from furnishing a formidable body of qualitative information, the evidence summarized in figures 25.2 and 25.3 may also offer clues to a quantitative assessment of biomass evolution through time.

Evolution of the Surficial Carbon Reservoir

A straightforward deduction derived from this evidence is that the early Earth had hosted a biosphere from the time the oldest sediments were deposited on its surface. The graphitized kerogen constituents of the Isua metasedimentary suite stand in continuity with the younger record, giving eloquent testimony to organic carbon burial as long as 3.8 Gyr ago (Schidlowski, 1982). An astounding corollary of the oldest record is that the C-org content of Archean rocks does not seem to be significantly lower than that of geologically younger sediments (cf. figure 25.2).

We may reasonably infer that the sole contributors to the Earth's oldest organic carbon pool were microbial (prokaryotic) ecosystems whose first undisputed morphological manifestations appear somewhat later in the record (≈ 3.5 Gyr ago) in the form of lithified microbial mats (stromatolites) and coeval microfossils of most probably cyanobacterial affinity (cf. Awramik et al., 1983; Walter, 1983; Schopf and Packer, 1987). In view of the fact that extant communities of benthic prokaryotes (specifically cyanobacteria) have been shown to sustain impressive rates of primary productivity with maxima between 8 to 12 g C-org/m² × day (Krumbein and Cohen, 1977; Cohen et al., 1980), the conspicuous accumulation of fossil biomass in the Earth's oldest sediments is perhaps not surprising. Such rates vividly demonstrate that microbial communities are among the most productive ecosystems of the contemporary biosphere, being comparable to those of tropical rain forests or selected agricultural crops like wheat or sugar beet. Given suitable environmental conditions, the performances of their Archean and Proterozoic precursors were probably not below these standards. It is, moreover, generally accepted that the Precambrian was the "Golden Age" of prokaryotic ecosystems (Cloud, 1976; Awramik, 1982; Schopf, 1983). If such high rates of primary production can be sustained by microbial photoautotrophs working on the prokaryotic level, a good case can be made that the rate of global production of biomass may not have increased very much since the first veneer of microbial life spanned the surface of the planet in Archean times.

A potentially quantitative clue to biomass evolution is provided by the isotope age functions of both sedimentary carbon species (figure 25.3). Apart from constituting the isotopic signature of autotrophic carbon fixation, the approximate constancy on Gyr-timescales of the δ¹³C-org and δ¹³C-carb functions entails straightforward information on the relative sizes of both carbon reservoirs within the constraints of an isotope mass balance—see equation (2). Specifically, the long-term averages of $\delta^{13}C\text{-org} = -25‰$ and $\delta^{13}C\text{-carb} = \pm 0‰$ would translate into C-org:C-carb ratios close to 0.2:0.8, indicating that roughly 20% of total carbon residing in the surficial exchange reservoir (where isotope fractionations between organic and inorganic carbon are established) end up as organic matter in the widest sense. With equation (2) inherently representing a *budget equation*, its results are largely independent of attendant background parameters such as fluxes, residence times, and so forth, indicating a gross C-org:C-carb partitioning of 20:80 in the surficial reservoir when sedimentary carbonates leave the system with δ¹³C-carb values around zero permil.

Students of the carbon isotope record had long been stunned by such manifestation of geochemical conservatism, a conservatism that implies that a largely fixed proportion of total carbon residing in the surficial exchange reservoir at all times $t < 3.8$

Gyr had been sequestered by the biosphere in the form of either living or dead biomass. Attempts to account for this conspicuously stable partitioning between C-org and C-carb have involved mainly a possible steering function of phosphorus as the ultimate critical nutrient whose availability would have set an upper limit for biomass production since the time reducing power had ceased to be limiting to the biosphere, that is, since water-splitting (cyanobacterial) photosynthesis had taken over as the principal biological carbon-fixing process. Assuming a model scenario with quasi-uniform turnover rates of phosphorus in the exogenic cycle and a concomitant stabilization of the principal phosphorus reservoirs inclusive of the surficial stationary PO_4^{3-} pool, this could have given rise to a constant C-org:C-carb partitioning, with the size of the stationary biomass (living and dead) constrained, for instance, by the requirement of the Redfield ratio that about 100 carbon atoms be fixed as organic matter for each phosphate molecule available for metabolization. In keeping with the axiom of an inherently boundless proliferation of living matter, we might expect biomass production to continue until the last vagrant phosphate molecule within the environment had come to be tied up in either living or dead biomass. With both an upper limit and a steady state thus attained for biological carbon fixation, the balance of surficial carbon was due to be retained in the oxidized reservoir (mostly as marine bicarbonate) and subsequently disposed of in the form of carbonate. Thus a most probable consequence of a phosphate control of the global biomass could have been an approximately constant partitioning of surficial carbon between a biological (reduced) and an inorganic (oxidized) carbon reservoir.

It should go without saying that the constancy of the environmental phosphate burden postulated by such model would be largely a statistical one, resting on the premise of globally averaged (uniformitarian) turnover rates in the exogenic cycle through geological time and an early stabilization of the reservoirs involved. Possible pulsations in the long-term operation of the geodynamic system would, however, not only permit but also predict moderate oscillations around a long-term mean that should have been immediately transcribed into corresponding oscillations of the total biomass (living and dead) and consequent shifts of the organic carbon-to-carbonate ratio in the surficial exchange reservoir. Moreover, a simplistic scenario of this type was bound to undergo severe modulation by other geochemical factors and constraints. It is well known, for instance, that the *internal* cycling of phosphate within the marine subcompartment (where upwelling waters periodically release phosphate previously trapped in deeper water bodies) makes an impact on the marine ecosystem that is significantly more pronounced than that exercised by the external (continental) input. Also, different efficiencies of phosphorus utilization by different groups of primary producers must introduce additional scatter in the amount of biologically fixed carbon. We know that land plants with a relative preponderance of phosphorus-depleted cellulose and lignin exhibit carbon-to-phosphorus ratios between two and eight times in excess of the Redfield ratio of 106:1. The Redfield ratio reflects the elemental composition of marine phytoplankton (i.e., of protein-rich microorganisms). This being the case, repercussions in the global C-org:C-carb ratio might be preferentially expected during periods of major evolutionary changes in the composition of the biosphere such as the time of the first extensive proliferation of land floras (Devonian and Carboniferous periods). Another difficulty for a phosphate control of quasi-constant C-org:C-carb ratios rests with the substantially increased CO_2 content of the atmosphere-ocean system assumed for part of the geological past. Under such conditions, a proportionately smaller fraction of total carbon in the exchange reservoir would come to be tied up as organic matter if the phosphorus burden of this reservoir were to remain constant, with the resulting decrease of global C-org:C-carb apt to be monitored by a negative shift in the marine δ^{13}C-carb signal.

In glaring contrast to the potential vicissitudes in the operation of these steering variables, the actually observed near-time-invariance on the Gyr-scale of the δ^{13}C-org and δ^{13}C-carb age functions argues for a correspondingly constant C-org:C-carb ratio through geological time. In any case, it is most surprising that neither the increased pCO_2 levels that presumably prevailed in the early Precambrian nor the advent since the Devonian of lush continental floras (with a carbon-to-phosphorus almost an order of magnitude higher than that of marine primary producers) have made a sizeable impact specifically on the marine δ^{13}C-carb function that is likely to integrate most faithfully over the different subcompartments of the surficial carbon reservoir. Though an increase in δ^{13}C-carb is indeed evident over the interval Silurian to Permian, this positive

excursion is ostensibly comparable to analogues from the earlier record such as the terminal Precambrian (cf. Veizer et al., 1980; Schidlowski, 1982). Moreover, the amplitude of this isotopic signal is unlikely to accommodate a quantum jump in the increase of the global C-org:C-carb ratio such as is implied by both the rapid proliferation of continental floras and the concomitant rise in the efficiency of phosphorus utilization by land plants. Given a phosphate control for total organic carbon in the surficial compartment, the maintenance of C-org:C-carb ratios around a long-term mean, and notably the absence of unidirectional trends with time as demonstrated by the isotope record, would seem to be contingent on the operation of a delicately tuned compensation mechanism that had exercised a dampening effect offsetting, on a global scale, major disturbances in selected subcompartments of the cycle.

As for the possible implications of a limiting nutrient control by phosphate of the size of the standing (living) biomass, it is appropriate to point out that the rate of phosphorus supply affects primary production rather than stationary biomass densities. The latter are related primarily to the residence time (or longevity) of standing crops or vegetations. With no quantitative link thus existing between the supply of phosphorus and the amount of carbon fixed in the *living* biomass, the C-org component of the potentially phosphorus-controlled C-org:C-carb ratios that are monitored by the isotope record obviously comprises the totality of biologically processed reduced carbon constituents stored in the exchange reservoir. It is well known that the bulk of organic matter residing in this reservoir belongs to the nonliving realm, consisting principally of dissolved organic matter in the deep ocean or humic substances in soils. Hence although the isotope age functions shown in figure 25.3 are likely to give information on the relative proportions of reduced and oxidized carbon in the surficial reservoir as a whole, they surely withhold any definitive information on the quantity of living biomass (currently equivalent to some 10^{18} g carbon; cf. Bolin et al., 1979).

Evolution of the Sedimentary Organic Carbon Reservoir

Although the information contained in figures 25.2 and 25.3 provides only limited clues for a quantitative assessment of the living biomass through time, the data are decidedly more conclusive with regard to estimates of the quantity of fossil organic carbon. It is well established that both carbonate and organic matter have been continuously transferred from the Earth's surface to the crust as constituents of newly formed sediments. In the fullness of time, these fluxes have piled up within the sedimentary shell huge reservoirs of C-org and C-carb on the order of 10^{22} g, which surpass the amount of total carbon (Σ C-carb + C-org + C-CO_2 $\approx 10^{19}$ g) residing at the Earth's surface by three orders of magnitude. Specifically, with a sedimentary mass totaling 2.4×10^{24} g (Garrels and Mackenzie, 1971), the average C-org content of sedimentary rocks (0.5% to 0.6%) would translate into an organic carbon reservoir between 1.2 and 1.4×10^{22} g, which makes the $\approx 10^{18}$ g C-org of the surficial biosphere a negligible quantity. Accordingly, almost all biologically processed carbon present on this planet has come to be stored in the sedimentary shell in the form of kerogen and related substances.

Utilizing the carbon isotope mass balance introduced in equation (2) and current models for the growth of the sedimentary shell as a function of time, a reasonable approximation may be derived for the quantitative evolution of this sedimentary C-org reservoir. As has been detailed before, an interpretation of the data base assembled in figure 25.3 in terms of equation (2) would prompt the conclusion that the relative proportions of C-org and C-carb did not undergo much variation during the whole of the earth's history, with organic carbon always accounting for approximately 20% of total sedimentary carbon as from 3.8 Gyr ago (accepting that the oldest isotope record has been reset by metamorphism). Because, according to the "principle of geochemical uniformitarianism" (Garrels and Mackenzie, 1971, p. 276), the total carbon content of the sedimentary shell had been always fixed at roughly 3%, the isotope mass balance would indicate that the C-org content of the average sediment is about 20% of this and largely time-invariant, fluctuating around a mean of 0.5% to 0.6% (cf. figure 25.2). Hence, the principal unknown in attempts to trace the growth of the sedimentary organic carbon reservoir through time is the quantitative evolution of the stationary sedimentary mass as a whole, of which C-org has apparently constituted a fixed proportion since the onset of the record 3.8 Gyr ago.

It is well established that sediments are formed in a kind of global titration process by the reaction of primary (igneous) rocks with acid volatiles that are discharged from the Earth's interior. Therefore, we may view the increase of the sedimentary mass through time in terms of two limiting models that are rooted in corresponding limits for the terrestrial degassing process (cf. Garrels and Mackenzie, 1971, p. 255; Li, 1972). These are known as the constant mass model and the linear accumulation model (figure 25.4). In the former case, a virtually modern-size sedimentary mass had originated, as a result of early catastrophic degassing, at the very beginning of the Earth's history, and had subsequently persevered through time as a stationary quantity. The second model is characterized by a linear growth of the sedimentary mass based on a linear release function of the sediment-forming volatiles. According to this latter scenario, the sedimentary shell would have attained its present size

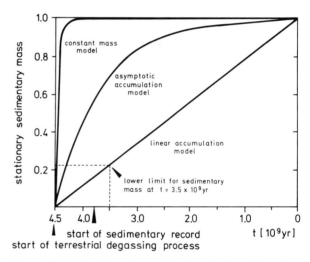

Figure 25.4 Possible pathways for the evolution of the stationary sedimentary mass as a function of different terrestrial degassing scenarios (the present mass of 2.4×10^{24} g = 1). The maximum possible mass is determined in each case by the quantity of acid volatiles provided by the degassing process that is available for sediment formation; hence early catastrophic degassing and linear degassing define an upper and lower boundary condition for the growth of the sedimentary shell with time and are reflected by the constant mass and linear accumulation models, respectively. The actual growth curve probably occupied a position between these extremes (asymptotic accumulation model), approaching the constant mass rather than the linear accumulation model (the function shown is based on a value of 1.16×10^{-9} yr^{-1} for the time-averaged terrestrial degassing constant; cf. Li, 1972). With carbon accounting for 3% of the sedimentary mass and the isotope record indicating that 20% of this total carbon had been organic carbon as from 3.8 Gyr ago, the above functions also constrain the quantitative evolution of the sedimentary C-org reservoir through time (for further details see text).

in the recent geological past, with the last 10% of its mass added during Phanerozoic times.

Because these two models are based on upper and lower boundary conditions for the terrestrial degassing process, it is reasonable to conjecture that the actual growth curve of the Earth's sedimentary shell has followed a path between these extremes. In fact, a good case can be made for a terrestrial degassing process characterized by exponentially decreasing degassing rates (Li, 1972). Therefore, the actual growth curve probably comes close to that defined by the asymptotic accumulation model depicted in figure 25.4. According to this function, the bulk of the sedimentary mass (almost 90%) would have been formed during the first 1.5 Gyr after the Earth's formation, the remainder having been added in the form of progressively smaller increments with an asymptotic approach to the present mass.

The consequences of such a scenario for the buildup of the sedimentary C-org reservoir are straightforward. Because the linear accumulation model defines an absolutely lower limit, the total sedimentary mass obviously could not have been less than 20% of the present one as from 1 Gyr after the start of the degassing process (i.e., 3.5 Gyr ago; figure 25.4). With 3% of this mass being total carbon (ΣC-carb + C-org), and both direct assays and isotope mass balance calculations indicating that about 20% of this (i.e., 0.5% to 0.6%) was always organic carbon, the minimum size of the sedimentary C-org reservoir at this time should have also amounted to 20% of its present size. Because the factual growth of this reservoir has probably followed the asymptotic rather than the linear function shown in figure 25.4, we may reasonably conclude that the quantity of organic carbon stored in the sedimentary shell has stayed almost within the same order of magnitude ($\approx 10^{22}$ g; figure 25.5) during the last 3.5 Gyr of geological history.

Summing up, we may state with reasonable confidence that a sedimentary organic carbon reservoir of almost modern size (approaching 10^{22} g) existed already in Archean times and subsequently persisted as a stationary quantity with only small increments added during later geological history. With the bulk of sedimentary organic matter stored in argillaceous rocks, the residence time of C-org in the sedimentary shell is largely determined by the mass half-age of shales, approaching 0.6 Gyr. Once trapped in the rock section of the cycle organic carbon is, accordingly, apt to be retained in the crust

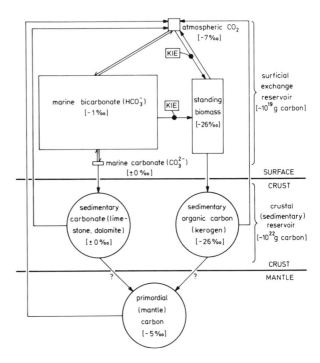

Figure 25.5 Overview of the global carbon cycle showing its conspicuous bipartition into an inorganic (left) and an organic branch (right); numbers in angular brackets give δ^{13}C averages (in ‰) of individual reservoirs. Simple arrows denote unidirectional flows (inclusive of assimilatory pathways) and double arrows stand for inorganic exchange equilibria. Carbon fluxes into the biosphere are beset with kinetic isotope effects (KIE) responsible for a marked enrichment of ^{12}C in biogenic matter relative to the inorganic feeder pool (mostly CO_2). Over the ages, biological processing of inorganic carbon has caused a large-scale accumulation of the light carbon isotope in the organic carbon reservoir (kerogen), with the heavy species (^{13}C) ultimately retained in sedimentary carbonate. Note that the total amount of carbon residing in the sedimentary shell ($\approx 10^{22}$ g) surpasses that stored in the three surface reservoirs ($\approx 10^{19}$ g) by three orders of magnitude (surficial reservoirs are drawn approximately to scale).

for geologically long intervals before being transferred to other geochemical reservoirs (inclusive of a possible return to the surficial compartment). The implications of the storage in the crust since Archean times of sizeable quantities of reduced carbon for the global redox balance and the early oxygenation of the atmosphere have been discussed elsewhere (Schidlowski, 1984).

Biogeochemical Record: Possible Gaian Implications?

In conclusion, it seems appropriate to assess briefly the significance of the biogeochemical evidence and the deductions thereof for the Gaia concept. Although the subsequent discussion certainly will not settle the issue, it may bring the following three points into sharper focus that will ultimately flow into any definitive assessment of the Gaia hypothesis:

1. There is no doubt that a microbial (prokaryotic) biosphere potentially capable of imposing a Gaian-type homeostatic control on terrestrial near-surface environments existed since the onset of the presently known sedimentary record 3.8 Gyr ago, and possibly before. Accordingly, the biological hardware needed for running a hypothetical global homeostatic machine would have been available very early in the Earth's history.

2. It is, moreover, firmly established that the basic configuration of the global carbon cycle with the characteristic bipartition of total sedimentary carbon between a reduced (organic) and an oxidized moiety (figure 25.5) reflects clearly the impact of the Earth's biota. Continuous biological processing in the exogenic exchange reservoir (atmosphere, ocean) of CO_2 primarily degassed from the Earth's interior is ultimately responsible for a dichotomized carbon flux into the crust, which consequently gave rise to the formidable reservoirs (on the order of 10^{22} g) of organic and carbonate carbon. An inherent corollary of this partitioning is a large-scale isotopic disproportionation of terrestrial carbon into isotopically light and heavy fractions because biogenic substances preferentially concentrate the light isotope (^{12}C), leaving the heavy species (^{13}C) to accumulate in the residual inorganic phases (bicarbonate and carbonate). As a whole, the geochemical cycle of carbon as represented by the box model of figure 25.5 figures as the very paragon of an element cycle that bears the mark of the Earth's biosphere.

3. Although it is self-evident that the huge reservoir of organic carbon stored in the crust in the form of kerogenous substances has once been processed by, and flushed through, the Earth's biosphere, it should be noted that other crucial controls of the carbon cycle have been exercised by purely inorganic processes. For instance, the input of CO_2 into the atmosphere-ocean system appears to be solely governed by volcano-tectonic activity. Also, the removal of oxidized carbon from the surficial exchange reservoir in the form of limestone and dolomite is, in principle, inorganic solution chemistry controlled by the kinetics of carbonate precipitation in an aqueous medium (irrespective of the fact that relevant reaction rates may be speeded up

by orders of magnitude as a result of an additional biological mediation).

Due consideration of these facts in the context of a general circulation model of terrestrial carbon (figure 25.5) cautions against an explanation of the basic features of the carbon cycle in terms of an exclusively biological control. Although the conspicuous bipartition of the cycle between reduced and oxidized compartments and the concomitant redistribution of ^{13}C:^{12}C ratios surely reflect the influence of the biosphere, the key junctions in the inorganic (oxidized) branch of the cycle are subject to inorganic controls. Summing up the performance of life processes in the global carbon cycle, it seems justified to state that the Earth's biota stars at a very prominent level, but certainly does not run the whole show.

References

Awramik, S.M. 1982. The pre-Phanerozoic fossil record. In: Holland, H.D., and Schidlowski, M., eds. *Mineral Deposits and the Evolution of the Biosphere*. Berlin: Springer, 67–81.

Awramik, S.M., Schopf, J.W., and Walter, M.R. 1983. Filamentous fossil bacteria from the Archaean of Western Australia. In: Nagy, B., Weber, R., Guerrero, J.C., and Schidlowski, M., eds. *Developments and Interactions of the Precambrian Atmosphere, Lithosphere and Biosphere (Devel Precambrian Geol, 1)*. Amsterdam: Elsevier, 249–266.

Bolin, B., Degens, E.T., Duvigneaud, P., and Kempe, S. 1979. The biogeochemical carbon cycle. In: Bolin, B., Degens, E.T., Kempe, S., and Kettner, R., eds. *The Global Carbon Cycle*. New York: Wiley, 1–56.

Broda, E. 1975. *The Evolution of the Bioenergetic Processes*. Oxford: Pergamon.

Broecker, W.S. 1971. A kinetic model for the chemical composition of sea water. *Quaternary Res*, 1, 188–207.

Broecker, W.S. 1973. Factors controlling CO_2 content in the oceans and atmosphere. In: Woodwell, C.M., and Pecan, E.V., eds. *Carbon and the Biosphere*. Washington, D.C.: U.S. Atomic Energy Commission, 32–50.

Cameron, E.M., and Garrels, R.M. 1980. Geochemical compositions of some Precambrian shales from the Canadian Shield. *Chem Geol*, 28, 181–197.

Cloud, P.E. 1976. Beginnings of biospheric evolution and their biogeochemical consequences. *Paleobiology* 2, 351–387.

Cohen, Y., Aizenshtat, Z., Stoler, A. and Jorgensen, B.B. 1980. The microbial geochemistry of Solar Lake, Sinai. In: Ralph, J.B., Trudinger, P.A., and Walter, M.R., eds. *Biogeochemistry of Ancient and Modern Environments*. Berlin: Springer, 167–172.

Degens, E.T. 1969. Biogeochemistry of stable carbon isotopes. In: Eglington, G., and Murphy, M.T.J., eds. *Organic Geochemistry*. Berlin: Springer, 304–329.

Deines, P. 1980. The isotopic composition of reduced organic carbon. In: Fritz, P., and Fontes, J.C., eds. *Handbook of Environmental Isotope Geochemistry,* Vol. 1. Amsterdam: Elsevier, 329–406.

Des Marais, D.J., and Moore, J.G. 1984. Carbon and its isotopes in mid-oceanic basaltic glasses. *Earth Planet Sci Lett,* 69, 43–57.

Ehrenberg, C.G. 1854. *Mikrogeologie—das Erden und Felsen schaffende Wirken des unsichtbar kleinen selbständigen Lebens auf der Erde.* Leipzig: Voss.

Garrels, R.M., and Mackenzie, F.T. 1971. *Evolution of Sedimentary Rocks.* New York: Norton.

Hayes, J.M., Kaplan, I.R., and Wedeking, K.W. 1983. Precambrian organic geochemistry: Preservation of the record. In: Schopf, J.W., ed. *Earth's Earliest Biosphere: Its Origin and Evolution.* Princeton, N.J.: Princeton University Press, 93–134.

Holland, H.D. 1978. *The Chemistry of the Atmosphere and Oceans.* New York: Wiley.

Holland, H.D. 1984. *The Chemical Evolution of the Atmosphere and Oceans.* Princeton, N.J.: Princeton University Press.

Hunt, J.M. 1972. Distribution of carbon in crust of Earth. *Bull Am Assoc Petrol Geol,* 56, 2273–2277.

Junge, C.E., Schidlowski, M., Eichmann, R., and Pietrek, H. 1975. Model calculations for the terrestrial carbon cycle: Carbon isotope geochemistry and evolution of photosynthetic oxygen. *J Geophys Res,* 80, 4542–4552.

Krumbein, W.E., and Cohen, Y. 1977. Primary production, mat formation and lithification chances of oxygenic and facultative anoxygenic cyanophytes (cyanobacteria). In: Flügel, E., ed. *Fossil Algae.* Berlin: Springer, 37–56.

Lerman, A. 1979. *Geochemical Processes: Water and Sediment Environments.* New York: Wiley.

Li, Y.H. 1972. Geochemical mass balance among lithosphere, hydrosphere and atmosphere. *Am J Sci,* 272, 119–137.

Mattey, D.P., Carr, R.H., Wright, I.P., and Pillinger, C.T. 1984. Carbon isotopes in submarine basalts. *Earth Planet Sci Lett,* 70, 196–206.

Redfield, A.C. 1958. The biological control of chemical factors in the environment. *American Scientist* 46, 205–222.

Reimer, T.O., Barghoorn, E.S., and Margulis, L. 1979. Primary productivity in an Early Archaean microbial ecosystem. *Precambrian Res,* 9, 93–104.

Ronov, A.B. 1958. Organic carbon in sedimentary rocks (in relation to the presence of petroleum). *Geochemistry,* 1958, 510–536.

Ronov, A.B. 1980. *Osadochnaya Obolochka Zemli (Earth's Sedimentary Shell),* in Russian. 20th Vernadsky Lecture. Moscow: Izdatel'stvo Nauka.

Schidlowski, M., 1978. Evolution of the Earth's atmosphere: Current state and exploratory concepts. In: Noda, H., ed. *Origin of Life.* Tokyo: Center Acad. Publ. Japan, 3–20.

Schidlowski, M. 1982. Content and isotopic composition of reduced carbon in sediments. In: Holland, H.D., and Schidlowski, M., eds. *Mineral Deposits and the Evolution of the Biosphere.* Berlin: Springer, 103–122.

Schidlowski, M. 1984. Early atmospheric oxygen levels: Constraints from Archaean photoautotrophy. *J Geol Soc London,* 141, 243–250.

Schidlowski, M. 1987. Application of stable carbon isotopes to early biochemical evolution on Earth. *Ann Rev Earth Planet Sci,* 15, 47–72.

Schidlowski, M., Appel, P.W.U., Eichmann, R., and Junge, C.E. 1979. Carbon isotope geochemistry of the 3.7×10^9 yr old Isua sediments, West Greenland: Implications for the Archaean carbon and oxygen cycles. *Geochim Cosmochim Acta,* 43, 189–199.

Schidlowski, M., Hayes, J.M., and Kaplan, I.R. 1983. Isotopic inferences of ancient biochemistries: Carbon, sulfur, hydrogen and nitrogen. In: Schopf, J.W., ed. *Earth's Earliest Biosphere: Its Origin and Evolution.* Princeton, N.J.: Princeton University Press, 149–186.

Schopf, J.W., ed. 1983. *Earth's Earliest Biosphere: Its Origin and Evolution.* Princeton, N.J.: Princeton University Press.

Schopf, J.W., and Packer, B.M. 1987. Early Archaean (3.3 billion to 3.5-billion-year-old) microfossils from Warrawoona Group, Australia. *Science,* 237, 70–73.

Todd, Lord A.R. 1981. Where there's life there's phosphorus. In: Kageyama, M., Nakamura, K., Oshima, T., and Uchida, T., eds. *Science and Scientists—Essays by Biochemists, Biologists and Chemists.* Tokyo/Dordrecht: Japan Scientific Society Press/Reidel, 275–279.

Trask, P.D., and Patnode, H.W. 1942. *Source Beds of Petroleum.* Tulsa: American Association of Petroleum Geologists.

Veizer, J., Holser, W.T., and Wilgus, C.K. 1980. Correlation of $^{13}C/^{12}C$ and $^{34}S/^{32}S$ secular variations. *Geochim Cosmochim Acta,* 44, 579–587.

Verhulst, P.F. 1845. Recherches mathématiques sur la loi d'accroissement de la population. *Nouv Mem Acad Roy Sci Belle-Lettr Bruxelles,* 18, 1–38.

Vernadsky, V.I. 1930. *Geochemie in ausgewählten Kapiteln.* Leipzig: Akademische Verlagsgesellschaft.

Walter, M. 1983. Archean stromatolites: Evidence of the Earth's earliest benthos. In: Schopf, J.W., ed. *Earth's Earliest Biosphere: Its Origin and Evolution.* Princeton, N.J.: Princeton University Press, 187–213.

G. H. Kohlmaier, Matthias Lüdeke, Alex Janecek, Günther Benderoth, Jürgen Kindermann, and Axel Klaudius

26

Land Biota, Source or Sink of Atmospheric Carbon Dioxide: Positive and Negative Feedbacks Within a Changing Climate and Land Use Development

Humans have had a significant influence on the biosphere in the past by converting natural ecosystems to life-supporting systems for ourselves both in the agricultural sector and in the forest product sector, particularly by claiming space for urban and industrial development and the infrastructures of these systems. With a growing world population, the effect of human activities on natural ecosystems is ever increasing, and now includes, in addition to the direct impacts of land use changes, the impact of air pollution and a globally changing climate. With respect to the source-sink function for atmospheric CO_2, the land biota have been in the past and probably will be in the future a significant reservoir of carbon that interacts with the atmosphere. As previously reported (Kohlmaier, 1988) we distinguish three areas of major concern:

1. *Deforestation,* both in the past in the now industrialized nations and presently in the tropical regions of America, Africa, and Asia, has had and will continue to have a significant impact on the atmospheric carbon budget (Seiler and Crutzen, 1980; Lanly, 1982; Houghton et al., 1983, 1987; Detwiler and Hall, 1988).

2. *Land biota and their soils respond to climatic changes* in two ways: in the long term by vegetation migration and in the short term by vegetation die-back and soil degradation. Temperature increases, such as those resulting from the CO_2 greenhouse effect, tend to result in the release of CO_2 to the atmosphere (Schleser, 1981; Kohlmaier et al., 1981; Buringh, 1984), thus amplifying the greenhouse effect in a positive feedback loop.

3. *Intact land and marine biota* are hypothesized to have a regulating and stabilizing effect on our atmospheric environment and climate (as stated, for instance, in the Gaia hypothesis by Lovelock and Margulis, 1974; Lovelock and Watson, 1982; Lovelock, 1987). Destruction of the naturally occurring biota by deforestation or by air or water

pollution may alter or stop this stabilizing negative feedback control. Conservation and plantation of the forests of the tropical, temperate, and boreal regions can lead to additional storage of atmospheric CO_2 in the form of wood and organic matter in the underlying soils. There are indications that the present atmospheric levels of CO_2, about 25% above the preindustrial value, already have led to a CO_2 fertilization effect (Strain and Cure, 1985; Kohlmaier et al., 1987; Kohlmaier et al., 1989) of significant magnitude for the atmospheric carbon budget.

In this chapter, we develop a biosphere model with a minimum set of free parameters to describe the above-mentioned effects on the atmospheric CO_2 budget and its consequent feedbacks on the expected global surface temperature.

Because of the large range of uncertainties for each of the three processes—deforestation, temperature-induced responses of the biota-soil system, and CO_2 fertilization of the living biota—the model and its parameters are tested against the information available regarding the development of the biosphere and the atmosphere in the past 120 years, ranging from the beginning of the industrialization in 1860 to 1980. Because the emphasis in this study is on the feedback of direct and indirect climatic variations (development of the atmospheric CO_2 content and the global surface temperature) on the biota, we rely here on the very detailed time-series studies of deforestation and carbon release to the atmosphere as presented by Houghton and colleagues (1983, 1987). We show in the following sections that the net CO_2 release from deforestation is consistent with the deconvolution studies of the atmospheric CO_2 development obtained from tree rings (Peng, 1985) and from ice core measurements only if CO_2 fertilization of the vegetation and a temperature effect on the biota-soil system are included in the analysis.

In particular, Siegenthaler and Oeschger (1987) have used the atmospheric data obtained from ice core measurements and the Mauna Loa record and the fossil fuel release to determine a net biogenic source by inferring a net carbon uptake by the oceans, calculated by either a box diffusion or an outcrop diffusion model. As this biogenic source flux is very different from Houghton's deforestation flux, an unidentified sink function for atmospheric CO_2 is postulated by Siegenthaler and Oeschger to explain this discrepancy.

As we are able to show that a combined CO_2 fertilization and temperature effect on the biota and soils can explain this discrepancy, we were confident that .his model with the corresponding parameter combinations would be able to make some predictions on the biota-soil response to a future CO_2 greenhouse climate. With the model and parameter combinations tested we investigate the possible ranges of a future development, identifying the biospheric feedbacks in a self-consistent way. We would like to mention here that our approach is complementary to that of Lashof (1988, 1989) in as much as we consider the specific processes leading to the feedback, both in stationary state and using dynamic calculations.

Model Description

The role of the biota and soils within the global carbon cycle has been described by a number of investigators using a variety of biospheric models that have been recently summarized by Harvey (1989). Because we wanted to explore the effect of the three processes described above, namely (1) land transformations associated in particular with deforestation and increased land need for agriculture; (2) response of the living biota and soils to a temperature change expected within the incipient greenhouse climate; and (3) the direct effect of increasing levels of atmospheric CO_2 on plant production and change in plant and soil biomass, processes that are each by themselves described by wide parameter and uncertainty ranges, we searched for the simplest possible model applicable at the same time to all three effects.

In figure 26.1 we show a simple three-compartment model of the biosphere assuming one compartment for the living biota and two compartments for the soil. Because there are large differences in turnover time of carbon we distinguish a compartment for the litter and top soil with a short carbon residence time and a compartment for the deep soil with a corresponding long residence time.

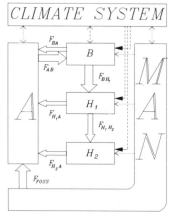

A : Atmosphere
B : Biota
H_1 : litter and upper soil
H_2 : lower soil humus
F_{AB} : flux A to B (NPP)
F_{BA} : flux B to A
F_{BH_1} : flux B to H_1
F_{H_1A} : flux H_1 to A
$F_{H_1H_2}$: flux H_1 to H_2
F_{H_2A} : flux H_2 to A
F_{FOSS} : fossil fuel CO_2 flux to A

Figure 26.1 Response of the atmosphere-biota-soil system to a climatic change.

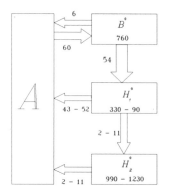

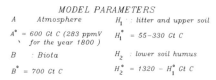

MODEL PARAMETERS

A Atmosphere H_1 : litter and upper soil

A^o = 600 Gt C (283 ppmV for the year 1800) H_1^o = 55–330 Gt C

B : Biota H_2 : lower soil humus

B^o = 700 Gt C H_2^o = 1320 – H_1^o Gt C

Figure 26.2 Initial steady-state fluxes and reservoir sizes in 1800.

In figure 26.2 we present the assumed initial steady-state configuration for both the living biomass and the two soil compartments. The living biomass compartment (B) is characterized by a net input flux of carbon, the net primary productivity (NPP), which at least in principle can be determined in an ecological assessment through the net annual increment in growth and the annual litter production. NPP is to be distinguished from the gross primary production (GPP), which includes the autotrophic respiration. This quantity, however, which is estimated (from dark respiration measurements) to be about two to three times as large as NPP, is not directly accessible through ecological measurements.

Two food chains are considered in the model: the

herbivory food chain, in which, together with natural fires, about 10% of the annual production is consumed; and the detritus food chain, in which the corresponding 90% of NPP is consumed or respired through the soil organisms including the microflora and fauna. Part of the litter and the upper soil organic components of compartment H_1 are oxidized directly to atmospheric CO_2 while a smaller part is transformed into organic compounds with longer residence times that enter into the deeper soil compartment H_2. In some biota-soil models (see Harvey 1989, model 1) the compartments B and H_1 are aggregated to one compartment with fast carbon turnover, contrasted with a slow carbon turnover of the compartment H_2. Because the CO_2 fertilization effect has been characterized with respect to NPP, the aggregation level, where only the net flux from the atmosphere to the combined compartment of B and H_1 is considered, a flux that is only 10% to 20% of the NPP, is not opportune for our study.

A further disaggregation of the living biota into leaf and woody material is certainly possible; our own investigations as well as these of Harvey (1989), however, having the large range of uncertainty of the parameters used to describe climate response and CO_2 fertilization, showed that more compartments do not yield more insight into the problem. Similarly, a consideration of different biomes (i.e., a subdivision into tropical and temperate forests and grasslands) seems justified only if the different environmental and climatic changes and their corresponding responses are known in better detail.

We construct our model so as to distinguish between the climatic and atmospheric CO_2 influences on the one hand and the direct impacts of humans through land transformations on the other hand. It is our goal to explain the past and future biospheric influence on the global carbon cycle with the same model structure. By calibrating the climatic sensitivity and the CO_2 fertilization response to the past, we hope to produce a reliable instrument for predicting the future positive and negative biospheric feedbacks within a given energy or CO_2 scenario.

In order to assess the direct effect of increasing levels of atmospheric CO_2 on NPP, we adopt Keeling's original β-factor concept (Keeling, 1973) by setting

$$NPP(CO_2) = (1 + \beta \cdot \ln(CO_2/CO_2^0))NPP^0(CO_2^0) \qquad (1)$$

Here β is a specific CO_2 fertilization factor describing the response of NPP of different plants to increases in atmospheric CO_2. This equation presupposes that the plants do not adapt to the higher atmospheric CO_2 levels in a compensating way either by reduction of the number of stomata on the leaves (Woodward, 1986, 1987; Körner, 1988), by stomata closure, or by any other plant physiological processes that cancel the increased supply of CO_2 (Körner, 1987). The logarithmic function agrees qualitatively with the observed behavior of diminishing returns on increasing levels of one nutrient component. Most of the CO_2 fertilization experiments have been done with CO_2 step-function experiments on single plants for relatively short-term periods up to a maximum of three years. The relative increase in NPP compared with the relative increase in CO_2 can be characterized by a linear β-factor, which in accordance with our former evaluation of β-factors (Kohlmaier et al., 1987) range between 0.15 and 0.60 (mean value, 0.375). As almost no long-term study on an open forest ecosystem in response to additional CO_2 has been done, we can only suppose that the positive response of tree seedlings to CO_2 (Kimball, 1983) is also valid for these natural ecosystems. More recently, Conroy et al. (1990) investigated the long-term response of several families of *Pinus radiata* in glasshouses to high CO_2 levels and found at the end of a 2-year enrichment period an average increase of 30%. They found that wood density was increased at elevated CO_2 and that the exponential growth phase was considerably faster at sites where phosphorus was not acutely deficient. They concluded that if the potential to store more carbon as wood at high CO_2 is widespread among other conifers then the net flux of CO_2 from the atmosphere to the forests should increase.

We do not distinguish in this study the detailed effects of CO_2 fertilization on C_3, C_4, and CAM (Crassulacean acid metabolism) plants as we will use a set of β parameters for the global ecosphere representing a mean value of all species. We do this realizing that most of the C_3 species, which constitute more than 90% of the total plant biomass, are affected more strongly by CO_2 than are the other groups of plants.

Because the concentration of CO_2 in the soils is 10 to 100 times larger than atmospheric CO_2, we do not expect that small changes in atmospheric CO_2 will greatly influence the CO_2 environment of the soils; as there are no other known biological processes in the soil that depend sensitively on CO_2, we neglect this factor for the soil processes.

Temperature and soil moisture and changes in these variables in the past and future climate will certainly influence both NPP and the various transfer rates to the litter- and soil-compartments and the heterotrophic respiration from the compartments H_1 and H_2. In this study we do not consider soil moisture changes because no data are available for the past or future on the aggregated level considered here. Esser and colleagues (1982) have shown that there is an optimum level of soil moisture with regard to litter and humus decomposition that lies between the extreme dry and wet regimes. Depending on the reference point with respect to this scale, a dryer soil moisture regime can lead to increased decomposition, as is expected, for instance, for the tundra and bog ecosystems, whereas on the other hand drought and dry conditions in the middle latitudes can decrease decomposition.

The response of NPP to a small temperature increase is indicated in the ecological literature (Larcher, 1983) to be positive in ecosystems that are not soil moisture–limited. For large increases in temperature, however, the total production, GPP, increases less than the corresponding autotrophic respiration (Enoch and Sacks, 1978), making the resultant NPP decrease.

We suggest here that it is reasonable to model the temperature dependence of NPP for small temperature increments by the following equation:

$$\text{NPP}(\text{CO}_2, T^0 + \Delta T) = \text{NPP}(\text{CO}_2, T^0) \qquad (2)$$
$$\cdot (1 + \bar{Q}_{AB}/10 \cdot \Delta T)$$

with $\bar{Q} = Q_{10} - 1$.

We use here the concept of linearized rate responses to a temperature increase ΔT:

$$\text{Rate}(T^0 + \Delta T) = (1 + (Q_{10} - 1)/10 \cdot \Delta T)\,\text{Rate}(T^0) \qquad (3)$$

in which the Q_{10} value describes the rate increase of a given process for a temperature increase of $10°K$. If, for example, a temperature change of $2°$ is to be

Table 26.1 Differential Equations of the Simplified Biota-Soil System

$$\frac{dB}{dt} = \text{NPP}^0 \cdot \left(1 + \frac{\bar{Q}_{AB}}{10} \cdot \Delta T + \beta \cdot \ln \text{CO}_2/\text{CO}_2^0\right) \cdot \left(1 - \alpha \cdot \frac{\Delta L_f(t)}{L_f^0}\right)$$
$$\bar{n}\,\frac{\text{NPP}^0}{B^0} \cdot B - (1 - \phi_{H1} - \phi_{H2}) \cdot F_{DEF}(t) \qquad (T1)$$

$$\frac{dH_1}{dt} = (1 - \varepsilon) \cdot \frac{\text{NPP}^0}{B^0}\,B - (1 - \kappa) \cdot \left(1 + \frac{\bar{Q}_{H1A}}{10} \cdot \Delta T\right) \cdot \frac{(1 - \varepsilon)\text{NPP}^0}{H_1^0}\,H_1$$
$$- \kappa \cdot \left(1 + \frac{\bar{Q}_{H1H2}}{10} \cdot \Delta T\right) \cdot \frac{(1 - \varepsilon)\text{NPP}^0}{H_1^0}\,H_1$$
$$- \phi_{H1} \cdot F_{DEF}(t) \qquad (T2)$$

$$\frac{dH_2}{dt} = \kappa \cdot \left(1 + \frac{\bar{Q}_{H1H2}}{10} \cdot \Delta T\right) \cdot \frac{(1 - \varepsilon)\text{NPP}^0}{H_1^0}\,H_1$$
$$- \kappa \cdot \left(1 + \frac{\bar{Q}_{H2A}}{10} \cdot \Delta T\right) \cdot \frac{(1 - \varepsilon)\text{NPP}^0}{H_2^0}\,H_2$$
$$- \phi_{H2} \cdot F_{DEF}(t) \qquad (T3)$$

Biogenic netflux into the atmosphere

$$F_{NET} = F_{DEF}(t) + F_{BIO}(t) \qquad (T4)$$

$$F_{BIO} = (1 - \kappa) \cdot \left(1 + \frac{\bar{Q}_{H1A}}{10} \cdot \Delta T\right) \cdot \frac{(1 - \varepsilon)\text{NPP}^0}{H_1^0}\,H_1$$
$$+ \kappa \cdot \left(1 + \frac{\bar{Q}_{H2A}}{10} \cdot \Delta T\right) \cdot \frac{(1 - \varepsilon)\text{NPP}^0}{H_2^0}\,H_2$$
$$+ \varepsilon \cdot \frac{\text{NPP}^0}{B^0}\,B - \text{NPP}^0 \cdot \left(1 + \frac{\bar{Q}_{AB}}{10} \cdot \Delta T\right.$$
$$+ \beta \cdot \ln \text{CO}_2/\text{CO}_2^0\Big) \cdot \left(1 - \alpha \cdot \frac{L_f(t)}{L_f^0}\right)$$

Additional Equations for the Calculation into the Future

$$\text{CO}_2(t) = \frac{1}{2.12} \cdot A \qquad \begin{array}{l}\text{Conversion of total atmospheric}\\ \text{carbon content (Gt C) into}\\ \text{concentration units (ppm CO}_2)\end{array}$$

$$\Delta T(t) = \gamma \cdot \ln \frac{\text{CO}_2(t - \tau)}{\text{CO}_2^0} \qquad (T5)$$

$$\frac{dA}{dt} = [F_{DEF}(t) + F_{BIO}(t) + F_{FOS}(t)] \cdot a_f \qquad (T6)$$

considered along with a Q_{10} value of 3, we expect, according to the above equations:

Rate(T^0 + 2°K) = (1 + (3 − 1)/10°K · 2°K) Rate (T^0)
= 1.4 rate(T^0)

For the top and deeper soil compartments, H_1 and H_2, we define an analogous temperature dependence as in the NPP where the flux F_{HA} describes the CO_2 release to the atmosphere:

$$F_{HA}(T^0 + \Delta T) \approx (1 + \tilde{Q}_{HA}/10 \cdot \Delta T) \cdot NPP^0/H^0 \cdot H \qquad (4)$$

where H stands either for H_1 or H_2. The Q_{10} values for heterotrophic respiration and soils are in the range of 1.3 to 4.0 (Edwards, 1975; Havas and Mäenpää, 1972; Kohlmaier et al., 1981; Schleser, 1981; Dörr and Münnich, 1987; Fung et al., 1987).

The transfer rate from H_1 to H_2 is modeled in analogy to equation (4) with an assumed Q_{10,H_1H_2} equal to Q_{10,H_1A}. The transfer rate of living biomass to the litter is assumed to be only indirectly dependent on temperature inasmuch as the litter production is assumed to be linearly dependent on B, which in turn is dependent on T through NPP.

The model equations for compartment B, H_1, and H_2 are summarized in table 26.1 (equations 1 to 3) and illustrated in figure 26.3 for the case of land use changes only, by introducing the deforestation flux,

F_{DEF}. In order to make our modeling results consistent with the very detailed studies of land transformations by Houghton and colleagues (1983) we incorporated their results in our model by removing carbon from the compartments B, H_1, and H_2 such that the net removal of carbon equals Houghton's net flux of carbon to the atmosphere, as illustrated in figure 26.3. The relative contributions of the carbon fluxes from the three compartments are modeled by introducing the fractions ϕ_{H1} and ϕ_{H2}. As the total NPP becomes reduced when forests are converted into farm or grasslands we add a factor to the NPP formulation:

$$NPP = NPP(CO_2, \Delta T) \cdot (1 - L(t)/L^0 \cdot \alpha) \qquad (5)$$

where $L(t)$ is the total forested area at time t, and L^0 is the initial forested area, and α is an efficiency factor that can be derived by accounting for the differences in productivities.

In equation (2) we assumed implicitly that NPP depended on both CO_2 and ΔT and could be modeled as a product function of the corresponding factors in equations (1) and (2), which then is simplified in equation 1 in table 26.1 by keeping only the first-order terms in ΔT and ΔCO_2.

The fraction ε is introduced to describe the part of carbon that is introduced directly by the herbivores and fire into the atmosphere, and the fraction κ describes the material that is resistant to oxidation in the top soil and enters into the deep soil.

With the requirement that all Q_{10} values are 1 and the corresponding β factor is zero, the baseline can be set for the biosphere contributing only through the direct human land use impact. The set of parameters α, ϕ_{H1}, and ϕ_{H2} is chosen self-consistently such that the total reduction of the biota-soil compartments (i.e., the net carbon flux from the biota to the atmosphere, F_{NET}—see equation 4 in table 26.1) equals F_{DEF} as given by Houghton and colleagues in this case. The values of the employed parameters together with their ranges of uncertainty are given in table 26.2.

Comparison of the Net Biogenic Input Flux as Deconvoluted from Atmospheric Data and as Calculated from the Biosphere Model

For our biospheric model both the temperature and CO_2 evolution during the past 120 years are of importance. We show in figure 26.4 the mean surface air temperature in its development from 1860 to 1980 using a smoothed temperature record as given

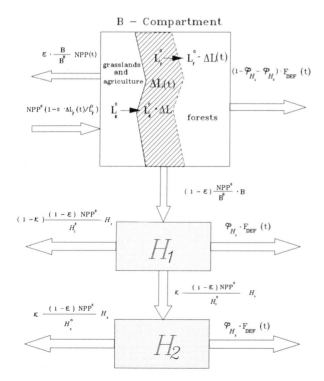

Figure 26.3 Consideration of land use changes (for temperature and CO_2 dependence of carbon (fluxes, see table 26.1).

Table 26.2 List of Parameters

		Estimate		
		Low	Medium	High
Q_{10}—values of temperature dependence of the carbon fluxes (Q_{ij}: i—donor, j—acceptor compartment):	Q_{AB}	0.5	1.25	1.5
	Q_{BHI}		1.0	
	$Q_{HIA} = Q_{HIH2}$	1.5	2.5	4.0
	Q_{HIH2}	1.5	2.0	3.0
Fertilization factor	β	0.15	0.375	0.6
Fraction from efflux from H_1 directed to H_2	κ	0.02	0.1	0.2
Fraction of NPP that reaches A immediately	ε	0.05	0.1	0.2
Reduction of NPP per area transformation	α	0.3	0.7	0.9
Preindustrial forest area (10^6 ha): Fraction of F_{DEF} subtracted from the	A_0		6350	
H_1 compartment	ϕ_{HI}		0.2	
H_2 compartment (chosen so that F_{NET} equals F_{DEF} if there is no CO_2 and temperature dependence)	ϕ_{H2}		0.5	

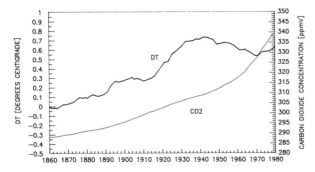

Figure 26.4 Solid line represents annual temperature anomalies, DT of the Northern Hemisphere (from Hansen and Lebedeff, 1987). Dashed line represents annual atmospheric CO_2 concentration (from Siegenthaler and Oeschger, 1987).

by Hansen and Lebedeff (1987). We also present the increase in atmospheric CO_2 concentration in the past 120 years as given by Siegenthaler and Oeschger (1987) based on air trapped in ice cores from Siple Station Antarctica and on the direct air measurements from Mauna Loa Observatory, starting in 1958. Using the atmospheric data, Siegenthaler and Oeschger were able to determine a total annual input flux from fossil fuels and biogenic sources by calculating the uptake of atmospheric CO_2 by the

oceans through a corresponding ocean model. Because the fossil fuel flux has been relatively well documented by Rotty and Marland (1986) the corresponding biospheric component of the total flux to the atmosphere was obtained by subtraction. The results of this calculation are shown in figure 26.5 for two different ocean models, which approximate the possible range of ocean uptake and resulting biospheric flux. It should be mentioned here that the indirect evaluation of atmospheric CO_2 by deconvolution of tree ring isotopic data as performed by Peng and colleagues (1983) yields essentially a similar result for the years 1940 and later, while the biospheric input function before 1940 is characterized by two strong maxima occurring in 1850 and 1910. This is in contrast to the result of Siegenthaler and Oeschger. It is clear from figure 26.5 that the net biospheric flux is in contrast to the deforestation flux determined by Houghton and colleagues (1983, 1987), not only in magnitude but also in the shape of the curve.

We ask now whether the additional components, namely CO_2 fertilization and temperature response of the biota-soil system, can modify the deforestation flux in such a way that it becomes consistent

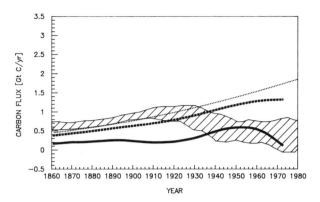

Figure 26.5 Calculated net flux F_{NET}—equation (T4)—from the biota to the atmosphere considering the fertilization only. Hatched area shows range of biogenic carbon net flux into the atmosphere as deconvoluted by Siegenthaler and Oeschger (1987). Dotted line shows $F_{NET} = F_{DEF}$, deforestation flux only, with no temperature and CO_2 dependence. Dashed line shows $F_{NET} = F_{DEF} + F_{BIO}$ (ΔCO_2), deforestation plus fertilization ($\beta = 0.15$). Solid line shows $F_{NET} = F_{DEF} + F_{BIO}$ (ΔCO_2), deforestation plus fertilization ($\beta = 0.60$).

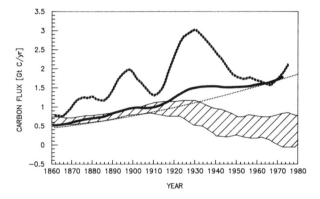

Figure 26.6 Calculated net fluxes F_{NET} considering the temperature effect only. Hatched area and dotted line as in figure 26.5. Dashed line shows that $F_{NET} = F_{DEF} + F_{BIO}$ (ΔT), deforestation and strong temperature dependence of soils: $\tilde{Q}_{AB} = 0.0$; $\tilde{Q}_{BHI} = 0.0$; $\tilde{Q}_{HIA} = 3.0$; $\tilde{Q}_{HIH2} = 3.0$; $\tilde{Q}_{H2A} = 2.0$. Solid line: $F_{NET} = F_{DEF} + F_{BIO}$ (ΔT), deforestation plus weak temperature dependence of soil: $\tilde{Q}_{AB} = 0.0$; $\tilde{Q}_{BHI} = 0.0$; $\tilde{Q}_{HIA} = 0.5$; $\tilde{Q}_{HIH2} = 0.5$; $\tilde{Q}_{H2A} = 0.5$.

with the net biospheric flux as measured by Siegenthaler and Oeschger (1987).

In figure 26.5 we show that the biospheric input of CO_2 into the atmosphere is considerably reduced if we assume that a fertilization factor of $\beta = 0.15$, corresponding to our estimated lower limit, or a β value of 0.6, corresponding to our estimated upper limit, is used. We also see, however, that neither one of the two curves corresponds to the shape of the biospheric net input flux derived by Siegen-

thaler and Oeschger, which shows a maximum in 1930.

In figure 26.6 we determine the effect of temperature alone using a combination of corresponding Q_{10} parameters that are characteristic of an intermediate and a high temperature response. It is interesting to see from figure 26.6 that a strong maximum occurs in the calendar year 1930 approximately corresponding to the temperature maximum shown in figure 26.4. We also find that the temperature response alone does not give a correct explanation of the discrepancy described above.

In figure 26.7 we present the combined effect of the two determinants, temperature and CO_2, for the best estimated mean values for the parameters and a corresponding high estimate of β and Q_{10}. We believe that we have been able to show that indeed a combination of the two effects yields a biogenic source function that is consistent with the atmosphere-ocean modeling results of Siegenthaler and Oeschger (1987). We are not surprised that the model also yields fluctuations in the early part of the record that are probably smoothed out in the determinations of the ice cores.

We are now confident that our biospheric model is able to give reliable results for the future atmosphere-biosphere development, provided that the corresponding scenarios for fossil fuel CO_2 emission and deforestation are given.

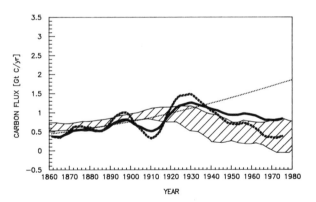

Figure 26.7 Calculated net fluxes F_{NET} considering a combination of fertilization and temperature effects. Hatched area and dotted line as in figure 26.5 and 26.6. Dashed line shows strong fertilization ($\beta = 0.6$) and strong temperature dependence of soils: $\tilde{Q}_{BHI} = 0.0$; $\tilde{Q}_{HIA} = 3.0$; $\tilde{Q}_{HIH2} = 3.0$; $\tilde{Q}_{H2A} = 2.0$ and biota: $\tilde{Q}_{AB} = 0.5$. Solid line shows medium fertilization ($\beta = 0.375$) plus weak temperature dependence of soils: $\tilde{Q}_{BHI} = 0.0$; $\tilde{Q}_{HIA} = 1.5$; $\tilde{Q}_{HIH2} = 1.5$; $\tilde{Q}_{H2A} = 1.0$ and biota $\tilde{Q}_{AB} = 0.25$.

Steady-State Consideration for the Soil Compartment in a Future Carbon Dioxide Greenhouse Climate

To get a first estimate of the response of the biota-soil system to a future greenhouse climate we look at a simplified version of the original biosphere model in which the two soil compartments H_1 and H_2 are combined to one compartment, H, and in which any change in B is neglected. In this one-compartment system we assume that the litter production is equal to the NPP and that the heterotrophic respiration is a function of the temperature change ΔT:

$$dH/dt = \text{NPP}(T, \text{CO}_2, L_f) \quad\quad (6)$$
$$- \text{NPP}^0/H^0 (1 + \bar{Q}_{HA}/10 \cdot \Delta T) \cdot H$$

We have chosen NPP to be a function of the three processes discussed above, temperature and CO_2 change as well as land use change, but in principle it may be any expected positive or negative change due to a variety of processes not included explicitly

in the original biosphere model, such as soil moisture change or acid rain.

Equation (6) may be solved in the quasi–steady state approximation ($dH/dt \approx 0$), provided there are no abrupt changes in NPP:

$$H^{ST} = H^0 \frac{\text{NPP/NPP}^0}{(1 + \bar{Q}_{HA}/10 \cdot \Delta T)} \quad\quad (7)$$

Using equation (7), the total soil carbon release, $H^{ST} - H^0$, is calculated for different values of equilibrium temperature change, Q_{10} values of the soil, and different assumptions on the net influence of temperature, precipitation, CO_2, and land use on NPP. The results are shown in table 26.3.

The fraction of carbon released and the total amount of carbon released or absorbed is given for a change in equilibrium temperature of 2°, 4°, or 8°C. For each change in temperature we distinguish the response for the possible Q_{10} values ranging between 2 and 4. The interpretation of table 26.3 is given as an example for a 2° change and a Q_{10} value

Table 26.3 Equilibrium Considerations for Soil Carbon Release in Response to a Change in Temperature and a Change in Net Primary Production (Temperature, Precipitation or CO_2 Fertilization Effect)

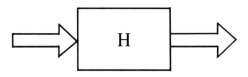

NPP   RES

$\Delta T_{eq} =$	2°C			4°C			8°C		
Q_{10} (soils) =	2	3	4	2	3	4	2	3	4
a) fraction released NPP = constant	0.17	0.29	0.37	0.29	0.45	0.55	0.45	0.71	0.78
b) fraction released NPP = 1.15 NPP_0	0.04	0.18	0.28	0.18	0.36	0.48	0.36	0.56	0.66
c) fraction released NPP = 1.30 NPP_0	−0.06	0.07	0.19	0.07	0.28	0.41	0.26	0.50	0.62
d) fraction released NPP = 0.85 NPP_0	0.29	0.39	0.47	0.39	0.53	0.61	0.53	0.67	0.75
case a) Gt C released H^0 = 110 Gt C	19	32	41	32	50	61	50	68	78
case a) Gt C released H^0 = 330 Gt C	56	96	122	96	149	182	149	205	234
case a) Gt C released H^0 = 1320 Gt C	224	383	488	383	594	726	594	818	937

of 3. If NPP remains constant such a temperature change will lead to a 29% loss (fraction, 0.29) of soil carbon, which amounts to 383 Gt C if the total soil carbon reservoir is taken to be $H^0 = 1320$ Gt C. We realize here that the total soil carbon is very difficult to assess with estimates ranging between 700 Gt C (Bolin, 1970) and 3000 Gt C (Bohn, 1976), with perhaps the most reliable value given by Schlesinger (1984) at 1500 Gt C. If only a partial equilibration with the total soil compartment is achieved, for instance, with the upper soil compartment H_1, then 32 to 96 Gt C are released. If on the other hand the net primary production is increased by 15% (case b) or by 30% (case c), then the higher-input flux of litter into the soil compartment leads to a loss of only 18% or 7%, respectively. There may be, however, reasons that the total NPP is decreased, for instance by a factor of 15%, then the expected loss of carbon from the soils will amount to 39% (case d). It is clear that higher equilibrium temperature changes, for instance, a change of 4°, and lower Q_{10} values, for instance, $Q_{10} = 2$ can lead to a mathematically equal result, as may be seen from the comparison of the corresponding rows in the table. We would like to summarize at this point that there is a strong positive feedback between temperature and soils if these effects cannot be compensated by an increased fraction of NPP, as may occur, for instance, through a CO_2 fertilization effect.

Feedback Analysis of Excess Atmospheric Carbon Dioxide, Temperature Change, and Carbon Change of the Land Biota and Soil System

In the above equilibrium considerations we calculated the CO_2 release or uptake for a given external temperature variation. In a complete analysis of the effect we must, however, consider the feedback between the additional CO_2 released and the corresponding additional temperature increase. Stimulated by the discussion of Lashof at the Chapman Conference in San Diego (1988) we include a feedback analysis in our results. The cybernetic feedback system between excess CO_2 and the temperature change ΔT is shown in figure 26.8a. The excess CO_2, XCO_2, will lead to a total temperature change (e.g., for CO_2 doubling, $2 \cdot CO_2^0$) that is larger than the temperature change computed without the feedback, provided the CO_2 release from the soils is stronger than the fertilization effect of the plants. In figure 26.8b we show a temperature analogue of the above feedback system with I being

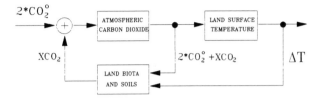

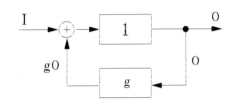

$$0 = I + g0 \qquad g: \text{gain factor} \qquad f = 1/(1-g) : \text{feedback factor}$$

Figure 26.8 Cybernetic feedback system between excess atmospheric CO_2 and temperature change ΔT.

the temperature change without and O being the temperature change including the biota-soil system. Within the nomenclature of the feedback theory we call g the *additional gain factor* of the biota-soil system and f the corresponding *feedback factor*.

Equilibrium Considerations

In our analysis we distinguish an equilibrium model, as many general circulation models do, and a corresponding dynamic model for the coupling of the atmosphere-climate system to the biota-soil system. Steady-state or equilibrium radiation models lead to a logarithmic dependence of the global temperature increase with increasing levels of atmospheric CO_2 (Tricot and Berger, 1987):

$$\Delta T(t) = \gamma \cdot \ln (1 + \Delta CO_2(t - \tau)/CO_2^0) \qquad (8)$$

where γ refers to the climatic sensitivity and τ to a time delay, set equal to zero in the equilibrium model. The parameter γ is determined by the complex and yet incomplete known climatic feedbacks (for instance through high and low clouds), water vapor content of the atmosphere, and atmosphere-ocean coupling; however, the coupling to the biota is still disregarded. Depending on the climate model assumptions the global surface air temperature increases between 1°K and 5°K have been suggested with a mean of 3°K for a CO_2 doubling. We choose here the parameter $\gamma = 4.55$, corresponding to a 3.15°K increase for our basic scenario, a value that allows a smooth transition from the past, including the Mauna Loa period, to the future.

The total atmospheric CO_2 increase, ΔCO_2, is considered to be composed of a fossil fuel contribution, a net deforestation contribution, and a biotic contribution that includes CO_2 fertilization and temperature response of the biota-soil system:

$$\Delta CO_2(t) = a_f(t) \cdot (\Delta CO_{2FOSS}(t) + \Delta CO_{2DEF}(t) \qquad (9)$$
$$+ \Delta CO_{2BIO}(t))$$

where the three terms in parentheses each represent the integrated flux up to time t, and where $a_f(t)$ is the corresponding air-borne fraction for the three inputs combined, which is different and smaller than the conventional air-borne fraction for fossil fuels only, which has been evaluated to be 0.56. For practical purposes we choose the air-borne fraction to be constant, that is, independent of CO_2 input, and equal to 0.50 with respect to the combined input, which is in accordance with the calculations between 1800 and 1980.

Extending the equilibrium considerations of the preceding sections we evaluate the CO_2 release from the soil system, disregarding the smaller changes in the living biota, from the equations (6) and (7):

$$XCO_2^{ST} = (H^0 - H^{ST}) \cdot a_f \qquad (10)$$
$$= H^0 \left(1 - \frac{NPP(\Delta T, CO_2, \Delta L_f)/NPP^0}{(1 + \bar{Q}_{HA}/10 \cdot \Delta T)}\right) \cdot a_f$$

where XCO_2^{ST} equals $\Delta CO_{2BIO} \cdot a_f$ and where the term in parentheses corresponds to the tabulated fractions in table 26.3 for a given externally fixed temperature change ΔT.

In the dynamic calculations, which are presented in a later section, the temperature rise ΔT_1, obtained for the standard fossil fuel scenario, is $4.27°K$ in the year 2100 while for the low fossil fuel scenario a temperature increase of $\Delta T_1 = 3.55°K$ is obtained.

In appendix to this chapter we define NPP as a function of a given temperature change ΔT, an atmospheric CO_2 concentration, and an assumed land use change, ΔL_f, which is needed to compute the ratio of NPP to NPP^0 in equation (10). Since the CO_2 and the temperature increase are related through equation (8), NPP can be expressed as a function of ΔT alone (equations A9 and A10 in the appendix). In equation (10), XCO_2 will thus depend on ΔT only. This relation together with equations (8) and (9) is used in equation (A12) to calculate the feedback temperature ΔT_2 in an internally consistent way, which is then related to the temperature change ΔT_1 without biotic feedback.

The temperature change with feedback ΔT_2 divided by the temperature change without feedback ΔT_1:

$$f = \Delta T_2/\Delta T_1 \qquad (A15)$$

is called the feedback factor of the biotic system while the gain factor g is defined by

$$g = (\Delta T_2 - \Delta T_1)/\Delta T_2 \qquad (A13)$$

Table 26.4 gives the results of the equilibrium biospheric feedback calculations for the year 2100 for two different fossil fuel and deforestation scenarios. The upper part of the table refers to the atmospheric CO_2 development until the year 2100 using the fossil fuel scenario suggested by Wuebbles (1984) from 1980 to 2050 and extending the same analytical form to the year 2100, and a constant deforestation flux of 1.9 Gt C annually, which incorporates the presumption that tropical deforestation will rather accelerate than come to an end within the future development. The lower part of table 26.4 refers to a low fossil fuel input scenario of a total cumulative increase of 500 ppm, described by a logistic function over the entire period from 1860 to 2100, the details of which are described in the appendix to this chapter. The low fossil fuel energy scenario is combined with a zero deforestation scenario after 1990.

For each of the two sets of energy and deforestation scenarios a combination of biospheric parameters ($\bar{Q}_{eff}$, $\bar{Q}_{HA}$, and 1) is analyzed. $\bar{Q}_{eff}$ is composed of two effects as described in the appendix—equations (A9) and (A10)—namely

$$\bar{Q}_{eff} = \bar{Q}_{AB} + 10 \cdot \beta/\gamma \qquad (A10)$$

For a given value of $\bar{Q}_{HA}$ (either 1 or 2) three values of $\bar{Q}_{eff}$ are chosen so as to represent the three cases of table 26.2 characterized by low, medium, and high parameter sets. The parameter 1 denotes the fraction of NPP remaining after a given land use change. The value $l = 0.95$ corresponds to a deforestation that is extended only until 1990, whereas the value $l = 0.82$ corresponds to a deforestation until 2100 and the value $l = 0.5$ to a deforestation as well as other severe environmental impacts on the biota (e.g., droughts, acid rain). It is seen that the feedback temperatures ΔT_2 lie in general 7% to 39% above the corresponding ΔT_1 values for the high-energy and high-deforestation assumption, whereas the low-deforestation scenario in the lower part of table 26.4 gives feedback values of $f = 0.91$ and 1.36. The effect of deforestation on the feedback factors becomes evident if one compares the

Table 26.4 Stationary Feedback Calculations

High-Energy Scenario
Non-feedback values: CO_2 = 715 ppm, $CO_2{}^0$ = 281 ppm, ΔT_1(715 ppm) = 4.27°K
Integrated input through deforestation (1800–2100): 276 Gt C

$\bar{Q}_{HA}$	$\bar{Q}_{eff}$	l	ΔT_2	g	f
1	−0.5	0.82	5.66	0.24	1.32
		0.5	5.87	0.27	1.37
1	0.33	0.82	5.27	0.19	1.23
		0.5	5.65	0.24	1.32
1	1.8	0.82	4.59	0.08	1.07
		0.5	5.26	0.18	1.23
2	−0.5	0.82	5.81	0.26	1.36
		0.5	5.96	0.28	1.39
2	0.33	0.82	5.53	0.22	1.29
		0.5	5.88	0.27	1.37
2	1.8	0.82	5.03	0.15	1.17
		0.5	5.51	0.22	1.29

Low-Energy Scenario
Nonfeedback values: CO_2 = 597 ppm, $CO_2{}^0$ = 281 ppm, ΔT_1 (597 ppm) = 3.55°K
Integrated input through deforestation (1800–1990): 80 Gt C; no deforestation after 1990

$\bar{Q}_{HA}$	$\bar{Q}_{eff}$	l	ΔT_2	g	f
1	−0.5	0.95	4.59	0.22	1.29
1	0.33	0.95	4.08	0.13	1.15
1	1.8	0.95	3.24	−0.09	0.91
2	−0.5	0.95	4.83	0.26	1.36
2	0.33	0.95	4.45	0.20	1.25
2	1.8	0.95	3.77	0.06	1.06

Above values for $\bar{Q}_{eff}$ are realized, for instance, through the following parameter sets:

$\bar{Q}_{eff}$ = −0.5	$\bar{Q}_{AB}$ = −0.5	β = 0.0
$\bar{Q}_{eff}$ = 0.33	$\bar{Q}_{AB}$ = 0.0	β = 0.15
$\bar{Q}_{eff}$ = 1.8	$\bar{Q}_{AB}$ = 0.5	β = 0.6

upper and the lower part of table 26.4. With the parameters $\bar{Q}_{HA}$ = 1 and $\bar{Q}_{eff}$ = 1.8 the value of f becomes smaller than 1 corresponding to a negative feedback—if at the same time the effect of deforestation on NPP is small corresponding to a factor l = 0.95. We also note that a comparison of two soils with a temperature sensitivity expressed through $\bar{Q}_{HA}$ = 1 and 2 gives a smaller difference of the feedback factors with the high-deforestation scenario than for the corresponding low-deforestation scenario, because deforestation itself is contributing relatively more to the feedback in the high-deforestation scenario. The next chapter shows that the equilibrium feedback factors are larger than the corresponding dynamic ones because the large soil reservoir with a long turnover time reacts relatively sluggishly to any given climatic change.

Dynamic Considerations

Tricot and Berger (1987) explained that the simple relation between the actual atmospheric CO_2 concentration and the corresponding temperature change can be maintained approximately in the dynamical calculations also if a corresponding time delay τ as given in equation (8) is introduced, where the time delay depends on the rate of atmospheric CO_2 increase, with values between ten and twenty years being typical for the present situation. We shall use here τ = fifteen years, which means that the atmospheric CO_2 concentration in the year 2085 is determining the observed temperature increase in 2100.

Equations (T1), (T2), and (T3) represent the time change of the reservoirs B, H_1, and H_2 for the past until 1980 as well as for the future extending until 2100. For a calculation of the CO_2 climate feedback we need to balance the atmosphere represented by equation (T6). In the latter equation we consider the contributions from deforestation, F_{DEF}, from CO_2-climatic feedbacks, F_{BIO}, and from fossil fuels, F_{FOSS}. The atmospheric increase is obtained by adding these fluxes and multiplying them by the total air-borne fraction a_f. Equations (T1), (T2), (T3), and

(T6) are integrated stepwise with the Eulerian procedure in which the temperature change ΔT and the CO_2 change, ΔCO_2, is calculated in equation (T6) as input for the next integration step of equations (T1) to (T3).

In figure 26.9 we present the results of the sum of the two fluxes: $F_{DEF} + F_{BIO}$ for a fixed deforestation scenario: $F_{DEF} = 1.9$ Gt C yr^{-1}. The dotted line in figure 26.9 represents just this flux, disregarding a temperature and fertilization effect. The dashed line, the solid line, and the dash-dotted line represent different combinations of the fertilization parameter β and the temperature response factors $\tilde{Q}$. This figure makes clear that the original deforestation flux (assumed to be 1.9 Gt C yr^{-1}) could be increased by as much as an additional 3 Gt C yr^{-1}, assuming a strong temperature dependence of the soils and a negative temperature response of the living biota. On the other hand a strong fertilization effect and a weaker temperature response of the deep soils will decrease the flux by about 3.5 Gt C in 2100.

In figure 26.10 the temperature change predicted for the corresponding scenarios as in figure 26.9 are shown and compared to a baseline calculation in which all biospheric feedbacks are neglected (short

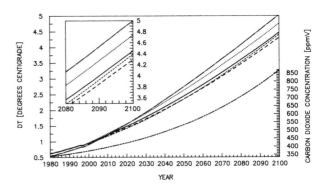

Figure 26.10 Calculated feedback temperature increase following the fossil fuel scenario for atmospheric CO_2 development from Wuebbles (1984), cited in Tricot and Berger (1987): Chain-dashed line. Short dashed line: no feedback, ΔT derived from logarithmic CO_2 dependence with time delay $\tau = 15$ years. Other lines as in figure 26.9, temperature development with biotic feedback.

dashed line). It is observed that the dynamic feedback factors up to the year 2100 are much smaller than the corresponding values derived in the equilibrium considerations; the strongest positive feedback factor increases the temperature by 18% in 2100 due to the fact that NPP was reduced both due to a deforestation effect, a negative temperature response, and a weak CO_2 fertilization effect, whereas a strong fertilization effect leads to a reduction of the transient temperature by 2%. The results of the calculated feedback and gain factors for the year 2100 are summarized in Table 26.5 for both the low and high fossil fuel scenarios. It is seen that for the parameter sets P1 to P4 nearly the same gain and feedback factors are obtained independent of the chosen scenario, if one disregards the small differences between the two scenarios, which can be attributed mainly to the higher proportion of CO_2 from deforestation relative to fossil fuel CO_2 in the low-energy scenario.

Discussion

In this study we distinguish between model results referring to the past 120 years, from 1860 to 1980, and corresponding results for the coming 120 years, extending from 1980 to 2100.

After defining a biosphere model with a minimum set of parameters and compartments (living biota B, upper soil compartment H_1, and lower soil compartment H_2), we identified a flux F_{BIO} (apart from the deforestation flux F_{DEF}) that is the result of CO_2 fertilization acting on net primary production and the temperature response of the biota-soil system.

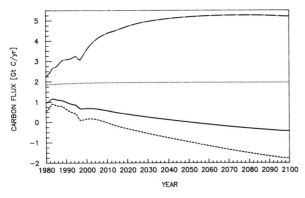

Figure 26.9 Calculated net flux F_{NET} (equation T4). $F_{NET} = F_{DEF} + F_{BIO}$ for the period 1980 to 2100, choosing $F_{DEF} = 1.9$ Gt C yr^{-1} = constant and varying the temperature and CO_2 dependence of F_{BIO}. Dotted line represents F_{DEF}. Dashed line represents $F_{DEF} + F_{BIO}$, assuming the optimum parameter set as for the past: strong fertilization ($\beta = 0.6$) and positive temperature response ($\tilde{Q}_{AB} = 0.5$) of NPP, strong temperature response of the soils with $\tilde{Q}_{BH1} = 0.0$; $\tilde{Q}_{H1A} = 3.0$; $\tilde{Q}_{H1H2} = 3.0$; $\tilde{Q}_{H2A} = 2.0$. Solid line represents $F_{DEF} + F_{BIO}$, using the suboptimum set of the past: medium fertilization with $\beta = 0.375$ and weaker temperature response of the biota ($\tilde{Q}_{AB} = 0.25$) and soils: $\tilde{Q}_{BH1} = 0.0$; $\tilde{Q}_{H1A} = 1.5$; $\tilde{Q}_{H1H2} = 1.5$; $\tilde{Q}_{H2A} = 1.0$. Dashed-dotted line represents $F_{DEF} + F_{BIO}$, small fertilization ($\beta = 0.15$) strong temperature dependence of the soils: $\tilde{Q}_{BH1} = 0.0$; $\tilde{Q}_{H1A} = 3.0$; $\tilde{Q}_{H1H2} = 3.0$; $\tilde{Q}_{H2A} = 2.0$ and high reduction of NPP ($\tilde{Q}_{AB} = -0.5$).

Table 26.5 Feedback and Gain Factors in 2100 From the Dynamic Calculations

a) low fossil fuel scenario: ΔT_1 (638 ppm) = 3.44°K

	Parameter Set			
	P1	P2	P3	P4
ΔT_2	3.42	3.56	3.84	4.31
g	−0.01	0.03	0.10	0.20
f	0.99	1.04	1.12	1.25
b) high fossil fuel scenario: ΔT_1 (838 ppm) = 4.28°K				
ΔT_2	4.19	4.33	4.62	5.04
g	−0.02	0.01	0.08	0.15
f	0.98	1.01	1.08	1.18

P1: $\beta = 0.6$ and $\bar{Q}_{AB} = 0.5$; $\bar{Q}_{BH1} = 0.0$; $\bar{Q}_{H1A} = 3.0$; $\bar{Q}_{H1H2} = 3.0$; $\bar{Q}_{H2A} = 2.0$
P2: $\beta = 0.375$ and $\bar{Q}_{AB} = 0.25$; $\bar{Q}_{BH1} = 0.0$; $\bar{Q}_{H1A} = 1.5$; $\bar{Q}_{H1H2} = 1.5$; $\bar{Q}_{H2A} = 1.0$
P3: $\beta = 0.0$ and $\bar{Q}_{AB} = 0.0$; $\bar{Q}_{BH1} = 0.0$; $\bar{Q}_{H1A} = 0.0$; $\bar{Q}_{H1H2} = 0.0$; $\bar{Q}_{H2A} = 0.0$
P4: $\beta = 0.15$ and $\bar{Q}_{AB} = -0.5$; $\bar{Q}_{BH1} = 0.0$; $\bar{Q}_{H1A} = 3.0$; $\bar{Q}_{H1H2} = 3.0$; $\bar{Q}_{H2A} = 3.2$.

We showed that neither of the two effects by itself was able to explain the discrepancy between the net biospheric flux evaluated by Siegenthaler and Oeschger (1987) and the net deforestation flux evaluated by Houghton and colleagues (1983, 1987).

However, in figure 26.7 we show that a combination of the two effects together with F_{DEF} describes reasonably well the net biospheric flux as deconvoluted by Siegenthaler and Oeschger.

The parameter sets required to give a best fit are described in the legend of figure 26.7. The optimum fit is obtained through a high fertilization effect ($\beta = 0.6$), a positive temperature response of NPP ($Q_{AB} = 1.5$), and a corresponding positive response of soil respiration. However, even moderate values of a CO_2 fertilization and equally moderate temperature responses of NPP and heterotrophic respiration lead to an acceptable result. It should be emphasized that in the model the most important effect of CO_2 fertilization is the increased litter production feeding into the soil system, which is thus depleted less rapidly with a temperature increase. We cannot at this point be sure whether other effects are operating on the biota that would make them an additional sink for atmospheric CO_2; thus Armentano and Hett (1980) have observed that the temperate forests of the world increased in carbon stock continuously from 1950 to 1975 for reasons not well identified up to now.

In the future interaction of the biosphere with the atmosphere-climate system we distinguish between equilibrium considerations and dynamic calculations. For a given temperature development as induced, for example, by the emission of CO_2 of fossil fuel origin, we calculate in table 26.3 the fraction and the amount of CO_2 released from the soil system. By looking at table 26.3 we recognize from row a) that a considerable fraction of the soil carbon can be released in an equilibrium situation where a 2°K, 4°K, or 8°K increase is attained, provided that the plant production, NPP, remains constant. If, however, as shown in row c), NPP is increased at the same time, then the fraction of carbon released may be considerably less or may even reverse sign if the temperature coefficient for the soil is relatively small. On the other hand, if NPP is decreased as shown in row d), then the soil fraction is even larger than in the reference case. As the turnover time in the upper soil compartment H_1 is of the order of only several years, while in the deeper soil compartment it is of the order of 100 years, we can expect that there will be only a small time delay in the dynamic response with respect to the CO_2 release from the upper soils. By comparing the last three rows of table 26.3 one can get an impression of the amounts of carbon released immediately by taking the upper soil compartment between 110 and 330 Gt C, while the last row gives the amount of carbon released after a long time. If these amounts are compared with the integrated fossil fuel input of CO_2 over the next 100 years, which are estimated to be between 500 and 1500 Gt C, then one realizes that the total soil carbon may have a considerable additional impact.

In the stationary feedback calculations of table 26.4, the effect of the CO_2 uptake or release by the biota-soil system on the surface temperature change is presented. In order to compare this with the corresponding dynamical calculations, which are driven by a low and a high fossil fuel input scenario, we chose a hypothetical stationary state in the year 2100 characterized by $\Delta T_1 = 3.55$°K (low) and

ΔT_1 = 4.27°K (high). The computed temperature increase ΔT_2 (3.8° to 4.8°K for the low- and 4.6° to 6.0°K for the high-energy case) is the result of the corresponding additional CO_2 increase in the atmosphere due to the coupling to the biota-soil system. Without going into the details of the results, which were described previously, we note that the calculated feedback factors f, which are equal to the ratio of $\Delta T_2/\Delta T_1$, are all larger than 1 except for one case in which a high stimulation of the NPP is combined with a low value of the temperature sensitivity of the soil.

In figures 26.9 and 26.10 we present the results of the dynamic calculations based on the high-energy scenario. It is shown in figure 26.9 that the deforestation flux F_{DEF} can be changed considerably through CO_2 fertilization and the response of the biota-soil system to increasing temperatures. In figure 26.10 we show the result of the coupling of the biota-soil system to the atmosphere with respect to the temperature development. When we apply the set of parameters that gives an optimum or suboptimum description for the past, we obtain a temperature development that lies only slightly below (or above) the reference curve derived from fossil fuel input only; that is, the climatic response of the biota-soil system nearly compensates the large deforestation flux. If one considers deforestation by itself, then one finds a feedback factor of 1.08, which is surpassed only by the case in which the NPP is decreased with increasing temperature, where we find a feedback factor of 1.18.

The results of the feedback calculation of the low fossil fuel scenario as opposed to the high fossil fuel scenario are summarized in table 26.5. It is noted that the feedback factors for the low fossil fuel scenario are slightly larger than for the corresponding high scenario, which can be explained by the fact that the same deforestation has a relatively larger impact on the low scenario.

Disregarding these small differences between the two calculations, we can state that the dynamic feedback and gain factors are considerably smaller than the corresponding steady-state values, a finding explained by the large turnover time for the deep soil carbon reservoir.

We have not presented here the wishful situation that the tropical forests can be maintained or even reforested in the coming years. In such a case we can expect that there is indeed a considerable negative feedback expressed by a feedback factor, which lies at perhaps 0.90 provided that the CO_2 fer-

tilization effect exists in the range of β = 0.15 to 0.60. We have performed additional sensitivity studies with respect to a disaggregation of the biota into zonobiomes and have found using the temperature data set of Hansen and Lebedeff (1987) that the higher latitude northern biomes contributed the largest CO_2 flux in the past 120 years, as was also true for the future projections, provided that the predictions of large temperature changes in the higher latitudes are valid.

In a future study we hope to consider the effect of precipitation and soil moisture change on the biota in addition to the described effects of temperature and atmospheric CO_2 concentration.

Acknowledgment

We should like to thank the German Minister of Research and Technology for financial support of this study. We are very grateful to Charles Hall, who reviewed this paper in detail and gave very helpful suggestions.

Appendix

Deforestation in the Past and in the Future

a. Past: Parametrization of the carbon flux into the atmosphere (F_{DEF}) and area transformations (ΔL_f, forest into farmland) as given by Houghton and colleagues (1983, 1987):

$$F_{DEF}(t) = \frac{3.75 \text{ Gt C yr}^{-1}}{1 + 11.93 \cdot e^{-0.02 \cdot (t - 1852)}} \tag{A1}$$

$$\Delta L_f = 112.4 \cdot 10^6 \text{ ha} \cdot e^{0.0098 \cdot (t - 1800)} \tag{A2}$$

$$1800 \leq t \leq 1980 \tag{A3}$$

Parameters are derived by a least square fit.

b. Future:

$$F_{DEF}(t) = 1.9 \text{ Gt C yr}^{-1} \text{ for } 1980 < t < 2100 \tag{A4}$$

$$\Delta L_f(t) = 11.3 \cdot 10^6 \text{ ha yr}^{-1} \cdot (t - 1980) + 657 \cdot 10^6 \text{ ha}$$
for $t > 1980$ $\tag{A5}$

Climate: Biota/Soil Feedback Analysis

The feedback analysis refers to the fact that additional CO_2 is

1. Absorbed through stimulation of NPP leading to an input of carbon into the biota and soils and

2. Released from the soils through the temperature increase. The change in NPP can be expressed

according to the development described in the model description section of this chapter.

$$NPP(\Delta T, CO_2, L_f) = NPP^0(1 + \bar{Q}(AB)/10 \cdot \Delta T \quad (A6)$$
$$+ \beta \cdot \ln(CO_2/CO_2^0)) \cdot l$$

The variable l is a variable in the dynamic calculation, which is defined by:

$$l = 1 - \alpha \cdot \Delta L_f(t)/L_f^0 \quad (A7)$$

with $L_f^0 = 6350 \cdot 10^6$ ha, $\alpha(t < 1980) = 0.8$ and $\alpha(t > 1980) = 0.53$.

For the steady-state calculations referring to the year 2100, l is fixed

i. $l = 0.82$ corresponding to the deforestation of tropical forests only

ii. $l = 0.5$ when referring to an additional reduction of NPP considering soil moisture defects and acid rain impact

iii. $l = 0.95$ if deforestation is stopped after 1990 and other environmental impacts are small.
   With the following relationship:

$$\Delta T(t) = \gamma \cdot \ln(CO_2(t - \tau)/CO_2^0) \quad (A8)$$

See also equation (8).

The terms describing temperature and CO_2 dependence of the NPP can be combined in one term, expressed either as a function of CO_2 or ΔT:

$$NPP = NPP^0 (1 + \bar{Q}_{eff}/10 \cdot \Delta T) \cdot l \quad (A9)$$

and

$$\bar{Q}_{eff} = \bar{Q}(AB) + 10 \cdot \beta/\gamma \quad (A10)$$

For a given future reference year, here the year 2100, different fossil fuel energy scenarios—equations (A16) and (A17)—yield a total atmospheric CO_2 concentration of $CO_2(t - \tau = 2085) = 715$ ppm and 597 ppm, which corresponds to a temperature change of:

$$\Delta T_1(2100) = \gamma \cdot \ln(CO_2(2085)/CO_2^0) \quad (A11)$$
$$= 4.27°K \text{ and } 3.55°K.$$

If one includes the important change of carbon in the soil layer, one obtains a temperature increase ΔT_2 that depends on the total atmospheric CO_2 from fossil fuel and biogenic sources—equations (9) and (10). As this CO_2 release can be expressed as a function of the temperature increase ΔT—equation (10)—one obtains an equation for this temperature change in complex form, which can be solved numerically:

$$\Delta T_2 = \gamma \cdot \ln \frac{1}{CO_2^0} \left[CO_2 + a_f \cdot \left\{ \Delta CO_{2,DEF} + \frac{H^0}{2.12} \right. \right. \quad (A12)$$
$$\left. \left. \left[1 - \frac{(1 + \bar{Q}_{eff}/10 \cdot \Delta T_2) \cdot 1}{1 + \bar{Q}_{HA}/10 \cdot \Delta T_2} \right] \right\} \right]$$

where CO_2 refers to the atmospheric CO_2 concentration considering fossil fuel only.

Following the feedback analysis of Lashof (1988) we obtain in accordance with figure 26.8 a gain factor g that is defined by the equations:

$$O = I + g \cdot O \quad \text{or} \quad \Delta T_2 = \Delta T_1 + g \cdot \Delta T_2$$
$$g = (\Delta T_2 - \Delta T_1) / \Delta T_1 \quad (A13)$$

and a corresponding feedback factor f that is defined by the equations:

$$f = O/I = 1/(1 - g) \quad (A14)$$
$$f = \Delta T_2/\Delta T_1 \quad (A15)$$

Scenarios of Atmospheric CO_2 Concentration (1980–2100) Based on Fossil Fuel Input (F_{FOSS}) only

The role of the oceans is considered by $a_f(t) = 0.5$, where a_f refers to the airborne fraction with respect to the total input.

High Fossil Fuel Scenario

$$CO_2(t) = 341.4 + 1.539(t - t_0) \cdot e^{9.173 \cdot 10^{-3}(t - t_0)} \quad (A16)$$

$$1980 \leq t \leq 2100, t_0 = 1983$$

This is the scenario proposed by Wuebbles and colleagues, as cited in Tricot and Berger (1987), extrapolated until 2100.

Low Fossil Fuel Scenario

$$CO_2(t) = \frac{500 \text{ ppm}}{1 + 146 \cdot e^{-0.025 \cdot (t - 1860)}} + 276.6 \text{ ppm} \quad (A17)$$

$$1980 \leq t \leq 2100$$

This more conservative scenario, proposed by Kohlmaier and colleagues (1990), assumes a sigmoid course of the CO_2 development within the period between 1980 and 2100.

References

Armentano, T.V., and Hett, J. eds. 1980. The role of temperate zone forests in the world carbon cycle—Problem definition and research needs. Washington, D.C.: United States Department of Energy CONF-7903105, 69.

Bohn, H.L. 1976. Estimates of organic carbon in world soils. *Soil Sci, Soc. Am. J.* 40, 468–470.

Bolin, B. 1970. The carbon cycle. *Sci Am,* 223(9), 124–132.

Buringh, P. 1984. Organic carbon in soils of the world. In: Woodwell, G.M., ed. *The Role of Terrestrial Vegetation in the Global Carbon Cycle: Measurement by Remote Sensing.* New York: SCOPE 23, Wiley, 91–109

Conroy, J.P., Milham, P.J., Mazur, M., and Barlow, E.W.R. 1990. Growth, dry weight partitioning and wood properties of *Pinus radiata* D. Don after two years of CO_2 enrichment. *Plant, Cell Environment,* 13:329–337.

Detwiler, R.P., and Hall, C.A.S. 1988. Tropical forests and the global carbon cycle. *Science,* 239, 42–47.

Dörr, H., and Münnich, K.O. 1987. Annual variation in soil respiration in selected areas of the temperate zone. *Tellus,* 39B, 114–121.

Edwards, N.T. 1975. Effects of temperature and moisture on carbon dioxide evolution in a mixed deciduous forest floor. *Soil Sci Soc Am Proc,* 39, 361–365.

Enoch, H.Z., and Sacks, J.M. 1978. An empirical model of CO_2 exchange of a C_3 plant in relation to light, CO_2 concentration and temperature. *Photosynthetica,* 12, 150–157.

Esser, G., Aselmann, I., Lieth, H. 1982. Modelling the carbon reservoir in the system compartment litter. *Mitt Geol Paläont Inst, (University of Hamburg),* 52, 39–58.

Fung, I.Y., Tucker, C.J., and Prentice, K.C. 1987. Application of advanced very high resolution radiometer vegetation index to study atmosphere-biosphere exchange of CO_2. *J Geophys Res,* 92, 2999–3015.

Hansen, J., and Lebedeff, S. 1987. Global trends of measured surface air temperature. *J Geophys Res,* 92, 345–372.

Harvey, L.D.D. 1989. Effect of model structure on the response of terrestrial biosphere models to CO_2 and temperature increases. *Global Biogeochem Cycle,* 3, 137–153.

Havas, P., and Mäenpää, E. 1972. Evolution of carbon dioxide at the floor of a Hylocomium Myrtillus Type Spruce Forest. *Aquilo Ser Bot,* 11, 4–22.

Houghton, R.A., Boone, R.D., Fruci, J.E., Honnie, J.E., Melillo, J.M., Palm, C.A., Peterson, B.J., Shaver, G.R., Woodwell, G.M., Moore, B., Skole, D.L., and Myers, N. 1987. The flux of carbon from terrestrial ecosystems to the atmosphere in 1980 due to changes in land use: Geographic distribution of the global flux. *Tellus,* 39B, 122–139.

Houghton, R.A., Hobbie, J.E., Melillo, J.M., Moore, B., Peterson, B.J., Shaver, G.R., and Woodwell, G.M. 1983. Changes in the carbon content of terrestrial biota and soils between 1860 and 1980: A net release of CO_2 to the atmosphere. *Ecol Monogr,* 53, 235–262.

Keeling, C.D. 1973. The carbon dioxide cycle: Reservoir models to depict the exchange of atmospheric carbon dioxide with the oceans and land plants. In: Rasool, S.I., ed. *Chemistry of the Lower Atmosphere.* New York: Plenum Press, 251–329.

Kimball, B.A. 1983. CO_2 and agricultural yield: An assemblage and analysis of 770 prior observations. Phoenix, Arizona: United States Department of Agriculture, WCL Report 14, 71.

Kohlmaier, G.H., Bröhl, H., Siré, E.O., Kratz, G., Fischbach, U., and Jiang Yunsheng. 1981. The response of the biota-soil system to a global temperature change. Proceedings of the contact group "Anthropogenic Climate Perturbations," Brussels, October 26 and 27, 1981, 1–20.

Kohlmaier, G.H., Bröhl, H., Siré E.O., Plöchl, M., and Revelle, R. 1987. Modelling stimulation of plants and ecosystem response to present levels of excess atmospheric CO_2. *Tellus,* 39B, 155–175.

Kohlmaier, G.H., Bröhl, H., Stock, P., Plöchl, M., Fischbach, U., Janecek, A., and Fricke, R. 1985. Biogenic CO_2 release and soil carbon erosion connected with changes in land use in the tropical forests of Africa, America and Asia. *Mitt Geol-Paläont Inst, (University of Hamburg),* 58, 132–136.

Kohlmaier, G.H., Janecek, A., and Kindermann, J. 1990. Positive and negative feedback loops within the vegetation/soil system in response to a CO_2 greenhouse warming. In: Bouwman, A.F., ed. Soils and the Greenhouse Effect. Proceedings of the International Conference 'Soils and the Greenhouse Effect", Wageningen, Netherlands, Aug. 14–18, 1989. Chichester: Wiley, 415–422.

Kohlmaier, G.H., Siré, E.O., Janecek, A., Keeling, C.D., Piper, S., and Revelle, R. 1989. Modelling the seasonal contribution of a CO_2 fertilization effect of the terrestrial vegetation to the amplitude increase in atmospheric CO_2 at Mauna Loa Observatory. *Tellus,* 41B, 487–510.

Körner, Ch., and Diemer, M. 1987. In situ photosynthetic responses to light, temperature and carbon dioxide in herbaceous plants from low and high altitude. *Funct Ecol,* 1, 179–194.

Körner, Ch. 1988. Does global increase of CO_2 alter stomatal density? *Flora,* 181:253–257.

Lanly, J.P. 1982. Tropical forest resources. FAO Forestry Paper 30, Rome: Food and Agriculture Organization United Nations Environment Programme 106.

Larcher, W. 1983. *Physiological Plant Ecology.* Berlin: Springer.

Lashof, D.A. 1988. The dynamic greenhouse: Feedback processes that may influence future concentrations of atmospheric trace gases. Paper presented at the Chapman Conference on Gaia Hypothesis. San Diego, March 7–11, 1988.

Lashof, D.A. 1989. The dynamic greenhouse: Feedback processes that may influence future concentration of atmospheric trace gases and climate change. *Climatic Change,* 14, 213–242.

Lovelock, J.E. 1987. Geophysiology: A new look at earth science. In: Dickinson, R.E., ed. *The Geophysiology of Amazonia: Vegetation and Climate Interactions.* New York: Wiley, 11–23.

Lovelock, J.E., and Margulis, M. 1974. Atmospheric homeostasis by and for the biosphere. *Tellus,* 26, 1–10.

Lovelock, J.E., and Watson, A.J. 1982. The regulation of carbon dioxide and climate. *Planet Space Sci,* 30, 795–802.

Peng, T.-H. 1985. Atmospheric CO_2 variations based on the tree-ring 13C record. In: Sundquist, E.T., and Broecker, W.S., eds. *The Carbon Cycle and Atmospheric CO_2: Natural Variations Archean to Present.* Geophysical Monograph 32. Washington, D.C.: American Geophysical Union, 123–131.

Peng, T.-H., Broecker, W.S., Freyer, H.D., and Trumbore, S. 1983. A deconvolution of tree ring based $\delta^{13}C$ record. *J Geophys Res,* 88, 3609–3620.

Rotty, R.M., and Marland, G. 1986. Fossil fuel combustion: Recent amounts, patterns and trends of CO_2. In: Trabalka, J., and Reichle, D., eds. *The Changing Carbon Cycle: A Global Analysis.* Berlin: Springer, 484–500.

Schleser, G.H. 1981. The response of CO_2 evolution from soils to global temperature changes. *Z Naturforsch,* 2, 38–45.

Schlesinger, W.H. 1984. Soil organic matter: A source of atmospheric CO_2. In: Woodwell, G.M., ed. *The role of Terrestrial Vegetation in the Global Carbon Cycle.* New York: Wiley, 111–127.

Seiler, W., and Crutzen, P.J. 1980. Estimates of gross and net fluxes of carbon between the biosphere and the atmosphere from biomass burning. *Climatic Change,* 2, 252–292.

Siegenthaler, U., and Oeschger, H. 1987. Biospheric CO_2 emissions during the past 200 years reconstructed by deconvolution of ice core data. *Tellus,* 39B, 140–154.

Strain, B.R., and Cure, J.D., eds. 1985. *Direct effects of increasing carbon dioxide on vegetation.* Washington, D.C.: Department of Energy Report, DOE/ER-0238, United States Department of Energy.

Tricot, C., and Berger, A. 1987. Modelling the equilibrium and transient responses of global temperature to past and future trace gas concentrations. *Climate Dynamics,* 2, 39–61.

Woodward, F.I. 1986. Ecophysiological studies on the shrub *Vaccinium myrtillus* L. taken from a wide altitudinal range. *Oecologia (Berlin),* 70, 580–586.

Woodward, F.I. 1987. Stomatal Numbers Are Sensitive to Increases in CO_2 from Pre-Industrial Levels. Nature 327:617–618.

Wuebbles, D.J. 1984. MacCracken, M.C., and Luther, F.M. 1984 *A Proposed Reference Set of Scenarios for Radiatively Active Atmospheric Constituents.* DOE/NBB-0066, TR015. Washington, D.C.: United States Department of Energy, 51. (See also citation in Tricot and Berger, 1987.)

Andrew J. Watson and Linda Maddock

27

A Geophysiological Model for Glacial-Interglacial Oscillations in the Carbon and Phosphorus Cycles

The Geophysiological Approach

Lovelock has introduced the term *geophysiology* to describe a systems approach to the science of the biosphere that is analogous to the physiological study of an organism (Lovelock, 1986). Though it fits in well with the Gaian view of the planet, geophysiology need not be the sole preserve of those who regard the Earth as a self-regulating system. The earth scientist does not have to believe that the Earth is alive before he or she can learn something from the approach that physiologists take to the study of organisms.

Organisms are complex entities with many sophisticated feedback systems that together regulate their metabolism. Physiological systems are characterized by feedbacks that are multiple, interlinked, distressingly nonlinear, and of both positive and negative varieties (Riggs, 1970). These same properties characterize interactions within the biosphere. For example, figure 27.1a is a cartoon, highly simplified, of a few of the possible interactions that link the earth carbon system. The global carbon cycle is physiological at least in this sense; like an organism, it is complex, multiply connected, and nonlinear.

How would a physiologist go about analyzing the system in the figure? The unpleasant truth about physiologists is that, given a new system to study, they quickly get to the stage of strapping the animal down to the laboratory bench. First they may subject it to various stimuli and measure its response, then as likely as not they will cut it into pieces and study the behavior of the parts in isolation from one another. With this kind of access to (literally) the guts of the system, they are soon able to construct and test elaborate theories.

Geophysiologists can neither dissect their animal nor perform controlled experiments on it, which gives them a moral edge but puts them at a severe practical disadvantage. The best they can do is to exploit unplanned perturbations like the burning of

fossil fuels, or study the imperfect proxy records of past changes in the earth system, in an attempt to deduce some of its basic properties. They can build models, but the models had better be simple because hard evidence of the dynamics of the biosphere is in very short supply.

In this chapter we build a simple model of quaternary fluctuations in the carbon and phosphorus cycles, from first geophysiological principles. Our textbook for the exercise was a delightful book written for physiology students (Riggs, 1970). The reason we chose the quarternary glaciations is that in the ice-core record of atmospheric CO_2, we have a rare example of high-quality data that shows the dynamic behavior of one component of the carbon cycle in response to a well-characterized excitation—namely, orbital forcing. In particular, the 160-Kyr record published by Barnola and colleagues (1987) shows that this response seems to have been reproduced over at least the last 1.5 glacial cycles, and that it is tightly correlated with changing temperature. Uniquely informative though it is, when compared to the quality of data available to the regular kind of physiologist, this raw material is not adequate to test more than the very simplest kind of model.

We emphasize the role of nonlinearity in the dynamics of geochemical systems. These systems have hitherto very frequently been assumed to be linear, largely because so few data have been available to test other assumptions. However, even very simple nonlinear systems can give rise to a great range of responses (multiple stable points, limit cycles, etc.) that are absent in linear models. It is important to recognize that, as a result of the close coupling of several nonlinear mechanisms, the system may have some unexpected properties, including reasonably homeostatic behavior that we can interpret as a Gaian mechanism (Watson and Lovelock, 1983).

The importance of nonlinearity in "the ice age

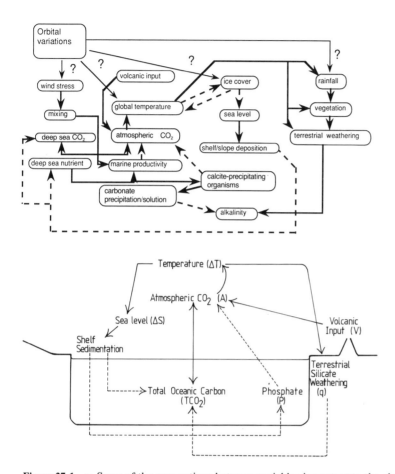

Figure 27.1 a, Some of the connections between variables important to the global carbon system. The diagram follows the conventions described by Riggs (1970); the arrows show the directions of causality between variables. Solid arrows stand for direct relationships, and broken arrows for inverse relationships. (For example, increased global temperature causes increased rainfall but decreased ice cover.) A feedback loop exists where a closed loop of arrows can be followed around the diagram; loops containing an odd number of broken arrows are negative feedbacks, whereas those containing zero or an even number of broken arrows are positive. **b,** Simplified version of a, showing only those interactions used in the model. The model contains three feedback loops of which two are negative and one is positive.

problem" has of course been recognized for some time (Imbrie and Imbrie, 1980). The system is thought to be forced by variations in the Earth's orbital parameters, predominantly at the precessional (1 per 22 Kyr) and obliquity frequencies (1 per 41 Kyr). The forcing function contains almost no power at the eccentricity frequency (1 per 100 Kyr) but is substantially amplitude modulated at this frequency. However, the dominant pattern in the response of the climatic system, as recorded by isotopic and CO_2 shifts, is of a saw-tooth oscillation with repeat frequency of order 100 Kyr. Linear models cannot produce a satisfactory match to this response from orbital forcing, and the models now being studied for the quarternary glaciations are substantially nonlinear (le Treut et al., 1988; le Treut and Ghil, 1983; Saltzmann and Sutera, 1987).

The Model

Rationale

We limit ourselves to a zero-order dynamical description specifically of the geochemical carbon-phosphorus cycle; in doing this we exclude or grossly simplify many processes that are vital to a complete understanding of the glacial-interglacial oscillations; our purpose is not to provide a comprehensive description of the phenomenon, but to discuss a possible subsystem. The ice-core record of CO_2 is *prima facie* evidence of a substantial disturbance in the global carbon cycle; the 100-Kyr dominant period of the oscillations is long enough that the dynamics of carbon and nutrients in the ocean are probably important, and it is that on which we concentrate.

Broecker (1982) first drew attention to the important role of ocean chemistry in explaining glacial-interglacial changes. According to his "shelf deposition" hypothesis, the flooding of the continental shelves at the close of glacial time was accompanied by a brief episode of enhanced burial of organic sediments on the shelves and slopes. The effect was to withdraw both organic carbon and phosphate from the oceans, with the reduction in nutrients causing an increase in atmospheric CO_2 by decreasing the capacity of the marine biota to lower the partial pressure of CO_2 in surface water. This is the mechanism we use as the basis for our model.

Subsequent to the publication of Broecker's idea, evidence was discovered in ice cores from Greenland of rapid excursions in both atmospheric CO_2 and climate during the last glaciation (Oeschger et al., 1985). The shelf-deposition hypothesis cannot explain changes in CO_2 on timescales much less than the ocean mixing period of 1000 years, so other mechanisms must be invoked, involving for example disturbances in the thermohaline circulation or marine productivity at high latitudes (Sarmiento and Toggweiler, 1984; Siegenthaler and Wenk, 1984; Knox and McElroy, 1984; Broecker et al., 1985). However, the rapid excursions are short-lived, geographically localized transients rather than sustained shifts. They appear to be spectrally distinct from the long glacial-interglacial cycle. It may be premature therefore to discard the shelf-deposition hypothesis entirely. As we shall see, shelf deposition (or indeed any mechanism involving wholesale removal of nutrients from the ocean) is incapable of explaining rapid variations, but on the other hand can help to explain the dominant periodicity.

Description

Figure 27.1b which is a stripped down version of figure 27.1a, shows in symbol-and-arrow form the relations between the variables in the model. Both phosphorus and carbon have residence times of order of magnitude 100 Kyr in the ocean, which is their principal reservoir in the biosphere (Broecker and Peng, 1982). Over this timescale, mechanisms must exist that tend to adjust their removal to sediments to be equal to the rates at which they are input to the biosphere. For P, the quantity of phosphorus in the ocean as a whole, we write

$$dP/dt = \frac{1}{\tau_P}(P_s - P) \qquad (1)$$

where τ_P is a characteristic time, and P_s is the steady-state value of P, taken to be 3 μM l^{-1}. The equation represents a simple balance between input by rivers and concentration-dependent removal to sediment as particulate detritus. In addition we model the removal of phosphorus during flooding of the continental shelves as an instantaneous drop in the value of P by 30% as sea level rises through some preset level, designated *shelf level* and set at 100 m below full interglacial sea level. The material buried on the shelves is assumed to have the standard Redfield ratio for carbon to phosphorus of 106 to 1.

The characteristic time τ_P is not a free parameter. The oceanic residence time of phosphorus against removal by all pathways is close to 70 Kyr (Froelich et al., 1982). The value of τ_P will be somewhat greater than this because it represents the residence time against removal by all processes except shelf deposition. We calculate that the appropriate value for τ_P is approximately 100 Kyr if a deposition event removes 30% of ocean phosphorus every 100 Kyr.

Ocean inorganic carbon chemistry is modeled using the equations of Skirrow (1975). These equations have two independent variables, but we can reduce the system to a single variable (which we take to be total carbon dioxide, TCO_2) by imposing one additional constraint, namely that the saturation index of calcium carbonate is held constant. This saturation index governs the depth in the oceans of the calcite lysocline, the level below which calcite in sediments tends to dissolve before it is buried. If the lysocline were to fall, for example, then the fraction of the ocean floor over which calcium carbonate accumulated would increase. Because of the large vertical flux of particulate carbonate from organisms, calcium carbonate would be removed from the ocean until within a few thousand years the saturation index was once again restored to nearly its former value (Broecker and Peng, 1987).

The properties of the CO_2 system under the assumption of constant carbonate saturation index are discussed in depth by Broecker and Peng (1982). In particular, they show that any change in TCO_2 must be accompanied by an almost equal shift in titration alkalinity (TALK). (Broecker's approximate treatment shows that $dTALK/dTCO_2 \approx 1$, whereas our calculations, which include the effect of borate and some variation in carbonate ion, give $dTALK/dTCO_2 = 0.94$.) The adjustment to the alkalinity occurs as, following removal of carbon to the shelves as organic material, the lysocline drops temporarily, allowing the deposition of excess calcium carbonate in the sediments in a *preservation event*. Such an event is well known to have accompanied the last deglaciation (Berger, 1977). Deposition of calcium carbonate removes two equivalents of TALK for each mole of TCO_2, until the system is restored to balance.

Our treatment of the carbon cycle is derived from the work of Walker and colleagues (1981) (we refer to their model as WHAK, for "Walker, Hays, and Kasting"); Berner and colleagues (1983) (we refer to their model as BLAG, for Berner, Lasaga, and Garrels); and other authors (Volk, 1987, Lovelock and Watson, 1982). The rate of input to the biosphere from vulcanism is designated V and is treated as a free parameter, of order 6×10^{12} moles carbon per year (a figure taken from the steady-state analysis of BLAG). Removal to sediments is accomplished by the periodic formation of shelf-slope organic-rich sediments in association with shelf flooding, and by the precipitation of carbonates in the ocean. However, because of the requirement that the calcium carbonate saturation index should remain constant, the ultimate rate-limiting step for carbon removal is the input of non-CO_2 alkalinity to the oceans, by continental weathering of silicate rocks. This process can be represented by reactions of the form:

$$XSiO_3 + 2CO_2 + 3H_2O \rightarrow$$
$$X^{2+} + 2HCO_3 + H_4SiO_4 \ldots . \qquad (2)$$

(where X may be Ca or Mg). The products of this reaction are washed to the ocean by rivers where they contribute one equivalent to TALK for each mole of bicarbonate formed.

Denoting the rate of carbon consumption by this reaction as q, the rate of carbonate burial by p, and the quantity of carbon in the biosphere as a whole by C, we can write

$$dC/dt = V - p$$
$$dTALK/dt = q - 2p \qquad (3)$$

Because C is dominated by inorganic carbon in the oceans, we can approximate C by $f \times TCO_2$, where f is about 1.06 at present. Then, eliminating p from these equations and substituting $dTALK/dTCO_2 \times dTCO_2/dt$ for $dTALK/dt$, we derive

$$\frac{dTCO_2}{dt} = (2V - q)/\left(2f - \frac{dTALK}{dTCO_2}\right) \qquad (4)$$

as the equation that governs TCO_2. In our abbreviated treatment we took f to be a constant, although it is apparent that it must change by a few percent between glacial and interglacial periods. We also ignored the weathering of carbonate rocks, on the grounds that carbonate weathering and precipitation is a null cycle that does not in total remove carbon from the biosphere.

Following WHAK, BLAG, and other models, we assume that the silicate weathering rate q is adjusted to keep the carbon budget in long-term balance by a feedback mechanism involving global temperature and atmospheric CO_2. The weathering rate is controlled by the partial pressure of CO_2 in soils and the rate of continental runoff, both of which may be expected to increase with temperature. In particular, soil CO_2 pressures are dominated by the effects of the terrestrial biota (Lovelock and Watson, 1982), the mass of which may have varied by a maximum of a factor of two between interglacial and glacial periods (Olson, 1985). We parameterized the weathering rate as a function of global temperature T:

$$q = q(T) \qquad (5)$$

and investigated two versions of this function; BLAG's version (Berner et al.; equation 28), and a linear variation that assumes that weathering was 25% slower during peak glacial than during peak interglacial time.

Three further relations are required to specify the model completely; we require the dependence of global temperature on the concentration of atmospheric CO_2 (denoted A), the dependence of A on TCO_2 and phosphate, and a relationship to specify sea level. Parameterizations of temperature in terms of atmospheric CO_2 are available in the literature (i.e., WHAK and BLAG models), though they have normally been used at values of A above the present level rather than below it. We used the BLAG equation, or a linear variation giving a 1.5°C change in T over the range 200 to 280 ppm CO_2, which covers the last glacial cycle. This variation in temperature is closer to the mean sea surface temperature change than the mean air temperature change. Our approach assumes that CO_2 alone can be used to completely specify temperature change, which is not the same as assuming that atmospheric CO_2 is the sole mechanism causing temperature change. This point is discussed more fully in our results section.

The dependence of A on TCO_2 and phosphorus was modeled in the manner described by Broecker and Peng (1982). The seawater CO_2 equations were used to calculate the pressure of CO_2 in equilibrium with surface water—the composition of which was calculated by adjusting deep sea total carbon and alkalinity to reflect phosphorus-limited production of organic material and calcium carbonate by the marine biota. Atmospheric CO_2 increases with total CO_2 in the oceans, but decreases with increasing phosphate, because this allows a more efficient biological carbon pumping. The calculation is sensitive to the Redfield ratios in which the biota produces phosphorus and organic and inorganic carbon; we kept these fixed at 1:106:26.

A physically accurate specification of sea levels would require a consideration of the rate of growth and break-up of the glacial ice sheets. Because the focus of our attention is on the biogeochemical cycles and on timescales of greater than 10 Kyr, we used an equilibrium model for sea level, assuming that it is a simple linear function of temperature and drops 100 m for each 1°C fall in T. This simplification means that the model cannot be used to examine phase differences between CO_2 and sea level variations, but it has the advantage that the number of ill-defined parameters is kept to a minimum. The final model has two free parameters: V, the rate of input of carbon to the biosphere, and the differential dq/dA, which controls the open-loop gain of the weathering rate feedback loop.

Results

The model displays rather complex behavior typical of simple nonlinear relaxation oscillators. A steady-state point always exists where the differentials of TCO_2 and P are zero, phosphate is equal to P_s and weathering rate equal to twice the tectonic input of CO_2. When integrated forward from given initial conditions, the system may approach this steady-state smoothly after passing through a maximum of one oscillation, provided it does not pass through a shelf-flooding episode. If the shelves do flood, the smooth evolution is interrupted but the temperature may still stabilize to the steady-state value. For a relatively restricted range of the free parameters, corresponding to conditions where the steady-state sea level lies 100 m or less above shelf level, the model may go into continuously repeated cycles. The period of these free oscillations lies between about 150 Kyr and 1 Myr depending on the values of the parameters, and is longer for the BLAG feed-

back relations than for our linear parameterization of temperature and weathering rate. In figure 27.2a the variation of steady-state sea level with tectonic input of carbon is shown for the two types of feedback. Example solutions for a single value of V are illustrated in figure 27.2b and c.

The behavior of the model and the tendency toward oscillation may be understood by comparing the relaxation times of carbon and phosphorus. For P, the $1/e$ response time is simply $\tau_P \approx 100$ Kyr in equation (1). For carbon, the relaxation time is dependent on all of the relations in the weathering rate feedback loop:

$$\tau_c = (2f - dTALK/dTCO_2)/[(dq/dA) \cdot (dA/dTCO_2)]$$

For conditions near those of the present day, we find that $dA/dTCO_2$, evaluated at constant carbonate saturation index, is about 2.5×10^{-16} ppm CO_2 per mole of carbon in the sea. If the BLAG relations are used for the functional dependence of q on T and T on A, then dq/dA is about 10^{16} moles ppm^{-1} Myr^{-1}, leading to a relaxation time for carbon of 480 Kyr. The linear model that we investigated has $dq/dA = 3.6 \times 10^{16}$ moles ppm^{-1} Myr^{-1}, giving $\tau_c = 130$ Kyr. In both models, therefore, carbon has

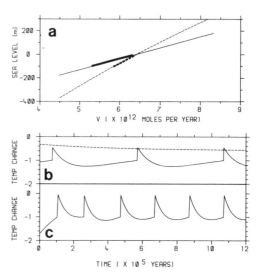

Figure 27.2 Unforced responses of the model. **a,** Sea level at steady state, as a function of the tectonic input of carbon to the biosphere, V, for the linear parameterization described in the text (solid line) and the BLAG relations (dashed line). Values of V over which continuous oscillations can be induced are shown by the thicker lines. **b,** Free oscillations using the BLAG feedback relations. $V = 6.1 \times 10^{18}$ moles Myr^{-1}. The dashed line shows a nonoscillating solution with the same parameters, but started from a different initial condition. **c,** Free oscillations using the linear feedback relations described in the text.

a significantly longer response time than phosphorus. After a shelf-flooding event, the recovery of phosphorus levels causes atmospheric CO_2 to fall, whereas the recovery of carbon tends to cause it to drift upwards, but on a slower timescale. Accordingly, temperature and sea level first decrease and then increase, which can lead to the shelf being exposed and then reflooded.

It is notable that unless the relaxation times governing the oscillation are shifted to values that seem unreasonably short, the free oscillation period cannot be made equal to the 100 Kyr observed between major glaciations. This contrasts with the approach of Saltzmann and Sutera (1987), who have investigated a rather more abstract model where the free oscillations *are* the glacial-interglacial cycle, the role of orbital forcing being merely to lock the phase of these oscillations to the Milankovich cycle.

To examine the response to orbital forcing, we suppose that some process, probably a high-latitude effect involving shifts in ocean circulation or marine productivity, modulates the concentration of atmospheric CO_2 in step with orbital variations. Figure 27.3a shows the forcing function, which was an additive input to atmospheric CO_2 having the form of the theoretical variation of summertime (July 21) insolation at 65°N (Berger, 1978), and a maximum peak-to-peak amplitude of 22 ppm. Figure 27.3b

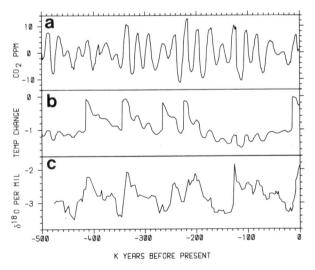

Figure 27.3 Forced oscillations. **a,** The forcing function, which has the form of the summertime insolation at 65°N in the Northern Hemisphere, calculated over the last 500 Kyr (Berger, 1978). It was converted into a fluctuation in atmospheric CO_2. **b,** Response of the model, with $V = 6.6 \times 10^{18}$ moles Myr^{-1}. The linear feedback relation was used. **c,** Oxygen-18 isotope record from deep sea cores RC11–120 and E49–18 (Hays et al., 1976).

shows an example of how the model responds. For a range of parameters the model will reproduce many of the major features seen in oxygen isotope records covering the last 500 Kyr (figure 27.3c). One notable feature of the model run shown in the figure is that although it does reasonably well at predicting four of five of the major termination events, it fails to predict the biggest event of all in the record, at about 130 Kyr BP (before present). This appears to be because the on-off nature of the model turns a feature at about 250 Kyr BP into a major deglaciation event. The effect of two shelf floodings separated by only about 60 Kyr is to remove sufficient carbon that the next glaciation is unusually severe; sea level drops well below the the shelf level and does not recover sufficiently to be able to flood the shelf in response to the excitation signal near 130 Kyr BP.

The model gives qualitatively the right sort of response because it contains the important elements of nonlinearity (especially in respect to the on-off response to shelf flooding) and a degree of low-pass filtering (due to the long residence times of carbon and phosphorus). As would be expected in such a simplistic approach, it is far from perfect. The most interesting problem is that the direct radiative effect of CO_2 variations on the global temperature is about an order of magnitude less than the observed glacial-interglacial excursions (Genthon et al., 1987). The close synchrony of the CO_2 and temperature shifts therefore does not occur simply because CO_2 causes the temperature change. There are two contrasting possibilities: at one extreme it may be that CO_2 dominates the 100-Kyr shifts in temperature but that other factors serve as slave amplifiers of the effect. Ice-albedo feedback and water-vapor feedback certainly could act in this way, and there may be more subtle effects also. At the other extreme it may be that atmospheric CO_2 and global temperature are both slave to some third common variable, and that the direct causal link between them is insignificant. Our model of course is only applicable to the first case.

To conclude, this investigation is meant to be geophysiological in that we consciously treated the system as being "like an organism." However, we used traditional geochemical ideas, and in particular, the useful trick of constraining the biota so tightly by its geochemical environment that it need not be explicitly treated at all. In this sense the model is weak Gaian—a halfway house on the road to building strong Gaian models in which biological dynamics would be properly included. The description "weak" may be something of a misnomer, however, because Gaia, even when treated as a metaphor, is still a powerful stimulant to creative thinking in earth systems science.

Acknowledgments

We thank J. E. Lovelock, D. R. Turner, and M. Whitfield for helpful discussions. The Marine Biological Association is funded in part by a grant-in-aid from the Natural Environment Research Council.

References

Barnola, J.M., Reynaud, D., Korotkevich, Y.B., and Lorius, C. 1987. Vostok ice core provides 160,000 year record of atmospheric CO_2. *Nature*, 329, 408–414.

Berger, A.I. 1978. Long term variations of daily insolation and quaternary climatic changes. *J Atmos Sci*, 35, 2362–2367.

Berger, W.H. 1977. Deep sea carbonate and the deglaciation preservation spike in pteropods and foraminifera. *Nature*, 269, 301–303.

Berner, R.A., Lasaga, A.C., and Garrels, R.M. 1983. The carbonate-silcate cycle and its effect on atmospheric carbon dioxide over the past 100 million years. *Am J Sci*, 283, 641–683.

Broecker, W.S. 1982. Glacial to interglacial changes in ocean chemistry. *Progr Oceanogr*, 11, 151–198.

Broecker, W.S., and Peng, T-H. 1987. The role of $CaCO_3$ compensation in the glacial to interglacial CO_2 change. *Global Biogeochem cycles*, 1, 15–30.

Broecker, W.S., and Peng, T.-H. 1982. *Tracers in the Sea*. Palisades, N.Y.: Eldigio Press, Lamont Doherty Geological Observatory.

Broecker, W.S., Peteet, D.M., and Rind, D. 1985. Does the ocean-atmosphere system have more than one stable mode of operation. *Nature*, 315, 21–26.

Froelich, P.N., Bender, M.L., Luedthe, N.A., Heath, G.R., and DeVries, T. 1982. The marine phosphorus cycle. *Am J Sci*, 282, 474–511.

Genthon, C., Barnola, J.M., Raynaud, J.M., Lorius, C., Jouzel, J., Barkov, N.I., Korotkevich, Y.S., and Kotlyakov, V.M. 1987. Vostok ice core: Climatic response to CO_2 and orbital forcing changes over the last climatic cycle. *Nature*, 329, 414–418.

Hays, J.D., Imbrie, J., and Shackleton, N.J. 1976. Variations in the earth's orbit: Pacemaker of the ice ages. Science, 194, 1121–1132.

Imbrie, J., and Imbrie, J.Z. 1980. Modelling the climatic response to orbital variations. *Science*, 207, 943–953.

Knox, F., and McElroy, M.B. 1984. Changes in atmospheric CO_2: Influence of the marine biota at high latitude. *J Geophys Res*, 89, 4629–4637.

Lasaga, A.C., Berner, R.A., and Garrels, R.M. 1985. In: Sundquist, E.T., and Broecker, W.S., eds. *The Carbon Cycle and Atmospheric CO_2, Natural Variations Archean to Present*. Washington, D.C.: American Geophysical Union, 397–411.

le Treut, H., and Ghil, M. 1983. Orbital forcing, climatic interactions and glaciation cycles. *J Geophys Res*, 88, 5167–5190.

le Treut, H., Portes, J., Jouzel, J., and Ghil, M. 1988. Isotopic modeling of climatic oscillations: Implications for a comparative study of marine and ice core records. *J Geophys Res*, 93, 9365–9383.

Lovelock, J.E. 1986. Geophysiology: A new look at earth science. *Bull Am Met Soc*, 67, 392–397.

Lovelock, J.E., and Watson, A.J. 1982. The regulation of carbon dioxide and climate: Gaia or geochemistry? *Planet Space Sci*, 30, 795–802.

Oeschger, H., Stauffer, B., Finkel, R., and Langway, C.C., Jr. 1985. Variations of the CO_2 concentration of occluded air and of anions and dust in polar ice cores. In: Sundquist, E.T., and Broecker, W.S., eds. *The Carbon Cycle and Atmospheric CO_2: Natural Variations Archean to Present*. Washington, D.C.: American Geophysical Union, 132–142.

Olson, J.S. 1985. Cenozoic fluctuations in biotic parts of the global carbon cycle. In: Sundquist, E., and Broecker, W.S., eds. *The Carbon Cycle and Atmospheric CO_2: Natural Variations, Archean to Present*. Washington, D.C.: American Geophysical Union, 377–396.

Riggs, D.S. 1970. *Control Theory and Physiological Feedback Mechanisms*. Baltimore: Williams and Wilkins Co.

Saltzman, B., and Sutera, A. 1987. The mid-quaternary climatic transition as the free response of a three-variable dynamical model. *J Atmos Sci*, 44, 236–241.

Sarmiento, J.L., and Toggweiler, J.R. 1984. A new model for the role of the oceans in determining oceanic CO_2. *Nature*, 308, 621–624.

Siegenthaler, U., and Wenk, T. 1984. Rapid atmospheric CO_2 variations and ocean circulation. *Nature*, 308, 624–626.

Skirrow, G. 1975. The dissolved gases—carbon dioxide. In: Riley, J.P., and Skirrow, G., eds. *Chemical Oceanography*, Vol 2, 2nd ed. London: Academic Press, 1–181.

Volk, T. 1987. Feedbacks between weathering and atmospheric CO_2 over the last 100 million years. *Am J Sci*, 287, 763–779.

Walker, J.C.G., Hays, P.B., and Kasting, J.F. 1981. A negative feedback mechanism for the stabilization of the earth's surface temperature. *J Geophys Res*, 86, 9776–9782.

Watson, A.J., and Lovelock, J.E. 1983. Biological homeostasis of the global environment: The parable. *Tellus*, 35B, 284–289.

Lee F. Klinger

28

Peatland Formation and Ice Ages: A Possible Gaian Mechanism Related to Community Succession

Hypotheses of biosphere-atmosphere feedback loops have mainly focused on the interactions between marine biota and climate (e.g., Charlson et al., 1987). However, land areas, which support over 99% of the earth's biomass, have considerable potential for being involved in Gaian regulation. The properties of landscapes that can significantly affect climate, such as albedo, evapotranspiration, and carbon content, can be readily altered by natural changes in the terrestrial vegetation caused by disturbance and succession. In order to identify possible Gaian mechanisms on land, one must consider these processes of landscape change.

Landscapes are areas of closely interacting biotic communities, and any change in the areal extent of these component communities constitutes landscape change. Landscape change often involves allogenic (environmental) factors such as climate change and physical disturbance. Landscapes also undergo autogenic (biologically controlled) change through community succession. Succession is a process whereby, in the absence of large-scale physical disturbance, biotic communities replace one another in a somewhat orderly and predictable chronosequence. The course and rate of succession can be altered or even reversed by the influence of allogenic factors. Succession, as an inherent mechanism of change in all landscapes (and perhaps also in all seascapes), has rarely been considered in discussions of possible biosphere-atmosphere interactions.

Following a brief discussion of the theoretical approach, this chapter presents a model of a possible Gaian mechanism related to landscape-level successional changes occurring over a glacial-interglacial cycle. Feedback mechanisms between the terrestrial biota and the atmosphere are proposed which should favor the initiation and maintenance of a relatively stable ice age climate. An important caveat is that ocean mechanisms are not considered in this model. Though oceans undoubtedly play a role in climatic change, to treat them here would require a

level of understanding of land-ocean-atmosphere interactions that scientists have not yet achieved. Therefore, any inadequacies in this model should be viewed in light of the fact that ocean dynamics are to some degree involved in all of the proposed feedback loops.

Successional Theory

Successional theory, which has been developed mainly from a vegetation perspective, is a central topic of debate among ecologists, who are divided, generally, between two viewpoints. The long-standing organismic viewpoint is that succession represents a developmental, ontogenic process in ecosystems (landscapes), analogous to the maturation process in an organism, which results in the formation of structurally and compositionally stable (climax) communities (Clements, 1916; Margalef, 1963; Odum, 1969). This view holds that succession toward a hypothetical climax community, usually old-growth forest, is a deterministic process of vegetation change in the sense that if the initial environmental and biological conditions are known the successional sequence can be predicted. Conversely, the more popular individualistic viewpoint considers succession to be an indeterministic process of change that varies according to both the physical environment and the life history traits of the individuals involved (Gleason, 1917, 1926). This view questions the existence of climax communities in light of numerous findings that old-growth forests do not exhibit structural or compositional stability (Jones, 1945; Raup, 1963). Also, early succession has been shown to progress along several different pathways within a given landscape due primarily to the influence of allogenic factors and is therefore not readily predictable (Connell and Slatyer, 1977).

The approach taken in this chapter, which draws from both of these viewpoints, is that early successional pathways are primarily under the control of allogenic factors and can, therefore, vary widely. However, as succession progresses the increasing importance of autogenic factors causes pathways ultimately to converge onto specific late-successional communities, and that, in the absence of large-scale physical disturbance, terrestrial successions converge on bryophyte-dominated communities with organic soils (bogs). Large-scale physical disturbance is defined here as any physical phenomenon resulting in the sudden ($\leq$ 1 year) decline or death of a majority of the individuals of one or more dominant or subdominant taxa in a community. Examples of physical disturbances are fire, landslide, blowdown, flooding, severe drought, heavy dust deposition, and volcanic ashfall. (By this definition of disturbance, arid and semi-arid landscapes are viewed as being continually maintained at early stages of succession due to the frequent occurrence of drought.)

The conclusion that bogs may be climax communities has been drawn for several regions including Siberia (Katz, 1926), southeast Alaska (Zach, 1950), subarctic Alaska (Viereck, 1966), and Great Britain (Walker, 1970a). The only test of the bog climax hypothesis has been done in southeast Alaska (Klinger, 1988, 1990; Klinger et al., 1990). Using several independent methodologies, it was concluded that, following the early stages of primary succession, closed-canopy coniferous forests progressed to open-canopy coniferous bog forests, and eventually to moss-sedge bogs over a period of about 2000 to 5000 years. Once formed, the bogs have remained structurally and compositionally stable on the order of 3000 to 8000 years. This transition from woodland (forest-dominated) to peatland (bog-dominated) landscapes, called *paludification,* is recognized as a widespread phenomenon that ranges from the arctic (shrubland to peatland) and subarctic to the tropics (Katz, 1926; Auer, 1928; Sjörs, 1948; Drury, 1956; Lawrence, 1958; Heinselman, 1963; Heilman, 1966; Ingram, 1967; Walker, 1970a; Moore and Bellamy, 1974; Flenley, 1978; Alhonen and Auer, 1979; Glaser, 1987). Pollen and stratigraphic evidence from northern Europe indicates systematic shifts from woodlands to peatlands through the course of several interglacial periods (Iversen, 1958, 1973; Andersen, 1966, 1969; West 1980). Though these studies do not prove the bog climax hypothesis, they are consistent with it. Because no data can be found that are clearly inconsistent with this hypothesis, it should be regarded, for now, as a plausible view of succession.

Peatland-Atmosphere Interactions

Positive Feedbacks

The organismic view of succession postulates that vegetation communities modify their physical environment to facilitate succession. For instance, acidification of soils by early successional species favors the establishment and spread of late-successional bog vegetation in southeast Alaska (Crocker and Major, 1955). However, vegetation communities may also have the capacity to alter atmospheric conditions to facilitate succession. Biogenic acid precipitation reported from certain peatland areas (Nriagu et al., 1987; Klinger, 1988) results from the release of sulfide (and perhaps nonmethane hydrocarbon) gases from peatland vegetation or soils. Acidic conditions tend to promote the establishment and growth of many bryophytes (Raeymaekers and Glime, 1986; Rochefort and Vitt, 1988), thus aiding the succession toward bog communities.

The succession from woodland to peatland is accompanied by changes in evapotranspiration, albedo, and carbon storage that may promote a cooler and moister regional climate, thus favoring the formation and maintenance of peatlands. Bryophytes, especially *Sphagnum* mosses, have the unique ability to strongly acidify soils and thus reduce microbial populations and decomposition rates. This results in the accumulation of peat, which impedes drainage and increases soil moisture storage. (Unhumified *Sphagnum* peat typically can hold thirty to forty times its dry weight in water.) Bryophyte mats are highly efficient ground insulators. Increased bryophyte cover lowers soil temperatures and (in permafrost regions) raises the permafrost table, thus further impeding drainage.

Evaporation rates from *Sphagnum* mats are extremely high, with some measured rates exceeding 1 mm min^{-1} (Clymo and Hayward, 1982). More typical evaporation rates from *Sphagnum* mats have been measured at 3 to 6 mm day^{-1} compared with 2 to 3 mm day^{-1} from an open water surface (Clymo, 1970). In peatlands dominated by *Sphagnum* mosses (which accounts for the majority of peatland areas) as much as 75% to 80% of the annual precipitation can be evaporated (Bay, 1969; Middeldorp. 1984; Boelter and Verry, 1977). The combination of high soil moisture capacity and high evaporation rates in peatlands compared with woodlands should increase atmospheric moisture, thus promoting the downwind incidence of dew, fog, and rain. This should favor the spread of bryophytes and should also decrease the likelihood of fires and droughts, which can prevent bog formation.

Where paludification extends over large regions, high levels of atmospheric moisture could promote increased cloud cover, the net effects of which could cause regional cooling. Increased surface albedo may be another important cooling mechanism associated with paludification. For instance, in boreal areas, the summer albedo of bogs ranges from 12% to 16%, compared with only 6% to 8% for forests (Larsen, 1980). During periods of snow cover, forest albedo increases to about 15% while bog albedo increases to over 80% (Larsen, 1980). Concerning the possibility that these conditions could promote ice ages, it is interesting to note that virtually all Pleistocene ice sheets were initiated in areas that are presently occupied or surrounded by extensive peatlands.

Peatlands constitute a significant pool of organic carbon, variously estimated at between 500 PgC (Houghton et al., 1985) and 860 PgC (Bohn, 1976) (1 Pg = 10^{15} g), and covering about 5 million km^2 (Matthews and Fung 1987). Large-scale changes in peat accumulation or decomposition rates would undoubtedly affect CO_2 and methane (CH_4) levels in the atmosphere. Because the process of early peat accumulation is slow, on the order of 10 g m^{-2} yr^{-1} in boreal regions, an increase in the extent of peatland formation could only account for a decrease in atmospheric CO_2 levels occurring over thousands to tens of thousands of years. During the early stages of peatland formation (< 2000 years), extensive forest dieback should result in the oxidation of large quantities of wood, which would augment atmospheric CO_2. Whether this source could result in an increase in atmospheric CO_2 would depend on shifts in fluxes of other carbon pools. Over the short-term, peatlands may accumulate carbon at roughly the same rate it is lost through forest dieback, so that the net effect of paludification, in these early stages, on atmospheric CO_2 may be nil. However, the long-term effect of peat accumulation should be a significant lowering of atmospheric CO_2. In fact, over tens of thousands of years, carbon would accumulate in peatlands to levels exceeding the total carbon in the atmosphere (700 PgC). Clearly, some sort of long-term negative feedbacks must be operating to prevent massive peat accumulation.

Emissions of CH_4 during the early stages of paludification should increase proportional to the increase in area and duration of anaerobic soil conditions. However, during the late stages of paludification when peat-forming mosses, such as *Sphagnum,* become dominant, the acidity of the organic soils becomes very high, which suppresses microbial activity. Methanogenesis should decrease as microbial populations decline. In addition, the net primary productivity (NPP) also decreases significantly in the late stages of paludification, and because CH_4 production is ultimately tied to NPP, CH_4 emissions should also decrease. Values for the absolute change in CH_4 emissions from vegetation and soils through the course of paludification are not yet known. The net effect of a long-term decrease in CO_2, and perhaps CH_4, due to widespread peatland formation would be to lower global atmospheric temperatures, thus promoting an ice age climate.

Negative Feedbacks

Paludification is dependent primarily on the growth of bryophytes. Therefore, any negative feedback mechanism must involve either limiting bryophyte establishment and growth or the outright death of the bryophyte layer. Bryophyte growth can be limited by high alkalinity or by low levels of moisture, nutrients, and perhaps CO_2. Death of the bryophyte layer occurs through physical disturbances, particularly fires, droughts, and heavy dust deposition.

One important negative feedback occurs with paludification on steep slopes where root death associated with tree death causes instability of the substrate, usually resulting in landslides. Primary succession is then initiated in these barren landslide areas. If this cycle keeps repeating itself, bog formation will not occur on steep slopes.

Most negative feedbacks involving peatland formation appear to occur over a glacial-interglacial cycle. Assuming peatlands play an important role in ice age initiation, several negative feedback mechanisms could be operating. During a glacial period, peatlands in areas of glaciation are physically destroyed by the advancing glaciers. The organic matter that is oxidized would contribute to atmospheric CO_2, partially offsetting the CO_2 decrease associated with paludification in nonglaciated regions. Peatlands may also be negatively affected by the heavy loess deposition that occurs downwind of ice sheets. Continued heavy loess deposition would kill the bryophyte layer, thus preventing further peat accumulation and exposing the peat to wind and water erosion.

During the late stages of a glacial period atmospheric CO_2 is known to decrease to about 200 ppm (Barnola et al., 1987). If this is partly a result of increased organic carbon in peatlands, as is proposed here, then it is possible that a negative feedback involving the reduction of bog vegetation growth (and, therefore, peat accumulation) due to CO_2 limitation could occur. However, little is known about the limiting effects of CO_2 on the growth of bryophytes and other bog vegetation.

Any effect of glaciation in changing atmospheric circulation patterns (e.g., shifting jet streams) causing the climate over a large region of peatlands to become warmer and drier could result in a negative feedback. Increased drought and fire disturbance in these regions would result in the degradation of peatlands, which would release CO_2 and eliminate the high levels of evapotranspiration and acidic deposition associated with the peatlands. CO_2-induced warming may lead to increased CH_4 emissions from peatlands and further greenhouse warming (Guthrie, 1986). If these peatlands are located in the tropics, then there is a great potential for very rapid turnover of this organic matter due to the higher temperatures for decomposition and due to the presence of humus-feeding termites (e.g., *Cubitermes*). Once surface peats are dry, humus-feeding termites can rapidly digest the organic matter releasing large amounts of CO_2 and, especially, CH_4 (Zimmerman et al., 1982; Zimmerman and Greenberg, 1983).

If any of these negative feedback mechanisms occur to the extent that significant global warming occurs, and to the extent that ice sheets begin to melt, then a short-term positive feedback can occur that would drive the global system into an interglacial period. During deglaciation, not only would there be enhanced peatland degradation due to the general warming of the climate, but the associated rise in sea level would inundate large areas of saline and freshwater peatlands, which preferentially develop in coastal regions. Much of this peat material would be destroyed and oxidized by marine transgression, though some would be preserved in the sediments. The rapid release of large quantities of CO_2 and CH_4 could result in a greenhouse warming that would drive the world toward an interglacial climate, thus closing a glacial-interglacial negative feedback loop.

A Model of Peatland Dynamics

Based on theoretical predictions and on the integration of results from numerous paleoecological and glaciological studies, a global model of landscape dynamics has been conceptualized. This model bears close resemblance to Iversen's (1958) model of cyclic vegetation change associated with glacial-interglacial cycles (figure 28.1). Iversen's model proposes that, at mid to high latitudes, landscape succession occurs from early successional grassland or woodland during the early interglacial to later successional woodland during the mid interglacial, then to peatland during the late interglacial. These changes are accompanied by increasing soil acidity and podzolization. Glacial periods are dominated by glaciers or arctic-alpine vegetation with soils undergoing solifluction and erosion. Pollen and stratigraphic evidence indicating systematic shifts from woodland to peatland landscapes in Europe through the course of several interglacial periods has lent support to Iversen's model (Andersen, 1966, 1969; Iversen, 1973; West, 1980). Although Iversen's model does not recognize bogs as climax communities (sensu Clements, 1916), it postulates, nonetheless, that natural landscape change from woodland to peatland (paludification) occurs extensively during the later part of an interglacial period. The main difference between Iversen's model and mine is that his is regional (northern Europe) whereas mine is global.

To illustrate the present model, total estimates of organic carbon in peatlands, as well as estimates for two latitudinal ranges (0° to 30° and 30° to 70°), are plotted over a glacial-interglacial cycle (Fig. 28.2). The two latitudinal ranges include both the Northern and Southern Hemispheres. These ranges are meant to delimit, roughly, the temperate and boreal areas from the tropics by considering the 30° latitudinal band of deserts as a natural landscape boundary. For reference, the general glacial chronology over the past 140,000 years, which represents the best described glacial-interglacial cycle, is presented.

The description of the hypothetical cycle of landscape dynamics controlling the organic carbon curves begins with early interglacial conditions. Early interglacial periods are characterized by warm and, at mid latitudes, dry climates (Cooperative Holocene Mapping Project [COHMAP], 1988), which are conducive to woodland expansion. In addition, rapid and extensive deglaciation of continental ice sheets would create large regions undergoing roughly synchronous successions. Those areas experiencing frequent fires or other physical disturbances would be maintained at early successional stages. However, sites such as small water

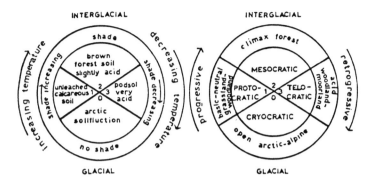

Figure 28.1 Iversen's model of ecosystem change in northern Europe during a glacial-interglacial cycle. The cycle of environmental change is on the left, the cycle of biotic community change is on the right. (From Iversen, 1958).

bodies and dryland areas not experiencing fires or other large-scale physical disturbances (particularly moist, coastal areas) would continue in the succession to peatland communities within about 2000 to 5000 years. This globally synchronous formation of peatlands may result in a sudden, but brief, change in climate toward cool, moist conditions associated with a leveling off or even lowering of atmospheric CO_2. Widespread peatland formation indicated from pollen analysis and basal peats from numerous glaciated areas in North America and Europe did, in fact, occur between 12,000 and 10,500 years BP (e.g., Heusser, 1960; Walker, 1970a; Iversen, 1973; Karrow et al., 1975; Tolonen and Tolonen, 1984). The climatic reversal (perhaps correlative to the Younger Dryas period) should be global, although it would probably be more intense near the regions of more extensive peatland formation. However, the continued release of greenhouse gases from the decay of tropical peatlands would promote the return of warm, dry climates. This hypothesis predicts that the Younger Dryas climate oscillations should be mainly CO_2 driven. Evidence that the Younger Dryas may have been caused by low atmospheric CO_2 and that it was a global phenomenon is presented by Kudrass et al. (1991).

Throughout the interglacial period, tropical peatlands continue to decay, and by the late interglacial they constitute only a fraction of the global peatlands. However, during the mid to late interglacial there is a cumulative increase in peatlands of higher latitudes (e.g., 50° to 70°) as more and more old-growth woodlands (or arctic shrublands) are paludified under the cool, moist conditions that prevail there. As discussed earlier, permafrost areas are particularly susceptible to paludification. To exemplify changes in peatland distribution during an interglacial period, estimates of the areal extent of

peatlands during the Holocene (which may or may not be representative of a typical interglacial) are plotted for an extensive, high-latitude permafrost region (western Siberia), as well as for mid and high latitude regions and subtropical and tropical regions (figure 28.3). Paleoecological evidence indicates that the increase in peatlands of mid and high latitudes is actually stepwise, or episodic (Davis, 1985). The reason for the episodic nature of paludification is not clear, though it may be related to cyclic variations in climate (Aaby, 1976) or to thresholds involving internal landscape dynamics. Tropical and subtropical peatlands are presumed to have decreased during the Holocene due primarily to peat degradation associated with warmer temper-

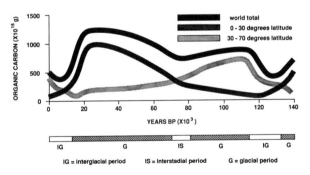

Figure 28.2 Estimated organic carbon in peatlands during an interglacial-glacial-interglacial cycle. The glacial chronology of the last 140,000 years is presented for reference. The light-shaded curve represents organic carbon in mid- and high-latitude areas (approximately 30° to 70° latitude). The dark-shaded curve represents organic carbon in low latitudes (approximately 0° to 30° latitude). The black curve represents the world total. Recent estimates of organic carbon in peatlands range from 500 (Houghton et al., 1985) to over 800 Pg (10^{15} g) C (Bohn, 1976).

atures causing an increased fire regime, to increased activity of humus-feeding termites, and to marine transgression inundating peatlands on continental shelves.

Once the previously described positive feedbacks involving peatland-atmosphere interactions gain control, a relatively rapid onset of glaciation can occur. Glacial onset should be characterized by widespread forest dieback, especially at higher elevations and latitudes, as paludification rate increases. This short-term source of CO_2 could temporarily prevent a decline in atmospheric CO_2 during the early onset of glaciation.

During the first half of a glacial period, peatland loss due to expanding continental ice sheets may be balanced by peatland formation at mid latitudes (e.g., 40° to 50°), where cooler and moister conditions occur from the equatorward shift in the jet streams. But as ice sheets continue to expand, the shifting jet streams would begin to influence regions of arid landscapes around 30° latitude. Increased moisture in these dry areas should tend to promote greater forest cover, but drought and fire may be frequent enough to prevent widespread paludification. If degradation of high-latitude peatlands by glaciers continues without the compensating effect of mid-latitude peatland formation during this period, warming trend, or interstadial, might be initiated (see 70- to 80-Kyr period in figure 28.2).

EXTENT OF PEATLANDS DURING THE HOLOCENE

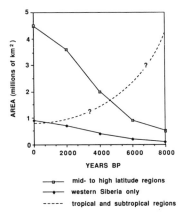

Figure 28.3 Estimated changes in the extent of peatlands in western Siberia (Neishtadt, 1977; Walter, 1977), mid- to high-latitude regions (Neustadt, 1982; Matthews and Fung, 1987), and subtropical and tropical regions during the Holocene. Estimates of subtropical and tropical peatland extent are highly tentative as they are based on sparse data.

Through the first half of the glacial period, the majority of the peatland formation is proposed to be occurring mainly at higher latitudes. Paludification, however, should also occur in tropical areas during this period, but peat accumulation would be much slower because warm temperatures favor high decomposition rates. Continued paludification in the tropics, even with low peat accumulation rates, could continue driving the global cooling trend, thus ending the interstadial warming. Global cooling and thus increased rates of tropical paludification may culminate in the dieback of tropical forests, and widespread tropical peatland formation. The maximum value of 1000 PgC in tropical peatlands is based on an estimated coverage of about 10 million km². This coverage value is based on a review of tropical paleoecological and soils literature (e.g., Walker, 1970b; Hope, 1976; Flenley, 1978; Sowunmi, 1981; Smith, 1982; Hansen et al., 1984; Yemane et al., 1985; Colinvaux and Liu, 1987; Salo, 1987; Bonnefille and Riollet, 1988), and includes tropical montane and alpine as well as lowland tropical areas. The lowering of sea level associated with glacial ice accumulation would expose continental shelves, which, following early succession, are excellent sites for peatland formation. Freshwater and saltwater peat deposits dating from the late Pleistocene and Holocene are commonly preserved in the shelf sediments of mid-latitude (Emery et al., 1967; Redfield, 1967; Delibrias and Guillier, 1971; Fujii and Mogi, 1971; Kaizuka et al., 1977), subtropical (Davies and Cohen, 1989), and tropical areas (Medvedev and Pavidis, 1987) and are evidence that shelves indeed supported peatlands prior to marine transgression. Due to the nature of these studies most radiocarbon dates are on the uppermost peat layers and, unfortunately, do not indicate when peat initiation occurred.

Whatever internal or external mechanisms initiated deglaciation, it is probable that the rapid decomposition of a significant fraction of tropical peatlands aided the process. The most likely candidate for initiation of deglaciation is the shift toward a warmer and drier climate caused by Milankovitch forcing (changes in the earth's radiation balance due to periodic orbital changes). This climatic change may have triggered a positive feedback response between peatland decomposition and greenhouse warming. However, there may be other factors, such as changes in ocean circulation, that also play an important role in the initiation of deglaciation.

Tropical peatland degradation should have continued throughout the ensuing interglacial period. The associated warming would have continued during the interglacial until such time as high-latitude peatland formation rates compensated or exceeded tropical peat decomposition rates, sometime around the mid-interglacial.

A detailed review of the evidence for the above model is beyond the scope of this chapter. However, a brief mention of ice core data for various carbon species is appropriate. In general there is remarkably good agreement between the predictions of this model and the ice core data for CO_2 (Neftel et al., 1982; Barnola et al., 1987) and CH_4 (Raynaud et al., 1988; Stauffer et al., 1988). Both of these atmospheric greenhouse gases show trends over the last 140,000 years that are inversely proportional to the relative extent of peatlands, as would be expected if peatlands are an important global sink for carbon. To remind the reader again, fully developed (climax) peatland communities are unlikely to be large sources of CH_4 because of low productivity and high acidity, and because, in tropical areas, peatlands inhibit termite activity, which is an important source of atmospheric CH_4. The glacial to interglacial transition is also characterized by a much greater increase in atmospheric CH_4 relative to CO_2, which supports the idea that termites may be important in the degradation of tropical peatlands. It should be noted, however, that in all of these studies alternative explanations, mainly dealing with changes in ocean circulation and productivity, are proposed. This model also does not yet incorporate carbon cycling changes associated with glacial-interglacial shifts in forest, grassland, and desert landscapes which may partly offset the effects of peatland dynamics.

Conclusions

In presenting a model of a possible terrestrial Gaian mechanism, I have attempted to describe natural landscape change over a glacial-interglacial cycle within a theoretical framework of succession. According to this model the succession from less stable woodland (or shrubland) to more stable peatland landscapes is primarily an autogenic process that promotes the initiation and maintenance of a relatively stable glacial climate. In this model interglacials are viewed as brief periods of instability imposed, in part, by Milankovitch forcing, though other, perhaps internal, factors may be involved.

This model may also have important implications in the forest decline and mass extinction phenomena.

Although it is based on considerable ecological and paleoecological evidence, this model is still rather speculative and remains mostly untested. The advantage of this model is that it is based on theoretical principles of succession that can be readily tested.

Acknowledgments

Thanks are extended to the many colleagues whose comments and criticisms of the ideas presented here have helped stimulate the development of this work. These include Karl Birkeland, David Gates, John Hollin, Scott Lehman, James Lovelock, Vera Markgraf, Ric Morrison, Stephen Schneider, Starley Thompson, Tom Veblen, Tyler Volk, Skip Walker, Pat Zimmerman, and two anonymous reviewers.

References

Aaby, B. 1976. Cyclic climatic variations in climate over the past 5,500 years reflected in raised bogs. *Nature*, 263, 281–284.

Alhonen, P., and Auer, V. 1979. Stratigraphy of peat deposits in Tierra del Fuego, South America: A review of the results of Finnish expeditions. In *Classification of Peat and Peatlands*. International Symposium in Hyytiälä, Finland, 273–282. (Published by the International Peat Society)

Andersen, S.T. 1966. Interglacial vegetational succession and lake development in Denmark. *Paleobotanist*, 15, 117–127.

Andersen, S.T. 1969. Interglacial vegetation and soil development. *Bulletin of the Geological Society of Denmark* 19, 90–102.

Auer, V. 1928. Some future problems of peat bog investigations in Canada. *Commentations Forestales*, 1, 1–31.

Barnola, J.M., Raynaud, D., Korotkevich, Y.S., and Lorius, C. 1987. Vostok ice core provides 160,000-year record of atmospheric CO_2. *Nature*, 329, 408–413.

Bay, R.R. 1969. Runoff from small peatland watersheds. *J Hydrol*, 9, 90–102.

Boelter, D.H., and Verry, E.S. 1977. Peatland and water in the northern lake states. USDA Forest Service General Technical Report NC-31.

Bohn, H.L. 1976. Estimate of organic carbon in world soils. *Soil Sci Soc Am J*, 40, 468–470.

Bonnefille, R., and Riollet, G. 1988. The Kashiru pollen sequence (Burundi) palaeoclimatic implications for the last 40,000 yr B.P. in tropical Africa. *Quaternary Res*, 30, 19–35.

Charlson, R.J., Lovelock, J.E., Andreae, M.O., and Warren, S.G. 1987. Oceanic phytoplankton, atmospheric sulphur, cloud albedo and climate. *Nature*, 326, 655–661.

Clements, F.E. 1916. *Plant Succession: An Analysis of the Development of Vegetation*. Publication 242. Washington, D.C.: Carnegie Institution.

Clymo, R.S. 1970. The growth of *Sphagnum:* Methods of measurement. *J Ecol,* 58, 13–49.

Clymo, R.S., and Hayward, P.M. 1982. The ecology of *Sphagnum*. In: Smith, A.J.E., ed. *Bryophyte Ecology*. London: Chapman and Hall, 229–289.

COHMAP. 1988. Climatic changes of the last 18,000 years: Observations and model simulations. *Science,* 241, 1043–1052.

Colinvaux, P.A., and Liu, K.-B. 1987. The late-Quaternary climate of the western Amazon Basin. In: Berger, W.H., and Labeyrie, L.D., eds. *Abrupt Climatic Change*. Dordrecht: D. Reidel, 113–122.

Connell, J.H., and Slatyer, R.O. 1977. Mechanisms of succession in natural communities and their role in community stability and organization. *American Naturalist,* 111, 1119–1144.

Crocker, R.L., and Major, J. 1955. Soil development in relation to vegetation and surface age at Glacier Bay, Alaska. *J Ecol,* 43, 427–448.

Davies, T.D., and Cohen, A.D. 1989. Composition and significance of the peat deposits of Florida Bay. *Bull Marine Sci,* 44, 387–398.

Davis, A.M. 1985. Causes and character of paludification in Newfoundland. *Can Geogr,* 29, 264–276.

Delibrias, G., and Guillier, M.T. 1971. Sea level on the Atlantic coast and the Channel for the last 10,000 years by the ^{14}C method. *Quaternaria,* 14, 131–135.

Drury, W.H., Jr. 1956. Bog flats and physiographic processes in the upper Kuskokwim River region, Alaska. *Contributions from the Gray Herbarium of Harvard University,* 177, 1–127.

Emery, K.O., Wigley, R.L., Bartlett, A.S., Rubin, M., and Barghoorn, E.S. 1967. Freshwater peat on the continental shelf. *Science,* 158, 1301–1307.

Flenley, J.R. 1978. *The Equatorial Rain Forest: A Geological History*. London: Butterworths.

Fujii, S., and Mogi, A. 1971. On coasts and shelves in their mutual relations in Japan during the Quaternary. *Quaternaria,* 14, 155–164.

Glaser, P.H. 1987. *The Ecology of Patterned Boreal Peatlands of Northern Minnesota: A Community Profile*. Fish and Wildlife Service Biological Report 85 (7.14). United States Department of the Interior.

Gleason, H.A. 1917. The structure and development of the plant association. *Bull Torrey Botanical Club,* 44, 463–481.

Gleason, H.A. 1926. The individualistic concept of the plant association. *Bull Torrey Botanical Club,* 53, 7–26.

Guthrie, P.D. 1986. Biological methanogenesis and the CO$_2$ greenhouse effect. *J Geophys Res,* 91(D), 10,847–10,851.

Hansen, B.C.S., Wright, H.E., Jr., and Bradbury, J.P. 1984. Pollen studies in the Junin area, central Peruvian Andes. *Geol Soc Am Bull,* 95, 1454–1465.

Heilman, P.E. 1966. Change in distribution and availability of nitrogen with forest succession on north slopes in interior Alaska. *Ecology,* 47, 825–831.

Heinselman, M.L. 1963. Forest sites, bog processes, and peatland types in the glacial Lake Agassiz region, Minnesota. *Ecol Monogr,* 33, 327–374.

Heusser, C.J. 1960. Late Pleistocene environments of north Pacific North America. Special Publication No. 35. American Geographical Society.

Hope, G.S. 1976. The vegetational history of Mt. Wilhelm, Papua, New Guinea. *J Ecol,* 64, 627–664.

Houghton, R.A., Schlesinger, W.H., Brown, S., and Richards, J.F. 1985. Carbon dioxide exchange between the atmosphere and terrestrial ecosystems. In: Trabalka, J.R., ed. *Atmospheric Carbon Dioxide and the Global Carbon Cycle*. Report DOE/ER-0239. United States Department of Energy.

Ingram, H.A.P. 1967. Problems of hydrology and plant distribution in mires. *J Ecol,* 55, 711–724.

Iversen, J. 1958. The bearing of glacial and interglacial epochs on the formation and extinction of plant taxa. *Uppsala Universitets Årsskrift,* 1958, 210–215.

Iversen, J. 1973. The development of Denmark's nature since the last glacial. *Geological Survey of Denmark,* V Series, No. 7-C. C.A. København: Reitzels Forlag.

Jones, E.W. 1945. The structure and reproduction of the virgin forest of the north temperate zone. *New Phytologist,* 44, 130–148.

Kaizuka, S., Naruse, Y., and Matsuda, I. 1977. Recent formations and their basal topography in and around Tokyo Bay, central Japan. *Quaternary Res,* 8, 32–50.

Karrow, P.F., Anderson, T.W., Clarke, A.H., Delorme, L.D., and Sreenivasa, M.R. 1975. Stratigraphy, paleontology, and age of Lake Algonquin sediments in southwestern Ontario, Canada. *Quaternary Res,* 5, 49–87.

Katz, N.J. 1926. *Sphagnum* bogs of central Russia: Phytosociology, ecology, and succession. *J Ecol,* 14, 177–202.

Klinger, L.F. 1988. Successional change in vegetation and soils of southeast Alaska. Doctoral dissertation. Boulder, Co.: University of Colorado.

Klinger, L.F. 1990. Global patterns in community succession. 1. Bryophytes and forest decline. *Memoirs of the Torrey Botanical Club,* 24, 1–50.

Klinger, L.F., Elias, S.A., Behan-Pelletier, V.M., and Williams, N.E. 1990. The bog climax hypothesis: Fossil arthropod and stratigraphic evidence in peat sections from southeast Alaska. *Holarctic Ecol,* 13, 72–80.

Kudrass, H.R., Erlenkeuser, H., Vollbrecht, R., and Weiss, W. 1991. Global nature of the Younger Dryas cooling event inferred from oxygen isotope data from Sulu Sea cores. *Nature,* 349, 406–409.

Larsen, J.A. 1980. *The Boreal Ecosystem*. New York: Academic Press.

Lawrence, D.B. 1958. Glaciers and vegetation in southeastern Alaska. *American Scientist,* 46, 89–122.

Margalef, R. 1963. On certain unifying principles of ecology. *American Naturalist,* 97, 357–375.

Matthews, E., and Fung, I. 1987. Methane emission from natural wetlands: Global distribution, area, and environmental characteristics of sources. *Global Biogeochem Cycles,* 1, 61–86.

Medvedev, V.S., and Pavlidis, Yu. A. 1987. New geological-geomorphological data on the shelf areas of the Seychelles Islands and Madagascar. *Oceanology, 27,* 729–734.

Middeldorp, A.A. 1984. Functional palaeoecology of raised bogs. Doctoral dissertation. *Amsterdam: University of Amsterdam.*

Moore, P.D., and Bellamy, D.J. 1974. *Peatlands.* New York: Springer-Verlag.

Neftel, A., Oeschger, H., Schwander, J., Stauffer, B., and Zumbrunn, R. 1982. Ice core sample measurements give atmospheric CO_2 content during the past 40,000 yr. *Nature, 295,* 220–223.

Neishtadt, M.I. 1977. The world's largest peat basin, its commercial potentialities and protection. *Bull Int Peat Soc, 8,* 37–43.

Neustadt, M.I. 1982. Bog-forming processes in the Holocene. *International Quaternary Union Meeting Proceedings,* Vol. 2, 212. Moscow, International Quaternary Union

Nriagu, J.O., Holdway, D.A., and Coker, R.D. 1987. Biogenic sulphur and the acidity of rainfall in a remote area of Canada. *Science, 237,* 1189–1192.

Odum, E.P. 1969. The strategy of ecosystem development. *Science, 164,* 262–270.

Raeymaekers, G., and Glime, J.M. 1986. Effects of simulated acidic rain and lead interaction on the phenology and chlorophyll content of *Pleurozium schreberi* (Bird.) Mitt. *J Hattori Botanical Lab, 61,* 425–443.

Raup, H.M. 1963. Some problems in ecological theory and their relation to conservation. *Br Ecol Soc Jub Symp, 1,* 19–28.

Raynaud, D., Chappellaz, J., Barnola, J.M., Korotkevich, Y.S., and Lorius, C. 1988. Climatic and CH_4 cycle implications of glacial-interglacial CH_4 change in the Vostok ice core. *Nature, 333,* 655–657.

Redfield, A.C. 1967. Postglacial change in sea level in the western North Atlantic Ocean. *Science, 157,* 687–692.

Rochefort, L., and Vitt, D.H. 1988. Effects of simulated acid rain on *Tomenthypnum nitens* and *Scorpidium scorpioides* in a rich fen. *Bryologist, 91,* 121–129.

Salo, J. 1987. Pleistocene forest refuges in the Amazon: Evaluation of the biostratigraphical, lithostratigraphical and geomorphological data. *Ann Zool Fennici, 24,* 203–211.

Sjörs, H. 1948. Mire vegetation in Bergslagen, Sweden. *Acta Phytogeogr Suecica, 21,* 1–299.

Smith, R.T. 1982. Quaternary environmental change in equatorial regions with particular reference to vegetation history: A bibliography. *Paleogeogr, Paleoclimatol, Paleoecol, 39,* 331–345.

Sowunmi, M.A. 1981. Palynological indications of Late Quaternary environmental changes in Nigeria. *Pollen et Spores, 23,* 125–148.

Stauffer, B., Lochbronner, E., Oeschger, H., and Schwander, J. 1988. Methane concentration in the glacial atmosphere was only half that of the preindustrial Holocene. *Nature, 332,* 812–814.

Tolonen, K., and Tolonen, M. 1984. Late-glacial vegetational succession at four coastal sites in northeastern New England:

Ecological and phytogeographical aspects. *Ann Bot Fennici, 21,* 59–77.

Viereck, L.A. 1966. Plant succession and soil development on gravel outwash of the Muldrow Glacier, Alaska. *Ecol Monogr, 36,* 181–199.

Walker, D. 1970a. Direction and rate in some British post-glacial hydroseres. In: Walker, D., and West, R.G., eds. *Studies on the Vegetational History of the British Isles.* London: Cambridge University Press, 117–139.

Walker, D. 1970b. The changing vegetation of the montane tropics. *Search, 1,* 217–221.

Walter, H. 1977. The oligotrophic peatlands of western Siberia—The largest peino-helobiome in the world. *Vegetatio, 34,* 167–178.

West, R.G. 1980. Pleistocene forest history in East Anglia. *New Phytologist, 85,* 571–622.

Yemane, K., Bonnefille, R., and Faure, H. 1985. Palaeoclimatic and tectonic implications of *Neogene* microflora from the northwestern Ethiopian highlands. *Nature, 318,* 653–656.

Zach, L.W. 1950. A northern climax, forest or muskeg? *Ecology, 31,* 304–306.

Zimmerman, P.R., Greenberg, J.P., Wandiga, S.O., and Crutzen, P.J. 1982. Termites: A potentially large source of methane, carbon dioxide, and molecular hydrogen. *Science, 218,* 563–565.

Zimmerman, P.R., and Greenberg, J.P. 1983. Termites and methane. *Nature, 302,* 354–355.

David J. Erickson III
29
Some Aspects of Air-Sea Carbon Dioxide Transfer During the Last Glacial Maximum

The air-sea exchange of CO_2 is critical in the partitioning of carbon isotopes between the atmosphere and ocean (Craig, 1957; Revelle and Suess, 1957; Keeling, 1973; Oeschger et al., 1975; Lal and Suess, 1983). Several models have examined variations in the magnitude and rate of change of carbon cycle parameters (Welander, 1959; Siegenthaler et al., 1980; Broecker, 1982; Siegenthaler and Wenk, 1984; Sarmiento and Toggweiler, 1984; Knox and McElroy, 1984; Keir, 1988). Oceanic circulation (Curry and Lohmann, 1986; Broecker and Peng, 1987; Boyle and Keigwin, 1987; Oppo and Fairbanks, 1987; Boyle, 1988), atmospheric circulation (Schneider and Mass, 1975; Kutzbach and Guetter, 1986), biological activity (Broecker, 1982; Pedersen, 1983; Keir, 1988), and air-sea exchange (Broecker et al., 1986; Etcheto and Merlivat, 1988; Erickson, 1989) all influence the carbon cycle on earth (Bard, 1988). Several mechanisms have been proposed to explain the apparent decrease in atmospheric CO_2 during the last glacial period (Barnola et al., 1987); however, none can explain the entire magnitude of the CO_2 concentration change (Curry and Crowley, 1987). Fortunately, new computer architectures available to the geophysical community allow a close global view of many parameters relevant to the past, present, and future cycle of carbon on Earth.

This work describes estimates of the global transfer velocity field of CO_2 ($K_w CO_2$) on a monthly basis as computed for the last glacial maximum, 18 Kyr BP. These calculations are based on the coupling of parameterizations of air-sea CO_2 exchange and global data fields from the National Center for Atmospheric Research (NCAR) Community Climate Model (CCM) (Williamson et al., 1987). The glacial version of the NCAR CCM is that of Kutzbach and Guetter (1986). The transfer velocity of CO_2 was obtained by computing the Schmidt number of CO_2 at the different surface water temperatures and scaling the values of transfer velocity computed from the Liss and Merlivat (1986) relationship. The CO_2 diffusivity data used was that of Jähne and colleagues (1987). The computational technique has recently been discussed elsewhere (Etcheto and Merlivat, 1988; Erickson, 1989).

Results

Figure 29.1 plots the glacial minus control CO_2 transfer velocity as computed for January. The Atlantic Ocean is associated with higher values from 45°N to 40°S, with the greatest changes from the equator to the North Atlantic ice edge. The North Pacific from 40°N to 60°N has substantially lower mean transfer velocities. As noted by Kutzbach and

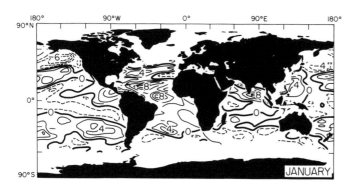

Figure 29.1 The difference in the transfer velocity of CO_2 from the glacial present as computed for January. The contouring interval is 2 cm hr^{-1}.

Guetter (1986), the core of the North Atlantic westerly jet was situated near the southern extent of the ice edge. The different air-sea interaction in the North Atlantic region may have resulted in an increased upwelling of nutrients through Ekman forcing of surface water away from the ice edge.

Figure 29.2 shows the zonal distribution of glacial-control $K_w CO_2$ as computed for glacial January. The CO_2 transfer velocity is increased between the equator and 35°N and from 20°S to 35°S. The Pacific Ocean makes up a large portion of values in the zonal average at mid-high latitudes and the decrease in wind stress over the North Pacific is quite apparent in figure 29.2.

The glacial minus control plot of CO_2 transfer velocity as computed for July is presented in figure 29.3. The North Atlantic again experiences increased CO_2 transfer velocities from the control, as does the Central and East Pacific north of 30°N. The monsoonal winds in the Indian Ocean are virtually absent, decreasing the CO_2 transfer velocity as well as possibly affecting productivity through decreased Ekman pumping.

The zonal average of the glacial-control $K_w CO_2$ as computed for July is presented in figure 29.4. The mid-high latitudes regions have $K_w CO_2$ values

somewhat higher during the glacial run whereas equatorial regions have remained the same or decreased. The absence of the monsoonal winds in the Indian Ocean results in a minium in the zonal average at roughly 10°N.

Discussion

There are significant differences in the global transfer of energy, atoms, compounds, and particles between the ocean and atmosphere during the last glacial maximum. The increased CO_2 transfer velocities over areas such as the North Atlantic are a result of increased mean wind speeds, a finding consistent with an increase in atmospheric sea-salt deposition observed in ice cores (Petit et al., 1981). However, the lower sea-surface temperatures may have resulted in a decrease in hurricane intensity and frequency (Hobgood and Cerveny, 1988). The differences in air-sea interaction may also have influenced the extent of Ekman forced upwelling on a local scale. The North Atlantic is an area that may have had increased nutrient supply to the surface water during the July run and receives a reasonable amount of solar energy during that month. Kutzbach and Guetter (1986) note that the solar energy reaching the ocean surface 18 Kyr BP was within 10% of present values. Due to higher mean wind speeds and mid-continent drying, increased atmospheric loading and deposition of iron-, copper-, and aluminum-laden atmospheric dusts to oceanic areas with ample nutrients and solar energy may have affected the biogeochemical cycling in those areas (Martin and Fitzwater, 1988). This combination of processes may have resulted in an increase in oceanic productivity that would serve to decrease the CO_2 content of the atmosphere (Broecker, 1982; Pedersen, 1983; Keir, 1988). A vertical reorganiza-

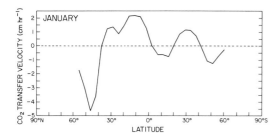

Figure 29.2 The zonal average of the difference in the transfer velocity of CO_2 from the glacial present as computed for January.

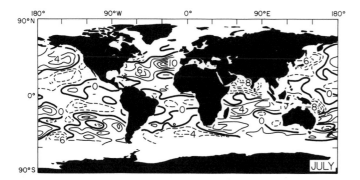

Figure 29.3 The difference in the transfer velocity of CO_2 from the glacial present as computed for July. The contouring interval is 2 cm hr^{-1}.

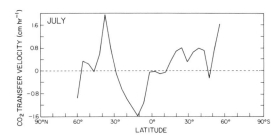

Figure 29.4 The zonal average of the difference in the transfer velocity of CO_2 from the glacial present as computed for July.

tion of nutrients would also result in a lowering of pCO_2 in the surface ocean, pulling down the atmospheric CO_2 concentration (Boyle, 1988). The CO_2 decrease proposed by this mechanism would redistribute carbon from the atmosphere to the ocean through the air-sea interface via the transfer coefficients shown in figures 29.1 to 29.4. This vertical chemical fractionation may be a result of changes in oceanic circulation unrelated to the wind-forced alterations discussed here.

An alternative possibility is that CO_2 was inhaled faster than it was exhaled by the ocean on a timescale of a few thousand years. This would be through a link to the carbon cycle involving oceanic circulation, atmospheric circulation, and earth surface temperature. This could be accomplished if the transfer velocities for CO_2 were increased over areas of CO_2 undersaturation and this effect was not compensated for over areas of supersaturation. The data presented here suggest that the magnitude of the source of CO_2 to the atmosphere from the ocean would be unchanged or slightly decreased in equatorial regions. However, at mid-high latitudes the resistance to transfer is significantly decreased during glacial periods. Should those waters be undersaturated, the flux of CO_2 from the atmosphere to the ocean would increase. This process would be especially effective in areas of active deep water formation or downwelling. In those regions the rate-limiting step from getting carbon from the atmosphere to the deep ocean is at the air-sea interface, different from the most common circumstance in which limiting step is transport across the surface ocean–deep ocean boundary. This scenario would serve to pull down the atmospheric concentration of CO_2 on relatively short timescales. This mechanism depends not only on the air-sea exchange of CO_2 but also on the distribution of surface ocean pCO_2 as controlled by glacial ocean circulation and biology.

Indeed, an additional factor is that the horizontal distribution of upwelling was probably quite different 18 Kyr BP than it is now. This would serve to bring CO_2-rich deep waters to the surface at different latitudes than occurs today. Thus should increased CO_2 transfer velocities occur over areas of CO_2 supersaturation, the ocean-to-atmosphere flux in those regions would increase. However, it should be noted that the global mean transfer velocity was only 10% larger during glacial times than at present. Furthermore, the productivity of the oceans is tied to this distribution of nutrient-rich waters in the euphotic zone. The calculations here suggest that certain areas of the North Atlantic and Southern Ocean may have experienced more upwelling and that areas associated with the Indian Ocean in July may have experienced less vertical nutrient transport to the euphotic zone during the last glacial maximum relative to today. A logical next step would be to force a three-dimensional ocean general circulation model with the atmospheric model used here (Kutzbach and Guetter, 1986) to quantitatively address the important atmosphere related changes associated with oceanic circulation in the geological past.

The distribution of carbon isotopes between the atmosphere and ocean is quite sensitive to the air-sea exchange rate. An equation relating the ^{14}C difference between the ocean and atmosphere to the transfer velocity has been proposed, via box modeling techniques (Oeschger et al., 1975; Heimann, 1978; Siegenthaler et al., 1980) and extended by Bard (1988). Bard notes that if the CO_2 transfer velocity changes by 50%, the age difference between surface ocean and atmosphere changes by 140 years. There are many areas in figures 29.1 and 29.3 where the transfer velocity is higher or lower than the control by more than 50% and several areas where the difference is a factor of 2. Over those areas with a factor of 2 increase in transfer velocity, the exchange of ^{14}C is increased and the surface ocean-atmosphere ^{14}C age difference is decreased by 280 years. These areas include the North Atlantic ocean and limited areas of the South Pacific. It appears that the largest change in ^{14}C content would be in the atmosphere, as the ^{14}C content of the surface ocean is controlled by oceanic circulation (Druffel and Linick, 1978).

Conclusions

The air-sea exchange of CO_2 was significantly different during the last glacial maximum than it is today. This difference is largely driven by stronger mid-latitude oceanic winds, which also may have influenced the extent of nutrient supply to the surface ocean via alterations of oceanic circulation. It appears that both physical and biological forcing could have contributed to the observed decrease in atmospheric CO_2 during the last glacial maximum. The distribution and exchange of natural ^{14}C between the atmosphere and ocean may have been very different during the last glacial maximum. Coupled ocean-atmosphere three-dimensional flows tuned for glacial boundary conditions may allow a more accurate portrayal of past biogeochemical cycles.

Acknowledgments

I would like to thank John Kutzbach for access to the Kutzbach and Guetter (1986) glacial run history tapes. I acknowledge support from the INCOR program between Scripps Institution of Oceanography, Lawrence-Livermore National Laboratory, and Los Alamos National Laboratory. The computational services were provided by the National Center for Atmospheric Research, which is supported by the National Science Foundation.

References

Bard, E. 1988. Correction of accelerator mass spectrometry ^{14}C ages measured in planktonic foraminifera: Paleoceanographic implications. *Paleoceanography*, 3, 635–645.

Barnola, J.M., Raynaud, D., Korotkevitch, Y.S., and Lorius, C. 1987. Vostok ice core provides 160,000 year record of atmospheric CO_2. *Nature*, 329, 408–414.

Boyle, E.A. 1988. Vertical oceanic nutrient fractionation and glacial/interglacial CO_2 cycles. *Nature*, 331, 55–56.

Boyle, E.A., and Keigwin, L.D. 1987. North Atlantic thermohaline circulation during the last 20,000 years: Link to high latitude surface temperature. *Nature*, 330, 35–40.

Broecker, W.S. 1982. Ocean chemistry during the glacial time. *Geochem Cosmochem Acta*, 46, 1689–1705.

Broecker, W.S., Ledwell, J.R., Takahashi, T., Weiss, R., Merlivat, L., Memery, L., Peng, T.-H., Jahne, B. and Munnich, K.O. 1986. Isotopic versus micrometeorological ocean CO_2 fluxes: A serious conflict. *J Geophys Res*, 91, 10,517–10,528.

Broecker, W.S., and Peng, T.-H. 1987. The oceanic salt pump: Does it contribute to the glacial-interglacial difference in atmospheric CO_2 content? *Global Biogeochem Cycles*, 1, 251–259.

Craig, H. 1957. The natural distribution of radiocarbon and the exchange time of carbon dioxide between atmosphere and sea. *Tellus*, 9, 1–17.

Curry, W.B., and Crowley, T.J. 1987. The $\delta^{13}C$ of equatorial Atlantic surface waters: Implications for ice age pCO_2 levels. *Paleoceanography*, 2, 489–518.

Curry, W.B., and Lohmann, G.P. 1986. Late Quaternary carbonate sedimentation of the Sierra Leone Rise (Eastern Equatorial Atlantic Ocean). *Marine Geogr*, 70, 223–250.

Druffel, E.M., and Linick, T.W. 1978. Radiocarbon in annual coral rings of Florida. *Geophys Res Lett*, 5, 913–916.

Erickson, D.J., III. 1989. Variations in the global air-sea transfer velocity field of CO_2. *Global Biogeochem Cycles*, 3, 37–41.

Etcheto, J., and Merlivat, L. 1988. Satellite determination of the carbon dioxide exchange coefficient at the ocean-atmosphere interface: A first step. *J Geophys Res*, 93, 15,669–15,678.

Heimann, M. 1978. Ueber ein geophysikalisches modell des globalen CO_2-kreislaufs. Thesis, Bern University.

Hobgood, J.S., and Cerveny, R.S. 1988. Ice-age hurricanes and tropical storms. *Nature*, 333, 243–245.

Jähne, B., Heinz, G., and Dietrich, W. 1987. Measurement of the diffusion coefficients of sparingly soluble gases in water. *J Geophys Res*, 92, 10,767–10,777.

Keeling, C.D. 1973. The carbon dioxide cycle: Reservoir models to depict the exchange of atmospheric carbon dioxide with the oceans and land plants. In: Rasool, I., ed. *Chemistry of the Lower Atmosphere*. New York: Plenum Press, 251–324.

Keir, R.S. 1988. On the late Pleistocene ocean geochemistry and circulation. *Paleoceanography*, 3, 413–445.

Knox, F., and McElroy, M.B. 1984. Changes in atmospheric CO_2: Influence of the marine biota at high latitudes. *J Geophys Res*, 89, 4629–4637.

Kutzbach, J.E., and Guetter, P.J. 1986. The influence of changing orbital parameters and surface boundary conditions on climate simulations for the past 18,000 years. *J Atmos Sci*, 43, 1726–1759.

Lal, D., and Suess, H.E. 1983. Some comments on the exchange of CO_2 across the air-sea interface. *J Geophys Res*, 88, 3643–3646.

Liss, P.S., and Merlivat, L. 1986. Air-sea gas exchange rates: Introduction and synthesis. In: Buat-Menard, P., ed. *The Role of Air-Sea Exchange in Geochemical Cycling*. Boston: Reidel, 113–127.

Martin, J.H., and Fitzwater, S.E. 1988. Iron deficiency limits phytoplankton growth in the North-east Pacific sub-arctic. *Nature*, 331, 341–343.

Oeschger, H., Siegenthaler, U., Schotterer, U., and Gugelmann, A. 1975. A box diffusion model to study the carbon dioxide exchange in nature. *Tellus*, 27, 168–192.

Oppo, D.W., and Fairbanks, R.G. 1987. Variability in the deep and intermediate water circulation of the Atlantic Ocean during the past 25,000 years: Northern hemisphere modulation of the Southern Ocean. *Earth Planet Sci Lett*, 86, 1–15.

Pedersen, T.F. 1983. Increased productivity in the eastern equatorial Pacific during the last glacial maximum (19,000 to 14,000 yr. B.P.). *Geology*, 11, 16–19.

Petit, J.-R., Briat, M., and Royer, A. 1981. Ice age aerosol content from East Antarctic ice core samples and past wind strength. *Nature*, 293, 391–394.

Revelle, R., and Suess, H.E. 1957. Carbon dioxide exchange between atmosphere and ocean and the question of an increase of CO_2 during the past decades. *Tellus,* 9, 18–27.

Sarmiento, J.L., and Toggweiler, J.R. 1984. A new model for the role of the oceans in determining atmospheric pCO_2. *Nature,* 308, 621–624.

Schneider, S.H., and Mass, C. 1975. Volcanic dust, sunspots and temperature trends. *Science,* 190, 741–746.

Siegenthaler, U., Heimann, M., and Oeschger, H. 1980. [14]C variations caused by changes in the global carbon cycle. *Radiocarbon,* 22, 177–191.

Siegenthaler, U., and Wenk, T. 1984. Rapid atmospheric CO_2 variations and ocean circulation. *Nature,* 308, 624–625.

Welander, P. 1959. On the frequency response of some different models describing the transient exchange of matter between the atmosphere and the sea. *Tellus,* 11, 348–354.

Williamson, D.L., Kiehl, J.T., Ramanathan, V., Dickinson, R.E., and Hack, J.J. 1987. Description of NCAR community climate model (CCM1). NCAR technical note. NCAR/TN-285 + STR.

William D. Bischoff and Collette D. Burke

30

Phanerozoic Carbonate Skeletal Mineralogy and Atmospheric Carbon Dioxide

Studies of inorganically precipitated carbonate minerals in limestones of the Phanerozoic Eon suggest a secular variation in the original mineralogy of the precipitates. Episodes of predominantly calcite precipitation have been distinguished from episodes of both calcite and aragonite precipitation (Sandberg, 1975, 1983, 1984, 1985; Mackenzie and Pigott, 1981; Wilkinson, 1982; Wilkinson et al., 1985; Wilkinson and Given, 1986). It is hypothesized that changes in seawater chemistry control the differences in the mineralogy of these abiotic carbonates. Seawater from which predominantly calcite is precipitated is termed a *calcite sea,* whereas that from which aragonite also is precipitated is termed an *aragonite sea.* An increase in the pCO_2 is postulated to change seawater chemistry such that the inorganic precipitation of aragonite is inhibited, producing a calcite sea (Mackenzie and Pigott, 1981; Sandberg, 1985; Wilkinson and Given, 1986). In turn, episodes of lower pCO_2 may give rise to aragonite seas. In both calcite and aragonite seas, skeletal organisms lived and secreted shells that consisted of calcite, aragonite, or magnesian calcite. Using the fossil record, we attempt to assess whether organisms of differing shell composition were affected positively or negatively by the ambient ocean water chemistry that existed during the episodes of calcite and aragonite seas.

During episodes of inorganic calcite precipitation, organisms producing aragonite shells are probably more stressed than those producing calcite shells because of the seawater chemistry inhibiting inorganic aragonite precipitation. Alternatively, aragonite-shelled organisms might possess an advantage in aragonite seas. To determine the effect of changing seawater chemistry on shelled invertebrates and calcareous algae, we organized these taxa into categorical groupings based on their shell mineralogies. Species-level diversification and generic level abundance data for each mineralogically designated taxon were examined as a function of geological intervals associated with the presence of calcite or aragonite seas.

A secondary goal of this study was to test the relative utility of the Gaia hypothesis (in any of its forms) and the theory of evolution (sensu, coevolution of organism and environment) as potential models or explanations of species diversification as a function of changing seawater chemistry. Before the diversification and abundance data of shell-secreting organisms are presented, controls on carbonate mineral stability, on atmospheric pCO_2, and on biological controls of skeletal precipitation are briefly reviewed.

Types of Carbonate Minerals and Their Stability

The most commonly occurring carbonate minerals forming today are calcite, aragonite, and magnesian calcites. These minerals are precipitated most abundantly to form tests and skeletons of marine invertebrates, but also are precipitated inorganically to form cements and ooids. Calcite and aragonite are polymorphs of $CaCO_3$, with calcite crystalizing in the rhombohedral system (space group $R\bar{3}c$, $z = 2$) and aragonite crystalizing in the orthorhombic system (space group Pmcn, $z = 4$). Magnesian calcites are solid solutions of $MgCO_3$ in $CaCO_3$ and are similar structurally to calcite, with magnesium probably randomly substituted in calcium lattice sites. Magnesian calcite compositions range naturally up to about 30 mole% $MgCO_3$.

The differences in chemistry and mineralogy of the carbonate minerals result in a difference in their solubility (stability). The solubility for calcite or aragonite can be represented by the following equilibrium relation:

$$K_{sp} = [Ca^{2+}] [CO_3^{2-}] \quad (1)$$

where K_{sp} is the solubility product, a constant corresponding to a value of the product of the activities (denoted by brackets) of the ions in a solution exactly saturated with respect to the solid. In a solution in equilibrium with calcite, the ion activity product (IAP) of Ca^{2+} and CO_3^{2-} is equal to the value of the K_{sp}. At 25°C and 1 atm total pressure, the value of the K_{sp} for calcite is $10^{-8.48}$ and that for aragonite is $10^{-8.34}$ (Plummer and Busenberg, 1982). Solutions with a value of the IAP less than the solubility product are undersaturated with respect to the solid, and those with an IAP greater than the solubility product are supersaturated with respect to the solid phase. Because the value of the K_{sp} for calcite is lower than that for aragonite, calcite is the most stable phase.

For the magnesian calcites, the solubility is a function of the magnesium concentration in the solid. Although the solubility product for solid solutions has been represented differently by a number of methods (cf. Mackenzie et al., 1983; Walter and Morse, 1984; Bischoff et al., 1987), the most commonly used expression is:

$$K_{sp} = [Mg^{2+}]^X[Ca^{2+}]^{(1-X)}[CO_3^{2-}] \qquad (2)$$

where the brackets again denote activities of the ions in solution and the X refers to the mole fraction of $MgCO_3$ in the solid phase (Bischoff et al., 1987; Mackenzie et al., 1983).

Tropical, shallow waters in the world ocean currently are supersaturated with respect to calcite, aragonite, and a range of magnesian calcites. In figure 30.1, the solubilities of calcite, aragonite, and magnesian calcites, and the saturation states of tropical, shallow seawater with respect to these minerals are illustrated. The values for the activities of the ions in solution were obtained from the Garrels's and Thompson's (1962) model of seawater, which is applicable at 25°C and 1 atmosphere total pressure. The solubility data for the biogenic magnesian calcites were obtained from the "best fit" curve of Mackenzie and colleagues (1983), and those for synthetic magnesian calcites from Bischoff and colleagues (1987). The saturation state of surface, tropical seawater with respect to calcite is about seven times greater than the IAP of equilibrium, whereas that for aragonite is about six times greater. With respect to biogenic magnesian calcites between 0 and about 22 mole% $MgCO_3$, tropical seawater is supersaturated. As a function of increasing latitude, however, seawater saturation with respect to carbonate minerals decreases (Broecker et al., 1979; Mackenzie et al., 1983). The difference in the stabilities between biogenic and synthetic magnesian calcites has been attributed to micro-

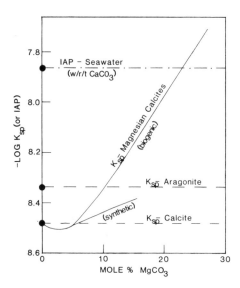

Figure 30.1 Solubilities of calcite, aragonite, and biogenic and synthetic magnesian calcites as a function of $MgCO_3$ concentration. Also illustrated is the saturation state of surface, tropical seawater with respect to calcite and aragonite. Data sources are referenced in the text.

structural complications and the presence of trace elements and carbonate ion positional disorder in the biogenic materials (Bischoff et al., 1987; Busenberg and Plummer, 1989). Few experiments have been performed on inorganic magnesian calcite cements and ooids to determine their stabilities, but their stabilities probably fall between the values for biogenic and synthetic magnesian calcites.

Secular Trends in the Original Mineralogy of Cements and Ooids

Ooids are concentric laminations of $CaCO_3$ precipitated around skeletal grains or other clastic particles in surf zones of tropical waters (Bathurst, 1975). Those forming today are composed mostly of aragonite, but some are composed of magnesian calcite. Cements precipitate in the pores of sediments during limestone formation. Today, cements are composed mostly of magnesian calcites, but aragonite cements also are prevalent (James and Ginsburg, 1979). During diagenesis, magnesian calcites and aragonite are converted to calcite or dolomite. It is possible to infer the original mineralogy of ooids and cements in limestones on the basis of texture and trace element composition after diagenetic alteration (Mackenzie and Pigott, 1981; Sandberg, 1983, 1984, 1985; Wilkinson et al., 1985).

Differences in texture and mineralogical origin

between ancient and modern ooids were noted by Sorby (1879). Sandberg (1975), however, first proposed that differences in seawater chemistry might account for the differences in original mineralogy of ooids. Because magnesium inhibits the precipitation of calcite (Berner, 1975) and can also affect crystal growth rates of aragonite and calcite (Folk, 1974), Sandberg (1975) proposed that an increase in the Mg:Ca ratio of post-Paleozoic seawater facilitated the precipitation of aragonitic ooids (an aragonite sea).

Further studies of ooid and cement texture and trace element chemistry (Mackenzie and Pigott, 1981; Sandberg, 1983, 1984, 1985; Wilkinson et al., 1985; Wilkinson and Given, 1986) led to the recognition of a secular variation throughout the Phanerozoic Eon of calcite and aragonite seas. Because the episodes of calcite and aragonite seas correspond to proposed variations in atmospheric CO_2 (Fischer, 1982), atmospheric CO_2 controls on ocean chemistry came to be regarded as the principal cause of the secular variation in abiotic carbonate mineralogy (figure 30.2) (Mackenzie and Pigott, 1981; Sandberg, 1983, 1984, 1985; Wilkinson and Given, 1986). There are minor episodes of calcite and aragonite seas recognized to be superimposed on the curve of figure 30.2 (Sandberg, 1985; Wilkin-

son et al., 1985) but the curve in figure 30.2 is considered the first-order variation (Sandberg, 1985).

The controls on atmospheric CO_2 over geological intervals of millions of years are attributed to tectonic processes (Mackenzie and Pigott, 1981; Walker et al., 1981; Fischer, 1982; Berner et al., 1983; Lasaga et al., 1985; Kasting, 1984; Berner and Barron, 1984; Kasting and Richardson, 1985; Kasting et al., 1986). Atmospheric CO_2 is increased during episodes of increased metamorphism, volcanism, and when continental areas are submerged so that the demand for CO_2 by continental weathering processes is diminished. Increased rates of volcanism, metamorphism, and flooding of continental areas occur during times of rapid sea floor spreading. This scenario produces a calcite sea.

If atmospheric CO_2 levels are indeed the cause of the change in ooid mineralogies, the mechanism most likely involves a change in the saturation state of seawater (Mackenzie and Pigott, 1981; Sandberg, 1985; Wilkinson et al., 1985; Wilkinson and Given, 1986). To decrease the saturation state of seawater with respect to carbonate minerals while increasing dissolved CO_2, carbonate alkalinity must be conserved with a concomitant decrease in pH. The following equation shows the reaction of dissolved CO_2 with CO_3^{2-} ions to increase the concentration of HCO_3^-:

$$CO_2 + H_2O + CO_3^{2-} = 2HCO_3^- \qquad (3)$$

At any pH, the ratio of HCO_3^- to CO_3^{2-} is fixed; and an increase in this ratio will lower the pH. The lowered concentration of CO_3^{2-} ion reduces its activity, and with constant Ca^{2+}, and Mg^{2+}, the saturation state of the ocean with respect to carbonate minerals is lowered. Lowering of the saturation state with respect to carbonate minerals could inhibit the formation of aragonite and would lower the concentration of $MgCO_3$ in a magnesian calcite that is in metastable equilibrium with seawater (see figure 30.1). As a result, calcite would be favored during episodes of high pCO_2.

It is likely that during times of rapid sea floor spreading, the Mg:Ca ratio of seawater also would be reduced. At spreading ridges, reactions that occur between hot seawater circulating through basalts result in an exchange of Mg in seawater for Ca in basalts (Wolery and Sleep, 1976, 1988; Holland, 1978; Edmond et al., 1979; Sundquist, 1985). Away from ridges, low temperature alteration of basalts also results in the exchange of seawater Mg for basaltic Ca (Perry et al., 1976; Gieskes and Lawrence,

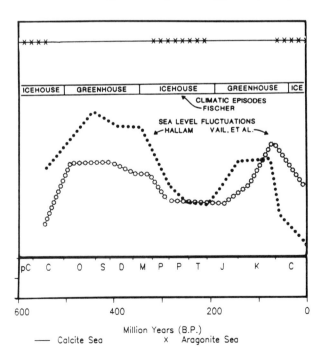

Figure 30.2 Episodes of calcite and aragonite seas, climate (Fischer, 1982), and sea level fluctuations of Hallam (1977) and Vail and colleagues (1977) for the Phanerozoic. (Figure modified from Sandberg, 1983).

1981). Thus it is likely that the Mg inhibition effect on the formation of calcite also is reduced during episodes of rapid sea floor spreading and high atmospheric pCO_2.

Several models have been developed for assessing the tectonic controls on atmospheric CO_2 and the consequent effects on oceanic concentrations of HCO_3^-, CO_3^{2-}, Ca^{2+}, and Mg^{2+} (Berner et al., 1983; Kasting, 1984; Lasaga et al., 1985; Kasting and Richardson, 1985; Kasting et al., 1986). Not all of these models specifically address the concentrations of each of these ions in seawater, and the results do not always indicate that the saturation state of seawater with respect to carbonate minerals is lowered during episodes of high atmospheric CO_2. Nevertheless, the current database used to hypothesize the presence of calcite or aragonite seas does correlate with independently inferred variations in atmospheric CO_2, and saturation state is the most likely controlling mechanism for the inhibition of aragonite precipitation.

Biomineralization

The mechanisms used by organisms to produce skeletal materials are too diverse and complex to be discussed in detail here. For our purposes, however, Lowenstam (1981) and Mann (1983) conveniently have classified these processes into two broad categories: biologically induced and biologically controlled mineralization. During biologically induced mineralization, an organism causes precipitation indirectly from a process not specifically designed for skeletal production. In this case, the precipitate is as much a product of the aqueous environment as of the biological process, and the mineralogy may change as a function of changing aqueous chemistry. During biologically controlled mineralization, the organism constructs a compartment in which precipitation occurs. The organism has limited to full control on the chemistry of the fluid in the compartment, nucleation, type of mineral precipitated, and rate of precipitation (Lowenstam and Weiner, 1989). The compartment also can be used to protect the skeletal material from dissolution. For biologically controlled mineralization, we hypothesize that organisms are stressed by changing ocean chemistries because energy expended by the organism to regulate the flow of ions into and out of these compartments would fluctuate.

Diversification and Abundance Data

To assess the possible effects of Phanerozoic calcite and aragonite seas on the diversity of organisms secreting carbonate minerals, plots of rates of speciation and generic abundances as a function of calcite and aragonite seas were constructed. Much of the data used to assess organism responses to calcite and aragonite seas is from Raup (1976a). Raup compiled listings of fossil species from the Zoological Record and tabulated them according to taxon (mostly at the class level) and according to the geological period during which they first appeared in the rock record. The data are listed as the number of new species in the taxon during each geological period. These data only include the number of new species in any geological period and do not represent the abundance of species living during the period. Unfortunately, these data have been presented incorrectly in the literature as species abundances (Wilkinson, 1982).

Raup also determined the total speciation rate for each geological period by dividing the total number of new species during the geological period by the length of the period (in millions of years). The rate of speciation or diversity was then plotted as a function of the geological timescale (figure 2 in Raup, 1976a). Because we treated Raup's data in a similar fashion, it is important to discuss his interpretation of this diagram. Raup noted maxima in diversity during the Devonian and the Cenozoic Periods. The occurrence of these maxima may be biased by the corresponding maxima in the volume of preserved Devonian and Cenozoic rocks (Gregor, 1970), the corresponding maxima in the area of exposure of rocks of these systems (Blatt and Jones, 1975), and paleontological sampling vagaries including the number of paleontologists working on a geological system or in a particular area (Raup, 1976b).

In this study, we have normalized the Raup data (1976a) to episodes of calcite and aragonite seas. The episodes of calcite and aragonite seas are classified according to the first-order secular variation of Sandberg (1985, fig. 2). Episodes of aragonite seas include the Cambrian, Pennsylvanian through Triassic, and the Tertiary and Quaternary Periods. Episodes of calcite seas (aragonite inhibiting) include the Ordovician through Mississippian, and the Jurassic and Cretaceous Periods. The number of new species for each period of the Raup data was summed for the duration of each calcite or aragonite episode. The number of new species was then divided by the length of each calcite or aragonite episode (in millions of years) to determine a speciation rate (number of new species per my^{-1}). Because Raup did not divide the Carboniferous into the Mississippian and Pennsylvanian Periods in his tabulation, we distributed the new species in the Carboniferous into the previous Ordovician-Mississippian calcite episode and the following Pennsylvanian-Triassic aragonite episode according to the relative length of the Mississippian and Pennsylvanian Periods during the Carboniferous. The geological timescale used was that prepared for the Decade of North American Geology (Palmer, 1983).

The procedures outlined here were completed for the total number of new species as well as for groups classified according to whether they secrete calcite, aragonite, magnesian calcite, or shells of mixed mineralogy (calcite and aragonite). Our mineralogical classification scheme (table 30.1) is based on data from Chave (1954), Milliman (1974), Lowenstam (1981) James and Klappa (1983), and Boardman and colleagues (1987). This mineralogical assignment is similar to that of Wilkinson (1982) except for gastropods and pelecypods. Whereas Wilkinson classified these organisms as aragonite secreting, many of these taxa secrete calcite or shells composed of both aragonite and calcite in varying proportions (cf. Milliman, 1974). Because these taxa are not subdivided below the class level in the Raup data (1976a), we could not separate groups that secrete shells of calcite or aragonite exclusively, and have lumped all the gastropods and pelecypods into the mixed mineralogy category.

Raup's data (1976a) do not include fossil algae. We have also tabulated generic abundances (not speciation rates) of the calcareous algae. Generic abundance data were extracted from the data of Johnson (1957, 1967) and Wray (1978). The mineralogy of the secreted carbonate of calcareous algae is also included in table 30.1 and was extracted from Milliman (1974), Chave (1984), and Agegian (1985).

Results

Diversification

All Fossil Species The rate of speciation for all fossil species from the data of Raup (1976a) is plotted as a function of the first-order variation in calcite and aragonite seas in figure 30.3. This plot may be compared directly to that of Raup's figure 2 (1976a), with the differences attributable to the interval over which the speciation rate is averaged. Raup used geological periods for intervals, whereas we have used the longer intervals associated with calcite and aragonite seas. The longer intervals used in our diagram tend to smooth the maximum and minimum observed by Raup for the Devonian and Triassic, respectively. The speciation rate as a function of calcite and aragonite seas is remarkably uniform except for the maximum of the Cenozoic era. This maximum is probably a bias resulting from the number of paleontologists working on rocks of this age as well as their widespread exposure at the surface (Raup, 1976b).

Also plotted in figure 30.3 is the speciation rate for all the carbonate-secreting organisms listed by

Table 30.1 Skeletal Mineralogy

	Number of Species or Genera*
Aragonite	
Cephalopoda	14613
Coelenterata (Mesozoic-Cenozoic)	8692
Chlorophyta (green algae)	43
Calcite	
Foraminifera	14447
Trilobitomorpha	10420
Brachiopoda	9035
Crustacea	12287
Coelenterata (Paleozoic)	8692
Porifera (Also SiO_2)	1951
Magnesian Calcite	
Bryozoa	5370
Echinodermata	6259
Rhodophyta (red algae)	26
Mixed Calcite and Aragonite	
Gastropoda	15255
Bivalvia	12629
Vermes and trace fossils	2602

*Species data from Raup (1976a); sources for generic abundances in text.

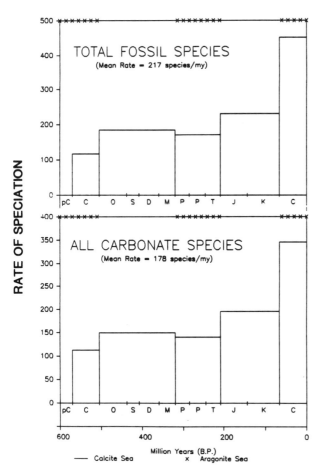

Figure 30.3 Rate of speciation (number of new species-myr^{-1}) for all fossil and carbonate-secreting species.

Raup (1976a). Because carbonate skeletal materials are fossilized easily and dominate the fossil record, it is not surprising that the shape of the speciation rate plot for carbonate secreters is similar to that for all fossil species. The average rate of speciation for carbonate secreters during the Phanerozoic (195 species-my^{-1}) is 90% of the average total fossil speciation rate (217 species-my^{-1}). Excluding the Cenozoic maximum, the rate of speciation for carbonate-secreting organisms is fairly smooth as a function of calcite and aragonite seas; perhaps with a slight increase during the Phanerozoic.

Calcite-Secreting Species   Throughout the Phanerozoic, the abiotic precipitation of calcite (probably originally magnesian calcite) is continuous and not inhibited by the occurrence of aragonite or calcite seas. Seawater saturation states with respect to calcite probably are never less than 1, because dropping seawater saturation states below this value would result in dissolution of limestones, thereby restoring the saturation state to equilibrium with calcite. Likewise, organisms that secrete calcite shells should not be adversely affected by the presence of calcite or aragonite seas. In figure 30.4, the speciation rate for all calcite-secreting organisms (trilobites, brachiopods, crustaceans, forams, and Paleozoic corals) is plotted as a function of calcite and aragonite seas. For all calcite species, there is a decline in speciation rate in the Paleozoic and Mesozoic eras, resulting from the decline in speciation rates for the trilobites and brachiopods. The usual maximum of the Cenozoic era is enhanced by the radiation of the foraminifera. Benthic forams are usually composed of magnesian calcite whereas the pelagic forms are calcite (Milliman, 1974). No distinction between these types of forams could be made using the Raup (1976a) data. The post-Paleozoic diversification of forams, however, involves pelagic types (Sandberg, 1975). Although the speciation rate for all calcite-secreting organisms is not smooth throughout the Phanerozoic, there is no obvious correlation with the presence of calcite or aragonite seas.

Aragonite-Secreting Species   The abiotic precipitation of aragonite mostly occurs during the high saturation states associated with the presence of aragonite seas. It is possible that the secretion of aragonite by organisms during episodes of calcite seas is inhibited by the lowered seawater saturation state. Our results indicate, however, that there is no correlation of the speciation rate of aragonite-secreting species with the presence of aragonite or calcite seas (figure 30.5).

It is difficult to extract exclusively aragonite-secreting species from the data of Raup (1976a). Post-Paleozoic corals are composed primarily of aragonite, but most of the Octocorallia secrete magnesian calcite. Cephalopods are also included in the exclusively aragonite-secreting group. Fossilized cephalopods usually show textures associated with original aragonite mineralogy. Our exclusively aragonite group, then, includes cephalopods and post-Paleozoic corals. The rate of speciation as a function of aragonite and calcite seas is plotted in figure 30.5. There is a general increase in speciation rate throughout the Phanerozoic up to the Cenozoic. The maximum in the Jurassic-Cretaceous calcite sea is the result of the diversification of the ammonites and corals. The shape of the curve for the speciation rate of aragonite organisms apparently is independent of the presence of calcite and aragonite seas, with the maximum occurring during

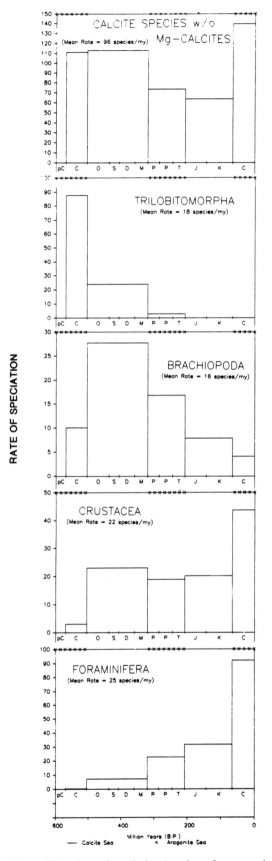

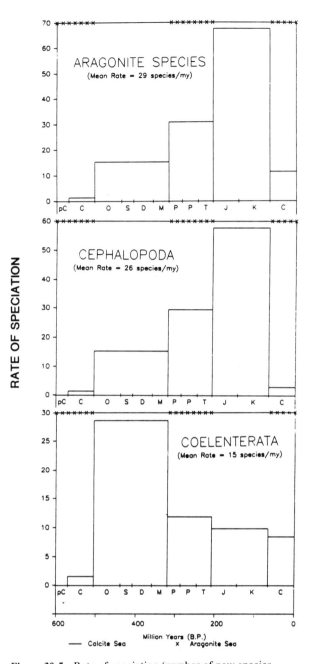

Figure 30.5 Rate of speciation (number of new species-my^{-1}) for aragonite-secreting species. Dominant taxa include post-Paleozoic coelenterates and cephalopods.

Figure 30.4 Rate of speciation (number of new species-my^{-1}) for calcite-secreting species excluding magnesian calcite secreters. Taxa include trilobites, brachiopods, crustaceans, and forams.

a calcite sea. If the exclusively aragonite-secreting pelecypods and gastropods could be extracted from the Raup (1976a) data, it is likely that the maximum in the rate of speciation for the aragonite-secreting species would occur during the Cenozoic.

Magnesian Calcite-Secreting Species Abiotic precipitation of magnesian calcite may be the dominant form of calcite precipitation during aragonite or calcite seas. It is possible that the $MgCO_3$ concentration in abiotic precipitates is lowered during episodes of calcite seas, as compared with aragonite seas, because of the lowered solubility achieved (figure 30.1). Magnesian calcite-secreting organisms, in general, do lower the amount of magnesium in their shells as a function of seawater saturation state (cf. Mackenzie et al., 1983; Agegian, 1985; Mackenzie and Agegian, 1989). Therefore, it is likely that the speciation rate of magnesian calcite-secreting organisms is unaffected by the presence of calcite or aragonite seas.

Magnesian calcite-secreting species included in the Raup (1976a) data are the echinoderms and bryozoans, although some bryozoans also secrete aragonite. The speciation rate data for species that secrete magnesian calcite are plotted in figure 30.6. After the initial aragonite sea in the Cambrian Period, the rate of speciation is uniform except for the maximum in the Cenozoic aragonite sea. The bryozoan and echinoderm subgroups follow similar trends. Echinoids, however, replaced Paleozoic crinoids and other early forms of echinoderms as the principal contributors to the echinoderm speciation rate in the Mesozoic and Cenozoic.

Mixed Aragonite and Calcite-Secreting Species The gastropods and the bivalves secrete carapaces with variable amounts of calcite and aragonite. Some studies suggest that the amount of calcite and aragonite is a function of temperature (cf. Chave, 1954; Milliman, 1974) and it is likely that the variation also is affected by saturation state. If these organisms that secrete shells of mixed mineralogy are capable of increasing the relative amount of calcite during episodes of calcite seas, it is unlikely that they would be affected adversely in either type of seawater.

Of all the carbonate-secreting organisms, as divided into subgroups here, the gastropods have the highest average speciation rate (27 species-my^{-1}) and the highest maximum during any calcite or aragonite sea, occurring during the Cenozoic ara-

gonite sea (figure 30.7). Both the speciation rates for gastropods and pelecypods show an increase throughout the Phanerozoic, with no apparent correlation with the presence of calcite or aragonite seas. Together, the bivalves and gastropods account for 25% of the average Phanerozoic carbonate speciation rate, increasing to 50% of the Cenozoic carbonate speciation rate (cf. figure 30.3).

Algal Abundances
Because the algae are important contributors to carbonate sediments, we tabulated generic abundance data for the red algae (Rhodophyta) that secrete magnesian calcite and the green algae (Chlorophyta) that secrete aragonite. The red algae include the magnesian calcite-secreting families of Solenoporaceae, Melobesieae, Corallineae, and the ancestral corallines. The green algae include the aragonite-secreting families of Dasycladaceae and Codiaceae. Generic abundances as a function of the geological periods and calcite and aragonite seas are presented in figure 30.8. This figure differs from the rate of speciation figures in that a decline in abundance truly represents extinction events. Note the general trends applicable to magnesian calcite-secreting red algae and the aragonite-secreting green algae, as well as for both groups together. During episodes of calcite seas, generic abundances increase, whereas for aragonite seas, generic abundances decrease. This trend suggests that factors relating to the generation of calcite or aragonite seas are correlated to algal abundances.

Discussion

In general, our results for speciation rates as a function of secreted carbonate mineralogy do not correlate with the presence of aragonite or calcite seas. Because organisms that precipitate aragonite are not inhibited during calcite seas (the speciation rate maximum occurs during a calcite sea), as is the abiotic precipitation of aragonite, shell protection mechanisms of these organisms are probably sufficient to prevent dissolution. Alternatively, it is possible that areas of tropical ocean water supersaturated with aragonite are extensive enough to allow for the diversification of these organisms during calcite sea events. It is also possible that during episodes of calcite seas the saturation state is lowered sufficiently to inhibit kinetically the abiotic precipitation of aragonite without decreasing the satura-

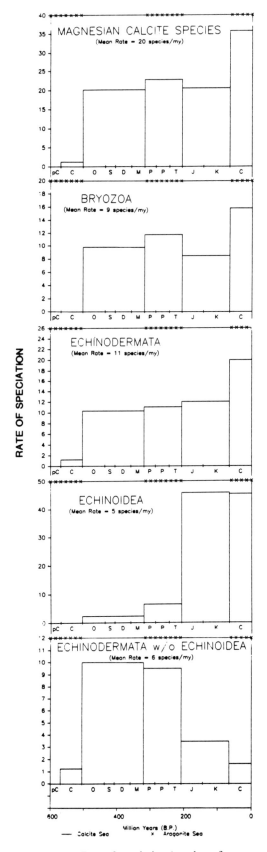

Figure 30.6 Rate of speciation (number of new species-my⁻¹) for magnesian calcite–secreting species. Taxa include bryozoans and echinoderms.

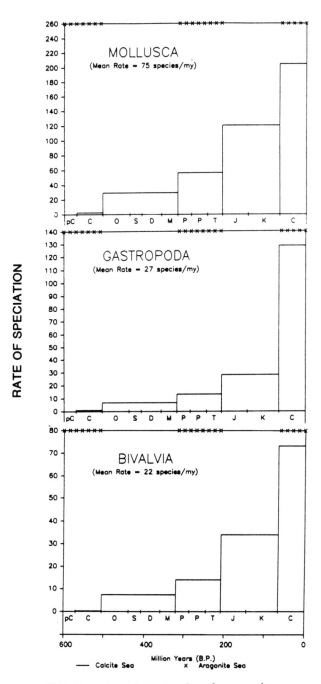

Figure 30.7 Rate of speciation (number of new species-my⁻¹) for groups containing species that secrete both aragonite and calcite. Dominant taxa are members of the phylum Mollusca and include gastropods and bivalves.

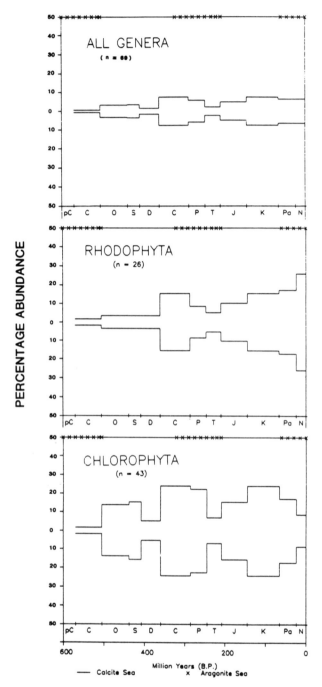

PERCENTAGE ABUNDANCE

Figure 30.8 Percentage abundance of algal genera that secrete magnesian calcite (i.e., Rhodophyta, red algae) and aragonite (i.e., Chlorophyta, green algae).

tion state with respect to aragonite below a value of 1. In such waters, biological mechanisms of shell calcification would not be affected and shell maintenance would not stress the aragonite-secreting organisms.

The Mesozoic-Cenozoic diversification of organisms secreting shells of mixed mineralogy may represent a competitive advantage for these organisms over those secreting aragonite or calcite alone. More data are needed, however, on the extent of mixed-mineralogy skeletal secretion for the bivalves and the gastropods throughout the Phanerozoic. It is also important to assess whether the organisms in this category that secrete calcite or aragonite alone also are capable of secreting mixed-mineralogy shells. Nevertheless, the bivalves, some of which secrete mixed-mineralogy shells, out-competed and virtually replaced calcite-secreting brachiopods. Phylogenetically, the rates of speciation during the Cenozoic for the gastropods and bivalves within the phylum Mollusca far exceed the rate for carbonate-secreting cephalopods. The ability to secrete a shell of mixed mineralogy is an adaptation that provides greater strength to the shell (Moore, 1969) and may eliminate the stress associated with changing seawater chemistry.

The decline in generic abundance of carbonate-secreting algae during aragonite seas and the increase associated with calcite seas is noteworthy. It is unlikely that saturation states control generic algal abundances because the aragonite-secreting algae also decrease during aragonite seas. A more likely controlling mechanism is the amount of shelf area associated with the occurrence of calcite and aragonite seas. During episodes of calcite seas, when volumes of oceanic ridges are large, high sea levels produce epicontinental seas. These submergent modes (Mackenzie and Pigott, 1981; after Sloss and Speed, 1974) provide vast areas of continental shelves in which the algae may radiate. Conversely, during episodes of aragonite seas when ridge volume is small (oscillatory modes), expansive shelf areas do not exist for algal radiation.

The algae may provide an interesting check on the expanse and degree of the saturation states of seawater associated with calcite or aragonite seas. Algal organization and calcification mechanisms are less specialized than those of metazoans, and as a result, their ranges are much more dependent on seawater saturation states. Seawater saturation states with respect to calcium carbonate minerals decrease with increasing latitude (Broecker et al., 1979). The green algae (aragonite-secreting) generally are found only in tropical waters where seawater saturation states with respect to carbonate minerals are highest. In contrast, the magnesian calcite-secreting rhodophytes are found in all surface waters including the Arctic (cf. Adey and Mac-Intyre, 1973; Milliman, 1974). In the more northerly latitudes where the temperature is lower and saturation states are lower, the skeletal secretions of the red algae contain less magnesium (Chave, 1954; Agegian, 1985). Thus if green algae always have had a distribution similar to that of the Holocene, an analysis of the geographic distribution of the green algae throughout rocks of the Phanerozoic may delimit the extent of seawater supersaturated with respect to aragonite for both calcite and aragonite sea episodes. If these studies are completed in conjunction with a study on the distribution of abiotic carbonates, it may be possible to delimit the paleogeography of seawater chemistry (with respect to carbonate saturation states).

Our study of the diversification of protozoans, metazoans, and algal abundances during the Phanerozoic does not easily lend itself to support of the Gaia hypothesis in its stronger forms. Our conclusion concerning the extent of shelf area and its effect on the algal abundances can readily be interpreted as an organismal response to environment, that is, substantiating evidence for synthetic evolutionary theory. Examples of biological control of environment from the Precambrian (e.g., evolution of an oxygen atmosphere replacing CO_2) and for stronger Gaianlike mechanisms today (e.g., planktonic production of dimethylsulfide and the link to cloud production and temperature modification [Liss, 1988]) are used to support the Gaia hypothesis. If the Gaia hypothesis is valid, then examples of Gaianlike mechanisms must be substantiated for the Phanerozoic. The only possible evidence that exists to test the Gaia hypothesis throughout the Phanerozoic is the fossil record. Without this substantive evidence, we are left with an hypothesis that explains earth processes only occasionally.

Within the context of our study, two Gaianlike mechanisms (sensu, biological generation of negative feedback loops) can be postulated. These Gaianlike mechanisms, however, are explained as easily in the context of coevolutionary processes. There exist biological controls on atmospheric CO_2 (photosynthesis) and oceanic saturation states (bio-

logical precipitation is the primary removal mechanism for Ca from the oceans) but long-term, global changes in the amount of atmospheric CO_2 and oceanic saturation states are readily explained by tectonic processes (Mackenzie and Pigott, 1981; Walker et al., 1981; Fischer, 1982; Berner et al., 1983; Lasaga et al., 1985; Berner and Barron, 1985; Kasting and Richardson, 1985; Kasting et al., 1986). Long-term global stability in atmospheric CO_2 on the order of 10^2 myr as suggested by variation in ooid mineralogy, have been attributed to geological processes of weathering and volcanism associated with plate tectonic activity (Sundquist, 1985; Walker and Drever, 1988). It is possible that carbonate-secreting organisms could ameliorate the changes in oceanic saturation state by increasing the production of carbonate skeletons. Also, changes in the amount of photosynthesis conducted by the algae could ameliorate the tectonically driven changes in CO_2. Neither biological process is sufficient, however, to maintain a steady state in atmospheric CO_2 or oceanic saturation state with respect to carbonate minerals on timescales longer than 10^2 years (Sundquist, 1985; Walker and Drever, 1988).

The database used in our study is insufficient to test either of these Gaianlike responses. Although generic abundances of the algae increase during episodes of high atmospheric CO_2, an increase in generic abundance does not necessarily correlate with an increase in individuals. A survey of the extent and individual abundance of algae throughout the Phanerozoic is necessary to estimate their contribution to global primary production. Likewise, an estimate of the carbonate skeletal production throughout the Phanerozoic is necessary to quantify organismal response to variations in oceanic carbonate saturation states.

Conclusions

1. Speciation rates of organisms as a function of the type of carbonate skeletal material secreted do not correlate with the occurrence of calcite and aragonite seas. The diversification of forams and metazoans during episodes of lower seawater saturation states with respect to carbonate minerals probably continues because of shell protection mechanisms. The extent and degree of seawater saturation with respect to carbonate minerals during aragonite and calcite seas, however, remain unknown.

2. The speciation rate of groups of organisms that include species capable of secreting both aragonite and calcite is greater than the rate for groups of organisms that secrete calcite or aragonite alone. The ability to secrete both carbonate minerals may provide these organisms with a competitive advantage over those that cannot.

3. Generic abundance of algae increases during episodes of calcite seas regardless of the type of carbonate mineralogy secreted by the organisms. The increase in abundance probably results from continental flooding and the concomitant increase in shelf area associated with higher rates of sea floor spreading during calcite sea episodes.

4. Although carbonate-secreting organisms may ameliorate changes in oceanic saturation state by changing rates of shell production, or modify atmospheric CO_2 by changing rates of photosynthesis, these biologically mediated events occur on timescales much shorter than those that affect the tectonically driven global changes in the carbon reservoirs. Nevertheless, carbonate-secreting organisms have adapted successfully to changes in oceanic saturation state. Further study of the rates of shell production and algal photosynthesis is necessary to test Gaianlike mechanisms for the Phanerozoic.

Acknowledgments

Many of the ideas presented in this paper were shaped by discussions with participants in the Chapman Conference on the Gaia Hypothesis. We also wish to thank Fred T. Mackenzie and William W. Hay for thoughtful reviews of the manuscript. Acknowledgment is made to the donors of The Petroleum Research Fund, administered by the American Chemical Society, for partial support of this research. Partial travel funds provided by the American Geophysical Union enabled us to participate in the Gaia Conference.

References

Adey, W.H., and MacIntyre, I.G. 1973. Crustose coralline algae: A re-evaluation in the geological sciences. *Geol Soc Am Bull,* 84, 883–904.

Agegian, C.R. 1985. The biogeochemical ecology of *Porolithon gardineri* (Foslie). Ph.D. Dissertation, University of Hawaii.

Bathurst, R.G.C. 1975. *Carbonate Sediments and Their Diagenesis.* Amsterdam: Elsevier.

Berner, R.A. 1975. The role of magnesium in the crystal growth of calcite and aragonite from sea water. *Geochim Cosmochim Acta,* 39, 489–504.

Berner, R.A., Lasaga, A.C., and Garrels, R.M. 1983. The carbonate-silicate geochemical cycle and its effect on atmospheric carbon dioxide over the past 100 million years. *Am J Sci,* 283, 641–683.

Berner, R.A., and Barron, E.J. 1984. Factors affecting atmospheric CO_2 and temperature over the past 100 million years. *Am J Sci,* 284, 1183–1192.

Bischoff, W.D., Mackenzie, F.T., and Bishop, F.C. 1987. Stabilities of synthetic magnesian calcites in aqueous solution: Comparison with biogenic materials. *Geochim Cosmochim Acta,* 51, 1413–1423.

Blatt, H., and Jones, R.L. 1975. Proportions of exposed igneous, metamorphic and sedimentary rocks. *Geol Soc Am Bull,* 86, 1085–1088.

Boardman, R.S., Cheetham, A.H., and Rowell, A.J. 1987. *Fossil Invertebrates.* Palo Alto: Blackwell.

Broecker, W.S., Takahashi, T., Simpson, H.J., and Peng, T.H. 1979. Fate of fossil fuel carbon dioxide and the global carbon cycle. *Science,* 206, 409–418.

Busenberg, E., and Plummer, L.N. 1989. Thermodynamics of magnesian calcite solid-solutions at 25°C and 1 atm total pressure. *Geochim Cosmochim Acta,* 53, 1189–1208.

Chave, K.E. 1954. Aspects of the biogeochemistry of magnesium. 1. Calcareous marine organisms. *J Geol,* 62, 266–283.

Chave, K.E. 1984. Physics and chemistry of biomineralization. *Ann Rev Earth Planet Sci,* 12, 293–305.

Edmond, J.M., Measures, C., McDuff, R.E., Chan, L.H., Collier, R., Grant, B., Gordon, L.J., and Covliss, J.B. 1979. Ridge crest hydrothermal activity and the balances of major and minor elements in the ocean: The Galapagos data. *Earth Planetary Sci Lett,* 46, 1–18.

Fischer, A.G. 1982. Long-term climatic oscillations recorded in stratigraphy. In: Crowell, J.W., ed. *Climate in Earth History.* Washington, D.C.: National Academy of Sciences, 97–104.

Folk, R.L. 1974. The natural history of crystalline calcium carbonate: Effect of magnesium content and salinity. *J Sediment Petrol,* 44, 40–55.

Garrels, R.M., and Thompson, M.E. 1962. A chemical model for sea water at 25°C and one atmospheric total pressure. *Am J Sci,* 260, 57–66.

Gieskes, J.M., and Lawrence, J.R. 1981. Alteration of volcanic matter in deep sea sediments: Evidence from the chemical composition of interstitial waters from deep sea drilling cores. *Geochim Cosmochim Acta,* 45, 1687–1703.

Gregor, B. 1970. Denudation of the continents. *Nature,* London, 228, 273–275.

Hallam, A. 1977. Secular changes in marine inundation of USSR and North America throughout the Phanerozoic. *Nature,* 269, 769–772.

Holland, H.D. 1978. *The Chemistry of the Oceans and Atmospheres.* New York: Wiley Interscience.

James, N.P., and Ginsburg, R.N. 1979. The seaward margin of Belize barrier and atoll reefs. *Int Assoc Sediment Spec Pub,* 3, 1–191.

James, N.P., and Klappa, C.F. 1983. Petrogenesis of early Cambrian reef limestones, Labrador, Canada. *J Sediment Petrol*, 53, 1051–1096.

Johnson, J.H. 1957. Bibliography of fossil algae: 1942–1955. *Colorado School Mines Q*, 52, 1–92.

Johnson, J.H. 1967. Bibliography of fossil algae, algal limestones, and the geologic work of algae, 1956–1965. *Colorado School Mines Q*, 62, 1–148.

Kasting, J.F. 1984. Comments on the BLAG model: The carbonate-silicate geochemical cycle and its effect on atmospheric carbon dioxide over the past 100 million years. *Am J Sci*, 284, 1175–1182.

Kasting, J.F., and Richardson, S.M. 1985. Seafloor hydrothermal activity and spreading rates: The Eocene carbon dioxide green house revisited. *Geochim Cosmochim Acta*, 49, 2541–2544.

Kasting, J.F., Richardson, S.M., Pollack, J.B., and Toon, O.B. 1986. A hybrid model of the CO_2 geochemical cycle and its application to large impact events. *Am J Sci*, 286, 361–389.

Lasaga, A.C., Berner, R.A., and Garrels, R.M. 1985. An improved model of atmospheric CO_2 fluctuations over the past 100 million years. In: Sundquist, E.T., and Broecker, W.S., eds. *The Carbon Cycle and Atmospheric CO_2: Natural Variations Archean to Present, Geophysical Monograph Series, 32*. Washington, D.C.: American Geophysical Union, 154–162.

Liss, P.S. 1988. The biogenic production of trace gases in surface seawater, their emission to the atmosphere and role in air chemistry. In: Abstract published in program for *Chapman Conference on the Gaia Hypothesis*. Washington, D.C.: American Geophysical Union, 19.

Lowenstam, H.A. 1981. Minerals formed by organisms. *Science*, 211, 1126–1131.

Lowenstam, H.A., and Weiner, S. 1989. *On Biomineralization*. New York: Oxford, 25–50.

Mackenzie, F.T., and Agegian, C.R. 1989. Biomineralization and tentative links to plate tectonics. In: Crick, R.E., ed. *Origin, Evolution and Modern Aspects of Biomineralization in Plants and Animals*. New York: Plenum Press, 11–27.

Mackenzie, F.T., and Pigott, J.D. 1981. Tectonic controls of Phanerozoic sedimentary rock cycling. *J Geol Soc London*, 138, 183–196.

Mackenzie, F.T., Bischoff, W.D., Bishop, F.C., Lojens, F.C., Schoonmaker, J., and Wollast, R. 1983. Magnesium calcites: Low-temperature occurrence, solubility, and solid-solution behavior. *Rev Mineral*, 11, 97–144.

Mann, S. 1983. Mineralization in biological systems. *Structural Bonding*, 54, 125–174.

Milliman, J.D. 1974. *Recent Sedimentary Carbonates 1*. New York: Springer-Verlag.

Moore, R.C. 1969. *Treatise on Invertebrate Paleontology, N, Mollusca 6*. Kansas, G.S.A., N 73–78.

Palmer, A.R. 1983. The Decade of North America Geology 1983 geologic time scale. *Geology*, 11, 503–504.

Perry, E.A., Gieskes, J.M., and Lawrence, J.R. 1976. Mg, Ca and $^{18}O/^{16}O$ exchange in the sediment-pore water system, hole 149, DSDP. *Geochim Cosmochim Acta*, 40, 413–423.

Plummer, L.N., and Busenberg, E. 1982. The solubility of calcite, aragonite and vaterite in CO_2-H_2O solutions between 0°C and 90°C, and an evaluation of the aqueous model for the system $CaCO_3$-CO_2-H_2O. *Geochim Cosmochim Acta*, 46, 1011–1040.

Raup, D.M. 1976a. Species diversity in the Phanerozoic: A tabulation. *Paleobiology*, 2, 279–288.

Raup, D.M. 1976b. Species diversity in the Phanerozoic: An interpretation. *Paleobiology*, 2, 289–303.

Sandberg, P.A. 1975. New interpretations of Great Salt Lake ooids and of ancient non-skeletal carbonate mineralogy. *Sedimentology*, 22, 497–537.

Sandberg, P.A. 1983. An oscillating trend in Phanerozoic non-skeletal carbonate mineralogy. *Nature*, 305, 19–22.

Sandberg, P.A. 1984. Aragonite cements and their occurrences in ancient limestones. In: Schneidermann, N., and Harris, P.M., eds. *Carbonate Cements: Special Publication 36*. Tulsa, OK.: Society Economic Paleontologists Mineralogists.

Sandberg, P.A. 1985. Nonskeletal aragonite and pCO_2 in the Phanerozoic and Proterozoic. In: Sundquist, E.T., and Broecker, W.S., eds. *The Carbon Cycle and Atmospheric CO_2: Natural Variations Archean to Present*. Washington, D.C.: American Geophysical Union, 585–594.

Sloss, L.L., and Speed, R.C. 1974. Relationships of cratonic and continental margin tectonic episodes. In: Dickinson, W.R., ed. *Tectonics and Sedimentation: Special Publication 22*. Tulsa, OK.: Society Economic Paleontologists Mineralogists.

Sorby, H.C. 1879. The structure and origin of limestones. *Proc Geol Soc London*, 35, 56–95.

Sundquist, E.T. 1985. Geological perspectives on carbon dioxide and the carbon cycle. In: Sundquist, E.T., and Broecker, W.S., eds. *The Carbon Cycle and Atmospheric CO_2: Natural Variations Archean to Present*. Washington, D.C.: American Geophysical Union, 5–60.

Vail, P.R., Mitchum, R.M., Jr., and Thompson, S. 1977. Seismic stratigraphy and global changes in sea level, part 4. In: Peyton, C.E., ed. *Seismic Stratigraphy, Mem. 26*. Tulsa, Ok.: American Association of Petroleum Geologists, 83–97.

Walker, J.C.G., and Drever, J.I. 1988. Geochemical cycles of atmospheric gases. In: Gregor, C.B., Garrels, R.M., Mackenzie, F.T., and Maynard, J.B., eds. *Chemical Cycles in the Evolution of the Earth*. New York: Wiley, 55–76.

Walker, J.C.G., Hays, P.B., and Kasting, J.F. 1981. A negative feedback mechanism for the long-term stabilization of Earth's surface temperature. *J Geophys Res*, 86, 9776–9782.

Walter, L.M., and Morse, J.W. 1984. Magensian calcite stabilities: A reevaluation. *Geochim Cosmochim Acta*, 48, 1059–1070.

Wilkinson, B.H. 1982. Cyclic cratonic carbonates and Phanerozoic calcite seas. *J Geol Educ*, 30, 189–203.

Wilkinson, B.H., and Given, R.K. 1986. Secular variation in abiotic marine carbonates: Constraints on Phanerozoic atmospheric carbon dioxide contents and oceanic Mg/Ca ratios. *J Geol*, 94, 321–333.

Wilkinson, B.H., Owen, R.M., and Carroll, A.R. 1985. Submarine hydrothermal weathering, global eustacy, and carbonate polymorphism in Phanerozoic marine oolites. *J Sediment Petrol*, 55, 171–183.

Wolery, T.J., and Sleep, N.H. 1976. Hydrothermal circulation and geochemical flux at mid-ocean ridges. *J Geol,* 84, 249–275.

Wolery, T.J., and Sleep, N.H. 1988. Interactions of geochemical cycles with the mantle. In: Gregor, C.B., Garrels, R.M., Mackenzie, F.T., and Maynard, J.B., eds. *Chemical Cycles in the Evolution of the Earth.* New York: Wiley, 55–76.

Wray, J.L. 1978. Calcareous algae. In: Haq, B.U., and Boersma, A., eds. *Introduction to Marine Micropaleontology.* New York: Elsevier, 171–188.

Michael A. Palecki

31

Feedbacks Between Climate and Carbon Dioxide Cycling by the Land Biosphere

The global carbon cycle is a complex system of sources and sinks that interact simultaneously at a variety of timescales. CO_2 in the atmosphere is one of the smaller reservoirs of carbon, but it has a crucial role in regulating the climate of the Earth through its radiative properties (Ramanathan, 1988). Large but nearly compensating exchanges of CO_2 occur annually between the atmosphere and both the ocean mixed-layer and land biosphere. Significant net source and sink imbalances in these exchanges may be caused by climate perturbations. Imbalances may be brief, such as those related to the occurrence of Warm Events of the Southern Oscillation (Bacastow, 1976; Gammon, et al., 1985). However, if net fluxes persist, they can act as a feedback to the climate system by altering the atmospheric CO_2 content significantly. This appears to have happened during the recent glacial period (Genthon et al., 1987).

Although considerable effort has been expended in looking at specific mechanisms for climate-carbon cycle interactions, many of the complex range of feedbacks are not well understood (Trabalka et al., 1985). Improved understanding is needed in light of the unprecedented rate of anthropogenic inputs of CO_2 to the atmosphere (Marland and Rotty, 1984). Because the anthropogenic CO_2 is perturbing both the natural carbon cycle and climate simultaneously, it is important to account for both of these effects. Although the studies of oceanic-atmospheric CO_2 flux processes are extremely important, they will not be discussed in detail here. The major focus here will be the examination of the empirically derived atmospheric CO_2 content and biotic flux changes in light of the effects of climate variations on the land biosphere.

First, the data used in this study are described. Then the two major pathways of land biosphere response to simultaneous climate change and CO_2 increases will be discussed: physiological adjustment and vegetative composition adjustment. The biosphere-climate-atmospheric CO_2 content relationship will be explored over the period of 1970 to 1984, for which high-quality background CO_2 data are available (Bacastow and Keeling, 1981; Komhyr et al., 1985). Over longer periods, estimates of the biotic flux of CO_2 to the atmosphere (Peng and Freyer, 1986; Houghton et al., 1983) are available for examination. Finally, the resulting inferences will be discussed in relation to future CO_2-warmed climates.

Data Preparation and Analysis

The two longest records of direct measurement of atmospheric CO_2 content are from stations located at Mauna Loa, Hawaii, and the South Pole. Monthly CO_2 data are available from published sources for the period 1957 to 1975 from the Scripps Institute for Oceanography (SIO) (Bacastow and Keeling, 1981). Newer data sets from the Geophysical Monitoring for Climate Change were made available for the period 1976 to 1984 (Conway and Tans, personal communication). These two combined data sets represent the background atmospheric CO_2 content recorded away from sources of localized contamination, and so reflect global variations. Data for the period 1970 to 1984 are used in order to avoid some measurement problems during the 1960s (Keeling, personal communication).

The detailed procedures for CO_2 data selection and interpolation are described by Palecki (1986). Following this step, the data are decomposed into a long-term trend, average seasonal component, and residual component. First, a 52-week running mean is subtracted from the data. The average seasonal component is identified by compositing these residuals by week of the year. Then a second long-term trend is synthesized by going back to the original data and subtracting the average seasonal cycle, giving a rough trend with all interannual variations intact. A least-squares fit of estimated fossil fuel usage (Marland and Rotty, 1984) with the rough trend is used to remove the exponential increase.

The remainder is the atmospheric CO_2 content anomaly time series, consisting of the variance that is of a nonseasonal and non–fossil fuel nature.

The first derivative curve of these interannual variations represents the rate-of-change of atmospheric CO_2 content, which is directly related to anomalous sources and sinks of CO_2. Atmospheric CO_2 content, being a cumulative variable, is related to physical forcings by its rate-of-change (Bacastow, 1976, et al., 1980). Figure 31.1 displays the derivative curve for the South Pole CO_2 record. The time series has been smoothed with a 39-week (9-month) running mean to emphasize interannual changes. The smoothed CO_2 derivative curves for Mauna Loa and the South Pole will be related to climate variables affecting the land biosphere. CO_2 exchange between the biosphere and atmosphere is quite complex, but is most responsive to changes in precipitation and surface air temperature. Therefore, precipitation and temperature data are used to bring forth climate-biosphere-CO_2 relationships.

For looking at short-term relationships, climate data are collected for large regions in the tropics. (The reasons for these selections will become apparent later.) Figure 31.2 indicates the regions for which temperature and precipitation data are gathered. The temperature data are from the Department of Energy grid-point surface air temperature data set (Jones et al., 1985). The precipitation data

are extracted from the DOE climate data bank station records (Bradley et al., 1985), which at the time of this study contained coverage only through 1980. Also, time series for equatorial African stations in this data set contain considerable gaps during the 1970s, and so are not utilized here. The selected data are detrended and standardized (precipitation with the gamma distribution), and both are smoothed with a 9-month running mean in order to emphasize interannual variations.

Prior to 1957, measurements of atmospheric CO_2 content are of low quality and spotty frequency. To examine climate-biosphere-CO_2 relationships, a proxy data set must be used. This information can come from two sources: studies of anthropogenic land use changes and examinations of isotopic carbon content of tree rings. Houghton and colleagues (1983) employ historical documents and records to reconstruct a land use history since the mid-1800s. Using this information and a biogeochemical model of the carbon cycle, they developed a time series of the expected CO_2 flux from the biosphere to the atmosphere involved in deforestation, agricultural, and silvacultural activities. An independent record of the net flux of CO_2 from the biosphere to the atmosphere has been developed by Peng and Freyer (1986) from the ^{13}C content of tree-ring wood. This takes into account all biospheric CO_2 fluxes, including CO_2 originating in natural changes of the biosphere as well as anthropogenic CO_2 fluxes. These time series are displayed in figure 31.3. Houghton (1986) suggests that the differences between the two reconstructions may be the climatically induced anomalies in biospheric CO_2 flux to the atmosphere. Unfortunately, the uncertainties contained in the reconstruction of net biotic flux through the analysis of land use records (Detwiler and Hall, 1988a, b; Houghton, 1988; Brown, 1988) or by tree-ring ^{13}C deconvolution (Francey and Farquhar, 1982; Leavitt and Long, 1988) preclude a quantitative comparison with climate records. However, a qualitative

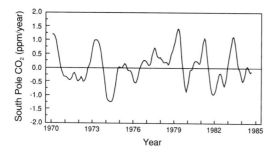

Figure 31.1 South Pole CO_2 derivative time series, 1970–1984.

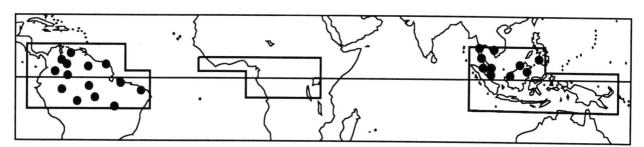

Figure 31.2 The areas represented by the tropical temperature averages are enclosed in boxes; the stations used in creating the precipitation averages are shown as dots.

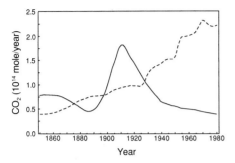

Figure 31.3 The dashed curve is the CO_2 flux from the biosphere estimated from global land use changes (Houghton et al., 1983). The solid line is the net biotic flux derived from ^{13}C analysis of tree rings (Peng and Freyer, 1986).

discussion of the long-term biotic flux of CO_2 to the atmosphere will be given later.

Biome Physiology and Vegetation Change

The distribution of the major vegetation categories, or biomes, is largely controlled by climate. A simple classification of biome type in terms of mean annual temperature and precipitation has been proposed by Whittaker (1975), while Holdridge (1947) has used a combination of temperature, precipitation, and evapotranspiration in a classification scheme. These biomes consist of myriad different community combinations, or ecosystems, but have some essential constitutional features that set them apart. The magnitudes of net carbon storage and other physiological rates probably denote the key biome differences in the present context. But these physiological processes occur over much shorter timescales than actual vegetation change. Therefore, there will be differential response of the biosphere CO_2 cycling to changes in climate, depending not only on the nature of the climate anomaly but also on its persistence. On relatively short timescales, one can assume that the biome structure is fairly constant, with the major natural biosphere-climate-CO_2 pathway being described by ecosystem physiology. Over longer periods, the vegetation populations will adjust to environmental change, affecting the CO_2 flux rate between the biosphere and atmosphere in a substantial way. Also, the atmospheric CO_2 content trends will become important, with plants adjusting to the additional CO_2 in relatively different manners. This will affect both physiological rates and competitive advantage within the ecosystem.

Physiology

A general model of plant physiology can be used as a simple tool for looking at a more complex ecosystem (Larcher, 1980). The basic processes of living plants include the fixing of CO_2 by photosynthesis (gross primary productivity, GPP), and the use of photosynthates in plant material construction (net primary productivity, NPP) or plant maintenance needs (autotrophic respiration, R_a). Therefore, the amount of CO_2 removed from the atmosphere is expressed by the equation, $NPP = GPP - R_a$. When thinking about more than one plant, a useful concept is the net ecosystem productivity (NEP) (Gates, 1985). This is the balance between CO_2 drawdown by NPP and the return of CO_2 to the atmosphere by organic litter decay (heterotrophic respiration, R_h): $NEP = NPP - R_h$. These various rates are dependent on the availability of light, nutrients, air temperature, and soil moisture. Temperature and precipitation anomalies will be the focus for examining the potential effects of climate variability on CO_2 cycling by an ecosystem.

Gross primary productivity and R_a rates of plants are governed by van Hoff's reaction-rate/temperature rule (Larcher, 1980). Both will increase at some exponential rate as temperature increases. However, availability of CO_2 will limit GPP to a maximum level, while R_a is limited only by the inhibition of enzymes at high temperature. Therefore there will be a temperature at which NPP will maximize, followed by a stabilization or even slight lowering of NPP with increasing temperature. Higher than normal temperatures could reach beyond this optimum. A key additional factor is the increase of R_h with temperature by a similar exponential-type function (Ford, 1982). Thus while NPP remains stable or decreases as temperature increases beyond optimum, NEP, the total ecosystem CO_2 storage flux, will decrease.

The carbon flux balance is much more sensitive to water stress. Water availability to a plant in a given physical environment (soils, nutrients, etc.) is dependent on both temperature and precipitation. Both increased evapotranspiration at higher temperatures and decreased precipitation will cause soil moisture levels to go down. As water stress occurs, stomatal openings close to limit evapotranspirative water loss, effectively reducing CO_2 influx. At a critical leaf water potential, NPP usually falls off rapidly. Under severe drought conditions, plants will drop increased amounts of litter. While R_h also decreases in a severe drought (Pomeroy and Service, 1986), this litter will be available for later return to the atmosphere, either when heterotrophs are moistened enough or through the agency of fire (Malingreau et al., 1985). In fact, the completeness and frequency of burns, both natural and anthropogenic, are greatly heightened during drought, even in tropical regions (Fearnside, 1984).

The best opportunity for climate-related physiological variations to impact global atmospheric CO_2 content would be in regions where NPP and R_h are usually very high. Fairly small climate perturbations could cause large biotic CO_2 flux anomalies. Also, regions with quite homogeneous climate anomalies over large areas would have an undiluted CO_2 signal. These criteria are met in the tropical regions. NPP is very high in general, especially in the rainforest regions (Lieth and Box, 1977; Box, 1978). Unlike the extratropics, the tropical land regions respond in a fairly uniform manner to the Southern oscillation, a tropical Pacific climate pattern associated with coherent climate anomalies over the major tropical land areas (Webster and Chang, 1988; Yarnal and Kiladis, 1985). This includes both a hot and dry phase (Warm Events) that could enhance biotic flux of CO_2 to the atmosphere and a cooler and wetter phase (Cold Events) with an opposite impact on global atmospheric CO_2 levels. Biosphere-climate-atmospheric CO_2 content linkages will be sought in the short term using the direct measurement records of Mauna Loa and the South Pole.

Biome physiology and CO_2 exchange with the atmosphere may also be affected directly by the increase in atmospheric CO_2 levels due to anthropogenic releases. Changes will take place in natural ecosystems over many years but have been assessed only in brief controlled experiments so far. Because photosynthesis in many plants is CO_2 limited, higher atmospheric CO_2 levels are likely to increase the GPP (and thus NPP) of standing vegetation. This is well known as the CO_2 fertilization effect, defined by a biotic growth factor that represents the fractional change in NPP that occurs with a change in atmospheric CO_2 content (Bacastow and Keeling, 1973). However, it is still unclear how much this will change NEP, as increased litter may still be returned naturally to the atmosphere by increased rates of heterotrophic activity (Oechel and Strain, 1985). Standing wood increases would be a long-lasting sink to atmospheric CO_2, however. A second and potentially more important biological

response to increased atmospheric CO_2 would be an increase in plant water use efficiency. Stomatal openings could remain partially closed while receiving all the needed CO_2 from the atmosphere, reducing plant evapotranspiration for each unit area of leaf. Increases in leaf size, though, may counteract much of this benefit by exposing more leaf area for evapotranspiration (Acock and Allen, 1985).

These combined physiological feedbacks to climate and to atmospheric CO_2 content change cannot be directly measured at large spatial scales. For shorter-term physiological feedbacks, direct comparison of tropical climate observations and atmospheric CO_2 content changes will be made. For the longer time record of net biospheric CO_2 flux, the physiological responses must be considered along with additional feedbacks related to the actual changes in vegetation composition over the last 130 years.

Vegetation Composition

Much research has focused on the evolution of vegetation distributions at the time of the deglaciation of North America. Especially noteworthy are efforts to reconstruct the changes of species locations through time using paleoecological data and models (Webb, 1985; Delcourt and Delcourt, 1987; Solomon and Tharp, 1985). These studies indicate that as temperatures moderated, boreal forests replaced tundra and ice cover, while higher NPP deciduous and evergreen forests expanded their coverage at the expense of grasslands. For the land biosphere as a whole, oceanic $\delta^{13}C$ records reveal that global land biosphere carbon storage may have increased by one-third coming out of the last glaciation (Keigwin and Boyle, 1985). An overall change to a warmer, moister global climate led to increased land biosphere carbon storage, slowly drawing down a net flux of atmospheric CO_2 over a long period. The opposite occurred at the beginning of the glacial advance; higher carbon storage biomes were reduced in extent and replaced with biomes of less carbon storage, releasing CO_2 to the atmosphere and oceans. Thus unlike the physiological processes mentioned earlier, vegetation composition changes associated with large, long-term climate changes act as a negative feedback to climate, releasing CO_2 during cooling and absorbing CO_2 during warming.

Over the last 130 years, one would not expect to see vast natural biome shifts, although anthropogenic land use changes have been ubiquitous. Vegetation change related to recovery from anthropogenic disturbance could result in a significant drawdown of CO_2 if climate change allows for accelerated plant regeneration. These processes will also be aided by increased atmospheric CO_2 levels (Trabalka et al., 1985). Unmanaged vegetation composition will adjust slowly within the context of succession. Modeling studies indicate that as a projected CO_2-induced warming occurs, large vegetation alterations at high latitudes may be expected (Emanuel et al., 1985a, b). This would involve some drawdown of atmospheric CO_2 as boreal forest limits move northward. Some simultaneous changes may work in the opposite direction, however. A model of carbon storage in eastern North America indicates that although storage is enhanced at northern latitudes, the southeast United States region may lose stored carbon due to vegetation decline and release of soil carbon (Solomon et al., 1984). This would be related to increased water stress in the warmer climate. It is therefore not clear in which direction vegetation composition changes will affect global CO_2 cycling due to climate change in the recent past.

Interannual Variations in Atmospheric Carbon Dioxide and Biosphere-Climate-Carbon Dioxide Cycling Linkages

Two main approaches are used to bring out the biosphere-climate-atmospheric CO_2 content relationships over interannual time periods. Lag correlations are employed to establish the phase between the climate variations and the CO_2 derivative changes. As mentioned earlier, the times of the strongest linkage between climate and CO_2 derivatives are during extreme events of the Southern Oscillation. Composites of the response of climate and CO_2 variables during Warm Events and Cold Events are presented that demonstrate very clearly the relationships indicated by the lag correlation results. Strong correlations with a leading phase manifest the large role played by climate variations in the carbon cycling of the tropical biosphere.

Lag Correlations

To facilitate comparison of the CO_2 and climate data, the South Pole CO_2 derivative (flux anomaly) time series is depicted alongside the tropical land surface air temperature and precipitation time series (figures 31.4a, b). A considerable correspondence is evident between the anomalous net CO_2 fluxes to the atmosphere and the tropical climate time series. The air temperature series is positively correlated with the CO_2 time series, but shows some phase shifts and amplitude incongruities. The precipitation series is apparently locked in phase, leading and negatively correlated to the CO_2 flux anomalies (troughs in precipitation lead peaks in atmospheric CO_2 derivatives). This is confirmed in calculating the lag correlations between the climate and CO_2 derivative time series (table 31.1). All correlations are significant, and the signs of the relationships are exactly as expected from the phys-

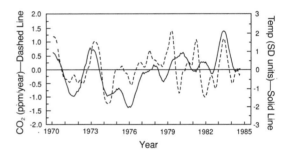

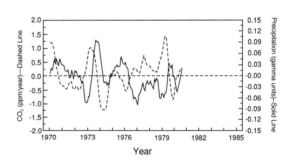

Figure 31.4 Comparisons of South Pole CO_2 derivatives (dashed) with (a) tropical land surface air temperature departures and (b) tropical land precipitation departures.

Table 31.1 Correlation of CO_2 Derivatives with Tropical Climate, 1970–1984

CO_2 Station	Climate Variable	Lag	Correlation
South Pole	Temperature	0, − 1	0.47
Mauna Loa	Temperature	0	0.47
South Pole	Precipitation	+ 5	− 0.77
Mauna Loa	Precipitation	+ 1	− 0.43

iological arguments given previously. A decrease in precipitation, augmented by an associated increase in temperature, causes a net anomalous flux of CO_2 to the atmosphere, as is indicated by a positive CO_2 derivative departure at nearly the same time.

The lag results indicate that the climate anomalies generally lead the CO_2 flux anomalies or occur simultaneously. One would expect CO_2 sources or sinks in the tropics to mix hemispherically within 1 to 2 months (Pearman and Hyson, 1980). Some ambiguity exists in the correlation lag relationships, which may have resulted from both analytic problems and the complexity of the global carbon cycle. Most simply, the averaging of place-specific climate anomalies over a very large region can include nonsimultaneous departures, especially when the Southern Oscillation is not at an extreme. Also important to consider is the exact timing of the biosphere physiological responses to climate perturbations, which would be affected by the phenology of the plants. There is some seasonality to leaf formation even in the tropical evergreen forests (Larcher, 1980). Finally, CO_2 anomalous sources and sinks elsewhere may complicate the global signal, including flux imbalances in the oceans (Bacastow, 1979; Hanson et al., 1981) or in extratropical land biota. In fact, the weaker correlations between the Mauna Loa CO_2 signal and tropical precipitation may be explained by the effects of flux imbalances in the large biomass of the Northern Hemisphere. Still, the correlation analysis indicates that water availability and temperature impacts on the tropical land biosphere cause a large portion of the interannual global net CO_2 flux anomalies.

Superposed Epoch Analysis
Superposed epoch analysis is a technique employed to create representative composites of climatological events that recur at irregular intervals (Bradley et al., 1987a). Segments of a climatological time series surrounding the dates of occurrence of an event type are aligned in time; following this, the individual data values corresponding to each time unit of the segment are averaged to create the composite time series of the event. In this case, composites of the South Pole CO_2 derivatives and tropical land surface air temperature and precipitation departures are produced, running from 24 months before to 24 months after April of the year during which a Southern Oscillation extreme occurs. The Warm Event base years used here are 1972, 1976, and 1982; the Cold Event base years are 1970, 1973, and

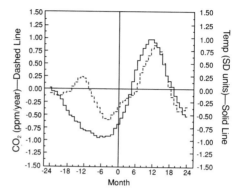

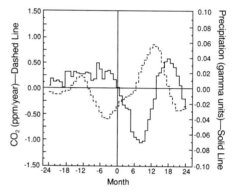

Figure 31.5 Composite Warm Event South Pole CO_2 derivatives for the events in 1972, 1976, and 1982 (dashed), in comparison with composite (a) tropical land surface air temperatures and (b) tropical land precipitation.

1975 (Bradley et al., 1987a). Precipitation data extend only to 1980, so this Warm Event composite is made from just the two earlier events.

For both the Warm and Cold Event times, the relationship between the South Pole CO_2 derivative and the temperature and precipitation composites are extremely clear. Looking at the Warm Events (figure 31.5a, b), it appears that precipitation varies first, with air temperature changes following and CO_2 flux anomalies responding to both. The same phase relationship is apparent with the Cold Event composites (figure 31.6a, b), perhaps even more clearly because the precipitation composite is based on the same three events as the CO_2 derivative composite. Correlations of the composite patterns (table 31.2) show that very strong relationships exist between the South Pole record of anomalous CO_2 fluxes and tropical climate, with proper phase lags predominating.

While correlations such as these do not provide absolute assurance of a causal relationship, such an interannual biosphere-climate-CO_2 cycling link is strongly indicated by these results. Direct measurements of the net biotic CO_2 flux to the atmosphere are now being made by analyzing changes in atmospheric ^{13}C content (Keeling et al., 1984). Considerable biotic flux anomalies have been observed during the 1982 and 1986 Warm Events, tending to confirm the statistical results (Keeling, personal communication).

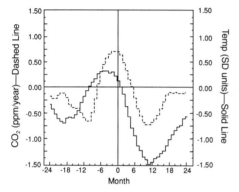

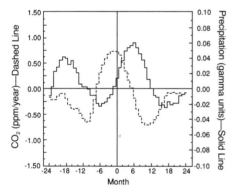

Figure 31.6 Composite Cold Event South Pole CO_2 derivatives for the events in 1970, 1973, and 1975 (dashed), in comparison with composite (a) tropical land surface air temperatures and (b) tropical land precipitation.

Discussion

The land biosphere is dynamically linked to the global carbon cycle, with especially rapid exchanges of CO_2 taking place between the biosphere and atmosphere. Biotic CO_2 flux rates are responsive to climate variability and climate change, but these fluxes can themselves affect climate if they persist. In the short term, interannual variations in global atmospheric CO_2 content are shown to be related to large-scale climate anomalies in the tropics. The physiological effect of above-normal temperatures and below-normal precipitation lead to anomalous releases of CO_2 from the biota to the atmosphere. Under these conditions, NPP is decreased while R_h and fire frequency increase greatly. The opposite appears to occur in conditions of ample rains and reduced temperatures, which allow for above-normal carbon utilization by plants. In both cases, it appears that water availability to plants is the key environmental factor.

At longer timescales, carbon storage in the land biosphere that is not being directly impacted by human land use changes may be increasing. The divergence between the biotic flux curves (figure 31.3) of Houghton and colleagues (1983) and Peng and Freyer (1986) may be caused by the changes in climate over the last 50 years (Houghton, 1986). While the accuracy of either estimation method is uncertain (Detwiler and Hall, 1988a, b; Houghton, 1988; Brown, 1988; Francey and Farquhar, 1982; Leavitt and Long, 1988), it seems likely that some biotic CO_2 flux has been partially compensating for the large land use changes that have occurred in the twentieth century. Another method of estimating net biotic flux (Siegenthaler and Oeschger, 1987) also finds only a small flux of CO_2 from the biosphere in recent times; this is in sharp contrast to expectations based on land use changes (Houghton et al., 1985). Some other segment of the biosphere

Table 31.2 Correlation of CO_2 Derivative and Tropical Climate Southern Oscillation Event Composites

CO_2 Station	Climate Variable	Lag	Correlation
	Warm Events		
South Pole	Temperature	$+1$	0.80
Mauna Loa	Temperature	$0, -1$	0.65
South Pole	Precipitation	$+5$	-0.88
Mauna Loa	Precipitation	$+3$	-0.77
	Cold Events		
South Pole	Temperature	$+2, +1$	0.75
Mauna Loa	Temperature	$+3, +2$	0.73
South Pole	Precipitation	$+6$	-0.81
Mauna Loa	Precipitation	$+5$	-0.55

must be utilizing atmospheric CO_2 at an increasing rate in order to keep the net biotic flux very small. The details of this drawdown of CO_2 into the biosphere are not completely clear, although it probably occurs in response to improved growing conditions in terms of climate and atmospheric CO_2 levels. In higher latitudes, vegetation expansion in response to significantly longer growing seasons may be important. At other latitudes the increase in biomass and carbon accumulation may be more subtle, taking the form of increased rates of forest regeneration by gap filling and increases in photosynthates stored as woody tissue. The combined effect of increasing atmospheric CO_2 (LaMarche et al., 1984) and precipitation in the Northern Hemisphere since the mid-nineteenth century (Bradley et al., 1987b) may result in more water being available to plants, even with the well-known temperature increase during this period (Jones et al., 1986). It is possible that a combination of CO_2 availability and climate change may have resulted in the enhancement of natural biospheric CO_2 sinks over long periods.

The shorter term biosphere-climate-CO_2 cycling linkages are of the nature of a positive feedback. A rapid interannual fluctuation in climate causes an anomalous CO_2 flux between the biosphere and atmosphere in a complementary sense. Warm and drier conditions lead to an increase in atmospheric CO_2, which would lead to conditions warmer still. However, the feedback loop is incomplete in practice, as the climate shifts independently to a cooler state before a sufficient amount of CO_2 is released to be radiatively effective in increasing temperatures. The longer-term enhancement in the drawdown of CO_2 by the biosphere noted above is potentially a response to increased atmospheric CO_2 levels and to warming and moistening climates. The biosphere-climate-CO_2 cycling linkages in this case are of the nature of a negative feedback. The ecosystems that are not being altered appear to be increasing net carbon storage; in taking advantage of improved growing conditions, the biosphere is also limiting the rate-of-change of atmospheric CO_2 content. This would be expected if the land bio-

sphere is acting as a Gaian regulatory agent to stabilize global environmental conditions (Lovelock, 1988).

The implications for the near future are important. In table 31.3, the feedback characteristics of biosphere-atmosphere CO_2 flux exchanges are broken down on several timescales. Rapid, brief climate fluctuations engender a positive biospheric CO_2 flux feedback, while long-term changes bring about a negative feedback. In the last 50 years, the negative feedback loop seems to have become increasingly important, compensating for much of the CO_2 flux to the atmosphere from land use changes. The natural land biosphere has acted as a negative feedback to the atmospheric CO_2 content and its radiative forcing. However, if rapid warming occurs as expected and is sustained for many years, severe water stress may result over large areas of the land biosphere. This could cause the positive feedback loop to become increasingly active over time. NEP may decrease despite the fertilization effect if climate conditions grow hostile faster than vegetation adjustments can take place. In addition, continuing reductions of the extent of the remaining biosphere by human usage could limit the ability of the remaining biosphere to absorb future atmospheric anthropogenic CO_2 releases (Lovelock, 1988). This would allow the rate of atmospheric CO_2 to increase even faster, with inherent acceleration of climate change.

Whether a biosphere-climate positive feedback loop will become activated is highly uncertain. This discussion has not examined the role of other components of the climate system and carbon cycle, such as the oceans. However, it has served to raise the warning flag that at least the land biosphere portion of planetary environmental regulation could be overwhelmed by the speed of the changes occurring due to the anthropogenic releases of CO_2 and reductions of land biosphere extent. This analysis, although not conclusive, indicates that considerably more attention needs to be paid to the land biosphere-climate-CO_2 cycling interactions and feedbacks in order to better model future environmental change.

Table 31.3 Climate-Biosphere-CO_2 Feedback Processes

Temporal Scale	Mode	Feedback Type
<10 Years	Physiology	Positive
>10 Years	Physiology and	Mixed
<100 Years	vegetation change	
>100 Years	Vegetation change	Negative

Acknowledgments

The early part of this project was supported by a grant from the United States Department of Energy, Oak Ridge National Laboratory (subcontract 19x-89685v) to Roger Barry, University of Colorado. The Geophysical Monitoring for Climatic Change program provided data and computer resources; the author thanks D. Gillette, J. Peterson, T. Conway, and P. Tans of GMCC for their assistance. Further technical aid given by researchers of the Climate Research Program of NOAA/ERL is also greatly appreciated. Funding from the American Geophysical Union and the Earth System Science Center at The Pennsylvania State University supported my travel to the Chapman Conference. B. Yarnal and J. Robinson substantially improved the paper with their comments and suggestions. Finally, thanks are extended to C.D. Keeling for his helpful commentary at the time of the presentation of this paper, and to the anonymous reviewer for his or her useful suggestions.

References

Acock, B., and Allen, L.H., Jr. 1985. Crop response to elevated carbon dioxide concentrations. In: Strain, B.R., and Cure, J.D., eds. *Direct Effects of Increasing Carbon Dioxide on Vegetation*. Washington, D.C.: United States Department of Energy, 53–97.

Bacastow, R.B. 1976. Modulation of atmospheric carbon dioxide by the southern oscillation. *Nature*, 261, 116–118.

Bacastow, R.B. 1979. Dip in the atmospheric CO_2 level during the mid-1960s. *J Geophys Res*, 84, 3108–3114.

Bacastow, R.B., Adams, J.A., Keeling, C.D., Moss, D.J., Whorf, T.P., and Wong, C.S. 1980. Response of atmospheric carbon dioxide to the weak 1975 El Nino. *Science*, 210, 66–68.

Bacastow, R.B., and Keeling, C.D. 1973. Atmospheric carbon dioxide and radiocarbon in the natural carbon cycle: Changes from A.D. 1700–2070 as deduced from a geochemical model. In: Woodwell, G.M., and Pecan, E.V., eds. *Carbon and the Biosphere* (CONF-720510). Washington, D.C.: Atomic Energy Commission, 86–135.

Bacastow, R.B., and Keeling, C.D. 1981. Atmospheric carbon dioxide concentration and the observed airborne fraction. In: Bolin, B., ed. *Carbon Cycle Modelling*, SCOPE 16. New York: John Wiley and Sons, 103–112.

Box, E. 1978. Geographical dimensions of terrestrial net and gross primary productivity. *Radiation Environmental Biophys*, 15, 305–322.

Bradley, R.S., Diaz, H.F., Eischeid, J.K., Jones, P.D., Kelly, P.M., and Goodess, C.M. 1987b. Precipitation fluctuations over Northern Hemisphere land areas since the mid-19th century. *Science*, 237, 171–175.

Bradley, R.S., Diaz, H.F., Kiladis, G.N., and Eischeid, J.K. 1987a. ENSO signal in continental temperature and precipitation records. *Nature*, 327, 497–501.

Bradley, R.S., Kelly, P.M., Jones, P.D., Goodess, C.M., and Diaz, H.F. 1985. *A Climatic Data Bank for Northern Hemisphere Land Areas, 1851–1980* (DOE/EV/10739-2). Washington, D.C.: United States Department of Energy.

Brown, S. 1988. Comments on "Tropical forests and the global carbon cycle." *Science*, 241, 1739.

Delcourt, P.A., and Delcourt, H.R. 1987. *Long-Term Forest Dynamics of the Temperate Zone*. New York: Springer-Verlag.

Detwiler, R.P., and Hall, C.A.S. 1988a. Tropical forests and the global carbon cycle. *Science*, 239, 42–47.

Detwiler, R.P., and Hall, C.A.S. 1988b. Response to comments on "Tropical forests and the global carbon cycle." *Science*, 241, 1738–1739.

Emanuel, W.R., Shugart, H.H., and Stevenson, M.P. 1985a. Climatic change and the broad-scale distribution of terrestrial ecosystem complexes. *Climatic Change*, 7, 29–44.

Emanuel, W.R., Shugart, H.H., and Stevenson, M.P. 1985b. Response to comment: Climatic change and the broadscale distribution of terrestrial ecosystem complexes. *Climatic Change*, 7, 457–460.

Fearnside, P.M. 1984. Simulation of meteorological parameters for estimating human carrying capacity in Brazil's Transamazon highway colonization area. *Tropical Ecol*, 25, 134–142.

Ford, M.J. 1982. *The Changing Climate: Responses of the Natural Fauna and Flora*. London: George Allen and Unwin.

Francey, R.J., and Farquhar, G.D. 1982. An explanation of $^{13}C/^{12}C$ variations in tree rings. *Nature*, 297, 28–31.

Gammon, R.H., Sundquist, E.T., and Fraser, P.J. 1985. History of carbon dioxide in the atmosphere. In: Trabalka, J.R., ed. *Atmospheric Carbon Dioxide and the Global Carbon Cycle* (DOE/ER-0239). Washington, D.C.: United States Department of Energy, 28–62.

Gates, D.M. 1985. Global biospheric response to increasing atmospheric carbon dioxide concentration. In: Strain, B.R., and Cure, J.D., eds. *Direct Effects of Increasing Carbon Dioxide on Vegetation* (DOE/ER-0238). Washington, D.C.: United States Department of Energy, 171–184.

Genthon, C., Barnola, J.M., Raynaud, D., Lorius, C., Jouzel, J., Barkov, N.I., Korotkevich, Y.S., and Kotlyakov, V.M. 1987. Vostok ice core: Climatic response to CO_2 and orbital forcing changes over the last climate cycle. *Nature*, 329, 414–418.

Hanson, K.J., Peterson, J.T., Namias, J., Born, R., and Wong, C.S. 1981. On the influence of Pacific Ocean temperatures on atmospheric carbon dioxide concentration at ocean weather station P. *J Phys Oceanogr*, 11, 905–912.

Holdridge, L.R. 1947. Determination of world plant formations from simple climate data. *Science*, 105, 367–368.

Houghton, R.A. 1987. Estimating changes in the carbon content of terrestrial ecosystems from historical data. In: Trabalka, J.R., and Reichle, D.E., eds. *The Changing Carbon Cycle, A Global Analysis*. New York: Springer-Verlag, 175–193.

Houghton, R.A. 1988. Comments on "Tropical forests and the global carbon cycle." *Science*, 241, 1736.

Houghton, R.A., Boone, R.D., Melillo, J.M., Palm, C.A., Woodwell, G.M., Myers, N., Moore, B., III, and Skole, D.L. 1985. Net flux of carbon dioxide from tropical forests in 1980. *Nature*, 316, 617–620.

Houghton, R.A., Hobbie, J.E., Melillo, J.M., Moore, B. III, Peterson, B.J., Shaver, G.R., and Woodwell, G.M. 1983. Changes in the carbon content of the terrestrial biota and soils between 1860 and 1980: A net release of CO_2 to the atmosphere. *Ecol Monographs,* 53, 235–262.

Jones, P.D., Raper, S.C.B., Bradley, R.S., Diaz, H.F., Kelly, P.M., and Wigley, T.M.L. 1986. Northern Hemisphere surface air temperature variations: 1851–1984. *J Climate Applied Meteorol,* 25, 161–179.

Jones, P.D., Raper, S.C.B., Santer, B., Cherry, B.S.G., Goodess, C., Kelly, P.M., Wigley, T.M.L., Bradley, R.S., and Diaz, H.F. 1985. *A Grid Point Surface Air Temperature Data Set for the Northern Hemisphere* (DOE/EV/10098-2). Washington, D.C.: United States Department of Energy.

Keeling, C.D., Carter, A.F., and Mook, W.G. 1984. Seasonal, latitudinal, and secular variations in the abundance and isotopic ratios of atmospheric CO_2. *J Geophys Res,* 89, 4615–4628.

Keigwin, L.D., and Boyle, E.A. 1985. Carbon isotopes in deep-sea benthic foraminifera: Precession and changes in low-latitude biomass. In: Sundquist, E.T., and Broecker, W.S., eds. *The Carbon Cycle and Atmospheric CO_2: Natural Variations from Archean to Present.* Washington, D.C.: American Geophysical Union, 319–328.

Komhyr, W.D., Gammon, R.H., Harris, E.B., Waterman, L.S., Conway, T.J., Taylor, W.R., and Thoning, K.W. 1985. Global atmospheric CO_2 distribution and variations from 1968–1982 NOAA/GMCC flask sample data. *J Geophys Res,* 90, 5567–5596.

LaMarche, V.C., Jr., Graybill, D.A., Fritts, H.C., and Rose, M.R. 1984. Rising atmospheric CO_2: Tree-ring evidence for growth enhancement in natural vegetation. *Science,* 225, 1019–1021.

Larcher, W. 1980. *Physiological Plant Ecology.* New York: Springer-Verlag.

Leavitt, S.W., and Long, A. 1988. Stable carbon isotope chronologies from trees in the southwestern United States. *Global Biogeochem Cycles,* 2, 189–198.

Lieth, H., and Box, E. 1977. The gross primary productivity of the land vegetation: A first attempt. *Tropical Ecol,* 18, 109–115.

Lovelock, J. 1988. *The Ages of Gaia—A Biography of Our Living Earth.* New York: W.W. Norton and Company.

Malingreau, J.P., Stephens, G., and Fellows, L. 1985. Remote sensing of forest fires: Kalimantan and North Borneo in 1982–1983. *Ambio* 14, 314–321.

Marland, G., and Rotty, R.M. 1984. Carbon dioxide emissions from fossil fuels: A procedure for estimation and results for 1950–1982. *Tellus,* 36B, 474–487.

Oechel, W.C., and Strain, B.R. 1985. Native species response to increased atmospheric carbon dioxide concentration. In Strain, B.R., and Cure, J.D., eds. *Direct Effects of Increasing Carbon Dioxide on Vegetation.* Washington, D.C.: United States Department of Energy, 117–154.

Palecki, M.A. 1986. An empirical and modeling study of the relationship between changes in physical variables of the ocean surface and the global carbon cycle. M.A. thesis, Department of Geography, University of Colorado, Boulder.

Pearman, G.I., and Hyson, P. 1980. Activities of the global biosphere as reflected in atmospheric CO_2 records. *J Geophys Res,* 85, 4468–4474.

Peng, T.-H., and Freyer, H.D. 1986. Revised estimates of atmospheric CO_2 variations based on the tree-ring ^{13}C record. In: Trabalka, J.R., and Reichle, D.E., eds. *The Changing Carbon Cycle, A Global Analysis.* New York: Springer-Verlag, 151–159.

Pomeroy, D., and Service, M.W. 1986. *Tropical Ecology.* Essex, UK: Longman Scientific and Technical.

Ramanathan, V. 1988. The greenhouse theory of climate change: A test by an inadvertent global experiment. *Science,* 240, 293–299.

Siegenthaler, U., and Oeschger, H. 1987. Biospheric CO_2 emissions during the past 200 years reconstructed by deconvolution of ice core data. *Tellus,* 39B, 140–154.

Solomon, A.M., and Tharp, M.L. 1985. Simulation experiments with late Quaternary carbon storage in mid-latitude forest communities. In: Sundquist, E.T., and Broecker, W.S., eds. *The Carbon Cycle and Atmospheric CO_2: Natural Variations from Archean to Present.* Washington, D.C.: American Geophysical Union, 235–249.

Solomon, A.M., Tharp, M.L., West, D.C., Taylor, G.E., Webb, J.W., and Trimble, J.L. 1984. *Response of Unmanaged Forest to CO_2-Induced Climate Change: Available Information, Initial Tests, and Data Requirements* (DOE/NBB-0053). Washington, D.C.: United States Department of Energy.

Trabalka, J.R., Edmonds, J.A., Reilly, J.M., Gardner, R.H., and Voorhees, L.D. 1985. Human alteration of the global carbon cycle and the projected future. In: Trabalka, J.R., ed. *Atmospheric Carbon Dioxide and the Global Carbon Cycle* (DOE/ER-0239). Washington, D.C.: United States Department of Energy, 247–288.

Webb, T., III. 1985. Holocene palynology and climate. In: A.D. Hecht, ed. *Paleoclimatic Analysis and Modeling.* New York: John Wiley and Sons, 163–195.

Webster, P.J., and Chang, H.-R. 1988. Equatorial energy accumulation and emanation regions. Impacts of a zonally varying basic state. *J Atmospheric Sci,* 45, 803–829.

Whittaker, R.H. 1975. *Communities and Ecosystems.* New York: Macmillan.

Yarnal, B., and Kiladis, G. 1985. Tropical teleconnections with El Nino/Southern Oscillation (ENSO) events. *Progr Phys Geogr,* 9, 524–558.

VII
Other Mechanisms

Raymond Siever

32

Silica in the Oceans: Biological-Geochemical Interplay

The geochemical cycle of silica at the surface of the Earth is an instructive example of the biological world interacting with the inorganic world in a system with moderately complex feedback loops. Organisms that secrete silica, from unicellular algae and foraminifera to flowering plants, are the agents of precipitation of a chemically simple but structurally complex set of mineral phases. How organisms thus mediate silica in the oceans and in so doing exert control on the chemistry of seawater gives insights into the current geochemical cycle on the global scale. It is also a story that has a history. The silica cycle went through a series of transformations as the earth changed and organisms evolved. The silica cycle illustrates a geochemical system that operates between continental surfaces and the oceans with negligible direct interactions with the atmosphere (recognizing that there is an indirect connection with CO_2 through weathering).

In the context of Gaia hypotheses it is appropriate to question the similarities between a set of complex chemical reactions like those of the silica cycle and the set of characteristics that we call an organism. An organism has a memory in the genetic substance that controls its life, a memory that ultimately goes back about four billion years. The Earth has no controlling memory in the same sense. It has records of past events in the rocks that geologists map and analyze, using anything from fossils to isotopes as tracers. The only overall control of geological events is the plate tectonics of the crust, driven by the internal dynamics of the planet, which evolved with a large element of randomness through geological time. The regime of the Earth's surface evolved as the interaction of the crust with the atmosphere and oceans, again with a large element of randomness in exactly where and when specific surface environmental characteristics arose. In tracing biological-geochemical interactions, we must respect the different ways in which organisms and the Earth evolve. Both are systems with elements of randomness but the two are very different in the ways in which memory controls dynamics.

Geological and geochemical reactions at the Earth's surface that are not biologically mediated, such as the sequence of salts precipitated by the evaporation of seawater, differ from those of an organism in their slow reaction rates and feedbacks. There are no enzyme-kinetic systems speeding up the rates of crystallization of sulphates and halides during evaporite formation. Earth's only equivalent of enzyme-kinetic systems speeding notoriously slow silicate chemical reactions at the low temperatures of Earth's surface is the complex interplay of biological and abiological processes during weathering and sedimentation. For example, the precipitation of opaline silica by diatoms in surface ocean waters is orders of magnitude faster than the growth of abiogenic opals in cavities in the weathering of volcanic rocks. Only when rocks are buried kilometers deep in the crust of the Earth do their temperatures rise sufficiently to speed up geochemical reactions. The feedbacks from a geochemical reaction, even those biologically mediated, are so insensitive, nonspecific, and slow-acting that they cannot meaningfully be compared to the sensors of an organism. Thus homeostasis of the Earth is a poorly to gently modulated combined biological-abiological system that includes significant perturbations such as the climatic conditions that provoke glaciation.

The Silica Cycle Today

Like any other geochemical cycle, the silica system transfers material from rocks on the continents to the oceans, where it is removed and buried as sediment (figure 32.1). The two sources of dissolved silica are weathering on the continents and hydrothermal alteration of basalts at midocean ridges. The latter can be seen as a form of weathering of newly extruded basalt by seawater at temperatures

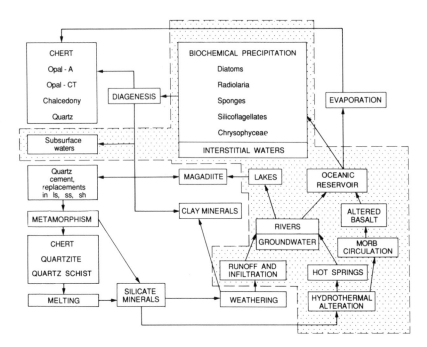

Figure 32.1 The global geochemical cycle of silica.

from 35°C to 350°C. These inputs to the oceanic reservoir are balanced, assuming the oceans are in a steady state, by sedimentation of solid silica as metastable amorphous or opaline silica.

Starting in the earliest stages of diagenesis, the postdepositional alteration of sediment, opaline silica starts a series of transformations that convert it ultimately to the stable phase at low temperatures, quartz. In the process chert (flint) is formed and diagenetic quartz is added to sandstones, shales, and carbonate rocks. Deep burial and involvement in plate tectonic collisions metamorphose the chert and quartz and ultimately may melt them. Both processes form new silicate minerals in these deep-seated rocks, which eventually are uplifted in mountains and exposed to surface weathering, completing the cycle.

Biological involvement in the weathering process is an essential component of the cycle under most conditions on Earth today. Bacteria, fungi, and higher plants all play an important role in weathering. Biology is equally important in the precipitation of silica. Some plants sequester silica, deposited in soils as opal phytoliths. Others, like petrified wood, are silicified by silica-rich waters derived from weathering, especially of volcanics. Biological interplay with basalt hydrothermal alteration is absent. The abundant biota of hydrothermal vents has no role in the high-temperature alteration of basalt that produces huge volumes of dissolved silica.

Biological control of the output from the oceans is virtually complete. The silica output of the oceans is almost entirely in the form of biochemical precipitates: the opal-A (essentially an amorphous form of silica) of diatom frustules, radiolarian tests, and sponge spicules. (The silica of other organisms, such as the silicoflagellates, is quantitatively unimportant.) A high proportion of these precipitates is recycled within the ocean system. Silica skeletal materials dissolve in the water column and the dissolved silica is brought back to surface waters by upwelling. The great quantities of siliceous oozes, primarily the remains of diatoms, that are finally deposited on the sea floor are in the deep sea, located beneath high primary productivity regions of surface waters.

The close link to high primary productivity is through the photosynthetic diatoms. Much of the total photosynthesis of the ocean is carried on by these algae and it is through this activity that the silica cycle is linked to the phosphorus and nitrogen cycles. Silica may be used to mark upwelling zones that return nutrients to surface waters. We shall see later that this was not always so during geological history.

Primary nonbiogenic deposits of silica are limited to a few occurrences in unusual peritidal environments. Although most diagenetic change in siliceous sediments is abiological, bacteria may play some role in the early diagenesis of silica by speeding up the dissolution of siliceous remains in the water column and in shallowly buried deposits (Stein, 1977). Evidence of biological interaction in the past is found in many chert nodules in ancient carbonate rocks that were localized by clumps of siliceous sponges acting as nucleation centers during early diagenesis (Maliva and Siever, 1989).

From this recital it is clear that the ocean is the major reservoir in which biological control is exerted on the silica cycle. A quantitative description of the inputs and outputs of the ocean is shown in figure 32.2. The efficiency of diatom precipitation is so great that the concentration of dissolved silica in seawater is extremely low, approximately two orders of magnitude undersaturated with respect to amorphous silica. This is the primary biological control on the silica chemistry of the ocean. Although seawater is fairly well mixed, there is a range of compositions of about one order of magnitude between the most depleted surface waters and slightly enriched bottom waters. The somewhat higher concentrations of some bottom waters is related to early diagenetic reactions of siliceous ooze materials with their interstitial waters, originally seawater buried in the pores of the sediment.

This diagenetic process, which ultimately transforms the original amorphous silica of diatoms and other organisms into siliceous rock, has important feedbacks into the ocean system. Amorphous silica is unstable and relatively soluble compared with more stable polymorphs of silica, especially quartz. The sedimented frustules of diatoms rapidly dissolve in the interstitial waters of the siliceous ooze to reach concentrations approaching saturation with respect to amorphous silica. As this happens, slow precipitation of a more stable phase, opal-CT (a disordered cristobalite-like silica), begins. At the same time, a powerful concentration gradient is set up between the interstitial waters and the seawater lying only a few centimeters above, the two reser-

voirs connected by an open-pore system. Diffusion from buried sediment to bottom seawater proceeds through this pore network and constitutes an important feedback loop that keeps bottom waters somewhat enriched over surface waters.

Biological processes play a role in this loop by speeding up the dissolution of silica in the sediment. Although bacterial activity is low in deep sea sediments, bacterial oxidative degradation of the organic matter intricately interwoven with the biochemical silica of diatom frustules speeds up the dissolution of the solid silica (Stein, 1977; Hurd, 1983). As silica-organic ligands are destroyed by degradation of the organic matter, the silica, now unprotected by an organic coating and more soluble because of its very high surface area, dissolves much faster than it would in a sterile environment. The bacterial system speeds up what would happen anyway by abiogenic processes. Unfortunately, we know little of the precise mechanisms by which organic matter in silica frustules is degraded and how the solid silica is affected.

Silica Deposits of the Past

Chert and other siliceous rocks were formed during all stages of the Earth's history, at least from the time of the earliest rocks known, about 3.8 billion years old. A perusal of the geological history and occurrence of cherts shows that in past times several different kinds of chert formed in different oceanic environments (Maliva et al., 1989). For the past 60 million years, during most of the Tertiary period, cherts were formed by the diagenesis of diatom and, to a lesser extent, radiolarian oozes. The geology and geochemistry of these formations indicates conditions much like those of today in Baja, California, sedimentary basins formed in deep waters off highly productive continental borderlands. These accumulations of siliceous skeletons

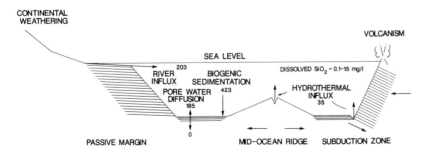

Figure 32.2 The present dissolved silica budget of the oceans (fluxes modified from Wollast and Mackenzie, 1983).

are distinctively rhythmically bedded, more or less pure cherts alternating with siliceous shales on a scale of a few to a few tens of centimeters.

Explanations for this rhythmic bedding fall into four groups: (1) a steady sedimentation of silica with clay sedimentation turning off and on; (2) a steady sedimentation of clay, with silica turning off and on; (3) deposition by turbidity currents with fluid dynamic settling differences segregating coarser diatoms from finer clay particles; (4) diagenetic segregation by which silica is chemically transferred to separate beds (Iijima and Utada, 1983; Steinberg et al., 1983). Explanation (1) would be driven by climatic and weathering cycles on land abruptly turning off and on the supply of clay, a mechanism for which there is little evidence. Explanation (2) would involve the turning off and on of primary productivity in the surface waters of the basin. This explanation has been favored for the Monterey Formation of California and similar formations (e.g., Compton, 1986) and invokes interaction of diatom primary productivity with rates of nutrient recycling by upwelling, which in turn is related to the effects of climatic change on oceanic circulation. Explanation (3) accounts for a large number of orogenic belt–bedded cherts (Iijima and Utada, 1983; Hein and Karl, 1983). Diagenetic segregation, as in (4), probably accounts for a smaller number of bedded cherts. Rhythmically bedded chert-shale sequences are not all exactly alike and probably arise from a multiplicity of causes, some biological, some tied also to climate. All involve the biological sedimentation of diatom frustules as a beginning.

As we go back in time, into the Cretaceous period, we find a change in chert occurrence. There are numbers of radiolarian chert formations that are similar in most respects to the Cenozoic diatom cherts. Some diatoms are present but it is the radiolarians that are the bulk of the bedded cherts. At the same time we see many occurrences of nodular cherts in carbonate rocks. In the latest part of the Cretaceous the nodular cherts are found in the chalk formations of western and northern Europe. These formations were formed largely of the carbonate skeletons of coccolithophores that settled to the bottom of a moderately deep water basin, one whose bottom was well below wave base in most areas. These cherts are formed at least in part from the redistribution of the silica of sponge spicules. The Cretaceous, then, was a time of transition, the sponges and radiolaria giving way to diatoms as the chief biological mediators of the silica cycle in the oceans.

The pre-Cretaceous world of silica was one dominated on shallow continental shelves and epicontinental seas by sponges and in the open ocean by radiolaria. The relatively few preserved bedded chert formations associated with the deeper waters off continental margins are remnants of sea floor radiolarian oozes. Deformed and altered cherts of ophiolites are the fragmentary records of sea floor cherts scraped off at subduction zones. In contrast, siliceous sponges were numerous in the subtidal quiet waters of shallower seas.

The picture changes again when we move back into the Precambrian, when no silica-secreting organisms had yet evolved. There are abundant cherts in the later Precambrian, superficially similar to the biogenic rocks of later times. But a great many of these are silicified carbonate rocks, with some textural similarities to the chert nodules of later times but not at all like the bedded cherts of the Phanerozoic. Many Precambrian rocks of all kinds show evidence of wholesale silicification, in which large masses of carbonate and silicate rock were replaced by chert. No truly bedded cherts similar to the radiolarian and diatom bedded cherts of later periods are found, even in the most likely places for their occurrence, the ophiolite suites.

Considering the middle and early Precambrian we find a distinctive form of bedded chert, the banded iron formations of interbedded hematite or other iron minerals and chert. In some ways, the banded iron formations are similar to the rhythmically bedded chert-shale formations, with the hematite taking the place of shale. Other banded iron formations are arenites, which have an essentially detrital, current-bedded character (Simonson, 1985). Earlier Precambrian iron formations probably involve interaction of extensive hydrothermal activity with the oceans and oceanic sediment. Regardless of the many possible origins of banded iron formations, which remain controversial, they are abiological responses to the oceans and atmosphere that had evolved by that time.

This brief survey of different silica rock types provides the geological background for a reconstruction of the silica regime of the oceans during geological time as it was affected or controlled by the biological world.

Dissolved Silica Concentrations of the Oceans

The concentration of dissolved silica in today's oceans is extremely low, varying from about 0.1 $mgSiO_2/L$ in productive surface waters, to over 10 $mgSiO_2/L$ in some deep waters (Spencer, 1983). The highest concentrations of a few deep waters are close to saturation with respect to quartz but the vast bulk of deep and surface sea waters are at least one order of magnitude undersaturated with respect to quartz, and close to two orders of magnitude undersaturated with respect to the amorphous silica of diatoms and other biogenic silica. Long ago, I pointed out that neither mineral equilibria nor kinetics could provide an adequate explanation for such low concentrations and that it could only be the efficiency of the diatoms that was responsible (Siever, 1957).

As noted earlier, the patterns of silica concentration in the ocean are governed by depletion by diatoms in surface waters, regeneration by dissolution as the organisms sink to the bottom, and diffusion from more concentrated interstitial waters of bottom sediments. The distribution of Tertiary siliceous deposits and the abundance of diatom frustules in them are evidence that the oceans have been poised at their present concentrations throughout this latest period of Earth history.

The siliceous sediments of the Cretaceous and earlier periods do not support that assumption. Both geology and biology seem to point to higher concentrations in the oceans of the past. Although the diatoms had evolved in the latest Jurassic and underwent a period of species radiation during the Cretaceous, the steady-state biomass of all species of these organisms was not high until the Paleocene-Eocene. This is evidenced by the frequency of their remains in sediments of the Deep Sea Drilling Program (DSDP) (Riech and von Rad, 1979) and in formations now exposed on the continents. Thus the oceans were controlled biologically mainly by the radiolaria and sponges, both far less efficient today as silica secreters than were the diatoms. There is no biological evidence that pre-Tertiary radiolaria and sponges were more efficient silica secreters than they are today. There is evidence from the paleontological record that radiolaria were generally more robust in the earlier Tertiary (Moore, 1969). Harper and Knoll (1974) have inferred that the efficiency of the diatoms for silica precipitation put selective pressure on the radiolaria to evolve tests that required less silica.

The geological argument on former concentration levels of silica in the oceans relates to the mechanism of nodular chert formation (Siever, 1986). These early diagenetic products formed by intra- or interformational diffusion toward centers of precipitation (Siever, 1962; Maliva and Siever, 1989). Elevated concentrations supporting diffusion gradients are thought to have been provided by the dissolution of sponge spicules in interstitial waters undersaturated with respect to amorphous silica. Unfortunately, we cannot generally make a mass balance between the amount of silica now in the chert nodules and the amount of spicules once present in the surroundings (now dissolved but to some extent preserved by calcite replacement). In many abundantly cherty formations it is doubtful that there were enough silica spicules in the diffusional collecting region around the growing nodule to account for the mass of silica in the nodule.

If seawater were more concentrated in silica than it is today, the chertification mechanism would be somewhat different (Siever, 1986). Interstitial waters would be initially the same as seawater, poised at concentrations much higher than today's by the balance between inputs and biogenic precipitation by sponges and radiolaria. Early diagenetic precipitation of opal-CT in a nucleating nodule would draw down the concentration in the immediate vicinity of the nodule. Silica would then diffuse in from surrounding regions, powered not only by dissolution of spicules but by downward diffusion from seawater. This diffusion from an infinite reservoir would solve the mass balance problem.

How high would oceanic silica concentrations have been during the long reign of sponges and radiolaria, the approximately 500 million years between the beginning of the Cambrian and the end of the Cretaceous? We can estimate this from the concentrations needed to power diffusion to an opal-CT precipitating nodule, about 50 to 60 $mgSiO_2/L$, much higher than the highest bottom waters of today.

The silica cycle would have been very different from today's. Because the sponges lived in relatively shallow waters, the cycle of settling to the bottom through a deep water column and regeneration by dissolution would have been supported only by the radiolaria. Because radiolaria are separated from primary productivity by at least one trophic level and because their silica tests are much slower to dissolve (Hurd and Theyer, 1975), dissolved silica would have been tied less directly to nutrient recycling and regions of upwelling. There would have been no diffusional input to the ocean from highly concentrated interstitial waters; instead diffusion into bottom sediments would have constituted an output. Dissolution of sponge spicules at the sediment-water interface would have contributed to some regeneration of dissolved silica in shallow platform waters. The effects of higher silica concentrations on inorganic mineral reactions, such as those of clay minerals and zeolites, would have been significant.

Because the silica concentrations of the oceans would have been more influenced by inorganic reactions relative to biological control, the silica of the ocean may have been more variable. Secular variation of inputs by rivers and midocean ridges would have been less damped than those of more recent times, when variation was inhibited by the activities of diatoms.

Finally, we turn back to the Precambrian, when no silica secreters existed. At that time, the oceans could operate solely as a balance between various mineral reactions, with no direct biological controls (figure 32.3). There was a biological world at that time, eukaryotic after about 1.5 billion years ago, only prokaryotic before that.

Here I point out only that there still may have been some connection of biology and the silica cycle, primarily via the effects of organic matter of the unicellular organisms of the time. We know that there are organic matter–silica complexes (Bennett, 1987; Bennett and Siegel, 1987) and that organic matter affects the solubility and precipitation of free silica (Siever, 1962). The mechanism for localization of silicification by organic matter is not clear but must involve a stage of sorption by labile organic compounds followed by a stage of bacterial destruction of those compounds and liberation of the silica to interstitial waters. These effects are more pronounced in the later parts of the Proterozoic. In earlier times, silicification may have been completely dominated by hydrothermal and other

geochemical sedimentation processes. The concentration of silica in sea water during the Precambrian was poised at high levels compared with those of today, perhaps as much as 80 to 90 mgSiO$_2$/L as a kinetic balance between seawater, basalt, clay minerals, zeolites, and diagenetic opal-CT.

Macroevolution and the Silica Cycle

The macroevolutionary changes that dominated the silica cycle over the last 600 million years are shown in figure 32.4. Although a large and diverse biota evolved during the Precambrian, it appears that there was no direct use of silica by organisms. Thus there was no significant interaction between the biosphere and the silica cycle other than some chemical reactions of labile organic matter produced by unicellular organisms. In the late Proterozoic, more complex faunas appeared—the Ediacara fauna—but these metazoans had not evolved any mechanism for secreting silica. The biosphere and the silica cycle remained disjunct.

With the arrival of the Cambrian, the picture started changing dramatically. The newly evolved radiolaria and siliceous sponges began to utilize large quantities of silica. After an initial low-level startup in the Cambrian, the dominant pattern of the earlier part of the Phanerozoic was set: the pelagic ocean became the scene of radiolarian activity, the shallow platform seas the place for sponges. Together these two groups helped control the silica output of the oceans and localized the sediments in two very different environments (though there are transitions and mixtures of the two). The silica concentrations of the oceans at this time were depressed over those of the Precambrian, probably to levels a little higher than the most disordered opal-CT saturation, about 60 mgSiO$_2$/L.

In the Mesozoic, important evolutionary developments began that were later to modify the silica cycle. Most important, the diatoms evolved in the

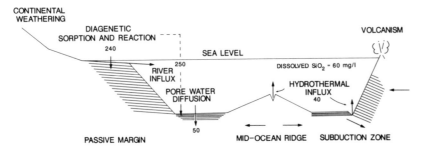

Figure 32.3 An estimate of the later Precambrian dissolved silica budget of the oceans.

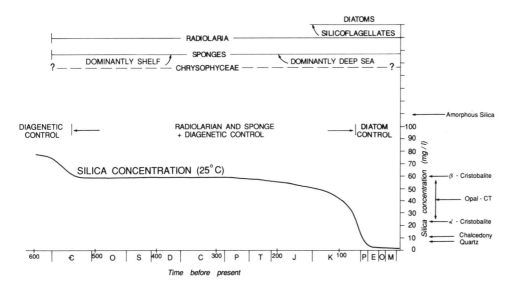

Figure 32.4 The evolution of the silica cycle from the latest Precambrian to the present, showing the ranges of silica-secreting organisms and hypothesized silica concentrations of the ocean. The saturation values for relevant silica minerals are shown on the same concentration scale.

late Jurassic. So too did the silicoflagellates, but they were and have remained quantitatively unimportant in silica sedimentation. On land, and in small part migrating to marine environments, the angiosperms evolved, and with them, a variety of silica secreters, especially the grasses and relatives. During the Mesozoic the large populations of siliceous sponges that in the Paleozoic had lived in the shallow waters of continental shelves and epeiric seas waned to the low levels of today, while other species continued in the deeper parts of the oceans. As a result, chert nodules in shallow water limestones became far less abundant in the later Mesozoic and Tertiary. Regardless of these qualitative changes in silica-secreting populations, the distribution of cherts suggests that for most of the Mesozoic the oceans remained at much the same levels as during the earlier Phanerozoic.

The diatoms became globally dominant in the silica cycle near the beginning of the Tertiary, following intense radiation of species through the Cretaceous. By the beginning of the Eocene, diatoms had become abundant throughout the surface waters of the ocean and especially so in the highly productive regions of upwelling of bottom waters. The link of diatoms to silica thus linked the silica cycle directly to the phosphorus and nitrogen cycles. Though radiolaria and sponges continued to play roles, they became bit players compared with the diatoms. The extraordinary efficiency of diatoms in reducing silica in seawater further de-

pressed silica concentrations to their present very low level, undersaturated with respect to any common silica or silicate mineral.

There were effects on land, too, as angiosperms spread and diatoms became important in lakes and soils. It is arguable whether these developments slightly affected weathering rates, but it is improbable that we could quantitatively recognize any such effect from oceanic sediments.

Conclusions

The effects of the interaction of the biological world of silica with the oceans are thus seen to be a reaction of several different life forms to inputs of silica to the ocean. In earlier times, the sponges and radiolaria reacted as mediators of silica concentrations as they became the primary output agencies of oceanic silica. Moderately efficient at silica secretion, they were able to reduce oceanic silica concentrations from their Precambrian levels. When the diatoms evolved and eventually took over, the silica concentrations dropped dramatically to very low levels.

The organisms react to the input rather than controlling it by any feedback. The primary controls on inputs from continental weathering and midocean ridges are tectonics and weathering, neither of which is in any way affected by the output. Although lowered seawater silica concentrations would enhance the leaching rate of basalt, silica leaching in moderate- and high-temperature hydrothermal environments is so extensive that the small difference in initial seawater silica concentrations would make differences in basalt alteration negligible.

It is possible that the evolution and adaptation of silica secreters to marine waters is in part affected by their silica concentrations. Early sponges and radiolaria found high silica concentrations and were able to continue as their own activities lowered silica levels. When the diatoms arrived, they found relatively abundant silica levels and promptly reduced them further. The sponges and radiolaria tolerated this extreme drop in silica concentration but became less abundant. Perhaps future silica secreters will have to be even more efficient than the diatoms to be successful in the oceans.

From this analysis, it seems clear that the organisms evolve and alter their oceanic environment significantly, all the while reacting to the inputs controlled by the larger forces of the Earth, on which they have no effect. A possible exception is climate and its modification by atmospheric gases. Because the diatoms are heavily involved in primary productivity, they contribute to the carbon-oxygen-sulfur cycle that has such an important set of relations to the atmosphere (Berner et al., 1983). We have no reason to believe that the diatoms are more or less efficient at photosynthesis than their nonsiliceous forerunners. Nor have we any reason to infer changes in the ratio of buried to oxidized organic carbon—and consequently atmospheric changes—that relate to silica sedimentation. Yet we know that the end of the Mesozoic was a significant period in the evolution of land and sea plant and animal life and their effects on the environment of Earth's surface. What we do not know is the extent to which evolutionary events may have had significant feedbacks on climate.

Finally, we come back to the beginning: the silica cycle cannot be understood without explicit recognition of the importance of interactions of the biological world and the inorganic geological world. The biological world modifies its environment but the major controls on the rate of recycling depend on the larger physical forces of earth's interior.

Acknowledgments

Work done under National Science Foundation Grant EAR-86-06410. A.H. Knoll read the manuscript and made many valuable suggestions.

References

Bennett, P.C. 1987. The accelerated dissolution of quartz in aqueous organic acid solutions at 25°C. *Geol Soc Am Abstracts with Programs,* 19, 586.

Bennett, P.C., and Siegel, D.I. 1987. Increased solubility of quartz in water due to complexing by inorganic compounds. *Nature,* 236, 684–686.

Berner, R.A., Lasaga, A.C., and Garrels, R.M. 1983. The carbonate-silicate geochemical cycle and its effect on atmospheric carbon dioxide over the past 100 million years. *Am J Sci,* 283, 641–683.

Compton, J.S. 1986. Early diagenesis and dolomitization of the Monterey Formation, California. Ph. D. thesis, Harvard University.

Harper, H.E., and Knoll, A.H. 1974. Silica, diatoms, and Cenozoic radiolarian evolution. *Geology,* 3, 175–177.

Hein, J.R., and Karl, S.M. 1983. Comparisons between open-ocean and continental margin chert sequences. In: Iijima, A., Hein, J.R., and Siever, R., eds. *Siliceous Deposits in the Pacific Region.* New York: Elsevier, 25–44.

Hurd, D.C. 1983. Physical and chemical properties of siliceous skeletons. In: Aston, S.R., ed. *Silica Geochemistry and Biogeochemistry.* London: Academic Press, 187–244.

Hurd, D.C., and Theyer, F. 1975. Changes in the physical and chemical properties of biogenic silica from the central equatorial Pacific. I. Solubility, specific surface area, and solution rate constants of acid-cleaned samples. In: Gibb, T., ed. *Analytical Methods in Chemical Oceanography.* Advances in Chemistry, Series No. 147. *American Chemical Society,* 211–230.

Iijima, A., and Utada, M. 1983. Recent developments in the sedimentology of siliceous deposits in Japan. In: Iijima, A., Hein, J.R., and Siever, R., eds. *Siliceous Deposits in the Pacific Region.* New York: Elsevier, 45–64.

Maliva, R., Knoll, A.H., and Siever, R., 1989. Secular change in chert distribution: A reflection of evolving biological participation in the silica cycle. *Palaios,* 4, 519–532.

Maliva, R.G., and Siever, R. 1989. Nodular chert formation in carbonate rocks. *J Geol,* 97, 421–433.

Moore, T.C., Jr. 1969. Radiolaria: Change in skeletal weight and resistance to solution. *Geol Soc Am Bull,* 80, 2103–2108.

Riech, V., and von Rad, U. 1979. Silica diagenesis in the Atlantic Ocean: Diagenetic potential and transformations. In: Talwani, M., Hay, W., and Ryan, B.F., eds. *Deep Drilling Results in the Atlantic Ocean: Continental Margins and Paleoenvironment.* Washington, D.C.: Geophysical Union Maurice Ewing Series 3, 315–341.

Siever, R. 1957. The silica budget in the sedimentary cycle. *Am Mineralogist,* 42, 821–841.

Siever, R. 1962. Silica solubility, 0-200;, and the diagenesis of siliceous sediments. *J Geol,* 70, 127–150.

Siever, R. 1986. Oceanic silica geochemistry and nodular chert formation. *Geol Soc Am Abstracts with Programs,* 18, 750.

Simonson, B. 1985. Sedimentological constraints on the origins of Precambrian iron-formations. *Geol Soc Am Bull,* 96, 244–252.

Spencer, C.P. 1983. Marine biogeochemistry of silicon. In: Aston, S.R., ed. *Silicon Geochemistry and Biogeochemistry*. New York: Academic Press, 101–142.

Stein, C.L. 1977. Dissolution of diatoms and diagenesis in siliceous sediments. Ph.D. thesis, Harvard University.

Steinberg, M., Bonnot-Courtois, C., and Tlig, S. 1983. Geochemical contribution to the understanding of bedded chert. In: Iijima, A., Hein, J.R., and Siever, R., eds. *Siliceous Deposits in the Pacific Region*. New York: Elsevier, 193–210.

Wollast, R., and Mackenzie, F.T., 1986, The global cycle of silica. In: Aston, S.R., ed. *Silica Geochemistry and Biogeochemistry*. London: Academic Press, 39–76.

Robert B. Chatfield

33

Ephemeral Biogenic Emissions and the Earth's Radiative and Oxidative Environment

The Gaia conference was concerned with the co-evolution of life and the physicochemical state of the Earth over the last four billion years. Many examples of chemical change in the environment are played out over hundreds or millions of years (e.g., those that concern CO_2). Compounds that have radiative importance usually have long atmospheric lifetimes, so that large concentrations build up. CO_2 and CH_4 have atmospheric lifetimes of years, N_2O of decades. However, this chapter is concerned with the most ephemeral trace gas emissions, dimethylsulfide (DMS), methyl iodide, nitric oxide, and isoprene, whose lifetimes in the air range from fifteen minutes to two or three days. These biological emissions fuel element cycles in the atmosphere that typically last a few days more. Nevertheless, they appear to have important effects on the Earth's radiative environment, and affect the temperature, moisture supply, and oxidative environment of living species. The constant repetition of these cycles can make them important, and their short timescales may make them somewhat more rapidly susceptible to inadvertent modification by humankind.

I begin with a description of rapidly reactive sulfur, starting with microorganism excretion within the ocean to the maintenance of a distribution of aerosol particles that nucleate cloud and rain droplets. I will take the cycle until it determines the number of cloud condensation nuclei, which can then determine the reflectivity of clouds, and therefore the heat budget of the Earth. This is just one part of a feedback cycle, the CLAW cycle (described by Charlson, Lovelock, Andreae, and Warren, 1987), that helped bring the Gaia conference about. The general influences in this portion of the cycle are well known, to zero order. However, when we ask if the cycle is strong enough to be significantly stabilizing or destabilizing for global temperature, it is important to quantify the influences. It turns out that the details of the chain of influence, involving both chemical and microphysical processes, are uncertain to a significant degree. The possibility of interspecies competition through a sort of gentle chemical warfare in the atmosphere is illustrated with the potential role of methyl iodide in the atmosphere. Incidentally, methyl iodide and dimethylsulfide were both first identified in the atmosphere by Lovelock et al. (1972, 1973) and were attributed to biological emissions.

The overview progresses from ocean to land, where, in nearly pristine rainforest conditions, the aerosol cloud nuclei appear to be primarily carbon compounds. The heterogeneous collection of material contains an important contribution from the prime natural organic emission of the forests, isoprene. A role for isoprene emission from trees is as yet unknown. This chapter describes the possibilities that it controls the production of ozone over the forest, and that human actions are overwhelming and are reversing this control.

Dimethylsulfide Emissions to Cloud Condensation Nuclei Spectra: The Complex Chain

Cloud-Albedo Feedback Strength

The CLAW (Charlson et al., 1987) bioclimatic feedback loop achieves some efficiency in controlling atmospheric temperature by changing the reflectivity of marine clouds by changing the number of cloud condensation nuclei (CCN) and hence the number of cloud droplets among which cloud liquid water is distributed. That cycle is described in their paper in *Nature*, in Lovelock (1988), and elsewhere in this volume. Figure 33.1 shows that loop with an emphasis on the chemistry and microphysics involved. The details of the chain from the point of S excretion from the coccolithophores and other microscopic oceanic flora to the shape of the aerosol CCN distribution is my subject here. These details are not quantitatively understood, but involve processes that are ripe for quantitative study.

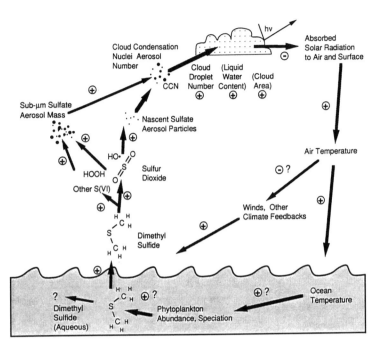

Figure 33.1 General characterization of the CLAW (Charlson et al., 1987) climatic feedback loop, with added emphasis to the portions introducing sulfur to the atmosphere and modifying its oxidation to form those sulfate aerosol particles that nucleate cloud droplets. Positive signs on the effects loop indicate a positive relationship between variables, negative signs the opposite. Successive signs are composed by multiplication; if the effects multiply all the way around the loop to give a negative sign, then the loop tends to stabilize the system; if positive, then it tends to destabilize the system.

Two Effects of Sulfur Oxidation on Cloud Nuclei

The ephemeral-sulfur-cycle portion of the CLAW feedback loop has several fundamental points of impact on activity of CCN. The properties of the aerosols that make them CCN are essentially (1) strong solubility and (2) sufficient mass distributed throughout a (3) sufficient number of particles to allow water to condense. As described by Pruppacher and Klett (1980), nucleation of cloud droplets in an updraft is a competitive phenomenon among aerosol particles of various sizes in which the smallest particles never acquire sufficient water to become cloud droplets. The largest particles are too rare and hard for water to reach to allow nucleation of many droplets. Sulfate can be added to the appropriate type of aerosol, called the *submicron mode,* in several ways. It can be added by the production of *new* tiny sulfuric acid–water–ammonia particles which then accumulate together as mass is added. These depend on the production of monomeric gas-phase sulfuric acid molecules. (Monomers are isolated single chemical compounds which may potentially become aerosols.) Alternatively, gas-phase sulfuric acid may condense onto the preexisting aerosol. The first processes can add

new particles, potentially CCN, to the atmosphere, but the second process (condensation) modifies the number of CCN in a more complex way. In the marine atmosphere, they may also acquire mass during their passage through clouds (Andreae et al., 1986). That is, sulfate may also be formed by aqueous oxidation of dissolved sulfur dioxide within cloud droplets. If the sulfate is not rained out or removed from the boundary layer by these clouds, the evaporating droplet leaves an aerosol particle with a bit more sulfate, and therefore a better CCN.

Actually, the term *sulfate* in the previous paragraph is a bit of a misnomer; *hexavalent sulfur* is the more appropriate word. Remote marine CCN-sized aerosols contain several forms of oxidized sulfur-VI. Approximately 90% of the sulfur is present as sulfuric acid (sulfate); most of the remainder is methane sulfonic acid (MSA), with only one ionization possible (Savoie, 1984). A small amount (less than 1%) may be in a polar but nonionic form, dimethyl sulfone (Watts et al., 1987). The MSA is unlikely to nucleate new aerosol, but can contribute to the mass of the aerosol and to its efficiency as a CCN.

In any case, to understand the reaction of the CCN to changes in sulfur input, it is necessary to understand the response of two processes, gas-phase sulfuric acid monomer production rate, and a total hexavalent sulfur production rate due to all processes.

Dimethylsulfide from Ocean Reservoir to Atmosphere

Let us begin our focus on the CLAW loop at the point of origin of reactive sulfur DMS, from the living organism. Figure 33.2 is a conceptual picture of the process: the DMS are dimethylsulfide propiothetin (DMSP) excreted from certain phytoplankton and appear to distribute rather freely within the oceanic mixed layer (Andreae et al., 1985; Bates et al., 1987). It is not immediately available to the atmosphere, but must pass through the thin interfacial layers of the ocean and the atmosphere, where mixing is restricted (Liss and Slater, 1974). As Andreae (chapter 15, this volume) indicates, the DMS is exposed to oxidation and ingestion within the ocean mixed layer, but these processes are not yet quantitatively understood; it appears that the processes may well compete effectively with transfer to the atmosphere. The transfer of DMS to the atmosphere is favored with certain kinds of weather, primarily when the wind speed is high. At other times, DMS may begin to accumulate in the ocean. If there were no consumption or oxidation within the ocean, all the DMS would eventually be emitted, and details of transfer need not concern us. The physics requires that the time-integrated flux be the same, in the absence of other sinks. That is, the locations and times of emissions would vary, but not the total DMS emitted, so that effects on clouds might not be so great.

More interesting and more likely is the possibility that the alternate fates tend to consume the DMS. In that case, the increased wind speeds prevalent in the Northern Hemisphere during the glacial times would increase the delivery of sulfur to the atmosphere. A strong effect would be the stirring of the oceanic mixed layer; even stronger is the effect of increased transport through the submillimeter interfacial layer (Liss and Merlivat, 1986). This process in isolation would tend to brighten clouds and preserve the cooling of the oceans and atmosphere, as figure 32.2 indicates. If the original CLAW feedback loop is climate-stabilizing, this process is destabilizing. The fact that ice-core analyses contain elevated MSA, an incompletely understood product of DMS oxidation, during the ice ages suggests some sort of causal link between oceanic DMS

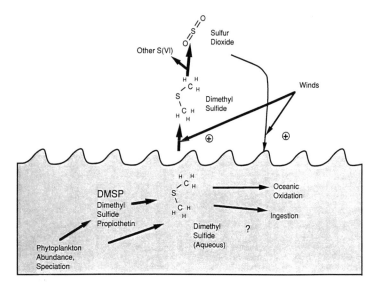

Figure 33.2 A closer view of the complexities of the sea-to-air transfer processes in which marine biology and chemistry, atmospheric chemistry, and climate (temperature, wind speed) interact. If DMS has other fates than transfer to the atmosphere, then higher wind speeds (e.g., during glacial periods) would increase sulfur emission to the atmosphere. Higher wind speeds would also slightly increase the removal of SO_2 to the ocean, lowering the rate of production of new sulfate aerosol particles. However, if essentially all DMS produced in the ocean has only one fate, emission to the atmosphere, DMS fluxes are not affected by wind speed in the long-term mean. However, the SO_2 fluxes are.

emissions and climate (Saigne and Legrand, 1987; Legrand et al., 1988). Alternative explanations for the MSA are suggested in the next section. Recent work by Legrand and colleagues (1991) also recognizes several of these uncertainties.

Sulfur Oxidation Pathways in the Atmosphere
Brief descriptions of the CLAW feedback loop may imply that the DMS emitted from the ocean all makes its way to sulfate in the CCN aerosol. In fact, as figure 33.3 and figure 33.1 show, the path from DMS to cloud droplet is chemically complex and

has several possibilities for diversions, diversions that may be modulated by changing climatic conditions. MSA plays an even more complex role. All that is currently certain is that it arises from DMS, but the reaction process and its climatic dependences are essentially unknown.

Alternate Fates for Dimethylsulfide   Figure 33.3 shows that oxidation of dimethylsulfide is initiated mostly by hydroxyl radical, HO•, the primary oxidizer and cleanser of the troposphere. (The presence of the radical dot is an optional reminder that

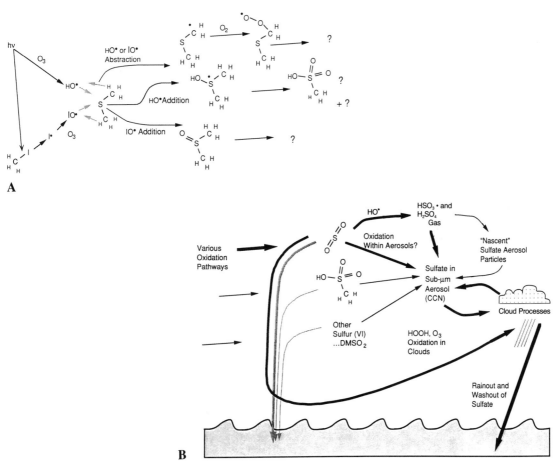

Figure 33.3 The oxidation pathways of sulfur in the marine atmosphere. A, initial stages, showing the possible interaction of the iodine and sulfur cycles that result from the emissions of DMS and methyl iodide. Two main sorts of pathways are shown. Addition of the oxygen to the sulfur atom, as S-O-H or S = O, leads to differing products, with partial yields, described in the text. The abstraction or removal of an H by either HO or IO would lead to similar sulfur products, also described in the text. B, Various DMS oxidation pathways tend to lead to sulfur dioxide, MSA, or dimethylsulfone, which have different effects. While much SO$_2$ redissolves to the ocean, some may produce new sulfate aerosol particles, which most simply accumulates on existing particles, adding to their mass and making them more likely CCN. Oxidation of SO$_2$ in cloud droplets or on existing aerosol (mostly large sea salt particles) also contributes to aerosol sulfate mass, but not particle number. The other hexavalent sulfur species simply add to the mass of S (VI) in aerosol, contributing to CCN with somewhat less efficiency.

the chemical species has an unpaired electron. This commonly implies that the species is highly reactive, and will rapidly participate in one-electron oxidations, or radical reactions.) DMS may differ from other tropospheric reduced gases; it may have another important oxidation via the more exotic species, iodine monoxide radical, IO$^\bullet$. Another oxidation, by NO$_3$$^\bullet$ radical, appears to be very small, except when fresh, day-or-two old anthropogenic nitrogen oxide pollution affects oceanic emissions (Chatfield and Crutzen, 1990; Andreae at al., 1985). In each case, there are indications that the chemical attack is complex. Basically, there are two sites for radical attack. One of the hydrogens may be abstracted from a methyl group, leaving an organic radical. The fate of this organic radical is not known, but it is likely to be the same no matter which initiating radical attacks. Alternatively, the sulfur atom itself may attract the initiating radical. This additional pathway offers various subsequent reaction pathways, with the additional d orbitals of the heavy sulfur atom available for various kinds of bonding. Laboratory experiments suggest a variety of products, depending on the attacking radical and the environmental conditions.

Oxidation of DMS by IO$^\bullet$ radical has been reported to lead mostly to an intermediate species dimethyl sulfoxide (DMSO) in a process that destroys a very small amount of ozone, and also regenerates the IO$^\bullet$.

$$IO^\bullet + DMS \rightarrow DMSO + I \quad (1)$$

$$I + O_3 \rightarrow IO^\bullet + O_2 \quad (2)$$

DMSO is only an intermediate compound, reacting rapidly with hydroxyl radicals in what appears to be a complex manner. Using the data of Barnes and colleagues (1987), Chatfield and Crutzen evaluated the products of this reaction as

$$HO^\bullet + DMSO \rightarrow 0.6\,SO_2 + 0.4\,SO_4^= + 2\,HCHO. \quad (3)$$

To do this, it was necessary to discriminate against the product dimethyl sulfone, (CH$_3$)$_2$SO$_2$, found in the laboratory chambers but whose measured concentrations are vanishingly small in the atmosphere (Watts et al., 1987), and attribute this remainder to an uncharacterized sulfur-VI compound listed simply as SO$_4^=$. It is the SO$_2$ that is likely to be on the main pathway to forming new CCN aerosol particles. Although hydroxyl is still part of the oxidation chain in this situation, it is the competition between

HO$^\bullet$ and IO$^\bullet$ in the initial oxidation step that will determine the products. The HO oxidation of DMSO in the gas phase is so rapid as to allow little other fate.

At this time, there appear to be several difficulties in the geochemistry of sulfur that are hard to explain if the IO$^\bullet$ reaction proceeds to oxidize DMS in large measure (Chatfield and Crutzen, 1990). HO$^\bullet$ appears to be the prime oxidizer.

The Role of HO$^\bullet$ Similar uncertainties lead us to write general overall reactions for the direct reaction of DMS with hydroxyl, writing for abstraction,

$$HO^\bullet + DMS \rightarrow 0.6\,SO_2 + 2\,HCHO \quad (4)$$

and for the complex addition reaction, a strongly temperature-dependent additional pathway

$$HO^\bullet + (CH_3)_2S \xrightarrow{O_2} \ldots \rightarrow 0.75\,SO_2 + 0.25\,MSA + 1.5\,HCHO \quad (5)$$

which also depends on the number density of molecular oxygen present. It is also quite possible that DMSO is a consequential product of this pathway; if it is, then DMSO production via the iodine cycle must be even less. The assignment of a MSA yield for this route was made in accord with chemical intuition, limited laboratory data, and simply in an attempt to match model results to observations of the MSA general abundances and latitudinal distributions. Those results were as expected, but other problems appeared, namely in the predicted vertical distribution of MSA (Chatfield and Crutzen, 1990). So much for the virtues of chemical intuition and model tuning. MSA behavior appears more complicated than they allow.

The Formation of Aerosol Sulfate
The SO$_2$ formed by the reactions described here does not all make new aerosol particles. Let us concentrate our attention on the lowest 500 to 1000 m above the ocean surface, the marine boundary layer and low-cloud layer, which interchange material rapidly with the surface layers above the ocean. (Timescales of .5 to 6 hours are common.) Refer back to figure 33.2 Four competitive fates for SO$_2$ are known. The most significant is likely to be returned to the ocean by solution

$$SO_2 \rightarrow HSO_3^- \text{ (oceanic)} + H^+ \quad (6)$$

limited again by transfer near the interface. This process increases significantly as wind speed increases (Liss and Merlivat, 1986). The effect is that during those times when DMS is being vented strongly into the atmosphere, the critical species, sulfur dioxide, is being removed more effectively. Another large portion may be oxidized by hydrogen peroxide or ozone with clouds. Low clouds will return the sulfate rapidly to atmospheric layers that communicate with the subcloud layer. Overall,

$$SO_2 + HOOH \rightarrow SO_4^= + 2\,H^+ \tag{7}$$

$$SO_2 + O_3 \xrightarrow{H_2O} SO_4^= + 2\,H^+ \tag{8}$$

in a process that is essentially limited only by the time for a SO_2 molecule to reach a cloud. It appears reasonable that the same processes can occur throughout the marine boundary layer on water that is contained in solution on deliquescent sea salt particles:

$$SO_2 + HOOH \rightarrow SO_4^= + 2\,H^+ \text{ (on sea salt)} \tag{9}$$

$$SO_2 + O_3 \xrightarrow{H_2O} SO_4^= + 2\,H^+ \text{ (on sea salt)} \tag{10}$$

Most of this sulfate is concentrated on a very few heavy particles. Sea salt concentrations also have a large wind-speed dependence that has the same effect on SO_2 as direct dissolution into the ocean, described above. Finally, there is a rather slow process proceeding homogeneously in the gas phase,

$$SO_2 + HO^\bullet \rightarrow HSO_3^\bullet \rightarrow H_2SO_4 \tag{11}$$

It is only this process that can produce gas-phase sulfuric acid, and to our knowledge, has the possibility to nucleate new particles, and thereby increase the CCN number. This is a key process. The nucleation of nascent accumulation-mode aerosol particles must compete with absorption of sulfur-VI onto existing particles.

Note that only the second and fourth processes—equations (7), (8), (11)—actually add sulfate mass to the accumulation-mode aerosol. The third process makes airborne sulfate, but most of that sea salt sulfate is in the 1-μm-diameter or larger particles, which accounts for few particles, nucleates few cloud droplets, and removes sulfate rapidly back to the ocean by sedimentation and similar processes (Slinn, 1982; Erickson and Duce, 1988). Adding to the ionic sulfur-VI in the aerosol, of course, is the MSA.

Sulfur Dioxide and Cloud Condensation Nuclei Creation in the Free Troposphere The reactions described above occur mostly within the marine atmospheric boundary layer. However, a small and significant fraction of that material may escape to the middle and upper troposphere. Here, occasional high values of SO_2 have been repeatedly reported, even in very clean air (Maroulis et al., 1980; Griffith and Schuster, 1987; Berresheim et al., 1989). These may be explained by the Staubsauger effect in atmospheric chemistry (Chatfield and Crutzen, 1984), in which compounds that are very reactive near the surface, like DMS, nitrogen oxides, or organics, may be transported rapidly to the upper troposphere, where chemical destruction rates may be lower. (Staubsauger is German for vacuum cleaner, and describes the rapid sucking upward of material from the lowest layers.) The most effective rapid transport is through cumulonimbus clouds, although midlatitude frontal storms also frequently have regions of rapid vertical motion.

These motions are frequently not considered in models of the chemical climatology, which use an eddy diffusion parameterization that has proved adequate in modeling less reactive trace gases like CO_2, CH_4, and N_2O. Because these infrequent, vigorous transports allow SO_2 to be produced in the free troposphere, they also contribute strongly in determining the sulfate CCN production in that region. This illustrates a common theme in biogeochemistry: not all the details of transport need be correct in detail. However, the modeled processes must accurately capture the significant timescales. In this case, both the rapid timescale of cloud motions and that of large-scale transport and subsidence must be captured for the rapid sulfur cycle to be simulated adequately.

The Climate-Chemical Interactions
Although the exact nature of the pathways are not yet clear, several complexities in the chains connecting DMS emissions to CCN are clear. First, there are a variety of pathways, and they have sensitivities to climatic conditions like temperature (affecting the relative rate of addition of $HO^\bullet$ to DMS), water vapor, ultraviolet mean intensity (which determine how much SO_2 oxidizes by $HO^\bullet$ in the gas phase to nucleate particles, in competition with other fates). Secondly, while MSA would seem to be an ideal climatic tracer, reflecting proportionally the history of the DMS to CCN sulfate cycle (Le-

grand et al., 1988), it is presently unclear which pathway makes MSA, what temperature effects operate, and whether and how it may oxidize.

Gaian Homeostasis or Natural Selection? It is immediately suggestive that both DMS and methyl iodide are broadly distributed natural emissions present over the oceans. The methyl iodide produces a compound, IO•, which may modify the oxidation of the DMS, altering the fundamental feed stocks of the aerosol size spectra in a way that could modify the number of effective CCN. Could this be a form of positive or negative interaction of the emitting organisms? Granting that the cycle would be strong enough to help control the oceanic climate for some reasonably short period, could this be a form of species competition, a subtle form of chemical warfare between species with alternate climatic optima, or, possibly, an exploitation of an already present chemical process, making the mechanism more sensitive to changes in temperature?

The problems with conjectures along these lines are the following. The evidence is (Chatfield and Crutzen, 1990) that the iodine cycle may be somehow short-circuited in the troposphere, so that IO• is not able to play the role that once seemed possible (Chameides and Davis, 1980). Either IO• is sequestered somehow into an unreactive species, or as newly published data suggests (Daykin and Wine, 1990), the IO• + DMS reaction rate coefficient may be very slow. Methyl iodide is thought to originate strongly from macroalgae, associated with near-shore environments (Lovelock and Wade, 1973). However, it has a detectable concentration of 1 to 3 ppt over the open oceans (Lovelock et al. 1973; Singh, 1983), with a presumed biological source that is not clear. The oceanic concentrations of both species in the North Sea appear to have both a near-shore and an open-sea component (Nightingale and Liss, personal communications). Additionally, the alternate pathways appear only mildly to change the manner in which sulfur-VI gets into the aerosol phase.

The interaction of the species can be attributed to local evolution rather than some sort of purposeful behavior if the effects are suitably local to the organisms secreting both methylated compounds. That timescale is not yet completely clear. Apparent local effects on aerosol populations have been noted (Bates et al., 1987), but the timescale for CCN to adjust to typical concentrations appears to

be several days, and that would typically take the sulfur species beyond the local region with oceanic emissions.

Perhaps the most basic conclusions to be drawn from the complexities that this chapter describes are these. Some sort of rough positive relationship between DMS secretion and CCN production may be expected. This relationship could be expected over many days as the production of CCN and its rainout continue to adjust to local conditions. However, other, possibly correlated phenomena, such as the variation of wind speed and the emission of methyl iodide and its possible consequent chemistry, complicate the picture and allow for the CCN to be controlled by completely different processes.

Effects of Cloud Condensation Nuclei Spectra on Climate

What if increased DMS emissions do change the number of CCN? What effects does this have on climate? Figure 33.1 shows the familiar chain of consequences described by Charlson and colleagues (1987) with a few additional effects. The CLAW hypothesis is that the effect that is most worthy of attention is a marginal brightening of clouds, clouds that are considered, for simplicity, to have the same area and liquid water content in any case. In fact, there are reasons to believe that both of these should be significantly affected by the CCN population.

The liquid water content of a cloud depends on the water vapor distribution below and around the cloud and the rain efficiency of the cloud. Here, the rain efficiency is taken to be a gross system property of a cloud, relating the flux of liquid water, precipitation, reaching the surface to the water vapor flux moving up through the cloud base. Clearly, the water vapor distribution of typical environments in the troposphere depends in some direct way on the rain efficiencies of clouds in the troposphere. At steady state, the rain removal of water from the atmosphere must equal the evaporative input. If physical conditions, for example the number of effective CCN, cause a lower rainfall efficiency, then atmospheric water and the cloud base water vapor flux must rise until the precipitation again equals evaporation. The lower the rain efficiencies, the more water vapor must be present in the troposphere to balance precipitation to evaporation. An important detail should be added: moister environmental air should also commonly tend to increase the rainfall efficiency.

Figure 33.1 indicates several effects of increasing the CCN number, including the CLAW hypothesis. Two of these involve another property of increased CCN number, namely a tendency to lower the rainfall efficiency of the cloud by marginally decreasing the colloidal instability of the cloud droplet population (Pruppacher and Klett, 1980). Albrecht (1989) has begun to quantify a strong effect on low clouds. Decreasing the drizzle efficiency of low cloud decks tends to increase the water vapor in the region and retard evaporation of cloud (more reflective cloud area), and also increases the liquid water content (brighter clouds). Both of these effects can add to the effects described by CLAW, with the same sign. The effects on atmospheric radiation are also tied fairly closely to the local ocean surface and the factors controlling its emission of DMS: Boundary-layer transport of sulfur species and their cycling through low clouds occurs on a day-or-so timescale comparable to the production of CCN.

Cloud Condensation Nuclei and the Principal Greenhouse Gas: $H_2O(v)$

The amounts and persistence of low cloud are also dependent in some complex way on water vapor and temperature (stability) in the lower middle troposphere above the low-cloud layer. Water vapor in this region has a much longer history, depending on details of convection and subsidence over planetary-scale distances (Manabe et al., 1965). Specific humidities are dependent primarily on the predominant cloud detrainment heights and rainfall efficiencies of distant, towering clouds. In many cases the humidity is set by conditions thousands of kilometers, even tens of thousands of kilometers, away. *If* CCN enrichment decreases the rainfall efficiency of *these* cloud systems, then the whole middle troposphere must have increased water vapor, by conservation of water substance. That is, there may be a change in the most significant greenhouse gas, water. For example, Smith and Vonder Haar (1991) have noted that the National Center for Atmospheric Research Community Climate Model has an immediate and large response to changes in the rainfall efficiency assumed. Contrary to the previous effects, the increased water vapor tends to warm the atmosphere when sulfur emissions increase. The simulation does this because of the very large infrared absorption-emission properties of

water vapor, which is by far the most effective greenhouse gas. The assessment of the whole system response to all these effects is not simple. It requires simulations of the general circulation, with accurate description of water vapor, and with a convective rainfall parameterization that responds to microphysical parameters like the CCN number and large-scale features like environmental humidity. In the meantime, we are left with generalizations about the relative humidity structure of the atmosphere whose physical and chemical underpinnings are simply not understood. A prime and to date useful example is the observation of 75% relative humidity as a tropospheric "characteristic state" (Manabe and Wetherald, 1967).

Reactive C and N Compounds, Ozone, and the Forest Environment

The focus now moves to the continental atmosphere, and the habitability of that region as affected by the atmospheric environment, chemical and physical. The initial question is the potential role of biogenic emissions on clouds and rain; then I turn to other potential chemically mediated feedback processes that could operate to stabilize the biosphere-atmosphere system. The focus is exclusively on the tropical rainforest environments, because those regions, along with the drastically simplified environments of the true deserts, tundras, and icecaps, are the only continental environments in which we can even glimpse the chemical "state of nature" not overwhelmed by humankind. There are several appealing potential feedback loops whose links are not completely clear.

Rainforest Aerosol and Effects on Clouds In transition, it must be pointed out that sulfur emissions do *not* play the major role as CCN in the cleaner forest areas that have been investigated. When there is minimal human influence, the submicrometer aerosol particles are predominantly organic acids, with a smaller amount of sulfate derived from DMS and hydrogen sulfide. However, even the remote central Amazon basin frequently shows pervasive influence from anthropogenic burning during the dry season, and then sulfate and nitrate become the principal anions of the bulk aerosol (Andreae et al., 1988; Andreae and Andreae, 1988). The understanding is that much of the organic material originates from forest emissions. These emissions may be particulate, like the relatively huge pollen particles, or they may be gaseous compounds. We know that, for the midlatitude and oceanic atmosphere, submicron aerosol is derived from gas-phase emissions by chemical reaction: it is secondary aerosol. Perhaps this is also true of the tropical rainforests. The dominant emission is isoprene, 2-methyl 1-3 butadiene, which has the following structure:

```
        H  H
         C
      H \  H
         C=C
   H      /     H
     C=C
   H    H
```

The placement of the reactive double bonds suggests that isoprene will rapidly break up into small oxygenated organic species when oxidized in the atmosphere, and this is true. Major identified soluble components of the submicrometer aerosol appear to be formic and acetic acid. The latter acids have been thought to originate as direct emissions (Graedel, 1987; Keene and Galloway, 1986), or through cloud liquid-phase chemistry (Jacob, 1986), but recent research shows how they may be produced more directly from isoprene in the gas phase (Madronich et al., 1990). More understanding of the formic acid sources is needed.

More complex organics, the terpenes, may yield heavier molecular weight aerosol. These $C_{10}H_{16}$ and related compounds are also emitted in relatively large quantity (Zimmerman et al., 1988), and some, like α-pinene, with double bonds internal to a carbon ring structure, typically produce polyfunctional aldehyde acids. This matter can become organic aerosol under favorable circumstances, for instance, high relative humidity and high preexisting aerosol surface area for condensation.

Cloud condensation nuclei typically have a smaller effect on cloud albedo and rainfall efficiency over most continental areas, for several reasons. Continental environments frequently have much higher CCN concentrations (Pruppacher and Klett, 1980), although these concentrations are related to very fine soil dust and to sulfate originating from the combustion of natural or fossil fuels, processes that are damped in the pristine rainforest environment. Furthermore, cloud updrafts are more vigorous over the forests than over the oceans, due to the greater heating of the earth's surface, and the

deeper clouds with cooler tops likely have more involvement of the ice-based cold-rain process. These clouds would not be sensitive to the colloidal instability or warm-rain process that depends on having relatively few cloud droplet nuclei, but rather to the production of ice crystals, a much less well understood process.

Could there be a continental cloud-abetted feedback loop? It is important not to omit the long-considered feedback through hydrology, transpiration, and water vapor itself (Charney et al., 1975; Bryson and Baerreis, 1967). That is, forests perpetuate a humid environment, moisture convergence, and rainfall. In this self-stabilizing situation, the character of tropical forests becomes susceptible to the driest months. Species are apparently selected along the forest margins for their ability to tolerate increasing periods of drought (Leith and Werger, 1989; Shukla et al., 1990). Feedback loops promoting forest stability would seem to be most susceptible to CCN effects that dominate during these months. The most commonly described effect is that due to cloud seeding from biogenic raindrop and ice nuclei (Schnell and Vali, 1976). These ice nuclei could promote rainfall through either microphysical or dynamic effects (Cotton and Anthes, 1989), that is, by making raindrops directly from accumulation of cloud water on ice crystals, or by releasing energy that enhances and prolongs the infrequent dry-season convective storms. Any role for isoprene emissions and cloud (not ice) condensation nuclei is harder to fathom. Analyses of the aerosol composition over the Amazon show a very large large-organic aerosol component, a component that is likely derived by abrasional or mechanical processes from plants, for example small hairs or bits of leaf wax. However, the submicron aerosol, apparently not usually made by these processes, is also organic. The only empirical evidence linking isoprene emission to the submicron organic aerosol is circumstantial: both are pervasive throughout the basin in all airflow conditions; either isoprene is the source or they share similarly distributed sources. The proper number of these, with a hydrophilic or soluble organic film, could serve to nucleate cloud droplets that are favored with a large size, broadening the cloud droplet size spectrum, favoring warm-rain production, and thereby be essentially rain nuclei (Pruppacher and Klett, 1980). In any case, sulfur compounds have very minor effects on the aerosol over these forests under pristine conditions; biomass burning upwind now influences the forests strongly in the dry seasons (Talbot et al., 1988).

The C and N Cycles and the Oxidative Environment

Isoprene in the atmosphere has been a puzzle since it was first reported (Sanadze, 1969; Rasmussen, 1970). The hydrocarbon is emitted from broadleaf trees predominantly during the day and when their stoma are open. Emission typically increases strongly at higher leaf temperatures (Zimmerman et al., 1988). The rate of emission is extremely species-dependent for midlatitude species, and continuing studies suggest the same is true for tropical plants (Zimmerman, personal communication). The isoprene is clearly being constructed in the leaf of the plant at a site where it can be emitted, and when it is emitted, it is at a consequential energetic cost to the plant (Monson and Fall, 1989). Those authors conclude, "At present, there are no obvious benefits to isoprene emission." They then speculate that the isoprene emission may be part of a regulation of precursor pools that are necessary for other leaf functions, as they found evidence that isoprene emission rates are linked to electron transport reactions of photosynthesis.

The emission of carbon by isoprene is two or three times larger than the emission of methane from these tropical forested regions (Bartlett et al., 1988; Zimmerman et al., 1988), and may be significant in the net cycling of carbon to and from the forest canopy. The isoprene emissions of rainforests do appear to be the most important control on hydroxyl radical in the air immediately above them in the subcloud layer (Jacob and Wofsy, 1988).

A role for isoprene that has always appeared appealing is in controlling ozone, O_3. Ozone is a phytotoxic gas that apparently causes damage within leaf mesophyll at ambient levels (Chameides, 1989), and therefore requires continuous repair, at a small energy cost. An obvious control for ozone would appear to be the well-known direct reaction

$$O_3 + C_5H_8 \rightarrow \text{products} \qquad (12)$$

which is, however, too slow to reduce ozone effectively, except at night. Indirect reactions, in which ozone reacts with hydroperoxy radicals involved in isoprene oxidation, are more important in some situations, but they do not affect ozone much more rapidly (Chameides, 1988). Isoprene can also affect the production of ozone. In high nitrogen–oxide environments, it can increase the production of ozone

(Chameides et al., 1988). However, rainforest environments have low sources of nitrogen oxides; the natural sources of NO are from soil emissions and lightning. Under these circumstances, the organic radicals produced in isoprene oxidation, for example, peroxyacetyl radical, can tie up nitrogen

$$NO + O_3 \rightarrow NO_2 \qquad (13)$$

into peroxyacetyl nitrate (PAN) so that local ozone production, which is catalyzed by the NO,

$$HOO^\bullet + NO \rightarrow NO_2 \qquad (13)$$

$$NO_2 \xrightarrow{h\nu} NO + O_3, \qquad (14)$$

is suppressed. Other organic nitrates may also participate, too. The tying up of nitrogen into these compounds is not yet fully understood, but appears to be substantial (Jacob and Wofsy, 1988; Madronich et al., 1990). This process may effectively limit ozone production, and thereby limit ozone to low values below 20 ppb, the typical concentrations observed in the wet season (Browell et al., 1988). Within the canopy of the forest concentrations fall to 5 parts per billion or less (Kirchoff et al., 1989).

The roles of isoprene emission for an individual plant or for the plant's larger environment remain unclear, but it appears to retain the potential to play a role in geochemical feedback loops. If it is an accidental accompaniment to the evolution of the forest environment, its biogeochemical consequences are nevertheless important.

Ozone has another important role in the bioclimatic system. Although essentially ephemeral itself, lasting from one to twenty days depending on conditions, tropospheric ozone is an important greenhouse gas, along with the biogenic reduced-gas emissions methane and nitrous oxide. The chemical lifetimes of the latter are decades, or centuries, allowing substantial, parts-per-million concentrations to accumulate within the atmosphere, and thus having sufficient optical depth to absorb and reradiate infrared radiation effectively. Nevertheless, some studies indicate that tropospheric ozone may have the greatest potential, after CO_2, to influence the earth's infrared radiative budget, and hence global temperatures (Ramanathan et al., 1985). This effect is based on the unique infrared absorption spectrum of ozone, and also on uncertainties in the projection of tropospheric ozone as human activities increasingly perturb the global trace-gas climatology. Certain models indicate a large effect of anthropogenic NO emissions, along with other compounds, upon the global tropospheric ozone levels (Crutzen and Gidel, 1983; and others).

Observational studies have suggested that this process is occurring, and quite visible, over the half of the tropics including the tropical rainforest (Delany et al., 1985; Fishman and Larsen, 1987; Logan and Kirchoff, 1986; Andreae et al., 1988) and model studies have suggested a possible ultimate origin: the burning of tropical biomass, both in forest clearing and in tropical agricultural practices. Both are increasing rapidly under the pressure of population and international economics. The chemistry following the emission of nitrogen oxides in combustion yields significant near-surface ozone enhancements. The modeling study of Chatfield and Delany (1990) gives a mechanism for such large-scale ozone production extending in the free troposphere from South America to eastern Africa. It also underlines the uncertainty of model projections of ozone by illustrating a pervasive tendency for models to overestimate ozone, due to numerical limitations, even if they have all the pollution sources, physics, chemistry, and meteorology correct.

The emission of isoprene from trees may decrease ozone in the pristine atmosphere, and even in many current rainforests. However, the process is paradoxically reversed in situations where human activity, industrial or agricultural, results in nitric oxides near one part per billion concentration. In this case, isoprene emissions increase the ozone production from the nitric oxides, according to a well-studied process illustrated by Chameides and colleagues (1988), and Trainer and colleagues (1987). This process is likely being observed in the heavily populated African continent (Andreae et al., personal communication). Whether isoprene emission is an accidental or evolutionarily adaptive method of ozone control may not matter as much as the fact that human activities are reversing it. The consequences for the climatic and oxidative environment for the Earth's flora, and for humankind, must be better understood.

Conclusions

As our understanding of the interaction within the biosphere advances, more potential feedback loops of the system emerge. Many will prove trivial, others very important. The selection of loops for more detailed investigation depends on an increasingly quantitative understanding of the links of the loop. This chapter presents a largely qualitative summary of quantitative work that has been done on the links of the sulfur cycle, from secretion within the oceanic mixed layer to the maintenance of a spectrum of aerosol sulfate particles that are the marine CCN. While an increase in secretion very likely tends to precede an increase in CCN, there are many interfering factors that could strongly modify the loop. These include climatic factors determining temperature and atmospheric hydroxyl radical, and also biological factors like the oceanic emitters of methyl iodide. The CCN resulting should affect atmospheric water vapor, and these effects may reinforce or contravene the main feedback loop described by Charlson and colleagues (1987), clouds may persist and contain more water vapor, but the above-cloud atmosphere may have more radiatively important water vapor.

Continental clouds should act very differently from marine clouds; in pristine environments like the tropical forests, organic materials, likely originating from the fauna, should predominate. Isoprene emissions may produce organic acids, which are the most important CCNs. Other effects of isoprene are to determine the hydroxyl radical and the ozone levels of the rainforest mixed layer. While isoprene is central in these atmospheres, no role, either physiological or as an interactive control mechanism within the forests' atmospheric environment, has been identified. Ozone levels appear to have important consequences for the global temperature as well as the oxidative environment of plant mesophyll. Human activities may be changing these substantially, so ozone deserves intense study, although the modeling and understanding of ozone will be very difficult.

Acknowledgments

Thanks to Michael Keller, David Erickson, M.O. Andreae, and Glenn Shaw for reading and discussing a draft of this paper, and to Bruce Albrecht for making available his paper before publication. The National Center for Atmospheric Research is funded by the National Science Foundation.

References

Albrecht, B.A. 1989. Aerosols, cloud microphysics, and fractional cloudiness. *Science*, 245, 1227–1230.

Andreae, M.O., and Andreae, T.W. 1988. The cycle of biogenic sulfur compounds over the Amazon Basin. 1. Dry season. *J Geophys Res*, 93, 1487–1497.

Andreae, M.O., Charlson, R.J., Bruynseels, F., Storms, H., Van Grieken, R., and Maenhaut, W. 1986. Internal mixture of sea salt, silicates, and excess sulfate in marine aerosols. *Science*, 23, 1620–1623.

Andreae, M.O., Ferek, R.J., Bermond, F., Byrdd, K.P., Engstrom, R.T., Hardin, S., Houmere, P.D., LeMarrec, F., Raemdonck, H., and Chatfield, R.B. 1985. Dimethylsulfide in the marine atmosphere. *J Geophys Res*, 90, 12,891–12,900.

Andreae, M.O., Talbot, R.W., Andreae, T.W., and Harriss, R.C. 1988. Formic and acetic acid over the central Amazon region, Brazil. 1. Dry season. *J Geophys Res*, 93, 1616–1624.

Barnes, I., Becker, K.H., Carlier, P., and Mouvier, G. 1987. FTIR study of the DMS/NO$_2$/I$_2$/N$_2$ photolysis system: The reaction of IO radicals with DMS. *Int J Chem Kin*, 19, 489–501.

Bartlett, K.B., Crill, P.M., Sebacher, D.J., Harriss, R.C., Wilson, J.O., and Melack, J.M. 1988. Methane flux from the central Amazonian floodplain. *J Geophys Res*, 93, 1571–1582.

Bates, T.S., Charlson, R.J., and Gammon, R.H. 1987. Evidence for the climatic role of marine biogenic sulphur. *Nature*, 329, 319–321.

Berresheim, H., Andreae, M.O., Ayers, G.P., Gillett, R.W., Merrill, J.T., Haris, V.J., and Chameides, W.L. 1989. Airborne measurements of dimethyl sulfide, sulfur dioxide, and aerosol ions over the Southern Ocean south of Australia. Submitted to *J Atmos Chem*, 1989.

Browell, E.V., Gregory, G.L., Harriss, R.C., and Kirchoff, V.W.J.H. 1988. Tropospheric ozone and aerosol distributions across the Amazon Basin. *J Geophys Res*, 93, 1431–1451.

Bryson, R.A., and Baerreis, D.A. 1967. Possibilities of major climatic modification and their implications: Northwest India, a case for study. *Bull Am Meteorol Soc*, 48, 136–142.

Chameides, W.L., and Davis, D.D. 1980. Iodine: Its possible role in tropospheric photochemistry. *J Geophys Res*, 85, 7383–7398.

Chameides, W.L., Lindsay, R.W., Richardson, J., and Kiang, C.S. 1988. The role of biogenic hydrocarbons in urban photochemical smog: Atlanta as a case study. *Science*, 241, 1473–1475.

Chameides, W.L. 1989. The chemistry of ozone absorption to plant leaves: role of ascorbic acid. *Environ Sci Technol*, 23, 595–600.

Charlson, R.J., Lovelock, J.E., Andreae, M.O., and Warren, S.G. 1987. Oceanic photoplankton, atmospheric sulphur, cloud albedo and climate. *Nature*, 326, 655–661.

Charney, J., Stone, P.H., and Quirk, W.J. 1975. Drought in the Sahara: A biogeophysical feedback mechanism. *Science*, 187, 434–435.

Chatfield, R.B., and Crutzen, P.J. 1984. Sulfur dioxide in remote oceanic air: Cloud transport of reactive precursors. *J Geophys Res*, 89, 7111–7132.

Chatfield, R.B., and Crutzen, P.J. 1990. Are there interactions of iodine and sulfur species in marine air photochemistry. *J Geophys Res*, 95, 22,319–22,341.

Chatfield, R.B., and Delany, A.C. 1990. Convection links biomass burning to increased tropical ozone: However, models will tend to overpredict O$_3$. *J Geophys Res*, 95, 18473–18488.

Cotton, W., and Anthes, R.A. 1989. *Storm and Cloud Dynamics*. San Diego: Academic Press.

Crutzen, P.J., and Gidel, L.T. 1983. A two-dimensional photochemical model of the atmosphere. 2. The tropospheric budgets of the anthropogenic chlorocarbons, CO, CH$_4$, CH$_3$Cl and the effect of various NO$_x$ sources on tropospheric ozone. *J Geophys Res*, 88, 6641–6661.

Daykin, E.P., and Wine, P.H. 1990. Rate of reaction of IO radicals with dimethylsulfide. *J Geophys Res*, 18,547–18,553.

Delany, A.C., Crutzen, P.J., Haagenson, P., Walters, S., and Wartburg, A.F. 1985. Photochemically produced ozone in the emission from large-scale tropical vegetation fires. *J Geophys Res*, 90, 2425–2429.

Erickson, D.J., III, and Duce, R.A. 1988. On the global flux of atmospheric sea salt. *J Geophys Res*, 93, 14,079–14,088.

Fishman, J., and Larsen, J.C. 1987. Distribution of total ozone and stratospheric ozone in the tropics: Implications for the distribution of tropospheric ozone. *J Geophys Res*, 92, 6627–6634.

Graedel, T.E. 1987. Atmospheric formic acid from formicine ants. *Eos Trans AGU*, 68, 273.

Griffith, D.W., and Schuster, G. 1987. Atmospheric trace gas analysis using matrix isolation—Fourier transform infrared spectroscopy. *J Atmos Chem*, 5, 59–81

Jacob, D.J. 1986. Chemistry of OH in remote clouds and its role in the production of formic acid and peroxymonosulfate. *J Geophys Res*, 91, 9807–9826.

Jacob, D.J., and Wofsy, S. 1988. Photochemistry of biogenic emissions over the Amazon forest. *J Geophys Res*, 93, 1477–1486.

Keene, W.C., and Galloway, J.N. 1986. Considerations regarding sources of formic and acetic acids in the troposphere. *J Geophys Res*, 91, 14,466–14,474.

Kirchhoff, W.W.J.H., Marinho, E.V.A., Dias, P.I.S., Calheiros, R., Andre, R., and Volpe, C. 1989. O$_3$ and CO from burning sugar cane. *Nature*, 339, 264.

Legrand, M.R., Delmas, R.J., and Charlson, R.J. 1988. Climate forcing implications for Vostok ice-core sulfate data. *Nature*, 334, 418–420.

Legrand, M.R., Feniet-Saigne, C., Saltzman, E., Germain, C., Barkov, N.I., and Petrov, V.N., 1991. Ice-core record of oceanic emissions of dimethylsulphide during the last climate cycle. *Nature*, 350, 144–146.

Leith, M., and Werger, M.J.A. 1989. Ecosystems of the world: Tropical rain forest ecosystems, vol. 14B. New York: Elsevier.

Liss, P.S., and Slater, P.G. 1974. Flux of gases across the air-sea interface. *Nature,* 247, 181–184.

Liss, P.S., and Merlivat, L. 1986. Air-sea gas exchange rates: Introduction and synthesis. In: Buat-Menard, P., ed. *The Role of Air-Sea Exchange in Geochemical Cycling.* Dordrecht: Reidel, 113–127.

Lovelock, J.E., 1988. *The Ages of Gaia.* New York: W.W. Norton.

Lovelock, J.E., Maggs, R.J., and Rasmussen, R.A. 1972. *Nature,* 237, 452.

Lovelock, J.E., Maggs, R.J., and Wade, R.J. 1973. Halogenated hydrocarbons in and over the Atlantic. *Nature,* 241, 194.

Logan, J.A., and Kirchoff, V.W.J.H. 1986. Seasonal variations of tropospheric ozone at Natal, Brazil. *J Geophys Res,* 91, 7875–7881.

Madronich, S., Chatfield, R.B., Calvert, J.G., Morrigat, G.K., Veyret, B. and Lesclaux, R. 1990. A photochemical origin of acetic acid in the troposphere. *Geophysical Research Letters,* 17, 2361–2364.

Manabe, S., Smagorinsky, J., and Strickler, R.F. 1965. Simulated climatology of a general circulation model with a hydrologic cycle. *Mon Weath Rev,* 93, 769–798.

Manabe, S., and Wetherald, R.T. 1967. Thermal equilibrium of the atmosphere with a given distribution of relative humidity. *J Atmos Sci,* 24, 241–259.

Maroulis, P.J., Torres, A.L., Goldberg, A.B., and Bandy, A.R. 1980. Atmospheric SO_2 measurements on project GAMETAG. *J Geophys Res,* 85, 7345–7349.

Monson, R.K., and Fall, R. 1989. Isoprene emission from aspen leaves. The influence of environment and relation to photosynthesis and photorespiration. *Plant Physiol,* 90, 267–274.

Pruppacher, H.R., and Klett, J.D. 1980. *Microphysics of Clouds and Precipitation.* Dordrecht: Reidel.

Ramanathan, V., Cicerone, R.J., Singh, H.B., and Kiehl, J.T. 1985. Trace gas trends and their potential role in climate change. *J Geophys Res,* 90, 5547–5566.

Rasmussen, R.A. 1970. Isoprene: Identified as a forest type of emission to the atmosphere. *Environ Sci Technol,* 4, 667–671.

Saigne, C., and Legrand, M. 1987. Measurements of methanesulphonic acid in Antarctic ice. *Nature,* 330, 240–242.

Sanadze, G.A. 1969. Light-dependent excretion of molecular isoprene. *Progr Photosynth Res,* 2, 701–706.

Savoie, D.L. 1984. Nitrate and non-sea-salt sulfate aerosols over major regions of the world ocean: Concentrations, sources, and fluxes. Ph.D. dissertation, (available from University Microfilms International). University of Miami.

Schnell, R.C., and Vali, G. 1976. Biogenic ice nuclei. Part I. Terrestrial and marine sources. *J Atmos Sci,* 33, 1554–1564.

Shukla, J., Nobre, C., and Sellers, P. 1990. Amazon deforestation and climate change, *Science,* 247, 1322–1325.

Singh, H.B. 1983. Methyl halides in and over the Eastern Pacific (40°N–32°S). *J Geophys Res,* 88, 3684–3690.

Slinn, W.G.N. 1982. Air-to-sea transfer of particles. In: Liss, P.S., and Slinn, G.N., eds. *Air–Sea Exchange of Gases and Particles.* Dordrecht: Reidel, 299–405.

Smith, L., and Vonder Haar, T.H. 1991. Cloud-radiative interaction in a general circulation model: Impact upon the planetary radiation balance. *J Geophys Res,* 96, 893–914.

Talbot, R.W., Andreae, M.O., Andreae, T.W., and Harriss, R.C. 1988. Regional aerosol chemistry of the Amazon Basin during the dry season. *J Geophys Res,* 93, 1499–1508.

Trainer, M., Hsie, E.Y., McKeen, S.A., Tallamraju, R., Parish, D.D., Fehsenfeld, F.C., and Liu, S.C. 1987. Impact of natural hydrocarbons on hydroxyl and peroxy radicals at a remote site. *J Geophys Res,* 92, 11,879–11,894.

Watts S.F., Watson, A., and Brimblecombe, P. 1987. Measurements of the aerosol concentrations of methanesulphonic acid, dimethyl sulphoxide and dimethyl sulphone in the marine atmosphere of the British Isles. *Atmos Env,* 21, 2667–2672.

Zimmerman, P.R., Greenberg, J.P., and Westberg, C.E. 1988. Measurement of atmospheric hydrocarbons and biogenic emission fluxes in the Amazon boundary layer. *J Geophys Res,* 93, 1407–1416.

Paul S. Mankiewicz
34

The Macromolecular Matrix of Plant Cell Walls as a Major Gaian Interfacial Regulator in Terrestrial Environments

The Thermodynamics and Physical Chemistry of Interfacial Regulation

This chapter provides a brief overview of classical thermodynamic and physical chemical descriptions of interfacial regulation, indicating the importance of interfaces between the phases of matter in the regulation of such parameters as temperature, redox chemistry, water flow and availability, and concentration of minerals and gases. Although by no means exhaustive, this overview includes the fundamental work on this subject, and the importance and relevance of interfacial regulation to discussions of global climatic regulation.

Physical-Chemical Regulation: Interfaces, Partition Functions, and Global Free-Energy Minima

J. Willard Gibbs, in the last century, demonstrated that the interaction of temperature, pressure, and concentration occurs at interfaces, the surface junctures between two different phases of matter such as liquid and solid water, or ocean surface and atmosphere.[1] Interfaces may thus be said to regulate the interactions between temperature, pressure, and concentration of components. This regulation occurs through the fundamental modes of condensation, evaporation, freezing, melting, and sublimation in phase change relations. The atmosphere, hydrosphere, lithosphere, and cryosphere are the interacting components of the climate (Schneider and Londer, 1984). It is not often appreciated that in quantitative terms all these climatic components comprise immense volumes with comparatively little surface area (i.e., interface).

Free energy, the ability to do mechanical or chemical work, is regulated by interfaces. An extreme but indicative example is that described independently by both Semenov and Hinshelwood,[2] where, above a specific temperature, the reaction between oxygen and hydrogen is no longer regulated by interaction with the reaction vessel walls, and proceeds explosively. At lower temperatures, the reaction rate is regulated by the interface between the reacting gases and the vessel wall.

Free-energy availability is, by definition, the universal circumstance on this far-from-equilibrium surface of the Earth. Reactions from processes associated with surfaces such as absorption and adsorption, as well as those chemical reactions dependent on enzyme kinetics, are driven by a decrease of free energy, measured as the increased likelihood or probability of a reaction to occur.

From these fundamentals, one can see that phase changes regulate temperature and concentration, because

$$dG = dn(\mu_1 - \mu_2) \tag{1}$$

where dG = free energy change, dn = mass transfer in moles, and μ_1 and μ_2 are phase states in contact under equilibrium conditions (following Morowitz, 1970). The extensiveness and activity of contact between phases are the key here, since equilibrium is never reached in biotic systems because free energy reduction itself drives the further elaboration of biological surfaces, which further effect the regulation of temperature, partial pressure, and concentration (which further reduce free energy, etc.). This argument is elaborated in the following section in the fundamental terms of partition functions.

"From a microscopic point of view, it is clear that the magnitude of surface tension reduction must be related to the binding energy of the adsorbed species" (Zangwill, 1988). Surface tension is a function of surface properties, and the extent of any given surface provides sites for processes of chemisorption. As land plants elaborate their cell wall matrix, their free-energy lowering capacity increases by partitioning of the atmosphere and hydrosphere, functional components of climate. The chemisorption surfaces of the Langmuir model (Zangwill, 1988) are described by the grand partition function, Ξ, as follows:

$$\Xi = 1 + Z_{vib}e^{\beta(\mu - e_b)} \qquad (2)$$

where Z_{vib} = the vibrational canonical partition function; e = the root of all natural logarithms; $\beta = 1/kT$; μ = chemical potential; e_b = binding energy. In basic terms, this equation is important to discussions of global regulation because it indicates that surfacial partitioning is functionally related to the chemical potential and binding energy of the surrounding fluid phase(s). By such ongoing functional relationships between the elaboration of biological interfaces and chemical potential, the dynamic of regulation is inherent in processes of development. This leads to the hypothesis that, where organisms elaborate Langmuir type checkerboard surfaces, where ". . . non-interacting particles adsorb . . . onto a checkerboard substrate" (Zangwill), the pattern of regulation of chemical potential is constrained by the functional relations of the grand partition function. While there are many larger-scale implications of these relations, the point here is that interfaces regulate in fundamental terms at the scale of macromolecules through processes of chemisorption.

Physisorption may be discussed in similar terms. Following the classic equilibrium approach we may write

$$\Delta G_s = \Delta H_s - T\Delta S_s \qquad (3)$$

where G_s = surface Gibbs potential; H_s = surface enthalpy; and S_s = surface entropy. Since the surfaces of organisms are continually elaborated in response to conditions of surface entropy and Gibbs potential, here too, surface properties regulate the relationship of available energy, modifying temperature and concentration in the process. The continually elaborating surfaces of organisms move these relations into an irreversible field where membranes and biological polymers are continually elaborated in response to concentration of components and temperature,[3] as well as charge and mechanical stress.

The Physics of Turbulent Flow and Surface Boundary Layers

Air moves slowly along surfaces (such as a smooth, flat water surface) in lamina, layers that do not mix with one another. When air velocity is rapid enough that we sense air motion as wind, eddies shear off from the flow, mixing air at different heights. Laminar flow thus creates thick boundary layers where exchange occurs only through diffusion between layers, while the more rapid flow of turbulent air

homogenizes concentration and temperature differences by breaking down any layering of strata of air. Unlike other terrestrial structures and climate components, the land plants literally grow into zones of turbulence, creating dramatic potentials for mass and momentum exchange, which further powers their growth and development while making the microclimate more suitable for organisms in general.

The Geometry of Water Conduction and Resistance: The Hagen-Poiseuille Equation

The Hagen-Poiseuille equation gives the essential relations between flow rate and scale.

$$Q = \frac{\pi \Delta P r^4}{8\,\mu l} \qquad (4)$$

where Q is flow rate, P is pressure, r is the radius of the capillary, l its length, and μ the viscosity of water. Following this relationship, for each tenfold increase in the radius of capillary conducting spaces, the conductive capacities of volume of flow increase 10,000 times. Resistance follows the inverse of this relation, indicated by the partial symmetries of relative resistance versus relative conductance around the capillary radius of some tens of microns in figure 34.1.

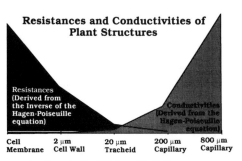

Figure 34.1 Capillary radii of various plant structures. Conductivity and resistance to flow form the functional basis of water regulation in plants. Relative values are derived from the Hagen-Poiseuille equation, where flow rate and resistance to flow depend on the fourth power of the radius of the conducting elements. On the far left, resistance to flow is at a maximum through cell membrane systems, and conductivity is at a minimum. The point on the far right marks the minimal resistance to flow and maximal conductivities of a small external capillary conducting space in a bryophyte colony. Resistance and conductivity extend across some twelve orders of magnitude, setting very broad bounds on water-regulating capacity of plant structures. Conductivities and resistances are approximately equal at around the scale of the tracheary cells of land plants. This would roughly minimize the energetic costs of regulating the movement of water through such structures.

Figure 34.1 describes the relation between biotic structures and the regulation of the fundamental variable of the terrestrial environment, water movement. These plant structures, with their associated conductivities and resistances to flow, form systems of regulators extending from the soil to the atmospheric interface. As indicated in figure 34.1, these systems are different in different plant taxa, especially between bryophytes (which primarily conduct water externally) and the rest of the land plants (which depend on internal tracheids to move water; see the section on the evolution of water-conducting strategies and regulatory capacities in the land plants). The structure and specific geometrical arrangement of materials of the plant body affect sets of unique capacities to absorb, hold, and transport water under various regimes of availability. The implication is that these structures regulate water, which regulates the environment from plant microhabitat to the biosphere.

The Magnitude of the Land Plant Cell Wall Interface

On the Earth's surface, only the biosphere is a continually elaborating, complicated, multiphase system that maintains, by a self-organizing process, a high relative ratio of surface area to volume. In general, the abiotic components of climate tend to minimize surface area, whereas only the biosphere is driven by intrinsic forces to continually elaborate surfacial connections with the climatic components. These connections are forged through development, differentiation, and reproduction of organisms. The largest such set of surfacial connections may well be the most important in terms of regulation.

"The most abundant biopolymer on the earth is the macromolecular matrix of land plant cell walls" (United States Department of Energy, 1988). The macromolecular matrix connecting plants, substratum, and atmosphere is here estimated to be, by orders of magnitude, the largest interface on the Earth's surface, according to the following calculations. The specific interface elaborated in leaf area is estimated to be about 4.3 times the continental area of the Earth (Lieth and Whittaker, 1975). The area of the mesophyll, the plant body–water film–atmospheric interface, is taken to be 10 to 50 times greater than the leaf surface (Nobel, 1983). Root surface area, although in general less well known,

is calculated at 20 to 100 times greater than the leaf surface (Nobel, 1983).

Mesophyll area, the exchange surface within cavities in the leaves, is calculated from the above to be between 10 and 90 times the surface area of the oceans, and roughly 40 to 200 times the surface area of the land masses. Similar calculations indicate that root surface area is between 20 and 180 times the area of the oceans, and between 80 and 400 times the area of the land masses (figure 34.2).

The effective size of this multiple interface is continually modified by plant growth and decay, modulating conditions reciprocally affecting and affected by evaporation, convection, wind velocity, weathering, metabolism, and the concentrations of water vapor, carbon dioxide, nitrates, sulfates, and organics in the atmosphere. Although estimates are

Operative Scale of Biological Climate Regulation by Land Plant Structures

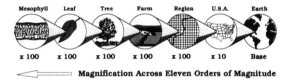

Plant Leaf and Root Surfaces as Multiples of Land Area of the Earth

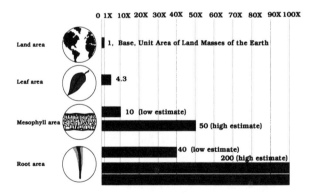

Figure 34.2 Regulation of the surface temperature of the Earth by land plants requires integrated behavior across several orders of magnitude, indicated by the magnification diagram covering eleven orders of magnitude. The land area of the Earth serves in this figure as the basic, functional unit of global response, providing a graphic estimate of the scale of the land plant interfaces in terms of the land areas of the Earth. Estimates of root surface area place it between 40 and 200 times that of the land area; leaf mesophyll area appears to be between 10 and 50 times the continental area; and leaf area is estimated to be about 4.3 times the total surface area of the land masses of the earth. (From Nobel, 1983 and Lieth and Whittaker, 1975).

necessarily approximate, and the Earth's surface is not smooth and regular, the figures given are probably very low because plants continually grow into steep gradients of flow and concentration.

Magnitude alone would suggest that the land plants have regulatory roles vis-à-vis the surface conditions on the planet. Different states, such as liquid-solid, solid-gaseous, liquid-gaseous, ". . . partition their free energy between the internal energy U(T) and the entropy S(T) in different ways" (Zangwill, 1988). The scale of the partitioning effected by the structure of the land plants, together with their anabolic and catalytic capacities and direct connections with the powerful surficial catalytic engines of the microbial world on their leaves (Corpe and Rheem, 1989) and in soils, assures them a prominent position among the regulators of the Earth's surface conditions.

Modes of Regulation by Terrestrial Plant Interfaces

Thus far, this paper has described interfacial regulation in terms of classical physical chemistry and thermodynamics, underscoring that interfaces are regulators, and that the land plant cell wall matrix is arguably the largest interface on the planet. How specifically might this interface modify and regulate global climatic parameters, affecting Gaian regulation? The following is a description of how, logically, this immense interface affects such parameters as water and mineral availability, temperature, and air flow patterns. According to the argument presented, interfacial regulation is effected by such processes as evaporation, chemisorption, physisorption, and control of resistance to the flow of water. The principles and equations described here will here be used to explicate the workings of this land plant interfacial surface.

Evaporative Surface: A Regulated
Free Energy–Lowering Interface

Evaporation rates are regulated by plant structures. Although there is a great deal of variation in evaporative rates, comparing a free water surface to a bryophyte (moss) colony and to a forest or agricultural field, plant communities commonly have water losses lower than the free water surface. However, from the early models of water relations of plants it became clear that these organisms are not passive with regard to evaporation. Specifically, surface properties, roughness in fluid dynamic terms, modifies evaporative rates and mass and mo-

mentum exchange, ". . . depending on the roughness of a crop, transpiration can exceed evaporation from a smooth surface of open water, a result which was not predicted by earlier works on the subject" (Blackwell, 1963). The significance of this effect has still not been fully appreciated: since evapotranspiration may be less *or* more than the evaporation from a free water interface, the presence and structural features of plant bodies must therefore modify the amount of water loss at any given interface, as compared with open water. Specific communities, such as salt marsh grasses, apparently utilize water uptake to modify oxygen penetration and redox state of the substratum (Dacey and Howes, 1984). In general, then, certain communities of larger land plants as well as some bryophyte colonies are able to modulate evaporative rates (table 34.1), indicating that plant communities actively modify the amount of water in the substratum and in the atmosphere.

Table 34.1 indicates that, in these experimental circumstances, and in models and measures of evaporation, the evaporative capacity of certain communities of vascular plants or bryophytes can exceed that of a free water surface, demonstrating that the resistance to the movement of water is considerably lower in bryophyte colonies than in larger plants and often lower than that of a free water surface itself. This together with other evidence indicates that the water-conducting strategies of bryophyte colonies are structured in terms of the flat gradients of evapotranspiration within the laminar flow boundary layer near the substratum, and that colony morphology is capable of moving water under quite unfavorable boundary layer conditions. Specifically, colony morphology regulates water movement. The larger land plants effect similar regulative capacities by rather different hormonally mediated processes, from guttation to stomatal control to the scaling of conducting tissue (figure 34.1).

Surface Tension, Physisorption, and Chemisorption:
Thermodynamic Free Energy–Lowering Capacity
and Regulation

The physical-chemical properties of the plant body matrix regulate redox state of the soil and plant-atmosphere systems (Dacey and Howes, 1984; Hutchinson, 1970; Morowitz, 1970). In the terms of surface physics, plant bodies actively partition the atmosphere, hydrosphere, and lithosphere, thereby regulating dynamically, and irreversibly, conditions at the Earth's surface. Organisms in general, and the land plants especially, utilize the processes of de-

Table 34.1 Evaporation As a Percentage of an Open Water Surface (Number of Trials = N > 15)

Species	Colony Growth Form	Percentage Evaporation	N
Bryum argenteum	Turf	113–116	33
Dicranum scoparium	Turf	133–143	37
Leucobryum glauca	Cushion	131–147	52
Eurynchium riparioides	Mat	111–127	19
Climacium dendroides	Canopy	58–90	26
Thuidium delicatulum	Weft	112–134	24
Hylocomium splendens	Weft	62–96	16
Rye grass field	—	60*	
Open water surface	Control	—	100

Evaporation with free water access
Bryophyte data from Mankiewicz, 1987a. Bryophyte colonies were set within perforated styrofoam discs floating in a water-filled container, 11.3 cm in height by 7.2 cm internal diameter. Percentages were calculated as the amount of water lost over time compared with the control (similar containers filled with water lacking bryophyte colonies).
*Calculated from Pruitt and Angus, 1961.

velopment to continually partition their surroundings through the elaboration of surface. On a local, regional, or global scale, the magnitude of these surfaces varies with time.

The capacity to increase surfacial area is inherent in the properties of plant development, cell division, differentiation, enlargement, and death. These processes elaborate specific surfacial ratios as a function of the stage of the life cycle, energy state, membrane potential, polarization, and constraints of order (Ruis and Goodwin, 1985). The macromolecular, extracellular matrix of the plant body may be described in such developmental or structural terms (Preston, 1974; Wainright et al., 1976). Within the plant body, and as a residuum in the soil, this macromolecular matrix provides unique surface properties that regulate their surroundings.

Although not often recognized in these terms, a liquid water film forms a surface-chemical complex with the cell wall matrix that dramatically increases the free energy–lowering capacity of the land plant body and their surroundings. Carbon dioxide and oxygen are orders of magnitude more soluble in liquid films. Plants, their humic and other byproducts, and associated microflora, provide a set of surface properties and energy states that radically increase the probability of solubilization of minerals. The presence of CO_2, water, and minerals within the plant body increases the probability of growth and surfacial elaboration. This autocatalytic process of the biosphere continues to elaborate surfaces which complex with films of liquid water, increasing the surfacial connection of atmosphere, lithosphere, and hydrosphere.

Air Flow Modification by Plant Structures

Plant bodies are complex surfaces that act to modify the velocity gradient of the atmosphere. Developmental processes and branching strategies thus regulate wind speeds near the ground because land plants entrain the fluid dynamic forces, which are prime movers of water, minerals, and CO_2 (Vogel, 1981; Zimmermann and Brown, 1971), thus regulating the forces that control mass and momentum transfer (Eagleson, 1982). At the same time, the land plants act as interfaces that enlarge and extend the surface boundary layer of the Earth, and increase its complexity and effective surface area.

The presence of the land plants in the velocity stream of the atmosphere adds several orders of magnitude of effective surface to these interfaces, because on the scale of seconds to minutes, meters of atmosphere move past land plant bodies, shearing parcels of air to and from the plant surface (Goldstein, 1938; Lemon et al., 1971; Mankiewicz, 1987a; Pruitt and Angus, 1961; Shapiro, 1961), displacing the interaction between plant and atmosphere far from equilibrium. The fluid dynamic entrainment of the atmosphere by land plant structures should be investigated in order to discover modes of regulation of momentum transfer in general circulation models (Eagleson, 1982). The presently largely noncausal models may be improved, even revolutionized, by researching specific relationships between surface roughness, leaf surface area, plant and community geometry, and momentum and mass transfer. This would provide definitive tests of the Gaia hypothesis in terms of *how much* plants structure the flow of energy and materials.

Resistance to Flow and Water Potential As Regulators of Water Conduction

The Hagen-Poiseuille equation provides essential relations between flow rate and scale, as discussed above, where, for each order of magnitude increase in the radius of a capillary conducting space, the volume of flow increases 10,000-fold. Table 34.2 describes the resistance to flow in plant structures in terms of the hydrostatic pressure required to move water through the plasmalemma, cell wall interstices, tracheid (woody conducting cell) lumen, and external capillary space in a moss colony. From the root-soil connection involving the movement of water through the membrane in the endodermis, to the tracheary cells of xylem, to the external capillary spaces between moss stems and leaves or peat systems, over twelve orders of magnitude of hydrostatic pressure are encompassed. This table is presented in the familiar terms of pressure differential per length rather than the more unwieldy dimensions of resistances (force times time divided by length raised to the fifth power!) to facilitate comparison with other data.

Hydrostatic resistances set rates of flow, and, more importantly, rates of exchange. Governed by fluid dynamic geometry, it is important to note that in each case, rates of water uptake and water loss will be different, depending on the hydration levels of the system. This general phenomenon of nonlinear behavior based on the history of the system is called *hysteresis*. It was discovered in soils by Haines (1925, 1927, 1930) and Fisher (1926, 1928). In general terms, hysteresis occurs at phenomenal scales across the twelve orders of magnitude of resistance covered in table 34.2. Such distinctly nonlinear behavior may be seen as a regulator of hydration levels and concomitant phenomena in bryophyte, peat, and soil systems (Hayward and Clymo, 1982; Mankiewicz, 1987b). Since the behavior of the system depends on its previous hydration level, it forms a simple kind of feedback system from which other regulatory capacities are derived. The structural organization and asymmetries of resistances and conductances for plant structures provide other examples of hysteresis.

Resistance occurs in series, from capillary and matric connections in soil up to membrane systems of leaf mesophyll cells. This, however, is only one of the polarly organized water distribution patterns in terrestrial vegetation. In all land plants, a film of liquid water extends from soil to leaf surface or mesophyll, with some 10^8 to 10^{13} parallel systems multiply branching off along the way, connecting this liquid water film with the membrane system of each cell within the organism. From bryophyte colonies to large trees, a continuous apoplast, the extracellular matrix, extends from base to tip (Raven, 1977), and cortex to epidermis. Since the osmotic pressure of each of some trillion cells in a large tree is more than twelve orders of magnitude greater than pressure in any hydrostatic system, the direction of flow and the capacity for water storage are governed by the physiological capacity of cells. Stomatal geometry and behavior (Lee and Gates, 1964; Gates, 1976) and cuticle resistance (Hadley, 1980) provide powerful controls of water loss. Thus an integration of structures and hormonally controlled processes acts to constrain the field of behavior set by the hydrostatic resistances of the plasmalemma.

Table 34.2 Water Conductivity and Resistance to Water Loss of Plant Structures

Plant Structure	Water Potential (MPa)
Plasmalemma	2×10^3
Cell wall interstices	2
6-μm thick (2×3 μm)	
Tracheid lumen	2×10^{-5}
r = 20 μm, L = 1 mm	
Small external capillary space in moss, peat, or soil	2×10^{-9}
r = 200 μm, L = 1 mm	

r = radius; L = length.
The first three pressures are from Nobel (1983) and the last is calculated from the Hagen-Poiseuille equation. For purposes of comparison, resistances to water movement are given in terms of pressure drop per unit length.

The Evolution of Water-Conducting Strategy and Regulatory Capacity in the Land Plants: Bryophytes and Tracheophytes

Terrestrial habitats may be divided into two functional size classes: (1) near the substratum where air flow is limited by viscosity to slow movement in sheets or lamina, creating a relatively surface boundary layer, the properties of which are determined by local surface properties of the Earth; and (2) above the substratum, (height $\geq$ 2 cm), where leaves and other plant structures extend into the freely moving atmosphere where flow is turbulent, the atmosphere is freely mixed, and boundary layers are relatively thin and determined by the scale of the plant structure itself.

Land plants embody two different strategies that exploit the differing limits and potentials of these habitats. Bryophytes largely inhabit the region within the surface boundary layer of the substratum, whereas the larger land plants or *tracheophytes,* extend into the portion of the atmosphere centimeters to meters above the substratum where more rapid movement and turbulence shear the boundary layer down to a minimal envelope surrounding each leaf. Within the laminar flow region, regulation of water movement is largely a matter of facilitating water holding and distribution rates across the plant colony–soil continuum (Walter and Stadelmann, 1968; Raven, 1977; Proctor, 1979; Mankiewicz, 1987 a and b; Klinger, Chapter 28). In turbulent shear, water regulation requires an integration of morphological modifications, from the atmospheric boundary layer around the leaf and stomates to root-soil connections (Raven, 1977; Zimmermann and Brown, 1971).

Terrestrial plant evolution itself has been partitioned between environments near the substratum within the laminar flow of the atmosphere and zones of turbulent shear. Plant bodies, colonies, and communities scale themselves differently for these two kinds of habitat. These spatial constraints and potentials also have temporal dimensions. Bryophytes occupy niches of similar scale to that of the earliest land plants (Gray and Boucot, 1977; Mankiewicz, 1987a). The functional spaces they inhabit, largely within the boundary layer of the terrestrial substratum, were first colonized by plants at least 420 million years ago. Diminutive land plants living within the laminar surface boundary layer evolved first, and larger plants exploiting zones of the tur-

bulent atmosphere came much later. From fossil evidence, land plants appear to have extended into the turbulent region of the moving atmosphere 350 million years ago. Since the middle of the Devonian, then, both of these different strategies have been in existence among the terrestrial biota. The time frame of the separation of these scales of plant differentiation encompasses at least tens of millions of years in evolutionary time (Chaloner, 1970; Gray and Boucot, 1977). On the basis of the Gaia hypothesis, investigations of the Silurian-Devonian boundary should uncover changes in global temperature regulation that may have accompanied these changes in plant structure.

Products of these evolutionary events, once distributed, would have changed the surface properties of the Earth. The origin and dispersal of organisms at the scale of the earliest land plants, in the millimeter-to-centimeter size range of mosses and liverworts, would modify the water-holding capacity of the terrestrial surfaces. We predict that biological activity, heat and mass exchange properties of the continental surfaces changed dramatically where these plants grew. Mineralized carbon burial and humic content of the oceans should increase with widespread distribution of land plants. The differentiation of tree forms more than fifty million years later in the Devonian permitted terrestrial vegetation to modify, in addition to these parameters, the geometrical and momentum exchange properties of the Earth's surface, such as increased surface roughness, increasing mass and momentum transfer, and decreasing water flow and erosion from terrestrial environments.

These evolutionary events can be interpreted in the context of the general circulation models discussed by Manabe (1982), Perrier (1982), and others. At global scale, these models have identified key regulators of surfacial conditions. According to Manabe (1982), "Some of the key processes in atmospheric circulation models are the exchanges of heat, moisture, and momentum between the earth's surface and the free atmosphere through the planetary boundary layer." As underscored here, at organismic scale in terrestrial environments, these key processes are differentially regulated by the land plants. Intriguingly, whereas radiative heat exchange may be quite similar amongst all land plants (Gates, 1980), moisture and momentum exchange are in large part functions of size, shape, and resistance. These two different water-conducting strategies—the bryophyte low-pressure, low-resistance, high water-holding capacity and the vascular plant high-pressure, high-resistance water transpiration system—act to regulate water content and humidity in various terrestrial ecosystems in different ways. By regulating gradients of liquid water in soil and peat systems, however, both of these plant groups establish redox gradients that further control weathering and other chemical processes. Thus these two strategies partition environments by differential capacities to modify biological, radiative, heat, mass, and momentum exchange. Simply, land plants differentially transform the fluid geometrical properties of landscapes. The components of climate and climate itself may be modified through the differential capacities of these two strategies vis-à-vis water retention and regulation, pH and eH modulation, mineralization, albedo, and the entrainment of atmospheric momentum.

Conclusion: Are Interfacial Regulatory Capacities Gaian?

The argument presented in this chapter is that the size and activity of the earth's liquid water interface is increased some two to seven orders of magnitude by the macromolecular matrix of the bodies of land plants, whereas resistance to water loss extends over some twelve orders of magnitude. By these means, the multiphase interface of the earth's crust, liquid water, and atmosphere are dynamically structured by the presence of the terrestrial vegetation and their cobionts. The magnitude and activity of this interface are regulated by growth and development. Because the presence of the liquid water interface itself regulates nutrient availability by functioning at once as the principle solvent on the planet, major transport system, and a primary governor of redox potential, it is the major candidate for regulator of surface temperature regulators. This line of investigation yields specific conclusions: if plants partition the components of climate, then the resulting phase change and concentration modifications will further change these climatic components, as well as the plant forms themselves. If these phase change and concentration modifications alter temperature and concentration favorably for the physiological requirements of plant and other organisms (and this is the largest and most active interface on the planet's surface), then by virtue of magnitude alone, it must form a regulatory feedback system of planetary proportions.

By Darwinian reasoning, we may view the bodies of land plants as organized such that flow rates of water and minerals from substratum to shoots, leaves, and atmosphere are modulated within the physiological bounds of these organisms. Darwin's law may thus be restated in physiological terms: where environments change, only those organisms that change their environment to fit their physiological requirements or change their physiological requirements can survive.

Moving from evolution to thermodynamics, this logic may again be applied. Since the cell wall matrix readily complexes with a film of liquid water, the high surface tension of water increases the free energy–lowering capacity of plant surfaces by increasing physisorption and chemisorption, and this partitions the environment locally and globally. While the research data summarized in table 34.1 derive from studies on evaporation, they are directly indicative of global free energy–lowering surfaces. Land plants extend the interface of liquid water from the mineralized soil into the freely moving gaseous atmosphere. In the process, the substratum-plant-atmospheric system acts as a free energy–lowering interface, mutually regulating the concentration of solutes and weathering rates in soils (Volk, 1987) and gases in the atmosphere. By acting to partition the components of climate, organisms provide free energy–lowering surfaces, gathering energy and materials for further environmental partitioning. Simply stated, surfaces structure the exchanges of mass and energy that drive organismic growth and reproduction. The growth- and humidity-regulating capacities of plants in general make the environment more amenable to their own physiological requirements and those of their cobionts. By capturing solar energy, mineralizing soil (Volk, 1987), producing and exchanging essential nutrients (Corpe and Rheem, 1989), and cropping, the assemblage of organisms appears to form together a feedback system that acts to regulate temperature and concentration of components in the terrestrial environment and establish and maintain conditions favorable to life (Chiariello et al., 1982; Safir et al., 1971; Schroth and Hancock, 1982; Seastedt and Crossley, 1984; Wood et al., 1984).

Surfaces, at global scale, effectively interconnect the components of the climate. Specifically, atmosphere, hydrosphere, cryosphere, and lithosphere are connected through interfaces that provide the surface energies that dynamically modify each in terms of the others. If these abiotic surface interactions acted to regulate temperature and concentrations of components such that these remain amenable to the physiological requirements of life, then the Earth would be regulated by nongaian interactions. Because land plants and their byproducts, as well as other organisms, provide orders of magnitude more surfacial interconnection between other components of climate than these components provide individually or together, Gaian regulation is much more probable.

Only processes of life continually elaborate interfacial connections between the multiple components of climate. In fact, because the structural development and evolution of organisms is an irreversible, far from equilibrium process (Brooks and Wiley, 1986; Webber et al., 1988), it may be argued that organismic surfaces have a tendency to increase in size and complexity over time, thereby increasing overall regulatory capacity (Raven, 1977; Vermeij, 1987), and like ecosystems, incorporating environmental variation (O'Neill et al., 1986). Such processes, occurring at various temporal and spatial scales of ecology and evolution, could well act as regulators of such regulatory capacity. By modulating the terrestrial water interface, land plants may regulate all processes and reactions dependent on the presence of this interface, an activity we calculate to be of global import.

The connection between land plant bodies, soil, and water potential has long been recognized in plant physiology. The novel perspective presented here relates the phenomenology of surface tension and films of liquid water with the thermodynamic fundaments of phase relations and partition functions. The purpose of these connections is to point out that we should expect the largest, most active interface on the planet to have maximum free energy–lowering and regulatory capacity. Clearly, this question cannot be fully answered here. However, the theoretical framework offered and supportive evidence presented suggest that water-conducting and water-holding strategies and capacities in terrestrial vegetation actively incorporate (in the sense of O'Neill et al., 1986) environmental variations. An inevitable conclusion, if this line of reasoning is correct, is that the hydrated carbon and interfacial af-

finity for water at surface hydration sites of the land plant body is the macromolecular instrument by which plants have transformed the land into the most catalytically active area of the planet.

Acknowledgments

Thanks are offered to William Kinsinger for helping design and create the figures. The comments of three anonymous reviewers were most helpful in making it clear to me where the manuscript did not manage to get essential points and relationships across. Thanks especially to Julie A. Downey for thoroughgoing discussions of strategies for the organization of this work.

Notes

1. A method of geometrical representation of the thermodynamic properties of substances by means of surfaces (Transactions of the Connecticut Academy, II. 382–404, Dec. 1873) is one early example among several of Gibbs' reasoning, which connects interfaces and regulation.

2. N.N. Semenov and C.N. Henshelwood shared the 1956 Nobel Prize in chemistry for their work on reaction mechanisms.

3. This point is well made in Lamprecht, I., and Zotin, A.I., eds. *Thermodynamics and Regulation of Biological Processes.* 1985. See especially Ruis, J.L.., and Goodwin, B.C. *Continuous phase transitions and morphogenesis.*

References

Blackwell, M.J. 1963. The role of evaporation in the surface energy balance. In: Ritter, A.J., and Whitehead, F.H., eds. *The Water Relations of Plants.* New York: Wiley.

Brooks, D.R., and Wiley, E.O. 1986. *Evolution as Entropy.* New York: Cambridge University Press.

Chaloner, W.G. 1970. The rise of the first land plants. *Biol Rev,* 45, 353–377.

Chiariello, N, Hickman, J.C., and Mooney, H.A. 1982. Endomycorrhizal role for interspecific transfer of phosphorus in a community of annual plants. *Science,* 217, 941–943.

Corpe, W.A., and Rheem, S. 1989. Ecology of the methylotrophic bacteria on living leaf surfaces. Federation of European Microbiological Societies. *Microbiol Ecol,* 62, 243–250.

Dacey, J.W.H., and Howes, B.L. 1984. Water uptake by roots controls water table movement and sediment oxidation in short *Spartina* marsh. *Science,* 224, 487–489.

Eagleson, P.S., ed. 1982. *Atmospheric General Circulation Models.* New York: Cambridge University Press.

Fisher, R.A. 1926. On the capillary forces in an ideal soil; correction of formulae given by W.B. Haines. *J Agricultural Sci,* 16, 492–505.

Fisher, R.A. 1928. Further note on the capillary forces in an ideal soil. *J Agricultural Sci,* 18, 406–410.

Gates, D.M. 1976. Energy exchange and transpiration. *Water and Plant Life: Ecological Studies,* 19, 137–147.

Gates, D.M. 1980. *Biophysical Ecology.* New York: Springer-Verlag.

Gibbs, J.W. 1961 (1906). *The Scientific Papers of J. Willard Gibbs.* New York: Dover Publications.

Goldstein, S. 1938. *Modern Developments in Fluid Dynamics: An Account of Theory and Experiment Relating to Boundary Layers, Turbulent Motion and Wakes. Vol. I and II.* New York: Dover Publications.

Gray, J., and Boucot, A.J. 1977. Early vascular land plants: Proof and conjecture. *Lethaia,* 10, 145–173.

Hadley, N.F. 1980. Surface waxes and integumentary permeability. *American Scientist,* 68, 546–553.

Haines, W.B. 1925. Studies in the physical properties of soil. II. A note on the cohesion developed by capillary forces in an ideal soil. *J Agricultural Sci,* 15, 529–535.

Haines, W.B. 1927. Studies in the physical properties of soil. IV. A further contribution to the theory of capillary phenomena in soil. *J Agricultural Sci,* 17, 264–290.

Haines, W.B. 1930. Studies in the physical properties of soil. V. The hysteresis effect in capillary properties, and the modes of moisture distribution associated therewith. *J Agricultural Sci,* 20, 97–116.

Hayward, P.M. and Clymo, R.S. 1982. Profiles of water content and pore size in *Sphagnum* and peat, and their relation to peat bog ecology. Proceedings of the Royal Society of London. Series B, 215:219–325

Hutchinson, G.E. 1970. The biosphere. *Scientific American,* 223, 44–53.

Lamprecht, I. and Zotin, A.I. eds. 1985. *Thermodynamics and Regulation of Biological Processes.* Berlin: Walter de Gruyter.

Lee, R., and Gates, D.M. 1964. Diffusion resistance in leaves as related to their stomatal anatomy and micro-structure. *Am J Botany,* 51, 963–975.

Lemon, E., Stewart, D.W., and Shawcroft, R.W. 1971. The sun's work in a cornfield. *Science,* 174, 371–378.

Lieth, H. and Whittaker, R.H., eds. 1975. *The Primary Production of the Biosphere.* New York: Springer-Verlag.

Manabe, S. 1982. Simulation of climate by general circulation models with hydrological cycles. In: Eagleson, P.S., ed. *Land Surface Processes in Atmospheric General Circulation Models.* New York: Cambridge University Press.

Mankiewicz, P.M. 1987a. *Hydrostatic and fluid dynamic constraints on external capillary water conduction in the diversification of the land plants: Bryophyte colonies, a model system.* Ph.D. thesis, City University of New York.

Mankiewicz, P.M. 1987b. The low pressure field porometer: A new, low cost technique for characterizing external capillary water conduction in whole colonies of bryophytes and other small plants. *Bryologist,* 90, 253–262.

Morowitz, H.J. 1970. *Entropy for Biologists.* New York: Academic Press.

Nobel, P.S. 1983. *Biophysical Plant Physiology and Ecology.* San Francisco: W.H. Freeman and Co.

O'Neill, R.V., DeAngelis, D.L., Wade, J.B., and Allen, T.F.H. 1986. *A Hierarchical Concept of Ecosystems.* Princeton, N.J.: Princeton University Press.

Perrier, A. 1982. Land surface processes: Vegetation. In: Eagleson, P.S., ed. *Land Surface Processes in Atmospheric General Circulation Models.* New York: Cambridge University Press.

Preston, R.D. 1974. *The Physical Biology of Plant Cell Walls.* London: Chapman and Hall.

Proctor, M.C.F. 1979. Structure and eco-physiological adaptation in bryophytes. In: Clark, G.C.S., and Duckett, J.G., eds. *Bryophyte Systematics.* New York: Academic Press, 479–509.

Pruitt, W.O., and Angus, D.E. 1961. Comparison of evapotranspiration with solar net radiation and evaporation from water surfaces. In *Investigation of Energy and Mass Transfers Near the Ground, Including Influences of the Soil-plant-atmosphere System.* First Annual Report, U.S Army Electronics Proving Grounds Technical Program, University of California, Davis.

Raven J.A. 1977. The evolution of vascular land plants in relation to supracellular transport processes. In: Woolhouse, H.W., ed. *Advances in Botanical Research.* New York: Academic Press.

Ruis, J.L., and Goodwin, B.C. 1985. Continuous phase transitions and morphogenesis. In: Lamprecht, I. and Zotin, A.I., eds. *Thermodynamics and Regulation of Biological Processes.* Berlin: Walter de Gruyter.

Safir, G.R., Boyer, J.S., and Gerdemann, J.W. 1971. Mycorrhizal enhancement of water transport in soybean. *Science,* 172, 581–583.

Schneider, S.H., and Londer, R. 1984. *The Coevolution of Climate and Life.* San Francisco: Sierra Club Books.

Schroth, M.N., and Hancock, G. 1982. Disease suppressive soils and root colonizing bacteria. *Science,* 216, 1376–1381.

Seastedt, T.R., and Crossley, D.A., Jr. 1984. The influence of arthropods on ecosystems. *Bioscience,* 34, 157–161.

Shapiro, A.H. 1961. *Shape and Flow: The Fluid Dynamics of Drag.* New York: Doubleday.

United States Department of Energy. 1988. Summary Report of a Workshop on Lignin Research: Needs and Opportunities. University of Illinois, April 18–19, 1988. CONF-880423–SUMM. Washington, D.C.: United States Department of Energy, Office of Energy Research, Division of Energy Biosciences.

Vermeij, G.J. 1987. *Evolution and Escalation.* Princeton, N.J.: Princeton University Press.

Vogel, S. 1981. *Life in Moving Fluids: The Physical Biology of Flow.* Boston: Willard Grant Press.

Volk, T. 1987. Feedbacks between weathering and atmospheric CO_2 over the last 100 million years. *Am J Sci,* 287, 763–779.

Wainwright, S.A., Biggs, W.D., Currey, J.D., and Gosline, J.M. 1976. *Mechanical Design in Organisms.* New York: Wiley.

Walter, H., and Stadelmann, E. 1968. The physiological prerequisites for the transition of autotrophic plants from water to terrestrial life. *Bioscience,* 18, 694–701.

Webber, B.H., Depew, D.J., and Smith, J.D. eds. 1988. *Entropy, Information, and Evolution.* Cambridge, Mass.: MIT Press.

Wood, T., Bormann, F.H., and Voigt, G.K. 1984. Phosphorous cycling in a Northern Hardwood Forest: Biological and chemical control. *Science,* 223: 391–393.

Zangwill, A. 1988. *Physics at Surfaces.* New York: Cambridge University Press.

Zimmermann, M.H., and Brown, C.L. 1971. *Tree Structure and Function.* New York: Springer-Verlag.

David Schwartzman, John Evans, Harold Okrend, and Soe Aung
35
Microbial Weathering and Gaia

This chapter discusses the role of soil microbes and other land biota in the operation of the carbonate-silicate climatic stabilizer and its implications for the Gaia hypothesis. We also report on experiments on laboratory weathering in soil substrates.

Weathering of calcium- and magnesium-bearing silicates and the temperature and rainfall dependence of weathering is a key part of the Walker climatic stabilizer (Walker et al., 1981). Weathering of these silicates acts as a sink for CO_2, balancing volcanic emissions, the source. The mechanism involves as well the precipitation of calcium carbonate, limestone in the ocean, and the control of temperature by the CO_2 level in the atmosphere and solar luminosity; the stabilizer operates by the increase of weathering with temperature. Is the role of soil microbes and other land biota incidental to operation of this stabilizer, or is their role crucial to maintaining habitable conditions? If the answer is yes to the latter question, then a real gaian (or a better term might be *geophysiological;* see Lovelock, 1987) mechanism would be demonstrated. This question has been addressed quantitatively in another study (Schwartzman and Volk, 1989).

Walker and colleagues (1981), the BLAG model group (Berner et al., 1983; Berner and Barron, 1984; Lasaga et al., 1985), and Kasting and colleagues (1988) recognize the role of plants and microbes in elevating pCO_2 (and hence increasing proton availability) in soil, promoting silicate weathering. But Kasting and colleagues (1988) maintain, in a provocative paper, that the carbonate-silicate climatic stabilizer would operate in absence of biota at only modestly higher temperatures:

We . . . suggest that the fundamental controls on atmospheric carbon dioxide levels are physical rather than biological. We would argue, for example, that if shelled organisms that now deposit calcium carbonate on the sea floor did not exist, the concentration of calcium and bicarbonate ions in seawater would rise. Once the ion concentrations reached a critical level, calcium carbonate would form without the intervention of organisms. Such must have been the case before about 600 million years ago, when shell makers first appeared.

Similarly, calculations show that the decrease in silicate weathering caused by a complete disappearance of land plants could be offset by a temperature increase of about 10 degrees C—a change that could be accomplished by the negative-feedback loop of the carbonate-silicate cycle. The increased greenhouse warming would produce a climate similar to that of 100 million years ago during the mid-Cretaceous period: warm, but nonetheless well suited for many forms of life, including the dinosaurs. Hence there is good reason to believe the earth would still have remained habitable even if it had never been inhabited. The carbonate-silicate cycle, acting alone, would have provided the necessary buffering mechanism.

We are critical of these arguments for the following reasons:

1. Algae facilitating limestone deposition were present in the ocean before 600 my ago, well into the Precambrian (stomatolites); their point that limestone formation in the oceans would occur under abiotic conditions, however, is well taken.

2. A land biota was also present well into the Precambrian (Campbell, 1979, cites a 2.4 by paleosol with reduced organic carbon).

3. The authors may be correct in estimating the climatic effects of vascular land plants, but they neglect the apparently important role of terrestrial microbial biota in enhancing weathering.

4. It would appear that in the absence of biota, a much higher pCO_2 in the atmosphere is needed to generate comparable carbonic acid levels in soils as now, a pCO_2 even higher than the level in present soils because of the diffusion problem (Lovelock, 1983).

5. The lack of a land biota, including vegetative cover and microbes, would presumably result in a reduction of evapotranspiration and rainfall (Lovelock, 1983). When it would rain, one would expect rapid erosion of any soils accumulated because of the absence of vegetative cover.

6. While the absence of soil would solve the diffusion problem, another more critical problem

would arise. The presence of a soil substrate seems to be demanded for water retention needed for carbonic acid availability and weathering. The likely absence of soils, which act as a sponge for the moisture needed for carbonic acid weathering and a reservoir of silicate grains with high surface area, would require much higher CO_2 levels in the atmosphere, and correspondingly higher temperatures, than those of the present day in order to balance the volcanic source of CO_2 (Schwartzman and Volk, 1989). Abiotic weathering rates may, as a first approximation, correspond to bare rock rates. Biotic enhancements on the order of 10^2 to 10^3 are suggested by the following data:

Rates on bare rock (not completely abiotic!): $< 2 \times 10^{-4}$ to $< 3 \times 10^{-5}$ mm/year, compared to rates > 12 to > 73 times that for lichen-covered rock (Hawaiian lava flows; Jackson and Keller, 1970)

Rind development on andesite/basalt clasts (western United States): average 5×10^{-6} mm/year (Colman and Pierce, 1981)

Chemical weathering rates in tropical soils, temperate saprolites: 4×10^{-3} to 5×10^{-2} mm/year (Colman and Dethier, 1986)

Other effects of biota and soil microbes contributing to higher rates of chemical weathering include their production of humic and other organic acids, chelating agents, and inorganic acids, acting as a sink for weathering products and acceleration of physical weathering through microfracturing of mineral grains (Silverman, 1979; Parfenova and Yarilova, 1965). Lasaga (1984) thinks that organic acids may be essential in producing observed weathering rates, because of the slow kinetics of the H_2O-CO_2 system.

The crucial question in relation to the Gaia hypothesis seems to be whether the absence of biotic enhancement of weathering would lead to such increases of CO_2 in the atmosphere that the climatic stabilizer would be reset at higher temperatures approaching the uninhabitability limit. The present juvenile CO_2 flux from volcanism (Des Marais, 1985) would double the CO_2 in the atmosphere-ocean system in 10^6 years. Although such an outcome would not result in a runaway greenhouse on Earth (Kasting and Ackerman, 1986), it could result in a much less habitable Earth throughout much of geological time. Temperatures fit for thermophilic microbes ($> 50°C$) and nothing else could result (Schwartzman and Volk, 1989 outline a scenario for the emergence of the geophysiological climatic stabilizer).

If soil microbes and land biota are essential to establishing weathering rates fast enough to keep the stabilizer operating at relatively cool conditions, then the climatic diversity of microbial soil populations, a product of natural selection, may be important. For example, ecological races of Bacteroides, a very widespread soil microbe, occur in different climatic zones, with temperature being one of the determinant influences (Volobuev, 1964; Mishustin, 1978).

Although there is a considerable literature on microbial involvement in weathering (see Silverman's review, 1979; Robert and Berthelin, 1986), further research seems warranted to clarify the relation of microbial involvement to weathering rates. Many studies have been done of biological and especially microbial involvement and on the role of biogenic organic acids in weathering, only a few have determined the comparative rates of silicate weathering in sterile versus nonsterile conditions in actual soil substrates (e.g., Berthelin et al., 1974). Silverman has noted the limitations of previous work:

The weathering of silicate rocks and minerals in nature is usually envisaged as a relatively slow process, taking place over geologic time. But biological and organic chemical weathering can be remarkably rapid in the laboratory where significant breakdown of silicates within days or weeks appears to be the rule rather than the exception. However, direct extrapolation of laboratory findings to natural events may be premature because of the many variables that cannot be controlled under natural conditions. Such variables as the number and different kinds of living organisms present, their interactions with one another, and with the kinds and amounts of organic matter present initially or as metabolic products, the availability of water and fluctuations in temperature, pH and eH, etc., all acting singly or in different combinations, make predictions of natural events uncertain. One can only acknowledge the great potential that exists for rapid and extensive biological and organic chemical weathering of silicate rocks and minerals in the natural environment.

With this caveat in mind, we experimentally tested the influence of sterilization (autoclaving) and humus levels on weathering rates by scanning electron microscopic (SEM) examination of silicate mineral grains placed in sterile and nonsterile moistened humus (A_1) and leached, humus poor subsoil (A_2) fractions of an argillic ultisol for varying times up to ten months, held at room temperature (figures 35.1–35.7). The pH of the humus was 4.5 to 5, the subsoil about 5. Cultures of the humus produced a spreading growth of bacteria and fungi that could

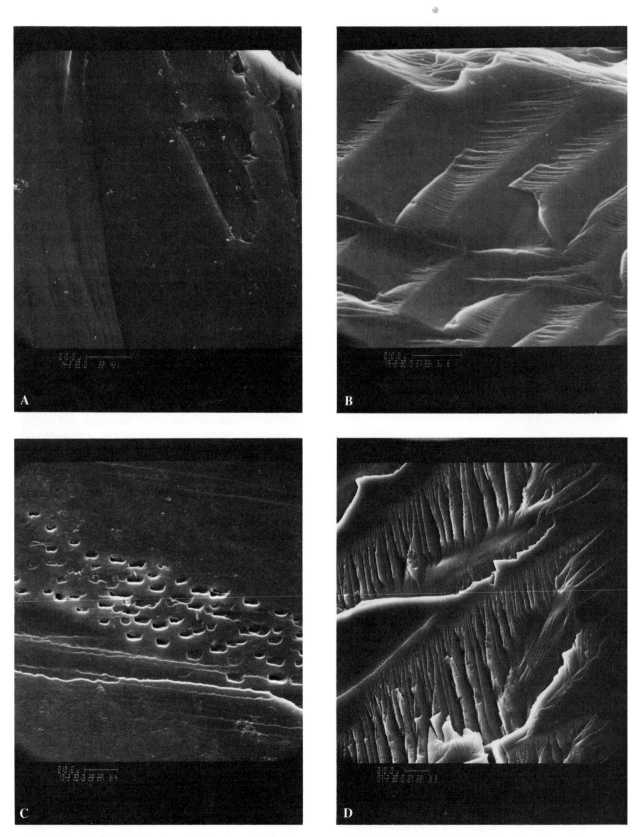

Figure 35.1 SEM photographs of anorthite grain surfaces
from a one-month experiment. **A,B,** fresh, unweathered grain. **C,D,** Nonsterile subsoil.

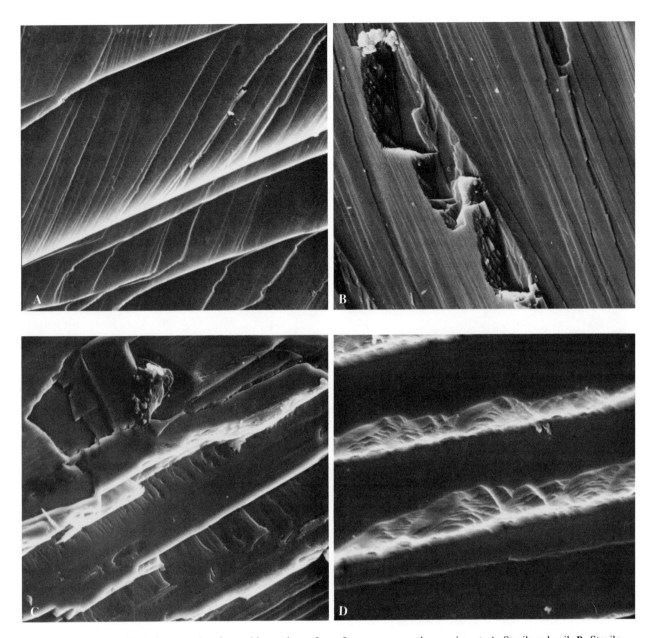

Figure 35.2 Further SEM photographs of anorthite grain surfaces from a one-month experiment. **A,** Sterile subsoil. **B,** Sterile quartz sand. **C,** Nonsterile subsoil, seeing (001) plane. **D,** Sterile subsoil, split from same grain as **C,** seeing (001) plane.

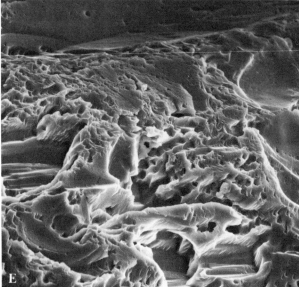

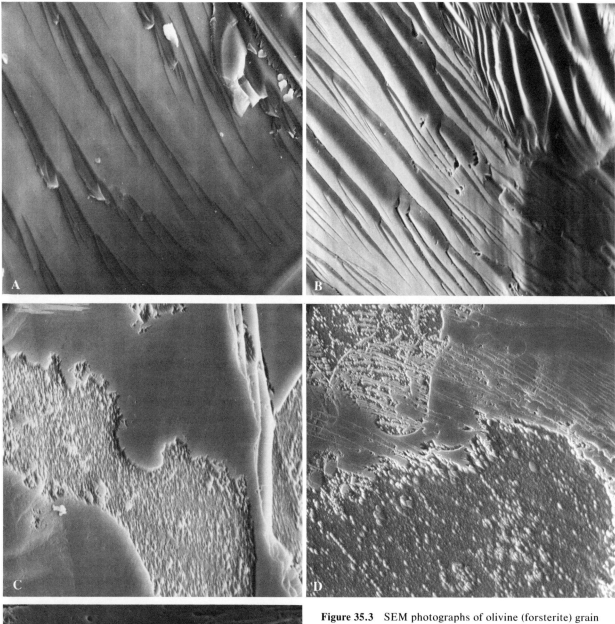

Figure 35.3 SEM photographs of olivine (forsterite) grain surfaces from a one-month experiment. **A,** Fresh, unweathered grain. **B,** Nonsterile subsoil. **C,** Sterile subsoil. **D,** Nonsterile humus. **E,** Sterile humus.

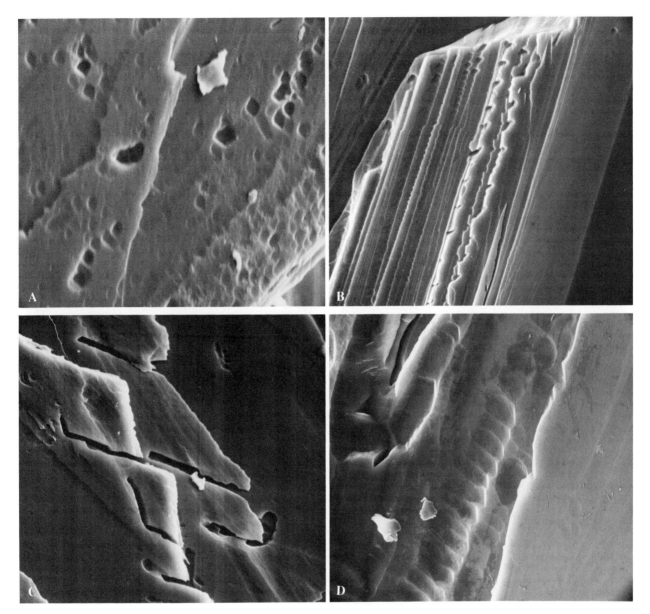

Figure 35.4 SEM photographs of anorthite grain surfaces from a six-month experiment. **A,** Nonsterile subsoil. **B,** Sterile subsoil. **C,** Nonsterile humus. **D,** Sterile humus.

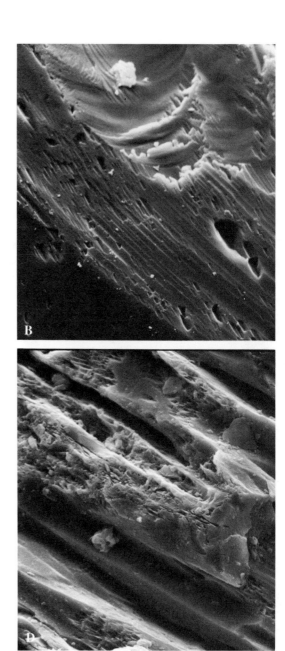

Figure 35.5 SEM photographs of olivine (forsterite) grain surfaces from a six-month experiment. **A,** Nonsterile subsoil. **B,C,** Sterile subsoil. **D,** Nonsterile humus. **E,** Sterile humus.

Figure 35.6 SEM photographs of anorthite grain surfaces ▶ from a ten-month experiment. **A,B,** Nonsterile subsoil; **B** shows possible microbial colonization. **C,** Sterile quartz sand. **D,** Sterile subsoil. **E,** Nonsterile humus; shows microbial colonization. **F,G,H,** Sterile humus.

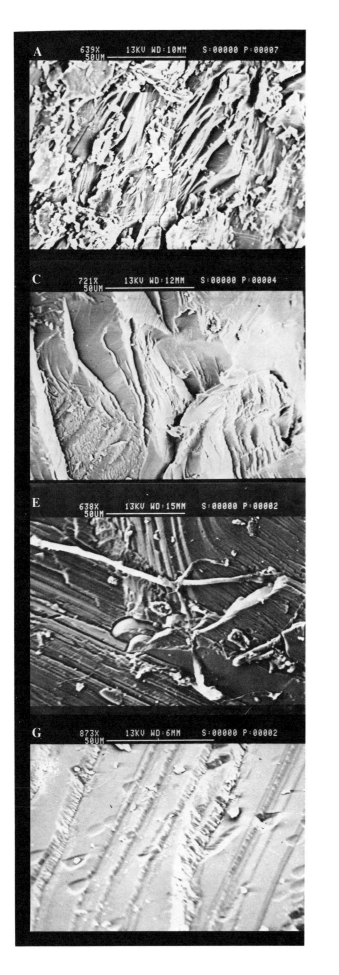
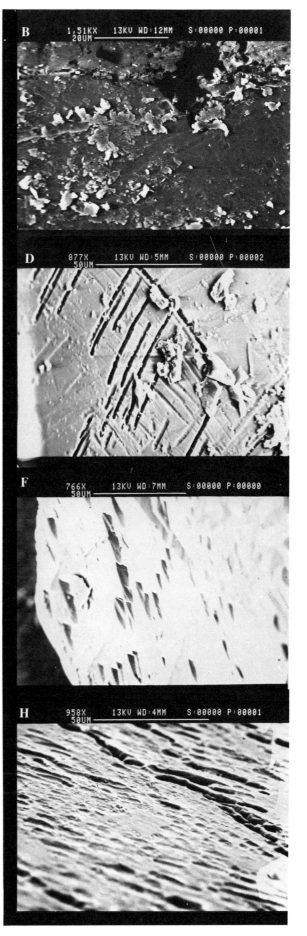

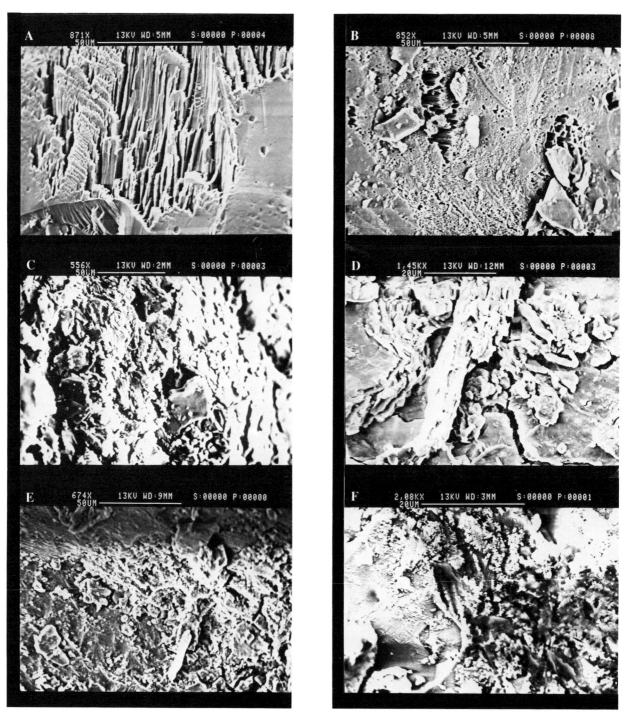

Figure 35.7 SEM photographs of olivine (forsterite) grain surfaces from a ten-month experiment. **A,B,** Nonsterile subsoil. **C,** Sterile subsoil. **D,E,** Nonsterile humus; shows microbial colonization (fungal hyphae) and alteration products. **F,** Sterile humus.

not be counted, the subsoil 2×10^6 colony forming units per gram. The results from an experiment of one month's duration pronounced pitting and etching found in anorthite and forsterite grains, possible effects in enstatite, none evident in diopside and grossular. Combined with results from experiments lasting six and ten months, we conclude that humic acids are the main factor in weathering in these experiments and not carbonic acid, because (1) sterile humus has weathering rates comparable to nonsterile; (2) no weathering of anorthite was observed in sterile quartz sand; and (3) greater effects were evident in the humus substrates than subsoil for both anorthite and forsterite samples. Some direct weathering activity of soil microbes is suspected in the anorthite experiments because significantly less pitting is evident in sterile than in nonsterile subsoil. Microbial colonization of both anorthite and forsterite grains is indicated in ten-month experiments. All these results are consistent with higher chemical weathering rates associated with microbial activity given that humic acids are themselves products of the latter. Possible microbial involvement in tropical weathering would be most interesting; fulvic acid may play an important role as a metal-complexing agent (Griffith and Schnitzer, 1975). We recommend an extensive research program to determine experimental weathering rates in soils of a variety of types, including tests of the effects of temperature, moisture levels, and other parameters. These experiments are needed to make assessments of the contribution of soil microbes to biotic enhancement of weathering.

Acknowledgments

We thank the Chapman Conference on the Gaia Hypothesis for travel assistance. The Department of Mineral Sciences, Smithsonian Institution of Washington, provided the mineral samples used in the experiments: anorthite (#137041), diopside (#105912), enstatite (#B18239), forsterite (#163641), grossular (#147798). Mobil Oil provided summer support for D. Schwartzman.

References

Berner, R.A., and Barron, E.J. 1984. *Am J Sci*, 284, 1183–1192.

Berner, R.A., Lasaga, A.C., and Garrels, R.M. 1983. *Am J Sci*, 283, 641–683.

Berthelin, J., Kogblevi, A., and Dommergues, Y. 1974. *Soil Biol Biochem*, 6, 393–399.

Campbell, S.E. 1979. *Origins of Life*, 9, 335–348.

Colman, S.M., and Dethier, D.P. 1986. In: Colman, S.M., Dethier, D.P. eds. *Rates of Chemical Weathering of Rocks and Minerals*. New York: Academic Press.

Colman, S.M., and Pierce, K.L. 1981. Weathering rinds on andesitic and basaltic stones as a Quaternary age indicator. *Western United States Geological Survey Professional Paper (U.S.)*, 1210, 1–56.

Des Marais, D.J. 1985. In: Sundquist, E.T., and Broecker, W.S., eds. *The Carbon Cycle and Atmospheric CO_2: Natural Variations Archean to Present*. Washington, D.C.: American Geophysical Union, 602–611.

Griffith, S.M., and Schnitzer, M. 1975. *Soil Sci*, 120, 126–131.

Jackson, T.A., and Keller, W.D. 1970. *Am J Sci*, 269, 446–466.

Kasting, J.F., and Ackerman, T.P. 1986, *Science*, 234, 1383–1385.

Kasting, J.F., Toon, O.B., and Pollack, J.B. 1988. *Sci Am*, 258, 90–97.

Lasaga, A.C. 1984. *J Geophys Res*, 89, 4009–4025.

Lasaga, A.C., Berner, R.A., and Garrels, R.M. 1985. In: Sundquist, E.T., and Broecker, W.S., eds. *The Carbon Cycle and Atmospheric CO_2: Natural Variations Archean to Present*. Washington, D.C.: American Geophysical Union, 397–411.

Lovelock, J.E. 1983. In: Westbroek, P., and de Jong, E.W., eds. *Biomineralization and Biological Metal Accumulation*. Dordrecht: Reidel, 15–25.

Lovelock, J.E. 1987. In: Dickinson, R.E., ed. *The Geophysiology of Amazonia*. New York: Wiley, 11–23.

Mishustin, E.N. 1978. In: Loutit, M.W., and Miles, J.A.R., eds. *Microbial Ecology*. Berlin. Springer-Verlag, 105–109.

Parfenova, E.I., and Yarilova, E.A. 1965. *Mineralogical Investigations in Soil Science*. Israel Program for Scientific Translations, Jerusalem

Robert, M., and Berthelin, J. 1986. In Huang, P.M., and Schnitzer, M., eds. *Interactions of Soil Minerals with Natural Organics and Microbes*. SSSA Special Publication Number 17. Madison, Soil Science Society of America: 453–495.

Schwartzman, D.W., and Volk, T. 1989. *Nature*, 340, 457–460.

Silverman, M.P. 1979. In: Trudinger, P.A., and Swaine, D.J., eds. *Biogeochemical Cycling of Mineral-Forming Elements*. Amsterdam, Elsevier, 445–465.

Volobuev, V.R. 1964. *Ecology of Soils*. Israel Program for Scientific Translations, Jerusalem.

Walker, J.C.G., Hays, P.B., and Kasting, J.F. 1981. *J Geophys Res*, 86, 9776–9782.

Diane M. McKnight

36

Feedback Mechanisms Involving Humic Substances in Aquatic Ecosystems

Humic substances are a general class of biologically derived, heterogeneous, organic compounds that are yellow to black in color, moderate to high in molecular weight, and recalcitrant to degradation in the environment (Aiken et al., 1985). Humic substances are ubiquitous, occurring at some concentration in most soil, sediment, and aquatic environments. In wetlands humic substances are generally abundant (e.g., McKnight et al., 1985), whereas in deep groundwater aquifers they may be present in trace quantities (e.g., Thurman, 1985a).

Humic substances are further classified as follows: fulvic acid (water soluble under all pH conditions); humic acid (insoluble in water below pH 2 and becoming soluble at greater pH values); and humin (insoluble in water at any pH) (Aiken et al., 1985). Each of these classes comprises a heterogeneous mixture of organic compounds that have similar chemical properties. In fact, it can be argued from an ecological perspective that heterogeneity is an inherent property of humic substances (McCarthy and Rice, chapter 37, this volume). The heterogeneity of humic substances makes the study of these ubiquitous materials quite challenging. Another challenging aspect of chemical characterization is the initial isolation of humic substances from aqueous or solid phases without substantial chemical alteration. For aquatic humic substances, preparative scale column chromatography has been used for isolation (Aiken, 1988), and for soil humic substances, various extraction procedures can be used (Hayes, 1985). However, the possibility of alteration has not been eliminated in these methods and yet the extent of alteration is equally difficult to measure. For these reasons, many aspects of humic substances in the environment, such as biological and chemical mechanisms of their formation, are unknown or subject to much speculation. For example, it is not known to what extent humic substances are residual products of degradation or result from polymerization of products released during degradation.

Although there is no one chemical structure that is representative of an aquatic fulvic acid molecule, there are general differences among soil humic acids and aquatic fulvic acids that can be illustrated diagrammatically. In natural waters, dissolved fulvic acid represents 30% to 80% of the dissolved organic carbon (DOC), whereas dissolved humic acid represents less than 1% to 5% of the DOC. Aquatic fulvic acids consist of moderately sized organic acids that are truly dissolved, and the number-average molecular weights for samples from different environments range from 500 to 1200 D (Aiken and Malcolm, 1987). The molecular size of aquatic fulvic acids is illustrated in figure 36.1, which is an idealized structure that is consistent with detailed chemical characterization of dissolved fulvic acid isolated from the Suwannee River in Georgia (Leenheer et al., 1990). This figure also illustrates some of the chemical characteristics that account for the reactivity of fulvic acid in natural waters. The four to five carboxylic-acid groups per molecule account for the weak acid behavior, and the average of two aromatic ring structures per molecule accounts for the yellow color and the interactions with solutes and surfaces through hydrophobic interactions (Leenheer et al., 1990).

In soils, humic substances are largely present in a solid phase and humic acids are more abundant

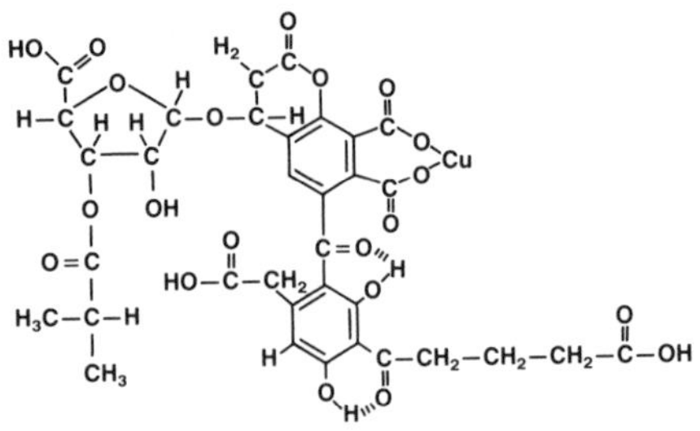

Figure 36.1 Possible chemical structure of a fulvic acid molecule that is consistent with measured properties of the Suwannee River fulvic acid (Leenheer et al., 1990), showing complexation of copper by carboxylic-acid groups.

than fulvic acids. Soil humic acids have high apparent molecular weights (10,000 to 100,000 D) (Stevenson, 1982), and may be present as molecular aggregates with inorganic materials, as illustrated in figure 36.2 (Wershaw et al., 1986).

Despite the many unknowns in the study of humic substances, it is generally recognized that their production corresponds to a conditioning of the environment, a modification of the physical and chemical properties of the habitat (Stevenson, 1982). In general, these modifications are beneficial and seem to enhance primary productivity in the ecosystem. This chapter describes a few of the mechanisms by which humic substances affect ecosystems. The main focus is on aquatic systems. This focus was chosen because (1) marine produc-

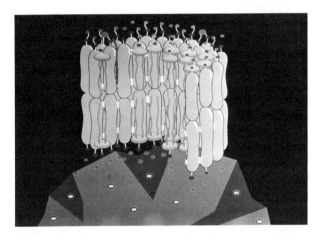

Figure 36.2 Possible membranelike structure of soil humic acid as an aggregate attached to a positively charged hydrous oxide surface in soil. A—nonlipid amphiphile; B—lipid amphiphile; and C—intercolated pollutant molecule. (From Wershaw, 1986.)

tivity may be affected by dissolved marine fulvic acid through light attenuation and trace metal complexation, and (2) a significant source of marine dissolved fulvic acid may be fulvic acid transported from continental freshwater and land-based ecosystems. Therefore, ecological aspects of humic substances in aquatic environments may be important on a global scale. It is the global-scale effects that are most relevant to the Gaia hypothesis, which is the hypothesis that the Earth in its entirety (biosphere, lithosphere, and atmosphere) has a structure and function that through many internal feedback mechanisms maintain a homeostasis in a manner comparable to that of a single organism.

Abundance of Humic Substances in the Environment

The definition of humic substances as refractory is based on the fact that such substances are observed to accumulate or persist in nature. Representative values for the residence time of humic substances in different environments as determined by carbon − 14 dating are presented in table 36.1. The average residence time for carbon in autotrophic organisms is also presented in table 36.1 as an indication of the temporal scale of carbon cycling in each ecosystem. The magnitude of the ratio of these two residence times is much greater in the marine ecosystems than in forest ecosystems, for example.

The refractory nature of humic substances is one reason that these substances are so ubiquitous. For example, dissolved humic substances in groundwaters from deep aquifers are likely to have been derived from buried organic deposits or transported from the land surface over long periods (Thurman,

Table 36.1 Residence Time (Age) of Organic Carbon Present in Autotrophs and in Humic Substances in Different Environments

Environment	Residence Time (years)	
	Autotroph	*Humic Substances*
Terrestrial*		
Forests	10–200	200–8,000
Prairies	1	200–8,000
Aquatic		
Ground water†		
Shallow	Not present	660
Deep	Not present	17,000
Wetland†	1–200	< 20
Lakes and rivers‡	< 1–2	?
Pacific Ocean§	< 1	3600

*From Stevenson, 1982.
†From Thurman, 1985b.
‡From Wetzel, 1983.
§From R.L. Malcolm, United States Geological Survey, unpublished data.

Table 36.2 Estimated Size of Major Pools of Carbon in the World Carbon Budget

Major Pool	Carbon $\times 10^{15}$ g
Atmosphere	640–700
Land	
Biota (plants)	800
Soil humus	700–3000
Oceans	
Biota	2
Organic (50% humic substances)	1700
Inorganic	38,600
Fossil fuels	10,000

1985b). Another reason that humic substances are ubiquitous is that they can be formed in the degradation of plant biomass and animal fecal material as well as microbial biomass.

Humic substances not only are ubiquitous, but also are significant in terms of the global carbon budget (table 36.2). The values in table 36.2 are only estimates and are subject to various uncertainties. For example, the concentration of dissolved organic carbon in marine surface waters may be underestimated by some analytical techniques (Sugimura and Suzuki, 1988). These estimates indicate that the quantity of organic carbon in soil humus, for example, is comparable to the quantity of organic carbon in the biota on the land surface. Also, the quantity of humic substances dissolved in the oceans is comparable to the quantity of organic material on land and much greater than that of the marine biota. The reason for this relationship is that although the concentration of humic substances in ocean waters is dilute, the volume of ocean water is large.

Ecological Effects of Humic Substances

The presence of humic substances affects the physical and chemical properties of the environment. Although this is true in aquatic and land-based ecosystems, the general nature of the effects is different. In land-based ecosystems, humic substances affect physical and chemical properties of soils, that is, texture, water retention, and nutrient availability (Foth, 1978; Hausenbuiller, 1978), which only directly affect plants and soil microbiota, and not the organisms of the higher trophic levels (McKnight and Feder, 1990). In contrast, in aquatic systems, dissolved humic substances affect the properties of the aquatic milieu in which organisms at all trophic levels exist.

Light Attenuation

One way in which dissolved humic substances affect the physical properties of aquatic ecosystems is absorbance of light, specifically photosynthetically active radiation (PAR 400 to 700 nm). Photosynthesis by algae or macrophytes is the dominant autotrophic process in lakes, rivers, streams, and oceans. Therefore, the intensity of PAR has a major effect on ecosystem structure and function. The importance of dissolved fulvic acid in light attenuation was demonstrated by James and Birge (1938), who determined the absorption of light per meter of lakewater as a function of wavelength by the total water sample, by the dissolved organic color (fulvic acid), and by the suspended particulate material (figure 36.3). In the three lakes with measurable organic color, the proportion of light attenuated by dissolved fulvic acid was substantial.

One way of comparing light availability is to determine the lower boundary of the euphotic zone, which is defined by the depth at which the rate of respiration equals the rate of photosynthesis (Z_{eu}) and usually corresponds to the depth at which light intensity has been decreased to 1% of surface light intensity (Moss, 1980). These relationships are illustrated in figure 36.4a. The relationship between the lower boundary of the euphotic zone and the extinction coefficient, which is the fraction of light absorbed over a meter depth, is shown in figure 36.4b. Very small extinction coefficients correspond to clear, infertile lakes and the open ocean, and in this lower range of extinction coefficients (5.0 to 0.1), a large percentage of the light attenuation, and therefore, the lower boundary of the euphotic zone is controlled by the concentration of dissolved fulvic acid.

Light attenuation may either enhance or decrease productivity depending on other aspects of the ecosystem. For example, inhibition of photosynthesis

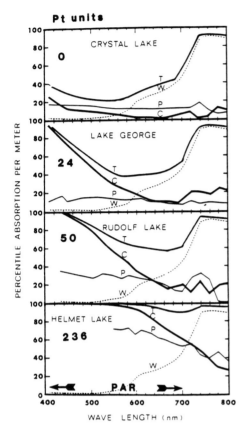

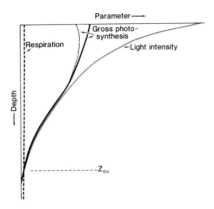

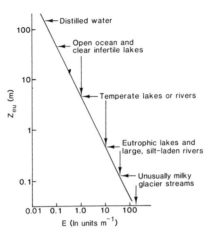

Figure 36.3 Percentile absorption of light at different wavelengths (including those of PAR) passing through 1 m of water of four lakes of northern Wisconsin. T—total absorption; C—absorption by dissolved organic color (humic substances); P—absorption by suspended particulate material; and W—absorption by pure water. The platinum color units of each lake also are indicated. (Modified from Wetzel, 1983.)

Figure 36.4 **A,** A representative relation between light (........), photosynthesis (————), and respiration (–––––) with depth in a lake. On sunny days photoinhibition (........) may occur. Z_{eu} is the depth of the euphotic zone. **B,** The dependence of Z_{eu} on the extinction coefficient, E, of natural water, indicating the range in E for different types of natural waters. (From Moss, 1980).

by intense light at the surface of lakes and oceans is commonly observed (figure 36.4a), and light attenuation by dissolved fulvic acid decreases the extent of this surface inhibition. However, light attenuation raises the lower boundary of the euphotic zone. The significance of such a change depends on the mixing depth of the system and the accessibility of nutrients.

Complexation of Trace Metals
An example of a process by which the presence of fulvic acid affects the chemical properties of the aquatic environment is complexation of trace metals. Trace metals can be required micronutrients or toxicants (Luoma, 1983; Morel and Hudson, 1985). In oceans and in alkaline lakes where the solubility of iron is minimal because the pH is above neutral,

an important question is how phytoplankton meet their requirement for iron, which is needed for photosynthesis and nitrogen fixation.

When considering the literature about the effects of trace metal complexation by humic substances, the two general effects that have been observed might seem to be contradictory. These effects are that (1) complexation of required micronutrients, such as iron and manganese, enhances their bioavailability; and (2) complexation of toxic trace metals by humic substances reduces their bioavailability and their toxicity. Although these two relationships would be expected from an evolutionary perspective, a consideration of the underlying chemical and biological processes indicates that these relationships can be explained.

Firstly, the toxicity of a given trace metal has

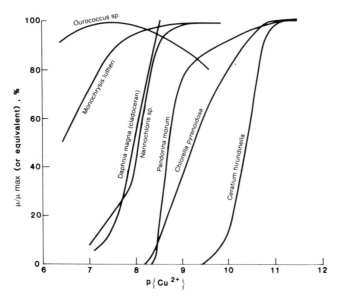

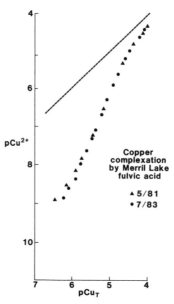

Figure 36.5 Inhibition of growth as a function of cupric ion activity for various species of freshwater (denoted by *), estuarine, and marine algae μ/μmax—growth rate divided by the maximum growth rate. (From McKnight, 1983.)

Figure 36.6 The change of free cupric-ion activity with addition of copper to solutions of Merril Lake fulvic acid with a concentration of 10 mgC/L at pH 6.0; the dashed line indicates the line for the free cupric-ion activity (Cu^{2+}) equal to the total dissolved copper concentration (Cu_T). (From McKnight et al., 1988.)

been shown to be largely dependent on the activity (concentration) of the free metal ion (Luoma, 1983). Further, for any particular metal, there is a wide range in the metal ion activity that is toxic to aquatic species (McKnight et al., 1983). The range of copper-ion activities that are toxic to species of freshwater, estuarine, and marine algae is illustrated in figure 36.5. The vertical axis in figure 36.5 is the growth rate relative to the maximum growth rate, which makes the data for the different species comparable. The range in toxic copper-ion activities is four to five orders of magnitude and encompasses much of the range of copper-ion activities in natural waters.

Complexation of trace metals by humic substances reduces toxicity by decreasing the free metal-ion activity (Sunda and Guillard, 1976; Anderson and Morel, 1978). The main copper-binding sites are likely to be bidentate carboxylic-acid sites, as illustrated in figure 36.1, because copper-carboxylate charge transfer complexes have relatively high formation constants (Piotrowicz et al., 1984). For copper concentrations that do not exceed the concentration of copper-binding sites of the fulvic acid, the copper-ion activity is less than the copper-ion activity in the absence of a complexing agent. This relationship is illustrated in the titration curve shown in figure 36.6. Depending on the ratio of metal to fulvic acid, complexation reduces the metal-ion activity by several orders of magnitude.

Complexation of trace metals by humic substances enhances the availability of required metal micronutrients by a mechanism that may not depend directly on the free metal-ion activity. Complexation increases the solubility of the metal, that is, the total concentration of metal in solution. In contrast to metals that are toxic, the availability of these required metals is determined by the free metal-ion activity and also by the rate at which the organism (e.g., algal cell) can assimilate the metal. In the instance of metal micronutrient limitation, the rate of uptake may not be directly limited by the free metal-ion, which becomes only a trace intermediary species, but by the rate of dissociation or supply of unbound metal, that is, the rate at which the equilibrium free metal-ion concentration is approached. If the metal-ion is complexed by dissolved fulvic acid, the rate of iron uptake is essentially determined by the rate of dissociation of the iron–fulvic acid complex. This rate is generally much faster than the rate at which hydrous or crystalline iron oxides dissolve (Wells et al., 1983). By enhancing uptake rate, formation of iron-humic complexes increases the bioavailability of iron. This increased bioavailability occurs even under conditions in which the concentrations of dissolved fulvic acid are very dilute, because the concentration of these required metals also is very dilute (Gordon et al., 1982).

Feedback Mechanisms Involving Humic Substances

In the context of the Gaia hypothesis, the question becomes whether these and other processes involving humic substances correspond to feedback mechanisms. As with many other questions in ecology, the answer depends on where the boundaries of the ecosystem are placed. For ecosystems of the scale of a forest or a wetland, there are many examples of how the production of humic substances acts as a feedback mechanism. As an example, Thoreau's Bog in Concord, Massachusetts is an ombrotrophic bog that receives input of only rainwater and other atmospheric deposition (Hemond, 1980). Therefore, all the organic material present in the bog was originally produced by the mosses and other plants in the bog. Dissolved humic substances and other dissolved organic compounds are elevated in bog water compared with other fresh waters, and during the fall, after the summer growth of *Sphagnum,* these concentrations increase (McKnight et al., 1985). The high concentrations of dissolved fulvic and humic acids in bog water are, in turn, responsible for the acidity of the water (pH about 4.0), which is typical of such bogs (Gorham et al., 1985). The acidic conditions, as well as the reducing conditions, contribute to the harshness of these bogs to other plants in the surrounding forests, and serve to maintain the dominance of the *Sphagnum* moss. This enhancement of the growth of *Sphagnum* relative to other plants by the humic-rich water is an internal feedback mechanism. Given this self-regulating nature of the bog ecosystem, it is interesting to note that Henry David Thoreau, for whom the bog is named, thought of the bog as a living organism.

In contrast to wetlands, the humic substances in lake water are not primarily produced within the water column of the lake, and their effects on biological processes in the lake do not directly feed back upon the humic substance concentration. For example, in most temperate lakes, the dissolved humic substances come into the lake from the surrounding watershed, originating in the vegetation and soils (Steinberg and Muenster, 1985).

However, there are some lakes in which the dissolved humic substances are generated from degradation of algal biomass occurring either in the water column or lake sediments, and the potential for an internal feedback mechanism exists. Such is the sit-

uation for permanently ice covered lakes in the McMurdo Dry Valleys of South Victorialand, Antarctica, another appropriate place for consideration of the Gaia hypothesis. The watershed surrounding these lakes is completely barren of vegetation, and the dissolved humic substances are derived solely from the degradation of algal and bacterial biomass produced within the lakes. The concentration of algal biomass, as measured by cell abundance, is substantial (1×10^5 cells/mL), despite the low light intensities resulting from the 4.5 m of ice (figure 36.7). This algal material settles to the lake bottom and continues to degrade in the sediments (Ishiwatari, 1985). In these lakes, the water column is very stable because of the ice cover, and salinity markedly increases with depth. The concentration of DOC has a similar profile (figure 36.7), which indicates that the DOC diffuses upward in the water column from the sediments (McKnight et al., 1990).

This upward diffusion of dissolved fulvic acid may affect the phytoplankton abundance by affecting the availability of iron. Below 9.5 m, the lake is anoxic and has extremely high sulfide concentrations, which limit iron solubility by formation of iron sulfides. Therefore, inorganic iron does not diffuse upward through this zone. However, the phytoplankton in the euphotic zone are receiving their requirement for iron by some mechanism. It is possible that the complexation of iron by the dissolved fulvic acid transports low concentrations of iron to the euphotic zone from the sediments, or that the presence of fulvic acid in the euphotic zone enhances the dissolution of iron from the inorganic

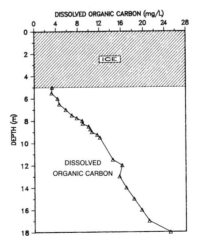

Figure 36.7 Depth profile of dissolved organic carbon in Lake Fryxell, a polar desert lake in the Dry Valleys, South Victorialand, Antarctica (From McKnight et al., 1990.)

particulate material settling through the ice and water column.

Humic Substances and Global Scale Processes

The two previous examples illustrate for local-scale ecosystems the ways in which humic substances can regulate ecosystem function. From an ecological perspective, the first step towards understanding the structure and function of the global ecosystem is to define the boundaries of the ecosystem. In defining the ecosystem, the designation of the boundaries cannot be judged as correct or incorrect but can be judged only in terms of their usefulness in developing an understanding of the ecosystem being studied. In the definition of the biosphere as the surface of the Earth and the oceans that are affected by the biota, the ecosystem boundaries fall just above and below the land surface and the oceans. In the Gaia hypothesis, the entire Earth is included in the ecosystem, and the boundaries are designated to be in the troposphere. For consideration of the function of humic substances in the global ecosystem, it does not matter whether the biosphere or Gaian boundaries are used. In either approach, the production of humic substances will influence ecosystem productivity and structure through several pathways, and some of these pathways correspond to feedback mechanisms that have a global scale.

Processes involving dissolved fulvic acid in ocean waters have an influence at a global scale because of the many processes that link the oceans and the atmosphere. For example, changes in the concentrations of marine fulvic acid could cause changes in iron availability and therefore changes in phytoplankton composition, and indirectly influence atmospheric processes.

In turn, there are several possible causes of a change in the concentration of marine fulvic acid. However, this question of how marine fulvic acid concentrations might change depends on whether the rivers of the world are an important source of DOC to the oceans in the present. The source of marine dissolved fulvic acid currently (1991) is as controversial as the correct concentration of marine DOC (Williams and Druffel, 1988). It is known that marine fulvic acid has chemical characteristics that are consistent with their production from marine phytoplankton biomass (Harvey and Boran, 1985). However, there also is substantial evidence that dissolved fulvic acid originates in land-based and freshwater systems (Mulholland and Watts, 1982) and is transported conservatively through estuaries (Mantoura and Woodward, 1983). A mass-balance calculation for the oceans indicates that a large percentage of dissolved marine fulvic acid could be entering from river and estuarine systems (Mantoura and Woodward, 1983). In figure 36.8, the transport of DOC derived from continental land-based and

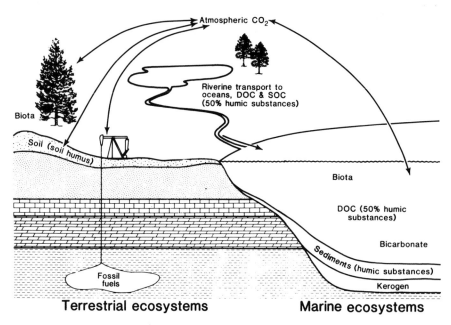

Figure 36.8 The global carbon cycle. Arrows indicate the transport of dissolved humic substances.

fresh water systems to the oceans is shown in relation to other carbon fluxes, and the magnitude of this estuarine flux relative to the pool of marine fulvic acid is not currently known. However, the relative magnitude and the significance of this estuarine flux have probably varied throughout geological time. For example, if we consider periods when terrestrial biomass was much greater, such as the Cretaceous, then this flux may have been greater.

Summary

Humic substances are produced through the degradation of plant and animal detritus in both land-based and aquatic ecosystems. Although humic substances are biologically refractory, their presence alters the chemical and physical properties of the environment. For aquatic ecosystems, regulation of pH, attenuation of light, and trace metal complexation are important processes involving humic substances. In the oceans, humic substances transported from the continents may influence productivity through these processes. In this case, the dissolved humic substance transport from the continents to oceans may be one step in a global-scale feedback process.

Acknowledgment

I thank R.L. Malcolm, E. Sundquist, and an anonymous reviewer for the helpful reviews on the manuscript.

References

Aiken, G.R. 1988. A critical evaluation of the use of macroporous resins for the isolation of aquatic humic substances. In: Frimmel, F.H., and Christman, R.F., eds. *Humic Substances and Their Role in the Environment*. New York: Wiley, 15–30.

Aiken, G.R., and Malcolm, R.L. 1987. Molecular weight of aquatic fulvic acids by vapor pressure osmometry. *Geochim Cosmochim Acta*, 51, 2177–2184.

Aiken, G.R., McKnight, D.M., Wershaw, R.L., and MacCarthy, P. 1985. *An Introduction to Humic Substances in Soil, Sediment, and Water*. New York: Wiley, 1–9.

Anderson, D.M., and Morel, F.M.M. 1978. Copper sensitivity to *Gonyaulex tamarensis*. *Limnol Oceanogr*, 23, 283–295.

Foth, H.D. 1978. *Fundamentals of Soil Science*, 6th ed. New York: Wiley, 157–173.

Gordon, R.M., Martin, J.H., and Knauer, G.A. 1982. Iron in north-east Pacific waters. *Nature*, 299, 611–612.

Gorham, E., Eisenriech, S.J., Ford, J., and Santelmann, M.V. 1985. The chemistry of bog waters. In: Stumm, W., ed. *Chemical Processes in Lakes*. New York: Wiley, 339–361.

Harvey, G.R., and Boran, D.A. 1985. The geochemistry of humic substances in seawater. In: Aiken, G.R., McKnight, D.M., Wershaw, R.L., and MacCarthy, P., eds. *Humic Substances in Soil, Sediment and Water*. New York: Wiley, 233–248.

Hausenbuiller, R.L. 1978. *Soil Science*. Dubuque, Iowa: Wm. C. Brown, Co.

Hayes, M.H.B. 1985. Extraction of humic substances from soil. In: Aiken, G.R., McKnight, D.M., Wershaw, R.L., and MacCarthy, P., eds. *Humic Substances in Soil, Sediment and Water*. New York: Wiley, 329–362.

Hemond, H.F. 1980. Biogeochemistry of Thoreau's Bog, Concord, Massachusetts. *Ecol Monogr*, 30, 507–526.

Ishiwatari, R. 1985. Geochemistry of humic substances in lake sediments. In: Aiken, G.R., McKnight, D.M., Wershaw, R.L., and MacCarthy, P., eds. *Humic Substances in Soil, Sediment and Water*. New York: Wiley, 147–180.

James, H.R., and Birge, E.A. 1938. A laboratory study of the absorption of light by lake waters. *Trans Wis Acad Sci Arts Lett*, 31, 1–154.

Leenheer, J.A., McKnight, D.M., Thurman, E.M., and MacCarthy, P. 1989. Structural components and proposed structural models for Suwannee River fulvic acid. In: *Humic Substances in the Suwannee River, Florida and Georgia—Interactions, Properties, and Proposed Structures*. United States Geological Survey Open-File Report 87-557, pp 331–377.

Luoma, S.N. 1983. Bioavailability of trace metals to aquatic organisms—a review. *J Sci Total Environ*, 287, 1–22.

Mantoura, R.F.C., and Woodward, E.M.S. 1983. Conservative behavior of riverine dissolved organic carbon in the Severn Estuary: Chemical and geochemical implications. *Geochim Cosmochim Acta*, 47, 1293–1309.

McKnight, D.M., Aiken, G.R., Andrews, E.D., Bowles, E.C., Smith, R.L., Duff, J.M., and Miller, L.G. 1988. Dissolved organic material in desert lakes in the McMurdo Dry Valleys of Antarctica. *U.S. Antarctic Journal*, XXIII, 152–153.

McKnight, D.M., Chisholm, S.W., and Harleman, D.R.F. 1983. CuSO$_4$ treatment of nuisance algal blooms in drinking water reservoirs. *Environ Manag*, 7, 311–320.

McKnight, D.M., and Feder, G.L. 1990. Ecological aspects of humic substances in the environment. In: MacCarthy, P., ed. *Humic Substances, Environmental Interactions*. New York: Wiley.

McKnight, D.M., Thorn, K.A., Wershaw, R.L., Bracewell, J.M., and Robertson, G.W. 1988. Rapid changes in dissolved humic substances in Spirit Lake and South Fork Castle Lake, Washington. *Limnol Oceanogr*, 33, 1527–1541.

McKnight, D.M., Thurman, E.M., Wershaw, R.L., and Hemond, H. 1985. Biogeochemistry of aquatic humic substances in Thoreau's Bog, Concord, Massachusetts. *Ecology*, 66, 1339–1352.

Morel, F.M.M., and Hudson, R.J.M. 1985. The geobiological cycle of trace elements in aquatic systems: Redfield revisited. In: Stumm, W., ed. *Chemical Processes in Lake*. New York: Wiley, 251–282.

Moss, B. 1980. *Ecology of Freshwaters.* New York: Wiley.

Mulholland, P.J., and Watts, J.A. 1982. Transport of organic carbon to the ocean by rivers of North America: The synthesis of existing data. *Tellus,* 34, 176–186.

Piotrowicz, S.R., Harvey, G.R., Boran, D.A., Weisel, C.P., and Springer-Yound, M. 1984. Cadmium, copper, and zinc interactions with marine humic as a function of ligand structure. *Marine Chem,* 14, 333–346.

Steinberg, C., and Muenster, U. 1985. Geochemistry and ecological role of humic substances in lakewater. In: Aiken, G.R., McKnight, D.M., Wershaw, R.L., and MacCarthy, P., eds. *Humic Substances in Soil, Sediment and Water.* New York: Wiley, 105–146.

Stevenson, F.J. 1982. *Humic chemistry: Genesis, composition, reactions.* New York: Wiley-Interscience.

Sugimura, Y., and Suzuki, Y. 1988. A high temperature catalytic oxidation method of non-volatile dissolved organic carbon in seawater by direct injection of liquid samples. *Marine Chem,* 24, 105–131.

Sunda, W.G., and Guillard, R.R.L. 1976. The relationship between cupric ion activity and the toxicity of copper to phytoplankton. *J Marine Res,* 34, 511–529.

Thurman, E.M. 1985a. *Organic Geochemistry of Natural Waters.* Dordrecht: Martin Nijhoff/Dr. W. Junk.

Thurman, E.M. 1985b. Humic substances in groundwater. In: Aiken, G.R., McKnight, D.M., Wershaw, R.L., and MacCarthy, P., eds. *Humic Substances in Soil, Sediment and Water.* New York: Wiley, 87–104.

Wells, M.L.L., Zorkin, N.G., and Lewis, A.G. 1983. The role of colloid chemistry in providing a source of iron to phytoplankton. *J Marine Res,* 41, 731–746.

Wershaw, R.L. 1986. A new model for humic materials and their interactions with hydrophobic organic chemicals in soil water or sediment–water systems. *J Contaminant Hydrol,* 1, 29–45.

Wershaw, R.L., Thorn, K.A., Pinckney, D.J., MacCarthy, P., Rice, J.A., and Hemond, H.R. 1986. Application of a membrane model to the secondary structure of humic materials in peat. In: Fuchsman, C.H., ed. *Peat and Water Aspects of Water Retention and Dewatering in Peat.* London: Elsevier Applied Science Publishers, 133–157.

Wetzel, R.G. 1983. *Limnology.* Philadelphia: W.B. Saunders.

Williams, P.M., and Druffel, E.R.M. 1988. Dissolved organic matter in the ocean: Comments on a controversy. *Oceanography,* 1, 14–17.

Patrick MacCarthy and James A. Rice

37

An Ecological Rationale for the Heterogeneity of Humic Substances: A Holistic Perspective on Humus

The term *humus,* or *humic substances,* refers to organic material in the environment that results from the decomposition of plant and animal residues, but that does not fall into any of the discrete classes of compounds such as proteins, polysaccharides, polynucleotides, and so on (MacCarthy and Suffet, 1989). Some authors (e.g., Stevenson, 1982) assign a more general meaning to the term *humus,* using it to designate soil organic matter in general, including both humic and nonhumic substances. However, in this chapter the terms *humus* and *humic substances* are used interchangeably in the context of the first sentence of this paragraph. Because humic substances cannot be defined in specific chemical terms, they are operationally classified into three pragmatically useful categories on the basis of their solubility in aqueous systems (Aiken et al., 1985):

Humic acid: the fraction of humic substances that is not soluble in water under acidic conditions (pH < 2) but is soluble at alkaline pH values;

Fulvic acid: the fraction of humic substances that is soluble under all pH conditions;

Humin: the fraction of humic substances that is not soluble in an aqueous solution at any pH value.

The Chemical Nature of Humus: A Synopsis

Humus consists of a very complicated mixture of irregular molecules that has defied all attempts at separation into discrete components or even into relatively well defined chemical classes. Similarly, all attempts at describing humic substances in specific structural terms have been unsuccessful because of the enormous complexity of these materials. In like manner, relatively little is known, at the fundamental level, about the mechanism(s) of the formation of humus. Documentary evidence for the chemical view of humus as a heterogeneous mixture of irregular molecules is provided later in this chapter. For more detailed discussions of the chemistry of humus the reader is referred to the texts by Stevenson (1982), Aiken et al. (1985), Kononova (1966), and Schnitzer and Khan (1972).

The Ecological Role of Humus

Humus constitutes a major component of soil organic matter, and is one of the most abundant forms of organic matter in the biosphere (Woodwell and Houghton, 1977; Woodwell et al., 1978). The ecological functions of humus in the soil are well documented. For example, humus serves to retain micronutrients that are necessary for plant growth; it maintains the water regime of the soil environment; it is essential for the development of a soil structure that is suitable for plant growth; and it acts as a pH buffer preventing rapid fluctuations in soil acidity. These multiple roles of humus in the environment are possible because of the reactivity of the humus molecules.

Humus is a pervasive material and is found in all terrestrial and aquatic environments. The widespread occurrence and persistence of humus result from its resistance to microbial decomposition. Swaby and Ladd, more than twenty years ago, suggested that this resistance to microbial decomposition is due to the molecular irregularity of the humic molecules (Swaby and Ladd, 1962, 1966). Basically, they suggested that because of the disordered nature of humus molecules no enzyme would be capable of rapidly degrading this material. We find it curious that so little attention has been devoted to a hypothesis that appears to explain satisfactorily a fundamental property of humus.

The properties that soil organic matter must possess in order to satisfy its ecological role will now be examined. In order to retain micronutrients and moisture, to provide buffer capacity to soil, and to maintain a viable soil structure for plant growth, it is necessary that the organic material be hydrophilic, acidic, and capable of complexing with metal ions. It is interesting to note that these ecologically desirable attributes are rather broad in character and do not require the participation of a unique compound, or a mixture of unique compounds, in order to be fulfilled. In fact, one could visualize many synthetic chemicals that potentially would contribute these and other necessary characteristics to soil. For example, polyacrylic acid or similar polymers could act as complexing agents that are capable of bridging mineral particles in the soil. Likewise, proteins and other biological polymers possess these desirable characteristics. There is, however, an essential requirement for soil humus that cannot, in general, be satisfied by discrete polymers or mixture of polymers, and in particular by biopolymers: it must persist in the soil for prolonged periods. Most biopolymers such as proteins, polysaccharides, and polynucleotides undergo relatively rapid decomposition in the soil environment, largely through the mediation of microorganisms. The orderly sequence of monomer units in these biological polymers facilitates their decomposition by specific enzymes. As already noted, humus possesses an inherent resistance to such degradation, and consequently persists for prolonged periods in the environment.

It is clear that in the development of soils there is a need for the evolution of an organic material that is resistant to microbial decomposition as well as possessing the other desirable properties described here. Because of the susceptibility of known biopolymers to microbial decomposition, and because of the tendency for the evolution of organisms capable of decomposing substrates having regular, polymeric structures, the lack of a discrete, orderly structure in humus is not surprising; on the contrary, it is very desirable, if not necessary, ecologically. The generation of a random mixture of irregular polyelectrolytic molecules satisfies, in a most elegant manner, the necessary requirement of environmental persistence as well as providing a material with average properties capable of supplying the necessary chemical characteristics to the soil. The very nature of humus, which many investigators find so frustrating is, in fact, precisely what allows this material to serve its vital ecological functions. In view of this ecological rationalization for the nature of humus, it is clear that one would be faced with a greater dilemma if humus consisted of anything other than a highly complex mixture of disordered organic molecules. The molecular complexity and irregularity of humus constitute its very essence. In the case of humus, molecular disorder, rather than order, provides the key to an important process in nature.

Hypothesis

It is proposed that the generation of a highly complex mixture of disordered, polyelectrolytic molecules, in the form of humus, is ecologically desirable and that this irregularity serves a vital role in nature. This hypothesis is consistent with what is known about the chemical nature of humus and is supported by extensive documentary evidence from the literature.

Supporting Evidence

Humus as a Mixture

Despite the fact that hundreds of papers have been published on the fractionation of humus, no material that could be termed a pure humic substance has yet been isolated. Some quotations from the literature aptly portray the enduring status quo in this area. Dubach and Mehta (1963) have stated that ". . . in spite of intensive efforts . . . no discrete fractions have ever been isolated from humic substances," and Dubach et al. (1964) pointed out that "the methods used to characterize the fractions . . . show rather a continuous variation"; Felbeck (1965) stated that "At the present time there has been no evidence presented to indicate that a definite fraction has ever been isolated from a humic substance. Each fraction can be refractionated into subfractions and this can be repeated, apparently, *ad infinitum*." According to Hurst and Burges (1967), "The concept of purity, so easy to apply to simple molecules, has a less precise meaning when applied to mixed polymers and is especially difficult to apply to humic acid." Perhaps the most intriguing statement in this regard is that of Dubach and Mehta (1963), who stated that "perhaps no two molecules of humic substances are alike." Similar statements continue to appear in the humus literature; for example, Gamble (1970) said that ". . . one must assume . . . that no two carboxyl groups are inherently chemically identical" in fulvic acid and Gjessing (1976) stated that "every molecule of humus could be different." Although the latter three statements may at first appear rather exaggerated, the not-improbable basis underlying such a conclusion, based on statistical calculations, is discussed later in this chapter. The recent literature shows that the situation has not changed during the past twenty years. For example, Swift (1985) concluded that humic substances consisted of "a broad spectrum of related molecules, each one differing almost imperceptibly from the next in terms of one or other of its properties . . . the most that can be expected of a fractionation procedure is to decrease the heterogeneity of the system as much as possible." Perdue (1985) stated that ". . . humic substances are indisputably a highly complex mixture that has thus far been essentially unresolvable into significant amounts of pure components." In the words of Stevenson (1985) ". . . each fraction (humic acid, fulvic acid, etc.) came to be regarded as being made up of a series of molecules of different sizes, few having precisely the same structural configuration or array of reactive functional groups." None of the recent books (Stevenson, 1982; Aiken et al., 1985; Suffet and MacCarthy, 1989; Hayes et al., 1989) on humus provides any method for the isolation of pure humic substances, nor do they provide any evidence that such does exist. The inescapable fact remains that humic substances continue to frustrate the efforts of scientists attempting to fractionate them, not only into discrete chemical compounds, but even into chemically homogeneous classes. Such a legacy of repeated failures to satisfactorily fractionate humus provides the perfect documentary evidence for the complicated, multicomponent nature of this material, and is consistent with the hypothesis proposed here. This conclusion concerning the highly complicated, multicomponent nature of humus based on the current status of separation attempts will continue to be valid regardless of any future success in fractionating these substances. Perhaps the time has come to stop referring to such unsuccessful fractionation attempts as *failures*, and to recognize what the data are, in fact, telling us: that humus represents the epitome of molecular irregularity and heterogeneity. It is for this reason that we are constrained to define humus and its fractions in operational terms.

Structural Irregularity in Humus

The study of the chemical structure of humus cannot be divorced from the fractionation studies in that both are intimately interwoven. To put this subject into perspective, a review of the history of biochemistry reveals that many of the major advances that have been made over the past half-century were predicated upon the development of methods for the isolation, fractionation, and purification of proteins, polysaccharides, polynucleotides, and other biopolymers. As discussed in the previous section, no corresponding advances have been made in the fractionation of humus, a fact that can be attributed to its structural irregularity and pronounced polydispersity. As stated by Gjessing (1976), "Humus is obviously not a definable organic compound, and it is unlikely that the composition will be clarified within the foreseeable future." We are thus confronted with a circular difficulty—the molecular heterogeneity of humus renders the question of its ultimate fractionation difficult, if not, in fact, moot. And, the lack of a satisfactory fractionation makes definitive structural determination impossible. Regardless of the sophistication of modern chemical and physical methods for structure determination, the ability to interpret the experimental data from these techniques is severely limited when the sample under investigation is anything other than a reasonably pure substance. The mixture problem and the difficulties it imposes on the interpretability of data have been discussed in more detail elsewhere (MacCarthy and Rice, 1985); when embarking on a structural study of a complex heterogeneous mixture it is necessary first to define clearly the meaning of structure in this context.

A critical evaluation of what is definitively known about the chemical nature of humus is warranted at this time: the ranges of elemental contents are known; functional group compositions are known to some degree, average molecular weights are known; molecular weight distributions are known; the presence of other structural moieties such as aliphatic or aromatic entities within humus has been established. However, the fundamental quest for a structural backbone for humus has failed. While much is known about the functional group contents of humus it has not been possible to integrate this knowledge within the unified framework of a unique molecular structure or class of structures. Nevertheless, the literature is replete with structural models for humus. These models are generally consistent with the known major properties of humus; they account reasonably well for the elemental and functional group contents, acidity, aliphatic and aromatic character, and so forth. In fact, all of these proposed structures are consistent with the functions of humus in the soil such as pH buffering, metal complexation, and water retention capacity. Despite these common features of the different structural models, the models are, nevertheless, dramatically different from one another in terms of the structural backbone and juxtaposition of functional groups and other chemical features. No convincing evidence has been presented favoring the adoption of any one of these models as providing a unique structural picture of humus. The failure of one generally accepted structural model to emerge from the literature can be viewed as overwhelming evidence for the nonexistence of extended structural regularity in humus. And, as suggested above, the existence of a single chemical structure for humus would actually pose a dilemma in terms of the persistence of this material throughout the environment. Humic substances continue to be related to operational definitions simply because we do not know how to describe them in discrete chemical terms. The literature data relating to structural studies of humus are consistent with the hypothesis proposed here.

The molecular irregularity of humus presents a confusing microscopic panorama to organisms; such disorder apparently preempts humus from serving as a fixed template for guiding the evolution of future generations of organisms capable of rapidly decomposing this material.

Ubiquity and Uniformity of Humus
Hardly any adjective has been more often used to characterize humus than *ubiquitous*. Humus is a pervasive substance found in extremely diverse environments throughout the world. Despite the molecular irregularity and heterogeneity of humus emphasized in the two preceding sections of this chapter, there is, nevertheless, a pronounced uniformity among humus samples regardless of their source. As paradoxical as it may at first appear, this uniformity is as much a feature of humus as are its molecular irregularity and heterogeneity. Although there are differences between humus samples obtained from different sites, the general similarities are more striking than the differences. For example, humic acids are generally similar in terms of elemental and functional group contents and acidic character. Based on a literature survey of over 400 humic acids representing a diversity of sources from around the world (soil, sediment, stream, lakewater, seawater, peat, and coal) the average carbon content was found to be 55.1% ± 5.1% where the error represents one standard deviation. This is a small value for standard deviation considering the diversity of sources from which the humic acids were derived. A similar result was found for the other major elements showing the remarkable sim-

ilarity in the elemental composition of humic acids from a wide diversity of sources (Rice and MacCarthy, 1991). The infrared spectra of humic acids, which provide an integrated picture of many of the structural characteristics of humus, are remarkably similar.

Ultraviolet–visible absorption spectra of humic substances are also very similar though lacking in structure. The composition and properties of old and recent humus samples display no major differences. This general uniformity exists despite the diversity of geographic location, biological origin, and climatic conditions from which the humus arises. The uniformity between humic samples has in the past been sometimes mistakenly attributed to a uniformity in discrete structure for humus samples. It must be recognized, however, that these common characteristics (elemental and functional group contents, acidic character, infrared and ultraviolet–visible spectra, etc.) represent average or net properties of the assemblage of molecules as a whole, and that uniformity in this context is not at all inconsistent with the occurrence of gross structural irregularity and heterogeneity within these substances. As stated by Gamble (1970), "Each fulvic acid sample taken from a given geographical location will be a unique mixture of the same molecular weight components." The ecological functions of humus in the environment require only that the average characteristics be confined to within certain limits. These functions do not require the presence of discrete molecular structures and are readily accommodated by a heterogeneous mixture with a set of suitable average properties, consistent with the hypothesis presented here.

Persistence of Humus
Whereas most biopolymers are decomposed rather rapidly by microorganisms in the soil environment, humus is capable of persisting for prolonged periods. The persistence of humus and its ubiquity as discussed in the previous section are, of course, complementary. As stated by Stevenson (1982), "The resistance of humus to biological decomposition has long been known." The mean residence times, as determined by ^{14}C dating, reported by Campbell and colleagues (1967) for fulvic acid, humic acid, and humin fractions from a Chernozemic black soil were (in years): 495 ± 60, 1235 ± 60, and 1140 ± 50, respectively. According to Stevenson (1982), these "findings attest to the high re-

sistance of humus to microbial attack." The data of other authors also attest to the persistence of soil and aquatic humus in the environment (Stevenson, 1982; Malcolm, 1985). The ability of a material of biological origin to persist in vast quantities by resisting microbial decomposition is vital for the continuance of plant life. The hypothesis proposed here explains how humus satisfies this function by existing as a highly complex mixture. Humus can also inhibit the decomposition of discrete biopolymers by forming a protective coating around the material (Mathur and Farnham, 1985).

Some synthetic polymers are known to be extremely refractory in the environment, at least in the short term. However, these are generally chemically inert materials. Part of the enigma of the persistence of humus is that this material is not chemically inert but possesses an abundance of reactive functional groups; the presence of these functional groups in humus is essential for the performance of its various natural functions in the environment, which were discussed earlier. Interestingly, in the case of humus, persistence and chemical reactivity are not antagonistic qualities.

Formation of Humus

The precise pathways through which humus is formed in the environment are not definitively known. Extensive investigations by many researchers over a long period have failed to yield a clear picture of the formation process. As in the case of structural ideas on humus, models and theories attempting to describe the formation of humus are rampant; proofs are nonexistent. Felbeck (1971) summarized four hypotheses, all of a biological nature, relating to the formation of humus. The irony is not that there are as many as four hypotheses (there are, in fact, many more, and numerous variations thereof) but that the individual hypotheses are remarkably different. These hypotheses differ in terms of the extent to which the precursor plant material is decomposed, as to whether the formation of humus occurs intracellularly or extracellularly, and so forth, and yet modern techniques do not allow us to establish which, if any, are the dominant pathways in the formation of humus. As also suggested by Felbeck (1971) it is possible that more than one mechanism operates simultaneously. Numerous theories for the formation of stream humic substances have been outlined by Malcolm (1985). If humus does indeed consist of a heterogeneous

mixture of irregular molecules, and if humus is not biologically predisposed to participate in unique biochemical interactions, then there should be no need for a specifically defined biological pathway for its formation. Humus could be formed by a combination of chemical and biochemical reactions involving a certain degree of randomness. The molecular irregularity that promotes the persistence of humus thus has its origin in the lack of biological specificity during its formation. It appears that the simplest route to the production of a biologically refractory material has been adopted in nature, namely, production of a complex, heterogeneous mixture by limiting the biological control of the formation processes. Entropy may be a significant driving force in this scheme. The lack of a specific pathway, or of a set of specific pathways, provides a simple explanation for the failure of researchers to elucidate the precise mechanisms of formation of humus. The proposed lack of specificity in the formation of humus is consistent with its ability to form from extremely diverse types of plant precursors and with the fact that climatic and other conditions do not appear to be critical factors in its formation. Swaby and Ladd (1966) proposed that humus "is not synthesized enzymatically, but by heterogeneous chemical catalysis . . ." involving ". . . chaotic chemical combination of monomers produced enzymatically," and Stevenson (1982) stated that "the number of precursor molecules is large and the number of ways in which they can combine is astronomical, thereby accounting for the heterogeneous nature of the humic material in any given soil."

Statistical Considerations in the Formation of Humus

Humus forms from virtually all types of plant precursors and in the presence of a wide variety of microbial populations. In any particular environment the number of potential building blocks for humus is very large and the number of potential ways for combining these units into a molecule of even moderate molecular size is staggering. A perspective on the number of molecular combinations that are possible can be obtained from a paper by Speiser and colleagues (1945), who pointed out that the number of isomers of a relatively simple polymer, partially demethylated pectinic acid, is "astronomical." Speiser and colleagues went on to say, "For an average sample of pectinic acid, the number of structures calculated . . . is many times the magnitude of Avogadro's number, which makes it highly improbable that a given sample could contain two identical molecules. . . ." This statement adds credence to those cited above (Dubach and Mehta, 1963; Gamble, 1970; Gjessing, 1976) that perhaps no two molecules of humic substances are alike! However, the analogy between pectinic acid and humus stops there—pectinic acid is a true polymer and is subject to rapid enzymatic degradation as discussed by Speiser and colleagues. The opportunity for molecular complexity is vastly greater for humus than it is for pectinic acid. Due to the complexity of humus and our ignorance of its molecular constitution, there is no way to calculate a reasonable estimate of the number of different molecules present in a given sample. However, based on this discussion one can easily envisage humus possessing a degree of molecular complexity consistent with the hypothesis proposed here.

Recapitulation

The discussions in the preceding sections can be summarized as follows: There are no specific structural controls or unique precursors in the formation of humus, and consequently a given molecule of humus displays a high degree of molecular irregularity due to the random juxtaposition of its structural components. As a result, an assemblage of humus molecules must constitute a mixture. Such a mixture of irregular molecules displays a natural resistance to enzymatic decomposition and consequently humus is persistent and ubiquitous. The average properties of humus samples are similar in many respects. This model for the nature of humus is consistent with its vital ecological role in the environment, which requires the existence of certain gross, average characteristics rather than mediation of unique molecular structures, in a material that is resistant to microbial degradation.

Concluding Comments

Although humus is resistant to decomposition, it is not totally recalcitrant and it does decay slowly; otherwise humus would accumulate indefinitely in the environment. An equilibrium condition is evidently attained in most environments where a balance between the rate of accumulation of humus and its rate of mineralization is reached.

Humus differs from all biopolymers in terms of its molecular irregularity and the lack of biologically induced specificity in its formation. This does not mean that microbial activity is not important in the formation of humus; microbial processes involving both degradative and synthetic reactions may be occurring, but the molecular structure of the overall, final product is not specifically controlled. The biopolymer lignin, although considerably simpler than humus, does display some degree of molecular irregularity. However, in the case of lignin the fundamental building blocks and their modes of connection are known. The irregularity of lignin may contribute to the fact that it is more resistant to microbial degradation than most biopolymers, but it is still considerably more susceptible to degradation than humus (Swaby and Ladd, 1966).

Most of the examples in this chapter relate to soil humus; however, we believe the hypothesis applies to humus in all environments. Although there are differences between aquatic and soil humus and between various humus fractions (MacCarthy et al., 1985) the overall similarities are profound. Aquatic humus displays a pronounced resistance to decomposition similar to soil humus (Malcolm, 1985) and persists in the environment. It has been shown that the humus in a selection of streams across the United States is uniform regardless of the botanic input to the stream or the sampling season (R.L. Malcolm, U.S. Geological Survey, personal communication).

In conclusion, the hypothesis proposed here is consistent with a large body of data from the literature. The holistic overview presented by the hypothesis provides an ecologically based rationale for the chemically heterogeneous nature of humus: in the case of humus the mixture is the message.

References

Aiken, G.R., McKnight, D.M., Wershaw, R.L., and MacCarthy, P., eds. 1985. *Humic Substances in Soil, Sediment, and Water: Geochemistry, Isolation, and Characterization.* New York: Wiley.

Campbell, C.A., Paul, E.A., Rennie, D.A., and McCallum, K.J. 1967. Dynamics of soil humus using C dating techniques. *Soil Sci,* 104, 217–224.

Dubach, P., and Mehta, N.C. 1963. The chemistry of soil humic substances. *Soils Fert,* 26, 293–300.

Dubach, P., Mehta, N.C., Jakab, T., Martin, F., and Roulet, M. 1964. Chemical investigations on soil humic substances. *Geochim Cosmochim Acta,* 28, 1567–1578.

Felbeck, G.T. Jr., 1965. Structural chemistry of soil humic substances. *Adv Agron,* 17, 327–368.

Felbeck, G.T. 1971. Chemical and biological characterization of humic matter. In: McLaren, A.D., and Skujins, J., eds. *Soil Biochemistry, Vol. 2.* New York: Marcel-Dekker, 36–59

Gamble, D.S. 1970. Titration curves of fulvic acid: The analytical chemistry of a weak polyelectrolyte. *Can J Chem,* 48, 2662–2669.

Gjessing, E.T. 1976. *Characterization of Aquatic Humus.* Ann Arbor, Mi.: Ann Arbor Science.

Hayes, M.H.B., MacCarthy, P., Malcolm, R.L., and Swift, R.S., eds. 1989. *Humic Substances. II. In Search of Structure.* Chichester, Wiley.

Hurst, H.M., and Burges, N.A. 1967. Lignin and humic acids. In: McLaren A.D., and Peterson, G.H., eds. *Soil Biochemistry.* New York: Marcel-Dekker, 261–286.

Kononova, M.M. 1966. *Soil Organic Matter* (translated by Nowakowski, T.Z., and Newman, A.C.D.) Elmford, N.Y.: Pergamon.

MacCarthy, P., DeLuca, S.J., Voorhees, K.J., Malcolm, R.L., and Thurman, E.M. 1985. Pyrolysis-mass spectrometry/pattern recognition on a well-characterized suite of humic materials. *Geochim Cosmochim Acta,* 49, 2091–2096.

MacCarthy, P. and Rice, J.A. 1985. Spectroscopic methods (other than NMR) for determining functionality in humic substances. In: Aiken, G.R., McKnight, D.M., Wershaw, R.L., and MacCarthy, P., eds. *Humic Substances in Soil, Sediment, and Water: Geochemistry, Isolation, and Characterization.* New York: Wiley, 527–559.

MacCarthy, P., and Suffet, I.H. 1989. Aquatic humic substances and their influence on the fate and treatment of pollutants. In: Suffet, I.H., and MacCarthy, P., eds. *Aquatic Humic Substances: Influences on Fate and Treatment of Pollutants.* Washington, D.C.: American Chemical Society, xvii–xxx.

Malcolm, R.L. 1985. Geochemistry of stream fulvic and humic substances. In: Aiken, G.R., McKnight, D.M., Wershaw, R.L., and MacCarthy, P., eds. *Humic Substances in Soil, Sediment, and Water: Geochemistry, Isolation, and Characterization.* New York: Wiley, 181–209.

Mathur, S.P. and Farnham, R.S. 1985. Geochemistry of humic substances in natural and cultivated peatlands. In: Aiken, G.R., McKnight, D.M., Wershaw, R.L., and MacCarthy, P., eds. *Humic Substances in Soil, Sediment, and Water: Geochemistry, Isolation, and Characterization.* New York: Wiley, 53–85.

Perdue, E.M. 1985. Acidic functional groups of humic substances. In: Aiken, G.R., McKnight, D.M., Wershaw, R.L., and MacCarthy, P., eds. *Humic Substances in Soil, Sediment, and Water: Geochemistry, Isolation, and Characterization.* New York: Wiley, 493–526.

Rice, J.A., and MacCarthy, P. 1991. Statistical evaluation of the elemental composition of humic substances. *Org Geochem,* in press.

Schnitzer, M., and Khan, S.U. 1972. *Humic Substances in the Environment.* New York: Marcel-Dekker.

Speiser, R., Hills, C.H., and Eddy, C.R. 1945. The acid behavior of pectinic acids. *J Phys Chem,* 49, 328–343.

Stevenson, F.J. 1982. *Humus Chemistry: Genesis, Composition, Reactions.* New York: Wiley.

Stevenson, F.J. 1985. Geochemistry of soil humic substances. In: Aiken, G.R., McKnight, D.M., Wershaw, R.L., and

MacCarthy, P., eds. *Humic Substances in Soil, Sediment, and Water: Geochemistry, Isolation, and Characterization.* New York: Wiley, 13–52.

Suffet, I.H., and MacCarthy, P., eds. 1989. *Aquatic Humic Substances: Influences on Fate and Treatment of Pollutants.* Washington D.C.: American Chemical Society.

Swaby, R.J., and Ladd, J.N. 1962 Chemical nature, microbial resistance, and origin of soil humus. In: Neale, G.J., ed. *Transactions of Joint Meeting Comms. IV & V.* International Society of Soil Science, Palmerston North, New Zealand, 197–202.

Swaby, R.J., and Ladd, J.N. 1966. Stability and origin of soil humus. In: *The Use of Isotopes in Soil Organic Matter Studies,* Report FAO/IAEA, Brunswick-Volkenrode, Sept. 1963. New York, Pergamon, 197–202.

Swift, R.S. 1985. Fractionation of soil humic substances. In: Aiken, G.R., McKnight, D.M., Wershaw, R.L., and MacCarthy, P., eds. *Humic Substances in Soil, Sediment, and Water: Geochemistry, Isolation, and Characterization.* New York: Wiley, 387–408.

Woodwell, G.M., and Houghton, R.H. 1977. Biotic influences on the world carbon budget. In: Stumm, W., ed. *Global Chemical Cycles and Their Alterations by Man.* New York: Wiley, 61–72.

Woodwell, G.M., Whittaker, R.H., Reiners, W.A., Likens, G.E., Delwiche, C.C., and Botkin, D.B. 1978. The biota and the world carbon budget. *Science,* 199, 141–146.

The Gaia hypothesis in its many manifestations invokes the biological regulation of the composition and redox state of the atmosphere (Margulis and Lovelock, 1974), oceans (Whitfield, 1981), and sediments (Brown et al., 1985). The biota function as an interactive system with homeorrhetic tendencies capable of responding to external pressures and stress in order to maintain the habitability of the biosphere (Lovelock, 1982, 1988). These stresses, which result in both short- and long-term changes in the Earth's surface environment include external (cosmological), internal (planetary), and biological processes (Mackenzie and Agegian, 1989). External processes may be gradual (e.g., increase in solar luminosity), periodic (orbital procession and eccentricity), or episodic (cometary impact). Internal processes include variations in endogenic heat production and plate tectonics (Mackenzie and Agegian, 1989). Biological processes include evolutionary innovations in biochemical pathways such as biomineralization and the diversification of life into five kingdoms (prokaryotes, protoctists, fungi, animals, and plants). In the face of these perturbations, the thread of life has remained unbroken. Biomineralization, or the biological formation of minerals, is an important part of maintaining the continued availability of biologically essential elements, and is involved in the regulation of surface temperature. This chapter discusses biomineralization and its role in biogeochemical cycling, climate regulation, and the maintenance of plate tectonics.

Biomineralization

Over sixty different minerals are now known to be precipitated by organisms (Lowenstam and Weiner, 1989). These include carbonates (aragonite, calcite, vaterite, siderite, rhodochrosite), silicates (opal), iron oxides (goethite, lepidocrosite, hematite, ferrihydrite, magnetite), manganese oxides (todorokite, birnessite), phosphates (francolite, dahlite, ap-

atite, brushite, vivianite), sulfates (gypsum, celestite, barite), and sulfides (pyrite, hydrotroilite, sphalerite, wurtzite, greigite, galena), as well as halides (fluorite), oxalates (whewellite, weddelite, glushkinskite), and citrates (Lowenstam and Weiner, 1983, 1989; Lowenstam, 1986; Krumbein, 1986).

Mineral formation through biomineralization may occur as a result of metabolic processes (biologically induced) or directly, under conditions determined by the organism and under genetic control (biologically controlled) (Lowenstam, 1986; Lowenstam and Weiner, 1983, 1989; Weiner et al., 1983). Biologically induced mineralization occurs when the conditions for precipitation of a mineral result from biological activity (e.g., change in pH, byproducts of metabolism). Pyrite is formed in sedimentary environments by the reaction of bacterially produced hydrogen sulfide (e.g., by *Desulfovibrio* sp.) with iron oxides (Jorgensen, 1983). Biologically controlled biomineralization occurs when a mineral is formed under conditions that are determined by the organism (usually in an organic matrix) and where the composition, shape, and size of the mineral are essential to its function. Magnetotactic bacteria produced ultra fine grained, single-domained crystals of pure magnetite intracellularly within a membrane-bounded structure called the *magnetosome* (Blakemore, 1982). If the crystals were larger or smaller, they would cease to function as a dipole magnet (Chang and Kirschvink, 1989).

Biogenic minerals may be produced under physical and chemical conditions that preclude the precipitation of the mineral in the absence of life. The ocean is undersaturated in strontium sulfate and yet *Acantharia* (unicellular protists) form a celestite test that dissolves rapidly after the death of the organism (Lowenstam and Weiner, 1989). The rates at which a mineral is precipitated may also be affected by biological activity. Manganese-oxidizing bacteria catalyze the precipitation of manganese oxide (e.g., birnessite) enzymatically or by producing organic compounds that enhance autooxidation of manganese both inside and outside the cells (Nealson, 1983b).

Biogeochemical Cycling

The continued availability to all organisms of biologically important elements is necessary for the long-term survival of life. Carbon, nitrogen, and phosphorous (in a ratio of 106:16:1 in most organisms), as well as sulfur, oxygen, and hydrogen are the six major elements, and more than a dozen others are needed in trace amounts (e.g., calcium, magnesium, iron, sodium, potassium, copper, cobalt, nickel, chlorine) (Stolz et al., 1989a). These elements must also be in a chemical form that can be used by organisms. Although dinitrogen gas is abundant in the atmosphere, it is unavailable to most of the biota and must be transformed into nitrates or ammonia by bacteria. The availability of these elements depends on the geological and biological effect on the chemical state of the element, namely its role within biogeochemical cycles.

Life not only depends on biogeochemical cycles but also affects the biosphere through the flow and transformation of chemical compounds (Moore and Dastoor, 1984; Vernadsky, 1929; Lapo, 1982). The formation of the opaline frustules of diatoms and siliceous spicules of sponges affect the concentration of silica in the ocean (Lowenstam, 1974; Whitfield, 1981). The biological control of biogeochemical cycling is most apparent in the paradoxical phenomenona of oxidative processes in anoxic environments and reductive processes in oxic environments (Sieburth, 1986). The oxidation of organic compounds can occur in the absence of molecular oxygen through anaerobic respiration. Iron-reducing bacteria oxidize fatty acids to carbon dioxide by reducing ferric iron to ferrous iron (Lovley and Phillips, 1986). Methane and methylotrophic bacteria (which live by oxidizing methane) have been discovered in the upper ocean (Sieburth, 1980; Sieburth et al., 1987).

Biological transformations also regulate the concentration of the various elements. Because phosphorus-containing gases have not been detected in the atmosphere, phosphorus has been thought to cycle as organic particulates or as phosphate ion in solution. Recently, however, Dèvai and colleagues (1988) have shown that bacteria can volatilize inorganic phosphate to phosphine.

An example of how processes of biomineralization control the availability of an element is the biogeochemical cycle of iron. Iron is found in a variety of biological molecules (e.g., cytochromes, ferredoxins, nitrogenase) (Nealson, 1983a). It is soluble and readily available to organisms in its ferrous form ($Fe++$), under anoxic conditions. However, it is oxidized to its insoluble ferric form ($Fe+++$) in the presence of oxygen. Iron-oxidizing bacteria (e.g., *Leptothrix* sp., *Gallionella* sp.) also convert ferrous iron to ferric-producing deposits of ferrihydrite and lepidocrocite (Nealson, 1983a; Lowenstam, 1986; Krumbein, 1986). Because of the insolubility of oxized iron, aerobic microorganisms have evolved iron sequestering compounds called siderophores, which have a high affinity for ferric iron (Nealson, 1983a). These compounds are excreted by the cell, and once the iron is bound are then reabsorbed.

Iron is so reactive with free oxygen that its reduction does not occur in natural environments without the activity of microbes (Lovley, 1987). Iron is reduced directly by iron-reducing bacteria (Lovley and Phillips, 1986, 1988; Lovley et al., 1987) or as a result of microbial metabolism, which consumes oxygen or produces reduced gases (e.g., hydrogen sulfide) (Nealson, 1983a). Although both of these biological processes convert ferric iron to ferrous iron, whether the ferrous iron remains available depends on the form of the ferric iron reduced. For example, when iron-reducing bacteria reduce amorphous ferric oxide, the liberated ferrous iron quickly reacts with the ferric oxide to produce magnetite (Lovley and Phillips, 1986; Lovley et al., 1987). The remaining ferric iron in the magnetite cannot be further reduced by the bacteria (Lovley and Phillips, 1986). It has been calculated that 10 g of iron-reducing bacteria can produce 1 kg of magnetite (Frankel, 1987)!

As mentioned above, magnetite is also formed, through iron reduction, by magnetotactic bacteria (Blakemore, 1982). These bacteria differ from magnetite-producing, iron-reducing bacteria in that they usually require oxygen for metabolism (dissimilatory iron-reducing bacteria are strict anaerobes) and deposit the magnetite intracellularly through a biologically controlled process (Blakemore, 1982). Although magnetotactic bacteria produce only 0.2 g of magnetite per 10 g of cells, they have been shown to contribute a significant amount of magnetite (10^{-9} to 10^{-7} g/cm^3) to marine sediments (Stolz et al., 1986, 1989b; Chang et al., 1987) and can sequester large concentrations of iron in the water column (nM to μM concentrations). The eventual fate of the magnetite depends on postdepositional events. In environments where there is a high content of total organic carbon (e.g., near-shore ocean basins), this magnetite is quickly dissolved with depth, due to the activity of sulfate-reducing bacteria (Stolz et al., 1986). However, when the total organic carbon content is low, the magnetite is preserved and buried (Chang et al., 1987).

Microbial iron reduction may date back well into the Precambrian. Putative magnetofossils (magnetite formed by magnetotactic bacteria) have been found in 700-my carbonate sediments and in 2.0-Ga siliceous cherts (Chang et al., 1989; Chang and Kirschvink, 1989). It has also been proposed that banded iron formations (e.g., Hamersley Group, Australia), which contain interbanded layers of oxidized and reduced iron and date back even further into the Precambrian, are the result of bacterial metabolism (Baur et al., 1985), in particular iron-reducing bacteria (Lovley et al., 1987).

Climate

Kasting and colleagues (1988) have postulated how climate evolved on the terrestrial planets and the role of CO_2. Climate is regulated by the carbonate-silicate cycle on a timescale greater than 500,000 years. In their model carbonate is weathered from carbonate-silicate rocks by carbonic acid in rain water, formed from CO_2 in the atmosphere. Carbonate is precipitated by plankton and deposited on the ocean floor where it is subducted (at a subduction zone) and recycled as CO_2 via outgassing at mid-ocean ridges and volcanism. The feedback mechanism for climate control in this model is changes in the rate of weathering against the constant outgassing of carbonate. A decrease in temperature results in less evaporation, thus less chemical weathering, and the amount of atmospheric CO_2 increases, warming the earth. Conversely, increased temperature results in increased weathering and more CO_2 is removed from the atmosphere, cooling things. Although they do concede that the present biota are important in CO_2 cycling, in their model the fundamental controls of CO_2 in the atmosphere must be physical rather than biological. This is because carbonate shell-forming organisms did not evolve until 600 my ago and plants only 400 my ago. Although historically this is true (Lowenstam & Margulis,

1980), prokaryotes have been producing deposits of both carbonate and organic carbon for over three billion years. Although climate may already have been affected by the biotic enhancement of weathering in the early Archean (Schwartzman and Volk, 1989), the biological processes involved in the calcium-silicate system (i.e., carbonate biomineralization) evolved by the early Proterozoic.

In today's ocean, carbonate precipitation is primarily attributed to biologically controlled biomineralization (e.g., coccolithophores, forams); evidence for biologically induced carbonate precipitation, however, is as old as the first appearance of life. Stromatolites are organosedimentary structures built by the activity of microorganisms that trap, bind, and precipitate sediment (Awramik, 1982). They first appeared over 3.4 by Ga and reached maximum extent about 850 Ma my ago (Awramik, 1982, 1984; Walter, 1983; Knoll, 1984). Today, their distribution is restricted and they occur in hypersaline lagoonal complexes (Margulis et al., 1980; Stolz, 1990a,b); intertidal flats (Walter, 1983); and subtidal shelf (Dill et al., 1986). Stromatolites are produced by complex microbial communities, the most abundant type dominated by phototrophic bacteria (Cohen et al., 1984; Stolz, 1984, 1990a,b). Cyanobacteria like *Microcoleus chthonoplastes* trap and bind the sediment while converting CO_2 and water to oxygen and organic carbon through photosynthesis. In carbonate-rich waters, microbial mats precipitate carbonate via biologically induced mineralization as a result of CO_2 assimilation during photosynthesis (Krumbein, 1986). This precipitation is further enhanced by the increase in pH caused by microbial species (e.g., cyanobacteria) using bicarbonate (Golubic, 1973).

Although the rock record suggests carbonate stromatolites were scarce in the Archean, they were widespread and abundant throughout the Proterozoic (2.5 to 0.6 Ga) (Awramik, 1984; Walter, 1983). During this time, carbonate precipitation by microbial activity was the major mechanism of stromatolite formation. The great diversity of stromatolite morphologies (e.g., domal, columnar branching, conophyton) indicates that microbial communities were directly involved in their construction. In fact, certain stromatolite morphologies are restricted to specific periods, and are used to subdivide the last 1000 Ma of the Proterozoic into four periods (early, middle, late Riphean, and Vendian) (Awramik, 1984). It seems plausible, then, that significant biological removal of carbonate ions from seawater did not begin with the first shell-forming phytoplankton in the Cambrian, but rather, with stromatolite-forming cyanobacteria in the early Proterozoic.

Prokaryotes are also an important component of the global organic carbon budget. They participate in the fixation of CO_2 into organics and biomass, and organic carbon burial. Autotrophic (carbon-fixing) bacteria are believed to be as old as the oldest life (Walter, 1983). Estimates based on the amount of organic carbon buried in shales (Swaziland, South Africa) suggest rates of primary production and carbon burial during the Archean to be approximately equal to those of extant ecosystems (Reimer et al., 1979). Today between one half and two thirds of global ocean productivity is by prokaryotes (Platt et al., 1983; Sieburth, 1986; Chisolm et al., 1988). Microbial communities can produce massive amounts of organic carbon in short periods through the coupling of photoautotrophy with chemoautotrophy. Mangrove Lake is a small marine karstic lake in Bermuda where in the last 4000 years, over 11 m of sapropel has accumulated ($\sim$ 1.06×10^6 kg; Hatcher et al., 1982). This organic ooze has been produced by cyanobacteria and sulfur-oxidizing bacteria. The high sulfide concentration, produced by sulfate-reducing bacteria and concomitant anoxia inhibit the degradation of the residual organics.

Having demonstrated the mechanisms of CO_2 removal and burial by prokaryotes, what possible evidence is there for the biotic regulation of climate through biomineralization. Changes in oceanic sediment composition, temperature regimes (based on oxygen isotope), and sea level are indicative of past glacial and interglacial periods (Herbert and Fischer, 1986). The periodicity of these events has been correlated with the Earth's orbital procession ($\sim$ 21,000 years) and eccentricity (100,000 years; Herbert and Fischer, 1986). Glacial periods are characterized by low oceanic temperature with a strong gradient, mixing, and sea level regression. During glacial periods there is less biogenic carbonate and more eolian-derived sediment, suggesting a greater amount of physical weathering (Robinson, 1986; Bloomendale et al., 1988; Broecker et al., 1988). Interglacial periods are characterized by a higher, more uniform, global ocean temperature ($10°C$ to $12°C$), stratification and anoxic sediments. Biogenic carbonate deposition is less restricted and during global ocean anoxia, more organic carbon (sapropel) is buried (Fischer and Arthur, 1977; Herbert and Fischer, 1986). This secular variation in

sediments suggests a biological mechanism for climate changes induced by the Earth's orbital procession and eccentricity. The deposition of biogenic carbonate during interglacials and organic carbon during global anoxic events would promote a decrease in atmospheric CO_2. During glacial periods, the decrease in biogenic carbonate and increased oxidation (due to well-circulated oceans) would promote an increase in atmospheric CO_2. This mechanism is not contingent on eukaryotes (plants and shell-forming plankton), but could have originated with prokaryotes as the major players in the early Proterozoic.

Plate Tectonics

Plate tectonic processes are essential for the continued survival of the biota. Carbonate buried in the ocean floor is recycled through subduction and outgassing. Orogeny and craton formation provide the land masses for the terrestrial biota. Although a primitive type is believed to have existed during the Archean, plate tectonics in its current form appeared in the early Proterozoic, around the time wide spread carbonate precipitation as stromatolites began (Awramik, 1984). Anderson (1984) has suggested that the biota may help promote plate tectonics, by precipitating carbonate and maintaining a moderate climate. In his model, the crust of the terrestrial planets consists of a basaltic surface underlain by dense eclogite. The thickness depends on where the geothermal gradient intersects the basaltic-eclogite transition. Venus, a planet with greenhouse heating, is believed to have a deep basalt-eclogite transition and a thick crust. Because of its thick atmosphere and high surface temperature, the crust on Venus is buoyant and cannot sink (Anderson, 1989). On Earth, the cool temperature causes the basalt-eclogite transition to lie closer to the surface. This results in a thin, fragile crust. Anderson (1984) postulates that "Thus there is an interesting possibility that plate tectonics may exist on the earth because of limestone generating life." Anderson further remarks that if the CO_2 in the atmosphere of Venus were converted into limestone, the temperatures of the surface and upper mantle would drop, decreasing the depth of the basalt-eclogite transition. It has been argued that the Archean Earth's atmosphere was stable against a runaway greenhouse (Kasting and Ackerman, 1986), and that abiotic carbonate would eventually precipitate when the concentration of calcium and bicarbonate in the sea reached a critical level (Kasting et al., 1988). However, others have argued that the biota played a major role in reducing surface temperature in the Archean (Schwartzman and Volk, 1989), and that biogenic carbonate formation has been significant since the early Proterozoic (see above).

Secular variation in plate tectonic activity, with concomitant eustatic change, appears to have a 10^8-year cycle and may affect climate and biomineralization (Mackenzie and Agegian, 1989). During periods of rapid sea floor spreading, midocean ridge volume is large, tectonic CO_2 is increased (opposed to being relatively constant as in the Kasting et al. model) and the sea level is high. Conversely, sea level drops when sea floor spreading and ridge volume subsides. High sea level leads to poor ocean circulation and stratification, and the CO_2 increase results in temperature increase, conditions indicative of an interglacial period. During the mid-Cretaceous, the last episode of high ridge volume (Mackenzie and Agegian, 1989), there were no large-scale glaciations, less pole-to-pole climate variability, and deep water temperatures were 10°C to 12°C warmer (Herbert and Fischer, 1986). As a result of global anoxic events during this period, increased sapropel deposits occurred (Herbert and Fischer, 1986). This is consistent with the biogenic precipitation of carbon in response to the increase of tectonically generated carbon dioxide.

Conclusions

Biomineralization has an integral part in biogeochemical cycles, climate control, and plate tectonics. The biota affects the composition of the atmosphere, oceans, and sediments as all biologically important elements are actively cycled through them. This activity is most apparent in the occurrence of paradoxical redox processes. The process of biomineralization evolved early in life's history. Carbonate biomineralization, and thus a major mechanism of CO_2 regulation, was at first biologically induced. As biologically controlled biomineralization evolved so too did the potential for better CO_2 regulation. It is apparent that the surface features of the Earth are affected by cosmological, internal, and biological phenomenon. The biota may respond to some of these events by regulating carbon mineralization. In the long term (10^8 years), the modulation of a moderate climate contributes to continued tectonic activity. On the short term (e.g., orbital variation, 21 kyr, 100 kyr) life

may regulate climate through the cycling of biogenic carbonate and organic carbon. Biomineralization may therefore represent a Gaian mechanism, regulating biogeochemical cycles by forming biominerals under physical and chemical conditions that preclude their formation without life, and at different rates.

References

Anderson, D.L. 1984. The Earth as a planet: paradigms and paradoxes. *Science,* 223, 347–355.

Anderson, D.L. 1989. Where on Earth is the crust. *Physics Today,* 42, 38–46.

Awramik, S.M. 1982. The Prephanerozoic fossil record. In: Holland, H.D., and Schidlowski, M., eds. *Mineral Deposits and the Evolution of the Biosphere.* Berlin: Springer-Verlag, 67–82.

Awramik, S.M. 1984. Ancient stromatolites and microbial mats. In: Cohen, Y., Castenholz, R.W., and Halvorson, H.O., eds. *Microbial Mats: Stromatolites.* New York: A.R. Liss, 1–22.

Baur, M.E., Hayes, J.M., Studley, S.A., and Walter, M.R. 1985. Millimeter-scale variations of stable isotope abundances in carbonates from banded iron-formations in the Hamersley Group of Western Australia. *Economic Geol,* 80, 270–282.

Blakemore, R.P. 1982. Magnetotactic bacteria. *Ann Rev Microbiol,* 36, 217–238.

Bloemendal, J., Lamb, L., and King, J. 1988. Paleoenvironmental implications of rock magnetic properties of late Quaternary sediment cores from the eastern equatorial Atlantic. *Paleoceanography,* 3, 61–87.

Broecker, W.S., Andree, M., Klas, M., Bonani, G., Wolfli, W. and Oeschger, H. 1988. New evidence from the South China Sea for an abrupt termination of the last glacial period. *Nature,* 333, 156–158.

Brown, S., Margulis, L., Ibarra, S., and Siqueiros, D. Desiccation resistance and contamination as mechanisms of Gaia. *Biosystems,* 17, 337–360.

Chang, S-B.R., and Kirschvink, J.L. 1989. Magnetofossils, the magnetization of sediments, and the evolution of magnetite biomineralization. *Ann Rev Earth Planet Sci,* 17, 169–195.

Chang, S-B.R., Stolz, J.F., and Kirschvink, J.L. 1987. Biogenic magnetite as a primary remanence carrier in limestones. *Phys Earth Planet Inter,* 46, 289–303.

Chang, S-B.R., Stolz, J.F., and Kirschvink, J.L., 1989. Biogenic magnetite in stromatolites. II. Occurrence in ancient sedimentary environments. *Precambrian Research* 43, 305–315.

Chisholm, S.W., Olson, R.J., Zettler, E.R., Goericke, R., Waterbury, J.B., and Welschmeyer, N.A. 1988. A novel free-living prochlorophyte abundant in the oceanic euphotic zone. *Nature,* 334, 340–343.

Cohen, Y., Castenholz, R.W., and Halvorson, H.O., eds. 1984. *Microbial Mats: Stromatolites.* New York: A.R. Liss.

Dèvai, I., Felföldy, L., Wittner, I., and Plòsz, S. 1988. Detection of phosphine: New aspects of the phosphorous cycle in the hydrosphere. *Nature,* 333, 343–345.

Dill, R.F., Shinn, E.A., Jones, A.T., Kelly, K., and Steiner, R.P. 1986. Giant subtidal stromatolites forming in normal saline waters. *Nature*, 324, 55–58.

Fischer, A.G., and Arthur, M.A. 1977. Secular variations in the pelagic realm. *Soc Econ Paleoleontologists and Mineralogists Special Publication* 25, 19–50.

Frankel, R.B. 1987. Anaerobes pumping iron. *Nature*, 330, 208.

Golubic, S. 1973. The relationship between blue-green algae and carbonate deposits. In: Carr, N.G. and Whitton B.A., eds. *"The Biology of Blue-green Algae."* Boston: Blackwell Scientific, 434–472.

Hatcher, P.G., Spiker, E.C., Szeverenyi, N.M., and Maciel, G.E. 1982. Selective preservation and origin of petroleum-forming aquatic kerogen. *Organic Geochem*, 4, 93–112.

Herbert, T.D., and Fischer, A.G. 1986. Milankovich climatic origin of mid-Cretaceous black shale rhythms in central Italy. *Nature*, 321, 739–743.

Jorgenson, B.B. 1983. The microbial sulfur cycle. In: Krumbein, W.E., ed. *Microbial Geochemistry*. Boston: Blackwell Scientific, 91–124.

Kasting, J.F. and Ackerman, T.P. 1986. Climatic consequences of very high carbon dioxide levels in the Earth's early atmosphere. *Science*, 234, 1383–1385.

Kasting, J.F., Toon, O.B., and Pollack, J.B. 1988. How climate evolved on the terrestrial planets. *Scientific American*, 258, 90–97.

Knoll, A. 1984. Review of the Earth's earliest biosphere: Its origin and evolution. *Paleobiology*, 10, 286–292.

Krumbein, W.E. 1986. Biotransfer of minerals by microbes and microbial mats. In: Leadbeater, B., and Riding, J., eds. *Biomineralization in Lower Plants and Animals*. Oxford: Clarendon Press, 55–72.

Lapo, A.V. 1982. *Traces of Biogone Biospheres*. Chicago: Mir Publishers.

Lovley, D. 1987. Organic matter mineralization with the reduction of ferrous iron: A review. *Geomicrobial J*, 5, 375–399.

Lovley, D., and Phillips, E.J.P. 1986. Availability of ferric iron for microbial iron reduction in bottom sediments from the freshwater tidal Potamac River. *Appl Environ Microbiol*, 52, 751–757.

Lovley, D., and Phillips, E.J.P. 1988. Novel mode of microbial energy metabolism: Organic carbon oxidation coupled to the dissimilatory reduction of iron and manganese. *Appl Environ Microbiol*, 54, 1472–1480.

Lovley, D., Stolz, J.F., Nord, G.L., Phillips, E.J.P. 1987. Anaerobic production of magnetite by a dissimilatory iron-reducing microorganism. *Nature*, 330, 252–254.

Lovelock, J. 1982. *Gaia, a New Look at Life on Earth*. Oxford and New York: Oxford University Press.

Lovelock, J. 1988. *The Ages of Gaia*. New York: Norton Publishers.

Lowenstam, H.A. 1974. Impact of life on chemical and physical processes. In: Goldberg, E., and Wiley, J. eds. *The Sea. Marine Geochem*, 5, 715–796.

Lowenstam, H.A. 1986. Mineralization processes in monerans and protoctists. In: Leadbeater, B., and Riding, J., eds. *Bio-*

mineralization in Lower Plants and Animals. Oxford: Clarendon Press, 1–17.

Lowenstam, H.A., and Margulis, L. 1980. Evolutionary prerequisites for the early Phanerozoic calcareous skeletons. *BioSystems*, 12, 27–41.

Lowenstam, H.A. and Weiner, S. 1983. Mineralization by organisms and the evolution of biomineralization. In: Westbroek, P., and DeJong, E.W., eds. *Biomineralization and Biological Metal Accumulation*. Boston: Reidel.

Lowenstam, H.A., and Weiner, S. 1989. *On Biomineralization*. New York: Oxford University Press.

Mackenzie, F.T., and Agegian, C.R. 1989. Biomineralization and tentative links to plate tectonics. In: Crick, R.E., ed. *Origin, Evolution and Modern Aspects of Biomineralization in Plants and Animals*. New York: Plenum.

Margulis, L., and Lovelock, J. 1974. Biological modulation of the Earth's atmosphere. *Icarus*, 21, 471–489.

Margulis, L., Barghoorn, E.S., Ashendorf, D., Banerjee, S., Chase, D., Francis, S., Giovannoni, S., and Stolz, J. 1980. The microbial community in the layered sediments at Laguna Figueroa, Baja California, Mexico: Does it have Precambrian analogues? *Precambrian Res*, 11, 93–123.

Moore, B., and Dastoor, M. 1984. The interaction of global biochemical cycles. *National Aeronautics and Space Administration Publication* 84-21.

Nealson, K.H. 1983a. The microbial iron cycle. In: Krumbein, W.E., ed. *Microbial Geochemistry*. Boston: Blackwell Scientific.

Nealson, K.H. 1983b. The microbial manganese cycle. In: Krumbein, W.E., ed. *Microbial Geochemistry*. Boston: Blackwell Scientific, 191–222.

Platt, T., Subba Roa, D.V., and Irwin, B. 1983. Photosynthesis of picoplankton in the oligotrophic ocean. *Nature*, 301, 702–704.

Reimer, T.O., Barghoorn, E.S., and Margulis, L. 1979. Primary productivity in an Archean microbial ecosystem. *Precambrian Res*, 9, 93–104.

Robinson, S.G. 1986. The late Pleistocene paleoclimatic record of North Atlantic deep-sea sediments revealed by mineral-magnetic measurements *Phys Earth Planet Int* 42, 22–47.

Schwartzman, D.W., and Volk, T. 1989. Biotic enhancement of weathering and the inhabitability of Earth. *Nature*, 340, 457–459.

Sieburth, J. McN. 1986. Dominant microorganisms of the upper ocean: Form and function, spatial distribution and photoregulation of biochemical processes. In: Burton, J.D., Brewer, P.G., and Chesselet, R. eds. *Dynamic Processes in the Chemistry of the Upper Ocean*. New York: Plenum Press, 173–195.

Sieburth, J. McN. 1987. Contrary habitats for redox-specific processes: Methanogenesis in oxic waters and oxidation in anoxic waters. In: Sleigh, M.A., ed. *Microbes in the Sea*. Chincester: Ellis Horwood Limited, and New York: Wiley, 11–38.

Sieburth, J. McN., Johnson, P.W., Eberhardt, M.A., Sieracki, M.E., Lidstrom, M., and Laux, D. 1987. The first methane-oxidizing bacterium from the upper-mixing layer of the deep ocean: *Methylomonas pelagicum* sp. nov. *Current Microbiol*, 14, 285–293.

Stolz, J.F. 1984. Fine structure of the stratified microbial community at Laguna Figueroa, Baja California, Mexico. II. Transmission electron microscopy as a diagnostic tool in studying microbial communities in situ. In: Cohen, Y., Castenholz, R.W., and Halvorson, H.O., eds. *Microbial Mats: Stromatolites*. New York: A.R. Liss, 23–38.

Stolz, J.F. 1990a. Ecology of phototrophic prokaryotes. In: Stolz, J.F., ed. *Structure of Phototrophic Prokaryotes*. Boca Raton: C.R.C. Press, 105–124

Stolz, J.F. 1990b. Distribution of phototrophic microbes in the stratified microbial community at Laguna Figueroa, Baja California, Mexico. *BioSys,* 23, 345–357.

Stolz, J.F., Botkin, D.B., and Dastoor, M.N. 1989a. The biosphere: A system of integrated parts. In: Rambler, M., Margulis, L., and Fester, R., eds. *Global Ecology.* New York: Harcourt Brace Jovanovich, 31–50.

Stolz, J.F., Chang, S.R., and Kirschvink, J.L. 1986. Magnetotactic bacteria and single-domain magnetite in hemipelagic sediments. *Nature,* 321, 849–851.

Stolz, J.F., Chang, S.R., and Kirschvink, J.L. 1989b. The effect of magnetotactic bacteria on the magnetic properties of marine sediments. In: Crick, R.E., ed. *Origin, Evolution and Modern Aspects of Biomineralization in Plants and Animals.* New York: Plenum, 497–506

Vernadsky, W. 1929. *La Biosphere.* Paris: Alcan. (English translation, Chicago: Mir Publishers, 1987).

Walter, M.R. 1983. Archean stromatolites: Evidence of the Earth's earliest benthos. In: Schopf, J.W., ed. *Earth's Earliest Biosphere: Its Origin and Evolution.* Princeton, N.J., Princeton University Press, 214–239.

Weiner, S., Traub, W., and Lowenstam, H.A. 1983. Organic matrix in calcified organic matrix. In: Westbroek, P., and DeJong, E.W., eds. *Biomineralization and Biological Metal Accumulation.* Boston: Reidel, 204–224.

Whitfield, M. 1981. The world ocean, mechanism or machination? *Interdisciplinary Sci Rev,* 6, 12–35.

Joel S. Levine

39
The Biosphere as a Driver for Global Atmospheric Change

The most unique feature of our planet is the presence of an active biosphere. The biosphere has exerted a major influence on the composition and chemistry of the atmosphere and on the climate over the history of the planet. This influence is just as strong in the present atmosphere. Since the appearance of the first living systems on the planet at least 3.8 billion years ago, the biosphere has significantly impacted the chemical composition of the atmosphere. The biosphere is a major source of many atmospheric gases (Lovelock and Margulis, 1974; and Margulis and Lovelock, 1974). Some of the most important atmospheric gases of biogenic origin are summarized in table 39.1.

In addition to the production and emission directly into the atmosphere of gases of biogenic origin, biogenic gases impact the composition, chemistry, and physics of the atmosphere in other ways (Levine and Augustsson, 1985; Levine, 1989). For example, the buildup of oxygen in the atmosphere, resulting from photosynthetic activity, had a very significant impact on the composition, chemistry, and physics of the atmosphere. The buildup of atmospheric oxygen led to the photochemical production of ozone (O_3). Ozone absorbs solar ultraviolet radiation (200 to 300 nm) and, hence, shields the

biosphere from this lethal radiation. The photolysis of ozone by solar radiation (300 to 310 nm) in the troposphere leads to production of excited oxygen atoms [$O(^1D)$]. The reaction of excited atomic oxygen with ever-present atmospheric water vapor (H_2O) leads to the formation of the hydroxyl radical (OH). The hydroxyl radical is the most significant chemical scavenger of the troposphere and initiates almost all of the chemistry of the troposphere that results in the chemical transformation of most biogenic and abiogenic gases.

In addition, both oxygen and ozone control the rate of photolysis of many atmospheric gases and, hence, further impact the photochemistry and chemistry of the atmosphere. The buildup of oxygen in the atmosphere also controlled and still controls the oxidation state of the soil and oceans. The oxidation states of the soil and oceans govern the metabolic biochemical processes of microorganisms, such as nitrification, denitrification, and methanogenesis, that lead to production of biogenic gases. Finally, the buildup of atmospheric oxygen led to the existence of fire as a global phenomenon. The burning of living and dead biomass is a very significant global source of many atmospheric gases, including carbon dioxide, carbon monoxide, methane, nitrous oxide, and nitric oxide. Due to its role as a source of atmospheric gases via biogenic production and biomass burning, which impact the chemical and radiative properties of the atmosphere, the biosphere has been and remains today an important driver for global atmospheric change.

The Evolution of Atmospheric Oxygen

Oxygen (O_2) is produced as a byproduct of the photosynthesis process, which can be expressed by the following reaction:

$$nH_2O + mCO_2 + h\nu \xrightarrow{\text{chlorophyll}} C_m(H_2O)_n + mO_2 \quad (1)$$

In this equation, $C_m(H_2O)_n$ represents carbohydrate produced by photosynthetic activity from water vapor (H_2O) and CO_2 in the presence of sunlight, rep-

Table 39.1 Some Atmospheric Biogenic Gases

Gas	Surface Concentration*
Nitrogen (N_2)	78.08%
Oxygen (O_2)	20.95%
Carbon dioxide (CO_2)	345 ppmv
Methane (CH_4)	1.7 ppmv
Nitrous oxide (N_2O)	330 ppbv
Ammonia (NH_3)	0.1–1 ppbv
Methyl chloride (CH_3Cl)	0.7 ppbv
Carbonyl sulfide (COS)	0.5 ppbv
Dimethylsulfide ((CH_3)$_2$S)	0.4 ppbv
Nitric oxide (NO)	5–1000 pptv
Dimethyl disulfide ((CH_3)$_2$S$_2$)	100 pptv
Carbon disulfide (CS_2)	15–30 pptv
Methyl bromide (CH_3Br)	30 pptv
Methyl iodide (CH_3I)	10–20 pptv

*ppmv = parts per million by volume = 10^{-6}
ppbv = parts per billion by volume = 10^{-9}
pptv = parts per trillion by volume = 10^{-12}.

resented by $h\nu$, where h is Planck's constant and ν is the frequency of the incident visible solar radiation.

There is a general agreement that photosynthetic activity and the subsequent biogenic production of O_2 were responsible for transforming the oxidation state of the early atmosphere from a mildly reducing atmosphere of CO_2, nitrogen, and water vapor to the present, strongly oxidizing mixture of nitrogen and oxygen (Levine, 1982, 1985). However, some O_2 was produced abiotically in the prebiological paleoatmosphere due to the photolysis of H_2O and CO_2, the two major components of volcanic outgassing (Levine et al., 1982; Canuto et al., 1982; Levine, 1985). The photochemical reactions leading to the abiotic production of O_2 can be expressed as[1]:

$$H_2O + h\nu \rightarrow OH + H; \quad \lambda \leq 240 \text{ nm} \tag{2}$$

followed by:

$$OH + OH \rightarrow O + H_2O \tag{3}$$

and

$$CO_2 + h\nu \rightarrow O + CO; \quad \lambda \leq 230 \text{ nm} \tag{4}$$

The atomic oxygen (O) produced in reactions (3) and (4) forms O_2 via the following reactions:

$$O + O + M \rightarrow O_2 + M \tag{5}$$

and

$$O + OH \rightarrow O_2 + H \tag{6}$$

where OH is the hydroxyl radical, CO is carbon monoxide, H is atomic hydrogen, and M is any molecule to absorb excess energy or momentum of the reaction. The abiotic production of O_2 via reactions (2) to (6) is very sensitive to atmospheric levels of H_2O and CO_2, and to the flux of solar ultraviolet radiation, all of which may have varied significantly over geological time (Canuto et al., 1982). The vertical distribution of O_2 in the prebiological paleoatmosphere for present atmospheric levels of H_2O, CO_2, and solar ultraviolet radiation is shown in figure 39.1 (Levine et al., 1982). For present values of these parameters, the surface mixing ratio of O_2 is about 10^{-15}.[2] Note that in the prebiological paleoatmosphere, O_2 was not uniformly distributed with altitude in the troposphere and stratosphere, as it is in the present atmosphere, but varied significantly with altitude. The altitude distribution of O_2 reflects its chemical production and destruction terms. For enhanced levels of CO_2 and solar ultraviolet radiation, the surface mixing ratio of O_2 may have approached the parts per billion by volume level (ppbv $= 10^{-9}$) (Canuto et al., 1982). However, the surface

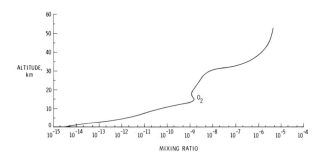

Figure 39.1 The vertical distribution of oxygen (O_2) in the prebiological early atmosphere. Prior to the origin and evolution of photosynthetic organisms, atmospheric oxygen resulted from the photolysis of volcanic H_2O and CO_2 by solar ultraviolet radiation. (From Levine et al., 1982).

mixing of O_2 was still significantly below the present atmospheric level of 21% by volume (21 parts per hundred by volume). It should be noted that in addition to the production reactions shown in equations (2) to (6), the calculation shown in figure 39.1 also includes various O_2 loss reactions (i.e., the photolysis of O_2 and losses due to various physical and chemical processes).

The Evolution of Atmospheric Ozone

In addition to transforming the early atmosphere from a mildly reducing mixture to a highly oxidizing one, the growth of biogenic O_2 in the atmosphere had another important effect. It led to the photochemical production of ozone (O_3), which eventually resulted in the shielding of the Earth's surface from biologically lethal solar ultraviolet radiation. The photochemical production of O_3 is initiated by the photolysis of O_2, forming oxygen atoms, which then recombine to form O_3. These reactions can be expressed as:

$$O_2 + h\nu \rightarrow O + O; \quad \lambda \leq 242 \text{ nm} \tag{7}$$

followed by:

$$O + O_2 + M \rightarrow O_3 + M \tag{8}$$

The calculated vertical distribution of O_3 as a function of atmospheric O_2 level, expressed in present atmospheric level (PAL) of O_2, is shown in figure 39.2 (Levine, 1982). For biological shielding of solar ultraviolet, the critical parameter is the total atmospheric burden or column density (O_3 molecules cm^{-2}) of O_3, as opposed to the vertical profile of O_3 shown in figure 39.2. The total O_3 column density as a function of atmospheric O_2 level expressed in PAL is given in table 39.2 (Levine, 1982). Biological shielding is obtained for a total O_3 column density of about 6×10^{18} O_3 molecules cm^{-2} (Berkner and

Marshall, 1965), which is approximately half of the present total O_3 column density of about 10^{19} O_3 molecules cm^{-2}, which varies somewhat with latitude and season. The calculations given in figure 39.2 and table 39.2 include the various O_3 loss reactions (i.e., the photolysis of O_3 and the chemical losses due to reactions with oxides of nitrogen, hydrogen, and chlorine) as well as the production reaction given in equation (8).

In the present atmosphere, O_3 not only shields the surface of the Earth from biologically lethal solar ultraviolet radiation, but is a strong oxidizing agent and also initiates a photochemical reaction that leads to the formation of OH, which is responsible for the chemical transformation of almost every biogenically produced gas. Almost all atmospheric biogenic and abiogenic gases are transformed via oxidation by OH. Two notable exceptions are the oxidation of nitric oxide (NO), which is controlled by ozone rather than OH—see reaction (14)—and the oxidation of nitrous oxide (N_2O), which is con-

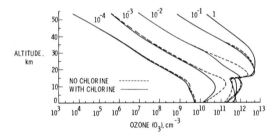

Figure 39.2 The vertical distribution of atmospheric ozone (O_3) as a function of the level of atmospheric oxygen expressed in terms of present atmospheric level, PAL = 1 with and without the inclusion of chlorine chemistry. (From Levine, 1982).

Table 39.2 Atmospheric Ozone as a Function of Evolving Oxygen Levels*

O_2 Level (PAL)	O_3 Column Density (cm^{-2})	Height of O_3 Peak (km)	O_3 Density at Peak (cm^{-3})
Without Chlorine Species Chemistry			
1	9.93 (18)†	20.5	5.53 (12)
10^{-1}	6.07 (18)	19	4.57 (12)
10^{-2}	2.47 (18)	16	2.48 (12)
10^{-3}	1.88 (17)	11.5	1.92 (11)
10^{-4}	5.58 (15)	0	5.63 (09)
With Chlorine Species Chemistry			
1	9.70 (18)	20.5	5.40 (12)
10^{-1}	5.94 (18)	19	4.62 (12)
10^{-2}	1.59 (18)	10	1.16 (12)
10^{-3}	6.98 (16)	9	5.72 (10)
10^{-4}	5.18 (15)	0	5.42 (09)

†9.93 (18) is read as 9.93×10^{18}.
*From Levine, 1982.

trolled by excited atomic oxygen—see reactions (12) and (13). OH is produced by the reaction of the excited oxygen atom [$O(^1D)$] with water vapor—reaction (10). Excited oxygen results from the photolysis of O_3—reaction (9). These processes can be represented by the following reactions:

$$O_3 + h\nu \rightarrow O(^1D) + O_2; \quad \lambda \leqslant 310 \text{ nm} \tag{9}$$

$$O(^1D) + H_2O \rightarrow 2 \text{ OH} \tag{10}$$

It should be pointed out that O_3 may also be photolyzed by solar radiation of wavelength greater than 310 nm, but this reaction leads to the production of ground state atomic oxygen rather than the more energetic excited oxygen [$O(^1D)$]. Reaction (10) is the overwhelming OH production process in the present troposphere since solar photons between about 290 and 310 nm reach the Earth's surface (stratospheric O_3 absorbs solar photons less than about 290 nm). However, in the O_2- and O_3-deficient paleoatmosphere, solar photons less than 290 nm could easily reach the surface, and the direct photolysis of H_2O in reaction (2) with the subsequent gravitational escape of atomic hydrogen was a major source of OH in the prebiological paleoatmosphere.

The Impact of Oxygen and Ozone on Atmospheric Photolysis Rates

As oxygen and its photochemical product, ozone, evolved to their present atmospheric levels, these gases controlled the rate of photolysis and, hence, the chemistry of other gases. The rate of photolysis, the chemistry, and the distribution of nitrous oxide (N_2O) are good examples of this effect. Nitrous oxide is produced in the soil by microorganisms via the biochemical processes of denitrification and nitrification. Nitrous oxide, while chemically inert in the troposphere, diffuses up to the stratosphere where it is destroyed by two different mechanisms. About 90% of stratospheric nitrous oxide is destroyed by direct photolysis by solar radiation:

$$N_2O + h\nu \rightarrow N_2 + O; \quad \lambda \leqslant 337 \text{ nm} \tag{11}$$

The remaining 10% of stratospheric nitrous oxide is lost by reaction with excited atomic oxygen [$O(^1D)$], with two reaction paths of equal probability:

$$N_2O + O(^1D) \rightarrow N_2 + O_2, \quad \text{and} \tag{12}$$

$$N_2O + O(^1D) \rightarrow 2 \text{ NO} \tag{13}$$

Reaction (13) is the major source of nitric oxide in the stratosphere. Nitric oxide leads to the photochemical destruction of stratospheric ozone through the NO_x (NO_x = NO + NO_2 [nitrogen dioxide]) catalytic cycle:

$$NO + O_3 \rightarrow NO_2 + O_2 \qquad (14)$$

$$NO_2 + O \rightarrow NO + O_2 \qquad (15)$$

This catalytic cycle results in a net reaction of:

$$O_3 + O \rightarrow 2O_2 \qquad (16)$$

To investigate how evolving atmospheric levels of oxygen and ozone controlled the distribution of nitrous oxide, we have calculated the vertical distribution of nitrous oxide as a function of atmospheric oxygen level (expressed in PAL of O_2) with the corresponding vertical distribution of ozone shown in figure 39.2. These calculations are given in figure 39.3. All of these calculations include the destruction of nitrous oxide due to reactions (14) through (16) and all assume a surface flux of nitrous oxide into the atmosphere of 1.7×10^9 N_2O molecules cm^{-2} s^{-1}, which corresponds to a flux of nitrous oxide of 13×10^{12} g N/yr, the global source strength of N_2O. These calculations show that in the oxygen- and ozone-deficient early atmosphere ($O_2 = 10^{-4}$ PAL), the mixing ratio of nitrous oxide was more than six orders of magnitude lower than in the present atmosphere ($O_2 = 1$ PAL) at 50 km. These calculations indicate that in the oxygen- and ozone-deficient early atmosphere, the photolysis of nitrous oxide in reaction (14) was the overwhelming destruction mechanism for nitrous oxide and that the oxidation of nitrous oxide in reaction (16) was not a significant source of nitric oxide as it is in today's atmosphere.

Oxygen and the Biogenic Production of Nitrous Oxide and Nitric Oxide

In addition to regulating the photochemistry of nitrous oxide and nitric oxide, atmospheric oxygen also controls the biogenic emissions of these gases in soil. Nitrous oxide and nitric oxide are produced in soils by microorganisms via nitrification and denitrification (Anderson and Levine, 1986, 1987). Anderson and Levine (1986) have shown that the availability of oxygen in soil controls both the microorganisms and the metabolic biochemical pathways responsible for the biogenic emissions of nitrous oxide and nitric oxide. As atmospheric oxygen diffuses downward into the upper centimeters of the soil, it controls the oxygen level in the soil. Hence, to a first approximation, the level of oxygen in the atmosphere controls the level of oxygen in the

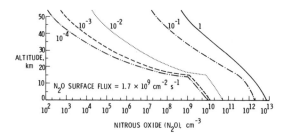

Figure 39.3 The vertical distribution of atmospheric nitrous oxide (N_2O) as a function of the level of atmospheric oxygen expressed in terms of present atmospheric level, PAL = 1. For all calculations, the same upward surface flux of nitrous oxide was specified. (From Levine and Augustsson, 1985).

soil. However, water or moisture in the upper layers tends to inhibit the diffusion of oxygen into the soil and form anaerobic zones in the soil. To better understand the influence of oxygen on the biogenic production of nitrous oxide and nitric oxide in soil, Anderson and Levine (1986) investigated the effect of oxygen partial pressure in soil on the production of nitrous oxide and nitric oxide by a wide variety of common soil-nitrifying and -denitrifying bacteria under laboratory conditions. Some of the results of the Anderson and Levine (1986) study are summarized here. They found that the production of nitric oxide per cell was highest by autotrophic nitrifiers and independent of soil oxygen level, whereas nitrous oxide production was inversely proportional to soil oxygen level. Nitrous oxide production was highest in the denitrifier, *Pseudomonas fluorescens,* but only under anaerobic conditions. The molar ratio of nitric oxide to nitrous oxide produced was usually greater than unity for nitrifiers and much less than unity for denitrifiers. Hence, the level of oxygen in the soil controls the microorganisms and the metabolic biochemical pathways responsible for the production of nitric oxide and nitrous oxide.

Oxygen, Fire, and Biomass Burning

In addition to its impact on atmospheric composition and photochemistry, as discussed in the previous sections, the buildup of atmospheric oxygen to present levels permitted the occurrence of fire as a global phenomenon (Watson et al., 1978). The burning of living and dead biomass in the diverse ecosystems of our planet is a significant source of many radiatively and chemically active atmospheric gases, including CO_2, carbon monoxide, methane, the nonmethane hydrocarbons, and the oxides of nitrogen (Levine, 1990; Levine, 1991). On a global scale, the burning of living and dead biomass may

Table 39.3 Gas Emission Ratios Due to Biomass Burning in Different Global Ecosystems (Emission ratios in % normalized with respect to carbon dioxide [CO_2]: Emission ratio $= \Delta x/\Delta CO_2$, Where $x =$ Gas Under Consideration, $\Delta =$ Enhancement Due to Production in Biomass Burn)

Gas	Tropical Forest		Chaparral Forest		Boreal Forest	Wetlands
	Crutzen et al. (1985)	Andreae et al. (1988)	Cofer et al. (1988a)*	Cofer et al. (1989)†	Cofer et al. (1989)‡	LeBel et al. (1988)
CO	12.1 (6.0–24)	8.5 (6.0–16.0)	5.1 ± 0.8 6.0 ± 3.1	6.4 ± 2.0 6.6 ± 1.6 8.2 ± 1.4	6.9 ± 0.4	
NMHC	1.1 (0.4–2.8)		0.39 ± 0.06 0.41 ± 0.08	0.68 ± 0.23 0.67 ± 0.19 1.17 ± 0.33	0.61 ± 0.17	
CH$_4$	0.8 (0.3–2.0)		0.36 ± 0.06 0.43 ± 0.10	0.76 ± 0.24 0.61 ± 0.19 0.87 ± 0.23	0.67 ± 0.07	
N$_2$O	0.018 (0.006–0.058)		0.014 ± 0.002 0.021 ± 0.012	0.015 ± 0.004 0.019 ± 0.005 0.039 ± 0.008	0.019 ± 0.004	
COS	0.00047 (0.00015–0.0015)					
NO$_x$		0.208 (0.066–0.348)				
NO		0.051 (0.017–0.085)				
NH$_3$		0.092 (0.059–0.13)				0.006–0.124
H$_2$			2.1 ± 0.4 2.3 ± 1.0	2.3 ± 0.8 2.5 ± 0.6 2.5 ± 0.6	1.8 ± 0.2	
HNO$_3$						0.012

*First number represents emissions from flaming stage of fire. Second number represents emissions from both flaming and smoldering stages, called *mixed emissions*.
†Same as above. Third number represents emission from smoldering stage of fire.
‡Represents emissions from flaming stage of fire.

cover as much as 5% of the land area of our planet each year (National Academy of Sciences, 1984). Most of these fires are human-initiated, such as the fires started for deforestation and land clearing in the tropical rain forests and the burning of vegetative stubble after harvesting in temperate latitudes. Prior to the last few years, almost all of the measurements of the gaseous and particulate emissions resulting from biomass burning were based on fires in the tropical rainforests, particularly Brazil (Crutzen et al., 1979; Greenberg et al., 1984; Crutzen et al., 1985; Andreae et al., 1988). Recently, measurements of the gaseous and particulate emissions associated with fires in other ecosystems have been made, including midlatitude chaparral forests (Cofer et al., 1988a,b, and 1989), Canadian boreal forests (Cofer et al., 1989, 1990b, 1991), and wetlands (LeBel et al., 1988; Cofer et al., 1990a). Measurements of the gaseous emissions produced by fires in these diverse ecosystems are summarized in table 39.3.

Fire and Biogenic Production of Gases

In addition to producing significant amounts of gases and particulates as a direct result of the combustion of living and dead biomass (Levine, 1990; Levine, 1991), fires have recently been found to have a significant impact on the biogenic emissions of nitric oxide and nitrous oxide from soils (Anderson et al., 1988; Levine et al., 1988) and on the emissions of methane from wetlands (Levine et al., 1990). Following prescribed fires in chaparral ecosystem in southern California, soil emissions of nitric oxide were found to increase by factors ranging from two to three compared to preburn emissions (Anderson et al., 1988; Levine et al., 1988). Measurements indicate that the postburn enhancement may persist for at least six months following the burn (Anderson et al., 1988). Prefire measurements failed to detect any nitrous oxide emissions, indicating a flux below 2 ng N m^{-2} s^{-1}, the minimum detection limit of the instrument. Postfire emissions of nitrous oxide at the same site exceeded 20 ng N m^{-2} s^{-1} (Levine et al., 1988). The postfire emissions of nitric oxide exceeded the postfire emissions of nitrous oxide by factors ranging from 2.7 to 3.4 (Levine et al., 1988). Pre- and postburn measurements of the soil indicated a significant increase of ammonium and a decrease of nitrate after the fire (Anderson et al., 1988; Levine et al., 1988). Laboratory measurements have indicated that the ratio of nitric oxide to nitrous oxide emissions for nitrifying bacteria ranges from about 1.0 to 8.5, whereas the ratio for denitrifying bacteria is less than unity (Anderson and Levine, 1986). This finding, coupled with the measurements that show soil ammonium, the substrate for nitrification, increasing after burning, and soil nitrate, the substrate for denitrification, decreasing after burning, suggests that the postburn enhancement in nitric oxide and nitrous oxide emissions probably results from the action of nitrifying bacteria (Levine et al., 1988).

Following prescribed fires in wetlands at the National Aeronautics and Space Administration Kennedy Space Center in Florida, the biogenic emissions of methane were found to exceed 30×10^{-3} g m^{-2} day^{-1}. Prefire measurements at the same site failed to detect any methane emissions, indicating a flux below 0.3×10^{-3} g m^{-2} day^{-1}, the minimum detection limit of the instrument (Levine et al., 1990). It is believed that the enhanced methane emissions following the fires is due to production of CO_2, acetate, and formate as combustion products of biomass burning. All three compounds are used by methogenic bacteria in the biogenic production of methane (Levine et al., 1990).

Nitrous Oxide

In addition to leading to the chemical destruction of ozone in the stratosphere as outlined in reactions (13) to (16), nitrous oxide is a greenhouse gas. Theoretical calculations indicate that a doubling of nitrous oxide from about 330 ppbv to 660 ppbv will increase the global surface temperature between 0.3°C to 0.4°C (Wuebbles and Edmonds, 1988). Atmospheric levels of nitrous oxide are increasing at a rate of 0.2% to 0.3% per year (Wuebbles and Edmonds, 1988). Biogenic emission is the major source of atmospheric nitrous oxide. This is especially true in light of recent findings indicating that the combustion of fossil fuels and biomass burning once believed to be major sources of nitrous oxide, may not be a significant source of nitrous oxide at all (Muzio and Kramlich, 1988; Cofer et al., 1990b; Levine, 1990; Cofer et al., 1991).

The total global production of nitrous oxide was believed to be about $13.4 \pm 6.7 \times 10^{12}$ g/year divided among the following sources: biogenic soil emissions: $7.5 \pm 4 \times 10^{12}$ g/year; biomass burning: $1.5 \pm 0.5 \times 10^{12}$ g/year; fossil fuel burning: $2 \pm 1 \times 10^{12}$ g/year; and emissions from the oceans and estuaries: $2 \pm 1 \times 10^{12}$ g/year (Seiler and Conrad, 1987). This budget will have to be reexamined in light of the finding that fossil fuel and biomass burning are not significant sources of nitrous oxide. A likely candidate to make up the production of ni-

Table 39.4 Estimated World Use of Industrially Fixed Nitrogen Fertilizer: 1940–1980*

Year	World Fertilizer Usage (10^6 Mt N/yr)
1940	3
1950	5
1960	10
1970	26
1980	55

*Data from Delwiche, 1981.

trous oxide previously attributed to fossil fuel burning and biomass burning is the enhanced biogenic soil emissions of nitrous oxide following fires (Anderson et al., 1988; Levine et al., 1988). Biogenic emissions of nitrous oxide (and nitric oxide) are significantly enhanced by the application of industrially fixed nitrogen fertilizers (Anderson and Levine, 1987) and by natural fertilization associated with the combustion products of biomass burning, such as ammonium (Anderson et al., 1988; Levine et al., 1988). Both the global usage of industrially fixed nitrogen fertilizers and the number of acres worldwide that burn each year appear to be increasing with time. The estimated worldwide use of industrially fixed nitrogen fertilizer from 1940 to 1980 is summarized in table 39.4.

Nitric Oxide

Nitric oxide is a chemically active gas that impacts the chemistry of both the troposphere and stratosphere. As already discussed, in the stratosphere, nitric oxide leads to the chemical destruction of ozone—reactions (14) to (16). In the troposphere, nitric oxide leads to the chemical production of nitric acid (HNO_3), the fastest growing component of acid rain. The nitrogen dioxide formed by the oxidation of nitric oxide by ozone—reaction (14)—reacts with OH in the presence of any third body (M) to form nitric acid:

$$NO_2 + OH + M \rightarrow HNO_3 + M \quad (17)$$

Once in the troposphere, water-soluble nitric acid has a characteristic atmospheric residence time of less than five days before it is lost by rainout. The loss of nitric acid by rainout and dry deposition is a source of fixed nitrogen in the form of nitrate (NO_3^-) to the biosphere. Once in the biosphere, nitrate is recycled back into the atmosphere in the forms of molecular nitrogen (N_2), nitrous oxide, and nitric oxide via denitrification.

Biogenic emissions and biomass burning are significant global sources of nitric oxide. Of the total global production of nitric oxide estimated to range between 22 to 92 $\times$ 10^{12} gN/year, biogenic emissions may account for 8 $\times$ 10^{12} gN/year, with a range of 1 to 15 $\times$ 10^{12} gN/year, and biomass burning may account for 12 $\times$ 10^{12} gN/year, with a range of 4 to 40 $\times$ 10^{12} gN/year (Wuebbles and Edmonds, 1988; Levine, 1990). Other important global sources of nitric oxide are fossil fuel combustion (20(15–25) $\times$ 10^{12} gN/year) and atmospheric lightning (8(1–10) $\times$ 10^{12} gN/year) (Wuebbles and Edmonds, 1988).

Methane

Methane is both a radiatively active and chemically active atmospheric gas. On a molecule-per-molecule basis, methane is twenty-five times more efficient than CO_2 as a greenhouse gas. Theoretical climate calculations indicate that a doubling of methane from about 1.7 to 3.4 ppmv will increase the global surface temperature between 0.2°C to 0.4°C (Wuebbles and Edmonds, 1988). Methane is responsible for more than 15% of the total destruction of OH in the troposphere; hence, together, carbon monoxide and methane control more than 95% of the total destruction of this very chemically active tropospheric gas (Levine et al., 1985). The reaction of methane with OH initiates the methane oxidation chain, which in the presence of nitrogen oxides leads to the chemical production of ozone in the troposphere (Levine et al., 1985). Methane is increasing in the atmosphere at a rate of about 1.1%/year (Wuebbles and Edmonds, 1988).

Atmospheric methane is produced by methanogens in anaerobic environments and by biomass burning. Methane production in anaerobic environments by methanogens include rice paddies (120 $\pm$ 50 $\times$ 10^{12} g/year); swamps and wetlands (47 $\pm$ 22 $\times$ 10^{12} g/year); and enteric fermentation in ruminants (86 $\pm$ 13 $\times$ 10^{12} g/year) (Seiler and Conrad, 1987). Global biomass burning produces 79 $\pm$ 23 $\times$ 10^{12} g/year (Seiler and Conrad, 1987; Levine, 1990). Hence, biogenic activity and biomass burning produce 332 $\pm$ 108 $\times$ 10^{12} g/year of the total global methane budget of 428 $\pm$ 131 $\times$ 10^{12} gC/year (Seiler and Conrad, 1987). Several of the global sources of methane appear to be increasing with time, including the number of acres worldwide that burn each year, the number of the world's cattle, and the global production of rice. The number of the world's cattle from 1940 to 1980 is estimated in table 39.5. The global production of rice from 1940 to 1980 is estimated in table 39.6.

Table 39.5 Number of Cattle in World

Year	Number of Cattle (10^6 Head)
1940	700
1950	800
1960	950
1970	1100
1980	1200

*Data from World Meteorological Organization, 1985.

Table 39.6 Global Production of Rice*

Year	Rice Production (10^6 Mt/yr)
1940	170
1950	170
1960	240
1970	300
1980	410

*Data from World Meteorological Organization, 1985.

Other Atmospheric Gases Produced by Biogenic and Biomass Burning Activities

Carbon Dioxide

Carbon dioxide is an important atmospheric greenhouse gas. Theoretical calculations indicate that a doubling of CO_2 from about 345 to 690 ppmv will result in a global average surface temperature increase of 2°C to 4.5°C (Wuebbles and Edmonds, 1988). Carbon dioxide is increasing in the atmosphere at a rate of 0.3 to 0.4%/year (Wuebbles and Edmonds, 1988). The production of CO_2 due to biogenic respiration and decay is almost exactly balanced by its loss via photosynthetic activity. Respiration and decay produce about 100 $\times$ 10^{15} gC/year of CO_2, which is about the exact amount of CO_2 consumed by photosynthetic activity each year. The measured atmospheric increase is attributable to CO_2 produced during the burning of fossil fuels and living and dead biomass. At the present time, the CO_2 produced by global biomass burning is estimated to range between 2 to 5 $\times$ 10^{15} gC/year (Levine, 1990; 1991), with global fossil fuel burning contributing between 5 to 6 $\times$ 10^{15} gC/year (Seiler and Crutzen, 1980; Mooney et al., 1987). The emissions of CO_2 from changes in land clearing and burning and fossil fuel combustion have increased with time. The CO_2 emissions due to land clearing and burning from 1860 to 1980 are summarized in table 39.7. The CO_2 emissions due to the combustion of fossil fuels from 1950 to 1980 are summarized in table 39.8. It is interesting to note that deforestation and biomass burning have been responsible for the high cumulative emissions of CO_2 over the period from 1860 until 1980, with estimates

Table 39.7 Carbon Dioxide Emissions to the Atmosphere from Changes in Land Use*

Year	CO$_2$ Emissions (Mt C/yr)
1860	340
1880	450
1900	525
1920	450
1940	800
1960	1300
1980	1500

*Data from Marland, 1988.

Table 39.8 Emissions of Carbon Dioxide to the Atmosphere by Fossil Fuel Combustion*

Year	CO$_2$ Emissions (Mt C/yr)
1950	1500
1960	2500
1970	4000
1980	5500

*Data from Rotty and Reister, 1986.

ranging from 135 to 260 $\times$ 10^{15} gC, compared with 170 $\times$ 10^{15} gC resulting from fossil fuel combustion (Woodwell et al., 1983; Bolin, 1986; Smith, 1988).

Carbon Monoxide

Carbon monoxide is an important player in the chemistry of the troposphere. Carbon monoxide is responsible for about 80% of the total destruction of OH in the troposphere, the major chemical scavenger in the troposphere (Levine et al., 1985). Carbon monoxide is increasing in the atmosphere at a rate of 1% to 5%/year (Wuebbles and Edmonds, 1988). Global biomass burning is responsible for between 110 to 450 $\times$ 10^{12} gC/year of carbon monoxide of the total global production of between 1500 to 4000 $\times$ 10^{12} gC/year (Logan et al., 1981; Levine, 1990).

Since the appearance of the first living systems on our planet and the evolution of the biosphere some 3.8 billion years ago, the composition, chemistry, and radiative properties of the atmosphere have been significantly altered by the production and emission of gases in the biosphere. Today, atmospheric gases produced by biogenic processes in the soil and ocean and by the burning of living and dead biomass are major sources of atmospheric gases. These gases control the temperature of our planet via their greenhouse effect and significantly regulate the chemistry of the troposphere and stratosphere.

Acknowledgments

The research performed at the National Aeronautics and Space Administration (NASA) Langley Research Center described in this chapter dealing with the production and emission of atmospheric gases due to biogenic processes and biomass burning and how these emissions and atmospheric composition and chemistry have varied over the history of our planet has been supported by two program offices in the NASA Life Sciences Division, Office of Space Science and Applications. It is a pleasure to acknowledge the continued support and counsel of Dr. Maurice Averner, Manager of the Biospherics Research Program, and Dr. John D. Rummel, Manager of the Exobiology Program.

Notes

1. The wavelength corresponds to the photodissociation threshold for the reaction, or the minimum energy required for the reaction to occur.

2. Trace species concentrations are usually given in terms of surface mixing ratio: parts per million by volume (ppmv = 10^{-6}), parts per billion by volume (ppbv = 10^{-9}), or parts per trillion by volume (pptv = 10^{-12}). The surface species mixing ratio is defined as the ratio of the surface number density of the species (atoms or molecules cm^{-3}) to the total surface number density of the atmosphere (2.55 $\times$ 10^{19} molecules cm^{-3}).

References

Anderson, I.C., and Levine, J.S. 1986. Relative rates of nitric oxide and nitrous oxide production by nitrifiers, denitrifiers, and nitrate respirers. *Appl Environ Micro*, 51, 938–945.

Anderson, I.C., and Levine, J.S. 1987. Simultaneous field measurements of biogenic emissions of nitric oxide and nitrous oxide. *J Geophys Res*, 92, 965–976.

Anderson, I.C., Levine, J.S., Poth, M.A., and Riggan, P.J. 1988. Enhanced biogenic emissions of nitric oxide and nitrous oxide following surface biomass burning. *J Geophys Res*, 93, 3893–3898.

Andreae, M.O., Browell, E.V., Garstang, M., Gregory, G.L., Harriss, R.C., Hill, G.F., Jacob, D.J., Pereira, M.C., Sachse, G.W., Setzer, A.W., Silva Dias, P.L., Talbot, R.W., Torres, A.L., and Wofsy, S.C. 1988. Biomass-burning emissions and associated haze layers over Amazonia. *J Geophys Res*, 93, 1509–1527.

Berkner, L.V., and Marshall, L.C. 1965. On the origin and rise of oxygen concentration in the Earth's atmosphere. *J Atmos Sci*, 22, 225–261.

Bolin, B. 1986. How much CO$_2$ will remain in the atmosphere: The carbon cycle and projections for the future. In: Bolin, B., Dous, B.R., Jager, J., and Warrick, R.A., eds. *The Greenhouse Effect, Climatic Change, and Ecosystems*. SCOPE 29. Chichester, UK: Wiley, 93–155.

Canuto, V.M., Levine, J.S., Augustsson, T.R., and Imhoff, C.L. 1982. Ultraviolet radiation from the young Sun and levels of oxygen and ozone in the prebiological paleoatmosphere. *Nature*, 296, 816–820.

Cofer, W.R., III, Levine, J.S., Riggan, P.J., Sebacher, D.I., Winstead, E.L., Shaw, E.F., Jr., Brass, J.A., and Ambrosia, V.G. 1988a. Trace gas emissions from a mid-latitude prescribed chaparral fire. *J Geophys Res,* 93, 1653–1658.

Cofer, W.R., III, Levine, J.S., Sebacher, D.I., Winstead, E.L., Riggan, P.J., Brass, J.A., and Ambrosia, V.G. 1988b. Particulate emissions from a mid-latitude prescribed chaparral fire. *J Geophys Res,* 93, 5207–5212.

Cofer, W.R., III, Levine, J.S., Sebacher, D.I., Winstead, E.L., Riggan, P.J., Stocks, B.J., Brass, J.A., Ambrosia, V.G., and Boston, P.J. 1989. Trace gas emissions from chaparral and boreal forest fires. *J Geophys Res,* 94, 2255–2259.

Cofer, W.R., III, Levine, J.S., Winstead, E.L., LeBel, P.J., Koller, A.M., Jr., and Hinkle, C.R. 1990a. Trace gas emissions from burning Florida wetlands. *J Geophys Res,* 95, 1865–1870.

Cofer, W.R. III, Levine, J.S., Winstead, E.L., and Stocks, B.J., 1990b. Gaseous emissions from Canadian boreal forest fires. *Atmospheric Environment,* 24A, 1653–1659.

Cofer, W.R., III, Levine, J.S., Winstead, E.L., and Stocks, B.J. 1991. New estimates of nitrous oxide emissions from biomass burning. *Nature,* 349, 689–691.

Crutzen, P.J., Delany, A.C., Greenberg, J., Haagenson, P., Heidt, L., Lueb, R., Pollock, W., Seiler, W., Wartburg, A., and Zimmerman, P. 1985. Tropospheric chemical composition measurements in Brazil during the dry season. *J Atmos Chem,* 2, 233–256.

Crutzen, P.J., Heidt, L.E., Krasnec, J.P., Pollock, W.H., and Seiler, W. 1979. Biomass burning as a source of atmospheric gases CO, H_2, N_2O, NO, CH_3Cl, and COS. *Nature,* 282, 253–256.

Delwiche, C.C. 1981. The nitrogen cycle and nitrous oxide. In: Delwiche, C.C., ed. *Denitrification, Nitrification, and Atmospheric Nitrous Oxide.* New York: Wiley, 1–15.

Greenberg, J.P., Zimmerman, P.R., Heidt, L., and Pollock, W. 1984. Hydrocarbon and carbon monoxide emissions from biomass burning in Brazil. *J Geophys Res,* 89, 1350–1354.

LeBel, P.J., Cofer W.R., III, Levine, J.S., Vay, S.A., and Roberts, P.D., 1988. Nitric acid and ammonia emissions from a mid-latitude prescribed wetlands fire. *Geophys Res Lett,* 15, 792–795.

Levine, J.S. 1982. The photochemistry of the paleoatmosphere. *J Molec Evol,* 18, 161–172.

Levine, J.S. 1985. The photochemistry of the early atmosphere. In: Levine, J.S., ed. *The Photochemistry of Atmospheres: Earth, the Other Planets, and Comets.* San Diego: Academic Press, 3–38.

Levine, J.S. 1989. Photochemistry of biogenic gases. In: Rambler, M.B., Margulis, L., and Fester, R., eds. *Global Ecology: Towards a Science of the Biosphere.* San Diego: Academic Press, 51–74.

Levine, J.S. 1990. Global biomass burning: Atmospheric climatic, and biospheric implications. *EOS,* 71, 1075–1077.

Levine, J.S. 1991. *Global Biomass Burning.* Cambridge, Massachusetts: MIT Press.

Levine, J.S., and Augustsson, T.R. 1985. The photochemistry of biogenic gases in the early and present atmosphere. *Origins of Life,* 15, 299–318.

Levine, J.S., Augustsson, T.R., Natarajan, M., 1982. The prebiological paleoatmosphere: Stability and composition. *Origins of Life,* 12, 245–259.

Levine, J.S., Cofer, W.R., Sebacher, D.I., Rhinehart, R.P., Winstead, E.L., Sebacher, S., Hinkle, C.R., Schmalzer, P.A., and Koller, A.M., Jr. 1990. The effects of fire on biogenic emissions of methane and nitric oxide from wetlands. *J Geophys Res,* 94, 1853–1864.

Levine, J.S., Cofer, W.R., Sebacher, D.I., Winstead, E.L., Sebacher, S., and Boston, P.J. 1988. The effects of fire on biogenic soil emissions of nitric oxide and nitrous oxide. *Global Biogeochem Cycles,* 3, 445–449.

Levine, J.S., Rinsland, C.P., and Tennille, G.M. 1985. The photochemistry of methane and carbon monoxide in the troposphere in 1950 and 1985. *Nature,* 318, 254–257.

Logan, J.A., Prather, M.J., Wofsy, S.C., and McElroy, M.B. 1981. Tropospheric chemistry: A global perspective. *J Geophys Res,* 86, 7210–7254.

Lovelock, J.E., and Margulis, L. 1974. Atmospheric homeostasis by and for the biosphere: The Gaia hypothesis. *Tellus,* 26, 2–12.

Marland, G. 1988. *The Prospect of Solving the CO_2 Problem Through Global Reforestation.* Department of Energy Report DOE/NBB-0082. Washington, DC: United States Department of Energy.

Margulis, L., and Lovelock, J.E. 1974. Biological modulation of the Earth's atmosphere. *Icarus,* 21, 471–489.

Mooney, H.A., Vitousek, P.M., and Matson, P.A. 1987. Exchange of materials between terrestrial ecosystems and the atmosphere. *Science,* 238, 926–932.

Muzio, L.J., and Kramlich, J.C. 1988. An artifact in the measurement of N_2O from combustion sources. *Geophys Res Lett,* 15, 1369–1372.

National Academy of Sciences. 1984. *Global Tropospheric Chemistry: A Plan for Action.* Washington, DC: National Academy Press.

Rotty, R.M., and Reister, D.B. 1986. Use of energy scenarios in addressing the CO_2 question. *Journal of the Air Pollution Control Association,* 36, 1111–1115.

Seiler, W., and Conrad, R. 1987. Contribution of tropical ecosystems to the global budgets of trace gases, especially CH_4, H_2, CO, and N_2O. In: Dickinson, R.E., ed. *The Geophysiology of Amazonia.* New York: Wiley.

Seiler, W., and Crutzen, P.J. 1980. Estimates of gross and net fluxes of carbon between the biosphere and the atmosphere from biomass burning. *Climatic Change,* 2, 207–247.

Smith, I.M. 1988. *CO_2 and Climate Change.* Report IEACR/07. London: IEA Coal Research.

Watson, A., Lovelock, J.E., and Margulis, L. 1978. Methanogenesis, fires, and the regulation of atmospheric oxygen. *BioSystems,* 10, 293–298.

Woodwell, G.M., Hobbie, J.E., Houghton, R.A., Melillo, J.M., Moore, B., Peterson, B.J., and Shaver, G.R. 1983. Global deforestation: Contribution to an atmospheric carbon dioxide. *Science,* 222, 1081–1086.

World Meteorological Organization. 1985. *Atmospheric Ozone 1985.* Global Ozone Research and Monitoring Project Report No. 16. Switzerland, World Meteorological Organization, Geneva.

Wuebbles, D.J., and Edmonds, J. 1988. *A Primer on Greenhouse Gases.* Report DOE/NBB0083. Washington, DC: United States Department of Energy.

Life on Earth is abundant and the atmosphere is itself almost wholly a biological contrivance. . . . It is possible that grass and forest fires are the regulators of oxygen concentration although this suggestion seems an insult to the subtlety of biological contrivance.
Lovelock and Lodge, 1972, pp 575, 577.

Life defies entropy by channeling solar energy into information-rich, self-replicating systems of molecules. Fire, in essence, is entropy's revenge. Massive exothermic chain reactions are a basic problem for a carbon-based land biota in an oxygen-rich atmosphere. The propensity to burn increases with increasing the mixing ratio of O_2 in a strong, nonlinear fashion. Fire has many biological and chemical consequences, some of which should be apparent in the geological record, and some of which may feed back to affect O_2 level.[1]

Fire as an Indicator of Oxygen Variation

Lovelock and colleagues assert that Gaia controlled Phanerozoic O_2 level, and hence pyricity, to a narrow range of variation (Lovelock, 1979, 1988; Watson et al., 1978). Specifically, they claim that O_2 has deviated from its present values of 21% by no more than a few percent. In contrast, geochemical modelers conclude that O_2 may have exceeded 30% or even 35% at various times in geological history (Berner and Canfield, 1989; Budyko et al., 1987; Garrels and Lerman, 1981). These arguments are reviewed here in turn.

Oxygen Thresholds

Lovelock and Lodge (1972), Lovelock (1979, 1988), and Watson et al. (1978) argue that the upper threshold for atmospheric O_2 is around 25%. Above this threshold, they claim, fires would raze the terrestrial biosphere. Because there is no indication that this has happened, they conclude that O_2 levels have never greatly exceeded present values. The experimental basis for this claim is Watson's dissertation (1978).

People citing Watson have regularly omitted caveats and overstated his conclusions. Curves showing Watson's "ignition component" (a unitless index of the probability of ignition upon exposure to simulated lightning) as a function of O_2 mixing ratio and fuel moisture have been reproduced in at least three places (Lovelock, 1979; Funnell, 1983; Kump, 1989) without noting that Watson used paper as a fuel, and without recognizing that even the soggiest of Watson's paper specimens contained water amounting to 80% of its dry weight, whereas equivalent figures for living foliage and wood are normally above 100%, and may reach 400% (Robinson, 1989a).

Watson tried to account for the effects of green fuels and fuel bed geometry on fire behavior by using fire prediction models developed by the United States Forest Service. This stretched models far beyond the range of conditions for which they were validated. Watson was well aware of the limitations of his work, and restricted his conclusions to a statement that 25% O_2 would "disturb the ecology of the rainforest." Moreover, he allowed as well that disturbance of O_2 and fire was probable in the Carboniferous.

If O_2 level falls below some minimum threshold, fire is snuffed out. Because fusain (fossil charcoal) has been found from the Devonian onward, Cope and Chaloner (1980, 1985) conclude that O_2 did not fall below this minimum in Phanerozoic time. The O_2 threshold for combustion is not well established. Table 40.1 presents alternative candidates. As discussed below, these data come from studies that were not designed to establish the O_2 minimum for combustion, and it is unclear how they should be interpreted.

Variable Oxygen, Variable Pyricity

As shown in figure 40.1, calculations based on sedimentary burial of reduced carbon (C-org) (Berner and Canfield,[2] 1989; Budyko et al., 1987) indicate that O_2 level has varied over the Phanerozoic, and

Table 40.1 Alternative Specifications of Minimum Oxygen Required to Support Combustion

Source	O_2 (%)	Basis for Determination
Cope and Chaloner, 1980	7	Combustion of CO in an $N_2 + O_2$ atmosphere
Gundar, 1976	5–10	Smoldering of peat . . . theoretical computation
Cope and Chaloner, 1985	13	Diffusion flames
Watson, 1978	16	Burning of shredded paper

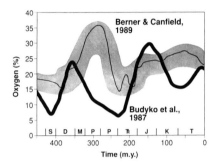

Figure 40.1 Computed trends in O_2 history over Phanerozoic time. Berner and Canfield (1989) "best estimate"; Budyko et al., 1987. In light of the substantial uncertainties involved in computation of the above curves, the results should be regarded as semiquantitative indicators. The tendency of O_2 to vary, however, is a robust feature of model behavior. Uncertainty bands shown as grey shading in Berner & Canfield and lack thereof in Budyko et al. reflect the presentations used in the original sources.

has been high in periods centered on the Cretaceous and Carboniferous. I examined the fossil record for signs of ecological disturbance in putative high-O_2 periods and found many indications of major disturbance that could plausibly be ascribed to fire (Robinson, 1989a). For example, the Pennsylvanian coal ball floras share many morphological and architectural features with modern floras that are subjected to frequent burning. The origin of the angiosperms in the Cretaceous, and the expansion and filling in of canopy layers in multistratal forest in the Paleocene suggest a frequently disturbed environment followed by a more stable environment. The presence, in Cretaceous, Pennsylvanian, and Permian coals, of large amounts of fusain in coals further supports the notion that fire was involved.

If O_2 history has followed patterns as predicted in figure 40.1, fusain contents should decline by the late Permian (early Permian according to Budyko et al., 1987). To the contrary, Chinese coals from the late Permian (Wang, 1984) have extremely high fusain contents, as do many Indian and Australian

coals of Gondwanan age (Edwards, 1975; Navale et al., 1983).

Cybernetics

Fire sets up numerous feedback interactions between the biota and the atmosphere. These feedbacks have been discussed separately by various authors, but to my knowledge, have not been collected into a unified hypothesis. In this section, I chart the feedbacks proposed by others, and add some feedbacks of my own to work toward a systems perspective. I use definitions and notation borrowed from the system dynamics method, and ultimately, from control engineering (see Forrester, 1968). These are reviewed briefly in the following section.

Feedback occurs when a change in a system variable sets in motion changes that feed back to the variable itself. If the perturbation of a target variable propagates around a feedback loop in a fashion that dampens the perturbation, the loop is, by definition, negative. If a perturbation feeds back so as to amplify its own effect, the feedback is positive. The sign of a loop pertains throughout the loop. If the loop dampens an impulse to one variable, it will also dampen an impulse to any other variable.

Positive feedback is destabilizing, and tends toward exponential growth or decay, or possibly divergent oscillation. Negative feedback tends to be stabilizing, but all negative feedbacks are not the effective homeostats described in Gaia *(Lovelock, 1979, chapter 4) or studied in* Daisyworld *(Watson and Lovelock, 1983). Negative feedback can produce damped oscillations, as in commodity cycles (Meadows, 1970) or predator prey cycles, or lead to stability only at an extreme condition, such as extinction.*

A feedback loop's sign can be determined by Boo-

lean algebra as follows. A sign is attached to each link $(A \rightarrow B)$ in the loop separately. If an increase in A causes an increase in B, the sign is positive $(+)$. If an increase in A causes a decrease in B, the sign is negative $(-)$. If B is unaffected by A, the loop is broken and no feedback occurs. Setting positive signs to zero, and negative signs to one, take the Boolean sum of the signs around the loop. If the result is zero, the loop is positive. If the result is one, the loop is negative.

For example, figure 40.2 charts feedback in the dynamic interaction of a population and a limiting resource. In the uppermost loop, a larger population causes more progeny $(+)$, and more progeny results in a larger population $(+)$. The loop has two positive and no negative signs, hence its Boolean sum $(1 + 1)$ is zero, and it is positive. In the outside loop, higher population causes greater resource consumption $(+)$, greater resource consumption reduces resource availability $(-)$, greater resource availability causes greater reproductive success $(+)$, and reproductive success increases population numbers $(+)$. The loop has four positive signs and one negative sign. Its Boolean sum $(4 \times 0 + 1)$ is one, and its sign is negative.

Feedback diagrams are useful for looking at interconnections, but explaining the behavior of a complex system requires far more than a chart of its feedback loops. In particular, loop behavior depends on the form, magnitude, and response times of the functional relationships in the loop, and on the state of the system within which it operates. Natural relationships are often nonlinear if the full range of their dynamic behavior is considered. When external forcings change, the nonlinear relations in a loop move into different regions of the curve. This causes individual loops to get stronger and weaker and may cause control to shift among

loops. Crossing an inflection point causes a loop to change sign; flattening of the curve linking two variables causes the loop to weaken and become inoperative. Strong positive relationship can overpower the modulating effects of negative feedback. This is important with respect to fire. The extreme sensitivity of combustion to O_2, H_2O, and the fuel availability are dominant factors defining the importance and behavior of fire as a player in the earth system.

Fire Feedbacks

The existence of free O_2 in the atmosphere depends on the balance of burial of reduced compounds—principally C-org—and oxidation of reduced compounds stored in the biosphere and crust (e.g., Walker, 1977). Therefore, any mechanism by which fire increases the average lifetime of C-org in the environment leads to increased O_2, and thus to more fire, that is, it sets up positive feedback.

Various authors, including Wong (1978a,b), Lovelock (1979, 1988), Seiler and Crutzen (1980), and Cope and Chaloner (1980), have noted that because fire forms char, and because charred C-org is largely inert, fire augments C-org burial. Lovelock further noted (personal communication 1984, 1988) that increased C-org burial sets up the positive feedback shown in the heavy inner loop of figure 40.3. C-org burial causes O_2 buildup, stimulating more fire and more charring.

Feedback does not end in this loop. Presumably, the completeness of char combustion increases with O_2 level. Experiments with combustion of coal and coke in O_2-limited environments have shown marked increase in the amount of carbon residual as O_2 concentration goes from 21% to 9% (Koizumi, 1956). In these experiments it was found that in-

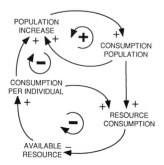

Figure 40.2 Positive feedbacks in the redox balance created by the presence of fire.

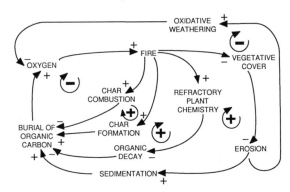

Figure 40.3 Negative feedbacks in the redox balance created by the presence of fire.

complete combustion in low-O_2 atmospheres resulted from a reduction of the depth to which O_2 diffused into the fuel, and hence a narrowing of the combustion zone. This results in a negative feedback (innermost loop, figure 40.3).

Fire, as an agent of natural selection, tends to favor thick bark and stem tissues that are rich in unreactive, nonvolatile compounds such as lignin and tannins. Such compounds retard both high temperature oxidation and biological decomposition. By skewing evolution toward higher production of refractory organics, fire may increase C-org burial, and contribute to O_2 buildup, as shown in the positive loop third from the center in figure 40.3. This may have contributed to the high rates of C-org burial in the putative high-O_2 period of the Late Paleozoic. Periderm (bark)-to-wood ratios for tree-lycopod floras of the Carboniferous coal swamps, for example, are often on the order of 8:1 (Phillips et al., 1985).

High O_2, by inducing severe burning and by decreasing the efficiency of photosynthesis,[3] reduces vegetative cover (disvegetation) and increases erosion. Increased erosion causes increased sedimentation. Increased sedimentation leads to increased C-org burial (Berner and Canfield, 1989) and therefore, to further O_2 increase. The result is an additional positive feedback, as represented in the outer loop to the left of figure 40.3. Erosion exposes new surfaces to oxidative weathering, and thus increases the O_2 sink. This sets up a negative feedback that mitigates the positive feedback from enhanced sedimentary burial (left outer loop, figure 40.3).

Kump (1988, 1989) proposed that fire stabilizes atmospheric O_2 through the paired outer loops in figure 40.4. Oxygen, by causing fires, increases the flow of phosphorus to the ocean from land systems, thereby lifting the constraints on marine productivity and C-org burial imposed by phosphorus deficiencies. This increases C-org burial and therefore increases atmospheric O_2 level—thus it is a positive feedback. Negative feedback is imposed by the next loop in: fire-induced phosphorus losses make land systems less productive. This reduces burial of C-org, reduces the O_2 source, and thus reduces fire incidence.

The pair of loops cannot stabilize O_2 unless the inner (terrestrial) negative loop overpowers the outer (marine) positive feedback, which is unlikely. Ecologists and agronomists have long suspected

phosphorus losses from ecosystems subjected to burning. However, field observations have failed to find consistent or large losses of phosphorus associated with burning (Tiedemann et al., 1979). Burning of watersheds does not greatly elevate phosphorus levels in runoff or lead to eutrophication of water systems. Even if fire resulted in increased phosphorus loss from land systems, it has yet to be demonstrated that this would lead to a decline in terrestrial burial of reduced carbon. It is thought that nutrient deficiency leads to increased synthesis of tannins and lignin, both of which are refractory (Loveless, 1961; Medina et al., 1990). Nutrient deficient (Verhoeven et al., 1988), and for that matter, fire-prone (Cohen, 1974), swamp environments can have high C-org burial fluxes; phosphorus-rich ecosystems with well-aerated soils do not, in general, accumulate C-org.

The ultimate control on O_2 and fire is probably the fact that fire literally burns itself out. Frequent fires reduce fuel loadings, which in turn result in less intense fires (Olson, 1981—negative loop at top center loop).

Figure 40.4 also includes two feedbacks that have been proposed as regulators of pO_2, and that do not include fire: (a) increased pO_2 results in lessening of the area of anoxic sedimentary environments, and therefore reduces C-org burial (Walker, 1977—leftmost loop) and O_2 production; and (b) increased pO_2 causes more rapid oxidation of rock and speeds the O_2 sink (Budyko et al., 1987—upper left loop). Others argue that these feedbacks are inconsequential for three reasons. First, rock weathering is limited by the rate of exposure of fresh sediments, not by atmospheric pO_2 (e.g., erosion; Berner and Canfield, 1989). Second, the feedbacks would lead to

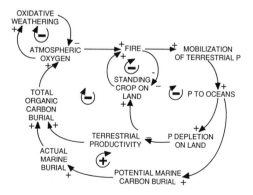

Figure 40.4 Negative feedbacks that may regulate O_2 without modulation by fire.

results that are contradicted by the isotopic record. Third, organic decay in marine environments is rarely limited by O_2 (Berner, 1989; Kump, 1989). Budyko and colleagues' incorporation of feedback from pO_2 to rock weathering probably contributes to the fact that they predict lower O_2 levels through most of the Phanerozoic than do Berner and Canfield (see figure 40.1).

Quantification and Hypothesis Testing

In dynamic systems, long-term dynamic behavior is determined by the state variables in the system, the forms and approximate magnitudes of functional relationships linking them, and the nature of exogenous forcings. If these can be specified the system can be modeled. Dynamic understanding can thus be achieved without precise quantitative understanding of all system relationships. In the next section, I review what is known about forms and functions of key relationships in fire-related systems, with emphasis on places where even the form of relationships is not known.

How Does Oxygen Affect Char Formation?
Information on the effects of O_2 level on charcoal yield is required to evaluate feedbacks involving char (e.g., inner loops, figure 40.3), and to reconstruct O_2 history based on fusain abundance or morphology. It would also be useful to know if O_2 affects the chemical behavior or morphology of char.

Little work has been done along these lines. A cacophony of definitions for char based, alternately, on blackness, reflectance properties, insolubility in strong solvents, cellular morphology, and chemical composition has the effect of rendering incomparable the results of research in different disciplines. Char formation in natural fires is poorly understood as a physical process. The variation of char chemistry and morphology with thermal history and air influx has been studied in the context of quality control for commercial charcoal manufacture and it is known that char yield is positively correlated with lignin content in the fuel (CETEC, 1981). Gross char yield (i.e., creation of char irrespective of its subsequent combustion) in natural fuels burned under laboratory conditions has been studied, but the results do not provide a basis for predicting net char yields under field conditions (Susott, 1980, and personal communication).

As for the relations among O_2 concentration, fuel moisture, fuel chemistry, fuel geometry, and other factors in affecting char yield from biofuels, even signs are often in doubt, to say nothing of the forms and strength of functional relationships. For example, it is unclear whether an O_2-stimulated fire in wet fuel will result in prolific charring or near complete combustion.

Almost nothing is known about variation in char yield and char deposition as a function of ecosystem type and fire severity. It is unclear whether char yields are higher in intense, or in mild burns; in grassland fires, or in coniferous crown fires; in coniferous surface fires, or in chaparral fires. Nor can we say whether some systems are more prone than others to export char to sedimentary burial sites.

We know less about the past than the present. The char yields, combustibility, and carbon and oxygen partitioning behavior in general, for paleofloras dominated by now-minor taxa such as lycopods, ferns, cycads, and ginkgoes may have been considerably different from that of modern systems. In particular, these floras were probably richer in lignin than are modern systems (Robinson, 1990) and might, therefore, have been expected to produce more char.

To What Extent, and Under What Conditions, Is Char Inert?
The O_2-fire-char feedback (central loop, figure 40.3) cannot be evaluated without knowing the extent to which char is inert. The abundance of fossil char shows a high propensity for preservation, but does not prove that char is always and completely inert. Some decay is likely. First, the assumption of complete inertness leads to improbably large estimates of the size of the char carbon pool (Goldberg, 1985). Second, decay seems possible, biologically. Various bacterial genera, including *Pseudomonas*, *Micrococcus*, and *Flavobacterium* are known to oxidize hydrocarbons. Straight-chain aliphatic compounds ranging from methane (CH_4) to octacosane ($C_{28}H_{58}$), and a variety of asphalts, waxes, and mineral oils can sustain bacterial growth over a range of temperature, redox, and pH conditions (Harris et al., 1956; Phillips and Traxler, 1963).

Two experimenters purport to have documented microbial oxidation of charcoal (Potter, 1908, cited in Goldberg, 1985; Schneour, 1966). In both cases oxidation was slow, and neither isolated the hypothesized organism. Furthermore, neither case excluded the possibility that the oxidized carbon belonged, not to the char per se, but to associated molecular features that might be considered impurities.

The absence of char in expected places further suggests decay. Charcoal is not generally found in old human habitation sites in the tropics, despite other evidence of fire use. According to archeological dogma, charcoal decays in wet sites (Gowlett et al., 1981; Yellen, 1986). The absence of char is also notable in Oligocene to Miocene savanna and prairie soils from South Dakota (Retallack, 1982). Pollen, not charcoal, was used as evidence for fire disturbance of pine woodland in a Miocene excavation on the Oregon/Idaho border (Taggart et al., 1982). These studies, however, identified char by a combination of soil screening and visual examination under low-power magnification. If char was present as submicroscopic fragments it would have been overlooked. It is possible that charlike substances survive as humified molecular fragments. For example, Kumada (1987), through spectral absorption studies and elemental analysis, isolated a class of dark-colored humic acids that is exceptionally resistant to decay. These are especially common in the soils of frequently burned grasslands and seem to be products of incomplete combustion of biotic carbon. It is also likely that wind and water erosion remove so much of the char formed in the burning of herbaceous vegetation that few fire traces are left in the soil.

Is Enough Char Buried to Affect Oxygen Balance?

Isotopic evidence indicates that total C-org burial fluxes have ranged, over Phanerozoic time, from 2 to 9×10^{18} moles my^{-1}, or 2 to 6 if the Carboniferous is excluded (Berner and Canfield, 1989). Seiler and Crutzen (1980) estimated present char creation rates to be 90 to 180 Tg C yr^{-1}. This amounts to 7.5 to 15×10^{18} moles C my^{-1}; that is, it exceeds total carbon burial flux for most of Phanerozoic time. Recent measurements (see Robinson, 1989b for review) suggest that Seiler and Crutzen's estimates of char yield are high by an order of magnitude, and a large portion of present biomass burning is anthropogenic. A reasonable figure for char formation, without the influence of humans and under 21% O_2, would be 0.05 to 1×10^{18} moles my^{-1}; and some part of the char created is eliminated by decay and reburning.

The rock record suggests that 1% to 10% of the organic carbon that is buried is in charred form, although this finding is not based on a statistically de-

rived sample, and may not be representative of Phanerozoic history as a whole. Fusinite (a maceral,[4] some portion of which is fossil charcoal) and semifusinite average about 10% of the mass of Cretaceous and Carboniferous coals but only 5% of Eocene coals (calculated from PSUCSBDB, 1988). Summerhayes (1981) presents extensive data on fusinite incidence in kerogens in Cretaceous marine sediments. The data show that except under anoxic condition, when marine organic carbon deposition is dominated by marine organics, fusinite is commonly above 10% of total C-org flux.

In sum, char formation seems to be of a magnitude that could be a significant contributing factor, but probably not a principal cause, of the bulges in C-org burial and O_2 excursion centered around the Carboniferous and Cretaceous (figure 40.1).

Can Fusain Be Used as Evidence?

Fusain (fusinite, when considered as a maceral) is a brittle, blackened, charcoallike substance widely found in coals and sedimentary rock from the late Devonian onward. Fusinite is often associated with semifusinite, a substance with similar but less extreme properties. Fusinite and semifusinite have been known since the early days of geology (Crickmay, 1935). A fire origin for fusain was proposed by Daubree (1846) in the mid 19th century. Whether the resemblance between fusain and charcoal is coincidental or indicative of fire origin has been debated ever since.

Fusinite and semifusinite are attractive evidence for study of O_2 variation because maceral composition is routinely evaluated in coal petrographic studies, and fusinite content has been evaluated for many thousands of coals. These data are not perfect: different researchers employ different criteria for distinguishing between fusinite and semifusinite, and between fusinite and other macerals (e.g., inertodetrinite). Observations are scattered, and many are unpublished, or have been published only in Slavic languages or Chinese. Information is scarce for periods, such as the Triassic and Mississippian, that produced little economically extractable coal.

The argument over the fire origin of fusain has recently quieted due to the death of the leading opponent of fire origin (see Schopf, 1975). A considerable body of evidence has accumulated to support fire origin (cf. Scott and Collinson, 1978 and appended comments by Fisher and Hancock; Cohen, 1974; Harris, 1981; Scott, 1989). For example, close

Table 40.2 Evidence of Correspondence Between Fusain and Char

Form	Evidence
Morphology	Width-to-length ratios in fusinite are several-fold lower than those of modern or fossil woods. Cellular morphology, as shown by advanced microscopic techniques, is very similar.
Chemistry	C:H:O ratios in fusinite closely match those of charcoal and contrast with those of coals.
Laboratory simulation	Charring of leaves, needles, fronds, and woods produces material that closely resembles fusinites.

correspondence has been found between fusinite and charcoal (table 40.2).

Spackman (personal communication, 1989), on the basis of examination of premacerals in modern peat, and Chaloner (personal communication, 1989), on the basis of observation of fusains of different ages, both conclude that all fusinite is pyrofusinite. Taylor and colleagues (1989), however, note that fusinite and semifusinite in Gondwannan coals from Australia have a very different morphology than that of other coals. They postulate that this fusinite originated in the freeze-drying of humic material, not from fire. Until methods are developed for differentiating pyrofusinites from fusinites formed by processes other than fire, ambiguity will plague reconstructions of fire history based on fusain.

The needed research has not been done because fusain has been considered uninteresting by most researchers studying paleobotany, paleosols (personal communication, DiMichele, 1989; personal communication, Retallack, 1986), and clastic sediments (Skolnik, 1958). Fusain is rarely collected; its presence is not consistently noted. Recently this attitude has begun to shift. Phillips, DiMichele, and associates working with late Paleozoic coal ball material, for example, have systematically reported fusain amount and location in depositional sequences, and regard fusain as a potential indicator of greater exposure of peat to oxidizing conditions through changes in climate or in water level (e.g., Phillips et al., 1985; various authors in Phillips and Cecil, 1985). Hunt and colleagues (e.g., Hunt, 1988) likewise, have begun piecing together spatial patterns of fusain richness in Australian coals from the Permian age.

Can Fire History Be Reconstructed from Sedimentary Cores?

A few percent of the char formed in burning is exported in smoke (Stith et al., 1981); additional char is exported over a period of months by wind and water erosion. Some char enters the soil pool, lake sediments, and so forth, only to be removed, over millennia to epochs, by glaciation and large-scale erosive processes, particularly during orogenic uplift. The char exported from burn sites and deposited in sediments (allochthonous char) provides evidence of past fire. Attempts have been made (Herring, 1977, 1985) to reconstruct global fire history, and to infer the broad zonal features of global fire regimes, by evaluating the flux of black carbon to marine sediments, as represented in deep sea sedimentary cores.

Although this approach offers the advantage that it records fire on a temporally and spatially integrated and broadly dispersed basis, and hence is not subject to noise from localized fire events, it poses other problems. The extension to times of putative high O_2 (e.g., the Late Paleozoic) is precluded by the lack of old sea floor. The sedimentary record convolves char source strength with the distance, direction, speed, and efficiency of transport, and with the rate of char decomposition. Data for deconvolution are grossly inadequate. Little is known about rates and conditions of char mobilization and transport. The respective roles of wind, water, and glaciation in char transport are unclear (Patterson et al., 1987; Robinson, 1987); there are no data on the fraction of char that remains on the fire site nor the rate of char export.

Furthermore, if char is truly inert, dating will be confused by recycling of sediments. The Pliocene and Pleistocene glaciations, for example, may have eroded much of the char formed at high latitudes in previous periods onto continental shelves. Such displacements may be common. Char from surface sediments in the Santa Barbara Basin typically produces radiocarbon dates of 2900 years, apparently as result of contamination of modern material with weathered char from Miocene sediments in the surrounding mountains (Byrne et al., unpublished data); the greater fraction of the kerogen in the sediments of the Ross Sea, Antarctica, appears to be recycled, by glacial action, from C-org in rocks of earlier origin (Sackett et al., 1974). Spores from recycled Paleozoic coals have been found in Cretaceous marine sediments (Hacquebard, 1989).

Moreover, zonal reconstructions are subject to question. By Stokes law, a spherical particle a few microns in diameter will take years to hundreds of years to sink to average deep ocean depths. Thus small particles will drift considerably, following azonal vectors established by ocean circulation, before being deposited on the bottom. Escape of Stokes settling by planktonic ingestion of particles and formation of fecal pellets may (Honjo and Roman, 1978) or may not (Pilskaln and Honjo, 1987) be important.

Herring's works (1977, 1985) shows that Pliocene and Quaternary char fluxes are higher, by orders of magnitude, than char fluxes for most of the Tertiary fluxes in general. Herring interpreted his data as showing that fire has become more common in more recent time, presumably for climatic reasons. The idea that O_2 level has risen slightly, at least since the Miocene, might also be entertained. Alternate hypotheses that might explain increased char flux in the Pliocene and Pleistocene include (a) glacial scouring of former depositional environments and recycling of char particles, (b) stronger wind circulation in glacial periods resulting in a greater proportion of the char that is formed reaching marine burial sites, and (c) artifacts of char decay.

Herring (1977) dismisses decay on the grounds that decay would first eliminate small particles, and he found no trend for char particle size to increase with age. The argument is unconvincing. The sample sizes presented are small and variances are high. Moreover, it is surface-to-volume ratio, not particle size, that controls decay processes. Char is extremely porous, and surface-to-volume ratio is almost independent of particle size. If anything, char decay would be expected to increase small particle populations by causing large particles to crumble.

There is evidence for high efficacy of eolian transport for the periods in which Herring found large char flux. For example, peak loess deposition rates during the Quaternary glaciation were around 100 times present values (Ruhe, 1969, cited in Jackson et al., 1973) and typical particle diameters for loess sediments in the Pleistocene were 10 to 70 μm, as compared to modes for aerosol dust in the present of 1 to 10 μm (Jackson et al., 1973).

In sum, it is hard to deduce changes in char source strength (e.g., changes in fires that yield char) from char in marine sediments. The difficulty of deconvolving source strength from transport, in combination with the scarcity of marine sediments that date to periods of putative high O_2, makes deep sea cores problematic as a primary source of data for looking for trends in fire over geological time.

How Much Fire (and Oxygen) Could the Land Biota Tolerate?

We know too little about the effect of O_2 on the combustion behavior of natural fuels to specify whether, or at what level, the fire hazards of high O_2 pose a fundamental threat to life. Experimentation is needed to establish the level of O_2 (if any) that will make living foliage or the bark of isolated upright stems flammable. Experimentation is also badly needed to test the assertion that fire creates a maximum tolerable O_2 level, to establish what that value is, and to identify the symptoms of a biosphere that is approaching a critical O_2 value.

The basis for specifying an O_2 floor is also weak. The behavior of fire in solid fuels is sufficiently complex that theoretical computations are of little value. The experimental evidence is inadequate. The effective O_2 threshold will vary depending on the geometry, moisture content, and chemistry of the fuel, and on whether flaming or smoldering combustion is used as a criterion. No study to date addresses these issues.

Conclusions

There are many tantalizing suggestions that fire was significant in the cybernetics of the earth system in Phanerozoic time. Present information is adequate to look for signs of variation of pyricity, and hence O_2, over geological time. Gaps in the available information, however, leave much room for speculation, and do not permit quantitative assessment of the importances of the several feedbacks that could operate through fire.

The primary problem is lack of attention, not lack of evidence. Fire has left abundant traces in the fossil record; but neither paleontologists, nor geochemists, nor geologists have paid much attention to those traces. Thus the basic research needed to interpret fusains and other possible indicators of fire has not been done. Lines of research that especially need work include (1) systematization and clarification of the chronology of fusain and semifusian deposition, including determinations as to the amounts of fusain formed through processes other than fire; (2) study of the qualitative and quantitative properties of fusain (morphology, chemistry, nuclear magnetic resonance NMR signature, etc.) as affected by the conditions of char formation (material burned, moisture content, ambient O_2 level); (3) study of the effects of O_2 level on the burning of various natural fuels; and (4) study of the decomposition of char.

Notes

1. Because combustion is much more sensitive to O_2 mixing ratio than to pO_2, I use O_2 *level* to mean O_2 *mixing ratio.*

2. Berner and Canfield consider both carbon and sulfur.

3. Photosynthetic efficiency declines with a change from 2% to 21% O_2 (c.f., Edwards and Walker, 1983). Thus we know that the hypothetical Gaia does not select O_2 equilibration states for the best interests of land plants.

4. Macerals are microscopically identifiable organic constituents of coal.

References

Berner, R.A. 1989. Biogeochemical cycles of carbon and sulfur and their effect on atmospheric oxygen over Phanerozoic time. *Global Planetary Change*, 1, 97–122.

Berner, R.A., and Canfield, D.E. 1989. A model for atmospheric oxygen over Phanerozoic time. *Am J Sci*, 289, 177–196.

Budyko, M.I., Ronov, A.B., and Yanskin, A.L. 1987. *History of the Earth's Atmosphere*. New York: Springer-Verlag.

Byrne, R., Michaelsen, J., and Soutar, A. *Fossil Charcoal From Varved Sediments in the Santa Barbara Channel: An Index of Wildfire Frequencies in the Los Padres National Forest (735 A.D. to 1520 A.D.)*, n.d. Undated manuscript, first author is at Dept. Geography, U. of Calif., Berkeley, CA 94720.

CETEC. *1981. Uso da Madeira para Fins Energticos*. Belo Horizonte, MG, Brazil: Fundação Technologic de Minas Gerais.

Cohen, A.D. 1974. Evidence of fires in the ancient everglades and coastal swamps of southern Florida. In: *Environments of South Florida: Present and Past*. Miami Geologic Society Memoir No. 2, 213–218.

Cope, M.J., and Chaloner, W.G. 1980. Fossil charcoal as evidence of past atmospheric composition. *Nature*, 283, 647–649.

Cope, M.J., and Chaloner, W.G. 1985. *Wildfire: An interaction of biological and physical processes*. In: Tiffney, B.H. ed. *Geologic Factors and the Evolution of Plants*. New Haven: Yale University Press, 257–277.

Crickmay, C.H. 1935. The nature and origin of fusain. *Am Midland Naturalist*, 16, 94–98.

Daubree, A. 1848. Examen de charbons produits par voie ignee a l'epoque hoille et a l'epoque liassique. *Bull Soc Geol France*, 2, 153–157.

Edwards, G.E. 1975. Marketable resources of Australian coal. In: Cook, A.C., ed. *Australian Brown Coals*. Wollongong, New South Wales, Australia: Australian Institute of Mining and Metallurgy—Illawarra Branch, 85–108.

Edwards, G. and Walker, D.A., 1983. C_3, C_4: *Mechanisms, and Cellular and Environmental Regulation of Photosynthesis,* especially chapter 13, Photorespiration. Oxford: Blackwell, 368–409.

Forrester, J.W., 1968. *Principles of Systems*. Cambridge Mass: Wright-Allen Press.

Funnell, B.M. 1983. Paleophysiology: The geochemical context. *J Geol Soc London*, 140, 1–4.

Garrels, R.M., and Lerman, A. 1981. *Proc Natl Acad Sci*, 78, 4652–4656.

Goldberg, E.D. 1985. *Black Carbon in the Environment: Properties and Distribution*. New York: Wiley Interscience.

Gowlett, J.W.K., Walton, D., and Wood, B.A. 1981. Early archaeological sites, hominid remains and traces of fire from Chesowanja, Kenya. *Nature*, 294, 125–129.

Gundar, S.V. 1976. Determination of the minimum oxygen concentration in flameless combustion of soil. In Russian. *Teknicheskii Zhur*, 8, 53–54.

Gutschick, V.P., and Gilbert, D.L. 1980. Discussion: What Controls Atmospheric Oxygen? *BioSystems*, 12, 123–125. (Review of Watson et al., 1978, with reply by Watson et al.)

Haquebard, P.A., 1989. The wanderings of *Donsexinis* Starch, 1957, alias *Densosporites* S.W. & B., 1944 in The North Atlantic Ocean. A forensic geology investigation. *Int J Coal Geol* 14, 15–28.

Harris, J.O., Kline, R.M., and Crumpton, C.F. 1956. A study of the presence of hydrocarbon utilizing bacteria at the soil-asphalt interface of Kansas highways. *Trans Kansas Acad Sci*, 59, 495–499.

Harris, T.M. 1981. Burnt ferns from the English Wealden. *Proc Geol Assoc*, 92, 47–58.

Herring, J.R. 1977. Charcoal Fluxes into Cenozoic Sediments of the North Pacific. Ph.D. Dissertation, earth science. San Diego, University of California.

Herring, J.R. 1985. Charcoal fluxes into sediments of the North Pacific Ocean: The Cenozoic record of burning. In: Sundquist, E.T., and Broecker, W.S., eds. *The Carbon Cycle and Atmospheric CO_2: Natural Variations, Archean to Present*. Washington, DC: American Geophysical Union, 419–442.

Honjo, S., and Roman, M.R. 1978. Marine copepod fecal pellets: Production, preservation and sedimentation. *J Marine Res*, 36, 45–54.

Hunt, J.W. 1989. Permian coals of eastern Australia: Geologic control of petrographic variation. *Int J Coal Geol* 12, 589–634

Jackson, M.I., Gilette, D.A., Danielsen, E.F., Blifford, I.H., Bryson, R.A., and Syers, J.K. 1973. Global dustfall during the Quaternary as related to environments. *Soil Sci*, 116, 135–145.

Koizumi, M. 1956. The combustion of solid fuels in fixed beds. The Combustion Institute, Sixth International Symposium on Combustion. New York: Reinhold Publishing Co., 577–583.

Kumada, K. 1987. *Chemistry of Soil Organic Matter*. Tokyo: Japan Scientific Society Press.

Kump, L.R. 1988. Terrestrial feedback in atmospheric oxygen regulation by fire and phosphorus. *Nature*, 335, 152–154.

Kump, L.R. 1989. Chemistry stability of the atmosphere and ocean. *Global Planetary Change*, 1, 123–136.

Loveless, A.R. 1961. A nutritional interpretation of sclerophylly based on differences in the chemical composition of sclerophyllic and mesophyllic leaves. *Ann Bot*, (London) 25, 168–184.

Lovelock, J.E. 1979. *Gaia*. Oxford: Oxford University Press.

Lovelock, J.E. 1988. *The Ages of Gaia*. New York: Norton.

Lovelock, J.E., and Lodge, J.P., Jr. 1972. Oxygen in the contemporary atmosphere. *Atmos Environ*, 6, 575–578.

Meadows, D.L. 1970. *The Dynamics of Commodity Production Cycles*. Cambridge, MA: Wright Allen Press.

Medina, E., Garcia, V., and Cuevas, E. 1990. Sclerophylly and oligotrophic environments: Relationships between leaf structure, mineral nutrient content, and drought resistance in tropical rainforests of the Upper Rio Negro region. *Biotropica*, 22, 51–64.

Navale, G.K.B., Misra, B.K., and Anandra-Prakash. 1983. The microconstituents of Godovari coals, South India. *Int J Coal Geol*, 3, 31–61.

Olson, J.S. 1981. Carbon balance in relation to fire regimes. In: Mooney, H.A., Bonnicksen, T.M., Christensen, N.L., Lotan, J.E., and Reiners, W.A., eds. *Fire Regimes and Ecosystem Properties*. Alexandria, VA: USDA Forest Service, 327–378.

Patterson, W.A., III, Edwards, K.J., and Maguire, D.H. 1987. Microscopic charcoal as a fossil indicator of fire. *Quaternary Sci Rev*, 6, 3–23.

Phillips, T.L., and Cecil, C.B. 1985. Special issue on paleoclimatic controls on coal resources of the Pennsylvanian system of North America. *Int J Coal Geol*, 5, 1–2.

Phillips, T.L., Peppers, R.A., and DiMichele, W.A. 1985. Stratigraphic and interregional changes in Pennsylvanian coal-swamp vegetation: Environmental inferences. *Int J Coal Geol*, 5, 43–109.

Phillips, U.A., and Traxler, R.W. 1963. Microbial degradation of asphalt. *Appl Microbiol*, 11, 235–238.

Pilskaln, C.H., and Honjo, S. 1987. The fecal pellet fraction of biogeochemical particulate fluxes to the deep sea. *Global Biogeochem Cycles*, 1, 31–48.

PSUCSBDB. 1988. *The Penn State Coal Sample Bank and Data Base*. Energy and Fuels Research Center, College of Earth and Mineral Sciences, 513 Deike Building, University Park, PA, 16802.

Retallack, G. 1984. Completeness of the rock and fossil record: Some estimates using fossil soils. *Paleobiology*, 10, 59–78.

Retallack, G. 1982. Paleopedological perspectives on the development of grasslands during the Tertiary. *Proceedings: Third North American Paleontological Convention*, 2, 417–421.

Robinson, J.M. 1987. *The Role of Fire on Earth: A Review of the State of Knowledge and a Systems Framework for Satellite and Ground-Based Observations*. Ph.D. Dissertation, Santa Barbara, Department of Geography, University of California.

Robinson, J.M. 1989b. On uncertainty in the computation of global emissions from biomass burning. *Climatic Change*, 14, 243–262.

Robinson, J.M. 1989a. Phanerozoic O_2 variation, fire, and terrestrial ecology. *Global Planetary Change*, 1, 223–240.

Robinson, J.M. 1990. Burial of organic carbon and the evolution of land plants. *Historical Biol*, 3, 189–201.

Sackett, W.M., Poag, C.W., and Eadie, B.J. 1974. Kerogen recycling in the Ross Sea, Antarctica. *Science*, 185, 1045–1047.

Schneour, E.A. 1966. Oxidation of graphitic carbon in certain soils. *Science*, 151, 991–992.

Schopf, J.M. 1975. Modes of fossil preservation. *Rev Paleobot Palynol*, 20, 27–53.

Schroeder, M.J., and Buck, C.C. 1970. *Fire Weather: A Guide for Application of Meteorological Information to Forest Fire Control Operations*. Handbook 360 USDA Forest Service. Washington, DC: United States Government Printing Office.

Scott, A.C. 1989. Observations on the nature and origin of fusain. *Int J Coal Geol*, 12, 443–475.

Scott, A.C., and Collinson, M.E. 1978. Organic sedimentary particles: Results from scanning electron microscope studies of fragmentary plant materials. In: Whalley, W.B., ed. *Scanning Electron Microscopy in the Study of Sediments: A Symposium*. Norwich, UK: Geo Abstracts, 137–168.

Seiler, W., and Crutzen, P.J. 1980. Estimation of gross and net fluxes of carbon between the biosphere and the atmosphere from biomass burning. *Climatic Change*, 2, 207–247.

Skolnick, H. 1958. Observations on fusain. *Bull Am Assoc Petrol Geol*, 42, 2223–2236.

Stith, J.L., Radke, L.F., and Hobbs, P. 1981. Particle emissions and the production of ozone and nitrogen oxides from the burning of forest slash. *Atmos Environ*, 15, 73–82.

Summerhayes, C.P. 1981. Organic facies of Middle Cretaceous black shales in deep North Atlantic. *Am Assoc Petrol Geol Bull*, 65, 2364–2380.

Susott, R.A. 1980. Effect of heating rate on char yield from forest fire. USDA Forest Service Research Note INT-295, Intermountain Forest and Range Experiment Station, Ogden, Utah, 84401.

Taggart, R.E., Cross, A.T., and Satchell, L. 1982. Effects of periodic volcanism on miocene vegetation distribution in Western Oregon and Western Idaho. *Proceedings: Third North American Paleontological Convention*, 2.

Taylor, G.H., Liu, S.Y, and Diessel, C.F.K. 1989. The cold-climate origin of inertinite-rich Gondwana coals. *Int J Coal Geol*, 11, 1–22.

Teichcmuuller, M. 1982. Origin of the petrographic constituents of coal. In: Stach, E., ed. *Stach's Textbook of Coal Petrology*. Berlin: Gebruder Borntraeger, 219–283.

Tiedemann, A.R., Conrad, C.E., and Dieterich, J.H. 1979. The effects of fire on water: A state-of-knowledge review. Forest Service National Fire Effects Workshop, Denver CO 1978. Washington, DC. General Technical Report, U.S. Dept of Agriculture Forest Service.

Verhoeven, J.T.A., Kooijman, A.M., and vanWirdum, G. 1988. Mineralization of N and P along a trophic gradient in a freshwater mire. *Biogeochemistry,* 6, 31–43.

Walker, J.C.G. 1977. *The Evolution of the Atmosphere.* New York: McGraw Hill.

Wang, Jie. 1984. *Petrography of the coal seam No. 1, Wangjaizhai Formation, Upper Late Permian, at Wangjaizhai Mine, Schuicheng, Guizhou, S.W. China.* China Institute of Mining and Technology, Paper presented at the 37th International Committee on Coal Petrology Meeting.

Watson, A.J. 1978. Consequences for the Biosphere of Grassland and Forest Fires. Thesis. UK: Reading University.

Watson, A.J., and Lovelock, J.E. 1983. Biological homeostasis of the global environment: The parable of Daisyworld. *Tellus,* 35B, 284–289.

Watson, A.J., Lovelock, J.E., and Margulis, L. 1978. Methanogenesis, fires and the regulation of atmospheric oxygen. *BioSystems,* 10, 293–298.

Wong, C.S. 1978a. Atmospheric input of carbon dioxide from burning wood. *Science,* 200, 197–200.

Wong, C.S. 1978b. Carbon dioxide—a global environmental problem into the future. *Marine Pollut Bull,* 9, 257–264.

Yellen, J.E. 1986. The longest human record. *Nature,* 322, 774.

VIII
Gaia, Catastrophes, and Other Planets

Christopher P. McKay and Carol R. Stoker
41
Gaia and Life on Mars

It is difficult to develop a complete scientific understanding of a class of objects when there is only one example available for study. The Gaia hypothesis of J. Lovelock presents such a difficulty. The Gaia hypothesis can be cast in many different versions, as discussed by Kirchner (1989), but the essence of this hypothesis is that life on Earth acts on the planet in such a manner as to provide optimal conditions for life (Lovelock and Margulis, 1973; Lovelock, 1979, 1988; Watson and Lovelock, 1983). The difficulties associated with configuring the Gaia hypotheses as a set of well-posed and predictive questions in a scientific context arise primarily from the fact that the Gaia hypothesis considers the entirety of life on Earth. The Gaia hypothesis has already been applied to other planets in a negative sense, in that Lovelock predicted (1990), prior to *Viking,* that Mars would be completely lifeless due to the absence of atmospheric indications of life. Unfortunately, there seems to be no opportunity for a positive test because there is no evidence from the reconnaissance of the solar system that life exists on any planet other than Earth. Thus we may need to wait for the exploration of extrasolar planetary systems before a natural example of a life-bearing planet can be investigated. Nonetheless, many useful insights regarding Gaia can be gained from comparative studies of the planets in our solar system.

Of all the other planets in the solar system, Mars is the most comparable to Earth in terms of surface climate. It is not surprising, then, that Mars provides the most relevant comparison for Gaia on Earth. There is extensive geological evidence that, early in the history of the planet, liquid water habitats existed on the surface of Mars and hence conditions may have been conducive to the origin of life there (McKay and Stoker, 1989; McKay and Davis, 1991). Furthermore, the possibility of constructing a planetary-scale biosphere on Mars is being seriously investigated (McKay, 1982; McKay et al., 1991b) and would provide a possible future experiment in Gaia on Mars.

In this chapter we compare the Earth with the other planets in the solar system with a view toward understanding Gaia. We first list those overall questions about life on Earth, including the Gaia hypothesis, that are difficult to address without another example of life to study. We also consider the abiotic atmospheric chemistry of the other planets and compare this to the biogenic chemistry of the Earth. We then consider how Mars—in particular, studies of past life on Mars—could help further our understanding of these questions. Finally we consider the implications of Gaia for planetary ecosynthesis on Mars.

Comparative Planetary Biology

The Gaia hypothesis is an example of a broader category of questions about life on Earth. In this section we briefly discuss how analysis of other planetary-scale biological systems is required for the successful investigation of these questions about life on Earth. By comparison we suggest that Gaia can best be tested in the context of life on more than one planet.

One of the profound scientific discoveries of the last few decades is the unity of biology. Biochemical analysis has indicated that all life on Earth is composed of the same basic building blocks: twenty amino acids, eight nucleic acids, and so forth (e.g., Goldsmith and Owen, 1980). All earthly life has the same fundamental genetic code based on DNA. From *Escherichia coli* to the blue whale, life on Earth is the same stuff. Molecular phylogenies (Woese, 1987) have mapped the tree of life, indicating the genetic relationships between all organisms and pointing the way to the universal ancestor.

The standard theory for the origin of life on Earth begins with abiotic organic matter, produced either in situ on Earth or carried here from the outer solar system by comets (Huebner and McKay, 1990). Prebiotic chemical evolution, in the presence of water, results in ever more complex structures until life itself begins and biological evolution commences. On Earth we have definitive evidence for microbial ecosystems by 3.5 Gyr ago (Schopf, 1983). The geological record provides an incomplete record of the early Earth, and life may have originated much earlier than 3.5 Gyr ago. In fact, there is suggestive evidence for life at 3.8 Gyr ago (Schidlowski, 1988). The determination as to whether life is a natural, emergent property of matter in Earth-like environments and would develop quickly on any similar body will probably require biological investigation of other planets that had an environment similar to that on the early Earth. There is a competing theory for the origin of life that postulates that life arose initially on clays (Cairns-Smith, 1982) and only later developed the complex organic machinery in use today. Again, the testing of such an hypothesis may require investigations of more than one example of the origin of life.

The energy source for the first organisms on Earth could have been based on heterotrophy (consumption of organic material) or autotrophy (production of organic material via photosynthesis or chemosynthesis). It is possible that the geological and phylogical record on Earth will allow us to determine which was the case. However, it will probably require more than one data point, to place this into a broader context of life's origins.

On Earth, there is evidence that the ancient microbial lineage split long ago into the three major taxonomic groups of the bacterial world (Woese, 1987). The universal pregenetic ancestor common to all three lines is the so-called progenote (e.g., Woese, 1981, 1987). Based on the comparison of molecular sequences (primarily RNA), phylogenetic trees have been constructed that suggest that the organisms ancestral to all modern organisms were sulphur-metabolizing thermophiles (Woese, 1987; Lake, 1988). With only one example of life to study, it is difficult to tell if this is due to chance or if there is some evolutionary reason for this initial combination of properties. If the earliest organisms on another planet—for example, Mars—also turn out to have been sulphur-utilizing thermophiles, the discovery would be a significant advance in our understanding of life as a planetary phenomenon.

Proceeding later in evolutionary time, an important event for life on Earth was the endosymbiosis that created the eukaryotic cell (Margulis, 1970). Was this development that would ultimately be the seed for all plants and animals merely a chance event or would similar circumstances in a similar environment produce similar developments? In addition, there is the question of the rise of the eukaryotic cell and tissue multicellularity, oxygenic photosynthesis, and the buildup of oxygen in the atmosphere. The answers to such questions may have to await the study of extant life on other planets.

As we have demonstrated in the preceding discussion, studies of life on Earth are intrinsically limited by the fact that there is only one fundamental life form on this planet. Thus questions such as the Gaia hypothesis that deal with the properties or history of life as a whole are limited in their applicability and testability. However, such limitations do not place them outside the realm of science, as has been claimed (Kirchner, chapter 6 this volume).

Even planets with no biological potential can be useful for testing the Gaia hypothesis. Oxygen on the present Earth is clearly of biological origin. Its role in the history of life on Earth is a central question in the interpretation of the Gaia hypothesis. In addition, the concentration of trace gases such as H_2 and CH_4 in the atmosphere of Earth is often used as an example of Gaian control mechanisms (Margulis and Lovelock, 1974), since even at trace concentrations these biogenic gases are grossly out of thermodynamic equilibrium with the O_2-rich atmosphere. However, the atmospheres of the outer planets and Titan show that such gross disequilibrium conditions can arise without indicating a Gaian mechanism, and in fact arise abiotically. In the atmosphere of Jupiter and Saturn, hydrocarbons, nitriles, and phosphoric compounds are all out of thermodynamic equilibrium (Strobel, 1985). On Titan, CO and CO_2 exist as trace gases in gross disequilibrium with an atmosphere in which CH_4 is a major species (Hunten et al., 1984). In interstellar clouds the concentrations of organic molecules are also significantly out of equilibrium (e.g., Irvine and Knacke, 1989). Although certain biological processes leave their mark on the atmosphere, comparative planetology suggests caution when assigning profound implications to observation of such disequilibrium gas concentrations, particularly in trace concentrations.

Life on Mars

Within our solar system, Mars is the most likely subject of study for addressing questions of planetary biology. There is evidence (summarized in table 41.1) that Mars had a water-rich and probably warmer climate early in its history (McKay and Sto-

Table 41.1 Comparison of Early Earth and Early Mars

Property	Early Earth	Early Mars
Water	Oceans	Evidence for surface liquid water and possibly a hydrological cycle
Temperature	$> 0°C$	$\cong 0°C$
Atmosphere	CO_2, N_2, $H_2O > 1$ atm	CO_2, N_2,† $H_2O \cong 1$ atm
Geochemical carbon cycle $CO_2 \rightarrow$ carbonate rocks	Reactions in water	Reactions in water
Carbonate rocks $\rightarrow CO_2$	Tectonics and volcanism	Early volcanism and impacts only
Duration of thick atmosphere	4.2 Gyr ago $\rightarrow$ present	4.2 Gyr ago $\rightarrow$ 3.5 Gyr ago (?)
Preservation of rock record	Highly altered and reworked	⅔ of the surface dates back to 3.8 Gyr ago
Biology	Diverse life by 3.5 Gyr ago, possibly 3.8 Gyr ago	?–?

†The N_2 concentration on early Mars is uncertain and may have limited the development of a biota (McKay and Stoker, 1989).
*Adapted from McKay and Stoker, 1989.

ker, 1989; McKay et al., 1991a). This evidence takes the form of runoff channels in the ancient cratered terrain (figure 41.1). Together with the outflow channels, these features suggest that Mars had a large inventory of water and that the liquid water was fairly stable at the surface. The maintenance of environmental conditions that allow for liquid water probably required a thicker atmosphere composed of one to a few bars of CO_2 (Pollack et al., 1987). However, it is important to note that the potential presence of liquid water habitats on early Mars is, by and of itself, motivation for study of the possible origin of life on that planet regardless of how such habitats were maintained. The key question is how long such liquid water habitats were in existence compared with the time required for the origin of life.

The environmental conditions on Mars' surface deteriorated from an initial warm state with liquid water habitats to the present harsh state in which liquid water is absent. Models of atmospheric evolution (Kahn, 1985; Pollack et al., 1987; McKay and Davis, 1991) suggest that the initial CO_2 atmosphere would have been depleted due to the formation of carbonate sediments by reaction in liquid water. The absence of tectonic activity precluded any long-term recycling of carbonates and Mars eventually lost its atmosphere. Pollack et al. (1987) have suggested that the thick atmosphere could be maintained by the recycling of CO_2 due to increased volcanic activity and geothermal heat flow on early Mars. When high geothermal heat flow is combined with an extended outgassing model, their results indicate that temperatures above freezing could have

been maintained for approximately 10^9 years. Carr (1989) has suggested that CO_2 was pumped into the atmosphere by impacts associated with the late bombardment and that the thick atmosphere would have dissipated quickly after the cessation of impacts, 3.8 Gyr ago. It is also possible that Mars lost a considerable fraction of its early atmosphere as a result of erosion by high-velocity impacts (Melosh and Vickery, 1989).

McKay and Davis (1991) have developed a model of ice-covered lakes on early Mars based on the climate model of Pollack et al. (1987) and studies of the thermodynamics of ice-covered lakes in the Antarctic dry valleys (McKay et al., 1985). As shown in figure 41.2, they conclude that liquid water habitats could have been maintained under perennial ice covers for several hundred million years *after* mean annual temperatures fell below the freezing point due to the fact that the peak perihelion temperatures remain above freezing. From the fossil record on Earth, we know that life evolved early in this planet's history, certainly before 3.5 Gyr ago. This implies that life arose sometime within the first few hundred million years—the time between the last reformation of the Earth's surface by impacts (Maher and Stevenson, 1988) and 3.5 Gyr ago, the age of the oldest sophisticated fossil evidence of life. Thus the timescale for liquid water on early Mars seems to be comparable to this upper limit on the timescale for life to have originated on Earth.

If life did originate on Mars, has it become extinct? The question of extant life on Mars is, strictly speaking, still open. The *Viking* landers carried ex-

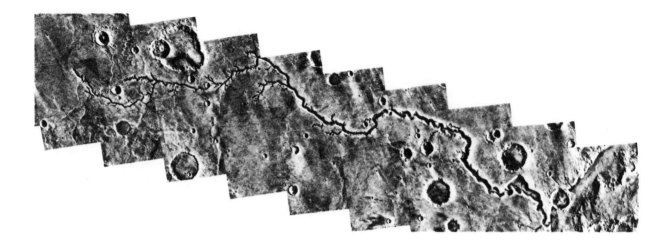

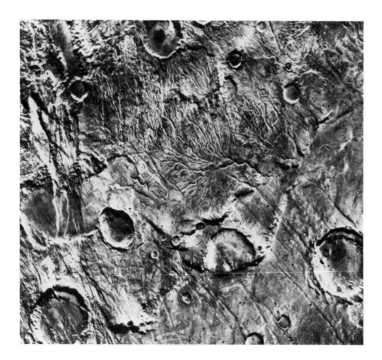

Figure 41.1   Runoff valleys on the surface of Mars. The morphology and length of such valleys suggest that liquid water was stable at the surface of Mars sometime in the past, unlike present conditions. The upper panel shows Nirgal Vallis (28°S, 40°W), which may have been caused by sapping of ground water. The more dendritic pattern of other valleys, such as shown in the bottom panel (48°S, 98°W), may indicate drainage after rainfall. If life arose on Mars during this wet, presumably warmer, period, its eventual extinction may have been deferred by Gaian mechanisms, a record of which may be preserved in the Martian fossil record—providing a test for the Gaia hypothesis.

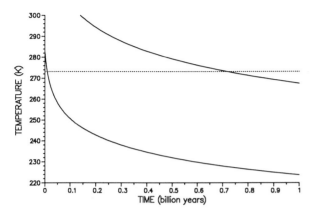

Figure 41.2 Temperature history on early Mars from McKay and Davis (1991). The lower curve is the mean planetary temperature and the upper curve is the peak temperature, which occurs at the subsolar point at perihelion. By analogy with the Antarctic dry valley lakes (mean temperature = −20°C), liquid water habitats could have persisted on early Mars as long as the peak temperatures were above freezing.

periments specifically designed to search for signs of microbial life on Mars. Interpretation of the results of the *Viking* biology experiments has been controversial, but most investigators suggest that they do not indicate biological activity at the landing sites (Klein, 1978, 1979; Horowitz, 1986; for an opposite view see Levin and Straat, 1981; Levin, 1988).

If life does exist on Mars at the present time, it does not cover a significant fraction of the planet's surface nor does it have obvious effects on the atmospheric composition. Lovelock and Margulis (1973; see also Lovelock, 1989) have argued, based on Gaia, that life can only be planet-wide and influential or it will not be present at all. The *Viking* biology experiment results have led to the widespread belief that Mars is indeed a dead planet at the present time. However, the *Viking* results can be questioned in two important ways (Klein, personal communication, 1989). First, the sites selected for the *Viking* biology experiments were far from ideal for biology. The sites were chosen based on the criteria for a safe landing and are poor choices for the search for life. Much better locations would be near the polar ice cap, near volcanic units that may still be recently active (as suggested for the Valles Marineris by Lucchitta, 1987), at locations of possible water or brine activity (Zisk and Mouginis-Mark, 1980; Zent and Fanale, 1986), and so forth. The second limitation of the *Viking* results is the fact that these experiments sought to investigate microbial metabolism of Martian organisms but did not search

for a potentially very relevant set of microbial metabolisms: anaerobic chemoautotrophs. One possible example of such a microbial ecosystem on Mars would be a group of bacteria, similar to methanogenic bacteria found on Earth, that utilized H_2 or H_2S emissions from a still active volcanic region together with atmospheric CO_2. Liquid water could be supplied from the melting of permafrost. Although there is no indication of such hydrothermally active regions on Mars, neither is the possibility ruled out. Thus it is conceivable that a future mission to Mars will find a restricted niche containing life. If extant life of limited extent is found on Mars, this will be a violation of a clear prediction made utilizing the Gaia hypothesis.

More likely, investigation of Mars will not find any evidence for extant life, but may find fossil evidence of life. The fossil record of early life on Earth provides a basis for speculating on what form a fossil of early life on Mars might take (McKay, 1986; McKay et al., 1991a). Of particular interest are stromatolites, which form when microbial mat communities trap and bind sediments deposited on them. To reach sunlight for photosynthesis, the microbial community moves upward through the sediments and leaves a distinctively layered remnant that becomes a stromatolite upon lithification.

If life did originate on Mars it would presumably have become extinct as the surface temperatures dropped and liquid water was no longer present. On the early Earth, the total loss of atmospheric CO_2 was prevented by the subduction of carbonate (and organic) sediments followed by the reconstitution of CO_2 at depth and its subsequent release through volcanos and geothermal emissions (Berner et al., 1983). Mars appears to be a one-plate planet (i.e., nontectonic) and hence was unable to recycle carbon-bearing sediments. It was thus doomed to lose its atmosphere and freeze.

How could life on Mars have forestalled this eventuality? One method would have been the inception of plate tectonics. Lovelock (1979) has suggested that plate tectonics on the Earth is strongly influenced, if not actually driven, by the biota in an essentially Gaian mechanism. Perhaps more realistically, the early Martian biota could have fostered conditions on that planet (such as low pH) that would have dissolved carbonate material and prevented the loss of atmospheric CO_2. In addition, organic matter would have to have been efficiently recycled. Even if such biological control mechanisms were applied, they might have only been able to forestall and not prevent the demise of the Martian biosphere. Even extreme versions of the Gaia hypothesis must admit the possibility that some events are beyond biological control.

Thus we suggest that the Gaia hypothesis predicts that the fossil record of life on early Mars, if it exists, should show signs of biological adaptation and attempted control of the deteriorating Martian environment. The persistence of life on Mars, via Gaia, should greatly exceed that expected from purely physical considerations. Life on Mars should have gone out with a Gaian bang, not a uniformitarian whimper.

Planetary Ecosynthesis on Mars

Scientific hypotheses can be tested not only by applying them to explanations of natural and historical events but also by using them to guide experiments and predict the outcomes. The Gaia hypothesis leads naturally to the prediction (McKay, 1982) that, if Mars could be artificially altered into a habitable planet and endowed with a complex and planetary-scale biology, then the planet would maintain a Gaian homeostasis.

If Mars sustained a habitable climate at some point in its early history, and if the volatiles (H_2O, CO_2, N_2) that composed the habitable state were retained over the subsequent eons, then it is possible that through remobilization of these volatiles Mars could once again enjoy clement conditions (McKay, 1982; McKay et al., 1991b). Current understanding of the climate history and volatile inventory of Mars bode well for such a proposal, but the information available is insufficient to make a definitive assessment (McKay et al., 1991b).

McKay and colleagues (1991b) identified two possible habitable states for Mars. In one state, possibly reminiscent of the early climate, there would be a thick CO_2 atmosphere with a surface pressure of about 1 to 2 bars, small amounts of O_2, and some N_2. Such an environment—similar to the Precambrian period which spanned approximately 80% of Earth's history—would be suitable for plants and anaerobic microorganisms. A central question concerning such an atmosphere is its stability, because there would be a strong positive (i.e., destabilizing) feedback between the amount of atmospheric CO_2 and the surface temperature. Furthermore, such an atmosphere would decay in the manner described here for its counterpart on early Mars. Would Gaian

mechanisms stabilize and prolong the life of such an atmosphere?

A second possible habitable state is one in which the atmosphere would be breathable by humans. Because in this case the level of CO_2 would be greatly reduced, the surface temperature would be extremely low, necessitating the addition of other, nontoxic greenhouse gases (Lovelock and Allaby, 1984). McKay and colleagues (1991b) have suggested that certain mixtures of chlorofluorocarbons, artificially produced or produced by genetically altered microorganisms, could maintain surface temperatures well above freezing. Again, the control mechanism for maintaining the surface temperature within desirable limits is unclear. Perhaps, if the production of the exotic greenhouse gases is under biological influence, Gaian mechanisms will again be the thermostat that achieves and maintains stability.

Conclusion

The Gaia hypothesis concerns the interaction between life and planetary evolution. Unfortunately, we have only one example of a planet with life on it—the Earth. This makes it difficult to address an entire range of scientific questions and hypotheses (of which the Gaia hypothesis is just one) dealing with the origin, evolution, and sustenance of life on a planet. However, recent studies of the planet Mars suggest that there is a reasonable possibility that life arose early in its history during an epoch of warmer, wetter surface conditions. If so, the investigation of the fossil record of this Martian life may provide critical tests for the Gaia hypothesis. Extending forward in time, we suggest that planetary climate engineering and synthesis of a planetary-scale biology on Mars may provide an opportunity for an experiment in Gaian mechanisms. Thus progress on the assessment of the Gaia hypothesis regarding life on Earth may require extended trips to Mars.

References

Berner, R.A., Lasaga, A.C., and Garrels, R.M. 1983. The carbonate-silicate geochemical cycle and its effect on carbon dioxide over the past 100 million years. *Am J Sci*, 283, 641–683.

Cairns-Smith, A.G. 1982. *Genetic Takeover and the Mineral Origins of Life*. Cambridge: Cambridge University Press.

Carr, M.H. 1989. Recharge of the early atmosphere of Mars by impact induced release of CO_2. *Icarus,* 79, 311–327.

Goldsmith, D., and Owen, T. 1980. *The Search for Life in the Universe.* Menlo Park, CA: Benjamin Cummings Publishing Co.

Horowitz, N.H. 1986. *To Utopia and Back: The Search for Life in the Solar System.* New York: W.H. Freeman and Co.

Huebner, W.E., and McKay, C.P. 1990. Implications of comet research. In: Huebner, W.F., ed. *Physics and Chemistry of Comets.* Berlin: Springer-Verlag, 305–331.

Hunten, D.M., Tomasko, M.G., Flaser, F.M., Samuelson, R.E., Strobel, D.F., and Stevenson, D.J. 1984. Titan. In: Gehrels, T., and Matthews, M.S., eds. *Saturn.* Tucson: University of Arizona Press, 671–759.

Irvine, W.M., and Knacke, R.F. 1989. The chemistry of interstellar gas and grains. In: Atreya, S.K., Pollack, J.B., and Matthews, M.S., eds. *Origin and Evolution of Planetary and Satellite Atmospheres.* Tucson: University of Arizona Press, 3–34.

Kahn, R. 1985. The evolution of CO_2 on Mars. *Icarus,* 62, 175–190.

Kirchner, J.W. 1989. The Gaia hypothesis: Can it be tested? *Rev Geophys,* 27, 223–236.

Klein, H.P. 1978. The Viking biological experiments on Mars. *Icarus,* 34, 666–674.

Klein, H.P. 1979. The Viking mission and the search for life on Mars. *Rev Geophys Space Phys,* 17, 1655–1662.

Lake, J.A. 1988. Origin of the eukaryotic nucleus determined by rate-invariant analysis of rRNA sequences. *Nature,* 331, 184–186.

Levin, G.V. 1988. A reappraisal of life on Mars. Proceedings of the NASA Mars Conference. *Am Astron Soc,* 71, 187–207.

Levin, G.V., and Straat, P.A. 1981. A search for a nonbiological explanation of the Viking labeled release life detection experiment. *Icarus,* 45, 494–516.

Lovelock, J.E. 1979. *Gaia.* Oxford: Oxford University Press.

Lovelock, J.E. 1988. *The Ages of Gaia.* New York: W.W. Norton.

Lovelock, J.E. 1989. Geophysiology, the science of Gaia. *Rev Geophys,* 27, 215–222.

Lovelock, J.E. 1990. Hands up for the Gaia hypothesis. *Nature,* 344, 100–102.

Lovelock, J.E., and Allaby, M. 1984. *The Greening of Mars.* New York: Warner.

Lovelock, J.E., and Margulis, L. 1973. Atmospheric homeostasis by and for the biosphere: The Gaia hypothesis. *Tellus,* 26, 1–10.

Lucchitta, B.K. 1987. Recent mafic volcanism on Mars. *Science,* 235, 565–567.

Maher, K.A., and Stevenson, D.J. 1988. Impact frustration of the origin of life. *Nature,* 331, 612–614.

Margulis, L. 1970. *Origin of Eukaryotic Cells.* New Haven: Yale University Press.

Margulis, L., and Lovelock, J.E. 1974. Biological modulation of the Earth's atmosphere. *Icarus,* 21, 471–489.

McKay, C.P. 1986. Exobiology and future Mars missions: The search for Mars' earliest biosphere. *Adv Space Res,* 6, 269–285.

McKay, C.P. 1982. Terraforming Mars. *J Br Interplanet Soc,* 35, 427–433.

McKay, C.P., Clow, G.A., Wharton, R.A., Jr., and Squyres, S.W. 1985. Thickness of ice on perennially frozen lakes. *Nature,* 313, 561–562.

McKay, C.P., and Davis, W.L. 1991. The duration of liquid water habitats on early Mars. *Icarus,* in press.

McKay, C.P., Mancinelli, R.L., Stoker, C.R., and Wharton, R.A. 1991a. The possibility of life on Mars during a water-rich past. In: Kieffer et al., eds. *Mars.* Tucson: University of Arizona Press.

McKay, C.P., and Stoker, C.R. 1989. The early environment and its evolution on Mars: Implications for life. *Rev Geophys,* 27, 189–214.

McKay, C.P., Toon, O.B., and Kasting, J.F. 1991b. On terraforming Mars. *Nature,* in press.

Melosh, H.J., and Vickery, A.M. 1989. Impact erosion of the primordial atmosphere of Mars. *Nature,* 338, 487–489.

Pollack, J.B., Kasting, J.F., Richardson, S.M., and Poliakoff, K. 1987. The case for a wet, warm climate on early Mars. *Icarus,* 71, 203–224.

Schidlowski, M. 1988. A 3,800-million-year isotopic record of life from carbon in sedimentary rocks. *Nature,* 333, 313–318.

Schopf, J.W., ed. 1983. *Earth's Earliest Biosphere; Its Origin and Evolution.* Princeton, N.J.: Princeton University Press.

Strobel, D.F. 1985. The photochemistry of the atmospheres of the outer planets and their satellites. In: Levine, J.S., ed. *The Photochemistry of Atmospheres.* New York: Academic Press, 394–437.

Watson, W.J., and Lovelock, J.E. 1983. Biological homeostasis of the global environment: The parable of Daisyworld. *Tellus,* 35, 284–289.

Woese, C.R. 1981. Archaebacteria. *Scientific American,* 244, 98–122.

Woese, C.R. 1987. Bacterial evolution. *Microbiol Rev,* 51, 221–271.

Zent, A.P., and Fanale, F.P. 1986. Possible Mars brines: Equilibrium and kinetic considerations. *J Geophys Res,* 91, D439–D445.

Zisk, S.H., and Mouginis-Mark, P.J. 1980. Anomalous region on Mars: Implications for near-surface liquid water. *Nature,* 288, 735–738.

Michael R. Rampino

42

Gaia Versus Shiva: Cosmic Effects on the Long-Term Evolution of the Terrestrial Biosphere

In the past few years, two concepts regarding the nature and history of life on Earth have been much debated. The first is the Gaia hypothesis, which suggests, in its most far-reaching interpretation, that the biosphere actively regulates the Earth's climate and atmosphere and ocean chemistry in such a way as to "optimize" conditions for life on the planet (Lovelock and Margulis, 1973; Lovelock, 1979; Lovelock, 1988). The other is what has come to be known as the *Shiva theory,* involving periodic or episodic catastrophic destruction of life by comet or asteroid impacts (Goldsmith, 1985, 1986). This theory is an outgrowth of the impact hypothesis to explain mass extinctions (Alvarez et al., 1980), and the idea of periodic comet showers caused by quasi-regular perturbations of the Oort cloud comets (Rampino and Stothers, 1984a,b; Whitmire and Jackson, 1984; Davis et al., 1984; Alvarez and Muller, 1984; Whitmire and Matese, 1985).

These discoveries have produced a new scientific mythology. Gaia, the Greek embodiment of Mother Earth, represents a model in which the Earth's life, air, oceans, and land surface form a complex system that can be seen as a single organism with the power to keep the planet a fit place for life. As Lovelock (1979) writes: "We have . . . defined Gaia as a complex entity involving the Earth's biosphere, atmosphere, oceans and soil; the totality constituting a feedback or cybernetic system which seeks an optimum physical and chemical environment for life on this planet." On the other hand, Shiva, the Hindu god of destruction and rebirth, brings periodic mass extinctions caused by factors external to the Earth, and clears the way for new species that evolve in the aftermath of destruction (Gould, 1984, 1989; Goldsmith, 1985, 1986). The theories seem to occupy two ends of the spectrum of our view of the natural environment. In one the environment is cared for and preserved by the biosphere, which is capable of responding to relatively slow geological and astrophysical changes (overcoming changes in atmospheric composition and the faint early sun

problem, for example). In the other, the biosphere is overwhelmed by sudden catastrophes from space that could, theoretically, snuff out life on Earth entirely, and perhaps has in other places in the Universe.

In the past decade, new and ingenious computer models of the Earth's biogeochemical cycles and climate are allowing us to probe more deeply into the interrelationships among the various aspects of the earth system (Berner et al., 1983; Lasaga et al., 1985; Walker et al., 1981; Kump, 1988; Volk, 1987, 1989a,b; Caldeira et al., 1990). We are beginning to see that the oceans, atmosphere, biosphere, and solid-earth systems are all interlocked through a series of complex feedback loops. There is no doubt that the composition of the atmosphere and oceans is greatly influenced by life; after all, the physical environment and life on Earth have coevolved over billions of years (Schneider and Londer, 1984). The cycling of the key elements oxygen, carbon, nitrogen, phosphorus, and sulfur involves important steps through the biosphere. But the claim that the biosphere is capable of regulating conditions on Earth at an optimum for living things is difficult to accept (Volk, 1987).

The differentiation of "hard" Gaia and "soft" Gaia that came out of the discussions at the Chapman Conference has changed the rules of the game somewhat, with even Lovelock retreating from the "hard" Gaia position of regulation in the "best interests" of the biosphere to the softer position of biospheric regulation of the environment within certain limits favorable for life. Caldeira (chapter 8, this volume), using the dimethylsulfide (DMS) system, has shown that hard Gaia feedback systems are difficult to evolve on the basis of individual or group selection. A possibly promising direction is that of treating evolution in terms of entropy and information, and the idea of ecosystem selection for those systems (Wicken, 1987). In these cases natural selection would include "an efficiency principle that promotes a maximization of resource flow into metabolic costs. The effect of this principle is to minimize specific entropy production in ecosystems" (Wicken, 1987). But many biologists over the years have pointed out the difficulty in defining just what an ecosystem is, let alone how it may evolve through competition with other ecosystems.

Soft Gaia is palatable as a metaphor for a style of scientific research rather than a completely testable hypothesis. According to Lovelock (1979), "The Gaia hypothesis is for those who like to walk or simply stand and stare, to wonder about the Earth and the life it bears, and to speculate about the consequences of our own presence here." Life is here because it is here, it has created the conditions for its own survival and spread, and the rise of complexity was inevitable once we add Margulis' (1981) ideas of endosymbiotic cell development. We can easily accept that the Earth and life on it represent a single system that has coevolved, but the idea of purposeful evolution stands outside of mainstream science.

Gaia and Mass Extinctions

Even if we were to accept that hard Gaia were possible, episodes of massive extraterrestrial impacts, with all of the possible disastrous consequences (Alvarez, 1986) would disrupt the Earth system in ways that the biosphere (or Gaia) could not possibly "foresee" or prepare for in any evolutionary sense. A major question must then be asked: How has the biosphere continued to survive and even flourish for some four billion years under the circumstances of episodic cosmic destruction? What are the methods and timescales of the recovery of the biosphere after catastrophic events?

According to Sepkoski (1986), "A mass extinction is any substantial increase in the amount of extinction (i.e., lineage termination) suffered by more than one geographically widespread higher taxon during a relatively short interval, resulting in an at least temporary decline in their standing diversity." Jablonski (1986) has commented that, "The fossil record near the end-Cretaceous and other extinction events suggest that large-scale evolutionary patterns are shaped by two macroevolutionary regimes. Microevolutionary and macroevolutionary processes of the background regime are occasionally disrupted, presumably by external forcing factors, and replaced by the mass extinction regime. Many traits of individuals and species that had enhanced the survival and proliferation of species and clades during background times become ineffective

during mass extinctions, and other traits that were not closely correlated with survivorship differences become influential. The mass extinction regime is apparently relatively short-lived—1 or 2 million years at most for the end-Cretaceous event, and perhaps considerably less." These results imply that mass extinctions play a larger role than is generally appreciated in creating opportunities for faunal change, removing dominant taxa and thereby enabling other groups—previously unimportant but with traits enhancing survivorship during mass extinctions—to undergo adaptive radiation.

Raup (1986) agrees that, "If mass extinctions are the result of environmental stresses so rare as to be beyond the 'experience' of the organisms, extinction may be just a matter of the chance susceptibility of the organisms to these rare stresses. . . . The result would be a highly selective extinction, but one having no constructive effect in terms of the general success of organisms in normal times." Some authors, however, have concluded that mass extinction events are qualitatively similar to background extinctions, and hence reflect similar non–impact related processes (e.g., McKinney, 1987). Raup (personal communication) has recently gone further in a kind of statistical experiment suggesting that perhaps *all* mass extinction events of various intensities are the result of impacts of various sizes.

In Lovelock's own words (Allaby and Lovelock, 1983) in discussing mass extinctions, "Very evidently, life is extremely resilient, recovering rapidly from injuries, so that the conditions necessary for life are restored. They are restored, as they were established originally, by living organisms themselves, and the entire surface of the planet, from the depths of the oceans to the top of the atmosphere, has been shaped by biological processes." He has even gone further and uses the survival of the biosphere during impact disasters to argue that, "it is very unlikely that anything we do will threaten Gaia" (Lovelock, 1988). This is not a popular stance with environmentalists. He adds, however, as an important afterthought, that Gaian alterations may not be to our (humans') advantage. But few explicit details are given as to how life can be prepared for and adjust to sudden catastrophic events that may not recur for periods of tens of millions of years.

For Alvarez (1987), survival during mass extinctions is largely the accident of the members of any species being so numerous or widespread that, even with very high "kill rates," some of the population manages to escape destruction. It helps to have the luck of being "preadapted to" or able somehow to avoid the heat blast and wildfires, cold, darkness, volcanic eruptions, acid rain, and various other possible shocks to the biosphere precipitated by impacts. In the sea, for example, some widespread but insignificant planktonic foraminifera managed to survive the mass extinction of zooplankton, while on land some of the small but ubiquitous mammals persisted, along with birds, lizards, alligators, turtles, insects, and other groups that somehow avoided annihilation.

One must apparently be content with accepting survival of the "luckiest" in the case of catastrophic mass extinctions (Alvarez, 1987), in marked disagreement with conventional Darwinian concepts of speciation as a result of competition among organisms for food and living space, as outlined recently by Hsu (1986 a,b,c). Gould (1989) has called this new form of evolution "evolution by lottery," and admits that it might be the most important form of evolution in terms of defining the major currents of the history of life on Earth.

In the Darwinian view of natural selection, as Gould (1989) quotes Darwin, the arena of competition is compared to "a yielding surface, with ten thousand sharp wedges packed close together and driven inwards by incessant blows, sometimes one wedge being struck, and then another with greater force." Here, each wedge corresponds to a variety or species, and the blows represent the driving force of natural selection. Because there is a finite area of surface into which each wedge can be pushed, one that manages to dig in will force out a previously stuck wedge. In this way, a more fit organism forces out a less fit one (fitness represents reproductive success). Darwin stressed the gradual nature of evolution by the slow accumulation of mutations; more recently Eldredge and Gould (1972) proposed that speciation occurs rapidly, with the intervals between speciation marked by a general stasis, with little evolutionary change. In this view, any mutations during the equilibrium stage would be eliminated by the restoring force of the general ecological equilibrium. This "punctuated equilibrium" model of speciation has generated many discussions pro and con, but with the caveat that rapid speciation events occur at times of rapid environmental changes and selective pressures, the model falls within the scope of Darwin's ideas.

By contrast, evolution by catastrophe means speciation through an entirely different mechanism; every so often, many species are killed off in a global catastrophe, niches are vacated en masse, and the survivors are free to speciate to fill the many empty niches. This goes even further than the debatable concept of punctuated equilibrium; a better term might be "punctured equilibrium" (suggested by Volk). The entire biosphere is shocked, and the process of speciation following the catastrophe is intimately related to the recovery of the biosphere as a whole. Thus the "normal mode" of speciation that takes place between mass extinctions, which never involves a recreation of the whole biosphere or a major portion of it, must be overridden for a period of time until the biosphere sorts itself out.

In fact, Hsu (1986a,b,c) has gone so far as to reject entirely the notion of Darwinian fitness, and has proposed instead a kind of Taoist view of life on Earth. He writes that, "The concept of rational causes and ultimate purposes may be built into our root perception of the world, an artifact of our own unique evolution. If the great happenings of life's history, even the fact that we are here at all, is happenstance . . . , then how are we to bear the apparent accident of our existence?" (Hsu, 1986a). He further suggests that, "Survival of the luckiest can be grasped, can be accepted. . . . There is a way, a principle, a truth in what has happened on this earth of ours that can't be found, and can't be talked about, but that nevertheless exists." Hsu seems to be implying a retreat from the standard scientific method to a semimystical interpretation in discussing the long-term evolution of the biosphere. Thus along with the new scientific mythology has come a call, from at least one researcher, for a new scientific philosophy based on Taoism.

The Record of Mass Extinctions

Several quite severe reductions in global diversity have occurred during the Phanerozoic, and these may be considered first-order mass extinctions (the Ordovician-Silurian boundary, the Frasnian-Fammenian boundary, the Permian-Triassic boundary, the late Triassic, and the Cretaceous-Tertiary boundary) (figure 42.1). These are all major upheavals in the history of life, the Cretaceous-Tertiary boundary (66 Myr BP) is marked by the extinction of some 75% of marine species. The Permian-Triassic boundary (250 Myr BP) involved the remarkable extinction of about 96% of marine species (Raup, 1979). In the latter case, we may well ask what prevented the remaining 4% of the species from dying

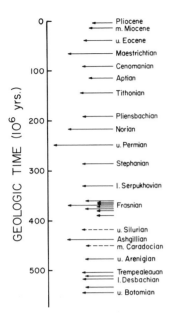

Figure 42.1 Major and minor marine extinctions during the Phanerozoic. The length of arrows represents the approximate estimated magnitudes of the extinction events. (After Sepkoski, 1986).

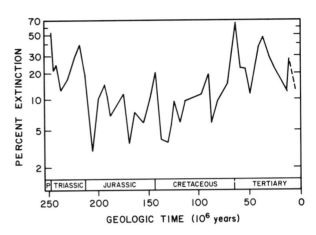

Figure 42.2 Mass extinction events of the last 250 million years. (After Raup and Sepkoski, 1984).

off as well? Luck? Or Gaia? Could a future mass extinction, by whatever cause, wipe out life totally on this planet, or would Gaian mechanisms somehow prevent this from happening?

The record of mass extinctions over the last 600 Myr is shown in figure 42.1 (Sepkoski, 1986); this contains the first-order extinctions mentioned here, and second-order mass extinctions of somewhat lesser magnitude that have been recognized using a new compilation of the ranges of families and genera (Sepkoski, 1982). Over the last 250 Myr (the Mesozoic and Cenozoic eras), where the geological record is best, eight or nine mass extinction events of varying severity at the family and genus level have been noted (figure 42.2), and these appear to occur periodically or quasi-periodically with a twenty-six- to thirty-million year period (Raup and Sepkoski, 1984, 1986; Rampino and Stothers, 1984a,b, 1986; Stothers, 1989) with at least approximate synchroneity in the marine and nonmarine realms.

The end-Cretaceous extinction event has been studied in the most detail, and has become the model of a geologically rapid mass extinction (Alvarez, 1987). The physical evidence for a geologically sudden event of worldwide extent is well established. The boundary interval is commonly marked in marine sections by a zone of clay deposition, followed by a time of reduced rates of car-

bonate sedimentation in deep sea sediments. The so-called Cretaceous-Tertiary (K/T) boundary clay, initially interpreted as composed largely of fallout from the ejecta cloud (Alvarez et al., 1980), and perhaps fine ash from impact-related volcanism, has since been shown to consist largely of fine-grained sediments deposited during an interval when carbonate deposition ceased as a result of the mass disappearance of calcareous plankton. In the most complete and least bioturbated sections, only the basal layer of the boundary clay shows evidence of impact fallout, and is rich in iridium, microspherules, and shocked minerals. The immediate postboundary period is marked by a negative fluctuation in $\delta^{13}C$ in the carbonate shells of surface plankton, and a homogenization of the $^{13}C:^{12}C$ ratio in ocean surface to deep waters (Zachos et al., 1989). This indicates a severe decrease in surface water productivity, described as a "Strangelove Ocean." The oceanic biosphere does not recover, in terms of productivity and numbers of calcareous plankton, for a few hundred thousand to a million years, judging from the isotope and carbonate deposition record following the mass extinction event (Caldeira et al., 1990). Fluctuations in carbon-isotope ratios and oxygen-isotope ratios following the K/T boundary, and other geological boundaries, imply that biomass and climate oscillated markedly following the initial shock to the biosphere (Kauffman, 1988; Rampino and Volk, 1988).

In the nonmarine realm, the Cretaceous-Tertiary boundary is well exposed in western North America. The boundary clay consists of a basal layer as much as 3-cm thick containing hollow spherules, overlain by a 2- to 3-cm thick "magic layer" containing shocked minerals and an iridium anomaly (Bohor et al., 1987), and appears to be composed largely of impact fallout. This layer is close to the last occurrence of in-place dinosaur fossils, and seems to be coincident with the final extinction of the great reptiles. The boundary layer is marked by the disappearance of many types of Cretaceous pollen, and a spike of fern spores, possibly marking a disaster event. Diversity of angiosperms takes about 1.5×10^6 years to recover. Iridium and shocked minerals, the best evidence of impact, have been found at more than eighty sites around the world in marine and terrestrial sections. Glassy tektites have now been found in Haiti (Sigurdsson et al., 1991). The combined evidence strongly supports the idea that the Cretaceous-Tertiary mass extinction of life was related to the impact of a cosmic object or objects (Alvarez, 1986).

Unfortunately, much of the evidence presented in a number of papers invoking volcanism, sea level changes, and other purely terrestrial events as the primary cause of the K/T mass extinctions involves the inclusion of misinterpreted, misleading, and erroneous data, and the exclusion of much relevant data (e.g., known impact craters described as terrestrial "cryptovolcanic structures," shocked minerals from volcanism, critiques of statistical analysis with no statistics, the construction of rival "paradigms" to impact based on little more than arguments that the impact hypothesis must be wrong because all of the loose ends are not tied up as yet (Kerr, 1988; Chapman, 1989; Ginsburg et al., 1989). The recently discovered presence of stishovite in the boundary clay (McHone et al., 1989) is clearcut evidence for impact. Sea level and climate changes may be of secondary importance, but are not the main cause of the K/T perturbations. No one has explained satisfactorily exactly how K/T sea level changes could cause catastrophic mass extinctions on land and in the sea when no extinctions accompanied the many Quaternary swings of sea level, and the evidence for explosive volcanism at various places in the world at K/T time is no more impressive than evidence for explosive volcanism at other times including the Quaternary, when no great mass extinctions on land and sea occurred. Volcanism may be involved in the K/T crisis period, but almost certainly as a secondary phenomenon, perhaps related to the impact process itself (Rampino, 1987, 1989). Flood basalt eruptions show a similar cycle of about thirty million years (Rampino and

Stothers, 1988). Perhaps mantle plumes are triggered or perturbed by large impacts.

The method of geology has traditionally been one of multiple working hypotheses (Gilbert, 1886). But this has been largely because in many cases no single explanation has been powerful enough to explain existing facts and make hard predictions that could be tested quantitatively. The Alvarez impact theory has changed that situation as far as the K/T mass extinctions are concerned, a fact that many geologists still do not accept. Consider the following, written by a well-known vertebrate paleontologist on a Wyoming morning: "I suppose a nononsense laboratory scientist, clad in his white lab coat and steely eyed objectivity, might think I was wasting my time communing with the spirit of the fossil beast" (Bakker, 1987). And what are the results of such musings? Disease perhaps, some form of Mesozoic Rinderpest brought about by mixing of fauna. The perfect theory! No physical evidence to confirm or disprove it.

Periodicity and Comet Showers

Raup and Sepkoski (1984, 1985), using Sepkoski's (1982) compendium of ranges of marine families and later genera, were the first to report rigid statistical analysis of the mass extinction record that showed a periodicity of about 26 million years over the last 250 million years. Rampino and Stothers (1984a) and Stothers (1989) have shown that a period near thirty Myr BP is the best one can determine considering the different timescales available. A number of studies have since supported the Raup-Sepkoski analysis, whereas others have questioned the results, often on the limited basis of "my group of organisms does not fit your picture of periodicity." At present, the periodicity of mass extinctions seems to be robust, but the exact periodicity and the significance level of the statistical analyses remain subjects of debate (Stothers, 1989; Stigler and Wagner, 1987; Raup and Sepkoski, 1988).

The idea of periodicity or quasi-periodicity in the geological record is not a new one. It goes back to early arguments over the nature of the stratigraphic and tectonic records (see Rampino and Stothers, 1986). Some early scientists saw periodic or at least episodic upheavals on a global scale, whereas others perceived merely a scattered and incomplete geological record, with much time and fossil record missing from the natural archives. This argument continues to some extent today, especially around geological boundaries, but for many geologists the high-resolution stratigraphic techniques developed over the past decade (Kauffman, 1986, 1988; Elder, 1988) have quite convincingly shown that many sections are remarkably complete, and that individual strata can be traced across depositional basins, and in a number of cases on a global basis (Walliser, 1986; Kauffman, 1988). Major perturbations show up as a widespread change in depositional conditions and biotic turnover (Kauffman, 1988). The concept of global bioevents has been clearly demonstrated through high-resolution stratigraphic methods, and seems to involve large-scale changes in ocean chemistry, periods of anoxia, and other effects of ocean circulation that require triggering events of massive scale.

The discovery of stratigraphic evidence for impacts makes it clear that global bioevents of the first order are driven or triggered by events originating outside of the normal processes of the Earth itself. This should not be seen as heresy to most geologists and paleontologists, because the community has often in the past considered global forces involving tectonics, sea level changes, oceanic turnover events, and severe climatic change outside of the normal interactions between biota and environment occurring at times of little or gradual change in the biological and geological records. It is only one more step to consider that those global changes may be triggered by extraterrestrial impacts, for which we have evidence in the form of craters and stratigraphic impact debris (Rampino and Stothers, 1986; Shoemaker and Wolfe, 1986).

The Long-Term History of Diversity

Despite the occurrence of mass extinctions, the record of familial diversity in the oceans shows a generally monotonic increase since the beginning of the Phanerozoic (Valentine and Moores, 1970). On a family level at least, most of the mass extinctions appear as minor setbacks in the climb toward greater diversity over the last 600 Myr (figure 42.3). Only the great late Permian extinction event (96% species extinction) shows up as a considerable readjustment in familial diversity, with a drop from more than 400 to less than 200 marine families in the late Permian. Numbers of marine families did not recover to the 400 level until the late Jurassic, some 90 Myr later (figure 42.3) (Erwin et al., 1987). But

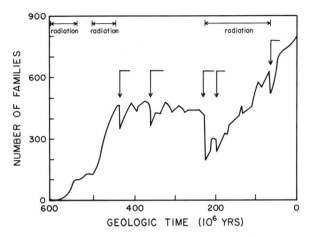

Figure 42.3 Phanerozoic record of diversity of families of skeletonized marine animals. Stippled areas represent the two major intervals of diversification (Erwin et al., 1987). Three principal radiations are indicated at the top. Arrows mark the five major mass extinctions, and the bars delineate the recovery time for family diversity. (After Erwin et al., 1987).

family-level diversity may be somewhat misleading, because many families that survived the mass extinction events were decimated at the genus and species levels (Raup and Sepkoski, 1986).

Various workers have interpreted the diversity curves in different ways. The early Valentine and Moores (1970) study proposed that marine diversity was related to continental shelf area and sea level, and hence times of continental accretion marked a reduction of shelf area and decrease in diversity, whereas times of continental breakup afforded more shelf area, and the possibility of greater marine diversity. Wilde and Berry (1986) have correlated the major changes in diversity over the last 600 Myr with overturn of oxic and anoxic ocean waters, brought about by glacial-evaporite cycles and major changes in sea level. Thus they view diversity as dependent on oceanographic and climatic conditions, which are driven by tectonics and climatic change. The diversity curve has also been interpreted in terms of equilibrium dynamics (Carr and Kitchell, 1980; Sepkoski, 1979, 1981). Three distinctive major marine faunas occur during the Phanerozoic. Fauna I was dominant during the Cambrian with a low equilibrium diversity. Fauna II replaced fauna I in dominance during the Ordovician. Fauna II reached a higher equilibrium level, forming a broad diversity plateau through the rest of the Paleozoic. Fauna II lost its dominance at the end of the Paleozoic at the time of the Permian extinction event, and was replaced by fauna III, which is climbing toward a higher equilibrium level. The plateau reached by fauna II suggests either that some carrying capacity exists that can support only so much diversity (Valentine and Walker, 1986), or that there is a long-term inertia in the system that prevents the kind of biological innovation that leads to increased diversity of life. Stasis during the Paleozoic may have been the results of (1) environments filled with life; (2) the evolution of increasingly effective predators, making it difficult for new forms to evolve; (3) existing organisms being too specialized to give rise easily to other totally new types. Erwin and colleagues (1987) observe that "One obvious feature shared by the biospheres of the late Vendian and Early Triassic is that they were both largely empty and that subsequent radiations filled them, although not necessarily to the brim" (figure 42.3). The opening of adaptive space on a large scale would result from mass extinctions. A prime example is the tremendous radiation of mammals following the K/T dinosaur extinctions. Had the dinosaurs not disappeared the mammals would have probably remained insignificant and marginally successful.

The Role of Major Perturbations

This leads to the question of whether episodic or periodic disturbances of the global biota actually have helped to drive the movement toward greater diversity seen over the last 600 Myr. The clearing out of adaptive space may be the primary factor in the rise of evolutionary novelties among metazoans (Erwin et al., 1987). Is the continued existence and viability of the biosphere as a whole dependent in some way on major physical disturbances, such as those that produce mass extinction events? Do these events represent challenges to Gaia, and a form of external modulation of the gaian system? The continued viability of many ecosystems is dependent on disturbances that lead to variations in properties such as productivity, biomass accumulation, species richness, and rates of nutrient cycling. On the geochemical side, impacts can promote nutrient recycling; for example, Kump (1988) has suggested that fires on land bring excess phosphorus to the oceans, where it is buried, eventually to show up again on land as phosphorus in continental rocks. It is then weathered and returned to the sea as phosphates that can be utilized by phy-

toplankton. Weathering rates would also increase from acid rain, climate warming, and deforestation. The oxygen content of the atmosphere may also be decreased, along with a transfer of carbon dioxide from the oceans to the atmosphere. Increased weathering could also lead to increased trace metals in the oceans, while volcanism would add trace metals, sulfur, and chlorine to the environment. On the biological side, mass extinctions allow radiation of new groups, create new niches and promote novelty, and break up static ecosystems.

Many natural systems depend on disturbances to remain viable. But how does the biosphere recover after major perturbations? Walliser (1986) may be on the right track in suggesting that major events show the following sequence: Extinction—an unstable interval (Strangelove Ocean?)—and radiation. He proposes that extinctions lead to a decrease in selectional stress that creates an interval of instability, during which opportunistic species may temporarily dominate. Evolutionary rates increase, and rapid radiation takes place among the survivors of the mass extinction. As niches become filled with new species, competition increases and evolutionary rates decrease. Eventually evolutionary rates may return to background levels.

A Galactic Connection?

Periodic mass extinctions may be related to a larger astrophysical context (Rampino and Stothers, 1984a,b, 1986). The Earth system may be responding to an external galactic forcing. This would make earthly Gaia not only a planetary property but a property inherent in the Galaxy, and perhaps the Universe as a whole. Do Shiva and Gaia represent a coupled and coevolved system—the stability of one somehow dependent on disturbances caused by the other? If the cause of mass extinctions is periodic or quasi-periodic comet showers, with a mean interval of about thirty million years between showers, then the showers may be linked to a well-known astronomical cycle: the oscillation of the Solar System up and down through the central plane of the Milky Way Galaxy (Rampino and Stothers, 1984a). Lovelock's term "geophysiology" might therefore be better renamed *astrogeophysiology,* because the interplay between Gaia and Shiva should take place on other Earth-like planets in the Galaxy, with comet impacts coming with a similar periodicity in all planetary systems that move up and down through the galactic disc. Perhaps other coevolved systems of destruction and renewal have evolved on Earth-like planets across the Cosmos.

References

Allaby, M., and Lovelock, J.E. 1983. *The Great Extinction.* Garden City, N.Y.: Doubleday.

Alvarez, L.W. 1987. Mass extinctions caused by large bolide impacts. *Physics Today,* 40, 24–33.

Alvarez, L.W., Alvarez, W., Asaro, F., and Michel, H. 1980. Extraterrestrial cause for the Cretaceous-Tertiary extinction. *Science,* 208, 1095–1108.

Alvarez, W. 1986. Towards a theory of impact crises. *Eos Trans Am Geophys Union,* 67, 649–658.

Alvarez, W., and Muller, R.A. 1984. Evidence from crater ages for periodic impacts on the Earth. *Nature,* 308, 718–720.

Bakker, R.T. 1987. *The Dinosaur Heresies.* New York: William Morrow and Co.

Berner, R.A., Lasaga, A.C., and Garrels, R.M. 1983. The carbonate-silicate geochemical cycle and its effect on atmospheric carbon dioxide over the past 100 million years. *Am J Sci,* 283, 641–683.

Bohor, B.F., Triplehorn, D.M., Nichols, D.J., and Millard, H.T., Jr. 1987. Dinosaurs, spherules, and the "magic layer": A new K-T boundary site in Wyoming. *Geology,* 15, 896–899.

Caldeira, K., Rampino, M.R., Volk, T., and Zachos, J.C. 1990. Results of biogeochemical modeling at mass extinction boundaries: Atmospheric carbon dioxide and ocean alkalinity at the K/T boundary. In: Kauffman, E.G., and Walliser, O.H. eds. *Extinction Events in Earth History.* Berlin: Springer-Verlag, 333–345.

Carr, T.R., and Kitchell, J.A. 1980. Dynamics of taxonomic diversity. *Paleobiology,* 6, 427–443.

Chapman, C. 1989. Snowbird II: Global catastrophes. *Eos, Transactions of the American Geophysical Union,* 70, 217–218.

Davis, M., Hut, P., and Muller, R.A. 1984. Extinction of species by periodic comet showers. *Nature,* 308, 715–717.

Elder, W.P. 1988. Geometry of Upper Cretaceous bentonite beds: Implications about volcanic source areas and paleowind patterns, western interior, United States. *Geology,* 16, 835–838.

Eldredge, N., and Gould, S.J. 1972. Punctuated equilibria: An alternative to phyletic gradualism. In: Schopf, T.J.M., ed. *Models in Paleobiology.* San Francisco: Freeman Cooper, 82–115.

Erwin, D.H., Valentine, J.W., and Sepkoski, J.J., Jr. 1987. A comparative study of diversification events: The early Paleozoic versus the Mesozoic. *Evolution,* 41, 1177–1186.

Gilbert, G.K. 1886. The inculcation of scientific method by example. *Am J Sci,* 41, 284–299.

Ginsburg, R.N., Burke, K., and Sharpton, V. 1989. Scientists debate global catastrophes. *Geotimes,* March, 34, 14–16.

Goldsmith, D. 1985. *Nemesis, the Death Star and Other Theories of Mass Extinctions.* New York: Walker and Co.

Goldsmith, D. 1986. The Shiva theory or how life on earth was nearly destroyed. *Griffith Observer,* February, 2–10.

Gould, S.J. 1984. The cosmic dance of Shiva. *Natural History,* 8, 14–19.

Gould, S.J. 1989. The wheel of fortune and the wedge of progress. *Natural History,* 3, 14–21.

Hsu, K.J. 1986a. *The Great Dying.* New York: Harcourt Brace Jovanovich.

Hsu, K.J. 1986b. Darwin's three mistakes. *Geology,* 14, 532–534.

Hsu, K.J. 1986c. Sedimentary petrology and biologic evolution. *J Sediment Petrol,* 56, 729–732.

Jablonski, D. 1986. Causes and consequences of mass extinctions: A comparative approach. In: Elliott, D.K., ed. *Dynamics of Extinction.* New York: Wiley, 183–229.

Kauffman, E.G. 1986. High resolution event stratigraphy: Regional and global Cretaceous bioevents. In: Walliser, O.H., ed. *Global Bio-Events.* Berlin: Springer-Verlag, 279–335.

Kauffman, E.G. 1988. Concepts and methods of high-resolution event stratigraphy. *Ann Rev Earth Planetary Sci,* 16, 605–654.

Kerr, R.A. 1988. Snowbird II: Clues to earth's impact history. *Science,* 242, 1380–1382.

Kump, L.R. 1988. Terrestrial feedback in atmospheric oxygen regulation by fire and phosphorus. *Nature,* 335, 152–154.

Lasaga, A.C., Berner, R.A., and Garrels, R.M. 1985. An improved geochemical model of the atmospheric CO_2 fluctuations over the past 100 million years. Monograph 32. Washington, D.C.: American Geophysical Union, 397–411.

Lovelock, J.E. 1979. *Gaia: A New Look at Life on Earth.* Oxford: Oxford University Press.

Lovelock, J.E. 1988. *The Ages Of Gaia.* New York: W.W. Norton and Co.

Lovelock, J.E., and Margulis, L. 1974. Atmospheric homeostasis by and for the biosphere: The Gaia hypothesis. *Tellus,* 26, 2–9.

Margulis, L. 1981. *Symbiosis in Cell Evolution.* San Francisco: W.H. Freeman.

McHone, J.F., Nieman, R.A., Lewis, C.F., and Yates, A.M. 1989. Stishovite at the Cretaceous/Tertiary boundary, Raton, New Mexico. *Science,* 243, 1182–1184.

McKinney, M.L. 1987. Taxonomic selectivity and continuous variation in mass and background extinctions of marine taxa. *Nature,* 325, 143–145.

Rampino, M.R. 1987. Impact cratering and flood basalt volcanism. *Nature,* 327, 468.

Rampino, M.R. 1989. Dinosaurs, comets and volcanoes. *New Scientist,* 121, 54–58.

Rampino, M.R., and Stothers, R.B. 1984a. Terrestrial mass extinctions, cometary impacts and the sun's motion perpendicular to the galactic plane. *Nature,* 308, 709–712.

Rampino, M.R., and Stothers, R.B. 1984b. Geological rhythms and cometary impacts. *Science,* 226, 1427–1431.

Rampino, M.R., and Stothers, R.B. 1986. Geologic periodicities and the Galaxy. In: Smoluchowski, R., Bahcall, J.N., and Matthews, M.S., eds. *The Galaxy and the Solar System.* Tucson: University of Arizona Press, 241–259.

Rampino, M.R., and Stothers, R.B. 1988. Flood basalt volcanism during the past 250 million years. *Science,* 241, 663–668.

Rampino, M.R., and Volk, T. 1988. Mass extinctions, atmospheric sulphur and climatic warming at the K/T boundary. *Nature,* 332, 63–65.

Raup, D.M. 1979. Size of the Permian-Triassic bottleneck and its evolutionary implications. *Science,* 206, 217–218.

Raup, D.M. 1986. Biological extinction in earth history. *Science,* 231, 1528–1533.

Raup, D.M., and Sepkoski, J.J., Jr. 1984. Periodicity of extinctions in the geologic past. *Proc Natl Acad Sci USA,* 81, 801–805.

Raup, D.M., and Sepkoski, J.J., Jr. 1986. Periodic extinctions of family and genera. *Science,* 231, 833–836.

Raup, D.M., and Sepkoski, J.J., Jr. 1988. Testing for periodicity of extinction. *Science,* 241, 94–96.

Schneider, S.H., and Londer, R. 1984. *The Coevolution of Climate and Life.* San Francisco: Sierra Club Books.

Sepkoski, J.J., Jr. 1979. A kinetic model of Phanerozoic taxonomic diversity. II. Early Phanerozoic families and multiple equilibria. *Paleobiology,* 5, 222–252.

Sepkoski, J.J., Jr. 1981. The uniqueness of the Cambrian fauna. In: Taylor, M.E., ed. *Short Papers for the Second International Symposium on the Cambrian System.* United States Geologic Survey Open File Report 81-743.

Sepkoski, J.J., Jr. 1982. A compendium of fossil marine families. *Milwaukee Public Museum Contributions Biol Geol,* 51, 1–125.

Sepkoski, J.J., Jr. 1986. Phanerozoic overview of mass extinctions. In: Raup, D.M., and Jablonski, D., eds. *Patterns and Processes in the History of Life.* Berlin: Springer-Verlag, 277–295.

Shoemaker, E.M., and Wolfe, R.F. 1986. Mass extinctions, crater ages and comet showers. In: Smoluchowski, R., Bahcall, J.N., and Matthews, M.S., eds. *The Galaxy and the Solar System.* Tucson: University of Arizona Press, 338–386.

Sigurdsson, H., D'Hondt, S., Arthur, M.A., Bralower, T.J., Zachos, J.C., van Fossen, M., and Channell, J.E.T. 1991. Glass from the Cretaceous/Tertiary boundary in Haiti. *Nature,* 349, 482–487.

Stigler, S.M., and Wagner, M.J. 1987. A substantial bias in nonparametric tests for periodicity in geophysical data. *Science,* 238, 940–945.

Stothers, R.B. 1989. Structure and dating errors in the geologic time scale and periodicity of mass extinctions. *Geophys Res Lett,* 16, 119–122.

Valentine, J.W., and Moores, E.M. 1970. Plate-tectonic regulation of faunal diversity and sea level: A model. *Nature,* 228, 657–659.

Valentine, J.W., and Walker, T.D. 1986. Diversity trends within a model taxonomic hierarchy. *Physica,* 22D, 31–42.

Volk, T. 1987. Feedbacks between weathering and atmospheric CO_2 over the last 100 million years. *Am J Sci,* 287, 763–779.

Volk, T. 1989a. Sensitivity of climate and atmospheric CO_2 to deep-ocean and shallow ocean carbonate burial. *Nature,* 337, 637–640.

Volk, T. 1989b. Rise of angiosperms as a factor in long-term climatic cooling. *Geology,* 17, 107–110.

Walker, J.C.G., Hays, P.B., and Kasting, J.F. 1981. A negative feedback mechanism for the long term stabilization of the earth's surface temperature. *J Geophys Res,* 86, 9776–9782.

Walliser, O.H., ed. 1986. *Global Bio-Events.* Berlin: Springer-Verlag.

Whitmire, D.P., and Jackson, A.A. 1984. Are periodic mass extinctions driven by a distant solar companion? *Nature,* 308, 713–715.

Whitmire, D.P., and Matese, J.J. 1985. Periodic comet showers and planet X. *Nature,* 313, 36–38.

Wicken, J.S. 1987. *Evolution, Thermodynamics, and Information.* Oxford: Oxford University Press.

Wilde, P., and Berry, W.B.N. 1986. The role of oceanographic factors in the generation of global bio-events. In: Walliser, O.H., ed. *Global-Bio-Events.* Berlin: Springer-Verlag, 75–91.

Zachos, J.C., Arthur, M.A., and Dean, W.E. 1989. Geochemical evidence for suppression of pelagic marine productivity at the Cretaceous/Tertiary boundary. *Nature,* 337, 61–64.

IX
Policy Implications

Gaia on the Brink: Biogeochemical Feedback Processes in Global Warming

The increasing concentrations of greenhouse gases in the Earth's atmosphere have the potential to dramatically alter the global climate. Human activity is directly modifying the composition of the global atmosphere, and the response of the Earth system will depend on how geophysical and biogeochemical feedbacks act to enhance or diminish the initial forcing (Lashof, 1989a; Ramanathan et al., 1987; Bolin et al., 1986). For example, the emissions and atmospheric lifetimes of many important greenhouse gases are themselves affected by atmospheric composition and climate. The Gaia hypothesis may suggest that the predominant biogeochemical feedbacks are likely to be negative. The analysis presented here indicates, however, that faced with rapid anthropogenic forcing, biogeochemical feedbacks are likely to significantly enhance global warming in the immediate future (within about a century). The longer-term response of the system, and purposeful or forced changes in human behavior (which could be considered part of the system), are beyond the scope of this chapter.

Feedbacks and Climate Sensitivity

The concept of feedback has considerable intuitive appeal and is widely, if sometimes loosely, used in discussions of climate change. The term is derived by analogy to an electronic amplifier with output (ω) determined by the input signal (ι) and a feedback signal proportional to ω. The gain of this system is defined by

$$g = (\omega - \iota)/\omega \qquad (1)$$

This work was initially presented in preliminary form at the Chapman Conference on the Gaia Hypothesis. A more complete discussion of this analysis was subsequently published as Lashof (1989a) and a summary was published as Lashof (1989b).

The views expressed are the author's: They do not express official views of the U.S. Government or the Environmental Protection Agency.

and the amplification (often referred to as the *feedback factor*; e.g., Hansen et al., 1984, 1985) is

$$f = \omega/\iota = 1/(1 - g). \qquad (2)$$

Note that while g can take on any real value less than 1, f is strictly positive, and thus ω always has the same sign as ι. As g approaches 1, f approaches $+\infty$, while as g approaches $-\infty$, f approaches 0. These simple relationships are emphasized to make precise the meaning of commonly used terms such as *negative feedback* ($g < 0$), positive feedback ($g > 0$), and unstable system ($g \to 1$). A useful consequence of the way *gain* is defined is that the gain for a linear system with several feedbacks is simply the sum of the gains associated with each individual feedback loop.

The sensitivity of the climate system can be defined as the global temperature increase that would occur at equilibrium in response to a given perturbation, such as an increase in the concentrations of greenhouse gases. This sensitivity will be determined by a combination of feedbacks that amplify or damp the direct radiative effects of, for example, an initial doubling of the concentration of CO_2. If we let ΔT_0 represent the global temperature increase that would occur in the absence of feedbacks (1.2K to 1.3K for a doubling of CO_2 concentrations; Ramanathan et al., 1987) then the total temperature change will be given by

$$\Delta T = \Delta T_0/(1 - \Sigma g_i), \qquad (3)$$

where the sum is over all feedback loops, i, in the system. Current general circulation models (GCMs) of the climate contain the key geophysical climate feedbacks, such as changes in water vapor, clouds, and sea ice albedo, but biogeochemical feedbacks such as changes in methane emissions, ocean CO_2 uptake, and vegetation albedo are generally neglected. Although each of these feedbacks is modest compared with the water vapor feedback, the biogeochemical feedbacks in combination have the potential to increase substantially the climate change associated with anthropogenic emissions of greenhouse gases.

Geophysical Feedbacks

Geophysical feedbacks internal to the climate system are those due to physical processes (as opposed to chemical or biochemical processes) in the atmosphere-ocean-cryosphere system that alter the radiative characteristics of the system in response to the initial radiative or temperature perturbation. The most important of these feedbacks, at least on a short timescale, are probably the water vapor feedback, the cloud feedback, and the ice and snow feedback. These feedbacks are simulated in GCMs and their strength determines the sensitivity of the climate system to a change in radiative forcing. The strength of these feedbacks in climate models is determined both by how the processes are represented and by the control climate (Cess and Potter, 1988). For a review and comparison of climate models see, for example, Schlesinger and Mitchell (1985) and Dickinson (1986).

The water vapor feedback arises because warming the atmosphere increases absolute humidity (relative humidity is more or less constant) and water vapor is a potent greenhouse gas (related changes in the lapse rate are included with the water vapor feedback for the purposes of this discussion). Hansen and colleagues (1984) found that the water vapor feedback produced a gain of 0.40 by using a one-dimensional radiative-convective (RC) model to back-calculate the individual contributions to the sensitivity of their GCM. Although the significance of this feedback is not in doubt, its magnitude is uncertain because the radiative properties of atmospheric water vapor are difficult to model (Kiehl, chapter 11, this volume). Dickinson (1986) obtains a central estimate of 0.39 and a 2σ range of 0.28 to 0.52 (table 43.1).

Changes in ice and snow cover contribute a positive feedback because warming the earth reduces the planetary albedo and increases heat transfer from the ocean to the atmosphere by reducing the extent and persistence of sea ice and snow cover. The importance of the albedo feedback is limited by vegetation and cloud masking of the surface reflectance. It is also conceivable that increased precipitation in a warmer world could increase snow cover. Changes in thermal inertia due to reduced insulation between the sea surface and the air may play a more important role than reduced albedo

Table 43.1 Estimated Gain from Climate and Biogeochemical Feedbacks

Feedback	Gain	Source
Geophysical		
Water vapor*	0.39 (0.28–0.52)	
Ice and snow	0.12 (0.03–0.21)	Dickinson (1986)
Clouds	0.09 ($-$0.12–0.29)	
Subtotal†	0.64 (0.17–0.77)	
Biogeochemical		
Methane hydrates	0.1 (0.01–0.2)	After Revelle (1983)
Tropospheric chemistry	$-.04$ $-$(0.01–0.06)	Hameed and Cess (1983)
Ocean chemistry	0.008	$\delta\ln(pCO_2)/\delta T = 4\%$
Ocean eddy-diffusion	0.02	$1/K \propto (\delta T/\delta Z)^2$
Ocean biology and circulation	0.06 (0.0–0.1)	After Sarmiento and Toggweiler (1984)
Vegetation albedo	0.05 (0.0–0.09)	After Hansen et al. (1984), Dickinson and Hanson (1984)
Vegetation respiration	0.01 (0.0–0.03)	Flux = 0.5 Pg y^{-1}°C^{-1}
CO_2 fertilization	$-.02$ $-$(0.01–0.04)	15% biomass increase for 2 × CO_2
Methane from wetlands	0.01 (0.003–0.015)	Lashof and Fung, unpublished
Methane from rice	0.006 (0.0–0.01)	After Holzapfel-Pschorn and Seiler (1986)
Electricity demand	0.001 (0.0–0.004)	After Linder and Inglis (1990)
Subtotal‡	0.16 (0.05–0.29)§	
Total	0.80 (0.32–0.98)§	

*Includes the lapse rate feedback and other geophysical climate feedbacks not included elsewhere.

†Based on 1.5K–5.5K for doubling CO_2. The individual values do not sum to these values—see Dickinson (1986) for details.

‡Based on selected biogeochemical feedbacks, considering which could occur together during the next century. See discussion section for details.

§Ranges are combined using a least-squares approach. That is, by letting $C - L = [\Sigma(c_i - l_i)^2]^{0.5}$, where C is the central estimate for the total, c_i is the central estimate for feedback i, L is the lower uncertainty bound for the total, and l_i is the lower uncertainty bound for feedback i. A similar calculation is performed for the upper uncertainty bounds.

(Manabe and Stouffer, 1980; Robock, 1983). Overall Hansen and colleagues (1984) find that the ice and snow feedback contributes a gain of 0.09 to the sensitivity of their GCM and Dickinson (1986) obtains a central estimate of 0.12 and a range of 0.03 to 0.21 (table 43.1).

The cloud feedback is probably the most complex and uncertain geophysical feedback in the climate system (Cess et al., 1989). In general, increases in the fractional cover or optical depth of low clouds would produce a negative feedback whereas increases in high (cirrus) clouds and increases in cloud altitude would produce a positive feedback. Hansen and colleagues (1984) fix cloud optical properties and find a substantial positive feedback (0.22). Roeckner and colleagues (1987) and Somerville and Remer (1984) argue that the liquid water content of clouds will increase with warming, substantially altering their optical properties. In the model calculations of Roeckner and colleagues (1987) this produces a large negative feedback at the surface, more than offsetting the positive feedback from changes in cloud cover. However, comparison of recent results with and without cloud optical property feedbacks shows that including this mechanism can increase or decrease total cloud feedback, depending on related changes in other cloud properties (Cess et al., 1989). Dickinson's analysis gives a central estimate of the gain due to changes in clouds of 0.09 and a range of -0.12 to 0.29 (table 43.1).

It is the uncertainty in the net effect of the geophysical climate feedbacks that determines the quoted uncertainty in the equilibrium response of the climate system to a given perturbation, such as doubling CO_2, and this uncertainty appears to be dominated by the effect of clouds (Cess et al., 1989). The most widely cited uncertainty range for ΔT from doubling CO_2 is 1.5K to 4.5K (National Research Council, 1979, 1983; World Meteorological Organization, 1986), which implies a gain due to the geophysical processes of 0.17 to 0.72. Dickinson's careful review of feedback processes and recent GCM results suggest that 1.5K to 5.5K may be a more appropriate uncertainty range (Dickinson, 1986; Wilson and Mitchell, 1987), and this range implies a gain of 0.17 to 0.77 (table 43.1). The relatively modest temperature increase observed to date seems to argue for the lower end of this range in the absence of other forcings (Wigley, 1989), while the amplitude of the seasonal cycle and glacial-to-interglacial temperature changes seem to ar-

gue for the upper end of this range (Boston and Thompson, chapter 11, this volume).

Biogeochemical Feedbacks

Biogeochemical feedbacks are those that involve the response of the biosphere and components of the geosphere not considered in typical climate models. Included here, for example, are feedbacks that involve changes in the sources and sinks of greenhouse gases, and changes in surface properties such as albedo and transpiration that are mediated by the intermediate- and long-term response of land vegetation (figure 43.1). Potential physical effects of warming include release of methane from hydrates, changes in tropospheric chemistry, and changes in ocean circulation and mixing. Potential effects from biological responses include changes in biological pumping of carbon from the ocean surface to deeper waters, changes in vegetation albedo, increased flux of CO_2 and methane from soil organic matter to the atmosphere due to higher rates of microbial activity, and increased flux of CO_2 from the atmosphere to the biosphere due to CO_2 fertilization.

Release of Methane Hydrates
Potentially the most important biogeochemical feedback is the release of CH_4 from near-shore

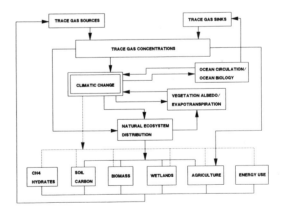

Figure 43.1 Biogeochemical feedback processes. Changes in trace gas concentrations produce climate change, which may affect ocean CO_2 uptake and the global distribution of natural ecosystems. Changes in ecosystem distribution affect surface albedo, evapotranspiration, the terrestrial component of the carbon cycle (both CO_2 and CH_4), and agriculture. Climate change can also directly affect these properties of the biosphere through the temperature and precipitation responses of given ecosystems. Global warming may also lead to methane emissions from hydrates and changes in energy use. Finally, changes in trace gas concentrations, particularly CO_2, directly affect natural and agricultural ecosystems.

ocean sediments. Methane hydrates are formed when a methane molecule is included within a lattice of water molecules; the ratio can be as small as 1:6, that is, one methane molecule for every six water molecules (Bell, 1982). The hydrate structure is stable under temperature and pressure conditions that are typically found under a water column of a few hundred meters or more in the Arctic and closer to a thousand meters in warmer waters. The region where hydrates are found can start at the sea floor and extend a few hundred meters into the sediment, depending on the geothermal temperature gradient (Kvenvolden and Barnard, 1984). Estimates of the total quantity of CH_4 contained in hydrates range from 2×10^3 to 5×10^6 Pg (Kvenvolden, 1988). Given the climatic change associated with a doubling of CO_2, Bell (1982; as corrected by Revelle, 1983) estimated that there could be a release of approximately 120 Tg CH_4/year from Arctic Ocean sediments, and Revelle (1983) calculated global emissions of approximately 640 Tg CH_4/year from continental slope hydrates. These estimates are, however, highly uncertain both because the total quantity of hydrates potentially subject to destabilization is not known and because bottom water may be insulated from surface temperature increases throughout much of the ocean (Kvenvolden, 1988). Nonetheless, a very strong positive feedback from this source is possible.

Assuming that a 2°C global warming causes a 1°C temperature increase at the water-sediment interface, I obtain a methane release rate of 220×10^{12} g/year (Tg/y). I further assume that the fractional change in the methane mixing ratio at chemical equilibrium is 1.5 times the fractional change in methane flux due to chemical interactions that increase the lifetime of methane with increasing emissions (Thompson and Cicerone, 1986). Thus an increase in the flux of methane by 220 Tg/y would increase the methane concentration by 1.2 parts per million (ppm). Finally I assume that the radiative forcing due to changes in the methane mixing ratio is enhanced by 70% to 0.17°C/ppm due to increased tropospheric ozone and stratospheric water vapor related to methane oxidation (Owens et al., 1985; Brasseur and De Rudder, 1987). Thus the gain from methane hydrate releases is given by

$$(1.2 \text{ ppm}) \times (0.17°\text{C/ppm})/2°\text{C} = 0.1 \qquad (4)$$

I subjectively assign a very wide uncertainty range of 0.01 to 0.2 to account for the large range in the estimates of total hydrates cited here, the possible

oxidation of some methane in the water column, and the possibility that most of the hydrate zone is bathed in water that is thermally insulated from the atmosphere, as argued by Kvenvolden (1988).

Tropospheric Chemistry

Climate-chemistry interactions have been reviewed recently by Ramanathan and colleagues (1987). In addition to the CH_4-CO-OH coupling and the stratospheric water vapor amplification discussed in the previous section, the chemical feedback with the largest climatic impact may be due to changes in OH resulting from changes in water vapor. A warmer Earth would have higher absolute humidity and thus more OH from the reaction $O(^1D) + H_2O \rightarrow 2OH$. This will, in turn, reduce CH_4 and tropospheric O_3 concentrations, resulting in a negative feedback on climatic change. Hameed and Cess (1983) find that climate-chemical feedback reduces tropospheric O_3 by 11% and CH_4 by 17%, assuming that CH_4, CO, and NO_x fluxes remain constant. This reduces the warming from doubling CO_2 in their model from 3.13K to 2.93K. Based on this result, the gain from this feedback is -0.04. This value depends strongly on the assumed background level of NO_x. In high-NO_x areas higher temperatures could increase O_3 formation, possibly reversing the sign of this feedback (Ramanathan et al., 1987). As current, and certainly future, NO_x distributions are highly uncertain, I assign a broad uncertainty bound to the gain from this feedback of $-(0.01$ to $0.06)$.

Another potentially important climate-chemical feedback is related to stratospheric O_3 chemistry. Surface warming from greenhouse gas buildup will be accompanied by strong stratospheric cooling. The altered temperature structure of the stratosphere will significantly influence O_3 chemistry, but both the sign and magnitude of the effect will depend strongly on the altitude as well as the magnitude of O_3 changes. These will, in turn, be influenced by future emissions of halocarbons and N_2O. A quantitative assessment of the impact of this feedback on climate is not available at this time (Ramanathan et al., 1987).

Oceanic Change

The oceans are the dominant factor in the Earth's thermal inertia to climate change as well as the dominant sink for anthropogenic CO_2 emissions. The mixed layer (approximately the top 75 m) alone contains about as much carbon (in the form of H_2CO_3, HCO_3^-, and $CO_3^=$) as does the atmosphere. Furthermore, the ocean biota plays an important role in carrying carbon (as organic debris) from the mixed layer to deeper portions of the ocean (e.g., Sarmiento and Toggweiler, 1984). Thus changes in ocean chemistry, biology, mixing, and large-scale circulation have the potential to substantially alter the rate of CO_2 accumulation in the atmosphere and the rate of global warming. And because the oceans are such an integral part of the climate system, significant changes in the oceans are likely to accompany a change in climate. For example, the oceans are responsible for about 50% of heat transport from the equator toward the poles (Dickinson, 1986), surface mixing is driven by winds, and deep circulation is driven by thermal and salinity gradients.

The feedbacks involving the ocean can be divided into three categories: the direct effect of temperature on carbonate chemistry, reduced mixing due to increased stability of the thermocline, and the possibility of large-scale reorganization of ocean circulation and biological activity.

Ocean Chemistry The most straightforward feedback is on ocean carbonate chemistry. As the ocean warms the solubility of CO_2 decreases and the carbonate equilibrium shifts toward carbonic acid; these effects combine to increase the partial pressure of CO_2 (pCO_2) in the ocean by 4% to 5%/°C for a fixed alkalinity and total carbon content. Hansen and colleagues (1984) used the box-diffusion formulation introduced by Oeschger and colleagues (1975) with the computation restricted to the mixed layer and thermocline to investigate the transient response of the climate to radiative forcing. I have modified this model to include equations for CO_2 solubility and carbonate chemistry from Takahashi and colleagues (1980) in order to investigate the coupling between climate change and ocean CO_2 uptake. Transport of excess carbon below the mixed layer is treated identically to transport of excess heat. The radiative forcing due to CO_2 increases is based on a parameterization of a one-dimensional RC model equivalent to that given by Hansen and colleagues (1988). I integrate this model from 1860 to 2100 using Rotty's (1982) record for fossil fuel emissions through 1980 and assuming 1%/y exponential growth from 1980 to 2100. Performing the calculation with and without coupling between temperature and carbonate chemistry, I find that the coupling produces a gain of 0.008 based on the temperature change realized in 2100.

Ocean Mixing As heat penetrates from the mixed layer of the ocean into the thermocline the stratification of the ocean will increase and mixing can be expected to decrease, resulting in slower uptake of both CO_2 and heat. This feedback raises the surface temperature that can be expected in any given year for two reasons: First, the atmospheric CO_2 concentration will be higher because the oceans will take up less CO_2. Second, the realized temperature will be closer to the equilibrium temperature due to reduced heat transport into the deep ocean. The strength of this feedback is estimated by letting the mixing parameter in the model described above be proportional to $(\delta T/\delta z)^{-2}$, where $\delta T/\delta z$ is the temperature gradient at the base of the mixed layer. The effect is to decrease the mixing coefficient 30% by 2100. This results in a gain of 0.02.

Ocean Biology and Circulation A more speculative, but potentially more significant, feedback involves a reorganization of the atmosphere-ocean circulation system, as suggested by Broecker (1987). This possibility is suggested by the apparently very rapid changes in the CO_2 content of the atmosphere during glacial-interglacial transitions as revealed by ice core measurements (e.g., Jouzel et al., 1987). Only shifts in carbon cycling in the ocean are thought to be capable of producing such large, rapid, and sustained changes in atmospheric CO_2. A number of studies have attempted to model the changes in ocean circulation or biological productivity required to account for the change in CO_2, emphasizing the importance of high-latitude processes (Keir, 1988; Sarmiento and Toggweiler, 1984; Seigenthaler and Wenk, 1984; Knox and McElroy, 1984). Because these changes in the ocean-atmosphere system may have been discontinuous (Broecker et al., 1985) the gain from this process in the future may be quite different from what it has been in the past; nonetheless, lacking coupled ocean-atmosphere GCMs, this is the only available basis for making an estimate. Assuming a glacial-interglacial temperature change of 5°C caused atmospheric CO_2 to increase by 80 ppm, the incremental radiative forcing was 0.56°C (based on the parameterization given by Hansen et al., 1988) and the gain from this feedback was 0.11. For the same relationship between temperature and CO_2 (16 ppm/°C) the gain would be lower in the future due to saturation of the CO_2 bands. For example, if the realized warming was 1°C by the time CO_2 reached 500 ppm, and if this triggered an additional increase in CO_2 of 16 ppm, the gain would be 0.06.

This calculation is consistent with the model of Sarmiento and Toggweiler (1984), assuming that the thermohaline circulation and the high-latitude particulate carbon flux decrease by about 10%/°C of warming. Given the arbitrary assumptions required to make this estimate, I assign an uncertainty range of 0.0 to 0.1 for the gain from the ocean circulation–biology feedback.

A fundamentally different and potentially highly significant feedback involving ocean biology has been proposed by Charlson and colleagues (1987). Dimethylsulfide (DMS) emitted by marine phytoplankton may act as cloud condensation nuclei (CCN) in remote marine locations where CCN are scarce, thereby affecting cloud optical properties. As noted above, changes in cloud optical properties can have a substantial influence on climate. Climate presumably affects biogenic DMS production, but the relationship is complex and poorly understood at this time (Charlson et al., 1987). DMS production is not directly related to primary productivity and interspecific differences in DMS production are large and may dominate direct climatic effects. Although this mechanism was originally proposed as a potential negative feedback consistent with the Gaia hypothesis, ice core data indicate that non–sea salt sulfate aerosol levels were higher during the last glacial maximum, suggesting that biogenic DMS production may act instead as a positive feedback (Legrand et al., 1988).

Terrestrial Biota

The terrestrial biota interacts with climate in a wide variety of important ways (figure 43.1). The discussion here emphasizes the effects of large-scale reorganization of terrestrial ecosystems as well as the direct effects of temperature and CO_2 changes. On a regional scale changes in surface roughness and evapotranspiration may be quite important, but such changes seem less likely to affect global climate than the processes discussed in more detail here.

Vegetation Albedo Probably the most significant global feedback produced by the terrestrial biota, on a decades-to-centuries timescale is due to changes in surface albedo (reflectivity) as a result of changes in the distribution of terrestrial ecosystems. Changes in moisture flux patterns may also be important, however, if they influence global cloudiness. Dickinson and Hanson (1984) examined the differences in albedo between the Climate Mapping and Prediction (CLIMAP) vegetation reconstruction for 18,000 years before present and current vegetation and found that the planetary albedo was 0.0022 higher at the glacial maximum due to differences in mean annual vegetation albedo. A similar result was obtained by Hansen and colleagues (1984), using a prescriptive scheme to relate vegetation type to climate in GCM simulations for current and glacial times. This represents about a 1% increase relative to the current albedo of 0.3, and results in a radiative forcing of 1 W/m^2. The gain associated with this albedo change is 0.06 to 0.08; this range was extended to 0.05 to 0.09 by Hansen and colleagues (1984) to account for uncertainties in the vegetation parameterization. Lacking other analysis, I assume that the low end of the range of gain calculated by Hansen and colleagues will apply in the future (namely, 0.05). This assumption is not unreasonable considering that the most important process—decreased albedo due to a poleward shift in the tundra–boreal forest boundary—should continue during the anticipated interglacial to superinterglacial transition. It is, however, also possible that increases in grassland and desert area, as a direct result of human activity or from climatic change, could increase albedo, partially compensating for decreased albedo at high latitudes. I therefore broaden the range assigned to this feedback to 0.0 to 0.09.

Carbon Storage Other significant feedbacks are related to the role of the terrestrial biosphere as a source and sink for CO_2 and CH_4. The carbon stored in live biomass and soils is roughly twice the amount in atmospheric CO_2, and global net primary production (NPP) by terrestrial plants absorbs about 10% of the carbon held in the atmosphere each year. On average this is nearly balanced by decay of organic matter, about 0.5% to 1% of which is anaerobic and thus produces CH_4 rather than CO_2. Small shifts in the balance between NPP and respiration, or changes in the fraction of NPP routed to CH_4 rather than CO_2, could therefore have a substantial impact on the overall greenhouse forcing, because CH_4 has a much larger greenhouse effect than CO_2 per molecule. Both NPP and respiration rates are largely determined by climate and NPP is directly affected by the CO_2 partial pressure of the atmosphere, thus the potential for a substantial feedback exists (e.g., Billings et al., 1982, 1983).

The relationship between climate and carbon

storage is not straightforward. Various approaches can be used to estimate changes in carbon storage resulting from climate change, including life-zone classification systems (Emanuel et al., 1985a,b), statistical models (Lashof, 1987), and dynamic models (Solomon, 1986; Kohlmaier and colleagues, chapter 26, this volume; Woodwell, 1986). Collectively these approaches suggest that increased soil respiration in the boreal zone is likely to cause a release of CO_2 on the order of 0.25 PgC y^{-1} $°C^{-1}$. Stress on other ecosystems globally seems likely to contribute an additional flux of perhaps the same magnitude. Modeling this feedback by inserting a flux of 0.5 PgC y^{-1} $°C^{-1}$ into the carbon-cycle–temperature model described above yields a gain of 0.01; a range of 0 to 0.03 probably characterizes the uncertainty.

Carbon Dioxide Fertilization Characterizing the global response of the biosphere to CO_2 fertilization is an equally thorny problem. Although the short-term response of a number species has been measured, generalizing to long-term carbon storage at the ecosystem or global level is difficult and controversial (e.g., Gates, 1985; Houghton, 1987, 1988; Idso, 1988). In a review of global biospheric stimulation by CO_2, Gates (1985) concludes that the fractional change in NPP will probably be 0.25 to 0.5 times the fractional change in atmospheric CO_2 (often referred to as the beta factor, after Bacastow and Keeling, 1973). NPP and biomass are not directly related, however, as is apparent from the difference between grassland and forest ecosystems, which may have similar annual productivity but vastly different carbon stocks. If it is assumed that forest biomass is limited by leaf area index and moisture transport, then maximum stand biomass may not increase with increasing CO_2. On the other hand, open areas within a forest—gaps—would be filled in faster, and average stand biomass should increase. This hypothesis was investigated by Shugart (1984) by arbitrarily increasing the intrinsic growth rate of all species in a number of gap dynamic stand simulation models. With modest growth stimulation the results were complex because of changes in species composition, but at stimulations of 50% to 100% results were nearly linear and showed that average biomass increased by 0.2 to 0.6 times the assumed increase in NPP. Using the center of both Shugart's and Gates' ranges implies that doubling CO_2 would lead to about a 15% increase in global biomass. Applying this relation-

ship in the carbon cycle model described above assuming no lag between CO_2 increases and biomass increases, I find that CO_2 fertilization produces a gain of -0.013. This calculation does not take into account increases in soil carbon storage resulting from the higher rate of organic matter input. Kohlmaier and colleagues (chapter 26, this volume) found this to be an important contribution to the net flux to the biosphere from CO_2 fertilization. Considering their result and the ranges given by Gates and Shugart, I adopt a central estimate for the fertilization feedback of -0.02 and a range of -0.01 to -0.04.

Methane Emissions The methane branch of the organic matter decay chain will also be perturbed by climatic change. Changes in water balance may be a critical factor, particularly in determining the land area subject to methanogenesis, as flooding seems to be the essential ingredient in producing the necessary anaerobic conditions. Unfortunately predicted changes in precipitation are highly uncertain and GCM soil moisture treatments are so far inadequate for drawing specific conclusions about ecological impacts. For simplicity I assume here that wetland area does not change and consider only the temperature effect on methanogenesis. For natural wetlands I further limit my attention to high-latitude bogs because coastal wetlands are not significant sources of methane and low-latitude wetlands tend to be carbon limited, suggesting that temperature change per se will not have a significant impact on their annual methane emissions.

Methane emissions from bogs can be expected to increase as the result of two complementary factors: the length of the emissions season will increase because the period when the ground is frozen will decrease and the average emissions rate will increase because of the direct temperature response of microbes. Rather than attempt to model absolute methane emissions, the perturbation to bog emissions is estimated as the product of the season length and temperature effects summed over latitude bands (Lashof and Fung, unpublished). Emissions estimates are based on bog area from Matthews and Fung (1987) aggregated to the latitude bands of the GISS GCM, and values for the season length and temperature changes were derived from zonally averaged surface temperature values over land from GISS $2 \times CO_2$ and $1 \times CO_2$ results (Hansen et al., 1983).

Given the uncertainty that emerges from reviewing the literature on the relationship between methane emissions and temperature (Koyama, 1963; Zeikus and Winfrey, 1976; Baker-Blocker et al., 1977; King and Wiebe, 1978; Svensson, 1980; Kelly and Chynoweth, 1981; Mayer, 1982; Cicerone et al., 1983; Hameed and Cess, 1983; Svensson and Rosswall, 1984; Svensson, 1984; Holzapfel-Pschorn and Seiler, 1986) I have estimated the strength of this feedback using values for Q_{10} (the factor by which the methane emission rate increases for a 10°C temperature increase) between 1 (no temperature effect) and 4. It seems unlikely that the higher values reported in some of the literature would apply to annual average emission rates. Very high Q_{10} values probably reflect either the low-temperature start-up of methanogenesis (Q_{10} approaches infinity as the soil temperature approaches the freezing point) or seasonal variations involving covariance between temperature and other controlling variables (e.g., moisture and organic matter availability). Using the amplification factors discussed under the section on "Release of Methane Hydrates," current bog emissions of 72 Tg/y from Matthews and Fung (1987), and $Q_{10} = 3$, I obtain 0.01 as the central estimate of the gain from wetlands methane emissions (table 43.1); the range (0.003 to 0.015) allows for the possibility that emissions from low-latitude wetlands could also increase somewhat as well as the range for Q_{10}. A similar estimate can be made for increased emissions from rice. My central estimate of 0.006 (table 43.1) assumes that $Q_{10} = 3$, current emissions are 100 Tg/y, and a global temperature increase of 4.2°C warms the major rice growing areas by 2.5°C. Assumptions based on the central estimate of Holzapfel-Pschorn and Seiler (1986)—$Q_{10} = 4$, current emissions = 120 Tg/y—yields a gain of 0.01, which is probably near the upper limit. I set the lower limit to 0, based on the possibility that emissions from rice paddies are carbon- rather than temperature-limited.

Other Terrestrial Biotic Emissions The biosphere plays an important role in emissions of various other atmospheric trace gases and these emissions are also likely to be influenced by climatic change. Although I make no attempt to quantify these effects here, it is worthwhile at least to note some of the potentially important processes. For example, as many as half of nitrous oxide emissions are attributed to microbial processes in natural soils (Bolle et al., 1986). Emissions of N_2O tend to be episodic, depending strongly on the pattern of precipitation events in addition to temperature and soil

properties (Sahrawat and Keeney, 1986). Thus it seems likely that climatic change would be accompanied by significant changes in N_2O emissions, although there may not be sufficient understanding of the microbiology to develop predictive models at present. The biosphere is also a key source of atmospheric nonmethane hydrocarbons (NMHCs), which play an important role in global tropospheric chemistry; the oxidation of NMHCs generates a substantial share of global carbon monoxide, therefore influencing the concentration of OH and the lifetime of methane (Mooney et al., 1987; Thompson and Cicerone, 1986), and NMHCs participate in tropospheric O_3 formation. As much as 0.5%–1% of photosynthate is lost as isoprene and terpene (Mooney et al., 1987). Lamb and colleagues (1987) found that biogenic NMHC emissions in the United States are about a factor of two greater than anthropogenic emissions. The ratio for the globe is probably greater. Emissions, at least for isoprene and α-pinene are exponentially related to temperature (Lamb et al., 1987; Mooney et al., 1987). The first-order impact of climatic change, then, is to increase NMHC emissions, producing a positive feedback through the CO-OH-CH_4 and tropospheric O_3 links. The actual impact when changes in ecosystem distribution are considered is uncertain, however, as different species have very different emissions (Lamb et al., 1987).

Energy Demand
The last biogeochemical feedback that I consider is mediated by one of the most interesting organisms on the planet—*Homo sapiens*. Climate change affects human activity in a myriad of ways, and thus influences anthropogenic emissions of greenhouse gases. Attempting to predict the magnitude (or even the direction) of these changes is beyond the scope of this chapter, but the particular case of electricity demand for heating and cooling has been examined. Linder and Inglis (1989) estimate that annual electricity consumption increases by -0.5% to 2.7%/°C for utilities in the United States, depending on the local climate and the saturation of electrical heating and air-conditioning equipment. If climate change leads to changes in saturation levels then substantially greater sensitivities are possible (Linder et al., 1987). Currently 37% of total CO_2 emissions from fossil fuels are produced by electric utilities and this share is expected to increase in the future (e.g., Rotty and Reister, 1986). Applying the U.S. average sensitivity of 1.0% obtained by Linder and Inglis

(1989) to the rest of the world, and taking the utility share of CO_2 emissions as 40%, I obtain a feedback on CO_2 emissions of 0.4%/°C. Applying this in the carbon cycle model yields a gain of 0.001; the range of demand sensitivities found by Linder and Inglis suggests uncertainty bounds of 0 to 0.004. Direct use of fuel for heating was not considered by Linder and Inglis, and decreases in emissions from this source will at least partially compensate for increased electricity demand.

Discussion

It is inappropriate simply to add all of the estimates displayed in table 43.1 because the feedback processes may not be independent and may not occur at the same time. Hansen and colleagues (1984, 1985) have shown, for example, that the heat capacity of the oceans makes the response time of the system proportional to the square of the amplification due to geophysical climate feedbacks that act essentially instantaneously. Consideration of biogeochemical feedbacks introduces additional time constants that may further delay the attainment of equilibrium. A best estimate of the overall impact of biogeochemical feedbacks over the next century therefore requires selectively combining the feedbacks in table 43.1.

The methane hydrate feedback was calculated based on an increased flux of methane as ocean sediments warm. The total amount of hydrate available is vast compared with the amount that would be released over a century; however, the onset of releases could be delayed relative to atmospheric warming. I have attempted to take this into account by assuming that the average temperature change at the top of the hydrate-containing sediments will be half of the atmospheric warming. The tropospheric chemistry feedback will act with a time constant similar to the lifetime of methane, and therefore can be considered operative over the period of interest here. The ocean chemistry and eddy-diffusion feedbacks are presumably largely subsumed by the overall ocean biology and circulation feedback deduced from changes that occurred during the last deglaciation. Reduced heat uptake by the ocean (part of the eddy-diffusion feedback) is an additional factor that could contribute to the rate of climatic change during the next century, but would not affect the equilibrium warming. For consistency, then, it seems appropriate to include only the biology and circulation feedback in the best estimate.

The vegetation albedo feedback assumes that boreal forest will invade the tundra, decreasing the surface albedo. Significant dieback of current boreal forests, resulting in substantial carbon releases (respiration feedback), could occur before the current tundra is colonized because of the limited dispersal rates of trees. Carbon losses from soils, however, could occur simultaneously with decreasing albedo due to shifts in live vegetation. The CO_2 fertilization feedback responds directly to changes in atmospheric concentrations, implying that it may occur more quickly than the feedbacks that respond to temperature and therefore involve the heat capacity of the oceans. The disruption of terrestrial ecosystems by climatic change, however, does seem likely eventually to overwhelm the effectiveness of CO_2 fertilization (assuming that anthropogenic emissions of greenhouse gases are unconstrained). Over a century, then, it may be best to assume that the respiration and fertilization feedbacks offset each other, and that the albedo feedback is only half realized. The methane feedbacks from wetlands and rice would be operative within this time frame, though it is worth noting again that the effect of changes in water status may overwhelm the effect of warming. Finally, increased emissions from higher electricity demand may be offset by decreased emissions from heating, so this (small) feedback is neglected in the best estimate given below.

Combining the feedbacks as reviewed in the previous paragraphs (methane hydrates, 0.1; tropospheric chemistry, −0.04; ocean biology and circulation, 0.06; vegetation albedo, 0.025; wetlands, 0.01; and rice, 0.006) yields a best estimate of 0.16 for the gain from biogeochemical feedbacks. Adding this estimate to the gain from geophysical feedbacks based on the review by Dickinson (1986) gives a total gain of 0.80, which would increase the climate sensitivity to an initial doubling of CO_2 from 3.5°C to 6.3°C. Quadratically combining the error estimates gives a range of 0.05 to 0.29 for the biogeochemical feedbacks and 0.32 and 0.98 for the system as a whole, implying a climate sensitivity of 1.9 to greater than 10°C.

Although the high end of the range calculated for the gain of the entire system implies an amplification factor of 50, this estimate cannot be taken seriously. Linearity, implicitly assumed in using gain to calculate amplification, is certainly not valid for temperature excursions much beyond the 2°C to 5°C range used to calculate the gains. Saturation of the H_2O, CO_2, and CH_4 absorption bands, geographical limits on the ice, snow, and vegetation albedo feedbacks, and limits on the supply of carbon for the vegetation respiration and wetland feedbacks all tend to stabilize the system near the upper limit of sensitivity. Nonetheless, the analysis presented here shows, as suggested by Kellogg (1983), that biogeochemical feedbacks have the potential to make the climate system substantially more sensitive to perturbations than is generally assumed.

Conclusion

The largest feedbacks that will come into play during the next century are almost certainly the geophysical climate feedbacks (water vapor, clouds, ice and snow albedo). The other feedbacks discussed here are individually rather modest in comparison—each probably has a gain of 0.1 or less, compared with 0.4 for the water vapor feedback. The most important biogeochemical feedbacks appear to be methane hydrates, ocean mixing and circulation, and vegetation albedo. In a high-gain system, however, the total amplification is very sensitive to small additional gains. Although there are many uncertainties, there is therefore the potential for the biogeochemical feedbacks discussed here to increase substantially the overall sensitivity of the climate system. A climate sensitivity as great as 8°C or even 10°C for an initial radiative forcing equivalent to doubling CO_2 cannot be ruled out. Thus this analysis suggests that rather than stabilizing the climate system, the biosphere is likely to amplify anthropogenic climate change.

The perturbations to global biogeochemical cycles reflected in the feedback processes discussed here are of great importance in their own right in addition to whatever gain they contribute to the climate system. The vegetation albedo feedback, for example, contributed only 0.3°C out of the 3.6°C global cooling in the ice-age analysis reported by Hansen and colleagues (1984), but this represented a massive reorganization of terrestrial ecosystems. A better quantitative assessment of both the impact of climatic change on biogeochemical cycles and the associated feedbacks is urgently needed and will require the incorporation of biogeochemical processes into transient models of the climate system.

Acknowledgments

This work would not have been possible without the help of I. Fung, who provided important discussions, much of the computer code used to construct the ocean model, data used to calculate the wetlands feedback, and critical comments on a draft of the manuscript. Helpful comments were also provided by R. Dickinson, J. Hoffman, P. Martin, P. Tans, D. Tirpak, and two anonymous reviewers.

References

Bacastow, R., and Keeling, C. 1973. Atmospheric carbon dioxide and radiocarbon in the natural carbon cycle: Changes from A.D. 1700 to 2070 as deduced from a geochemical model. In: Woodwell, G., and Pecan, E., eds. *Carbon and the Biosphere*. (CONF-720510). Washington, D.C.: Atomic Energy Commission. Available from National Technical Information Service, Springfield, Va.

Baker-Blocker, A., Donahue, T., and Mancy, K. 1977. Methane flux from wetlands areas. *Tellus,* 29, 245–250.

Bell, P. 1982. Methane hydrate and the carbon dioxide question. In: Clark, W., ed. *Carbon Dioxide Review: 1982.* New York: Oxford University Press, 255–277.

Billings, W., Luken, J., Mortensen, D., and Petersen, K. 1982. Arctic tundra: A source or sink for atmospheric carbon dioxide in a changing environment. *Oecologia,* 58, 7–11.

Billings, W., Luken, J., Mortensen, D., and Petersen, K. 1983. Increasing atmospheric carbon dioxide: Possible effects on arctic tundra. *Oecologia,* 58, 286–289.

Blake, D., and Rowland, F. 1986. World-wide increase in tropospheric methane, 1978–1983. *J Atmospheric Chem,* 4, 43–62.

Bolle, H., Seiler, W., and Bolin, B. 1986. Other greenhouse gases and aerosols. In: Bolin, B., Doos, B., Jager, J., and Warrick, R. eds. *The Greenhouse Effect, Climate Change, and Ecosystems.* Chichester: Wiley, 157–203.

Bolin, B., Doos, B., Jager, J., and Warrick, R. eds. 1986. *The Greenhouse Effect, Climate Change, and Ecosystems.* Chichester: Wiley.

Brasseur, G., and De Rudder, A. 1987. The potential impact on atmospheric ozone and temperature of increasing trace gas concentrations. *J Geophys Res,* 92, 10903–10920.

Broecker, W. 1987. Unpleasant surprises in the greenhouse? *Nature,* 328, 123–126.

Broecker, W., Peteet, D., and Rind, D. 1985. Does the ocean-atmosphere system have more than one stable mode of operation. *Nature,* 315, 21–26.

Cess, R., and Potter, G. 1988. A methodology for understanding and intercomparing atmospheric climate feedback processes in general circulation models. *J Geophys Res,* 93, 8305–8314.

Cess, R.D., Potter, G.L., Blanchet, J.P., Boer, G.J., Ghan, S.J., Kiehl, J.T., Le Treut, H., Li, Z.-X., Liang, X.-Z., Mitchell, J.F.B., Morcrette, J.-J., Randall, D.A., Riches, M.R., Roeckner, E., Schlese, U., Slingo, A., Taylor, K.E., Washington, W.M., Wetherald, R.T., and Yagai, I. 1989. Interpretation of cloud-climate feedback as produced by 14 atmospheric general circulation models. *Science,* 245, 513–516.

Charlson, R., Lovelock, J., Andreae, M., and Warren, S. 1987. Oceanic phytoplankton, atmospheric sulphur, cloud albedo and climate. *Nature*, 326, 655–661.

Cicerone, R., Shetter, J., and Delwiche, C. 1983. Seasonal variations of methane flux from a California rice paddy. *J Geophys Res*, 88, 11022–11024.

Dickinson, R. 1986. The climate system and modelling of future climate. In Bolin, B., Doos, B., Jager, J., and Warrick, R. eds. *The Greenhouse Effect Climatic, Change, and Ecosystems*. Chichester: Wiley, 207–270.

Dickinson, R., and Hanson, B. 1984. Vegetation-albedo feedbacks. In: Hansen, J., and Takahashi, T., eds. *Climate Processes and Climate Sensitivity*. Geophysical Monograph 29, Maurice Ewing Volume 5. Washington, D.C.: American Geophysical Union, 180–186.

Emanuel, W., Shugart, H., and Stevenson, M. 1985a. Climate change and the broad scale distribution of terrestrial ecosystem complexes. *Climatic Change*, 7, 29–43.

Emanuel, W., Shugart, H., and Stevenson, M. 1985b. Response to comment: Climatic change and the broad-scale distribution of terrestrial ecosystem complexes. *Climatic Change*, 7, 457–460.

Gates, D. 1985. Global biospheric response to increasing atmospheric carbon dioxide concentration. In: Strain, B., and Cure, J., eds. *Direct Effects of Increasing Carbon Dioxide on Vegetation*. Report DOE/ER-0238. Washington, D.C.: United States Department of Energy.

Hameed S., and Cess, R. 1983. Impact of a global warming on biospheric sources of methane and its climatic consequences. *Tellus*, 35B, 1–7.

Hansen, J., Fung, I., Lacis, A., Lebedeff, S., Rind, D., Ruedy, R., Russell, G., and Stone, P. 1988. Global climate changes as forecast by the GISS 3-D model. *J Geophys Res*, 93, 9341–9364.

Hansen, J., Lacis, A., Rind, D., Russell, G., Stone, P., Fung, I., Ruedy, R., and Lerner, J. 1984. Climate sensitivity: Analysis of feedback mechanisms. In: Hansen, J., and Takahashi, T. eds. *Climate Processes and Climate Sensitivity*. Geophysical Monograph 29, Maurice Ewing Volume 5. Washington, D.C.: American Geophysical Union, 130–163.

Hansen, J., Russell, G., Lacis, A., Fung, I., and Rind, D. 1985. Climate response times: Dependence on climate sensitivity and ocean mixing. *Science*, 229, 857–859.

Hansen, J., Russell, G., Rind, D., Stone, P., Lacis, A., Lebedeff, S., Ruedy, R., and Travis, L. 1983. Efficient three-dimensional global models for climate studies: Model I and II. *Monthly Weather Rev*, 111, 609–662.

Holzapfel-Pschorn, A., and Seiler, W. 1986. Methane emission during a cultivation period from an Italian rice paddy. *J Geophys Res*, 91, 11803–11814.

Houghton, R. 1987. Biotic changes consistent with the increased seasonal amplitude of atmospheric CO_2 concentrations. *J Geophys Res*, 92, 4223–4230.

Houghton, R. 1988. Reply to S. Idso, comment on 'Biotic changes consistent with increased seasonal amplitude of atmospheric CO_2 concentrations.' *J Geophys Res*, 93, 1747–1748.

Idso, S. 1988. Comment on 'Biotic changes consistent with increased seasonal amplitude of atmospheric CO_2 concentrations' by R. A. Houghton. *J Geophys Res*, 93, 1745–1746.

Jouzel, J., Lorius, C., Petit, J., Genthon, C., Barkov, N., Kotlyakov, V., and Petrov, V. 1987. Vostok ice core: A continuous isotope temperature record over the last climate cycle (160,000 years). *Nature*, 329, 403–418.

Keir, R. 1988. On the late Pleistocene ocean geochemistry and circulation. *Paleoceanography*, 3, 413–445.

Kellogg, W. 1983. Feedback mechanisms in the climate system affecting future levels of carbon dioxide. *J Geophys Res*, 88, 1263–1269.

Kelly, C., and Chynoweth, D. 1981. The contributions of temperature and of the input of organic matter in controlling rates of sediment methanogenesis. *Limnol Oceanogr*, 26, 891–897.

King, G., and Wiebe, W. 1978. Methane release from soils of a Georgia salt marsh. *Geochim Cosmochim Acta*, 42, 343–348.

Knox, F., and McElroy, M. 1984. Changes in atmospheric CO_2: Influence of the marine biota at high latitude. *J Geophys Res*, 89, 4629–4637.

Koyama, T. 1963. Gaseous metabolism in lake sediments and paddy soils and the production of atmospheric methane and hydrogen. *J Geophys Res*, 68, 3971–3973.

Kvenvolden, K. 1988. Methane hydrates and global climate. *Global Biogeochem Cycles*, 2, 221–229.

Kvenvolden, K., and Barnard, L. 1984. Hydrates of natural gas in continental margins. *Am Assoc Petro Geol Memoir*, 34, 631–640.

Lamb, B., Guenther, A., Gay, D., and Westberg, H. 1987. A national inventory of biogenic hydrocarbon emissions. *Atmospheric Environment*, 21, 1695–1705.

Lashof, D. 1987. *The Role of the Biosphere in the Global Carbon Cycle: Evaluation Through Biospheric Modeling and Atmospheric Measurement*. Ph.D. Dissertation, Energy and Resources Group. Berkeley, University of California (available from University Microfilms, Ann Arbor).

Lashof, D. 1989a. The dynamic greenhouse: Feedback processes that may influence future concentrations of atmospheric trace gases and climatic change. *Climatic Change*, 14, 213–242.

Lashof, D. 1989b. The dynamic greenhouse: Feedback processes that can influence global warming. In: Topping, J., ed. *Coping with Climate Change*. Washington, D.C.: Climate Institute, 102–110.

Legrand, M.R., Delmas, R.J., and Charlson, R.J. 1988. Climate forcing implications from Vostok ice-core sulphate data. *Nature*, 334, 418–420.

Linder, K., Gibbs, M., and Inglis, M. 1987. (December). *Potential Impacts of Climate Change on Electric Utilities*. Albany, N.Y.: Report New York State Energy Research and Development Authority 88-2.

Linder, K., and Inglis, M. 1990. *The Potential Impacts of Climate Change on Electric Utilities: Regional and National Estimates*. Washington, D.C.: U.S. Environmental Protection Agency.

Manabe, S., and Stouffer, R. 1980. Sensitivity of a global climate model to an increase of CO_2 concentration in the atmosphere. *J Geophys Res*, 85, 5529–5554.

Matthews, E., and Fung, I. 1987. Methane emission from natural wetlands: Global distribution, area, and environmental characteristics of sources. *Global Biogeochem Cycles*, 1, 61–86.

Mayer, E. 1982. *Atmospheric Methane: Concentration, Swamp Flux and Latitudinal Source Distribution.* Ph.D. Thesis. Irvine: University of California. As cited by Blake and Rowland (1986).

Mooney, H., Vitousek, P., and Matson, P. 1987. Exchange of material between terrestrial ecosystems and the atmosphere. *Science,* 238, 926–932.

National Research Council. 1979. *Carbon Dioxide and Climate: A Scientific Assessment.* Washington, D.C.: National Academy Press.

National Research Council. 1983. *Changing Climate.* Washington, D.C.: National Academy Press.

Oeschger, H., Seigenthaler, U., Schotterer, U., and Gugelmann, A. 1975. A box diffusion model to study the carbon dioxide exchange in nature. *Tellus,* 27, 168–192.

Owens, A., Hales, C., Filkin, D., Miller, C., Steed, M., and Jesson, J. 1985. A coupled one-dimensional radiative-convective, chemistry-transport model of the atmosphere. 1. Model structure and steady state perturbation calculations. *J Geophys Res,* 90, 2283–2311.

Ramanathan, V., Callis, L., Cess, R., Hansen, J., Isaksen, I., Kuhn, W., Lacis, A., Luther, F., Mahlman, J., Reck, R., and Schlesinger, M. 1987. Climate-chemical interactions and effects of changing atmospheric trace gases. *Rev Geophys,* 25, 1441–1482.

Revelle, R. 1983. Methane hydrates in continental slope sediments and increasing atmospheric carbon dioxide. In: National Research Council. *Changing Climate.* Washington, D.C.: National Academy Press.

Robock, A. 1983. Ice and snow feedbacks and the latitudinal and seasonal distribution of climate sensitivity. *J Atmospheric Sci,* 40, 977–986.

Roeckner, E., Schlese, U., Biercamp, J., and Loewe, P. 1987. Cloud optical depth feedbacks and climate modelling. *Nature,* 329, 138–140.

Rotty, R. 1982. Fossil fuel and cement production, 1860–1980. In: Clark, W., ed. *Carbon Dioxide Review: 1982.* New York: Oxford University Press, 456–460.

Rotty, R., and Reister, D. 1986. The use of energy scenarios in addressing the CO_2 question. *J Air Pollution Control Assoc,* 36, 1111–1115.

Sahrawat, K., and Keeney, D. 1986. Nitrous oxide emission from soils. *Adv Sci,* 4, 103–148.

Sarmiento, J., and Toggweiler, J. 1984. A new model for the role of the oceans in determining atmospheric pCO_2. *Nature,* 308, 621–624.

Schlesinger, M., and Mitchell, J. 1985. Model projections of the equilibrium climatic response to increased carbon dioxide. In: MacCracken, M., and Luther, F., eds. *Projecting the Climatic Effects of Increasing Carbon Dioxide.* Washington, D.C.: United States Department of Energy, 81–147.

Shugart, H. 1984. *A Theory of Forest Dynamics.* New York: Springer-Verlag, 203–206.

Siegenthaler, U., and Wenk, Th. 1984. Rapid atmospheric CO_2 variations and ocean circulation. *Nature,* 308, 624–626.

Solomon, A. 1986. Transient response of forests to CO_2-induced climate change: Simulation modeling experiments in eastern North America. *Oecologia,* 68, 567–579.

Somerville, R., and Remer, L. 1984. Cloud optical thickness feedbacks in the CO_2 climate problem. *J Geophys Res,* 89, 9668–9672.

Svensson, B. 1980. Carbon dioxide and methane fluxes from the ombrotrophic parts of a subarctic mire. *Ecol Bull (Stockholm),* 30, 235–250.

Svensson, B. 1984. Different temperature optima for methane formation when enrichments from acid peat are supplemented with acetate or hydrogen. *Appl Environment Microbiol,* 48, 389–394.

Svensson, B., and Rosswall, T. 1984. In situ methane production from acid peat in plant communities with different moisture regimes in a subarctic mire. *OIKOS,* 43, 341–350.

Takahashi, T., Broecker, W., Bainbridge, A., and Weiss, R. 1980. *Carbonate Chemistry of the Atlantic, Pacific, and Indian Oceans: The Results of the GEOSECS Expeditions, 1972–1978.* Report CU-1-80. Palisades, N.Y.: Lamont-Doherty Geological Observatory.

Thompson, A., and Cicerone, R. 1986. Possible perturbations to atmospheric CO, CH_4, and OH. *J Geophys Res,* 91, 10853–10864.

Wigley, T. 1989. Possible climate change due to SO_2-derived cloud condensation nuclei. *Nature,* 339, 365–367.

Wilson, C.A., and Mitchell, J.F.B. 1987. A 2 × CO_2 climate sensitivity experiment with a global climate model including a simple ocean. *J Geophys Res,* 92, 13315–13343.

Woodwell, G. 1986. Global warming: And what we can do about it. *Amicus J.,* 8, 8–12.

World Meteorological Organization. 1986. Report of the International Conference on the Assessment of the Role of Carbon Dioxide and of Other Greenhouse Gases in Climate Variations and Associated Impacts. Villach, Austria, 9–15 October 1985. WMO No. 661. (As quoted in Bolin, B., et al., eds. *The Greenhouse Effect, Climatic Change, and Ecosystems.* SCOPE 29. Chichester: Wiley, xx–xxiv.)

Zeikus, J., and Winfrey, M. 1976. Temperature limitation of methanogenesis in aquatic sediments. *Appl Environment Microbiol,* 31, 99–107.

Congressman George E. Brown, Jr.
and Anthony Ellsworth Scoville
44
The Greenhouse Civilization and the Gaia Hypothesis: A View from Congress

The Gaia hypothesis may become one of the philosophical foundations of the emerging Greenhouse Civilization, mankind's first global culture. The Greenhouse Civilization is the result of the twentieth-century information revolution driving our species' deep economic and technological penetration of the planetary cycles of energy and materials—cycles that created and sustained life on Earth for the past four billion years.

What are the political and economic implications of the new understanding of our living planet? How are some of these issues revealing themselves in the Congress? What economic levers might harmonize man's activities with global environmental cycles? And what fundamental changes in our political and social constitution might the Congress confront a century from now as the full effects of man's influence on the greenhouse effect and similar phenomena manifest themselves?

These questions suggest a deep connection between the global economy and the environment. Although this connection may seem apparent in the abstract, it is difficult to respect in the practice of scientific research, in daily commerce, and in political debates. As earth scientists study the faint early Sun paradox, the salinity balance of the oceans, or sulfide emissions of phytoplankton, it is unlikely that their thoughts are factoring in such matters as trade policy, savings and investment rates, banking regulations, and stock market speculation. But these economic variables are major factors affecting the future of the environment. We believe that the scientific community must involve itself early in economic, social, and political debates. Institutions

Congressman George E. Brown, Jr. is the Chairman of the House of Representatives Committee on Science, Space, and Technology.

Anthony Ellsworth Scoville is a Consultant on Science and Economic Policy to the Office of Congressman George E. Brown, Jr.

must be devised to give the scientific community a clear and effective voice in policy debates. In turn, the scientific community must speak out and offer solutions, on the basis of best available evidence. As in the case of climate warming, decisions must be made in anticipation of scientific certainty because certain evidence may herald irreversible environmental and social damage, or lost technological leadership.

In attempting to influence public policy, scientists must appreciate the difficulty of capturing the attention of Congress in the maelstrom of issues that confront its members daily. It is important to appreciate that the scale of environmental impacts relative to the economic currents that sweep our national and international political agenda is often small, especially in economic present values. This is true even for global problems such as greenhouse warming.

For example, capital investment is our lever on the future. Policies on investment affect the flow of trillions of dollars annually and define the general character of an economy, from education to energy use, for thirty to fifty years hence. Policy responses to the changed economic climate in the wake of the 1987 stock market crash may seem far removed from the subject of the conference but we believe they have a profound connection with the deliberations of the participants.

What is the relationship between the stock market crash and the greenhouse effect? How do the predicted effects of global warming compare with other events that buffet policy makers? It has been crudely estimated that the costs of a warmer climate associated with a doubling of carbon dioxide levels might amount to 3% of gross world product, or about $500 billion annually. This is a staggering sum and the costs will be felt by millions of people. However, consider that between August 15 and October 19, 1987, the value of stock listed on the New York Stock Exchange alone fell by $1 trillion and pension plan assets, upon which our elderly depend, declined by nearly $200 billion.

Given the magnitude of these losses, and more recently, the $100 billion required to rescue insolvent savings and loan banks, it should not be surprising when members of Congress seem deaf to pleas for action to avert climate change thirty years from now. To be heard over the din, scientists must ally themselves with other groups concerned with dramatically changing climates in the political and economic arenas, for example groups promoting trade competitiveness.

There is another important lesson to be drawn from the stock market crash. It concerns the timing of scientific advice in order to maximize its impact on policies. Political and economic leadership often requires that one must act when a society is ready to move even when one does not have perfect information about the future. Scientists must offer advice when society is ready to move on distantly related issues—not necessarily when scientists are ready to do so. Had scientists waited until proof of the ability to build an atomic bomb existed, the Manhattan Project would never have been undertaken. But the urgency of World War II compelled the leading physicists of the day to act upon the best available knowledge. Thus for better or worse, Einstein's letter to Roosevelt came to be written.

Congress is often criticized for reacting only to crises. But there are times when, in the course of meeting an immediate crisis, the resulting policies set the political and economic stage for generations to come. Fifty years ago, Franklin Roosevelt and the Congress were trying to meet the immediate problem of putting people back to work and providing a modicum of income security. They established Social Security, Unemployment Compensation, the Securities and Exchange Commission, government sponsorship of research and development, and Keynesian economic policies, which have provided the background for our economic growth from 1932 to the present day. We believe the 1987 crash is a strong indication that the United States has again entered one of those pivotal periods in its history when what we do today will endure through our children's lives well into the period when climate warming will become significant. It is also during this immediate future, and not much later, that investments to alleviate global warming could achieve sufficient market penetration to have a significant effect before substantial warming is expected. The scientific community must learn the lesson of economic and political timing if it hopes to affect policies on, for example, global energy use.

As mentioned previously, capital formation and investment are a society's lever on the future and are crucial to meeting problems like climate warming and the maintenance of technological leadership. Consider then a possible response to the 1987 crash. We believe that in the coming years the nation must stabilize its capital markets from panics and must increase savings for long-term investment in education and innovative technology necessary for United States' industrial competitiveness. To meet these needs we have proposed the creation of a National Retirement Account Bank (NRAB) capitalized by surpluses in the Society Security trust funds that will eventually amount to $13 trillion. Currently these surpluses can be invested only in U.S. Treasury bonds and serve to reduce the apparent budget deficit of the federal government. The proposed bank would be empowered to invest the surpluses throughout the economy in both public and private securities, with emphasis on new capital investment rather than simply trading in secondary issues. In times of panic or excessive speculation, the bank would buy or sell securities to moderate market gyrations, just as the Federal Reserve now protects banks from runs on deposits. Computer simulations conducted by one of us indicate that if these investments earn an 8.5% real return, the Social Security taxes could be repealed thirty years from now at the very time when Congress will be under great pressure to raise these taxes in order to pay benefits to the retiring children of the baby boom 1950s. By historical standards 8.5% is a high real return, but the figure has been exceeded for most of the 1980s by private pension funds, according to figures compiled by the Employee Benefit Research Institute.

This example may seem far removed from the concerns of earth scientists and environmental activists, but our point is that if Congress establishes such a bank or modifies the investment mandate of Social Security Trust funds, or if Congress establishes an equivalent set of private investment incentives, then the scientific community must speak out on the need to consider long-term environmental change like global warming when such investments are made.

Unfortunately, at the time of this writing, it appears that Social Security surpluses will continue to be invested in the federal deficit and nearly $100 billion dollars in annual savings will continue to be expended with no thought for the future except in the small portion of the budget that goes for civilian research and development. The examples could be multiplied. For example, we are unaware of any scientist or environmental group having argued that funds to bail out failed savings and loans should not be reinvested in oil field and related real estate speculation, which fueled the current bust. Such a policy would make sense both for banking prudence and for the alleviation of global warming. And we are unaware of any scientific organization's suggesting that reductions in capital gains taxes should be tied to the life cycle and timing of technological innovation rather than to arbitrary six-month or one-year periods. Although scientists would be eminently qualified to speak on these subjects, Congress has not heard from them.

It is often argued that the introduction of scientific and environmental factors in such areas as bank regulation will impair the economic efficiency of the free market. Many view environmental policies as unmitigated costs. We believe this view is mistaken. On the long timetable of capital investment, environmental policies could create immense and highly profitable markets if policy makers and business leaders anticipate, rather than resist, oncoming changes. However, just as is the case for normal economic competition, if the United States desires to capture markets created by the need to protect the global environment, then we believe it must create a banking system with a profitable investment horizon that includes the time when economic changes are expected, whether they come from the environment or from our international competitors.

For example, the reduction of world temperature increases will create a very large market for energy conservation devices as well as nonfossil forms of energy. In addition, adaptation to those moderate temperature increases to which the world is already committed will create substantial markets for new varieties of seeds, high-efficiency air conditioning, and new public water supplies. The beneficiaries of these markets will be the nations and businesses that invest in greenhouse technologies rather than pretending that we do not know enough about the

warming to begin the necessary technical and financial development. If we are correct in our belief that environmental protection creates economic markets, rather than costs, over a generation's time, then the day will come when industry pools funds for joint venture basic research on climate change, under the Federal Co-operative Research and Development Act of 1984, because it must do so in order to plan its investments!

Whether considering international competitiveness or climate change, however, in order to achieve the synergy between economic opportunity and societal and environmental needs, it is imperative that financial regulations create capital markets with investment horizons commensurate with the life cycle of new technologies and the time constants of environmental systems. Presently this is impossible because all investment analyses discount the value of future returns by market interest rates. A dollar of cost or benefit thirty years hence is worth about six cents today. In his book the *Coevolution of Climate and Life,* Stephen Schneider has an excellent example of the pernicious effect of discounting. There he notes that a $2.5 trillion loss of coastal property due to rising sea levels 150 years from now has a present value of only $75 million today (Schneider and Londer, 1984).

Discounting leads to absurd conclusions about the future. When the Federal Reserve raises interest rates to combat inflation, the present value of future costs incurred from climate change declines sharply. Are we really to believe that the economic costs of a warmer climate disappear if the Fed decides to take a hard line on inflation? Do the returns from investing in new conservation technology likewise decline and do they rise when interest rates decline because the economy is in a recession? That is what current investment theory and practice would have one believe. The old controversy between the virtues of planning and the free market is sterile because no one has ever tried to create a true free market for the future. Indeed, given present discounting practices, such a market is impossible today. One cannot have a market when all the goods, services, and costs in that market have no value.

We believe that one of the highest priorities for basic research on economics, technological innovation, and environmental policy should be developing new discount mechanisms that express the life cycle of new technologies and the life cycle of new knowledge and skills in the labor force. This type of interdisciplinary research is underrated by the National Science Foundation and by academic communities delimited by rigid departmental boundaries.

Researchers should find these topics of fundamental scientific as well as practical interest. Now that the global economy is a major factor in the operation of global environmental cycles, the rate of environmental and geological evolution will be substantially determined by savings and investment rates, fiscal policy, and discount rates governing the type of energy used and emission rates of pollutants. In short, natural evolution has become a component of economic history and vice versa. No longer can man act as though there were a natural environment and a separate human economy. They are combined in what we call the "greenhouse economy." Effective response to this new reality requires that scientists and technologists become integral parts of economic policy making.

How might scientific input to economic policy be effected? Currently, at both the national and international levels there is virtually no coordination between science and technology policy, environmental policy, and economic policy, even though Nobel economics laureate Robert Solow estimates that technological innovation has been the largest single contributor to economic growth over the past century. To rectify this situation, one of the authors has introduced legislation that would establish a cabinet-level Department of Science and Technology. In addition, the authors propose

(1) Merging the Office of Science and Technology Policy, the Council on Environmental Quality, and the Council of Economic Advisors;

(2) Requiring that at least some members of the Boards of Governors of the Federal Reserve banks have scientific and technical backgrounds;

(3) Requiring that the Federal Reserve Board consider investment in science and technology when making decisions on interest rates and money supplies; and

(4) Requiring that the International Monetary Fund explore new methods for refinancing developing nations debt so as to protect ecosystems like the tropical forests of the Amazon.

Concerning the fourth recommendation, at present, nations like Brazil are forced to exploit their natural resources in order to meet debt obligations. Yet Brazilian bankers have privately indicated their interest in a "debt for clean air and climate swap" along the lines of the innovative exchanges of debt for forest reserves that have occurred in Bolivia and Costa Rica. We were pleased to read James Lovelock's letter in *Geology* which made a similar proposal (Nisbet and Lovelock, 1987). In order to affect investment decisions, however, these ideas need to be published in the *Wall Street Journal* and the *Economist,* not *Geology.*

Opportunities for alliance with disparate political groups continue to arise and must be utilized by scientists and environmental activists. For instance, Latin American drug production is in part driven by the need to find alternate sources of hard currency income not committed to debt service. Scientists concerned about global ecosystems could and should find common cause with President Bush's war on drugs in attempting to find methods for reducing the debt burden that exacerbates both problems. But to our knowledge, the President's science advisor has not spoken out and is not in the decision-making loop on solutions to the social scourge of drug abuse.

In terms of international agreements, the Montreal agreement on stratospheric ozone is an enormously hopeful step in global cooperation on a serious environmental problem. It can be employed as a model for addressing climate change. Because of the inertia of capital investment in energy and agriculture, to address global warming with any success, we believe that the time has come to expand the Vienna-Montreal process to climate change as called for by Mostafa Tolba, executive director of the United Nations Environment Program. Given the importance of integrating science and economic policy, the authors urge that any convention on reducing greenhouse gases consider economic development and investment policies in addition to setting emissions targets.

In sum, the proposals enumerated here are just a few suggestions. These issues seem far removed from the earth sciences, but if the scientific community does not get involved, then momentous decisions will be made by economic institutions without any consideration for scientists' concerns. The time to act is now. The growing pressure of economic and financial problems together with the realignment of economic power away from the postwar dominance of the United States suggests to us that over the next few years Congress will set up new institutions and policies that will set the economic stage for many years to come. If the opportunity is missed, then it will be very difficult to respond in time either to climate warming or to the demands of international competitiveness.

The environmental issues raised by the emergence of a global information economy tapping a substantial fraction of the planet's net primary productivity and by our scientific knowledge of the coevolution of climate and life go far beyond matters of economic policy. They touch our deepest philosophical, spiritual, and ethical beliefs about the place of man in the community of life on Earth. As a result, law makers and citizens alike find themselves questioning the articles of the political constitution and social mores that are the basis for our laws and institutions.

For example, Congress has debated the regulation of biotechnology. Only in its infancy, biotechnology is reunifying the planet's gene pool, which has diverged since nucleated cells developed out of symbiotic colonies of unnucleated prokaryotes. As Lynn Margulis has pointed out, the free exchange of genes occurs routinely between prokaryotes. Now biotechnologists are learning how to transfer genes between eukaryotes. The geep, a cross between a goat and a sheep, is perhaps the most startling example of this genetic unification but is only the first of many that will occur. This is an extraordinary development in the history of life; it may prove as revolutionary as the appearance of nucleated cells and complex multicellular organisms approximately one billion, 400 million years ago. Not since that split has life constituted a global genetic community to the degree that one exists today through the mind of man.

The emergence of this new evolutionary direction is made possible by knowledge. With knowledge arises the opportunity for deliberate choice between alternative courses of action. However, as the biblical tale of Adam and Eve tells us, with choice arising from knowledge come questions of right and wrong, ethics, morality, law, and justice. In rudimentary form, Congress confronts this new form of evolution as it debates the patentability of new seeds and triploid oysters.

More generally, we find ourselves asking whether individual species and ecosystems have a right to survive and whether or not a single cell human embryo is protected by constitutional guarantees. Questions such as these tell us that knowledge of geophysical and biological laws has transformed what we believed to be a blind natural order into a civil and political society applicable to unicellular bacteria as well as to mankind. Before man, the mass extinction of species was apparently no more right or wrong than the drifting of continents or the chance collision of the Earth with comets that caused the extinctions. Now, man must decide whether we have the right to extinguish a quarter of all living species in the next fifty years as he clearcuts tropical forests.

But was the prehuman coevolution of life and the geosphere really blind? That is one of the sharpest controversies surrounding the Gaia hypothesis. Usually, the debate is framed in terms of evidence suggesting or refuting the contention that living species continually adjusted the composition of the atmosphere so as to produce an optimum environment for the survival and propagation of life on Earth. That is the "strong" Gaia hypothesis. Opponents suggest that the geosphere and biosphere merely adjusted to each other. That is the "coevolution" or "weak" form of the Gaia hypothesis.

We suggest that evidence for the resolution of this debate may be closer at hand than is commonly supposed. It may be found in the proceedings of this conference of scientists; it may be found in the debates of Congress, the calculations of engineers, and the investment analyses of bankers and venture capitalists. We suggest that the evolution of Gaia is not exclusively weak or strong but may be characterized by being both weak and strong depending on the perspective chosen. Stripped to its essence, the Gaia hypothesis asserts that the laws of biological evolution are themselves biological phenomena. In that light, one of the most obvious pieces of evidence that any theory of planetary evolution must account for is how human beings, as creatures of Gaia, could meet to discuss what they know about that evolution.

We suggest that the answer is implied by two remarkable theorems governing the limits of knowledge that were proved fifty years ago by the Austrian logician-philosopher Kurt Godel. Godel demonstrated that no formal system of axioms and rules of deduction, powerful enough to prove at least the theorems of the arithmetic of whole numbers, could be both complete and consistent. In other words, the laws of physics and biology, when applied to the whole evolution of the geosphere-biosphere, are examples of formal systems. As such they can never account for all biological or geological phenomena if they are rational or consistent in Godel's terms. In order for those laws to explain the evolution of all life to that life itself, they would have to contain an irrational, that is, contradictory element somewhere among their axioms.

Science is a biological phenomenon, and a fundamental tenet, indeed the precondition, of science is the belief that there is an order to nature that can be discovered by man. Yet if biological evolution can be modeled as a formal system with at least the deductive power of arithmetic, then there will always exist the *potential* for new dimensions in that evolution which cannot be explained by any finite and consistent set of principles until life is extinct. At which point science would no longer exist.

What does that tell us?

First, to the scientist, it should suggest that the coevolution of life and the geological Earth will be punctuated by the expansion of new forms of life into ecological niches created by their antecedents and often revealed by random nonbiological events such as cometary impacts. In other words, at any given time the past evolution of the geosphere-biosphere may be an ordered process amenable to scientific explanation; prospectively, however, it is not possible to define a universal goal for all life through all time since there are always possible future states that are undecidable in terms of past states. Rather, if the next step in evolution is to be a consistent product of previous evolution, then individuals, species, and life as a whole can only act to achieve an optimal condition defined over some restricted period of time in the future. Thus the weak form of the Gaia hypothesis must characterize the behavior of participants in Gaia (to those participants) even though after the fact the evolution of Gaia must appear to seek out some optimal state or condition and thus validate a strong form of the Gaia hypothesis if our knowledge of the past is sufficiently accurate.

Second, what is the significance of the limitations that Godel imposes on evolutionary goals, and on the possibility for rationally planning their achievement, to Congressmen and women and to all of us as citizens of the emerging planetary community that we earlier called the Greenhouse Civilization? Since the Gaia hypothesis claims that the planet

Earth is a complete system, including the changing flux of solar energy over time, then, at some time in the history of Gaia, we should expect to find the appearance of at least one form of life that is not rationally explicable or consistent with any preexisting order. The appearance of sentient human beings with their knowledge of biology, physics, and chemistry, and with their ability to apply this knowledge in technology, is living proof of the irrational completeness of life postulated by the Gaia hypothesis. It can be shown logically that knowledge of the laws of biological evolution, embedded in the mind of man, can no more be derived from those laws than the grammar of a language can be derived from a knowledge of its individual words. The attempt to do so immediately generates the paradoxes of self-reference that Godel has shown always exist in any complete system. Yet human beings are creatures of Gaia; our thoughts exist here and cause us to act upon Earth. That is the paradox of man on Earth.

Even if the coevolution of life and the planet Earth has been blind, with the appearance of the human mind that is no longer so. But our vision is limited. As scientists and engineers, politicians and investment bankers, we must always remember that goals and policies for achieving them are inherently suboptimal, if they are rational. So it shall be for the remainder of history. Under endless guises, in centuries to come, Congress will debate how to guard against the irrational capacity for destruction that human knowledge and its application have brought to the face of the earth. And Congress will also debate how to nurture those inexplicable creative solutions that knowledge provides to expand the domain of life from the oceans' abyss to the depths of space. Through it all, the watchwords must be tolerance and compassion for diversity—of species, environments, and thought.

As the twenty-first century dawns, we are calling ourselves as a species to a convention establishing a constitution for the Greenhouse Civilization. We come, in the words of the Preamble to the United States Constitution, to "form a more perfect (but not perfect) Union, establish Justice, insure domestic Tranquility, provide for the common defense, promote the general Welfare, and secure the Blessings of Liberty to ourselves and our Posterity." It is significant that the authors of the Constitution spoke of securing the Blessings of Liberty to ourselves, not capitalized, and our Posterity, in capital letters for it is in building the future that rationally irreconcilable conflicts arise. As we gather in the chambers of Congress, in our places of business and in our homes, we would do well to recall the words of James Madison, so prescient of Godel's deductions:

It is of great importance in a republic not only to guard against the oppression of its rulers, but to guard any part of society against the injustice of the other part.

If men were angels, no government would be necessary.

Postscript: January 16, 1990

Since this address was given in March 1988, five developments have occurred that reinforce points made at the conference.

First, scientific debate on the Gaia hypothesis has advanced with the publication of Schwartzman and Volk's (1989) paper on the biological enhancement of mineral weathering as a major factor reducing the surface temperature of the Earth to levels suitable for modern plants and animals (Weiss, 1989). To us the paper suggests that human beings could have a significant effect on the carbonate-silicate cycle responsible for sequestering carbon in ocean sediments. It appears that topsoil erosion, humus destruction, and desertification resulting from agriculture could inhibit the production and transport of calcium and bicarbonate ions in ground water, creating a bottleneck in the carbonate-silicate cycle. This bottleneck would tend to raise atmospheric CO_2 levels and climate warming beyond that caused directly by the combustion of fossil fuels.

Since there is no question that human activities have a significant effect on weathering and soil formation, if Schwartzman and Volk's findings are borne out by further research, it appears that human beings will play a role in one of the principal mechanisms by which the Gaia system controls the long-term habitability of the Earth. The extent and even the sign of humanity's effects will depend on the application of science and technology to agriculture and other land use practices.

Second, we are gratified to learn that the economist Charles Weiss concurs with our view that financial discounting severely restricts mankind's ability to factor the life cycle of technology and global environmental cycles that span a generation

or more into economic decisions. Writing in a recent issue of *Climatic Change,* Weiss (1988) remarks, "The events (sea-level rise and the loss of beach-front property) are a long way off (50 years), however, and the discount flow calculus we discussed earlier insures that they will not play a dominant role in the thinking of our banker despite the fact that (s)he is dealing in long-term financial instruments. The same is true of virtually any investment subject to discounting, regardless of the durability of the physical installation or the time span of the financial instrument."

Third, and relatedly, in our address we called for the "development of new discount mechanisms that express the life cycle of new technology." Capital gains taxes, which were so much in the news in 1989, are one method of affecting the discount rate because they alter the after-tax return to an investor. In 1990 there was again a strong push to reduce capital gains taxes and a reduction nearly passed in the Senate as well as the House.

What sort of reduction might be enacted in the future? Will there be a flat reduction in the tax rates or will a reduction reflect the life cycle of technology as we would hope? For example, capital gains taxes might be very high for the first three to five years that an investment is held; then they might decline sharply, perhaps becoming negative between ten and twenty years when a technology matures; finally, these taxes might rise to encourage reinvestment before a technology becomes obsolescent. Similar cyclical tax rates could be designed on a longer timescale for investments in forestry or agriculture. The rates could also be designed so that the life cycle cost of a capital gains tax reduction would be zero; however, the federal government would probably receive higher initial revenues as investors sought to liquidate short-term holdings in favor of long-term investments.

Clearly, the design of tax rates could have a significant effect encouraging both technical innovation to meet foreign trade competition and encouraging investors to consider the long-term environmental consequences of their decisions. Unfortunately, we heard very little from the scientific community concerning these issues. The time to speak out was in 1990 because a capital gains tax reduction would have been passed in 1990; it would not wait until 1995 or 2000 when the first unambiguous signal of a warming climate is detected. Between now and the year 2000 over $1 trillion will have been invested in the United States alone in industry and public infrastructure with regard to climate change.

Fourth, not only the timing but also the amount of investment is crucial to meeting climate change and other problems raised by man's impact on global environmental cycles. Once again, Social Security trust fund surpluses, which we discussed at the conference, are the subject of public debate. These surpluses are substantial and will amount to $100 billion annually in the 1990s. Senator Daniel Moynihan, a member of the 1983 Social Security reform commission and chairman of the Senate Finance subcommittee on Social Security, is proposing to reduce Social Security payroll taxes so as to prevent the use of trust fund surpluses to cover the federal deficit as is now the case. Senator Moynihan's measure may well pass since a tax cut is almost irresistible to Congress especially Democrats who would like to relieve middle-class taxes.

What should be done about the Social Security surpluses? One could continue the present policy, which amounts to enforced savings but provides little investment because the Federal government spends very little on public capital. One could reduce payroll taxes, as proposed by Senator Moynihan, in which case the individual taxpayers will save and invest about 5% of the refund. Finally, one could take steps to ensure that the surpluses are expended on capital investments throughout the public and private sectors as we advocated in our address to the Gaia conference and which has since then been separately endorsed by Federal Reserve Chairman Alan Greenspan. For example, we now propose that Social Security taxes be reduced through a tax credit that could only be taken if invested in an independent retirement account or similar long-term investment.

When coupled to a capital gains tax structure reflecting technological and environmental life cycles, the investment of Social Security surpluses would make an enormous contribution to our stewardship of the Gaia system far beyond the tweaking of National Science Foundation research budgets that preoccupies science policy analysts and professional societies.

Fifth and finally, since 1988, the development with probably the greatest impact on the future of Gaia is the revolution in eastern Europe and the Soviet Union. These nations are at last emerging from the destruction of World War II. For the first time they have the opportunity to build their own version of the development that occurred in western Europe and Japan over the last forty-five years. Will the revolution take this building as an opportunity to change from one of the most polluting and least energy-efficient regions on Earth to cleaner, more energy-efficient economies? The stakes are enormous and the effects of decisions made in the next few years will be felt for the next fifty years. When one considers that in a decade or two Comecon nations may have economies with the same growth rates as the market economy nations, surely the environment should be a factor as the Congress, Western European nations, and multilateral lending agencies grant loans or conclude trade agreements with them.

The cluster of opportunities raised by the Social Security surpluses and capital gains tax debates and by the revolution in eastern Europe illustrates one of the central points of our conference address: namely, that science policy and economic policy must be integrated to advance United States' economic competitiveness, to promote international economic development, and to safeguard the environment. In the Greenhouse Civilization, economic and environmental cycles are inseparable. As recent developments indicate, these issues are more alive today than they were in 1988. We believe that the research and vision of the scientific community will endure far longer than the speeches of congressmen and statesmen. But the time to act is now. To repeat some of our remarks at the conference:

Political and economic leadership often require that one must act when a society is ready to move even when one does not have perfect information about the future. Scientists must offer advice when society is ready to move on distantly related issues—not necessarily when scientists are ready to do so.—The United States has again entered one of those pivotal periods in its history when what we do today will endure through our children's lives well into the period when climate warming will become significant. It is also during this immediate future, and not much later, that investments to alleviate global warming could achieve sufficient market penetration to have a significant effect before substantial warming is expected. The scientific community must learn the lesson of economic and political timing.

References

Schneider, S.H., and Londer, R. 1984. *The Coevolution of Climate and Life*. San Francisco: Sierra Club Books, 439–440.

Nisbet, S.E., and Lovelock, J.E. 1987. "A Modest Proposal." *Geology*, 983.

Schwartzman, D.W., and Volk, T. 1989. Biotic enhancement of weathering and the habitability of earth. *Nature*, 340, 457–460.

Weiss, C. 1989. Can market mechanisms ameliorate the effects of long-term climate change? *Climatic Change*, 15, 303.

Anthony Ellsworth Scoville
Godel, Gaia, and Government

The connection between Godel, Gaia, and government mentioned in the latter part of the chapter deserves greater explanation than is appropriate for the published version of an address. This addendum seeks to fill that gap.[1]

Godel showed that any formal system either contains an inconsistency if it is powerful enough to prove all the theorems of arithmetic (that is, if it is complete), or, if such a system is consistent, then there are true theorems of arithmetic that are undecidable and cannot be proved within the system (that is, the system will be incomplete). A formal system is any finite set of axioms and a finite set of rules for combining these axioms so as to produce theorems.

A biological model for Godelian evolution of species is as follows: Assign to every living being up to the present time the status of an axiom of a formal system modeling biological evolution. For example, the axiom for an individual could be its genetic code; the rules of deduction would then be the rules for combining DNA. The whole model must satisfy at least the rules of Peano arithmetic. This model can be expanded to encompass the entire geobiological evolution of the Earth with each axiom being every atom on Earth from which we can derive all states of these atoms and their molecular combinations. In the vernacular of logic these derivable states or offspring are called theorems. In these terms, Gaia is a theorem-proving biological Turing machine.

Now start G running. Since G encompasses the entire Earth's history, necessarily G has the property that it lists all true and only true theorems (progeny) because those are the complete set of factual conditions that come to pass. Now suppose that Gaia produces the genetic code for an individual that utters the following remark: "Gaia will never produce the genetic code for the individual who makes this remark." If this statement is true then it is not true and if it is not true, then it is true. However, Gaia did produce the necessary code, that is, the author of this paper. If there is a correspondence between physiological conditions, like genetic codes, and thoughts, then, according to Godel it is impossible to derive the author's genetic code from any finite and consistent set of previous codes. The code corresponding to my statement is simply undecidable within G.

This model and example shed an interesting light on the conference debate between Kirchner, who contended that Gaia was not a valid theory because it cannot produce testable statements that distinguish between alternative theories, and the supporters of Gaia. In his critique, Kirchner never considered the possibility that Gaia might produce statements that are testable, in the sense of being observable, but are not decidable in Gaia and whose appearance cannot therefore be forecast from any previous history of Gaia. Recently it has been suggested that this situation may extend beyond Gaia to the cosmos as a whole.[2]

The possibility of testable but undecidable events within Gaia bears on the problem of evolutionary optimality or goal seeking that was the brunt of Kirchner's critique. The existence of undecidable events makes it impossible, even in principle, to define an optimum over the whole past and future of a system, until its history is finished. Optima or goals can only be defined over some restricted portion of the past and future history if they are also to be attainable through a sequence of logically consistent steps. Kirchner's critique is misplaced because even he cannot define a universal goal or optimum for any system that has a future. He can of course do so for any system that is extinct but then the definition of the goal is trivial (it is merely the last member of the species alive) and in no way distinguishes between alternative models of Gaia or evolution as Kirchner required.

It can be shown then that for any finite set of individuals a complete and consistent explanation for the evolution of one member into the other can be given. Where one gets into trouble is when one tries to explain the future evolution of a system. To do so requires reference to an infinite set of possible future states. One can have complete and consistent laws of biology or physics as long as time is reversible and the laws do not imply any successor relationship between specific historical states. However, the Gaia hypothesis and indeed all laws of geophysical and biological evolution violate this prohibition because they make reference to a specific starting point and specific conditions from which all others arise.

The first point is that past Gaian history may be explained but that future evolution cannot because one cannot prove that the life on Earth will end until

it does. At that time neither we nor our descendants, as individual actors in that history, will be able to prove it because we will have disappeared. Only a being observing the Earth from beyond could do so. As knowing individuals, we can have strong suspicions that the Earth will end but can never prove it. The ability to have those suspicions (knowledge) can be extremely disruptive, as is evident from the use of technology to burn fossil fuels and increase the greenhouse effect.

With regard to arguments over the optimality or homeostatic properties of Gaia, neither human beings nor Gaia can seek a goal that applies to all evolution through all time in a manner that logically builds upon preexisting conditions as a sequence of steps toward the goal. To do so involves reference to an infinite set of possible future states and is prohibited by Godel. However, one can restrict one's planning horizon and then develop a consistent plan involving a finite number of future possible states for achieving some state or phase space path that is considered optimal within that horizon. But then, except by coincidence in no way logically decidable, that goal is suboptimal with respect to evolution beyond the planning horizon.

The second point is that the incompleteness and the irrationality of evolution have nothing to do with our imperfect factual knowledge. Imperfect factual knowledge only means that one has a cloudy picture of the past and will make poorer "forecasts" than will Gaia, which, because it encompasses everything on Earth, necessarily produces all true and only true statements of fact. However, even with its perfect factual "memory" Gaia still cannot make perfect forecasts because, as Chaitin shows, there are some equations describing the computability of states in the evolution of a system for which it is impossible to prove either that the solutions exist or that they do not exist.[3] And if Gaia cannot make perfect forecasts of its whole future, then it cannot proceed on some optimal path toward a universal for all life on Earth except by accident.

The contrast, mentioned in the previous paragraph, between imperfect acquaintance with facts and the limits of knowledge (even with every possible fact at hand) reveals the fundamental reason why government is necessary. In the Greenhouse Civilization, the limits of knowledge reveal the role for government in the operation of global biogeochemical cycles and thus to the future of Gaia.

Upon reading the quotation by James Madison at

the end of the address, one's natural reaction is to assume that Madison is referring to human beings' imperfect factual knowledge or to their failure to live up to self-professed goals—that is, man is ignorant and the flesh is weak. The problem is far more profound. As mentioned above, the limits of rational action are posed by the infinite set of possible future goals; rational action toward a goal is possible only over some finite set of possible futures. Thus there will always be conflict between incompatible human goals no matter how perfect our knowledge.

Madison knew this. In the *Federalist Papers* he took direct issue with the mainstream of political thinking from Plato to Rousseau. Those thinkers sought to attain consensus, that is, the political will to make common social decisions, by homogenizing the population. Homogeneity necessitates reducing the size of a viable political entity. For that reason, the size of a republic was the subject of endless debates on whether the ideal state should have more or less than 5000 citizens. Following the Roman philosopher Polybius, Madison threw out these pointless arguments. Faced with the task of writing the constitution for a large and diverse nation riddled by divisions between states, he knew that one could never eliminate "factions," as he called parties with opposing goals. One could only blunt the ability of one group to tyrannize the others. For that reason he conceived the system of checks and balances between different branches of government embodied in our *Constitution*. The function of government is not to produce an homogeneous population with harmonious goals; rather it is to reconcile conflicting goals and the means for achieving them. The former (homogeneity) might suit a society of angels; the latter is required for the society of men. As applied to politics, Godel's main advance over Madison was to show that even angels would have irreconcilable differences and could not live in peace forever.

Madison intuitively sensed where the nub of the problem lies. As mentioned in our remarks to the conference, in the Preamble to the Constitution, Madison emphasizes the need to secure the blessings of liberty for our Posterity (capital "P") over ourselves (small "o"). His emphasis on posterity is not merely a moral exhortation that it is good to think of our kids not just ourselves. Rather, it recognizes that the most difficult conflicts in society arise out of differing views of the future, as well as

differing hopes and differing conceptions of how to realize them. But, as shown earlier in this addendum, it is the attempt to rationally derive the future from the past that causes any theory of evolution to run afoul of Godel. A theory of evolution and evolution itself, be it Darwinian or Gaian, can rationally explain the whole past (given all the facts) but cannot produce or derive all possible futures from the past with consistency or rationality. That is why government is necessary among men and women: namely, to reconcile logically inconsistent views of the future and the means to achieve them. And that is why, given at least partial responsibility for global cycles, mankind must treat the entire ecosphere as members of its world society, the Greenhouse Civilization. The Earth, with its atmosphere, biosphere, and geosphere, is not a mere natural resource to be treated as a passive subject for exploitation *or* for conservation.

These conclusions concerning the incompleteness or the inconsistency of evolutionary systems shed light on the role of scientific activism in public policy issues such as the greenhouse warming. We saw that, even with perfect data about the climate system and even with perfect data about the benefits and costs of fossil fuel consumption on economic development, there will always be prodevelopment and proenvironment groups with irreconcilable aims. That is, in Godel's terms, there are truths in each group's system of values and acceptable means for realizing them that are undecidable within the other's system. The extent then to which one group or another prevails can never depend solely on the facts of a situation even though they may help persuade unconvinced or uninterested third parties. Rather, political leaders must be convinced that one group cares more about an issue than the other does in inverse proportion to the size of its membership. Reconciliation ultimately occurs because at some higher level of values, such as the desire to preserve a society, one group accedes to the wishes of the other. But, we know from logical type theory, that this appeal to higher level values is an infinite regress. Because reconciliation requires terminating the regress, the possibility of civil war always lurks unless some common values can be found.

Politics is the art of comparing apples and oranges (mutual "undecidables," in Godel's terms). What Madison said is that a constitution must ensure that the majority who like oranges get to grow them but that it must not impede the right of the minority to grow apples. Considering the problem of climate change, the choice between a large warming and a small one is not a rational or decidable choice viewed from the perspective of society as a whole, although it is decidable within the separate perspectives of the environmentalist and the industrialist. The environmentalist wants little change; the industrialist believes that it will be possible to live with a warmer climate through technological adaptation. The environmentalist counters that technological optimism is naive given the complexity of nature; the optimist argues that answers have always been found in the past and can be found for any given problem that appears in the future. This argument is not subject to purely rational resolution even with the best possible data; the answer can only be proved, when and if, human beings become extinct. At which point it will be moot and still unprovable to the original debater, that is, the society making decisions, or Gaia (G).

Given this situation, scientists must be willing to express their concerns and they must be given institutional positions where their concerns can be heard on the relevant issues. Such is not the case today. Regardless of scientists' position in society, political argument will never be won by facts alone. Life will survive on Earth regardless of the extent to which human beings change the climate. But how it will survive depends very much on our choices. In this situation, the primary argument for reducing the buildup of greenhouse gases is not the usual one that the failure to do so will lead to flooding coastlines or other disasters. Rather, given the irreversibility of climate warming for at least a thousand years, unrestricted climate warming violates the basis of our society as embodied in the Constitution. No society can long survive in which the majority (our children and all future generations) are subject to the tyranny of the minority (those of us living today). To repeat the words of Madison, "It is of great importance in a republic not only to guard against the oppression of its rulers, but to guard any part of society against the injustice of the other part."

Notes

1. The discussion draws on Rucker's excellent treatment of Godel's theorems. See Rucker, R. 1982. *Infinity and the Mind.* Basel: Birkhauser, 267–295.

2. cf. Is the universe computable? *The Economist,* 9/16/89, 89f.

3. The application of Godel's theorems to the evolution of a system, and in particular to biological evolution, is the subject of theorems proved by Chaitin on the randomness of the logical structure of arithmetic. See the excellent review article: Stewart, I. 1988. The ultimate in undecidability. *Nature,* 332, 115–116. For a detailed exposition of Chaitin's ideas see Chaitin, G. 1987. *Algorithmic Information Theory.* Cambridge: Cambridge University Press.

List of Participants

David Abram
2320 Surrey Lane
Baldwin, NY   11510

Walter Alvarez
Department of Geology and Geophysics
University of California, Berkeley
Berkeley, CA   94720

Ian Anderson
New Scientist Magazine
3831 Carlson Circle
Palo Alto, CA   94306

Meinrat O. Andreae
Biogeochemistry Department
Max-Planck Institut fur Chemie
Postfache 3060
D-6500 Mainz
Germany

Soe Aung
Department of Geology & Geography
Howard University
Washington, D.C.   20059

Stanley Awramik
Department of Geological Sciences
University of California, Santa Barbara
Santa Barbara, CA   93106

Connie Barlow
1613 Eighth Avenue West
Seattle, WA   98119

Timothy S. Bates
NOAA/Pacific Marine Environmental Laboratory
OCRD
7600 Sand Point Way N.E.
Seattle, WA   98115

S.M.P. Benbow
Department of Geography
University of Liverpool
P.O. Box 147
Liverpool, L69 3BX
England

Jon C. Bergengren
National Center for Atmospheric Research
P.O. Box 3000
Boulder, CO   80307

Robert A. Berner
Department of Geology and Geophysics
Yale University
New Haven, CT   06511

E. Keith Bigg
12 Willis Avenue
Castle Hill NSW 2154
Australia

William D. Bischoff
Department of Geology
Wichita State University
P.O. Box 27
Wichita, KS   67208

Alistair Blachford
University of British Columbia
4460 West 11th Avenue
Vancouver, BC V6R 2MR
Canada

Jonathan Blair
National Geographic Society
1145 17th Street, N.W.
Washington, D.C.   20036

Stephen M. Bollens
School of Oceanography
WB-10
University of Washington
Seattle, WA   98195

Penelope J. Boston
Complex Systems Research Inc.
P.O. Box 1132
Boulder, CO   80301-0003

Daniel B. Botkin
Department of Biology
University of California, Santa Barbara
Santa Barbara, CA   93106

Nancy Ann Brewster
National Science Foundation
Science Policy and Planning
1800 G St. N.W. – Room 510
Washington, D.C.   20550

Collette D. Burke
Department of Geology
Box 27
Wichita State University
Wichita, KS   67208

Samuel S. Butcher
Chemistry Department
Bowdoin College
Brunswick, ME   04011

Kenneth G. Caldeira
Department of Applied Science
26 Stuyvesant Street
New York University
New York, NY   10003

William L. Chameides
School of Geophysical Sciences
Georgia Institute of Technology
Atlanta, GA   30332

David L. Chandler
The Boston Globe
135 Morrissey Boulevard
Boston, MA   02107

Robert J. Charlson
University of Washington
Department of Atmospheric Sciences
AK-40
Seattle, WA   98195

Robert B. Chatfield
NASA Ames Research Center
Moffett Field, CA   94035

Thomas M. Church
College of Marine Studies
University of Delaware
Newark, DE   19716

Ralph J. Cicerone
Geosciences Department
220 Physical Science Building
University of California, Irvine
Irvine, CA   92717

Fred Cole
Veritat Foundation Inc.
P.O. Box 29520
Los Angeles, CA   90027

Charles F. Cooper
Department of Biology
San Diego State University
San Diego, CA   92182

Curtis C. Covey
Mail Code L-262
Lawrence Livermore National Laboratory
Livermore, CA   94550

H. Nuzhet Dalfes
Institute of Environmental Sciences
Bogazici University
80815 Bebek Istanbul
Turkey

Wanda Davis
NASA/Ames Research Center
Mail Stop 239-12
Moffett Field, CA   94035

David DesMarais
NASA/Ames Research Center
MS 239-4
Moffett Field, CA   94035

Steve Deverel
U.S. Geological Survey
2800 Cottage Way
Sacramento, CA   95825

Andrew Dickson
Scripps Institution of Oceanography
University of California
Box S002
La Jolla, CA   92093

Jack Dymond
College of Oceanography
Oregon State University
Corvallis, OR   97331

Dieter Ehhalt
Institut für Chemie Der KFA(3)
Postfach 1913
D-5170 Julich
Germany

Anne H. Ehrlich
Department of Biological Sciences
Stanford University
Stanford, CA   94305

Paul R. Ehrlich
Department of Biological Sciences
Stanford University
Stanford, CA   94305

David J. Erickson
National Center for Atmospheric Research
P.O. Box 3000
Boulder, CO   80307

John R. Evans
MS-957 National Center
U.S. Geological Survey
12201 Sunrise Valley Dr.
Reston, VA   22092

Christopher W. Fairall
NEPRF
Airport Road
Monterey, CA   93943-5006

Brian Flannery
Exxon Research and Engineering
Route 22 East
Annandale, NJ   08801

Richard H. Gammon
NOAA/Pacific Marine Environmental Laboratory
7600 Sand Point Way, N.E.
Seattle, WA   98115

Filippo Giorgi
National Center for Atmospheric Research
P.O. Box 3000
Boulder, CO   80307

Indur Goklany
Department of the Interior, MS 4412
Office of Policy & Analysis
18th and C Street, N.W.
Washington, D.C.   20240

Allen L. Hammond
World Resources Institute
1709 New York Ave. N.W.
Washington, D.C.   20006

Richard Harris
National Public Radio
2025 M Street, N.W.
Washington, D.C.   20036

Thomas A. Harrop
Pennsylvania State University
1013 South Allen St. #408
State College, PA   16802

John Harte
University of California Berkeley
1180 Cragmont Avenue
Berkeley, CA   94708

Michalann Harthill
Minerals Management Service DOI
18th and C Streets, N.W.
Washington, D.C.   20240

David Hawkins
University of Colorado
Department of Philosophy
511 Mountain View Road
Boulder, CO   80302

Peter B. Heifetz
Center for Biochemical Engineering
Department of Mechanical Engineering
Duke University
Durham, NC   27706

Ann Henderson-Sellers
School of Earth Sciences
Macquarie University
North Ryde NSW 2109
Australia

Kaz Higuchi
Atmospheric Environment Service
4905 Dufferin Street
Downsview, Ont. M3H 5T4
Canada

Gregory J. Hinkle
Morrill Science Center
University of Massachusetts at Amherst
Amherst, MA   01003

Martin Hoffert
Department of Applied Science
New York University
26-36 Stuyvesant Street
New York, NY   10003

Heinrich D. Holland
Department of Earth & Planetary Sciences
Harvard University
20 Oxford St.
Cambridge, MA   01890

Sherwood B. Idso
U.S. Water Conservation Laboratory
4331 East Broadway Road
Phoenix, AZ   85040

Shirley Isakari
Scripps Institution of Oceanography
University of California
Box A-024
La Jolla, CA   92093

Brother John
Institute of Immortalism
2410 Dwight Way #8R
Berkeley, CA   94704

James E. Johnson
NOAA/PMEL
7600 Sand Point Way, N.E.
Seattle, WA   98115

Lawrence E. Joseph
Doubleday and Company
807 8th Avenue
Brooklyn, NY   11215

Joelee Joyce
National Science Foundation
1800 G Street, N.W.
Washington, D.C.   20550

James F. Kasting
Department of Geosciences
Pennsylvania State University
211 Deike Bldg.
University Park, PA   16802

Erle G. Kauffman
Department of Geological Sciences
Campus Box 250
University of Colorado
Boulder, CO   80309

Charles D. Keeling
Scripps Institution of Oceanography
A-020
La Jolla, CA   92093

Ralph F. Keeling
National Center for Atmospheric Research
P.O. Box 3000
Boulder, CO   80307-3000

Robin S. Keir
Scripps Institution of Oceanography
Geological Research Division
A-015
La Jolla, CA   92093

Russell C. Kelz
Pennsylvania State University
111 W. Marylyn Avenue
State College, PA   16801

Richard A. Kerr
Science Magazine
1333 H Street, N.W.
Washington, D.C.   20005

Haroon S. Kheshgi
Exxon Research and Engineering Co.
Route 22 East
Annandale, NJ   08801

Dale A. Kiefer
Department of Marine Biology
University of Southern California
Los Angeles, CA   90089-0371

Jeffrey T. Kiehl
National Center for Atmospheric Research
P.O. Box 3000
Boulder, CO   80307

John J. Kineman
NGDC/NOAA
Code E/GC1
325 Broadway
Boulder, CO   80303

Stagg L. King
School of Oceanography
WB-10
University of Washington
Seattle, WA   98195

James W. Kirchner
Department of Geology & Geophysics
University of California, Berkeley
Berkeley, CA   94720

Miriam Kittrell
Kingsborough Community College
2547 West 2nd Street
Brooklyn, NY   11223

Lee F. Klinger
National Center for Atmospheric Research
P.O. Box 3000
Boulder, CO   80307-3000

Gundolf H. Kohlmaier
Johann Wolfgang Goethe University
Post Box 11 1932
D-6000 Frankfurt am Main
Germany

James N. Kremer
Department of Marine Biology
University of Southern California
Los Angeles, CA   90089-0371

Lee R. Kump
Earth System Science Center
210 Deike Building
Pennsylvania State University
University Park, PA   16802

Justin Lancaster
Scripps Institution of Oceanography
Ritter Hall A-020
La Jolla, CA   92093

Daniel Lashof
Natural Resources Defense Council
1350 New York Ave., N.W.
Suite 300
Washington, D.C.   20005

John Laurmann
3372 Martin Road
Carmel, CA   93923

Allan Lazrus
National Center for Atmospheric Research
P.O. Box 3000
Boulder, CO   80307-3000

Caroline Leck
Department of Meteorology
University of Stockholm
S-10691
Stockholm
Sweden

Conway Leovy
Institute for Environmental Studies
FM-12
University of Washington
Seattle, WA   98195

Glen B. Lesins
Department of Oceanography
Dalhousie University
Halifax, Nova Scotia   B3H 4J1
Canada

Joel S. Levine
Atmospheric Sciences Division
NASA – Langley Research Center
Hampton, VA   23665-5225

David Lindley
Nature
1137 National Press Building
Washington, D.C.   20045

Peter S. Liss
School of Environmental Science
University of East Anglia
Norwich, Norfolk   NR4 7TJ
England

James A. Lovelock
Coombe Mill
St. Giles on the Heath
Launceston
Cornwall   PL15 9RY
England

Michael MacCracken
Lawrence Livermore National Laboratory
P.O. Box 808
L-262
Livermore, CA   94550

Kenneth P. MacKay
Department of Meteorology
San Jose State University
San Jose, CA   95192-0104

Paul Mankiewicz
The Gaia Institute
1047 Amsterdam Avenue at 112th
New York, NY   10025

Lynn Margulis
Morrill Science Center
University of Massachusetts at Amherst
Amherst, MA   01003

Sheila Marshall
202 New Mark Esplanade
Rockville, MD   20850

Philippe Martin
School of Earth Sciences
Macquarie University
North Ryde NSW   21097
Australia

Laura Lee McCauley
Arctic Research Consortium of the United States
P.O. Box 80684
Fairbanks, AK   99708

Christopher McKay
Space Sciences Division
NASA Ames Research Center
Mail Stop 239-12
Moffett Field, CA   94035

Heather I. McKhann
Department of Biology
University of California, Los Angeles
Los Angeles, CA   90027

Diane McKnight
U.S. Geological Survey
WRD Mail Stop 408
5293 Ward Road
Arvada, CO   80302

Linda Mearns
National Center for Atmospheric Research
P.O. Box 3000
Boulder, CO   80307

James Miller
Department of Meteorology and Physical
   Oceanography
Rutgers University
New Brunswick, NJ   08903

Judith B. Moody
J.B. Moody and Associates
25 West Washington St., Suite 10
Athens, OH   45701-2447

Cherilynn A. Morrow
Colorado Space Grant Consortium
University of Colorado
Campus Box 10
Boulder, CO   80309-0010

Richard D. Nance
Department of Geological Sciences
Ohio University
Athens, OH   45701

Euan G. Nisbet
Department of Geological Sciences
University of Saskatchewan
Saskatoon, Saskatchewan   S7N OWO
Canada

Jeffrey B. Noblett
Department of Geology
Colorado College
Colorado Springs, CO   80903

Walter C. Oechel
Systems Ecology Research Group
San Diego State University
6330 Alvarado Court, Suite 208
San Diego, CA   92120

Lorraine Olendzenski
Department of Botany
University of Massachusetts
Amherst, MA   01003

Theodore T. Packard
National Science Foundation
1800 G Street, N.W.
Washington, D.C.   20550

Michael A. Palecki
Department of Geography
Wilkeson Quad
State University of New York at Buffalo
Buffalo, NY   14261

Argyre S. Patras
Department of Applied Science
New York University
26 Stuyvesant Street
New York, NY   10003

Fred Pearce
New Scientist Magazine
42 Bramford Road
London   SW18 1AP
England

Brian H. Price
MITRE Corporation
7525 Colshire Drive
McLean, VA   22102

Michael R. Rampino
Department of Applied Science
New York University
26 Stuyvesant St.
New York, NY   10003

R.A. Rasmussen
Oregon Graduate Institute
19600 N.W. Von Neumann Dr.
Beaverton, OR   97006

William S. Reeburgh
Institute of Marine Science
University of Alaska
Fairbanks, AK   99775-1080

Michael Reeve
Ocean Science Division
National Science Foundation
1800 G St. N.W., Room 609
Washington, D.C.   20550

Alan Rice
University of Colorado
1200 Larimer Street
Denver, CO   80204

James A. Rice
Department of Chemistry
South Dakota State University
Box 2202
Brookings, SD   57007-0896

Elmer Robinson
NOAA/Mauna Loa Observatory
P.O. Box 275
Hilo, HI   96721

Jennifer M. Robinson
Department of Geography
Pennsylvania State University
302 Walker Building
University Park, PA   16802

Armand Ruby
University of Massachusetts
Rural Route 1
Box 296
Huntington, MA   01050

David B. Russell
Chemistry Department
University of Saskatchewan
Saskatoon, Saskatchewan   S7N OWO
Canada

Dorion Sagan
Boston University/Sciencewriters
P.O. Box 438
Allston, MA   02134

Wolfgang Sassin
Nuclear Research Center
KFA Julich
P.O. 1913
D-517 Julich
Germany

Manfred Schidlowski
Max-Planck Institut fur Chemie
Saarstr. 23
Postfach 3060
D-6500 Mainz
Germany

Stephen H. Schneider
National Center for Atmospheric Research
P.O. Box 3000
Boulder, CO   80307

David Schwartzman
Department of Geology and Geography
Howard University
Washington, D.C.   20059

Randolf W. Schweickart
Center for Biochemical Engineering
Department of Mechanical Engineering
Duke University
Durham, NC   27706

Anthony E. Scoville
1815 24th St., N.W.
Washington, D.C.   20008

Sybil P. Seitzinger
Academy of Natural Sciences
19th Street and the Parkway
Philadelphia, PA   19103

Glenn E. Shaw
Geophysical Institute
University of Alaska
Fairbanks, AK   99775-0800

Walter C. Shearer
United Nations Center for Science and Technology
    for Development
1 U.N. Plaza
New York, NY   10017

Ben Shedd
Shedd Productions Inc.
291 La Cienega Blvd.
Beverly Hills, CA   90211

Raymond Siever
Department of Earth & Planetary Sciences
Harvard University
Hoffman Laboratory 110
Cambridge, MA   02138

Richard C.J. Somerville
Scripps Institution of Oceanography
A-024
La Jolla, CA   92093

John F. Stolz
Department of Bioscience
Duquesne University
Pittsburgh, PA   15282

Jurgen Strehlau
Institut fur Geophysik
Christian-Albrechts-Universitat Kiel
D-2300 Kiel
Germany

Cornelius W. Sullivan
Marine Biology Research Section
Department of Biological Sciences
University of Southern California
Los Angeles, CA   90089-0371

Eric Sundquist
U.S. Geological Survey
Quissett Campus
Woods Hole, MA 02543

Rod Swenson
Center for Study of Complex Standards
84 Thomas St.
New York, NY   10013

Starley L. Thompson
National Center for Atmospheric Research
P.O. Box 3000
Boulder, CO   80307

Frances Vandervoort
Kenwood Academy
5015 S. Blackstone
Chicago, IL   60615

Michel M. Verstraete
Joint Research Center
Institute for Remote Sensing Applications
Ispra Establishment T.P. 440
I-21020 Ispra VA
Italy

John Visvader
College of the Atlantic
Eden Street
Bar Harbor, ME   04609

Tyler Volk
Earth Systems Group
Department of Applied Science
New York University
New York, NY   10003

Gosta Walin
Department of Oceanography
University of Gothenburg
Box 4038
S-400 40 Gothenburg
Sweden

James C.G. Walker
Department of Atmospheric and Oceanic Science
University of Michigan
2455 Hayward
Ann Arbor, MI   48109

Stephen Warren
Department of Atmospheric Sciences, AK-40
University of Washington
Seattle, WA   98195

Andrew J. Watson
Marine Biological Association
The Laboratory
Citadel Hill
Plymouth   PL1 2PB
England

Jonathan Weiner
3040 Yorkshire Rd.
Doylestown, PA   18901

Peter Westbroeck
Department of Biochemistry
University of Leiden
Wassenaarseweg 64
2333 Al Leiden
The Netherlands

John P. Wiley
Smithsonian Magazine
900 Jefferson Drive
Washington, D.C.   20560

George R. Williams
Division of Life Sciences
University of Toronto
1265 Military Trail
Scarborough   ONT M1C 1A4
Canada

Fred Bernard Wood
Computer Social Impact Research Institute
2346 Lansford Avenue
San Jose, CA   95125

Thomas R. Worsley
Department of Geological Sciences
Ohio University
Porter Hall
Athens, OH   45701

John B. Yoder
RD #4
Butler, PA   16001

Kevin Zahnle
NASA/Ames Research Center
Mail Stop 245-3
Moffett Field, CA   94040

Index

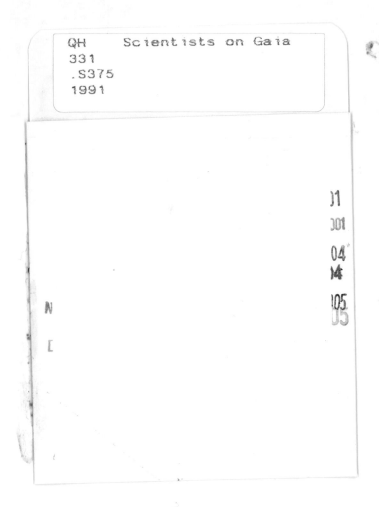